INVESTMENT BANKING AND INVESTMENT OPPORTUNITIES IN CHINA

INVESTMENT BANKING AND INVESTMENT OPPORTUNITIES IN CHINA

A COMPREHENSIVE GUIDE FOR FINANCE PROFESSIONALS

K. THOMAS LIAW

John Wiley & Sons, Inc.

Published by John Wiley & Sons, Inc., Hoboken, New Jersey.
Published simultaneously in Canada.

Wiley Bicentennial Logo: Richard J. Pacifico

For general information on our other products and services or for technical support, please contact our
Customer Care Department within the United States at (800) 762-2974, outside the United States at
(317) 572-3993 or fax (317) 572-4002.

Wiley also publishes its books in a variety of electronic formats. Some content that appears in print
may not be available in electronic books. For more information about Wiley products, visit our web site
at www.wiley.com.

Library of Congress Cataloging-in-Publication Data:

Liaw, K. Thomas.
    Investment banking and investment opportunities in China : a comprehensive
guide for finance professionals / K. Thomas Liaw.
        p.   cm.
    Includes bibliographical references and index.
    ISBN 978-0-470-04468-1 (cloth)
    1. Investment banking—China. 2. Investments, Foreign—China. I. Title.
HG5782.L535   2007
332.60951—dc22

                                                        2007002382

Printed in the United States of America.

10 9 8 7 6 5 4 3 2 1

To my family

Contents

Preface

This book is about China. It is written for market professionals and students who seek knowledge of China, which has become a magnet for business interests worldwide. Market professionals have great expectations in profiting from China's low manufacturing costs, huge consumer base, and opportunities in financial services. Students have interests in China for academic research and career opportunities. China's growing domestic demand and fast-rising foreign exchange reserves are having major impacts on international commodities prices and interest rates. China's foreign exchange policy is the center of attention of global financial markets. The 1.3 billion populations and the burgeoning economic growth result in exploding domestic markets. Financial services present profitable opportunities for foreign players to expand as well. The objective of this book is thus to provide a comprehensive analysis for the practicing professionals to advance professional development and for students interested in a career relating to China to gain relevant knowledge.

The book focuses on investment banking and investment opportunities in China. The book is dividend into three parts: Part I—Chapter 1 through Chapter 6—review China's financial markets and business environment. The coverage includes the economy, the financial markets, the WTO membership, opportunities and challenges of China investing, regulatory issues, and ways to invest in China.

Part II—Chapter 7 through Chapter 13—focus on investment banking in China. Large investment banks want to have a presence in China because privatization and market reforms present businesses in underwriting, advisory services, trading, derivatives, asset management, private equity, and restructuring. Goldman Sachs, Morgan Stanley, and several other institutions have invested in and established alliances with domestic firms. In addition, commercial banking and insurance presents great potentials. Many money center banks have taken strategic stakes in China's banks and insurance companies. Citigroup, Bank of America, and HSBC, for example, have invested billions and gained access to the burgeoning domestic financial markets.

Part III—Chapter 14 through Chapter 19—examine investment opportunities and the various means investors can use to profit from China's growth without venturing into China. Chapters in this part describe investment opportunities, growth investing, and value investing in China. This part also discusses financial instruments that foreign investors can use to invest in China's growth. Those include American depositary receipts (ADRs), Chinese country funds, and Chinese exchange-traded funds (ETFs).

In summary, this book is designed for use as a professional reference and an academic text suitable for business professionals and students interested in China's financial markets. For practitioners and investors, it demonstrates opportunities in China's economic growth and financial markets. The objective is to provide professionals with relevant and in-depth information in order to profit from doing business with China. For students, the text describes the full range of investment banking and investment opportunities in China. Such knowledge is helpful in today's global capital marketplace.

Acknowledgments

Writing this book has been an enjoyable journey. I have traveled to Beijing, Shanghai, Hangzhou, Chongqing, Hong Kong, and Taipei many times. I have also attended and presented at conferences about China and business in Asia at Harvard University and at annual meetings of academic associations. During those conferences, I have had the opportunities to discuss a wide range of issues relating to China's economy and financial markets with many business executives, government officials, and academic scholars. Over the past several years, I have also benefited from discussions with and comments by a number of other individuals. They all contributed greatly to the book. I would also like to thank my editor, Richard Narramore, for valuable suggestions in structuring the book coverage. In addition, I thank Tiffany Groglio and the Wiley editorial team involved in the project.

1

INTRODUCTION TO CHINA'S FINANCIAL MARKETS AND BUSINESS BASICS

An Overview of China's Powerful and Growing Economy

China is a magnet for business interests worldwide. It is one of the largest trading nations with annual imports and exports exceeding $1 trillion. It is the world's largest producer of many product categories. China's fast-rising foreign exchange reserves are having major impacts on international commodities prices and interest rates. China's foreign exchange policy is the center of attention for the global financial markets. The 1.3 billion population and the burgeoning economic growth have resulted in exploding domestic markets. Economic reforms, inflow of foreign direct investment, and membership in the World Trade Organization (WTO) are all major contributors to China's growth. In addition, China plans to gradually sell shares of stock of more than 1,300 largely state-owned companies to further the country's transition toward capitalism. This chapter provides an overview of China's economy, international trade, foreign exchange reserves, special economic zones, and effects of the accession into the WTO.

THE GLOBAL POWERHOUSE

From the initiation of the economic reforms in 1979 through 2006, China's gross domestic product (GDP) grew at an average rate of more than 9 percent. Many economists speculate that if China sustains this level of growth, it could become the world's largest economy by 2050. International trade has been a major part of China's booming economy. The large monetary flows of foreign direct investment and foreign-invested firms accounts for a significant portion of China's trade. The resulting surge in foreign exchange reserves has given rise to debates on China's currency policy and how the policy affects its economy and that of its trading partners.

3

China's Economic Development

Before the initiation of the economic reforms starting in 1979, China was an isolated, centrally planned economy. The economy was made up of predominantly Beijing-controlled, state-owned enterprises. Foreign-invested firms or private enterprises were virtually nonexistent. The Communist philosophy was "take what you need" not "what you deserve." There were no incentives to work hard. The economy was inefficient and stagnant.

Starting in 1979, China launched several economic reforms. The government permitted (and thus encouraged) price and ownership incentives for farmers by allowing them to sell a portion of their crops in the free market. Beijing also sought to decentralize economic policy making in several economic sectors. In addition, the government established special economic zones and development zones that offered tax and trade incentives to attract foreign investment (discussed in detail in a later section). The economy grew faster, from 5.3 percent pre-reform (1960–1978) to more than 9 percent post-reform (1979–2006).

The economic output of $2.26 trillion in 2005 sent China past France, Britain, and Italy to become the fourth largest economy in the world.[1] China's rapid growth and trade expansion could be sustained into the future, provided China is able to keep the economic reforms going, prevent the economy from over heating, and develop the tens of thousands of new managers crucial to continue the economic miracle.

China has emerged as an economic powerhouse with tremendous opportunities for all those who want to unleash this market's vast potential. Since 1980, China has grown faster for longer than any country in history. China now accounts for 13 percent of global outputs based on purchasing power parity (PPP) exchange rates. China's accession to the WTO and events like the awarding of the 2008 Olympics to Beijing attest to China's growing importance on the world economic stage. Key to China's economic growth is its entry into global markets, not only through foreign direct investment, but also through its impressive growth of exports and imports. Economic reforms also led to higher efficiency and enhanced productivity in the economy, boosting output and increasing resources for additional investments. Reform of the financial sector has moved up the policy agenda, especially after joining the WTO, to better support China's economic expansion.

This exceptional economic performance is leading to huge wealth creation. A growing number of Chinese people now have a net worth of more than $1 million. Chinese purchasing power now represents 12 percent of the global sales of luxury handbags, shoes, jewelry, and the like. Bentley Beijing is one of Rolls-Royce's top-selling dealerships. Shanghai hosted the Formula One Grand Prix in October 2005. Shanghai's Maglev, one of the world's fastest trains, began full operation in March 2004, covering the 20 miles from Shanghai to Pudong International Airport in a blistering 7 minutes and 20 seconds. With such economic power and rising visibility on the global stage, China attracts foreign investments of $60 billion a year. In addition, China's international trade (imports and exports) has exceeded $1 trillion per year since 2004 and its foreign exchange reserves crossed over the $1 trillion mark to $1.066 trillion at the end of 2006.

The 1.3 billion Chinese customers present tremendous market opportunities for all kinds of products and services. Multinationals use China not only as a manufacturing base to compete regionally or globally but also to compete in its burgeoning domestic market. The enormous workforce and the low wages give China huge cost advantages. Thus, China has been able to import materials and export products at very competitive terms. This results in trade surpluses year after year. The investment power of the foreign exchange reserves has significant impact on global interest rates. For example, the *Chicago Tribune* reported on January 14, 2006, that mortgage industry watchers were concerned about China's recent signal to diversify its foreign investments.[2] Market watchers were concerned that if China purchased fewer U.S. Treasury securities or agency securities (such as those issued by Freddie Mac and Fannie Mae), it might drive interest rates higher and substantially cool the real estate market.

Adding to those advantages are the high expectations of China that most people have. Such high expectations motivate investors and companies all over the world to allocate resources to China. Those investments are creating more opportunities, which in turn lead to higher expectations. To realize those expectations, investors and companies needed to have access to China. When China joined the WTO in 2001, it provided foreign institutions that access.

Profit from China's Burgeoning Growth

China's development has been a good thing for the West. Companies from all over the world buy, sell, and invest in China. They are profiting from China's competitive production costs, huge domestic markets, and direct investments in growing sectors.

Many domestic-focused companies in the West and Japan cannot compete with China in the production of computers, clothes, toys, and electronics. Thus, they established facilities in China to take advantage of low production costs. About half of the exports coming out of China are from big foreign multinationals that use the mainland as a production base. Multinationals hope to be able to compete with Chinese companies to sell their products and services in the Chinese domestic market.

The high-tech sector is highly penetrated by foreign firms. Many of the U.S. and European big names have established operations in China. For example, Motorola and Nokia see China as their biggest market. Microsoft, Yahoo, and Google are all big players. Automobile companies such as Volkswagen, General Motors, Toyota, Nissan, and Honda grab the majority of the market share. Although Volkswagen has represented the largest car sales for many years, other manufacturers are beginning to make inroads. For example, Cadillac plans to have 40 showrooms in China by year-end 2007.

In the rapidly growing banking and financial services markets, global financial institutions such as HSBC, Bank of America, Goldman Sachs, Morgan Stanley, Merrill Lynch, and Citigroup are expanding operations and buying stakes at large state-owned banks. Investments in other sectors, by way of venture capital or private equity, are booming as well.

Road Map to the Book

This book describes the super growth in China, presents what the opportunities are and how to profit from them, and discusses the potential risks. Part I introduces opportunities in China and business basics. We start by describing China's growing economy and financial markets. We then discuss the opportunities that come with the opening of China, how to position and profit from them, the business culture, and the risks. This part also covers business and financial regulations and how to enter the Chinese market.

Part II focuses on investment banking. Major activities include private equity, mergers and acquisitions, underwriting, derivatives, and asset management. Those operations are expected to bring in billions of dollars of income for financial companies from the United States, Europe, and Japan. Many large financial houses have already established a presence or formed strategic partnerships with Chinese institutions.

Large institutions can invest directly in China. Retail investors have other ways to get into the game as well. Part III describes the major vehicles investors use to "indirectly" invest in China by way of investing in Chinese stocks and funds traded outside China. Many Chinese companies list their shares in Hong Kong, London, and New York. Mutual fund companies have also established funds to specifically invest in China. Furthermore, exchange-traded funds representing the Chinese stock market or sector indexes provide foreign investors an efficient and liquid means to access the Chinese stock markets.

RAPIDLY EXPANDING INTERNATIONAL TRADE AND FOREIGN EXCHANGE RESERVES

Economic reforms have made China a major trading power. China's exports grew from $14 billion at the start of the economic reforms in 1979 to $762 billion in 2005 while imports increased from $16 billion to $660 billion. In 2005, the trade surplus was $102 billion. Much of the surplus came from exports to the United States and Europe. Excluding the United States, China actually had a deficit of $12 billion. As is clear from the Table 1.1, China's international trade surpassed $1 trillion in 2004 and continued to increase in subsequent years. China's foreign trade of $1.4 trillion in 2005 made it the third largest foreign trader behind the United States and Germany. If this pace of growth continues, it is likely to overtake the United States as the largest exporter by the end of the decade.

The expansion process has been facilitated by trade reforms and the general opening of the economy that have attracted surging foreign direct investment (see Table 1.2) and increased integration with the global trading system. Given China's size and substantial development potential, it will continue to have a large impact on the global economy. China's top-10 export destinations are the United States, Hong Kong, Japan, South Korea, Germany, the Netherlands, United Kingdom, Taiwan, Singapore, and Italy. Key import suppliers are mostly from Asia. The top import sup-

TABLE 1.1   China's International Trade

	Exports ($ Billions)	Imports ($ Billions)
1979	13.7	15.7
1980	18.1	19.5
1981	21.5	21.6
1982	21.9	18.9
1983	22.1	21.3
1984	24.8	26.0
1985	27.3	42.5
1986	31.4	43.2
1987	39.4	43.2
1988	47.6	55.3
1989	52.9	59.1
1990	62.9	53.9
1991	71.9	63.9
1992	85.5	81.8
1993	91.6	103.6
1994	120.8	115.6
1995	148.8	132.1
1996	151.1	138.8
1997	182.7	142.2
1998	183.8	140.2
1999	194.9	165.8
2000	249.2	225.1
2001	266.2	243.6
2002	325.6	295.2
2003	438.4	412.8
2004	593.4	561.4
2005	762.0	660.1
2006	961.1	791.7

Source: (1) International Monetary Fund, "Directions of Trade Statistics"; (2) *New York Times*, January 11, 2006; (3) News release, Embassy of the People's Republic of China in the United States, January 10, 2007.

pliers are Japan, South Korea, Taiwan, the United States, Germany, Malaysia, Singapore, Australia, Russia, and Thailand.

International Trade

China has emerged as a trade giant for imports and exports. On the export side, China has long claimed success as the world's factory for light industrial goods for export, such as textiles and toys, and continues to enjoy success in this area. At the same

TABLE 1.2 Foreign Direct Investments in China

	1990	1995	1996	1997	1998	1999	2000	2001	2002	2003	2004	2005
No. of Contracts	7,273	37,011	24,556	21,001	19,799	16,918	22,347	26,139	34,171	41,081	43,664	44,000
Amt. Contracted ($ Billion)	6.60	91.28	73.28	51.00	52.10	41.22	62.38	69.19	82.77	115.07	153.47	na
Amt. Utilized ($ Billion)	3.41	37.52	41.73	45.26	45.46	40.32	40.72	46.85	52.74	53.51	60.63	60.33
U.S. No. of Contracts	357	3,474	2,517	2,188	2,238	2,028	2,609	2,594	3,363	4,060	3,925	na
U.S. Amt. Contracted ($ Billion)	0.36	7.47	6.92	4.94	6.48	6.02	8.00	7.51	8.20	10.16	12.17	na
U.S. Amt. Utilized ($ Billion)	0.46	3.08	3.44	3.24	3.90	4.22	4.38	4.86	5.40	4.20	3.94	3.06
U.S. Share of Contracted Investment	5.40%	8.20%	9.44%	9.68%	12.44%	14.59%	12.83%	10.85%	9.91%	8.83%	7.93%	na

Source: The U.S.-China Business Council.

time, China has also focused on production of high value-added exports. This transformation is reflected in the significant shift in China's exports away from basic manufactured items and textiles into electronics and high-tech products, which now account for an increasing share of China's exports. For example, the customs figures showed that in 2005 China's high-tech exports rose 32 percent year-on-year to $218.3 billion. Exports of electronics products also rose 32 percent to $426.8 billion, accounting for 56 percent of total export value for the year. This move is further strengthened by the fact that Taiwanese manufacturers are making use of China's low-cost production as a base for high-tech manufacturing, more for re-importing into Taiwan than for China domestic sales. Table 1.3 lists China's market shares in Japan, the United States, and the European Union.

China has experienced a tremendous increase in infrastructure-related imports as it modernizes across the transportation, power, shipping, and telecom industries to foster the development of industry and sustain economic growth. Projects to develop infrastructure go hand-in-hand with China's efforts to support the surge in foreign direct investment. China has proven its ability to meet promised timeframes for order fulfillment and to satisfy the requirements of U.S. and European importers. High quality goods consistently delivered on time, along with access to markets and competitive pricing, have all contributed to China's success story. This success is reflected in an impressive real gross domestic product growth of 10 percent in the most recent three years, and a continued steady growth in trade, which reached $851 billion in 2003 and over $1 trillion in 2004.

As China broadens its production base to include higher-value products, the country's requirement for raw materials has grown in parallel with increased global demand. For example, oil demand is rising rapidly as the government works to diversify energy sources and move away from a reliance on coal. China accounts for about one third of the growth in global oil demand. There is also a rapid rise in demand for natural gas and hydropower. Companies in China, both multinational and state-owned enterprises (SOEs), need raw materials and semifinished goods for conversion to larger-ticket goods for sale in the domestic market and for re-export overseas. This, in turn, is driving an increased inflow of commodities.

TABLE 1.3   China's Export Market Shares (Percent)

	1970	1980	1990	1995	2000	2003	2005
Japan	1.4	3.1	5.1	10.7	14.5	18.5	11.03
United States	0.0	0.5	3.2	6.3	8.6	12.5	21.42
European Union	0.6	0.7	2.9	3.8	6.2	8.9	18.87

Source: International Monetary Fund, "Direction of Trade Statistics."

Note: Figures are imports from China divided by total imports, in percentage.

The immediate challenge is to keep up with China's voracious commodities appetite and the growing world demand for Chinese goods. These two demands are putting an upward pressure on pricing. For example, as the world's largest producer of steel, China requires a large inflow of iron ore and other ingredients for steel production. Commodity flows to China such as iron ore, copper, and oil have all seen price increases. With world pressure to keep the supply of raw materials apace with demand, the related challenge is to maintain competitive pricing for commodity imports. Upward pricing pressure must be kept in check to facilitate China's processing of raw materials to finished goods at competitive prices. This impacts China's ability to compete on big-ticket exports destined for large U.S. and European importers and importers in developing countries where China has made considerable inroads.

There has been a significant shift in share of total Asian exports into China. The fact that China has become increasingly prominent as an export destination for Asia as a whole underscores China's growing role as the Asian production hub. In addition, more intermediate products are being shipped to China for assembly before being shipped on to their ultimate markets. China's role in Asian regional trade has also become increasingly important. Imports from the region are growing rapidly, and China now is among the most important export destinations for other Asian countries (Table 1.4).

China's trade expansion in part reflects greater specialization in production within the Asian region. China now serves as the final processing and assembly platform for a large quantity of imports coming in from other Asian countries and then going out to the West. These changes have resulted in a shift in China's bilateral trade balances, with a significant portion of the surpluses with the West offset by the deficit with the neighboring countries, as evidenced by the trade statistics mentioned earlier that China ran a trade deficit with its trading partners excluding the United States. Reflecting this growing prominence and rising imports, China has been an important source of growth for the world economy. China's imports are growing rapidly from all trading partners and it is now the third largest importer of

TABLE 1.4   Imports to China (Percent)

	1980	1990	1995	2000	2003	2005
Asian	15.0	41.0	47.1	53.5	52.8	38.00
ASEAN	3.4	5.6	7.4	9.3	11.3	na
Japan	26.5	14.2	21.9	17.8	18.0	15.22
Korea	na	0.4	7.8	10.0	10.4	11.64
Taiwan	na	na	11.2	11.3	12.9	na
European Union	15.8	17.0	16.1	13.3	12.9	11.14
United States	19.6	12.2	12.2	9.6	8.2	7.42

Source: International Monetary Fund, Direction of Trade Statistics.

developing countries' exports after the United States and the European Union. It is the largest importer of copper and steel, and among the largest importer of other raw materials.

Foreign Exchange Reserves

China has accumulated more than $1 trillion in foreign exchange reserves. The allocation of those funds for investment purposes has huge implications on global financial asset prices and interest rates.

At the start of the economic reform in the late 1970s, China's foreign exchange reserves were minimal. In the early 1980s, export growth contributed to an initial increase in reserves that grew to $8.9 billion by 1983. Trade deficits in 1985 and 1986 eroded the reserves in those years (declined to $2.1 billion in 1986). In 1987, the surplus on trade in services slightly exceeded the merchandise trade deficit, producing a small current-account surplus, and a net capital inflow helped push reserves back up to $2.9 billion. The reserves were held above this level for another two years. The economic slowdown of 1989 to 1991 produced a sharp fall in imports in 1990, while exports continued to rise, producing a merchandise trade surplus for that year of $11.1 billion. The level of foreign exchange reserves crossed over the $100 billion mark in 1996 to $105.0 billion.

Joining the WTO in 2001 contributed to a rapid growth in China's imports and exports. Foreign direct investment inflows exceeded $50 billion a year in 2002 to 2003 and topped $60 billion a year in 2004 to 2006. Foreign exchange reserves reached a record $819 billion at the end of 2005 (see Table 1.5). By the end of 2006, the amount exceeded $1 trillion.

There has been much talk recently about stimulating private consumption in China, which is seen by a growing chorus of policy makers and analysts worldwide to be an important means of reducing China's growing external surplus. It is important for China to rebalance the economy away from heavy dependence on exports to lead growth toward self-sustaining domestic demand.

As companies have improved their performance, corporate savings have risen and now account for almost half of national savings. Corporations have an incentive to retain their earnings in order to finance their investment with internal funds. This is particularly true for private sector companies, which have limited access to bank financing and few domestic alternatives for raising money. State-owned enterprises that do make profits are generally not required to pay dividends to the government, and these companies naturally prefer to retain their earnings and plow them back into new investments.

By some measures, Chinese households have in recent years saved almost a third of their disposable income. One would expect a lower saving rate in an economy that still has a relatively low per capita income and, more importantly, good prospects for continued high income growth. So why do Chinese households save so much of their current income? Most observers believe the precautionary motive for saving is very strong among Chinese households because of the lack of an adequate pension system

TABLE 1.5   China's Foreign Exchange Reserves

Year	$ Billions
1977	1.0
1978	0.2
1979	0.8
1980	−1.3
1981	2.7
1982	7.0
1983	8.9
1984	8.2
1985	2.6
1986	2.1
1987	2.9
1988	3.4
1989	5.6
1990	11.1
1991	21.7
1992	19.4
1993	21.2
1994	51.6
1995	73.6
1996	105.0
1997	140.0
1998	145.0
1999	154.7
2000	165.6
2001	212.2
2002	286.4
2003	403.3
2004	609.9
2005	818.9
2006	1,066.0

Source: State Administration of Foreign Exchange, China.

and the sharply rising costs of health care. Demographic factors add to this saving motive. The one-child policy instituted in the 1970s to control population growth has led to a declining young working class to support the old generation. The need to finance education expenses has also bolstered saving.

The slow development of financial markets in China has meant limited availability of credit, so that households generally have to save in order to purchase big-ticket items, like houses and cars, rather than being able to borrow against future income. It also has meant that there are low returns on households' financial assets and limited opportunities for portfolio diversification, since there are few alternatives to depositing savings in state-owned banks.

All of this suggests that financial market reform and development is a key priority, which the Chinese authorities recognize. The pace of the reform has picked up since China joined the WTO in 2001. Enterprises might be less compelled to rely on internally generated funds if they have access to financial markets to raise capital. Increased access to credit for households, the availability of a wider range of saving instruments that would help them to diversify risk, and higher returns on their assets also could contribute to a reduction in household savings. Thus, building a broader-based, well-functioning financial market would help to rebalance China's economy by tilting domestic demand growth away from heavy reliance on investment toward consumption. Exchange-rate flexibility could have a role by providing more scope for monetary policy independence and helping cushion the economy from economic shocks. It could contribute to rebalancing the economy by improving investment decisions, and the appreciation of its currency raises consumption by bolstering households' real incomes. The government also has a major part to play in influencing saving and consumption, particularly through provision of education, health care, and pensions. Reducing uncertainties in these areas could substantially diminish the strong precautionary saving motive among Chinese households and give them the confidence to raise their consumption.

SPECIAL ECONOMIC ZONES

China's special economic zones (SEZs) are a unique approach to economic development. Chinese policy makers realized that international trade and commerce had the potential for improving China's overall economic situation. They also recognized that by inviting foreign investors into the country, they could learn about foreign technologies and business practices. The establishment of the SEZs allowed Beijing to try out unconventional market-oriented techniques to promote economic development in designated geographic areas. If the experiments were successful, they could be applied to other parts of the country. If the specific measures were not beneficial, the effect was minimized. This gradual approach has enabled the country to become more open and efficient while avoiding unwanted economic or social instability. As such, the objectives are to use innovative market techniques to develop the coastal areas, to attract foreign investment to modernize China's industries, and to serve as a window to the outside world. The establishment of the SEZs has unambiguously contributed to the super economy of China today.

The main SEZs are Shenzhen, Zhuhai, Shantou, Xiamen cities, and Hainan Province. The Hainan Province SEZ was established in 1988 although the other four zones were established in 1980. Jiang Zemin, former president, stated that "The development of SEZs is an important part of building socialism with Chinese characteristics" at a grand gathering in Guangdong Province in 2000 to mark the twentieth anniversary of the establishment of the Shenzhen SEZ.[3] However, SEZs open China to the world and are heavily influenced by capitalism. As a result, those zones probably will not contribute to "building socialism" but instead to transforming China into a capitalist market.

In addition to the five SEZs, the concept also includes open coastal cities, coastal economic open zones, high-tech industrial development zones, export-processing zones, bonded areas, and Shanghai Pudong New Area. Since 1984, China has opened coastal cities, including Dalian, Qinhuangdao, Tianjin, Yantai, Qingdao, Lianyungang, Nantong, Pudong Area of Shanghai, Ningbo, Fuzhou, Guangzhou, Zhanjiang, Beihai, and others. Connected by railways with inland, the open coastal cities serve as important trade ports. From 1984 to 2002, the State Council ratified 49 economic and technological development zones (including Dalian, Tianjin, Ningbo, Beijing, and Harbin) to attract foreign investment and speed up economic development. Likewise, coastal economic zones act as the bridge and window for foreign trade and the base for earning foreign exchange through exports. Furthermore, high-tech industrial development zones promote the development of science and technology that are key to international competition. The State Council has approved 53 state-level high-tech development zones. Another related area is export-processing zones. Those aim at more efficient processing and management of trade. The bonded area in Pudong New Area was established to promote the development of export-oriented services. In addition, the Shanghai Pudong New Area aims to develop Pudong as an export-oriented, multifunctional, and modern area for pushing China's economy into the future.

Development of the Special Economic Zones

The SEZs were initially established after the model of export-processing zones in Taiwan and Korea.[4] The first Asian export-processing zone was in Kaoshiung, Taiwan, as a key strategy for outward industrialization policy that was the foundation of Taiwan's economic achievement. The role of SEZs in China's development is similar to that of export-processing zones in high-performing East Asian countries. However, China's industrial development may not follow a pattern similar to the East Asian model because of China's socialism, its vast size of land, and enormous regional diversity.

Before the establishment of the SEZs in Guangdong Province, a small area in Shekou was marked out in Shenzhen as an export-processing zone. The SEZs were originally intended to serve as a place for testing new reforms of enterprise management, finance, and labor matters. This was a significant development because Beijing sought, for the first time, to link foreign investment with trade in those zones. By providing preferential treatment and facilities for foreign investment and trade, the SEZs turned the inward-looking strategy to an open-door policy. The five SEZs together with 14 other coastal cities constituted the front line of the open-door policy. The locations of four of the SEZs were selected because of their proximity to Hong Kong and Taiwan with easy access to information, technology, management know-how, and capital. In addition to economic factors, political considerations were also involved in selecting SEZs in Guangdong and Fujian Provinces. Selecting SEZs far away from the major centers of population confined the possible disruptions of the SEZs within the existing order.

Consequently, in August 1980, the People's Congress passed Regulations for the Special Economy Zone of Guangdong Province. The word "Special" refers to the special policies and flexible measures granted by the central government, allowing SEZs to utilize a special economic management system to:

- Experiment with and acquire of modern high-tech and management expertise
- Create employment
- Earn foreign exchange reserves through promotion of exports
- Promote economic development and regional development
- Create links with Hong Kong, Macao, Taiwan, and overseas Chinese communities
- Experiment with new economic reform with market forces

World Trade Organization Impact

The SEZs showed a great degree of flexibility in attracting businesses and allowing different types of arrangements for foreign investors. The zones provided investors with specific benefits that were not available elsewhere in the country. Those incentives along with infrastructure improvements and a legal and administrative system favoring the establishment of private and joint-venture enterprises led to a flood of foreign investments.

China's membership in the WTO presents challenges. With WTO membership, Beijing is trying to unify income tax rates for domestic and foreign corporations. Foreign enterprises enjoyed a 15 percent income tax rate versus the standard 33 percent national rate. Tax holidays of two or three years were common in the 1980s and 1990s. With the new policy, this dual tax scheme may no longer exist. How does the dismantling of these preferential treatments affect China's SEZs? Some argue that the loss of various incentives will cause foreign companies to locate in other parts of the country or in other parts of Asia. Others believe that membership in the WTO will not be the end of the SEZs but will require Beijing to reposition its policies to attract foreign investors.

MEMBERSHIP IN THE WORLD TRADE ORGANIZATION

China joined the WTO on December 11, 2001, as part of an ongoing process of integration into the global economy that started with the open door policies in the late 1970s. Membership in the WTO signified another stage of China's economic restructuring. It is also a political statement that the economic reforms and open-door strategies will continue. Membership indicates a broadening of international trade reform from a policy that had been focused on SEZs to a more comprehensive approach under which China agreed to change its laws, institutions, and policies so that they conform to the norms of international trade.

Process Leading to Membership

China applied to become a member of the General Agreement on Tariff and Trade (GATT) on July 11, 1986. From 1986 to 1989, GATT conducted meetings to settle problems with regard to China's application. During this period, GATT's contracting parties, including Japan, the European Community (EC), Australia, New Zealand, and Canada supported China's accession. The process was going smoothly without China agreeing to any major changes in its trade policy to meet GATT requirements.

However, all the goodwill GATT members showed toward China was lost after the Tiananmen Square incident on June 4, 1989. China's suppression of the democratic movement derailed the accession process, and most contracting parties withdrew their support. The United States made greater demands for economic reform as a condition for China's membership. As a result, China began to align its policy with GATT requirements.

By 1991, China's relationship with the United States had soured over disputes on China's handling of intellectual property rights (IPR), China's most-favored-nation (MFN) status in the United States, human rights violations on the mainland, and Beijing's military technology transfers to third-world countries. These issues created difficulties for China as it sought renewal of its MFN status by the United States. As a result, China changed its tactics and started to negotiate with smaller countries. China won the support of Belgium, Brazil, and Argentina, and soon had won over other, more important, contracting parties, such as Germany, Australia, and Great Britain. Bolstered by this new momentum of support, China was able to gain the support of still other countries.

The period from 1989 to 1992 marked two important themes: building a coalition of support outside the United States and internal policy changes to conform to GATT principles. During this period, China offered several significant concessions, including: (1) amendment of Sino-foreign investment law in December 1989, (2) publication of trade policies in December 1991, and (3) the establishment of a research institute to study international trade rules and to help the country rejoin GATT.

As GATT evolved into the WTO, China had the opportunity to gain a founding member status. Yet, China's contentious relationship and trade imbalance with the United States continued to hamper its quest for membership. After more than a year and a half of inactivity on China's part, it resumed negotiations with GATT in February 1992. Negotiations continued until December 1994 because both United States and other member countries demanded concessions from China in many areas. The primary focus of negotiations during 1992 to 1993 was on tariff reduction. In 1994, the emphasis shifted to other areas, such as intellectual property rights and market access by service sectors. China's desire to become a founding member led to many concessions on its part including: (1) concessions on human rights issues, (2) concessions covering sensitive areas, such as the automobile industry, and (3) extension of copyright protection.

With many major concessions addressed, the EU, Japan, and Australia supported China's admission into the GATT by the first half of 1994. To win the support of the United States, China offered concessions on a list of products that no longer needed import licensing and named 50 import categories whose tariffs were to be reduced.

After its bid for founding member status failed, China suspended formal negotiations. Both the United States and China came to loggerheads as neither was ready to back down from its position. The United States was upset over China's lack of action on U.S. copyright infringement issues and the growing trade deficit with China. The beginning of 1995 was the breaking point, when talks on copyright issues fell through, a trade war broke out between the countries.

Other areas of dispute soon erupted, including China's aggression toward Taiwan and continued disputes over developing country status, which drew opposition from the U.S. commercial and agricultural sectors. With regard to developing country status, the United States considered China to be a developed country due to its vast economic size and fast economic growth. Yet, China viewed this designation negatively and believed it would result in economic instability. Formal bilateral negotiations were stalled. The EU attempted to restart negotiations on China's behalf; it recognized China's developing country status and pushed for a transition period that would gradually change China's status to a full member. This approach received a lukewarm reception from the United States.

In 1996, the WTO's larger contracting parties, such as the EU, Canada, and Japan, resumed formal negotiations with China and sought to accelerate China's accession. The EU "transition period" approach for China received widespread support among WTO members and China. The EU now focused its negotiations on addressing which areas would be phased in, how long would the phases last, and which areas were to be immediately opened. The EU sought better terms on market access, subsidies, and tariffs. Access to the automobile sector was the most significant issue because the EU demanded drastic cuts in Chinese automobile tariffs and greater transparency of China's long-term policies in the automobile industry. During 1996, the relations between the United States and China soured even further as a result of the intellectual property rights disputes. In March, the United States called for $3 million dollars in preliminary sanctions against Chinese exports due to China's failure to protect U.S. intellectual property rights. In June, China and the United States reached an agreement over intellectual property rights. Yet, other areas of American concerns needed to be addressed, such as agricultural issues and the trade deficit. This led the United States to push for increased access to China's markets.

In 1997, China made a series of offers to WTO members and carried out many negotiations with member countries. The new offers covered tariff reduction in which China reduced the average tariff rate from 23 percent to 17 percent by October 1997. Regulations on distribution and production for foreign companies in China also were addressed. China promised to open the wholesale and retail sectors to foreign investment and to grant rights to all enterprises in China to import or export after a short transition period.

During 1997, the U.S. Congress took a tough stance on a variety of issues with China and proposed several stringent sanctions, including: (1) a ban on prison-labor products, (2) a ban on travel to the United States by Chinese officials who engaged in religious persecution or who forced women to have abortions as a means of population control, (3) inclusion of American human rights monitors in Beijing, (4) a ban on American trade with companies controlled by the Chinese military, and (5) denial of below-market-rate international loans to China.

In 1998, negotiations centered on China's liberalization of the agricultural and services sectors. Adding to WTO members' arguments was the fact that China had increased its share of exports over its Asian neighbors as a result of the 1997 Asian financial crisis. Members maintained that China's increased fortunes allowed it to increase its share of Western countries' imports drastically. As a result, China offered to reduce tariffs to 10.8 percent by 2005 and to eliminate import restrictions on 385 types of commodities over the next 10 years. Additionally, China provided concessions concerning the telecommunications and services sectors, including banking and insurance markets.

In 1999, China focused its attention on negotiations with the United States. China offered tariff cuts on beef and wheat. The United States had several additional concerns, including accusations that the Chinese were stealing nuclear secrets from the United States, a rising trade deficit with China, and apprehensions raised by both U.S. steel and information technology industries.

To further complicate issues, a NATO bomb hit China's embassy in Belgrade during the conflict in Bosnia. To curb internal dissent over the incident, China suspended negotiations with the United States. As this issue faded, China resumed negotiations with the United States. By November 1999, the United States and China were in accord and reached a bilateral agreement. In the same month, another bilateral agreement was signed by China and Canada.

In January 2000, China and the EU held bilateral talks on several outstanding issues covering market access, tariffs, investment, and industrial goods. Other unresolved issues included market access for telecom and insurance companies. In February, China and India signed a bilateral agreement, which increased the trade volume between both countries. By May, China had agreed to concessions pushed by the EU, which resulted in the signing of a bilateral agreement. China made a commitment to lift restrictions on insurance business, which would include allowing foreign operators to sell the same products as their Chinese competitors. Restrictions on location of foreign insurers were relaxed—previously foreign insurers were permitted only in the cities of Shanghai and Guangzhou. Also, foreign partners in Chinese life insurance joint ventures would be permitted to exercise effective management control, for they could choose their Chinese partners and secure a legal guarantee of freedom from any regulatory interference in private contracts on a fifty-fifty equity basis. Additionally, in May 2000, China signed a bilateral agreement with Australia, after reaching an agreement to liberalize access to 1,000 product categories across agricultural and manufacturing exports and to key service sectors.

In September 2000, China and Switzerland reached a bilateral agreement. This left only Mexican-Chinese negotiations as the last remaining obstacle before the WTO accepted China as a member. In September 2001, China and Mexico wrapped up bilateral negotiations. China made concessions to extend its current countervailing duties on 1,300 Chinese products in textiles, garments, footwear, and toys for six years. It also permitted an antidumping measure, which allowed Mexico to maintain the import duties after a six-year period if it discovered dumping. The eighteenth meeting of the WTO China working group finalized legal documents on China's accession; China was formally approved as a member at WTO's November Doha meeting.[5]

Regulatory Changes

China made a variety of commitments to the WTO for membership. A summary of the eight subject areas follows:[6]

1. *Trading rights and distribution services:* China agreed to grant full trade and distribution rights to foreign enterprises by the end of 2004 (with some exceptions, such as for certain agricultural products, minerals, and fuels).
2. *Import regulations:* Import regulations largely concern general and product specific import tariffs. In addition to a number of specific tariff reductions, Beijing agreed to reduce the average tariff imposed on industrial goods and agricultural products from 24.6 percent and 31 percent to 8.9 percent and 15 percent, respectively (with most cuts made by 2004 and all cuts completed by 2010).
3. *Export regulations:* China agreed to accept GATT Article XI, which generally prohibits export restrictions other than duties, taxes or other charges related to the cost of administering an export regime. Exceptions are made for certain sensitive products, such as those whose export could compromise national security.
4. *Internal policies affecting trade:* China agreed to abide by the core GATT 1994 principles of MFN nondiscrimination (known in the United States as normal trade relations) and national treatment, which requires that foreign firms operating in China would be treated no less favorably than Chinese firms for trade purposes, especially as such treatment relates to taxation, regulatory transparency, and price controls.
5. *Investment:* China agreed to eliminate local content and foreign-exchange balancing requirements from its laws, regulations, and other measures. Importantly, China also agreed that importation or investment approvals would not be conditioned on requirements such as technology transfer and export offsets.
6. *Agriculture:* China agreed to limit subsidies for agricultural production to 8.5 percent of the value of farm output and eliminate export subsidies on agricultural exports.

7. *Intellectual property rights:* China agreed to implement the WTO's Trade-Related Aspects of Intellectual Property Rights (TRIPS) Agreement immediately upon accession. The TRIPS agreement sets down minimum standards for most forms of intellectual property regulation—copyright and related rights, industrial designs, patents, trademarks, and trade secrets—within all member countries of the WTO.

8. *Services:* China agreed to open the banking system to full competition from foreign financial institutions by 2007. Beijing also agreed to permit various degrees of foreign ownership in joint ventures in insurance and telecommunications.

Status of China's World Trade Organization Commitments

China met four significant WTO commitments in 2005. These areas are advertising, banking, freight forwarding, and insurance. In advertising, it met the commitment by allowing wholly foreign-owned enterprises (WFOEs) in advertising services when the Regulation on Management of Foreign-Invested Advertising Companies took effect on December 10, 2005. With regard to banking, China met its commitment when the China Banking Regulatory Commission announced on December 5 that it would allow foreign banks to expand their local currency business into Ningbo, Zhejiang; and Shantou, Guangdong. China opened Shenyang, Liaoning; and Xi'an, Shaanxi, in December 2004. In fact, China went beyond its WTO commitments and opened five other cities—Changchun, Jilin; Harbin, Heilongjiang; Lanzhou, Gansu; Nanning, Guangxi; and Yinchuan, Ningxia—in December 2005. In the area of freight forwarding, China met its commitments by allowing WFOEs in freight-forwarding agency services and to apply national treatment to capitalization requirements for foreign-invested freight forwarders. Another fulfilled commitment is insurance. Foreign-invested insurers no longer need to cede to the China Reinsurance Corporation a portion of the lines of the primary risk for nonlife, personal accident, and health insurance. The China Insurance Regulatory Commission also lowered the minimum required total asset level for an insurance brokerage license from $300 million to $200 million. The lower asset requirement took effect on December 11, 2005.

In 2006, China's new commitments were:[7]

- *Architectural, engineering, and urban planning services:* China will allow WFOEs in architectural, engineering, and integrated engineering services. Urban planning WFOEs have been permitted since May 2003.
- *Banking:* China has to lift all geographic and customer restrictions on their local currency businesses on foreign-invested banks. Moreover, China is scheduled to eliminate any nonprudential measures that restrict the ownership, operation, and operational form of foreign-invested banks. The combined phase-in of these commitments should mark the full opening of China's banking sector to foreign companies. It will allow wholly foreign-owned banks to provide local currency services to any Chinese client in any city. Full implementation of these commitments is made particularly important by the likelihood of continuing

restrictions on foreign investment in domestic banks, which is capped at 25 percent for all foreign investors and less than 20 percent for any one foreign investor.

- *Distribution and retail:* China is scheduled to allow WFOEs and other foreign-invested wholesalers and commission agents to distribute chemical fertilizers, processed oil, and crude oil. Implementation of this commitment will remove the last remaining product prohibitions for foreign-invested distributors, except for restrictions on salt and tobacco, which are to remain under state control.

- *Retail:* WFOEs and other foreign-invested retailers with 30 or fewer outlets should be allowed to sell chemical fertilizers. Foreign majority-owned chain retailers with more than 30 outlets should be allowed to sell motor vehicles. Implementation of these commitments will mark the completion of WTO-mandated openings in China's retail sector, though China will retain the right to prohibit foreign-majority owned chain retail outlets with more than 30 stores from selling tobacco products, certain chemicals, some agriculture items, and specific processed oil products.

- *Insurance:* The last of China's WTO commitment in insurance requires it to allow wholly foreign-owned insurers to engage in reinsurance; international marine, aviation, and transport insurance; and brokerage for reinsurance and large-scale commercial risks, international marine, aviation, and transport insurance.

- *Telecom:* China is scheduled to lift all geographic restrictions on mobile voice and data telecom services for Sino-foreign joint ventures. Foreign-invested mobile voice and data telecom providers were restricted to operating in 17 cities, including Beijing, Chongqing, Guangzhou, and Shanghai. After the geographic restrictions are lifted, China will have fully implemented its WTO commitments in these services. China's WTO schedule does not require it to lift the 49 percent cap on foreign ownership in a mobile service provider. In domestic and international services, China is scheduled to expand the number of cities and regions in which Sino-foreign joint ventures may operate and raise the cap on foreign ownership. Foreign-invested fixed-line telecom providers could operate only in Beijing, Guangzhou, and Shanghai. China's 2006 WTO commitments allow these service providers to expand into many of China's most important business centers: Chongqing; Chengdu, Sichuan; Dalian and Shenyang, Liaoning; Fuzhou and Xiamen, Fujian; Hangzhou and Ningbo, Zhejiang; Nanjing, Jiangsu; Qingdao, Shandong; Shenzhen, Guangdong; Taiyuan, Shanxi; Wuhan, Hubei; and Xi'an, Shananxi. In addition, the cap on foreign ownership should rise from 25 percent to 35 percent and should rise again to 49 percent by the end of 2007.

BEIJING 2008 OLYMPICS

Several months before China gained WTO membership, the International Olympic Committee (IOC) named Beijing as the host city for the 2008 Olympic summer games (Table 1.6). Accession into the WTO gave China MFN status with all its trading partners. The prestige of the Olympics has provided the government an extraordinary opportunity to showcase Beijing and China. Immediately after winning the bid, the Beijing Organizing Committee for the Games of the Twenty-ninth Olympiad (BOCOG) released a $34 billion plan featuring new highways, new railways, urban regeneration, and environmental initiatives to become ready for hosting the games. The marketing slogan is "One World One Dream."

China plans to use the 2008 Olympics to focus on the urban development of Beijing. The massive improvements to infrastructure together with the enhanced image displayed on the world stage will lead to a long lasting economic lift. Beijing's $34 billion plan covers five areas that will, after the event, continue to serve a broad range of needs for the economic, social, and cultural life of Beijing. The five areas are specialized sports facilities, infrastructure, environmental initiatives, urban regeneration and cultural heritage, and tourism promotion and hotel development.

In its initial plan, the Beijing Olympics committee proposed 37 facility sites for the 2008 games. Among those sites, 15 are existing facilities with five requiring refurbishment and 22 new facilities. To improve infrastructure, Beijing has budgeted $11 billion for transportation addressing road systems, bus systems, urban rail, and airport. Along with an improved transportation system, China is also working on enhancing infrastructure for utilities and telecommunications, with an additional $5.4 billion budget. The Olympics has been an important stimulus to Beijing's actions to improve the environment in the city. Beijing has budgeted $8.6 billion to bring blue skies back to the city by 2008, promising cleaner air than Paris. Measures target reducing pollution, a new waste treatment system, water and sewage plants, and the 125-kilometer tree belt (the forested area surrounding the city). The tree belt is one component of the larger "Green Great Wall" to forestall desertification throughout China. The urban regeneration Beijing makes in preparation of the 2008 Olympics has significantly impacted the real estate market, residential as well as business.

TABLE 1.6   Olympics Hosting Cities

Year	City
1972	Munich
1976	Montreal
1980	Moscow
1984	Los Angeles
1988	Seoul
1992	Barcelona
1996	Atlanta
2000	Sydney
2004	Athens
2008	Beijing

Beijing will demolish several older, inner-city housing structures and build new ones. Beijing will also develop new areas of the city and expand the infrastructure to service this area. Furthermore, the BOCOG is calling the 2008 Olympics the People's Olympics to place its culture and heritage on display for the world. Hotels and tourism will certainly enjoy a sharp uptick during the extended period surrounding the Olympics.

CONCLUSION

China's economy grew 10 percent despite the serious setback by the Severe Acute Respiratory Syndrome (SARS) outbreak in 2003. The economy continued to expand at 10 percent in the subsequent three years. We reviewed the important elements of the Chinese economy and the growing influence of its rising foreign exchange reserves. The open-door policies and the establishment of the special economic zones were the foundation for the economy's expansion. The 2008 Olympics has presented an opportunity for China to upgrade Beijing's environment for long-term benefits of the economy.

2

Opening Financial Markets through World Trade Organization Membership

China's accession to the World Trade Organization (WTO) in December 2001 has sped up its reform of the financial system. China has committed to eliminating barriers and opening the financial sector to foreign investment. As a result, foreign institutions rushed to invest and tap into China's booming growth. Foreign entry will not only put pressure on domestic firms, but also will boost the efficiency of domestic institutions. Privatization of state-owned institutions will be a significant part of the process. This chapter outlines China's commitments in the financial sector, including banking, securities, and insurance. The coverage includes the markets that foreign financial institutions have participated in, anticipated growth areas, and the projected revenues.

CHINA'S TRADE COMMITMENTS

Trade reforms and commitments are crucial in promoting China's integration into the global trading system. Tariff reductions and the dismantling of nontariff barriers are largely the continuation of the reform policies. Past tariff reforms also included import tariff exemptions, especially for processing trade and foreign investment. Under China's WTO commitments, tariffs dropped to an average of 9 percent by 2005. In contrast, the opening of the markets to foreigners in services and other trade-related areas is a milestone. Foreign participation in areas such as telecommunications, financial services, and insurance was virtually nonexistent or marginal. China has also taken measures to lift restrictions on trading and domestic distribution for most products. In addition, China made commitments on national treatment and nondiscrimination principles.

China General Commitments

"International economic cooperation has brought about this defining moment in the history of the multilateral trading system," said Mike Moore, WTO Director-General, at the conclusion of the meeting of the Working Party on China's Accession.[1] As a result of the negotiations, China agreed to undertake a series of important commitments to open and liberalize its economy and industries. As a result, China will offer a more predictable environment for trade and foreign investment in accordance with WTO rules. A WTO news release at the conclusion of negotiations stated that some of the commitments undertaken by China are the following:

- China will provide nondiscriminatory treatment to all WTO members. All foreign individuals and enterprises, including those not invested or registered in China, will be accorded treatment no less favorable than that accorded to enterprises in China with respect to the right to trade.
- China will eliminate dual pricing practices as well as differences in treatment accorded to goods produced for sale in China in comparison to those produced for export.
- China will not use price controls for purposes of affording protection to domestic industries or services providers.
- China will implement the WTO Agreement in an effective and uniform manner by revising its existing domestic laws and enacting new legislation fully in compliance with the WTO Agreement.
- Within three years of accession, all enterprises will have the right to import and export all goods and trade them throughout the customs territory with limited exceptions.
- China will not maintain or introduce any export subsidies on agricultural products.

Under the agreement, China reserves the right of exclusive state trading for certain products such as cereals, tobacco, fuels, and minerals, and maintains some restrictions on transportation and distribution of goods inside the country. Many of the restrictions that foreign companies were subject to would be gradually eliminated or considerably eased after a three-year phase-out period. In other areas, such as the protection of intellectual property rights, China promised to implement the Trade-Related Aspects of Intellectual Property Rights (TRIPS) Agreement in full from the date of accession. On the other hand, prohibitions, quantitative restrictions, or other measures maintained against imports from China in a manner inconsistent with the WTO Agreement would be phased out or otherwise dealt with according to the mutually agreed terms and timetables specified in an annex to the Protocol of Accession.

China's Commitments in Goods and Services

The agreement further spells out China's specific commitments in goods and services. In the goods area, China committed to gradually eliminate trade barriers and expand market access to goods from foreign countries. After implementing all the commitments, China's average bound tariff level will decrease to 15 percent for agricultural products. The range is from 0 to 65 percent, with the higher rates applied to cereals. For industrial goods, the average bound tariff level will go down to 8.9 percent with a range from 0 to 47 percent, with the highest rates applied to photographic film, automobiles, and related products. Some tariffs would be eliminated and others reduced mostly by 2004 but no later than 2010.

The two largest categories in goods are textiles and agricultural products. Upon accession, China became a party to the Agreement on Textiles and Clothing and is subject to its rights and obligations. As for all WTO members, quotas on textiles ended on December 31, 2004, but there will be a safeguard mechanism in place until the end of 2008 permitting WTO member governments to take action to curb imports in case of market disruptions caused by Chinese exports of textile products. For agricultural products, China agreed to limit its subsidies for agricultural production to 8.5 percent of the value of farm output.

Three primary categories in services are telecoms, banking, and insurance. Since China's accession, foreign services suppliers have been permitted to establish joint-venture enterprises and provide services in several cities. Foreign investment in the joint venture was initially limited to a maximum of 25 percent. Within one year of accession, the areas were expanded to include services in other cities and foreign investment should be no more than 35 percent. Within three years of accession, foreign investment should be no more than 49 percent. After five years of accession, there would be no geographic restrictions.

In banking, foreign financial institutions would be permitted to provide services in China without client restrictions for foreign currency business. For local currency business, within two years of accession, foreign financial institutions started to provide services to Chinese enterprises. Within five years of accession, foreign financial institutions were allowed to provide services to all Chinese clients.

In insurance, foreign nonlife insurers would be permitted to establish a branch or a joint venture with 51 percent foreign ownership. Within two years of accession, China allowed foreign nonlife insurers to establish a wholly-owned subsidary. Upon accession, foreign life insurers were permitted 50 percent foreign ownership in a joint venture with the partner of their choice. For large-scale commercial risks, reinsurance and international marine, aviation, and transport insurance and reinsurance, upon accession, joint ventures with foreign equity of no more than 50 percent would be permitted; within three years of accession, foreign equity share would be increased to 51 percent; within five years of China's accession, wholly foreign-owned subsidiaries were permitted.

Benefits of China's Accession

China's accession to the WTO has been beneficial to China and its trading partners. China's membership means reduced distortion of trade as Chinese export subsidies are eliminated and the use of state trading to control imports is reduced. It will increase Chinese imports of bulk commodities that can be more efficiently grown or produced in other countries. As market forces play a greater role and as transparency in policy decisions increases, there will be greater predictability of China's import demand and export sales. In addition, as WTO accession leads to further economic growth and rising consumer incomes, Chinese consumption of high-value products will rise. Those benefits were best summarized by Long Yongtu, head of the Chinese delegation at the eighteenth session of the Working Party on China:[2]

> The outcome of China's accession to the WTO will be marked with the feature of a "win-win" and "all-win" for China as well as for the world. As for the rest of world, after China's accession, the great potential of China's market will be gradually translated into actual purchasing power, so as to provide a huge open market to all countries and regions in the world. This would be an important contribution to be made by China to the [sic] mankind. As for China, it will further improve the market economic system to be in line with the current international rules and the principles of the WTO. China will, in light of the WTO principle of market opening on reciprocal basis, strength[en] its economic and technological cooperation with all the WTO Members including developing members. China's economic reform towards market economy and its policy of further opening-up will greatly accelerate China's modernization drive and enhance its ability to participate into international economy.

COMMITMENTS IN FINANCIAL SERVICES

China's accession to the WTO promises unprecedented market access for foreign banks, securities firms, insurance companies, and other financial institutions. With among the highest savings rates in the world, Chinese citizens present huge untapped potential for a broad range of financial products and services. A 2005 poll conducted by Deloitte & Touche found that more than 40 percent of financial firms were already involved in the Chinese market in some form, and that almost 30 percent were exploring how to become involved.[3] Only 18 percent of institutions polled had no interest in entering the market. More than 70 percent of firms polled said they intend to enter either via a joint venture or by setting up a representative office or branch. The remaining banks were considering either a direct investment in a domestic Chinese institution or use of a Qualified Foreign Institutional Investor.

China has exceeded its commitments on market opening under the WTO. Beijing is eager to cooperate with Western banks that are considering the market, and to encourage strategic investments by them. Opportunities for big banks range from serving their existing corporate customers, many of which increasingly need support for their fast-growing operations in China, to bringing new products and levels of financial sophistication to China's emerging middle class. Further, by introducing Western practices, global banks have a chance to bring China's banking system into line with internationally accepted standards.

Banking

In the banking field, China committed to loosening domestic banking regulations with regard to foreign banking institutions. It ultimately hopes to strengthen its banking system by encouraging limited equity investment in domestic banks and educating its workforce in modern banking practices.[4]

China's commercial banking industry currently consists of four large state-owned commercial banks (SOCBs) that have enjoyed dominant market shares in loans and deposits. Exposure to poor-performing state-owned enterprises (SOEs) has led to high nonperforming loans (NPLs). China has established four asset management companies (AMCs) in 1999 to buy NPLs from commercial banks. The four state-run AMCs are China Orient AMC, Great Wall AMC, Huarong AMC, and Cinda AMC. As of late 2005, those four AMCs have acquired about $325 billion of NPLs from China's five largest commercial banks. They have disposed of about $90 billion, mostly to domestic investors and local governments buying back the debt of SOEs in their jurisdictions. Disposals to foreign buyers remain relatively insignificant.

China has made major commitments to reform its banking industry with respect to foreign banks. Over time, foreign banks gradually will be given permission to accept deposits and extend credit. The geographic coverage of foreign banking operations extend from Shanghai and Guangzhou to other cities in China. By the end of 2006, the geographical restrictions would be lifted.

Insurance

China's major concessions in the deregulation of its insurance industry include:

- *Geographic limitations:* China permitted foreign property and casualty insurers to insure large-scale risks nationwide immediately upon accession to WTO and pledged to eliminate all geographic limitations within three years.
- *Scope:* China agreed to expand the scope of activities for foreign insurers to include group, health, and pension lines of insurance, which represent about 85 percent of total premiums, phased in over five years.
- *Prudential criteria:* China consented to award licenses solely on the basis of prudential criteria, with no economic needs test or quantitative limits on the number of licenses issued.
- *Investment:* China agreed to allow 50 percent ownership for life insurance. Life insurers can choose their own joint venture partners. For nonlife, China pledged to allow branching or 51 percent ownership on accession, and to form wholly-owned subsidiaries within two years.
- *Effective management control:* This was negotiated for foreign insurers in life insurance joint ventures, through choice of partner, and a legal guarantee of freedom from any regulatory interference in private contracts on a fifty-fifty equity basis.

- *Licenses:* China made a commitment to immediately give seven new licenses to European insurers, in both the life and nonlife sectors. Further, two European Union (EU) firms would be permitted to establish operations in two new cities.
- *Property and casualty:* In this sector, the state-owned People's Insurance Co. of China (PICC) had some 80 percent of the market. Geographic restrictions on foreign insurers were lifted once China joined the WTO.
- *Life:* China demographics, shrinking state subsidies for social services (such as medical care), and rising incomes virtually guarantee huge market potential in life insurance and increasingly in pension and health insurance as well. Chinese firms, particularly state-owned China Life, dominate the market.

China's life insurers, like its banks, need foreign capital and expertise. Beijing's pragmatic approach to dealing with these needs has been to grant case-by-case approvals of foreign investment in Chinese life companies and new life insurance joint ventures.

Deregulation has granted life insurers a broader scope to offer flexible investment-type products in addition to the fixed-rate, savings-type products that have dominated the market. In this area, foreign firms have a competitive advantage. As Chinese financial-market deregulation continues, foreign investors can expect life insurance companies to begin providing active asset management, for example, for pension funds.

Securities

Making certain that its capital markets continue to facilitate a steady flow of private investment into reforming state and nonstate enterprises is among China's highest priorities. Upgrading the capabilities and professionalism of China's domestic securities industry is part of this process, as is nurturing an institutional investment industry.[5]

The domestic securities industry is consolidating. To survive in a more competitive and open marketplace, securities firms must expand their capital bases. Better companies will likely raise equity from private placements and, in some cases, through initial public offerings in the domestic market or by listing overseas.

Apart from developing listed mutual funds, China needs and wants to expand and professionalize its asset-management institutions. Institutional managers, now generally securities firms and trust companies, take money from institutional investors, principally state-owned enterprises and listed domestic companies. Qualified foreign financial institutions have been given opportunities to participate in this sector. Since what the Chinese want most is foreign business know-how and capital, foreign participation will be limited to joint-venture arrangements.

Implications for the Financial Industry

As China phases out its restrictions on foreign entities and sells off its state-owned enterprises, the influx of business and financial services to support these industries will grow.[6] WTO accession is a catalyst to push China's economic restructuring and movement toward its aim of establishing a socialist market economic structure.

Yet, some sectors are plagued by concerns about the potentially disastrous implications that the liberalization process could have on the Chinese banking system. China's domestic banks are burdened with huge NPLs, inadequate regulatory and credit-control systems, and insufficient capital on which to operate, resulting in very low profitability. Undoubtedly there will be major changes in this sector; either China's banks will push for joint ventures to increase their banking sophistication or weaker banks will be acquired or liquidated. Restrictions on banking that have limited competition in the industry have been lifted gradually. The market practice will have to move toward risk-based pricing.[7]

In the securities business, the continued development of the stock market will be difficult unless China takes steps to improve corporate governance, transparency, performance-based compensation, and a legal system that protects investor interests. Furthermore, the current practice of rationing initial public offerings must stop. Whether a company is able to go public should not be based on the company's political connections, but on future profitability.

It was anticipated that the change in the fixed-income market would be most dramatic after entry into WTO. As in most developing countries, China's focus has been on the stock market. The fixed-income market is underdeveloped. The size of the bond market is relatively insignificant, and the markets are very thin with poor liquidity. This has created two significant problems: (1) Corporations rely on the stock market and house banks for financing and (2) credit risk is not monitored by investors, which has contributed to the severity of the financial market crises in emerging markets. The entrance of foreign securities firms will introduce the fixed-income culture. The development of the fixed-income market is essential; it provides capital to corporations and it requires credit analysis. Rating agencies will assess the financial status of the instrument and/or the issuer.

The mutual fund business and insurance are changing as well. In the past, there were closed-end mutual funds only. The Chinese government allowed the establishment of open-end mutual funds in May 2001. Many well-known asset managers from the United States and other countries have applied for licenses to operate open-end mutual fund businesses. In insurance, both domestic (such as People's Insurance Company of China) and foreign insurers (such as AIG) will eventually offer life, health, property/casualty, and financial insurance.

In summary, in the financial industry, an improved foreign investment environment will facilitate the inflow of foreign capital, technology, and management expertise. Leaders in the financial industry will help to develop a depth of products for managing risk, raising capital, floating debt, and providing insurance. This is also key to the privatization of state-owned enterprises.

MARKET OPENING IN BANKING

To sustain the necessary growth to modernize the economy and create jobs for millions of workers entering the labor force each year, Beijing faces continuous pressure to improve economic performance. The financial system serves as the foundation for the real sector to achieve its potential. China will have to rely in large part on the banking sector to engage in commercial banking under the rule of market forces. Banks need to shift away from their traditional role as suppliers of credit to SOEs, and SOEs need to restructure to improve their operating efficiency and financial condition. The four state commercial banks account for the largest share of the banking market. Exposure to poor-performing SOEs has negatively impacted on bank performance. Thus, Chinese authorities have taken a number of steps to strengthen the banking sector so it will be able to support continued rapid rates of growth. Agreements with the WTO have aided in that reform process. Under the WTO requirements, China had to open the market to foreign banks by 2006. Consequently, HSBC Bank (China), Standard Chartered Bank (China), Citigroup Inc. (China), and Bank of East Asia (China) were given license in early 2007 to engage in all banking businesses, including RMB business on the mainland. This section reviews the current reform process, discusses foreign entry, and presents the areas of important opportunities for foreign banks.

Banking Market Reforms in 2005 and 2006

As the date (December 2006) for China to fully open its financial industry to the outside world moved closer, all Chinese commercial banks accelerated their reform. In 2005 and 2006, there was an unprecedented increase in reform of the banking industry.[8] To sustain the economic growth and integrate fully with the global economy, China could not afford to fail in its reform of the state-owned commercial banks. China Construction Bank has been successfully listed in Hong Kong. Listings of Bank of China and Industrial and Commercial Bank of China have been successfully completed as well. Also in reform are city commercial banks across the country and the joint-stock commercial banks. In addition, consideration is being made on including reform of the rural credit cooperatives into the entire financial system reform.

In the first three quarters of 2005, the gross assets of China's banking institutions increased from RMB 31.6 trillion to RMB 36.0 trillion, up 13.8 percent. During the same time period, their gross liabilities increased from RMB 30.3 trillion to RMB 34.5 trillion, up 13.6 percent. The total assets increased to RMB 43.9 trillion by year-end 2006. By the end of 2006, the total liabilities were RMB 41.7 trillion. In terms of NPLs, the total in 2006 was RMB 1.25 trillion.

After Beijing selected Bank of China and China Construction Bank to pilot shareholding restructuring reform in late 2003, the similar reform of Industrial and Commercial Bank of China (ICBC) kicked off in April 2005. By June 2005, ICBC had completed its financial reorganization. On October 27, 2005, China Construction Bank made a successful IPO in Hong Kong, issuing 26.49 billion H-shares globally at a price of HK$2.35.[9] According to the estimated figures for 2005, the price-net assets ratio was 1.96 times, and the price-earnings ratio was 13.9 multiples. The capital raised from the listing was about $8 billion. ICBC also floated its shares in 2006, raising $19 billion.

Corporate governance reform remained a main content in reform of the state-owned commercial banks, in which standardization of corporate governance, establishment of a sound independent director system, intensification of risk management, and reshuffle of business proceedings became the crucial issues. The ICBC, Bank of China, and China Construction Bank have established standardized corporate governance frames. They completed the drafting, voting, and reporting for approval of their articles of association, rules of procedures for the board of directors, board of supervisors, and general meeting of shareholders, rules of procedures for their boards' special committees, and operational mechanisms. The placement of committees under the board of directors of the three banks also was completed. In spite of the differences in names, the fields covered by the committees are basically similar, covering development strategy, audit, risk management, personnel and compensation, and related-party transactions.

There are still many challenges facing the development of China's state banks. In particular, there are some new challenges in development:

- After getting listed, the state banks face new requirements of supervision rules and information disclosure. Following supervision criteria of international financial markets, agendas of the banks have to be reformed to build standardized corporate governance and improve their information disclosure system.
- To sustain profitability, changes in market conditions will pose a challenge for the restructured banks to have their financial indicators reach the level of internationally advanced banks. It is a major strategic task of the state banks to improve their operating efficiency, and optimize business and income mix on the basis of intensifying capital, cost, and risk restraints.
- Enhancing risk management capacity will be a long-term challenge to the state banks. High growth will be a marked feature of China's financial market in the future. Effective management of the risks associated with such growth will be the key for China's state banks to improve their management capacity.

In 2006, China was to fully open up its financial sector in which a new era when the global banking industry competes in the same market would appear. As mentioned earlier, four foreign banks have been granted license to operate like a local bank. Some of the state-owned commercial banks have listed their shares outside China. The Chinese banking industry is now truly global. Under strong government policy backup, China's state-owned commercial banks will enter a fresh development stage.

Entry by Foreign Financial Institutions

The allure of the largest consumer market and the opening of the banking sector have created a mad rush by foreign banks to become shareholders in China's banks. In recent years, many have invested in strategic stakes in Chinese banks. As Table 2.1 shows, International Finance Corporation (IFC) and HSBC started to acquire stakes in Nanjing City Commercial Bank and Bank of Shanghai in 1999 and 2001. Citibank followed with a 4.62 percent investment in Shanghai Pudong Development in 2003.

TABLE 2.1 Foreign Investments in Chinese Banks (as of October 2005)

Chinese Bank	Foreign Investor	Date	Shareholding (%)
Bank of Beijing	ING Bank	March 2005	19.9
	IFC	March 2005	5.0
Bank of China	Royal Bank of Scotland	August 2005	5.0
	Merrill Lynch	August 2005	2.5
	Li Ka-shing Foundation	August 2005	2.5
	Temasek	August 2005	10.0
	UBS	September 2005	1.7
	Asia Development Bank	October 2005	0.3
Bank of Communications	HSBC	August 2004	19.9
Bank of Shanghai	HSBC	December 2001	8.0
	IFC	September 1999	5.0
	IFC	December 2001	2.0
Bohai Bank (Tianjian)	Standard Chartered Bank	September 2005	19.9
China Construction Bank	Bank of America	June 2005	9.0
	Temasek	June 2005	6.4
Hangzhou City Commercial Bank	Commonwealth Bank of Australia	April 2005	19.9
Huaxia Bank	Pangaea Capital Management	September 2005	6.9
	Deutsche Bank	October 2005	9.9
	Sal. Oppenheim	October 2005	4.1
ICBC	Goldman Sachs	August 2005	5.8
	Allianz	August 2005	3.2
	American Express	August 2005	0.8
Industrial Bank	Hang Seng	April 2004	15.98
Jinan City Commercial Bank	Commonwealth Bank of Australia	September 2004	11.0
Minsheng	Temasek	July 2004	4.55
	IFC	July 2004	1.08
Nanjing City Commercial Bank	IFC	November 2001	5.0
	BNP Paribas	October 2005	19.2
Shanghai Pudong Development	Citibank	January 2003	4.62
Shenzhen Development	Newbridge Capital	December 2004	17.89
	GE Commercial Finance	September 2005	7.0
Xian City Commercial Bank	Bank of Nova Scotia	September 2004	2.5
	IFC	September 2004	2.5

Source: PricewaterhouseCoopers. "NPL Asia." November 2005.

The majority of foreign investments in Chinese banks took place in 2004 and 2005, to position themselves to take advantage of the WTO 2006 market-opening schedule.

One of those pre-IPO investments in China's top-tier state-owned commercial banks has paid off handsomely for Bank of America and Temasek. China Construction Bank Corp. sold a total of 26.49 billion shares and raised $8.02 billion on October 20, 2005 (listed on the Hong Kong Stock Exchange). It was China's largest ever IPO and was the world's largest of the year. The offering was priced at HK$2.35 a share, or 30 cents, at the high end of the expected range due to strong demand. The retail tranche of the IPO was 42 times oversubscribed.

Two other big mainland banks have listed in Hong Kong. The Bank of China listed in early 2006 and the Industrial and Commercial Bank of China (ICBC) in October 2006. ICBC's IPO raised $19 billion, the largest IPO in history. ICBC's market capitalization is now second only to that of Citigroup.

Business Opportunities for Foreign Financial Institutions

Relaxation of entry, product, and market controls presents a unique and enticing banking opportunity. Foreign banks are expanding activities in China. They all know the risks of venturing into this market, but the biggest risks for many large institutions are non-engagement. In 2005, PricewaterhouseCoopers surveyed 35 foreign banks with regard to their strategic issues in China.[10] Among the 35 foreign institutions, HSBC topped the peer ranking in foreign exchange trading, treasury, corporate lending, trade finance, and retail banking. Citibank claimed the top spot in project financing, investment banking, asset management, and corporate finance. Standard Chartered ranked third in many categories. Table 2.2 lists the peer ranking.

The 35 participants in the survey commented on their experiences, important markets in the next three years, and the mode of expansion. Many banks made money in corporate banking, treasury, and trade finance. In terms of loan exposure, as Table 2.3 shows, at least 10 banks extended credit to manufacturing, electronics, energy and mining, chemicals, automotive, food and beverage, communications, and construction/real estate industries.

Most banks anticipated a growth rate of at least 30 percent in revenues in 2005 and 2008. Four banks projected a growth of at least 100 percent in 2008, one anticipated 150 percent, and another forecasted 300 percent. Other results pointed to the market development in the near term:

- Many have provided services in trade finance, foreign exchange, top-100 corporate lending and treasury, and small to medium-sized enterprise (SME)

TABLE 2.2   Peer Ranking of Foreign Financial Institutions in China

	First	Second	Third
Foreign Exchange Trading	HSBC	Citibank	Standard Chartered
Treasury	BSBC	Citibank	Standard Chartered
Corporate Lending	HSBC	Citibank	Standard Chartered
Project Financing	Citibank	HSBC	Standard Chartered
Investment Banking	Citibank	Goldman Sachs	Morgan Stanley
Asset Management	Citibank	HSBC	Deutsche Bank
Corporate Finance	Citibank	HSBC	Goldman Sachs
Mergers and Acquisitions	Morgan Stanley	HSBC	Citibank
Trade Finance	HSBC	Citibank	Standard Chartered
Retail Banking	HSBC	Citibank	Standard Chartered

TABLE 2.3 Loan Exposure by Foreign Banks

I	II	III	IV	V	VI	VII	VIII	IX	X	XI	XII	XIII	XIV	XV	XVI	Total
10		50				30					10					100
20		5				70						5				100
	10	10	20		40	10					5				5	100
	10				80		10									100
					50				30						20	100
	40				40				5				5		10	100
	20	10	10	20	10	10	10				10					100
			10		10				80							100
		10								80		10				100
				10						80			10			100
		10	10							70			10			100
					20					70					10	100
				25			5			60					5	100
	10	5	10			10				50			10			100
5	2			5	3	15	20			45			5			100
					33		33			34						100
	10		30		20					30	10					100
5	5	6			12	12			15	30					20	100

(continued)

TABLE 2.3 (Continued)

I	II	III	IV	V	VI	VII	VIII	IX	X	XI	XII	XIII	XIV	XV	XVI	Total
		5	10							25	10				50	100
	10	10		10		25	10			20	5	5	10	5		100
		5		60						20						100
	20	15	10	5	20	10	5			20		10	10	10	10	100
				10	50		10			15		10				100
0	5	6	4	10	10	10	4	1		14	11	11	3	3	9	100
20							60			10			10			100
	3					1				6					90	100
	10	10	10	20	20	10	5			5	10	10	10			100
		10	10	40		10		10		5	15	10	15	5		100

Source: PricewaterhouseCoopers. "Foreign Banks in China," September 2005.

Note: I = Agriculture, II = Automotive, III = Chemicals, IV = Communications, V = Construction/Real Estate, VI = Electronics, VII = Energy & Mining, VIII = Food & Beverage, IX = Knowledge Based Industries, X = Machines, XI = Manufacturing, XII = Paper & Forest Products, XIII = Retailers, XIV = Trading, XV = Transportation, and XVI = Other.

lending. Other services include: funds management, high net worth individuals, retail deposits, residential mortgage, and credit card marketing.

- The focused markets in the next three years (2005–2008) are foreign exchange, trade finance, money market, top-100 corporate treasury and lending, and SME lending. The emerging areas that present opportunities are funds management, high net worth individuals, credit cards, securities trading, retail deposits, consumer loans, Internet banking, and retirement products.
- The lines of businesses that banks are active in at present and plan to be in 2008 cover Renminbi, derivatives, funds management, transaction and custodian services, wealth management, and credit cards. Table 2.4 lists the markets where they had presence in 2005 and those they plan to service in 2008.
- Most of the banks in the survey indicated they would change their business model over the next three years. Regulatory changes and changes in product offerings are the primary driving forces that will affect their business model. Other areas of consideration include increasing customer demand, increasing competition, parent banking strategy, and state of the economy.
- In terms of expansion, the most preferred option is organic growth, followed by partnership with a commercial bank, and then with a Big Four; the large

TABLE 2.4   Banking Markets in 2005 and 2008

Market	2005	2008
Trade finance	33	33
Corporate Banking	31	31
Treasury/Foreign Exchange/Money Market	24	28
Project Financing	21	23
Correspondent Banking	21	22
Corporate Finance	19	21
Investment Banking	16	20
SME Lending	12	12
Term Deposits	10	15
Funds Management	7	12
Mortgages	6	12
Internet Banking	6	11
Bonds	6	16
Transaction & Custody	5	10
Private Banking	3	11
Wealth Management	2	4
Life Insurance/Risk Products	2	6
Credit Cards	1	9
SME Venture Capital	1	2

Note: Number in the second column under "2005" indicates the number of banks that provided services in the business line in 2005 and that in the third column under "2008" indicates the number of banks planning to be active in that market in 2008.

four state-owned commercial banks, including Bank of China, China Construction Bank, ICBC, and Agricultural Bank of China. Among those that indicated if they pursued a joint venture, the critical issues were the ability to exercise management control, protect the interests of foreign investors, raise stakes in domestic financial institutions, leverage to joint venture investment, build in exit mechanisms, and integrate nonbank financial services.

MARKET OPENING IN SECURITIES

Many investment banks see tremendous opportunities in China. Investment banking houses such as Goldman Sachs, Morgan Stanley, Citigroup, and UBS have all positioned themselves to take advantage of the market potentials. Access to China's market became a reality after China joined the WTO. Foreign securities houses now are able to establish joint-venture operations, become special members of all exchanges, and engage in underwriting A shares. In addition, they can engage in underwriting and trading B and H shares as well as government and corporate debt securities. At the same time, privatization of state-owned enterprises means many Chinese companies seek listing in foreign markets. For example, China Life, China Telecom, Suntech, China Construction Bank, Bank of China, and ICBC have listed their shares overseas.

Almost all major U.S. investment banks have operations in Hong Kong. However, an office in Hong Kong does not mean business in mainland China. The Chinese economy is growing at a record rate and many bankers see great potential. Some economists predicted China to be the second largest economy in the world after the United States by 2030. Even those who view the potential with less certainty cannot ignore it. Therefore, a growing group of global investment houses is setting up investment banking operations in mainland China, including Citigroup, JPMorgan Chase, Merrill Lynch, Goldman Sachs, Morgan Stanley, Lehman Brothers, HSBC, BNP, Credit Suisse, and UBS.

With the exception of Morgan Stanley's joint venture (China International Capital Corporation, CICC), the Chinese government has only recently granted permission to foreign investment banking houses to set up operations in China. Morgan Stanley and China Construction Bank set up a joint venture back in 1995, the first of this kind in China. The establishment of CICC gave Morgan Stanley a jump on its rivals. For example, it arranged a $1 billion global bond issue by China's Ministry of Finance in 1996. CICC later advised on China Telecom's purchase of Hong Kong Telecommunications for $1.2 billion and acted as co-underwriter for China Telecom's $3.9 billion public offering.

Citigroup bought 4.62 percent of Shanghai Pudong Development Bank for $67 million in 2003 and has invested in other Chinese financial operations as well. Goldman Sachs has a joint venture in China called Goldman Sachs Gao Hua Securities. Goldman Sachs owns 33 percent and Beijing Gao Hua holds 67 percent of the joint venture that focuses on underwriting A shares and RMB-denominated corporate debt. In addition, it also offers financial consulting services.

Merrill Lynch also has a joint venture with a one-third stake. Merrill negotiated the deal for more than a year with Huaan Securities. The objective of the joint venture is to engage in the mainland China underwriting business. Merrill and Royal Bank of Scotland led a group of investors in August 2005 to acquire 10 percent of Bank of China for $3.1 billion. Bank of America paid $3 billion for 9 percent of China Construction Bank. Furthermore, Goldman Sachs and Allianz have invested in Industrial and Commercial Bank of China. Table 2.5 lists joint-venture securities firms.

TABLE 2.5   Joint-Venture Securities Firms

Securities Firms	Major Shareholders/Promoters
1 China International Capital Corporation, Ltd.	China Jianyin Investment Limited
	Morgan Stanley International, Inc.
	China National Investment & Guaranty Co., Ltd.
	The Government of Singapore Investment Corporation
	Mingly Corporation
2 BOC International, Ltd.	BOC International Holdings
	China National Petroleum Corporation
	State Development & Investment Corporation
	China General Technology (Group) Holdings Limited
	Yuxi Hongta Tobacco (Group) Co., Ltd.
	Shanghai State-Owned Assets Operation Co., Ltd.
3 EVERBRIGHT Securities Co., Ltd.	China Everbright Group
	China Everbright Limited
	Xiamen Xinshiji Group Import & Export Co., Ltd.
	Dongguan Lianjing Industry Investment Co., Ltd.
	Nanjing Xinding Investment and Development Co., Ltd.
4 China Euro Securities Co., Ltd.	CLSA Asia-Pacific Markets
	Xiangcai Securities Co. Ltd.
5 Shanghai Daiwa SMBC Securities Co., Ltd.	Daiwa Securities SMBC Co. Ltd.
	Shanghai Securities Co., Ltd.
6 Goldman Sachs Gao Hua Securities Co., Ltd.	Goldman Sachs
	Beijing Gao Hua Securities Co. Ltd.

Source: China Securities Regulatory Commission.

Investment management industry started in China in 1998 when the CSRC approved 10 fund management companies for the first time. Unlike the United States, where the number of open-end funds dominates that of closed-end funds, there were no open-end funds in China until 2001. The lure of the Chinese markets lies in the country's high savings rate and low mutual fund penetration. In addition, the rising pension liabilities will also drive the growth of the fund management industry.

U.S. fund managers have entered the Chinese markets. Merrill Lynch established a joint venture with Bank of China International (investment banking arm of Bank of China). It began to sell the first fund in late 2004, listed on the Shenzhen Exchange in the first quarter of 2005. Despite it being the second listed open-end fund, the fund raised $130 million, less than half the amount hoped for. China Southern Fund Management launched the first listed open-end fund in August 2004, raising RMB 3.54 billion. The fund could generate interest simply because of its novelty. Investors can either trade listed open-end funds like regular stocks on an exchange, or redeem invested cash as with a regular mutual fund. American International Group, UBS, ING, Societe Generale, and Allianz have also established a presence to tap into the $1.5 trillion savings market. Table 2.6 lists joint-venture asset management companies in China.

Foreign banks have become active in domestic stock markets by way of qualified foreign institutional investors (QFIIs). As of year-end 2006, 52 firms have established QFIIs (see Table 2.7). According to a 2005 report from Merrill Lynch, fees from the securities business in China are projected to reach $12 billion in 2009. Morgan Stanley and Goldman Sachs could each book more than $1 billion in annual revenues there. Citigroup is thought to be able to capture the most revenue in the long run due to its commercial and consumer banking and finance businesses. Table 2.8 lists 2005 revenues from securities business and the projected levels in 2009.

MARKET OPENING IN INSURANCE

Under the WTO accession agreement, China is committed to opening its insurance market.[11] The main commitments of the Chinese government in opening the insurance business are discussed next.

Form of the Businesses

Immediately after China's entry to the WTO, nonlife insurers from abroad were allowed to set up branches or joint ventures in China. Foreign firms gained the permission to hold as much as 51 percent of the stake in the joint ventures. Two years after the entry, nonlife insurance firms from abroad would be allowed to set up solely funded subfirms in China, that is, there will be no restriction on the form of enterprise establishment. Immediately after the entry, foreign life insurers would be

TABLE 2.6 Joint Venture Asset/Fund Management Companies

Companies	Major Shareholders/Promoters
1 China Merchants Fund Co., Ltd	China Merchants Securities Co., Ltd. China Power Finance Co., Ltd. China Hua Neng Finance Co., Ltd. COSCO Finance Co., Ltd. ING Group
2 Fortune SGAM Fund Management Co., Ltd.	Fortune Trust & Investment Co., Ltd. SG Asset Management Co.
3 Guotai Junan Allianz Fund Management Co., Ltd.	Guotai Junan Securities Co., Ltd. Allianz AG.
4 Fortis Haitong Investment Management Co., Ltd.	Fortis Investment Management Haitong Securities Co., Ltd.
5 INVESCO Great Wall Fund Management Co., Ltd.	AMVESCAP Dalian Shide Group Co., Ltd. Great Wall Securities Co., Ltd. Kailuan Group Co., Ltd.
6 Fullgoal Fund Management Co., Ltd.	BMO Financial Group Haitong Securities Co., Ltd. Shenyin & Wanguo Securities Co., Ltd. Huata i Securities Co., Ltd. Shandong International Trust & Investment Company Fujian International Trust & Investment Company
7 ABN AMRO XIANGCAI Fund Management Co., Ltd.	ABN AMRO Xiangcai Securities Co., Ltd. Shandong Xinyuan Holding Co., Ltd.
8 Everbright Pramerica Fund Management Co., Ltd.	Pramerica Investment Management Everbright Securities Co., Ltd.
9 SYWG BNP PARIBAS Asset Management Co., Ltd.	BNP Paribas Asset Management Shenyin & Wanguo Securities Co., Ltd.
10 China International Fund Management Co., Ltd.	J.P. Morgan Asset Management (UK) Limited Shanghai International Trust and Investment Co., Ltd.
11 BOC International Investment Managers	Merrill Lynch Investment Managers BOC International (China) Limited BOC International Holdings Limited
12 Franklin Templeton Sealand Fund Management Co., Ltd.	Franklin Templeton Inventments Sealand Securities Co., Ltd.

(continued)

TABLE 2.6 (Continued)

Companies	Major Shareholders/Promoters
13 AIG-Huatai Fund Management Co., Ltd.	AIG Global Investment Corp Huatai Securities Co., Ltd. Suzhou New District Hi-tech Industrial Co., Ltd. Guohua Energy Investment Corporation (China) Jiangsu Communications Holding Co.
14 UBS SDIC Fund Management Co., Ltd.	UBS State Development & Investment Corp.
15 Harvest Fund Management Co., Ltd.	Deutsche Assets Management China Credit Trust Co., Ltd. Lixin Investment Co., Ltd.
16 ICBC Credit Suisse Asset Management Co., Ltd	Credit Suisse First Boston Industrial and Commercial Bank of China China Ocean Shipping (Group) Co.
17 Bank of Communications Schroder Fund Management Co., Ltd.	Schroder Investment Management Limited Bank of Communications China International Marine Containers (Group) Ltd.
18 CITIC Prudential Fund Management Co., Ltd.	Prudential Group CITIC Trust & Investment Co., Ltd. China-Singapore Suzhou Industrial Park Venture Co., Ltd. Suzhou Gao Xin Zone Economy Development Group Omni-Company
19 CCB Principal Asset Management Co., Ltd.	Principal Financial Services, Inc. China Construction Bank China Huadian Corporation
20 HSBC Jintrust Fund Management Co., Ltd.	HSBC Investments (UK) Limited Shan Xi Trust & Investment Corporation Ltd.
21 First State CINDA Fund Management Co., Ltd.	Colonial First State Group Ltd. China CINDA Asset Management Corporation
22 LORD ABBETT CHINA Fund Management Co., Ltd.	Lord Abbett & Co., LLC Changjiang Securities Co., Ltd. Tsinghua Holdings Co., Ltd.
23 Lombarda China Fund Management Co., Ltd.	BLP GuoDu Securities Co., Ltd. Pingdingshan Coal Co., Ltd.
24 KBC-GOLDSTATE Fund Management Co., Ltd.	Goldstate Securities Co., Ltd. KBC Asset Management Group

Source: China Securities Regulatory Commission.

TABLE 2.7   Qualified Foreign Institutional Investors

1   UBS Limited
2   Nomura Securities Co., Ltd.
3   Citigroup Global Markets Limited
4   Morgan Stanley & Co. International Limited
5   Goldman Sachs & Co.
6   The Hongkong and Shanghai Banking Corporation Limited
7   Deutsche Bank Aktiengesellschaft
8   ING Bank N.V.
9   JP Morgan Chase Bank
10 Credit Suisse First Boston (Hong Kong) Limited
11 Nikko Asset Management Co., Ltd.
12 Standard Chartered Bank (Hong Kong) Limited
13 Hang Seng Bank Limited
14 Daiwa Securities SMBC Co., Ltd.
15 Merrill Lynch International
16 Lehman Brothers International (Europe)
17 Bill & Melinda Gates Foundation
18 INVESCO Asset Management Limited
19 ABN AMRO Bank N.V.
20 Societe Generale Asset Management S.A.
21 Templeton Asset Management Limited
22 Barclays Bank PLC
23 Dresdner Bank Aktiengesellschaft
24 Fortis Bank S.A./NV
25 BNP Paribas
26 Power Corporation of Canada
27 CALYON S.A.
28 Goldman Sachs Asset Management International
29 Government of Singapore Investment Corporation
30 Martin Currie Investment Management Ltd.
31 AIG Global Investment Corp.
32 Temasek Fulllerton Alpha Pte Ltd.
33 JF Asset Management Limited
34 Dai-ichi Mutual Life Insurance Company
35 DBS Bank Ltd.
36 AMP Capital Investors Limited
37 The Bank of Nova Scotia
38 KBC Financial Products UK Limited
39 La Compagnie Financierr Edmond de Rothschild Banque
40 Yale University
41 Morgan Stanley Investment Management Inc.
42 Prudential Asset Management(Hong Kong) Limited
43 Stanford University
44 GE Asset Management Incorporated
45 United Overseas Bank Limited
46 Schroder investment Management Limited
47 HSBC Investments (Hong Kong) Limited
48 Shinko Securities Co., Ltd.
49 UBS Global Asset Management(Singapore) Ltd.
50 Sumitomo Mitsui Asset Management Company, Limited
51 Norges Bank
52 Pictet Asset Management Limited

Source: China Securities Regulatory Commission.

TABLE 2.8   Securities Business Revenues ($ Millions)

	2005	2009 (Projected)
Equity underwriting	700	1,300
Debt underwriting	100	800
M&As	200	600
Asset management	400	1,700
Brokerage	300	1,100
Sales and trading	2,200	6,300

Source: Merrill Lynch, April 2005.

allowed to set up joint ventures in China, and to hold up to 50 percent stake in the joint ventures. They could choose their partners independently. Investors of the joint ventures are allowed to make joint venture clauses independently within the scope committed. Immediately after China's WTO accession, the foreign stake in Sino-foreign joint venture insurance brokerage companies was limited to 50 percent, and the percentage was capped at 51 percent within three years after the accession. Five years after the WTO entry, foreign insurance brokerage companies would be permitted to set up solely funded subfirms. With gradual cancellation of geographical limitations, foreign insurance companies will, after approval, be permitted to set up branches. The qualification conditions for initial establishment do not apply to the establishment of internal branches.

Geographical Limitations

Immediately after the WTO entry, foreign life and nonlife insurance firms gained access to offer services in Shanghai, Guangzhou, Dalian, Shenzhen, and Foshan. Two years after the entry, their business could be extended to Beijing, Chengdu, Chongqing, Fuzhou, Suzhou, Xiamen, Ningbo, Shenyang, Wuhan, and Tianjin. All geographical restrictions were to be lifted three years after the entry.

Business Scope

Immediately after WTO entry in December 2001, nonlife insurers from abroad would be permitted to engage in "general insurance policies" and large-scale commercial insurance without any geographical limitation, and offer nonlife services to overseas enterprises, property insurance to foreign-funded enterprises in China, and related liability insurance and credit insurance services. Two years after the entry, nonlife insurers from abroad would be able to offer all kinds of nonlife insurance services to Chinese and foreign customers. Immediately after the entry, foreign life insurance companies would be permitted to provide individual (nongroup) life insurance services to foreign citizens and Chinese citizens. Two years after the entry, they would be permitted to provide health insurance, group insurance, pension insurance, and annual pay insurance services to Chinese and foreign citizens. Immediately after the entry, foreign reinsurance companies would be permitted to provide life and non-life reinsurance services in the form of branch company, joint-venture company, or solely funded subfirm. There are no geographical restrictions or quantity limits in license granting.

Business License

Immediately after the WTO entry, China committed to abolishing the restrictions on the number of licenses issued to foreign insurers. Foreign insurers must satisfy the following conditions before applying for licenses in China: a business history of more than 30 years in a WTO member country, operating a representative office in China for two consecutive years, and holding no less than $5 billion in total assets as of the end of the year prior to the application.

Large-Scale Commercial Insurance

Large-scale commercial insurance refers to insurance offered to large industrial and commercial enterprises. Its standards are: the annual premium paid by such an enterprise at the time when China entered the WTO exceeded RMB 800,000, and its investment topped RMB 200 million; one year after the WTO entry, the annual premium paid by the enterprise should exceed RMB 600,000 and its investment should exceed RMB 180 million; two years after the WTO entry, the annual premium paid by the enterprise should exceed RMB 400,000 and its investment should exceed RMB 150 million.

Legal Insurance Scope

China has committed that the 20 percent proportion for reinsurance provided by Sino-foreign direct insurance companies to Chinese reinsurance companies would not be changed immediately after the WTO entry. The percentage would be lowered to 15 percent one year after the entry, 10 percent two years after the entry, 5 percent three years after the entry, and eliminated four years after the entry. However, foreign capital insurance companies initially would not be permitted to engage in third-party liability insurance of motor vehicles, liability insurance for public transport vehicles, commercial vehicle drivers and carriers, and other legal insurance services.

General Insurance Policy Brokerage Service

National treatment will be granted. Foreign insurers would be allowed to do business in Shanghai, Guangzhou, Dalian, Shenzhen, and Foshan immediately after the WTO entry, in 10 more cities two years after the entry, and in all cities three years after the entry.

Application Qualification of Insurance Brokerage Companies

In addition to the requirements of a 30-year operating history and running representative office for two consecutive years, there are conditions for capital: in excess of RMB 500 million at the time of entry, in excess of RMB 400 million one year after the entry, in excess of RMB 300 million two years after the entry, and in excess of RMB 200 million four years after the entry.

In summary, the current major criteria for foreign insurance partners are as follows: The asset base is at least $5 billion in China. It has more than 30 years of experience in a WTO member country. The foreign insurer needs to have established a representative office in China for at least two years. In addition, the paid up capital is not less than RMB 200 million.

Opportunities in Life Insurance

Looking ahead, an aging population, social security reform, and the low levels of government support for health care and pensions are creating demand for insurance. The market is now open. China has lifted its previous restrictions limiting foreign insurers to 15 cities and prohibiting the sale of group policies. The potential for growth is immense as less than 4 percent of the 1.3 billion people have insurance.[12] Right now in the early stage of the market opening, domestic life insurers (China Life, Ping An, and Chain Pacific Life) dominate the market with more than 70 percent of the premium revenues, for example, in the first five months of 2005. The growing range of permissible investment assets, increasing consumer sophistication, and a lack of experience on how to grow a market opens doors for foreign insurers. AIG, founded in Shanghai in 1919, was awarded the first special license to operate as a wholly owned company. Others in the 1990s started to penetrate the life insurance market via joint ventures or investment in domestic insurers. Table 2.9 lists top domestic life insurers and foreign rivals and joint ventures.

For foreign insurers with an eye on the China market, joint ventures have been the most popular venue. Many of the joint ventures are with nonlife partners. One good reason is that the foreign insurer will control running the business, because the Chinese partner does not have the expertise. Foreign insurers also found it beneficial to be able to train a sales force from the bottom up without teaching new tricks to old dogs. Another entry format is to set up a boutique operation focusing on the growing number of rich Chinese. Brand name recognition is important. Thus, many joint ventures chose to list their Chinese partner first to leverage the local brand. Given the small market share for foreign operations, virtually everyone is in expansion mode. It may take five to seven years to break even or yield a profit.

Buying a stake in a domestic company is another route. For those control is crucial, a strategic investment with a limited ownership does not fit the objective. But for

TABLE 2.9   Life Insurers in China

Domestic	Foreign Capital and Joint Ventures
China Life Insurance	Generali China Life
Ping An Life Insurance	AIG
Pacific Insurance	Avia-Cofco Life
New China Life Insurance	CITIC-Prudential Life
Taikang Life Insurance	Pacific-Aetna Life
Taiping Life Insurance	Manulife-Sinochem Life
Shengming Life Insurance	

others, strategic investments offer an attractive vehicle. Domestic companies benefit from capital infusions and the foreign partners' expertise in operating and management techniques.

According to KPMG, foreign insurers make money on policies with an annual premium of at least $300. This clientele has been their target. As such, the foreign company's average customer is 20 to 25 years old, lives in large cities (Shanghai, Beijing, and Shenzhen), and has an annual income of more than $6,000. This is China's middle class.

In the past, health insurance and accident coverage was the exclusive province of the life insurers. In 2005, CIRC authorized four startups offering health care coverage. Nonlife insurers also started to offer accident products. Reform of state and corporate pension arrangements will determine the size of the private pensions industry. It is not clear how this will play out. But Ping An and Tai Ping were selected to participate in the trial of the new arrangements.

The number of domestic life insurers increased from 3 in 1992, to 5 in 1996, to 6 in 2001, and to 8 in 2003, and to 53 in April 2007. Foreign and joint-venture companies increased from 1 in 1992 to 20 by 2004. Foreign life insurers now can apply for licenses to sell anywhere in China and to offer group products. Individual regular premium policies sold through the agent channel offer the highest profit margin at about 8 percent. Individual policies sold through the bancassurance channel and group products yield lower margin at 3 to 4 percent range.

Opportunities in Nonlife Insurance

There are abundant opportunities for nonlife underwriters in every sector of industrial and agricultural activity, and transport, trade, and consumer sector. The market, like the life area, is dominated by the big Chinese companies. People's Insurance Company of China (PICC) enjoys a market share of more than 50 percent. Foreign companies tend to focus on limited areas, targeting multinationals in China who feel comfortable dealing with foreign insurers.

Foreign companies could enter the market by way of a joint venture, a strategic investment, or set up branches and upgrade them to wholly owned subsidiaries. Though China lifted the 15-city rule in December 2004, most foreigners are still not operating in locations outside those 15 cities. In the brokerage area, Willis Group has a joint venture in Shanghai, and Sumitomo, Sompo Japan Insurance, and Aioi Insurance have taken minority stakes in domestic brokers.

Among the foreign players, AIG was first into the market with its license in nonlife (American International Underwriter). AIG also acquired a strategic stake of 9.9 percent in PICC Property & Casualty. Hong Kong's Ming An Insurance has also set up branches. Tokyo Marine and Fire Insurance operates in Shanghai.

Domestic nonlife insurers increased from 6 in 1992, to 9 in 1996, to 11 in 2002, to 14 in 2004, and to 39 in April 2007. During the period, foreign and joint-venture companies increased from 2 in 1992 to 7 in 2001 and to 12 in 2004. During 2001 to 2004, PICC's average expense ratio was 23.75 percent and loss ratio was 72.75 percent. For Ping An, the annual averages were 29.5 percent and 73.25 percent. Thus, PICC was profitable but Ping An was not (due to a loss of 17 percent in 2001). All nonlife insurers want to grab a share of the automobile insurance, the largest of the nonlife market with about 60 percent premium.

CIRC has issued several new licenses in recent years. These include specialized agriculture insurance companies and the first motor insurance company. In the reinsurance area, Swiss Re, Munich Re, and General Cologne Re have been authorized to operate in the mainland. The only domestic reinsurers, China Life Re and China Property Re, have a strong client relationship and a large market share. To continue the development of the reinsurance market, CIRC restricts the freedom to reinsure directly overseas.

So far, more than 30 foreign and joint-venture insurance companies have been approved to operate insurance business in China. Among them, quite a few are large international banking and insurance integrated financial groups. Compared with foreign rivals, China's insurance industry is less competitive. According to a document released by the Beijing branch of the CIRC, the results of a survey of 5,000 residents in the Beijing insurance market showed that among those residents who have purchased life insurance, only 17 percent showed satisfaction with the after-sale service, 64.5 percent said "it is so-so and needs improvement," and 18.5 percent indicated dissatisfaction. Besides, the customers know little about their rights. Only 25.65 percent said they were very clear about the insurance clauses, 19.2 percent said they have not even read the clauses, 47.7 percent said they have read but do not fully understand the clauses, and 7.9 percent said they have tried to read but cannot understand the clauses. Also, a survey of 1,600 residents who have not purchased insurance showed that the respondents were reluctant to buy insurance on the grounds that "it is easy to buy insurance but difficult to claim for indemnity," "insurance is unnecessary for the moment," and "no suitable insurance products have been found." Poor service quality has become an important reason restraining the development of the insurance market in China. Thus, there is room to improve services and to offer new products. There are challenges, but opportunities are tremendous.

CONCLUSION

China has opened the financial markets, mostly on schedule with the WTO commitments. Chinese authorities have also taken measures to strengthen the financial sector to ensure that it is able to support the continued economic growth. Beijing has set up AMCs to take NPLs off bank balance sheets. Many foreign financial institutions have acquired stakes in 17 domestic banks. Foreign entry in securities business has resulted in six joint-venture securities firms and 24 fund management companies by year-end 2006. The insurance market has attracted foreign investments and China Life has listed on the New York Stock Exchange.

3

Huge Opportunities and Unique Challenges of Investing in China

The growth of the middle class is creating consumer demand. Improvements in infrastructure and relaxation of regulations, especially after the accession to the World Trade Organization (WTO), have made the Chinese markets more accessible. The emergence of mergers and acquisitions also allows foreign investors to buy local competitors and acquire a strategic stake. Doing business in China is still challenging, though. Shortage of management personnel is severe and violation of intellectual property right is rife. However, the great risk for multinationals is not competition or red tape, instead it is non-engagement. This chapter looks at several major sectors in which multinational companies have established operations and discusses the challenges those foreign firms now face.

THE NEW ENVIRONMENT

China is still an emerging market. But it is not just any emerging market; it is the most important emerging market. China has become one of the world's largest economies. Many chief executive officers make their way to the doors of Zhongnanhai leadership compound in Beijing. After meeting with Chinese leaders, they often praised the country's economic miracle and compete with each other to announce large investments. For years, many multinational companies have used China as a manufacturing base. Because China has also spent heavily to improve its infrastructure and develop its industries, it has become a large importer of raw materials for chemicals, plastics, steel, glass, and electronics.

In the past, many of those multinational companies soon realized that the domestic demand was not as large as expected. On top of that it was difficult to access the local market. However, some evidence has indicated that the market has changed. The

growth of the middle class is creating consumer demand. Thanks to continued reforms and WTO requirements, the market is also much more accessible. For many
big companies, China is becoming a major global market and a market that they cannot afford to ignore.

Turning to the Domestic Market

Economic growth leads to higher income and rising domestic demand. For example,
automobile sales were 500,000 in 1997 but by 2005, China was the second largest automobile market second only to the United States. Many consumer products, such as
shampoo and detergent, show similar trends. Multinational companies in China want
to compete in China's domestic market. Firms from the United States, Europe, and
other Asian countries all want a piece of the market. So do China's state-owned enterprises (SOEs) and the private sector. Competing in the domestic market requires a
different strategy. The low-cost advantage (when competing in the global market) is
non-existent because Chinese companies are able to operate at lower costs.

Foreign firms, taking advantage of the improved business environment, utilize sophisticated brand building and marketing strategies. The improved infrastructure has
made it possible for them to move production inland to second-tier cities for lower
costs. Furthermore, the emergence of a market for mergers and acquisitions allows the
large multinational companies to buy up local competitors.

Better-established firms have largely worked out systems and procedures to alleviate the challenges that remain (either red tape or formal restrictions). The focus for
executives has also shifted to strategic planning and development issues. Chinese operations are starting to make a real difference to the overall performance of global
firms. Many companies now place China as one of their top revenue sources. Staying
outside is fast becoming a risky strategy.

Changing Business Environment

Many multinational companies are seeking to sell their products in China because it
is emerging as a more mature market. Central to the process has been the continued
rapid growth of the economy. According to a survey by KPMG in 2004, 43 percent of
multinationals reported that their operations in China either outperformed or met
their original business plans.[1] Foreign companies have realized that they do not need
one billion customers to justify their presence. Low per capita income does not prevent China from becoming a major global market for many types of goods and services. The emergence of consumer markets is the result of the widening income
inequality. The poverty in the rural areas is a serious social problem facing the government. But in urban areas, the faster increase in incomes has generated a middle class
that has the financial means to buy the more expensive products that foreign firms
want to sell.

Tens of millions of people now can afford to buy and furnish a small apartment,
take a vacation, and buy a small car. The rising demand for these end products has

also created business-to-business opportunities. For example, rising car and home sales have generated additional paint, cement, plastics, and steel businesses.

Promising domestic demand and the appeal as an export base are no doubt attracting foreign companies. Equally important are changes contributing to an upgraded business environment, including improvements to infrastructure (hard and soft) and the WTO accession. The transport system has improved significantly. The railway system is better and China has the world's first magnetic levitation line connecting Shanghai and Pudong International Airport. The road network has been upgraded. Expressways, virtually non-existent before the mid-1990s, now reach many places near major cities. Air transport has also been vastly improved as construction of new airports and upgrades of the existing ones have been completed. New terminals have been opened in Shanghai, Beijing, Chongqing, and Guangzhou. Heavy investments have been made in the country's port infrastructure. Major ports now handle heavy container traffic.

The enhancement of the information technology network has allowed companies to improve operating efficiency. For example, Unilever moved from Shanghai to Hubei in 2003. Unilever now uses a centralized database to manage many of its human resource operations in its subsidiaries across the country.

The upgrading of hard infrastructure goes hand in hand with improvements in soft infrastructure. Customs regulations are being relaxed. More international shiplines include ports in China, connecting it with the rest of the world. China's air links with foreign cities have also been increasing. Though the state remains a big player in the economy, private sector companies are gaining influence. Beijing has been successful in promoting competition in many industries, including previously regulated industries.

China's accession to the WTO has accelerated the reform process. WTO membership was a significant formality for China's entry to the mainstream of the international community. Beijing bureaucrats use WTO membership to drive through programs of domestic economic restructuring.

OPPORTUNITIES FOR INVESTING

China's cost advantage as an export base, its growth in domestic demand, and the opening of the market has produced increasing activities of foreign firms. Annual foreign direct investment (FDI) reached and sustained a level of more than $60 billion in 2004 and 2006. The sources of FDI have diversified. In the early 1990s, the overwhelming majority of FDI came from Hong Kong, Macau, and Taiwan. Since then, the suppliers of foreign capital have diversified to other countries such as the United States, the European Union, Japan, Korea, and Singapore. The manufacturing investments have also moved up in the value chain. The 1980s and early 1990s were dominated by the toy and garment makers from Taiwan and Hong Kong. Then IT manufacturers arrived. Capital intensive firms with huge investment plans have also begun to arrive in China. For example, BP, Shell, and ExxonMobil are all involved in multibillion, long-term projects. Volkswagon (VW), Nissan, and Toyota have committed more than $10 billion. Furthermore, service-sector firms that were kept out by restrictions in the past are beginning to make their mark. International financial institutions and insurers have invested billions in state-owned commercial banks. Retail giants such as Wal-Mart and Carrefour are rolling out nationwide store networks.

Opportunities for Multinational Corporations

Foreign firms are establishing larger operations and are having greater influence on the local economy. The proportion of exports manufactured by foreign invested enterprises (FIEs) rose from an already high 41 percent in 1997 to 55 percent in 2003.[2] Foreign firms now also sell in the domestic market. VW has the largest market share in domestic automobile sales. Motorola and Nokia see China as one of the most significant revenue producers. VW's Chinese joint venture in 2003 generated net earnings of Euro 561 million, a big contribution to its overall group operating profit of Euro 1.78 billion. China is moving from the most important emerging market to an important profit center for many multinationals. The National Basketball Association and National Football League are heavily promoting their sports in China. In accordance to the WTO commitments, most segments of the markets are now open to foreign firms. Later sections of this chapter discuss opportunities for multinationals in the automotive, pharmaceutical, telecommunications, retail, finance, and logistics industries.

Stock Market Opportunities

Several investment vehicles are available to foreign portfolio investors wanting to gain exposure to China. There are both closed-end and open-end mutual funds that invest primarily in the equity of companies whose principal business is based in China or the greater China region. These funds can be purchased either on the stock exchange or from mutual fund companies. Currently, many investors are pouring money into China private equity or venture capital funds. These funds typically make investments in companies in China that have not yet listed their shares on any exchange. Although this is potentially a high return possibility, investors should be aware of some degree of illiquidity and lack of transparency. Other than those funds, investors may consider purchasing stocks of Chinese companies in Chinese domestic market (A shares and B shares) or outside in Hong Kong, London, or New York.

A unique feature of China's stock markets is that companies may issue A shares and B shares. A shares are primarily for Chinese residents and are denominated in renminbi (RMB). B shares were exclusively for foreign investors, but in February 2001, the People's Republic of China (PRC) government allowed Chinese residents to purchase B shares. B shares are not convertible to A shares, but both types of shares give their owners the same rights with one exception: dividends for B shares are in foreign currencies. The result is a segmented market in which A shares are much more numerous: more than 1,000 companies have issued A shares (1,310 as of February 2007), but only a little over 100 have issued B shares (109 as of February 2007). The total number of A and B shares listed has increased from 53 in 1992 to 1,419 by early 2007.

The special characteristics of B shares are:

- B shares are denominated in RMB, but are traded in foreign currency (in U.S. dollars in the Shanghai bourse and Hong Kong dollars in Shenzhen).
- Dividends and other payments are calculated and declared in RMB, but paid in foreign currency.
- B shares were only issued to foreign investors before 2001. After 2001, domestic individual investors could open B shares accounts and trade B shares.
- Dividends and capital gains from B shares can be sent abroad despite China's strict foreign exchange control.
- B shares provide foreign investors with access to China's equity market.
- B shares are traded on both exchanges.
- Before entering the WTO, foreign brokerage firms were only able to trade B shares through local brokers. In recent years, qualified foreign institutional investors are able to trade A shares.

In addition to B share transactions, foreign investors can participate in China's stock markets through several other alternatives, including shares listed in Hong Kong (H shares), New York (N shares), and London (L shares). H shares are listed on the Hong Kong exchange to tap offshore financing. They are traded in Hong Kong dollars and can only be traded by Hong Kong residents or overseas investors. In Hong Kong, there are also Red Chip stocks, which are issued by Hong Kong companies that either are controlled by Chinese corporations or derive considerable revenues from operations in China. N shares are listed in New York in the form of American Depositary Receipts (ADRs). Dividends are declared in RMB but paid in U.S. dollars. L shares are listed in London in accordance with a memorandum of understanding signed between the United Kingdom and China in 1996. As of February 2007, 86 companies have issued both A and B shares while 34 companies floated A and H shares.

FORMS OF FOREIGN INVESTMENTS

There are various approaches foreign companies can use to invest in China. The simplest form is a processing and assembly agreement under which the foreign company supplies the raw materials to a local entity to process. The foreign company pays the local entity a fee. The finished products are then returned to the foreign company. The second form is an equity joint venture. An equity joint venture is a limited liability company with a joint ownership with the local entity in China. The foreign company often provides capital investment, technical expertise, and management skills. The local firm offers land and buildings to facilitate the operation. Another approach is a cooperative joint venture. This is similar to an equity joint venture with a key difference in that the obligations of each party are spelled out in the contract. The contract typically specifies the minimum registered capital and the capital contribution of each party.

The fourth form is a wholly foreign-owned enterprise (WFOE). WFOEs are legal entities in China and are wholly owned by one or more foreign companies. One big advantage of WFOEs is that the foreign company has full autonomy in the management of the company. This is a preferred structure if the foreign company is concerned about its trade secrets.

Establishing a holding company in China is another possible form of entry. The holding company can trade the manufactured goods and also render some services such as marketing, personnel recruitment, and accountancy. In addition, foreign companies may set up representative offices. The permitted business scope is very limited. A representative office is prohibited from engaging in business operations. Alternatively, a foreign firm may set up branches in China.

Too Much FDI

China attracts large sums of foreign investment. The flow of foreign money together with other favorable factors has fueled China's spectacular economic growth. But some observers have indicated that China has one of the highest savings rates and personal savings are well in excess of $1.5 trillion. Some see the huge FDI inflows as a sign of policy failure. This is in part because the state-owned commercial banks have traditionally based their lending on government instruction rather than on market forces. As a result, they have lent too much to SOEs and other government projects. The resulting high nonperforming loans have made it difficult for the new, private sector to obtain credit from the banking sector, forcing those private enterprises to look to their networks of friends, families, and foreign money. This is an expensive form of financing because private firms have to pay with equity.

AUTOMOBILE MARKET

China is the fastest-growing automobile market in the world. China surpassed Japan as the second largest automobile market in the world in 2005, second only to the United States. Rising incomes and consumer access to finance has contributed to booming car sales. China's vehicle output grew to 7.22 million units in 2006. The top three automakers are First Automotive Works, Shanghai Automotive Industry Corporation, and Dongfeng Motor Corporation. The top 10 motor vehicle companies accounted for 80 percent of the market.[3]

WTO Commitments

China has agreed to gradually liberalize the domestic automotive market with respect to tariffs, nontariffs, investments, and trade, including:

Tariff and Nontariff Measures
- On July 1, 2006, the auto import duty was reduced to 25 percent on average and auto-parts tariffs fell to an average of 10 percent.
- The initial quota value of imported automobiles in 2002 was $6 billion. The quota increased by 15 percent per year. On January 1, 2005, all import licenses and quotas were eliminated.

Investment Measures

- The elimination and cessation of enforcing trade and foreign-exchange balancing requirements, local content requirements and export performance requirements, and offsets and technology transfer requirements.
- Amendments to ensure the lifting of all measures applicable to motor vehicle producers restricting the categories, types or models of vehicles permitted for production.
- Raising the limit within which investments in motor vehicle manufacturing were approved at the provincial government level from the $30 million to $60 million one year after accession; $90 million two years after accession, and $150 million four years after accession.
- With respect to the manufacture of motor-vehicle engines, the 50-percent foreign equity limit for joint ventures was removed upon accession.

Trade in Services Related to Automobiles

- Foreign investment would be permitted to enter the following fields: internal sale of automobiles and parts, import and export of automobiles and distribution services, transport companies for operation, installments on automobiles, leasing, and financing motor vehicles for production.

Foreign Investment in the Automobile Industry

The automotive industry has opened up to foreign investments in recent years. Foreign investors first entered China in 1983 when Beijing Jeep Automobile was established. Generally, foreign investors focus on regions with a concentration of motor vehicle enterprises and where the economy is more developed and prosperous.

The market is growing and is profitable. The global market margin is very thin, at 5 percent or so. In China, the average margin is in the range of 10 percent to 20 percent. General Motors, for example, reported earnings of $437 million in 2003 from China. VW reported about a quarter of group profits from China at Euro 561 million. Thus, investments in this sector continue to surge, by both domestic and foreign firms. Global automakers turn to China at a time when the industry in traditional markets in the United States, Europe, and Japan is mature. Most of the international big names are now present in China, including Nissan, BMW, Hyundai, Daimler-Chrysler, GM, and Ford. Big investments include VW (Euro 5.3 billion), PSA Peugeot Citroen (Euro 600 million), Kia ($645 million), and Toyota's alliance with FAW. Table 3.1 lists the major domestic automakers and foreign ventures.

Future Outlook

Automobile manufacturing and related industries account for one in every nine jobs in OECD nations. Thus, it has been one of China's top priorities to develop an automobile industry that supplies the domestic market and exports to foreign markets. With so many big-name global automakers already committed, China is moving to explore foreign markets.

TABLE 3.1   Domestic Automakers and Foreign Joint Ventures

Domestic Companies:
Chery
Dongfeng Automobile
First Auto works
Anhui Jianghuai
Shenyang Brilliance
BYD
Jianxi Changhe
Geely
Great Wall
Guizhou Skylark
Harbin Hafei
Hebei Zhongxing
Rongcheng Huatai
Soueast

Foreign Joint Ventures:
BMW-Brilliance Automotive
DaimlerChrysler-Beijing Jeep
Fiat Auto-Yuejin Automotive
Ford-Changan Automobile
GM-Jinbei Automotive
GM-Shanghai Automotive
Honda-Guangzhou Automobile
Honda-Dongfeng Motor
Honda China (export)
Hyundai-Beijing Automotive
Hyundai-Dongfeng Yueda Kia
Mitsubishi-Hunan Changfeng
Nissan-Dongfeng Motor
Nissan-Zhengzhou Light Automobile
PSA Peugeot Citroen-Dongfeng Motor
Suzuki-Chongqing Changan
Suzuki-Jiangxi Changhe
Toyota-Tianjin Automotive
Toyota-Sichuan
VW-First Auto Works
VW-Shanghai Automotive

China is pursuing a novel way to turn its automobile manufacturing industry into a global force: Buy one of the world's most sophisticated engine plants, take it apart, piece by piece, transport it halfway around the globe, and put it back together again at home. The failure of China to develop its own version of sophisticated, reliable engines has been the biggest technical obstacle facing Chinese automakers as they modernize and prepare to export to the United States and Europe. Buying that technology from overseas would not only remove this obstacle but would also put China's auto industry solidly in a position to produce roomy cars that are also fuel efficient.

Lifan, a Chinese automaker, wants to bring technology to Chongqing to start producing engines in 2008. Accustomed to producing lightweight, fuel-saving cars for cost-conscious Chinese families, Chinese automakers want to use that expertise as a competitive advantage around the world. Geely, another Chinese carmaker that surprised American and European manufacturers by announcing plans at a Detroit auto show to enter the U.S. market in 2007, was emphasizing gas mileage even before oil prices surged over the past several years.

Exports to the United States

Most foreign automakers in China have plans to export as well. But, with the exception of Honda whose Guangzhou plant is for export only, few are doing so. As General Motors, Ford, and Delphi struggle for survival amid a wave of plant closings and bankruptcies, would-be Chinese rivals are casting a hungry eye on the massive U.S. market. Experts say companies like Wanxiang, Geely Motors, and Chery Auto are moving more quickly than Japan's Toyota and Honda three decades ago. Chery is planning to export Chinese-built cars to the U.S. market beginning in 2007. The distributor for the cars will be Visionary Vehicles LLC, which is owned by Malcolm Bricklin, who brought Yugos and Subarus into the U.S. market.[4]

Automobile Financing

In recent years, Chinese domestic banks have been rushing to offer individual automobile loans. Chinese automakers, such as Shanghai Automotive Industry Corp., First Automotive Works Corp., and Dongfeng have already entered the business. Foreign auto giants, including General Motors, Ford, Volkswagen, Toyota, Daimler-Chrysler, and PSA Peugeot Citroen, have also started to offer loans to customers in China as well.

Vehicle financing is a new thing for Chinese automakers. At present, probably 10 percent or so of new car sales in China are financed, and most of those are using money from commercial banks, instead of specialized auto financing companies. In developed markets, more than 70 percent of vehicles are sold with the use of automobile financing. The biggest problem facing auto financing in China results from inadequate credit risk controls, which has increased defaults for some domestic commercial banks. Many commercial banks in China raised their standards for vehicle financing, and some even halted the business because of defaults. As automobile financing slowly becomes a normal purchase process, it is expected to contribute to the continued growth of the Chinese automobile market.

RETAIL AND CONSUMER MARKET

China is the largest consumer market in the world. With a population of 1.3 billion, China has more consumers than the United States and Europe combined. The vast population and high economic growth is translating into huge consumer spending. Domestic spending drives China's continued growth. Currently, a major portion of consumer spending is for food and necessities. Sales of high-quality consumer goods are just taking off. Following China's accession to the WTO, high-quality products are enjoying lower tariffs and a wider consumer base.

WTO Commitments in Retail

For retailing services (excluding tobacco), if the services are provided in the form of cross-border supply, there are no limitations except for mail order. If the services are provided in the form of commercial presence, foreign service suppliers initially could supply services only under joint ventures in five Special Economic Zones (SEZs; Shenzhen, Zhuhai, Shantou, Xiamen, Hainan) and six cities (Beijing, Shanghai, Tianjin, Guangzhou, Dalian, Qingdao). In Beijing and Shanghai, a total of no more than four joint-venture retailing enterprises were permitted. In each of the other cities, no more than two joint-venture retailing enterprises would be permitted. Two joint-venture retailing enterprises among the four to be established in Beijing might set up their branches in the same city.

Upon China's accession to the WTO, Zhengzhou and Wuhan were immediately open to joint-venture retailing enterprises. Within two years after China's accession, foreign majority control was permitted in joint-venture retailing. Retailing of chemical fertilizers was open within five years after the accession.

If the services are provided in the form of presence of natural persons unbound, there shall be no commitments except as indicated in the Horizontal Commitments, which says that there shall be no commitments except for measures concerning the entry and temporary stay of natural persons who fall into one of the following categories:

- Managers, executives, and specialists defined as senior employees of a corporation of a WTO Member that has established a representative office, branch, or subsidiary in the territory of the People's Republic of China, temporarily moving as intracorporate transferees, shall be permitted entry for an initial stay of three years;
- Managers, executives, and specialists defined as senior employees of a corporation of WTO Members, being engaged in the foreign invested enterprises in the territory of the People's Republic of China for conducting business, shall be granted a long-term stay permit as stipulated in the terms of contracts concerned or an initial stay of three years, whichever is shorter;
- Entry for salespersons is limited to 90 days. Service salespersons are persons not based in China and receiving no remuneration from a source located

within China, and who are engaged in activities related to representing a service supplier for the purpose of negotiation for the sale of such services of that supplier. Such sales are not directly made to the general public and the salesperson is not engaged in supplying the service.

With regard to limitations on national treatment, if the services are provided in the form of cross-border supply, there shall be no limitations except for mail order. If the services are provided in the form of consumption abroad, there shall be no limitations. If the services are provided in the form of commercial presence, there shall also be no limitations. If the services are provided in the form of presence of natural persons unbound, there shall be no commitments except as indicated in Horizontal Commitments and its contents shall be the same as the previously-mentioned commitments in the aspect of limitations on market access.

Consumer Spending

Total consumer spending grew from 5.6 trillion Yuan in 1997 to 9.2 trillion Yuan in 2003. The five items that accounted for most of the spending were food, education and entertainment, clothing and foot wear, housing, and household durable goods. Food was the biggest item, consistently more than 40 percent of the total (Table 3.2). Food spending was 41.2 percent of all consumer spending in 2003, down from 47.9 percent in 1997. The decline was expected because as the economy grew, the consumer had more discretionary spending power. Among the key spending items, housing enjoyed the biggest jump, from 7.6 percent to 10.1 percent. Medicine and health care rose slowly from 3.8 percent of total spending to 5.5 percent during the same period. Household durable goods increased from 7.4 percent to 8.6 percent. Transport and communications rose from 5.2 percent to 6.7 percent while services increased slightly from 4.4 percent to 4.8 percent.

As spending in housing rises, consumers spend more on household electronics and appliances. Most households have color televisions, washing machines, and

TABLE 3.2   Consumer Spending Share from 1997 to 2003 (Percent)

Item	1997	1998	1999	2000	2001	2002	2003
Food	47.9	45.9	44.0	43.0	42.6	41.5	41.2
Medicine/healthcare	3.8	4.3	4.6	5.2	5.1	5.4	5.5
Clothing/footwear	14.0	12.5	11.3	11.2	11.1	10.5	10.4
Household durables	7.4	8.1	8.8	8.5	8.4	8.7	8.6
Transport/communications	5.2	5.6	6.0	6.2	6.4	6.6	6.7
Education/entertainment	9.8	10.7	11.4	11.9	12.1	12.6	12.7
Housing	7.6	8.5	9.3	9.4	9.6	10.0	10.1
Services	4.4	4.5	4.6	4.7	4.7	4.8	4.8

Source: Deloitte, "China's Consumer Market: Opportunities and Risks." February 2006.

refrigerators. A large and growing number of Chinese, especially the younger generation, are technologically savvy and have access to the most recent information. These young people are an important target for global companies interested in China. Many are starting to enjoy the convenience of automobile ownership. The growth of the automobile market suffered a temporary setback when the default rate for automobile loans ran as high as 30 percent. Chinese traditionally use cash to purchase automobiles. Automobile financing started just recently. As credit becomes more available, it will make automobiles, a big-ticket item, more affordable.

Home ownership is on the rise, aided by the availability of consumer credit. Until recently, consumer transactions were overwhelmingly on a cash basis. Most consumers did not have debt of any kind. This has changed. Since 2001, the markets for mortgages and automobile loans have developed. Main forces contributing to the development of the mortgage market are housing privatization and bank's diversification of loan portfolios. Banks expanded to mortgage lending to improve their asset mix. Estimates suggest that consumer loans accounted for roughly 10 percent of bank loans in 2004 and 90 percent of which was mortgage lending. Default rate in mortgages is low, hovering around 2 percent to 3 percent, which is much lower than that of automobile loans that hit as high as 30 percent.

Housing privatization will contribute to domestic demand. First, the perception of wealth will influence consumer spending. As housing prices rise, homeowners' wealth increases. Greater wealth increases spending. In addition, homeowners spend more on their homes, from paint, furniture, electronics, to appliances. Thus, spending on home-related goods is expected to rise along with housing privatization.

Demographics are among the most important factors foreign firms should consider in planning their China strategies. The inequality in income and living standards corresponds to geographic differences. Major costal cities such as Beijing, Shanghai, Guangzhou, and Shenzhen are very affluent. There are also geographic differences in the way the Chinese people spend their money. People in Shanghai, for example, spend more on housing, food, services, and communication than those who live in Beijing or Guangzhou. China is also a diverse nation, with many languages and lifestyles. Foreign firms should take into account those differences in product offerings and in managing local employees.

The one-child policy has slowed population growth. The U.S. Census Bureau has projected China's population to increase from current 1.3 billion to 1.45 billion by 2025. As Table 3.3 shows, the under 20 population will drop by 12 percent over the next 20 years. The number of young adults (20 to 34) will decline by 13 percent. On the other hand, adults in the age group of 34 to 59 will increase by 20 percent. It is interesting to note that males consistently outnumbered females in every age group up to the age of 69 in 2005. Starting at age 70, the population mix reversed. This suggests females enjoy a higher life expectancy. In 2025, the male population is expected to be still more than the female population up to the age of 59 and then the mix reverses starting at age 60.

TABLE 3.3   Midyear Population by Age and Gender: 2005 and 2025 (Million)

Age	2005			2025		
	Total	Male	Female	Total	Male	Female
	1,306,314	672,717	633,597	1,453,124	738,940	714,184
0–4	82,175	43,792	38,383	81,227	41,757	39,470
5–9	93,898	50,053	43,845	90,685	46,840	43,845
10–14	103,108	54,290	48,818	95,581	49,853	45,728
15–19	124,613	64,833	59,780	87,453	46,029	41,424
20–24	101,864	52,482	49,381	80,393	42,655	37,738
25–29	94,483	48,416	46,067	91,395	48,367	43,028
30–34	117,304	60,098	57,206	99,836	52,090	47,746
35–39	123,620	63,438	60,182	120,687	62,219	58,468
40–44	101,383	51,811	49,572	98,338	50,176	48,162
45–49	80,750	41,774	38,976	90,924	46,145	44,779
50–54	81,948	41,867	40,081	11,734	56,612	55,121
55–59	58,791	30,304	28,487	115,132	58,151	56,981
60–64	43,092	22,158	20,933	90,917	45,302	45,615
65–69	36,773	18,678	18,095	67,167	33,296	33,871
70–74	29,141	14,264	14,877	61,284	29,213	32,071
75–79	18,540	8,579	9,961	36,357	16,769	19,588
80–84	9,742	4,089	5,653	19,231	8,289	10,942
85–89	3,833	1,413	2,420	9,948	3,790	6,158
90–94	1,062	331	731	3,823	1,174	2,649
95–99	178	43	136	884	196	688
100+	17	3	14	128	17	111

Source: U.S. Census Bureau, International Database, 2005.

Opportunities for Foreign Firms

Foreign companies such as Unilever, Procter & Gamble, Colgate, Gillette, Metro (of Germany), Tesco (United Kingdom), and Carrefour (France) have entered the market. They initially faced little domestic competition and were able to sell and even report profits. Times have changed. Chinese companies have spent massively on manufacturing equipment and are now making everything from shampoos to batteries. Domestic firms have slashed prices and claimed sizable market shares. With many consumers who base their purchases on price alone (especially those in the countryside or second-tier cities), those Chinese companies are certainly a threat. The top retailers are mostly Chinese names such as the Bailian Group, Beijing Gome Electrical Home Appliance, Dalian Dashang Group, Suning Electrical Goods Chain Store Group, and Beijing Hualian Group. Carrefour was the only foreign firm to be listed in the top 5 in 2003 and 2004 (see Table 3.4). Carrefour dropped to the number 9 spot in 2005. But, Wal-Mart is expanding fast in China. Thus, foreign retailers are capturing a small but growing share of China's retail market.

Foreign retailers held 2.6 percent of the market in 2004, up from 2.3 percent in 2002. More than 30 major foreign retailers operate in China, including Wal-Mart

TABLE 3.4   Top 20 Retail Companies in 2004

	Name
1	Bailian Group
2	Beijing Gome Electrical Home Appliance
3	Dailian Dashang Group
4	Suning Electrical Goods Chain Store Group
5	Carrefour
6	Beijing Hualian Group
7	Suguo Supermarket
8	Nong Gong Shang Supermarkets
9	Beijing Wumart
10	Sanlian Commercial Company
11	Shanghai Yongle Electrical
12	Chongqing General Trading Group
13	Hao You Duo Guan Li Zhi
14	Parkson Investment
15	China Resources Vanguard
16	Five Star Appliance
17	A.Best Supermarket
18	Wuhan Wushang Group
19	Jiangsu Wenfeng Great World Chain Development
20	Wal-Mart

Source: "Steady Growth Seen in China's Retail Industry Forerunners for Full Year 2004," press release, Ministry of Commerce, February 6, 2006.

and Carrefour. These retailers had a combined sales volume of 138.3 billion Yuan, or $16.7 billion, an increase of 48 percent from 2002. In December 2004, China eased restrictions to allow overseas retailers to own 100 percent of operations set up in the country, and also removed restrictions as to where operations could be based. In addition, the government cut the minimum registered capital to 300,000 Yuan, or $36,000, from 10 million Yuan. Top foreign retailers such as Wal-Mart and Carrefour plan to accelerate store openings in China to further strengthen their presence in the rapidly growing market.[5] Wal-Mart opened new stores throughout the country and acquired Trust Mart for $1 billion in 2006. Carrefour planned to add 20 stores and recruit 10,000 employees in 2006.[6] European leading decoration and construction material retailer B&Q will open more than 100 chain stores in China by the end of 2010.[7] Other examples of expansion by foreign firms include 7-Eleven, McDonald's, Hooters, and Starbucks, just to name a few.

MEDICINE AND PHARMACEUTICAL

China represents a fifth of the world population. It is a significant untapped opportunity. Multinational pharmaceutical companies cannot afford to ignore the real opportunities in China's fast-growing market. It is expected that China will be the fifth largest pharmaceutical market in the world. Many global pharmaceutical companies have regarded China as a priority and have already entered into China. Table 3.5 lists the top 100 pharmaceutical companies in China.

WTO Commitments

China's WTO commitments include the tightening of rules on intellectual property, tariff concessions, and market access of non-Chinese service suppliers engaging in the distribution of pharmaceuticals. All such moves will create additional business opportunities for non-Chinese pharmaceutical companies in China and, in turn, place an intense pressure on the Chinese pharmaceutical industry. From a long-term point of view, China's accession to the WTO will help improve industry performance and international competitiveness. From a short-term viewpoint, the accession has directly influenced the following three aspects: a decline in tariffs, protection of intellectual properties, and the opening-up of wholesale and retail medical services.

Foreign Investment in Medicine

In accordance with the China's regulatory measures, foreign investors are encouraged to invest in the following fields of medicine:

- Production of patent medicines or medicines protected by the government and those in need of importation, vitamins, amino acid production, production of fever-allaying, analgesic medicines, production of new anticancer and cardiovascular medicines, production of new and economic contraceptives;
- Production of new medicines by using bioengineering techniques, anti-HIV vaccines and contraceptive vaccines, exploitation and production of sea medicine, production of diagnosis agents of AIDS and radiating immune system diseases, pharmaceutics (production of new agents and products involving new techniques, such as timed release, control release, target, and skin penetration), exploitation and application of new medicinal auxiliaries;
- Processing and production of Chinese medicines, their extracts and medicaments of Chinese origin, production of biomedical materials and products, production of antibiotic material medicines for animals, exploitation and production of new products and agents of veterinary antibiotics, and pesticides.

Foreign investment is restricted in the following fields of medicine: production of nalectin, penicillin G, and so on; production of analginum, paracetamol, vitamins B1 and B2, vitamins C and E; production of state-planned vaccinum, vaccine, immunotoxin, toxoid, production of addicted anaesthetic and psychiatric drugs; production of blood products, production of disposable hypodemic syringes, the transfusion system, blood transfusion devices, and blood containers.

Foreign investment is prohibited in the following fields of medicine: processing traditional Chinese medicine from the list of state-protected resources, application of

TABLE 3.5 Top 100 Pharmaceutical Companies in China in 2004

Rank	Company	Sales (RMB Million)
1	Jiangsu Yangtze River Pharmacy Group Co.	8,055.64
2	North China Pharmaceutical Group Ltd.	7,630.79
3	Harbin Pharmaceutical Group Co., Ltd.	7,396.69
4	Shijiazhuang Pharmaceutical Group	6,220.31
5	Tianjin Pharmaceutical Group Co., Ltd.	4,113.89
6	Shandong Xinhua Pharmaceutical Group Co., Ltd.	3,394.10
7	Xi'an Janssen Pharmaceutical Ltd.	3,057.99
8	Shenghua Group Holdings Co.	3,027.97
9	Shandong Xiwang Group Co.	2,769.20
10	Tianjin Zhongxin Pharmaceutical Co., Ltd.	2,685.76
11	Jiangxi Huiren Group Co., Ltd.	2,542.66
12	Shandong Lukang Pharmaceutical Co., Ltd.	2,329.02
13	Shanghai Leiyunshang Pharmaceutical Co., Ltd.	2,162.71
14	Jilin Xiuzheng Pharmaceutical Group Co., Ltd.	2,106.00
15	Zhejiang Hisun Group Ltd.	2,008.08
16	North East General Pharmaceutical Factory	1,958.78
17	GE Hangwei Medical Systems Co., Ltd.	1,931.85
18	Nanjing Medicines Group Co., Ltd.	1,551.60
19	Hangzhou EastChina Medicine Group Co., Ltd.	1,496.15
20	Shenzhen Wanji Pharmaceutical Co., Ltd.	1,490.54
21	Hebei Gaoying Enterprise Group Co., Ltd.	1,454.82
22	Lijun Group Co., Ltd.	1,414.22
23	Beijing Tongrentang Co., Ltd.	1,275.51
24	AstraZeneca Pharmaceutical Co., Ltd.	1,272.74
25	Jiangsu Hengrui Pharmaceutical Co., Ltd.	1,222.75
26	Roche Shanghai Pharmaceutical Co., Ltd.	1,212.25
27	Zhejiang Pharmaceutical Co., Ltd. Xinchang Factory	1,181.51
28	Sino-American Shanghai Squibb Pharmaceutical Co., Ltd.	1,154.95
29	Zhejiang Xinhecheng Co., Ltd.	1,137.08
30	Tianjin SmithKline & French Laboratories Ltd.	1,128.73
31	Chengdu Di'ao Group	1,119.01
32	Chitai Qingchunbao Pharmaceutical Co., Ltd.	1,112.74
33	Hunan Jiuzhitang Co., Ltd.	1,070.00
34	OMRON Dalian Co., Ltd.	1,027.26
35	Taiji Group Peiling Pharmaceutical Factory	1,011.59
36	Shandong Dong'e Ejiao Co., Ltd.	1,006.15
37	Lunan Pharmaceutical Co., Ltd.	988.71
38	Beijing Tongrentang Sci-tech Inc. Ltd.	967.50
39	Weihai Weigao Group Co., Ltd.	912.70
40	Yishui Dadi Corn Developing Co., Ltd.	902.20
41	Pfizer (Dalian) Pharmaceutical Co., Ltd.	900.74
42	Hangzhou Minsheng Pharmaceutical Co., Ltd.	885.72
43	Beijing Bayer Healthcare Co., Ltd.	881.64
44	Shanghai Pioneer Pharmaceutical Co., Ltd.	877.06
45	Jilin Aodong Pharmaceutical Group Ltd.	876.82

(continued)

TABLE 3.5 (Continued)

Rank	Company	Sales (RMB Million)
46	Jiangsu Hongbao Group Co., Ltd.	845.78
47	GSK(Suzhou) Ltd.	831.20
48	Novo Nordisk (Tianjin) Biotechnical Co., Ltd.	827.20
49	Qilu Pharmaceutical Factory	814.79
50	Qingdao Guofeng Pharmaceutical Co., Ltd.	808.04
51	Jiangxi Jimin Kexin Group Ltd.	796.75
52	Hebei Xingtai Shahe Hengli Group Co.	795.95
53	Xinxiang Liuzhuang Agriculture Industry & Commerce General Company	781.50
54	Shandong Zibo Shanchuan Medical Instrument Co., Ltd.	780.60
55	Fujian Fukang Pharmaceutical Co., Ltd.	780.00
56	Beijing Novartis Pharmaceutical Co., Ltd.	755.02
57	Zhejiang Zhongbei Jiuzhou Group Co.	736.46
58	Zhejiang Xianju Pharmaceutical Co., Ltd.	731.98
59	Shijiazhuang Shenwei Pharmaceutical Co., Ltd.	703.00
60	Shandong Shansong Biotechnology Group Co., Ltd.	700.09
61	Roche (Shanghai) Vitamins Co., Ltd.	691.83
62	Zhuhai United Labs. Ltd.	672.73
63	Guilin Sanjin Pharmaceutical Group Co.	672.47
64	Novozymes (China) Biotechnology Ltd.	670.97
65	Jiangsu Jiangshan Pharmaceutical Co., Ltd.	650.50
66	Rexton (Suzhou) Hearing Systems Co., Ltd.	640.56
67	Shandong Luye Pharmaceutical Co., Ltd.	638.35
68	Zhejiang Conba Group Co., Ltd.	633.18
69	Xi'an Green-Valley Pharmaceutical Co., Ltd.	629.94
70	Henan Wanxi Pharmaceutical Co., Ltd.	628.29
71	Shanghai New Asiatic Pharmaceuticals Company	621.11
72	Shandong Ruiyang Pharmaceutical Co., Ltd.	607.36
73	Jiangsu Jichuan Pharmaceutical Co., Ltd.	603.35
74	Wuxi Sino-Swed Pharmaceutical Co., Ltd.	602.34
75	Wuhan Spring Biotechnology Co., Ltd.	598.07
76	Shandong Yuwang Industrial Co., Ltd.	596.26
77	Lianyungang Kangyuan Pharmaceutical Co., Ltd.	596.24
78	Suzhou Dawnrays Pharmaceutical Co., Ltd.	579.98
79	Heze Ruiying Pharmaceutical Group	577.57
80	Zhejiang Jingxin Pharmaceutical Co., Ltd.	576.59
81	Beijing Double-Crane Pharmaceutical Co., Ltd.	572.48
82	Guizhou Yibai Pharmaceutical Co., Ltd.	570.47
83	Henan Topfond Pharmaceutical Co., Ltd.	566.98
84	Wuhan Jianmin Pharmaceutical Co., Ltd.	553.43
85	Zibo Jincheng Industry Stock Co., Ltd.	551.60
86	Guangdong Kangmei Pharmaceutical Co., Ltd.	550.78
87	Wyeth-Whitehall (Suzhou) Ltd.	550.49
88	Shanghai Pharmaceutical Group Sine Pharmaceutical Factory	544.00
89	Jiangsu Chia Tai Tianqing Pharmaceutical Co., Ltd.	541.00
90	Beijing Double-Crane Pharmaceutical Management Co., Ltd.	536.97

(continued)

TABLE 3.5 **(Continued)**

Rank	Company	Sales (RMB Million)
91	Jiangsu Suzhong Pharmaceutical Co., Ltd.	536.19
92	Zhejiang Yadong Pharmaceutical Co., Ltd.	536.06
93	Red Heart K Group Co., Ltd.	531.19
94	Yunnan Baiyao Group Co., Ltd.	530.32
95	Lianyungang Hansoh Pharmaceutical Co., Ltd.	526.10
96	Shanghai Traditional Chinese Medieme Co., Ltd.	524.06
97	Shouguang Fukang Pharmaceutical Co., Ltd.	519.80
98	Guizhou Shenqi Pharmaceutical Co., Ltd.	518.81
99	Shandong C.P.Freda Pharmaceutical Co., Ltd.	514.30
100	Zhaoqing Xinghu Biotechnology Co., Ltd.	511.40

Source: Siracle Pharma Info.

the processing technique of prepared herbal medicine in small amounts ready for decoction, and the production of half-processed medicine using a secret recipe.

At present, 20 of the 25 biggest multinational pharmaceutical corporations have set up manufacturing enterprises of sole investment or JVs, and more than 1,800 other JVs have been established. The sales of the foreign-invested enterprises has accounted for 25 percent of total annual sales in the medicine industry. The medicine produced has accounted for 60 percent to 65 percent of annual sales in big city hospitals. Foreign investment has played an important role in China's medicine market.

Economic development and huge market potential are the factors attracting multinational corporations because their performance in the Chinese market has become a key factor for their development in the future. International corporation groups, such as Johnson and Johnson, Bristol Myers Squibb, Pfizer, and Novartis are expanding their businesses in China steadily, and the move to increase input by some transnational corporations needs special attention. For example, AstraZeneca, one of the leading corporations of the global medicine industry, has set up a $100 million production base in Wuxi, Jiangsu Province. The base has a large producing capability and can offer a complete list of pharmaceutical types, including troches, capsules, oral liquid, aerosol, and asepsis products. Their products include Losec, which is in the global medicine sale list, and Betaloc and Bricanyl. SmithKline invested $92 million in their Tianjin factory before the merger and the factory in Suzhou tallied an investment of $136 million by the former Glaxo. GlaxoSmithKline has also worked with Chinese scientific and research groups on several occasions. For example, at the beginning of the 1990s, it cooperated with a Chinese pharmaceutical research institute in the filtration and development process of an approximate 10,000 herbal medicines.

Entry by Foreign Firms

Pharmaceutical companies entered China for the same reason as other foreign businesses, to sell their products to as many as the 1.3 billion people. Bristol Myers

Squibb, Jansen, and SmithKline were among the first to enter in the 1980s. China today is already one of the world's top markets and the potential for long-term growth is great. The WTO opened up the market and rising income levels will increase demand.

The market is difficult to penetrate. The majority of the population cannot afford to buy expensive medicine. Preferences play a big part, too. Among those who can afford it, many prefer traditional Chinese medicine. In general, most seem to prefer Chinese medicine for long-term care and Western drugs for short-term treatments. This is deeply rooted because many believe that Chinese medicine is compatible with the human body and internal functions and that Western drugs are fine for a quick cure but damage human body internal systems in the long run. This cultural bias is changing, but it will take years to change the culture.

Another important change in the business environment is the ongoing improvement in the protection of intellectual property rights (IPR), especially patent recognition for drug companies. This is improving, but still inadequate. In the past, pharmaceutical companies marketed drugs that were going off patent in China because of the concern over lack of protection in IPR. In recent years, this has begun to change. Pfizer, Novartis, and other large firms now offer their new drugs in China. They now include China in their global launch of new products. For foreign firms, however, it is important to know that there is little point launching a drug in China if it does not get on the provincial and national reimbursement list or there is little chance of sales in the private market.

To expand business, foreign drug makers need to look beyond Shanghai, Beijing, and Guangzhou to include other first-tier and second-tier cities. In addition, creating demand is another way to boost sales. For example, Pfizer's Lipitor, a drug to lower cholesterol, came to the market late, behind Zocor and Pravachol. But, Pfizer reshaped the market by changing the approach to the clinical management of heart disease making Lipitor the best-selling drug. Another area for market reshaping is to create demand by spending resources to investigate strategies for changing the opinions about Western medicines versus Chinese medicines and building brand awareness.

TELECOMMUNICATIONS

With 1.3 billion citizens, China has the world's largest fixed-line and mobile network in terms of both network capacity and number of subscribers. Only one out of 10 Chinese citizens had a phone just several years ago. Today, more than one out of three have a fixed telephone subscription and more than 1.25 million cellular subscribers sign up in China every week. In a few years, there will be more than 950 million fixed and mobile subscriptions, three times more than the entire population of the United States.

China became the world's largest telecom market in 2002. For a foreign firm to succeed, it is helpful to understand the complex and multifaceted internal mechanisms of the fast-changing and competitive environment. As a result of China's entry to the WTO, a new regulatory regime has been gradually put into place and foreign firms have been gradually allowed to access the market. The former monopolistic market has given way to state-run competition and then to foreign competition.

Current Market Environment

In the first half of 2006, China had 365 million fixed-line subscribers and 426 million mobile customers. Service revenues grow slower than the number of subscribers. Although low average penetration rates clearly allow further growth, rates in Beijing, Shanghai, Canton, or Shenzhen, are already similar to those in Western Europe or North America.

Chinese telecom operators focus their business on voice. Revenues from data only account for 5 percent of the total. New technologies are being deployed to provide differential services. These technologies include Asynchronous Digital Subscriber Line (ADSL), Wireless Local Area Networks (WLAN), Internet Protocol (IP) telephony and services associated with mobile communications such as Short/Multimedia Messaging Service (SMS/MMS), and ring tone download. Lacking the know-how to develop new services, Chinese operators are often cautious in purchasing cutting-edge technologies.

Mobile communication, especially Global System for Mobile (GSM), is the most profitable subsector. Concerning the Third Generation (3G), three technologies are relevant. The American system CDMA2000 (Code Division Multiplex Access) is ahead of game, the European W-CDMA (Wideband CDMA) still needs two years to mature, and the home-grown TD-SCDMA (Time Division Synchronous CDMA) is behind due to equipment problems (principally handsets).

Halfway between mobile and fixed, "Xiaolingtong" is a limited mobile service based on Personal Access System/Personal Handy Phone System (PAS/PHS) technology. Xiaolingtong acts as the wireless extension for the wired telephone system in China, known as wireless local loop. The phone's range is limited to the single metropolitan area. It consists of a wireless local loop that provides access to the fixed-line network. With over 80 million users, Xiaolingtong competes in big cities head to head with traditional mobile services since prices are typically just a fraction of mobile services. China Telecom operates a PAS system in China. China Netcom, one of China's two licensed mobile network operators, also provides Xiaolingtong service. The largest vendors of the system are UTStarcom and ZTE.

Telecom Industry's WTO Commitments

China's telecoms industry presents great potentials. The booming industry is likely to maintain strong growth momentum for years to come. The WTO accession helped domestic telecom operators speed up their readjustment in recent years to become more competitive. China's major telecom operators have undergone restructuring to become public companies, including China Mobile, China Unicom, and China Telecom. Fueled by the enormous market potential, many foreign companies such as Vodafone, AT&T, British Telecom, Japan Telecom, and Hong Kong's PCCW and Hutchison Whampoa already are carving out niches in the market. There are several approaches that foreign firms have employed to enter China's telecom industry. These include purchasing shares of major telecom operators, establishing joint ventures with domestic firms, and forming research and development centers with Chinese counterparts. The following section discusses the major items of China's commitments when it joined the WTO.

Basic Telecommunication Services

For paging services, foreign suppliers will be able to establish joint-venture (JV) enterprises without quantitative restrictions and provide services in and between the cities of Shanghai, Guangzhou, and Beijing. Foreign investment in JVs would be limited to 30 percent.

One year after China's accession, areas were expanded to include services in and between the cities of Chengdu, Chongqing, Dalian, Fuzhou, Hangzhou, Nanjing, Ningbo, Qingdao, Shenyang, Shenzhen, Xiamen, Xi'an, Taiyuan, and Wuhan, and foreign investment was not to exceed 49 percent. Two years after China's accession geographic restrictions were removed and foreign investment was raisesd 50 percent.

In mobile services (analog/digital, cellular services, and personal communications services), upon China's accession, foreign firms were permitted to establish JVs without quantitative restrictions and offer services in and between the cities of Shanghai, Guangzhou, and Beijing. Foreign investment in the JVs was not to exceed 25 percent. One year after accession the geographic areas were expanded to include the cities of Chengdu, Chongqing, Dalian, Fuzhou, Hangzhou, Nanjing, Ningbo, Qingdao, Shenyang, Shenzhen, Xiamen, Xi'an, Taiyuan, and Wuhan, and the limit of foreign investment was raised to 35 percent. Three years after the accession, foreign investment was not to exceed 49 percent. Within five years of the accession (by the end of 2006) there were no geographic restrictions.

Within three years of China's accession, foreign service suppliers were able to establish JV enterprises without quantitative restrictions and offer services in and between the cities of Shanghai, Guangzhou, and Beijing in domestic services. The domestic services include voice services, packet-switched data-transmission services, circuit-switched data transmission services, facsimile services, domestic private-leased circuit services and international services, including voice services, packet-switched data-transmission services, circuit-switched data-transmission services, facsimile services and international closed user-group voice and data services. Foreign investment in the JVs was not to exceed 25 percent.

Within five years of accession the areas were expanded to include services in and between the cities of Chengdu, Chongqing, Dalian, Fuzhou, Hangzhou, Nanjing, Ningbo, Qingdao, Shenyang, Shenzhen, Xiamen, Xi'an, Taiyuan, and Wuhan. Foreign investment did not exceed 35 percent. Within six years of accession, there would be no geographic restrictions and foreign investment could rise to 49 percent.

Value-Added Services

Foreign companies are permitted to establish JV value-added telecommunications enterprises without quantitative restrictions and to provide services in the cities of Shanghai, Guangzhou, and Beijing. The service items cover electronic mail, voice mail, online information and database retrieval, electronic data interchange, value-added facsimile services (including store and forward, store and retrieve), code and protocol conversion and online information and/or data processing. Foreign investment in the JVs was capped at 30 percent.

Within one year of China's accession, the areas were expanded to include the cities of Chengdu, Chongqing, Dalian, Fuzhou, Hangzhou, Nanjing, Ningbo, Qingdao, Shenyang, Shenzhen, Xiamen, Xi'an, Taiyuan, and Wuhan. Foreign investment was limited to a maximum of 49 percent. Within two years of China's accession, there would be no geographic restrictions and foreign investment would not exceed 50 percent.

As for the presence of natural persons in the basic and value-added service sector, managers, executives, and specialists defined as senior employees of a corporation of a WTO Member that has established a representative office, branch, or subsidiary in China, will be granted entry for an initial period of three years.

Telecom Operators

Telecom operators in China are exclusively Chinese. China Telecom and China Netcom are two fixed-line operators with nationwide licenses. China Mobile (GSM) and China Unicom (GSM and CDMA) are two large mobile carriers. In addition, there are two minor players as well, China Satcom and China Railcom. The state has control and majority ownership of all of them. Many of them have listed shares overseas.

China Telecom operates mainly in the wealthy Southern provinces (including Shanghai and Canton) in addition to the less prosperous West. It runs domestic and international fixed-line networks and provides fixed-line voice, data, video, multimedia, and information services. It compensates the lack of a mobile license by deploying PAS/PHS very successfully. A second focal point is broadband based on Ethernet and ADSL. China Telecom is listed on the Hong Kong and New York stock exchanges.

China Netcom operates mostly in the Northern provinces but has a strategy to enter China Telecom's southern provinces. China Netcom is catching up quickly to compete against China Telecom because of its strength in broadband, WLAN, IP telephony, and PAS/PHS.

China Mobile not only operates basic GSM services but also value-added services such as GPRS (General Packet Radio Service) data transfer, IP telephony, and multimedia. It ranks the first in the world in terms of network scale and customer base. It is listed on the Hong Kong and New York stock exchanges.

China Unicom is the only licensed full telecom service provider in China. Its services include fixed-line, mobile, IP telephony, data and internet. Furthermore, China

Unicom is the third largest mobile operator in the world and the only one in China operating a CDMA network. It is concentrating its efforts on CDMA and little investment is expected in GSM. It is listed on the Hong Kong, New York, and Shanghai stock exchanges.

China Satcom is licensed to engage in all kinds of satellite-related services such as transponder lease, domestic television broadcasting, public Very Small Antenna Aperture (VSAT) communications, video conference, data broadcasting, IP telephony and satellite based high-speed Internet access.

China Railcom grows at a slow pace due to its lack of expertise in daily business operation in addition to the lack of funds to upgrade its existing private network so as to provide services to the general public.

The leading international suppliers of network equipment are Alcatel, Cisco, Lucent, Nortel, and Siemens. In addition, major international suppliers of portable phone sets, including Ericsson, Motorola, Nokia, Samsung, and Siemens are all well known in China.

A large number of Chinese companies have developed under the government's protection and compete now with foreign corporations not only in the Chinese market but also in third countries. Datang is the main TD-SCDMA manufacturer, UT-Starcom, the main PAS/PHS manufacturer, Huawei leads the SMS market, and Great Wall stands out in the broadband sector.

Other Chinese equipment suppliers include Shanghai Bell and Zhongxing Telecommunications Equipment (ZTE). Furthermore, Amoi, Konka, Ningbo Bird, and Keijan are among the most recognized names in Chinese mobile phone manufacturers.

Foreign Entry

Prior to its WTO accession, China's policy protected its telecom industry because it was and is a national priority sector. Only foreign equipment vendors were allowed to invest in China. Authorization for the investments was conditioned on technology transfer. International telecom carriers were banned from accessing the market.

The Chinese government has been gradually opening the carriers market to foreign companies. There have been some geographical limits to this opening but they are being relaxed. In 2005, foreign investors were allowed to form joint ventures, investing up to 50 percent in Internet services in the whole country, up to 49 percent in the mobile sector in 17 major Chinese cities, and up to 25 percent in fixed-line basic services in Beijing, Shanghai, and Canton (Guangzhou Province). For a foreign company wanting access to the Chinese market, finding a Chinese partner to form a joint venture is extremely important.

Foreign investments come from the United States, Canada, Sweden, Finland, Germany, France, Japan, and South Korea. Many companies from these countries already have one or more joint ventures.

FINANCIAL SERVICES

Foreign financial institutions are subject to tighter restrictions than companies in other sectors. Foreign firms also face domestic competitors that have huge branch networks and very aggressive pricing strategies. Chapter 2 described how China's accession to the WTO opened the financial services market to foreign competition. Many international large financial institutions have established operations and acquired strategic stakes to leverage their capital and expertise. For many, China's market today is relative small compared to their home market. But, most of them see China will emerge as one of their biggest global markets within 10 years.

Entry Strategies

Large international financial institutions such as HSBC, Citigroup, and AIG are taking every advantage and opportunity to increase their visibility and operations in China. They are aggressively rolling out branches. They are offering new products as fast as regulations allow, such as credit cards and consumer and RMB loans to domestic clients. In addition, as presented in Chapter 2, those global powerhouses have been taking stakes in domestic financial institutions. Under China's banking regulations, foreign banks are not allowed to own more than 20 percent of a Chinese lender, or have a combined 25 percent stake. Citigroup, led by its influential rainmaker Bob Rubin, has obtained permission and successfully acquired a majority stake and taken control of the Guangdong Development Bank.[8]

Other continental European institutions are taking a low-profile and more diversified approach. Allianz, for example, has its wholly owned Dresdner bank, a general insurance operation in Guangzhou, and a joint-venture life insurance company Dazhong Insurance. Fortis has a banking presence, a joint-venture fund management business, and a 24.9 percent stake in Taiping Life. ABN Amro has taken a similar strategy.

The specialist approach is the third route foreign financial services firms take to enter China. Franklin Templeton was the first to establish a fund management joint venture in China. Chubb and Royal Sun Alliance (U.K. insurer) have wholly owned general insurance ventures in Shanghai. Bermuda-based insurance firm ACE has one exposure, the stake in and alliance with Huatai insurance.

Competitive Advantages of Foreign Firms

Local players have huge distribution networks and low pricing. The big four state-owned banks have about 100,000 branches. Local banks have a lower cost structure as well. However, those local competitors have accumulated large numbers of nonperforming loans. Thus, their balance sheets are not as strong as those of foreign financial services firms. The competitive advantages of foreign firms also include management expertise and product development. Shortage of management personnel is a serious challenge to the domestic institutions and Wall Street still retains an edge in financial engineering. On top of all those, Chinese clients generally associate foreign firms with better service quality than their local counterparts.

MANY CHALLENGES

Doing business in China is not easy. Failure to take into account business risks, market differences from the West, and local competition, are among the biggest mistakes global consumer market companies continue to make when looking to expand or start-up in China. The reality is that the Chinese consumer is very price sensitive. Multinational companies who want to successfully compete in this market need to do their due diligence prior to going in because entering the Chinese market is no simple feat. Businesses entering the Chinese market need to be aware of the ferocity of the domestic competition. In addition to domestic competition, some of the important challenges are corruption, business culture, intellectual property rights, and recruiting for talent.

Corruption

Corruption is a widespread problem affecting all levels of Chinese society. For the average Chinese, corruption has become an element of daily life. It is common, or even expected, that the family of a sick person gives a "red envelope" filled with cash to doctors and nurses before an operation. Even though the government has announced it is determined to fight against corruption, many are not convinced because some of the high-ranking officials are part of the problem.

It is naive to believe corruption is a result of economic reform or the wealth created through the reforms. Corruption is present in all political systems and all places. The key question is how serious it is. In the past, small gifts and goods difficult to find in China served as the means to ease administrative difficulties in issuing documents, entering school, and other daily situations. Today the habit has changed because economic development has created social gaps and new economic ties in society. A part of the population, thanks to overseas families and successful business ventures, has become rich. Many utilize their new-found wealth to bribe officials. Since the state system still operates under a communist bureaucracy, in which a complicated administration process requires numerous permits and authorization forms that take a long time to obtain, bribing local administrators greases the wheels. A "red envelope" has become the euphemism for a bribe because money is always offered in a red envelope, a tradition carried out during the Chinese New Year. Today it is part of the business culture, both for national and foreign companies and it is considered unavoidable when operating in China.

Corruption at high levels is a threat to the authorities. The case of Beijing Party Chief Chen Xitong proved the Communist Party itself can be shaken by corruption and its image seriously affected.[9] Chen Xitong was ousted in 1995 and jailed for corruption, the most senior Chinese official removed over graft since the Communists came to power. For most Chinese, the main criticism they have of their government is of general corruption and privileges granted according to rank. A more specific and detailed coverage of corruption is provided in the next chapter.

Cultural Differences

There are many subtle differences between Chinese and Western practices. This example illustrates that even people who speak the same language often misunderstand each other:[10]

> A man walking down the street noticed a sign in the window of a restaurant that said, SPECIAL TODAY—RABBIT STEW. He said to himself, "That's a favorite of mine," and went to order the stew. After he had taken three or four bites, which did not taste right, he asked the waiter to call over the proprietor. "By any chance is there any horsemeat in this rabbit stew?" the customer asked. "Well, now that you ask, there is some," replied the owner. "What is the proportion?" asked the man. "Fifty-fifty," came the reply. Now most people would have felt that no further questioning was needed, that there was a clear understanding. But this man pursued the issue. "What do you mean by fifty-fifty?" he asked, and the proprietor replied, "One horse to one rabbit."

The complexity is many times more than that illustrated by this example. Many talk about the cultural differences in terms of Confucianism. That probably was correct years ago before the Communist Party took over China. The Cultural Revolution destroyed most of Confucius' teaching. With this said, there are key differences between Chinese and Western cultures. Several obvious and important ones are described here. The first obvious distinction is the convention of addressing and titles. In Western societies, you greet a gentleman named "Hu Dachung" as Mr. Dachung, taking for granted that the rules that apply to Americans and Europeans also apply to the Chinese. The opposite, however, is the case. In the West, the first-mentioned name is the first name and the second-mentioned stands for the last name or family name. In Chinese, the first-mentioned is the family name and the second is the first name. Thus, it is Mr. Hu, not Mr. Dachung. There is another subtle difference. In the West, it is the title followed by the last name, for example, Mr. Hu. In Chinese, it is the last name followed by the title, that is Hu xian sheng (xian sheng means Mr. in Chinese).

The increased Western influence over the past years has softened these rules. Many Chinese rearrange their names to make it easier for foreigners. But, confusion often occurs because some people have rearranged their names while others have not. Therefore, it is helpful to get oriented to Chinese rules. It is important to know that most Chinese last names are monosyllabic such as Lin, Li, Wang, Chen, Hu, and Jiang. It is also helpful to know that more and more young Chinese have monosyllabic first names such as Xia, Quin, or Wei. It is not easy to tell which is the family name and which is the first name if you are not fluent in Chinese. Most Chinese understand the common last names.

In China, gift giving is an art. Official policy forbids giving gifts because they are considered bribery. But gifts are an essential element to start a relationship and to keep it going. Presents are presented at many social opportunities. Most people go to a birthday party or visit someone in the hospital with a present. Relatives and good friends receive gifts during the major holidays and festivals. These presents have been influenced by fashion trends and people have started to give Western gifts. Traditionally, Chinese celebrate birthdays from 40 onward, and often only round number birthdays such as 50, 60, 70, or 80. It is also common to give cash, placed in a red envelope, at the New Year or a wedding. A gift must not only fit the occasion, but also fit the position of the recipient. To Westerners, it sometimes seems strange to observe the art of gift giving in China. The recipients initially almost always reject the present in the beginning. But it would be impolite to withdraw the present. It is expected that the gift giver remains firm, insisting that the present be accepted. After a period of hesitation and repeated insistence on the part of the guest, the host will finally accept the present but continues to state that it was not necessary. The host then puts the gift away unopened. The Chinese typically do not practice spontaneous unwrapping, except in the eastern coastal area where Western influence is quite strong. Another aspect crucial in gift giving is to avoid clocks, shoes, green porcelain, or four of anything. The reason is that the word clock in Chinese sounds like death (end), shoes are considered impure, green porcelain gives a hint of adultery, and the word four also means death in Chinese.

Bureaucracy is a fact of life everywhere, especially in China. Conducting business there is a challenge. Not only is dealing with various levels of hierarchy necessary, but there is also a strong need for technology transfer and managerial knowledge. Another aspect is the vast cultural divide, requiring a different form of communication. It is not practical to expect international standards of conducting business in China, but with increasing globalization, certain international practices are accepted. The Chinese system is based on strict hierarchies, an almighty bureaucracy, and a well-established nepotism. Appropriate gifts and right connections are certainly helpful in greasing the wheels and getting business done. This aspect of connections (or guanxi in Chinese) is covered in the next chapter.

Intellectual Property Rights

Since joining WTO, China has strengthened its legal framework and amended its IPR and related laws and regulations to comply with the WTO Agreement on Traded-Related Aspect of Intellectual Property Rights (TRIPs). Despite stronger statutory protection, China continues to be a haven for counterfeiters and pirates. Though we have observed commitment on the part of many PRC government officials to tackle the problem, enforcement measures taken to date have not been sufficient to deter massive IPR infringements. Several factors undermine enforcement measures. From a cultural standpoint, counterfeiting is seen as a legitimate way to make a living. Furthermore, many Chinese do not feel it is Beijing's responsibility to protect multinational companies from IPR violations. Some have indicated that multinational companies have enjoyed a host of tax benefits and manufacturing cost advantages already. It is the company's responsibility to protect its own intellectual property.

Geography plays a role in the prevalence of counterfeiting as well. Beijing faces obstacles in trying to control local administrators across the country and enforce IPR. Local protectionism represents an obstacle for anticounterfeiting efforts. Local officials and law enforcement agencies hoping to maintain order, increase employment and income in their jurisdiction area sometimes encourage or even participate in the illegal business. Some bureaucrats offer protection to counterfeiters in exchange for bribes.

Moreover, the counterfeiting business employs a significant number of people and generates much needed income in villages where counterfeiting plants are located. Cracking down on counterfeiting would mean firing workers and closing factories. That would cut off a valuable stream of income and disrupt the social order. As the dependence on small businesses in private sectors grows to generate jobs and income, government officials are more likely to turn a blind eye to those illegal activities.

Lost sales, damaged brand equity, and the proliferation of fake goods are major issues that companies face in China. In an effort to protect themselves, multinational companies have adopted a number of strategies. Some of them include differentiating products, packaging, educating stakeholders, advertising, conducting investigation, and surveillance. Some have taken offenders to court with limited success. Legislation and legal enforcement are key to protect IPR. But, this will take time and effort. A brief summary of China's patent, trademark, and copyright laws follows.

China's first patent law was enacted in 1984 and has been amended to extend the scope of protection. To comply with TRIPs, the latest amendment extended the duration of patent protection to 20 years from the date of filing a patent application. Chemical and pharmaceutical products, as well as food, beverages, and flavorings are all now patentable. China follows a first-to-file system for patents, which means patents are granted to those that file first even if the filers are not the original inventors. This system is unlike the United States, which recognizes the first-to-invent rule, but is consistent with the practice in other parts of the world, including the European Union.

China's trademark law was first adopted in 1982 and subsequently revised in 1993 and 2001. The new trademark law went into effect in October 2001, with implementing regulations taking effect on September 15, 2002. The new trademark law extended registration to collective marks, certification marks, and three-dimensional symbols, as required by TRIPs. China has a first-to register system that requires no evidence of prior use or ownership, leaving registration of popular foreign marks open to a third party. Foreign companies seeking to distribute their products in China are advised to register their marks and/or logos with the Trademark Office.

China's copyright law was established in 1990 and amended in October 2001. The new implementing rules went into force on September 15, 2002. Unlike the patent and trademark protection, copyrighted works do not require registration for protection. Protection is granted to individuals from countries belonging to the copyright international conventions or bilateral agreements of which China is a member. However, copyright owners may wish to voluntarily register with China's National Copyright Administration (NCA) to establish evidence of ownership should enforcement actions become necessary.

Recruiting for Talent

It is estimated that in about 10 years, China will need approximately 75,000 executive level managers who are competent in both Chinese and global settings. English skills and the ability to work with foreign clients are in such shortage among the locals, many Chinese executives are getting higher and higher salaries. But, higher compensation does not retain talent, as they use it as a revolving door to get better offers. Management programs such as MBAs and EMBAs are booming in China to produce managers as fast as they can. There is a strong push by Chinese state-owned companies to hire consulting firms or work with multinational firms to start training employees. Multinationals are getting serious about hiring smart local Chinese who are not fluent in English skills and training them. There is now a trend in importing management talent from India and the Philippines.

CONCLUSION

This chapter reviewed several of the key sectors in China that present opportunities to multinational corporations. It discussed the market potentials and the approaches that foreign firms have taken to enter the Chinese markets. The chapter also outlined some of the challenges that foreign firms face in doing business in China. The next chapter continues to explore business culture, risks, and corruption in China.

4

Navigating China's Business Culture, Political Risks, and Corruption

China is undergoing a political and economic transition. The business culture is different from Western practice and many believe corruption is part of business and plays a significant role in the current political and economic environment. Over the past few years, corruption cases involving Chinese government officials have been numerous. These waste valuable resources and in general have a negative effect on the welfare of the country. The Beijing government has introduced a "sunshine policy," putting all major activities of government officials under the scrutiny of the public to curb corruption and build a clean government.

BUSINESS CULTURE

The Chinese people do not speak one language. There are many different dialects from region to region. For example, someone from Beijing cannot understand residents of Guangdong or Hong Kong without learning Cantonese. Other regional languages and subcultures are also quite distinct. The Chinese attach great importance to cultivating and maintaining personal relationships, called guanxi, and are highly sensitive to maintaining face in everything they do.

Chinese business culture is different from Western business culture. In China, for example, it is a good practice to start a meeting with casual talk before moving on to business matters. During the meeting, it is customary to address your Chinese colleagues with the title that signifies their status, such as "Chairman Chen" or "President Chen" with the surname following the title. Smoking is part of the culture in China, be prepared to find few, if any, smoke-free environments.

Business card presentation is an essential part of business. It is customary to have one side of the business card in Chinese. Most Chinese people have their business cards engraved in gold. In China, this is a symbol of your status and prestige. When accepting a business card from your Chinese counterpart, show your interest by glancing at the details of the card before you put the card away. When presenting your position at a meeting, speak slowly with short pauses between sentences. It is an accepted custom to have pauses in a speech. Do not expect an immediate reaction from your Chinese colleagues. Patience is an essential element to a successful meeting. The subject of Taiwan is very sensitive. People in the People's Republic of China (PRC or mainland China) prefer to use the name Taiwan, so do not use the Republic of China (ROC). Beijing has insisted that Taiwan is part of the PRC, while Taiwan's government has long claimed that PRC and ROC are two separate countries.

Expensive gifts are interpreted as bribery. If, nevertheless, you want to give an expensive gift, it is better to present it in private. Inexpensive gifts are common. In this case, it is advisable to present your gift after, and not before, concluding your business. When presenting your gift, you should indicate that the gift is from the company and present it to the head of the group first. Great care should be taken in regard to the color of the gift wrapping. Chinese culture is very sensitive to colors. Red is the preferred color because this symbolizes luck. Gold is popular because it symbolizes fortune. It is helpful to ask the hotel staff, or the assistants in the store, to wrap the gifts that you want to distribute. It is recommended that you prepare a sufficient number of gifts in advance of your arrival in China.

There are several important holiday periods in China during which Chinese enjoy a weeklong holiday. Such holidays include labor-day week (May 1), the National Day (October 1), and the Spring Festival (Chinese New Year; the first day of the first lunar month). Table 4.1 lists Chinese holidays. Do not arrange business meetings around the times of these Chinese holidays. Similarly, it is important to remember that late arrival to a meeting is impolite to your host. It is recommended to bring a translator to the meeting who can translate for you and assist in explaining business customs according to Chinese formalities.

Chinese businesspeople from different regions have distinct characteristics. The following section describes the different styles of businesspeople from several areas of China.[1]

Beijing

Beijing is China's political capital. Beijing businesspeople treat seriously and with great respect someone whose business card displays the title chairperson or president, especially of a big corporation. Big companies, large business groups, and well-known brands tend to have an easier time here. On the other hand, Beijing's preoccupation with politics has resulted in a weaker market consciousness and slower reaction to market changes. Thus, Beijing business behavior often changes with government policy shifts, responding less to the market trend. Also related to Beijing's love of politics is the habit of talking about a wide variety of unrelated topics at the same time. Given these characteristics, foreigners conducting business in the PRC capital should be prepared to play "political cards" by cultivating connections with leading politicians.

TABLE 4.1 Holidays in the People's Republic of China

Date	English Name	Remarks
January 1	New Year	
May 1	Labor Day	
May 4	Youth Day	Commemorating the May Fourth Movement
July 1	CPC Founding Day	Formation of 1st National Congress on July 1, 1921
July 11	Maritime Day	The anniversary of Zheng He's first voyage
August 1	Army Day	Nanchang Uprising on August 1, 1927
October 1	National Day	Founding of PRC on October 1, 1949
1st day of 1st lunar month	Spring Festival (Chinese New Year)	Based on Chinese calendar
15th day of 1st lunar month	Lantern Festival	Based on Chinese calendar
5th Solar Term. Early April	Qing Ming Jie (Tomb Sweeping Day)	Based on Chinese calendar
5th day of 5th lunar month	Dragon Boat Festival	Based on Chinese calendar
7th day of 7th lunar month	Double Seven Festival	The Chinese version of Valentine's Day, based on Chinese calendar
15th day of 7th lunar month	Spirit Festival (Ghost Festival)	Based on Chinese calendar
15th day of 8th lunar month	Mid-Autumn Festival (Moon Festival)	Based on Chinese calendar
9th day of 9th lunar month	Double Ninth Festival	Based on Chinese calendar

Source: Wikipedia: the Free Encyclopedia.

Companies with good political skills and connections are regarded as more desirable business partners in Beijing.

Shanghai

Shanghai is China's economic and financial center. Because of Shanghai's history as an open city with strong foreign influence, it has developed a unique culture that combines West with East. This mix has given Shanghainese certain tendencies and characteristics, often called haipai, or Shanghai style. Their familiarity with Western culture makes them more adaptable to Western ways of business. For instance, many people have indicated that the rule of law is often observed in Shanghai. This is because most residents were from other parts of the country and could not rely on traditional social structures for support. They had to follow common rules to make a living. Thus,

Shanghai businesspeople are more likely to honor contracts. Furthermore, Shanghainese are inclined to maintain good relationships with social contacts over the short term and keep the level of socialization relatively shallow. Shanghainese do not mix emotions with business. Shanghainese tend to accept renqing (personal favor) reluctantly, return the favor quickly, and exchange favors of equal value. Shanghainese also tend to focus on economic interests, value individualism, and emphasize practicality. In Shanghai, business and money seem more important than personal relationships.

Finally, Shanghainese have a reputation for knowing how to obtain and protect personal rights and interests. In business negotiations, Shanghainese are generally professional, discreet, and attentive to details. Therefore, negotiations with Shanghainese over even minor issues can be lengthy.

Guangdong

Guangdong's geography and weather have contributed to the cultural differences that have evolved the Canton Province. Mountainous terrain separated Guangdong into various small, independent units and prevented much exchange with the culture and social systems of central China. Traditional Chinese culture, particularly Confucian ideals and the philosophy of moderation, weakened as they passed through Hunan, Jiangsu, and Zhejiang, and reached Guangdong in a modified form. Distance from mainstream Chinese culture has also led to a greater belief in local superstitious practices, such as face reading, belief in fate, and fengshui (a Chinese practice that configures office or home environments in ways that promote health, happiness, and prosperity).

Guangdong's location between mountains and seas contributed to the open and free cultural tradition of the Cantonese. Well-developed agriculture, along with convenient sea and river transportation, provided excellent conditions for commercial activities. Guangdong businesspeople have long traveled overseas for business.

In business, Cantonese prefer to take advantage of new opportunities, because it is relatively easy to obtain monopolistic profits from new business. In this sense, Cantonese are risk takers. Though many Cantonese make legitimate profits by following good business practices, some are notorious for counterfeiting and smuggling. Numerous underground workshops produce counterfeit branded products of all kinds. Counterfeit and lack of protection of intellectual property rights have been and will continue to be the dark side of business in many parts of China, not just Canton.

Sichuan

Sichuan is located in a basin, southwest of Shanghai, and is thus isolated. It is rich in natural environment. Its geographical isolation has fostered conservative attitudes and relative complacency. The Sichuanese were traditionally not as interested in business and pursuing commercial entrepreneurial efforts, compared with people in other parts of China.

After the opening and reform of China, the Sichuanese began to leave the basin for new opportunities. Some of them have become businesspeople and entrepreneurs. Only a small minority wanted to take the risk of leaving their homeland, however.

Sichuan is home to many of the firms that make up China's military-industrial complex because both the Nationalist and Communist governments considered Sichuan a safe base, far from foreign threats. For many years, Sichuan has been among the top regions in terms of scientific and technological innovation.

Credibility has been the central focus of dealings in this region. Once the Sichuanese have made a promise, they will do all they can to realize it. This emphasis on credibility spills over into business. Thus, borrowing and lending money among the Sichuanese was traditionally done orally, without contracts.

Sichuan has long been a center of Taoism and has been subject to strong Confucian influence. Thus, Sichuanese tend to emphasize harmony and moderation in their daily interactions. They tend to believe in the tenet of forgiveness. Even when they are right, they believe that they should not gloat. The Sichuanese are also known to emphasize practicality and have little vanity. Sichuan native Deng Xiaoping's reform slogan that "A good cat, whether black or white, is one that can catch mice," came from a popular Sichuan saying.

Zhejiang

Zhejiang people use their social skills to their advantage in business. During negotiations, for instance, they tend to say little about themselves, letting their prospective business partners speak first and thus feel more knowledgeable. In handling relationships, Zhejiang people excel in adjusting their tactics to the social status, position, purpose, and perspectives of their counterparts.

There are two prominent groups of Zhejiang businesspeople: those from Ningbo and those from Wenzhou. Ningbo businesspeople have a reputation for leaving home to seek their fortunes. Shanghai was traditionally the main base for Ningbo natives starting businesses in China, while Hong Kong was the main base for overseas Ningbo businesspeople. Like the Shanghainese, Ningbo businesspeople are familiar with both Western and Eastern cultures and thus are considered sincere and generally enjoy a good reputation among their clients.

Coastal Wenzhou is surrounded by mountains and open seas. Since ancient times, Wenzhounese have been successful in running businesses. They are well known for not fearing rejection and for selling their products throughout the country with smiling faces, endless persuasion, and worn-out shoes. Wenzhou businesspeople have spread out all over China and the world during the reform period. For example, they are extremely successful in the metropolitan New York area. People from Wenzhou are not picky about how they make their fortunes. They will deal in low-end items that others disdain, like buttons and cigarette lighters, and earn money quietly. Most of them also like being their own boss and are willing to take risks to do so. They are quite generous as well.

GUANXI

Good connections and close relationships with the right people are essential for success universally. Guanxi means relationships or connections; it is the cultivation of personal relationships with the possibility of material gain. Sometimes, the allocation of resources by the government is linked to personal connections among government officials and firm managers. Thus, the executives have to maintain good relations with relevant government officials and managers of other firms to ensure the provision of supporting resources and the timely delivery of necessary supplies. It is mutually beneficial. Therefore, guanxi is an important concept to understand when doing business in China. But, it is a mistake to assume that the cultivation of guanxi alone will lead to success.

Business and Guanxi

The right guanxi makes all the difference in ensuring a successful business. This is true everywhere, especially in China. By getting the right guanxi, the foreign company minimizes the risks, frustrations, and disappointments when doing business in China. Often it is acquiring the right guanxi with the relevant authorities that will determine the competitive standing of a firm in China. Moreover, the inevitable risks, barriers, and set-ups you are likely to encounter in China will be minimized when you have the right guanxi working for you.

Although developing and nurturing guanxi in China is a costly proposition both in terms of time and resources, the establishment of a strong network is well worth the investment. What your business gets in return is often much more valuable, especially in the long run. Even domestic businesses in China establish wide networks with their suppliers, retailers, banks, and local government officials. It is very common for individuals of a company to visit the residence of their acquaintances from other firms. This practice is central to successful Chinese commercial activity.

The Chinese culture is distinguished from the Western culture in many ways. For example, the Chinese prefer to deal with people they know and trust. This does not seem different from doing business in the Western world. But in reality, the heavy reliance on relationship means that Western companies have to make themselves known to the Chinese before any business can take place. Furthermore, this relationship is not simply between companies but also between individuals at a personal level. The relationship is not just before sales take place but it is an ongoing process. The company has to maintain the relationship if it wants to do more business with the Chinese.

Establishing Guanxi

Guanxi does not have to be based solely on money. Treating someone nicely could result in a good relationship. Second, it starts with and builds on the trustworthiness of the individual or the company. If a company delivers its promise, the company is showing trustworthiness and the Chinese would be more inclined to deal with them again. Third, being dependable and reliable definitely strengthens the relationship. It is like being friends, and friends can count on each other in good and tough times. Furthermore, frequent contacts with each other foster understanding and emotional bonds and the Chinese often feel obligated to do business with their friends first.

Relationships with government officials are beneficial for doing business in China. Political and administrative interference in business have declined. More and more companies have realized that good connection is helpful, but not the only factor in achieving success. If they are not getting any help from the government, they are more reluctant to be influenced by government officials. So government guanxi may have less influence with these companies. Since guanxi could function as an information network, foreign companies with wide guanxi and relationship networks often do better than companies with little or no relationship with the Chinese.

A Note on Guanxi

Guanxi can take on many forms. It is completely legal in the Chinese culture and not regarded as bribery in any way. So there is no need to feel uncomfortable about it. Trustworthiness of both the company and individual is an important component. Following through on promises is a good indication of this. Frequent contact fosters friendship as well. Chinese do business with their friends first. There are risks with this system, though. When something goes wrong, the relationships are challenged, and friendships quickly disappear. Moreover, guanxi and bribery are often linked. To maintain guanxi, it is sometimes difficult not to be corrupted in the exchange of expensive gifts and bribery.

POLITICAL STRUCTURE

The PRC is still an authoritarian and one-party state, ruled by the Communist Party with President Hu Jintao and Premier Wen Jiabao at the helm. China is committed to economic reform and opening to the outside world. The Chinese leadership has identified reform of state industries as a government priority. Beijing's strategies for achieving that goal include large-scale privatization of state-owned enterprises. To improve efficiency and credibility, the leadership has also downsized the government bureaucracy and taken measures to curb corruption.

China is a very large country. On top of the political hierarchy is the central government, which controls the next level consisting of the provinces and four largest cities. The next level is comprised of cities and counties, with townships and villages at the bottom. It is not correct to assume consistent and stable policy. There is tremendous variance in how the goals and policies of the central government are interpreted and implemented at the lower levels of government. Regional diversity is another factor. Policies from Beijing are sometimes vague and open to interpretation because Beijing wants local leaders to be able to adapt them to local conditions.

The Constitution

Since the establishment of the PRC on October 1, 1949, four constitutions have been adopted and amended in 1954, 1975, 1978, and 1982. The fourth constitution was adopted on the fifth Plenary Session on the Fifth National People's Congress on

December 4, 1982. It clearly stipulates the political system, economic system, the rights and obligations of citizens, setting up of state departments and their duties, and the basic tasks for future national development.

This constitution has five sections including preamble, general principles, the fundamental rights and duties of citizens, the structure of the state, the national flag, the national emblem, and the capital. There are four chapters and 138 articles in total. Since its adoption, this constitution has been amended several times.

The National People's Congress

The National People's Congress (NPC) is China's fundamental political system. Different from the legislative council under the Western system of "separation of three powers," the Constitution has made the NPC the most powerful entity of the country. In China, representatives of the local people's congress are elected directly from the local population. Above these levels, representatives are elected indirectly. The NPC is composed of representatives from provinces, autonomous regions, municipalities, and the military. The term for representatives in every level of the people's congress is five years.

At the annual meeting of the NPC, the representatives listen to the government reports and review other important documents. They examine these reports and make relevant resolutions and decisions. During the closing session of the NPC the standing committee of each level executes the power granted by the congress. The basic functions and powers of the NPC are to amend the Constitution, to supervise the enforcement of the Constitution, to enact and amend basic laws covering crucial matters, and to decide on the major national leaders. Strategic development plans for the national economy and social affairs have been vital for advancing China's social progress. But these plans require approval from the NPC. The premier of the State Council and ministers of the government must be appointed by the NPC. The NPC can also remove the chair of an NPC Standing Committee, the president, and the premier through legal procedures.

CORRUPTION

Studies have shown linkages between China's economic reform and corruption. The reform process presents opportunities because government plays an essential role in regulations and resources allocation. Corruption has become such a serious social and political issue that Beijing is taking a series of measures to fight it. Corruption is widespread throughout China.[2] For example, a bureaucrat from Beijing arrived at his new assignment in another city. His close subordinates gave him hints for taking bribes. They told him how often he could get sick and how often he could accept invitations to ribbon cuttings. Both occasions present opportunities to take "gifts." He also learned that those gifts could amount to thousands of U.S. dollars a year, more than his salary. Corruption involves many parties. It is systematic, not just an isolated incident.

Causes of Corruption

Selfish interests are the basic motive for economic transactions. People generally behave rationally. Economists define rent as a factor of income in excess of the competitive returns of the factor. Government intervention or regulation is one way to control rent. In other words, instead of enabling the free market to govern economic relations and transactions, the government steps in and regulates these relations.

The majority of government interventions on the market are prohibitive. That is, businesses or people are precluded from doing something, unless the government explicitly grants them permission to do so. Import licensing is one good example. Only the firms that have obtained import licenses are permitted to import a certain quantity of certain goods. If the quantity is limited or if few licenses are available, that will create a shortage in the market. Thus, the price will be substantially higher than the costs of its production/import, leading to excess profits or economic rent. By paying a bribe to get the import license, a portion of the rent is appropriated by the corruptor and the remaining is appropriated by the corrupted. The economic rent and the resulting corruption are the result of the regulation of import licenses.

In general, the more complicated and ambiguous the rules, the more opportunity there is for corruption. As an example, if the customs tariff rate for one product is 3 percent and for another similar product is 30 percent, there are strong incentives for corruption aimed at misclassification of the goods to pay a lower tariff rate. Furthermore, procedural legislation is very important for corruption. The complicated and nontransparent legislation giving discretion to government officials creates a tremendous opportunity for corruption.

Given that rent is the source of corruption and the government regulation that creates rent is an important factor of corruption, an effective strategy for fighting corruption is deregulation. Deregulation means abolishing government intervention that is prohibitive, thus allowing market forces to function effectively. Market forces will drive all the factors' returns to their competitive level and there will be no rent due to government intervention, hence eliminating one important factor contributing to corruption.

From another perspective, deregulation will decrease and in some cases eliminate corruption due to the lack of discretionary power of bureaucrats. There will be no incentive for private parties to bribe civil servants if they are not in a position to offer any favor to the corruptor. Deregulation and decreasing the role of the government has its limits, however. The basic reason for the government to exist is to provide and enforce the rule of law. For businesses, the most important aspect of the rule of law is protection of private property rights through efficient contract enforcement. In the case of rule of law, strict rule of law is one of the elements of an effective strategy for fighting corruption. Accordingly, all measures that improve the rule of law will definitely contribute to the fight against corruption. One of the crucial elements of strengthening the rule of law is the creation of transparent rules that are understood by all parties.

Streamlining procedural legislation and making it simple and transparent is important because it minimizes the uncertainty and reduces the discretionary power of government officials. The increased probability of apprehension and punishment creates a deterrent for civil servants to accept bribes, therefore raising the costs of corruption. Increasing the compensation of civil servants is another important element of the strategy for fighting corruption.

Fan and Grossman (2001) argued that "a large part of the success of the Chinese economic reform is attributable to the transformation of the typical local government official from being an unproductive political entrepreneur to being a productive economic entrepreneur." The motivation local officials have to become economic entrepreneurs is related to their income from the bribes. This is because their salaries are fixed and relatively low and taking bribes and appropriating public funds or property enrich them. This, in a strange way, has contributed to the economic performance. This is because those local officials who make the largest economic contribution are likely to extract the largest bribes. This phenomenon occurs typically in the early stages of economic development.

Types of Corruption

The root of corruption is either power or money. Corruption undermines protection of private property rights, deters potential investors, and drives entrepreneurial energy toward redistributive activities. Solutions to fight corruption include reducing opportunities for rent seeking through deregulation and simplifying procedures to reduce the discretion by officials.

There are two different theories to corruption. One is based on the principle-agent theory. This approach assumes that there is an asymmetry of information between principals (politicians or decision makers) and agents (civil servants or bureaucrats). This approach explains the existence of administrative corruption. However, this approach cannot explain political corruption. This approach assumes that the state is benevolent, so there is no possibility for political corruption. Only administrative corruption (corruption of civil servants) can be explained and predicted. However, the list of corrupted politicians and associated political scandals is lengthy all over the world. Political corruption simply cannot be explained within this methodological framework. The crucial feature of this approach is that corruption is exogenous to the political process and is not institutionalized. Nonetheless, if corruption is considered endogenous to the political process, corruption is institutionalized, and its level and pattern depend on the political regime in the country.

The second theory of corruption is rent appropriation by the ruler. Corruption is the answer to the problem of internal cohesion of predatory teams. Corrupt government officials are created to satisfy ruler desire to foster loyalty through patronage. Corrupt civil service is nothing but the extension of efficient rent appropriation by the ruler. The rent is extracted through sales of a limited number of permits and licenses for economic activity. Furthermore, endowing only a few civil servants with the power to grant licenses enables the diversion of the licensing proceeds from the budget toward private gains. Finally, civil servants are cooperative because they have their share in the spoils. Dictators often can find a reason as to why an uncooperative subordinate is guilty of corruption. Hence, there is both the carrot and the stick to strengthen loyalty.

In general, there are three basic types of corruption. The first is corruption for achieving or speeding-up materialization of some specific right that the citizen or legal entity is entitled to. Its specific and more aggressive version is bribing officials for jumping the queue for providing the service that is legal. In other words, civil servants are corrupted to do their job or to do it more quickly than they usually do, instead of not doing it. The frequency of this type of corruption is a good indicator of the capacity and effectiveness of a country's administrative process. It is important to note that a shortage of administrative services can be deliberately produced, aimed at creating the rent and its redistribution via corruption.

The second type of corruption violates the legal rules, or involves a very biased enforcement of the rules. This is administrative corruption. This type of corruption corresponds to the principle-agent model of corruption because the total supply of corruption (demand for the bribe for violating the rules) is provided by the civil servants. The most significant direct consequence of this type of corruption is that legislation and public policies are not justly enforced. A cynical approach to the issue within countries with widespread corruption is that some public policies are so bad, it is actually better for the society that they are not enforced. Accordingly, corruption is considered to be the second best solution. It would be better if these policies were not enforced at all. Nonetheless, since the political process resulted in bad policies, corruption is seen as a solution for bad public policies.

Finally, there is "state capture" corruption that is aimed at changing the rules and regulations into rules and regulations that favor the interests of the corruptor. The concept of state capture was developed by the World Bank primarily for explaining the reality of political life in transitional economies. The underlying assumption is that legislation and public policies are decisively influenced by the bribing of legislators by a few powerful businesspeople. In other words, public policies are inevitably formulated to favor them, not the public. There is no doubt that such a process exists, and that this type of corruption can explain some elements of public policy in many countries.

Subsequently, the crucial question is to what extent are the outcomes regarding public policies from legitimate lobbying and illegal corruption different. Additionally, the question is whether the social costs (in terms of the opportunity costs of resources used) of lobbying are greater or less compared with the social costs of corruption. In brief, although the type of corruption that influences public policy is very important to consider, the analytical framework of "state capture" should be substantially improved in order to better explain its mechanisms and for an enhanced understanding of the process.

The other important distinction in the case of corruption is its industrial organization, emphasizing centralized (monopolized) versus decentralized patterns of corruption. The crucial prerequisite for centralized corruption is the ability to enforce joint profit in bribe collection. It is closely related to the problem of enforcing collusion in oligopoly. It has been pointed out that when governments have an effective policing machine to monitor the action of civil servants, such as the KGB in the former Soviet

Union, corruption in the country is centralized. In decentralized corruption, a single corruptor is dealing with multiple, rather than single, corruption contracts (transactions), hence the transaction costs are multiplied. In other words, a monopolized corruption pattern is "better" than a decentralized one regarding the transaction costs.

In the case of China's corruption, Sun (2004) grouped corruption into several categories and types. Some of the categories are:

- *Embezzlement:* This refers to theft of public funds through fraudulent bookkeeping. Theft through contract fraud is by way of inflating the contract amount and taking a kickback. Theft through payment occurs when an official forwards funds to a self-employed merchant for purchase payment and then takes funds from the latter. Theft through receipt takes place when an official submits reimbursement by using receipt for personal purchases. Theft through managerial fraud is a scheme a manager uses to profit from overstating business expenses, employee salaries, or employee bonuses. Finally, theft through property transfer is to transfer some of the state properties under her/his control to a private business.
- *Misappropriation:* This involves unauthorized use of funds. This is a criminal offense if the amount is more than 5,000 Yuan.
- *Bribery:* This has evolved from gifts to other forms, such as taking money for granting permission, putting family members on the company's payroll, and expensive gifts. Some pay for the education expenses overseas for government official's children.
- *Illegal profiteering:* Public organizations and their employees are typical offenders. Funding for speculative activities fall into this category. Common speculation includes state-regulated goods, state-regulated permits, or illegal products or schemes.
- *Negligence:* This occurs when damages result from neglect of official duties. Sometimes profit incentive is behind deliberate or involuntary negligence, and public resources are usually involved. Areas of negligence include business ventures, supervision, or regulation.
- *Privilege seeking:* Seeking personal favors is a form of bribery. The economic reform has resulted in new problems such as allocating regulated goods to relatives or asking subordinates to pay for private tuition.

Measures to Fight Corruption

China's leadership in Beijing is firm in its stand to fight corruption. The death sentence handed down to Hu Changqing, a former provincial governor, and Cheng Kejie, a former NPC vice chairman, has signaled government's determination to fight corruption. Appendix A lists the U.S. Foreign Corrupt Practices Act: Antibribery Provisions. The act prohibits U.S. companies against bribery in dealings overseas.[3]

In recent years, the central leadership has adopted a series of measures to curb corruption. China's ruling Communist Party on February 17, 2004, published Regulations of Internal Supervision of the Communist Party of China (CPC) putting all the party's members under public supervision.[4] Under the regulations, the Political Bureau of the CPC Central Committee, the party's policy-making unit, must make a regular report to a plenary meeting of the Party Central Committee. The regulations aim to tighten supervision over the Party's officials at all levels across the country to fill up the existing supervision loopholes. The newly issued CPC regulations on internal supervision and disciplinary penalty have raised heated discussion among common people, who mostly believe they will lead to another bright stage for China's anticorruption movement. A random street survey by Xinhua indicated that more than 80 percent of the interviewed held the view that the regulations would enhance efforts against corruption and be fruitful.[5]

In 2003, at least 13 Chinese ministers or ministerial-level officials were prosecuted for corruption, including former Minister of Land and Resources Tian Fengshan and former Party chief of north China's Hebei Province Cheng Weigao. Therefore, to curb absolute power and prevent arbitrary behavior, the regulations make detailed stipulations on "collective leadership" and "power division" at all levels of the Communist Party structure.

Leaders of Party committees at all levels are required to submit an annual report on their work performance and how they are preventing corruption to the entire committee, while the media monitors Party organizations at every level.

The regulations guarantee that every ordinary Party member's supervisory rights will be fully respected and protected, stressing that Party organizations must handle all reports on corruption earnestly and in a timely way. Since the founding of the People's Republic of China in 1949, the CPC has never ceased its battle against corruption. However, official figures of disclosed corruption cases have been steadily rising over the past decade as the country shifts from a planned economy to a new socialist market economy.

From 1992 to 1997, statistics show 669,300 members of the CPC were punished for corruption, while from 1998 to 2002, the number rose to 846,150, a 26.4 percent increase. In 2006, China punished 97,000 CPC members amid a continuous campaign to build a clean party.

Beijing Olympics 2008

Construction and related preparations for the 2008 Olympics present businesses with opportunities to make large sums of money and the potential to corrupt government officials. Thus, China has introduced measures to fight corruption in preparing for the Beijing Olympics in 2008. This could become a blueprint for a wider campaign against graft.

In cooperation with international advisers, the Chinese government has instituted a range of procedures to minimize the potential for corruption in contracts for the Games, which will be worth up to tens of billions of dollars. These measures include more frequent audits of spending, last-minute selection of experts to decide on contract bids to reduce the possibility of bribery, threats of blacklisting for corrupt contractors, the opening of tenders to public scrutiny on the Internet, and establishing public hotlines for public complaints.

China has traditionally relied on the threat of serious punishment, including the death penalty, to deter graft. However, international advisers and specialists from Hong Kong have been advising the Chinese government that education, transparency, and preventative measures are also important.

Experts note that opportunities for graft often multiply in countries like China, where the political and economic systems are in transition between planned and market economies.

Similar problems were encountered in Eastern Europe after the breakdown of communism. In recent years the arrest and imprisonment of senior officials at the top of China's banking and financial system including the former head of the Bank of China in Hong Kong, Liu Jinbao, the former head of the China Construction Bank, Wang Xuebing, and the former chairman of the China Everbright Group, Zhu Xiaohua, suggests that corruption is deeply entrenched at the top levels of government and business.

Controversial Anticorruption Method in Nanjing

The Municipal Government of Nanjing, capital of east China's Jiangsu Province, issued a regulation requiring officials to report their extramarital affairs, with a belief that the stipulation could curb corruption.[6]

The new anticorruption method has sparked wide debate in China. According to estimates, 95 percent of China's convicted corrupt officials had mistresses. In south China's economic-booming cities of Shenzhen, Guangzhou, and Zhuhai, all the officials involved in the 102 corruption cases investigated in 1999 had mistresses. One of China's most notorious corruption cases also involved mistresses. Cheng Kejie, former vice-chairman of the National People's Congress (NPC) Standing Committee, and his mistress Li Ping, had conspired to take a bribe worth more than RMB 40 million for their planned marriage after divorcing their spouses. Cheng was sentenced to death and was executed in 2000.

CONCLUSION

Economic reform in China has been associated with an epidemic of corruption among local government officials. In recent years, the severe punishment and the threat of punishment have signaled Beijing's determination to fight corruption. Some have argued that Beijing also needs to implement deregulations to remove the power or discretion of government officials.

5

Chinese Business and Financial Law

The most direct approach to enter the Chinese market is to establish a local presence. For those who have evaluated the market and decided to enter China, one of the biggest challenges is compliance with regulations. Thus, it is helpful to gain a basic understanding of the relevant laws and then work with competent attorneys to ensure that you do not violate any regulatory provisions. This chapter provides a brief summary of regulations in banking, securities, and insurance. The chapter also lists the laws in each of these areas.

FOREIGN INVESTMENTS IN CHINA

China is one of the largest consumer markets in the world and is also an attractive operating area to export to other regions of the globe. There are several approaches to establishing a presence in China; each is subject to a different legal and administrative requirement. As described in a previous chapter, the options for a foreign company wanting set up a China presence include processing and assembly agreement, equity joint venture, cooperative joint venture, wholly foreign-owned enterprise, People's Republic of China (PRC) holding company, representative office, and branch. A representative office is the simplest form of a local presence, while a wholly foreign-owned enterprise gives you greater control and flexibility.

Investment Areas

At the start of the economic opening, most foreign investments clustered in the special economic zones (Shenzhen, Zhuhai, Xiamen, Shantou, and the New Area of Pudong in Shanghai) or the coastal area. By now, many foreign investments are in the special economic zones, national economic and technological development zones, national free trade zones, national high-tech industrial development zones, national Taiwanese investment zones, national border and economic cooperation zones, national export processing zones, and national tourist and holiday resort. In recent years, some foreign investors have selected the smaller cities to avoid competing with the big firms operating in the major cities.

The Process of Establishing Operations in China

Once your company has decided to go to China, the next step is to review the investment policies by the Chinese government. China has four categories of industrial projects for foreign investors: encouraged, permitted, restricted, and prohibited. The size and the area of investments will determine where to seek approval. Large investment projects require the approval by the central government, while local governments have the right to approve smaller investments in the unrestricted category.

As described in an earlier chapter, there are several approaches to investing in China. For joint ventures (JVs), the process involves several steps. It is crucial to prepare a project proposal and a feasibility study to submit to the regulatory authority for approval. If approved, the next step is to submit the signed contract and the articles of association for examination and approval. The relevant regulatory authority will issue a certificate for the joint venture if it is satisfied with the application. On receipt of the approval, you and the local partner will apply for registration to get a business license.

If the investment is to establish a wholly owned subsidiary, the procedures call for submission of the completed application form, the articles of association, and relevant legal documents. Article 14 of Detailed Rules for the Implementation of the Law on Wholly Foreign-Owned Enterprises requires the application to set up a wholly foreign-owned enterprise to include:

1. Name or title, address, and registered address of the foreign investor and name, nationality, and position of its legal representative
2. Name and address of the proposed wholly foreign-owned enterprise
3. Scope of operations, product type, and production scale
4. Total amount of investment in the proposed enterprise, amount of registered capital, source of capital, method of investment, and term of investment
5. Organizational format and structure and the legal representative of the proposed enterprise
6. Main types of production equipment to be used and respective age of equipment, production technology, level of technology, and source of supply
7. Product sales direction, regions, sales channels, and methods
8. Foreign exchange income and expenditure arrangements
9. Establishment provisions and personnel framework, arrangements for employee recruitment, training, wages, welfare benefits, insurance, and labor protection
10. Amount of environmental pollution likely to the caused and proposed measures for solution

11. Site selection and area of land to be used
12. Capital construction and capital, resources, and raw materials required for production and operations and supply measures
13. Progress plans for project implementation
14. Period of operation of the proposed enterprise

In addition, under the rules governing foreign invested enterprises, you must open a bank account for both the Chinese and foreign currencies, tax registration, customs registration, and foreign currency registration. In addition, the Chinese government imposes strict regulations on if and how the profits can be distributed. Article 58 states: "From the profit remaining after payment of income tax in accordance with Chinese tax law provisions, a wholly foreign-owned enterprise shall allocate money for a reserve fund and employee bonus and welfare funds. That allocated as the reserve fund shall be no less their 10 percent of the after-tax profit amount. If the accumulative total of allocated funds reaches 50 percent of an enterprise's registered capital, the enterprise shall not be required to make any further allocation. The allocation ratio for the employee bonus and welfare funds may be determined by a wholly foreign-owned enterprise itself." The regulation also prohibits a wholly foreign-owned enterprise from distributing dividends unless the losses of previous years have been made up.

BANKING

Foreign banks are keen to tap into the fast-growing Chinese market and the estimated US$1.5 trillion in savings there. With the WTO accession, foreign entry has speeded up and competition has intensified. The initial public offerings of the state-owned banks made early investors large sums of profits. So foreign financial institutions are in China for strategic expansions and for investment profits. Banking laws and the deregulatory process govern the way foreign institutions enter the market.

The banking regulatory authority is the China Banking Regulatory Commission (CBRC). The banking law aims at "improving banking regulation and supervision, standardizing banking supervisory process and procedures, preventing and mitigating financial risks in the banking industry, protecting the interests of depositors and other customers, as well as promoting a safe and sound banking industry in China."[1] The objectives are to promote safety and soundness of the banking industry and maintain public confidence in the financial system. Appendix B lists the Law of the People's Republic of China on Banking Regulation and Supervision.

The banking law is grouped into six chapters. Chapter I contains general provisions that lay out the objectives of the regulation and the institutions that are subject to this regulation, including banks, asset management companies, trust and investment companies, finance companies, financial leasing companies, and other financial institutions established in the People's Republic of China as authorized by the banking regulatory authority under the State Council.

Chapter II defines the banking regulatory authority. The regulatory authority, China Banking Regulatory Commission, operates under the State Council. The regulatory authority makes public the supervisory process and procedures and puts in place the supervisory system and monitoring mechanism. The personnel in performing their regulatory and supervision duties should maintain integrity and preserve confidentiality. Additionally, this chapter also states that local governments and relevant government departments at various levels shall provide assistance to facilitate banking regulation.

Chapter III outlines regulatory and supervisory responsibilities. The banking regulatory authority authorizes the establishment, changes, termination, or business scope of banks. It also has the responsibility to assess the source of capital and the financial strength of the banking institution. Other areas of regulation relate to the products and services a bank is permitted to offer, on site examination, establishment of a regulatory rating system, and an early warning system.

Chapter IV provides for supervisory methods and procedures. The CBRC requires banks to submit financial and statistical reports. It may take appropriate measures to conduct on-site examination and consult with bank directors and senior executives to inquire about the bank's business operations and risk management. If a bank is not in full compliance, the CBRC has the authority to impose remedial measures within a prescribed period of time or to take corrective measures, including closure of the banking institution.

Chapter V describes legal responsibility. When an employee of the regulatory authority commits a violation or bribery, relevant administrative sanctions or criminal liability will be imposed. The regulatory authority can impose fines or pursue criminal prosecution if a banking institution has violated banking regulations.

Finally, Chapter VI lists supplementary provisions.

SECURITIES REGULATIONS

The securities market regulator is China Securities Regulatory Commission. The securities market is now an important source of capital for companies by way of issuing securities. The market also provides a channel for speculators to trade and for investors to make a long-term investment. There are many domestic securities firms and foreign entry has added capital and enhanced management and product offerings.

The securities law contains 12 chapters (Appendix C). As stated in Chapter I, the purpose of the securities law is "protecting the lawful rights and interests of investors, safeguarding the economic order and public interests of the society and promoting the growth of the socialist market economy." This law applies to the issuance and transactions of debt instruments, equity securities, and other financial instruments. The auditing organ of the state shall carry out auditing supervision of stock exchanges, securities companies, securities registration, and clearing institutions.

Chapter II deals with issuance of securities. For an initial public offering (IPO) of stocks, a company shall satisfy the following requirements: (1) Having a complete and well-operated organization, (2) Having the capability of making profits successively and a sound financial status, (3) Having no false record in its financial statements over the latest three years and having no other major irregularity, and (4) Meeting any other requirements as prescribed by the securities regulatory authority under the State Council, which has been approved by the State Council. A listed company that makes any initial nonpublic offer of stocks shall satisfy the requirements as prescribed by the securities regulatory authority under the State Council, which have been approved by the State Council and shall be reported to the securities regulatory authority under the State Council for examination and approval. For a bond issue, a public issuance of corporate bonds shall satisfy the following requirements: (1) The net asset of a stock-limited company being no less than RMB 30 million and the net asset of a limited-liability company being no less than RMB 60 million, (2) The accumulated bond balance constituting no more than 40 percent of the net asset of a company, (3) The average distributable profits over the latest three years being sufficient to pay the one-year interests of corporate bonds, (4) The investment of raised funds complying with the industrial policies of the state, (5) The yield rate of bonds not surpassing the level of interest rate as qualified by the State Council, and (6) Meeting any other requirements as prescribed by the State Council. The funds as raised through public issuance of corporate bonds shall be used for the purpose as verified and may not be used for covering any deficit or nonproduction expenditure. The public issuance of convertible corporate bonds by a listed company must also meet the requirements of the present Law on public offer of stocks, and shall be reported to the securities regulatory authority under the State Council for examination and approval.

Chapter III sets forth regulatory provisions for transaction of securities. Only legally issued securities can be traded. All stocks, corporate bonds, or any other securities that have been publicly issued according to law shall be listed in a stock exchange to trade. The chapter also describes the conduct of the brokerage community.

Chapter IV lists regulations for the listing of securities. A company applying for listing of stocks needs to meet the following requirements: (1) The stocks shall have been subject to the examination and approval of the securities regulatory authority under the State Council and shall have been publicly issued; (2) The total amount of capital stock shall be no less than RMB 30 million; (3) The shares as publicly issued shall reach more than 25 percent of the total amount of corporate shares; where the total amount of capital stock of a company exceeds RMB 0.4 billion, the shares as publicly issued shall be no less than 10 percent thereof; and (4) The company may not have any major irregularity over the latest years and there is no false record in its financial statements. A stock exchange may prescribe the requirements of listing that are more strict than those as prescribed, which shall be reported to the securities regulatory authority under the State Council for approval. For a bond listing, the requirements are: (1) The term of corporate bonds shall be more than one year, (2) The amount of corporate bonds to be actually issued shall be no less than RMB 50 million, and (3) The company shall meet the statutory requirements for the issuance of corporate bonds when applying for the listing of its bonds.

Once the security is listed, the issuer has a reporting responsibility. Within two months as of the end of the first half of each accounting year, submit to the securities regulatory authority under the State Council and the stock exchange a midterm report indicating the following contents and announce it: (1) The financial statements and business situation of the company, (2) The major litigation involving the company, (3) The particulars of any change concerning the shares or corporate bonds thereof as already issued, (4) The important matters as submitted to the general assembly of shareholders for deliberation, and (5) Any other matter as prescribed by the securities regulatory authority under the State Council. Furthermore, the chapter also provides for regulations against trading on private information and mergers and acquisitions.

Chapter V contains regulations for stock exchanges. The formation of an exchange, the organization of an exchange, and the responsibilities of an exchange are covered.

Chapter VI sets forth regulations on securities companies. The requirements for setting up a securities firm are: (1) Having a corporation constitution that meets the relevant laws and administrative regulations, (2) The major shareholders having the ability to make profits successively, enjoying good credit standing and having no irregular or rule-breaking record over the latest three years, and its net asset being no less than RMB 0.2 billion, (3) Having a registered capital that meets the provisions of the present Law, (4) The directors, supervisors, and senior managers thereof having the post-holding qualification and its practitioners having the qualification to engage in securities business, (5) Having a complete risk management system as well as an internal control system, (6) Having a qualified business place and facilities for operation, and (7) Meeting any other requirement as prescribed by laws and administrative regulations as well as the provisions of the securities regulatory authority under the State Council, which have been approved by the State Council. Once approved, the firm can engage in (1) Securities brokerage, (2) Securities investment consulting, (3) Financial advising relating to activities of securities trading or securities investment, (4) Underwriting and recommendation of securities, (5) Self-operation of securities, (6) Securities asset management, and (7) Any other business operation concerning securities.

Chapter VII deals with securities registration and clearing institutions. The establishment of a securities registration and clearing institution shall fulfill the following requirements: (1) Its self-owned capital shall be no less than RMB 0.2 billion, (2) It shall have a place and facilities as required by the services of securities registration, custody, and settlement, (3) Its major managers and practitioners shall have the securities practice qualification, and (4) It shall meet any other requirement as prescribed by the securities regulatory authority under the State Council. The words "securities registration and clearing" shall be indicated in the name of a securities registration and clearing institution. A securities registration and clearing institution shall perform the following functions: (1) The establishment of securities accounts and settlement accounts, (2) The custody and transfer of securities, (3) The registration of roster of securities holders, (4) The settlement and delivery for listed securities trading of a stock exchange, (5) The distribution of securities rights and interests on the basis of the entrustment of issuers, (6) The handling of any inquiry relating to the aforesaid business operation, and (7) Any other business operation as approved by the securities regulatory authority under the State Council.

Chapter VIII contains provisions for securities trading service institutions including investment consulting institution, financial advising institution, credit rating institution, asset appraisal institution or accounting firm engages in any securities trading service. Such an institution needs to meet certain qualification requirements.

Chapter XI is for securities industry association.

Chapter X addresses provisions for securities regulatory bodies.

Chapter XI provides for regulations on legal liability when there is a violation.

Chapter XII contains supplementary articles.

INSURANCE REGULATION

The regulations of the insurance industry in China have changed over time in response to the development of the industry. The regulatory body is the China Insurance Regulatory Commission. Appendix D lists the current insurance law. The current insurance law covers insurance contract, life insurance, property insurance, insurance company, insurance operational rules, supervision of the insurance business, legal liability, and supplementary provisions.

Chapter I covers general provisions. It states that "This law has been formulated with a view to standardizing the insurance activities, protecting the legitimate rights and interests of parties to insurance activities, strengthening the supervision and administration of the insurance business and promoting its healthy development." It, in general terms, addresses the parties to an insurance contract. Another provision indicates that, under the law, the regulatory authority shall exercise supervision and administration of the insurance market.

Chapter II covers insurance contracts. Article 19 states that an insurance contract shall contain:

1. Name and domicile of the insurer
2. Names and residences of the insurant and the insured and the name and residence of the beneficiaries of life insurance
3. Objects of insurance
4. Insurance liability and liability exemption
5. Insurance term and the starting time of insurance liabilities
6. Insured value
7. Insured amount
8. Premium and the method of payment
9. The method of payment of insurance indemnity or insurance money
10. Liabilities for breach of contract and the handling of disputes
11. The year, month, and date in which the contract is signed

It also defines the rights and responsibilities of the insured and the insurer to the insurance contract. The chapter then addresses the specifics of property insurance contract and life insurance contract.

Chapter III covers "insurance company." The organizational form of an insurance company is limited to joint stock company or wholly state-owned company. The requirements for approval of an insurance company are:

- It shall have articles of association as provided for by this law and the company law.
- It shall have the minimum registered capital provided for in this law.
- It shall have senior management staff with professional knowledge and work experience.
- It shall have a sound organizational setup and management system.
- It shall have offices and other related facilities that are up to the requirements.

The regulatory authority will also consider the development of the insurance market and fair competition. The minimum capital amount is RMB 200 million.

Chapter IV provides for insurance operational rules. The business scope for a property company is property loss insurance, liability insurance, and credit insurance. Personal insurance line covers life insurance, health insurance, and accidental injury insurance. An insurer is permitted to engage in property insurance or life insurance, but not both.

Chapter V covers supervision and administration of the insurance business. The insurance clauses in the contract and the insurance rates for the areas that involve public interest need regulatory approval. In case an insurer fails to have sufficient reserves or reinsurance, the regulatory authority shall order insurance company to take corrective measures or the managing executives will be removed.

Chapter VI contains provisions that govern insurance agents and brokers. In life insurance, an agent is not permitted to work for two insurers at the same time.

Chapter VII covers legal liability. It lists various amounts of fines or other civil liabilities for different violations.

Finally, Chapter VIII is for supplementary provisions. The law described is applicable to Chinese-foreign joint equity insurance companies, solely foreign funded insurance companies, and branches of foreign insurers.

CONCLUSION

The chapter described the regulatory issues in banking, insurance, and securities. In banking, the chapter covered licensing, operations, and related issues. In securities business, requirements for listing and compliance in trading are discussed. The discussion also covered brokerage business and stock exchange. In insurance, life and nonlife are separated.

6

Greasing the Wheels and Entering the Chinese Markets

T he approach a company selects to establish a presence in China relates to the company's strategic considerations. A representative office is the easiest type to set up, but it is limited to liaison activities only. A joint venture is a more significant establishment, but the success in part depends on the Chinese partner. A wholly foreign-owned enterprise gives the foreign firm greater control over management, intellectual property rights, and marketing. It also avoids import restrictions. An alternative is to take advantage of the special treatment that Beijing has provided to goods that originate in Hong Kong.

POTENTIAL VEHICLES FOR INVESTING IN CHINA

There are two different approaches to investing in China. As mentioned in a previous chapter, financial market investors use vehicles such as closed-end China funds, open-end mutual funds, private equity funds, listed stocks, and bonds to get exposure to the China market. There are also several vehicles for establishing operations in China, which include processing and assembling agreements, joint ventures, wholly foreign-owned enterprises, holding companies, representative offices, and branches. Local companies with foreign investments are called foreign invested enterprises. The last part of the book describes how to make an investment in financial assets related to China. This chapter examines approaches to setting up real investments in the Chinese market as well as how to take advantage of the special access that Hong Kong companies enjoy under CEPA.

Real Investments

Establishing a presence in China serves three important purposes. First of all, the production costs are lower due to low labor costs and other expenses. It can be used as a base to export to other countries. In addition, China is the largest consumer market in the world, and thus, there is no need to export to China in order to reach this massive market.

Industries in Which to Invest

The company's strategic plan will mandate where and which industry to invest in. Beyond that strategic consideration, it is helpful to know that the Chinese government has policies that prioritize its targeted industries for foreign investments. Accordingly, Beijing has grouped foreign investments into categories: (1) encouraged, (2) restricted, and (3) prohibited. For several industries, certain areas of business are encouraged while others are restricted. Prohibited industries are in gambling, journalism, weapons, telecommunications, and broadcasting. Appendix E provides a detailed list of these groupings.[1]

Trade and Investment Zones

China has established investment zones to attract foreign investments. Those investment zones include special economic zones, open cities, economic and technological development zones, high-tech development zones, free trade zones, and export processing zones. China offers investors incentives for investing in those zones. Incentives include tax holidays, better infrastructure, and discount on the rent of business premises. It is important to note that this is changing because of China's accession into the WTO. It is a requirement of WTO membership that China should have a level playing field for both Chinese firms and foreign companies. It is, though, still possible that certain areas are exempt from the unified tax policy that imposes the same tax rate across the board.

REPRESENTATIVE OFFICES

A representative office is easy to set up, but its activities are limited to provision of services that do not lead to earnings or profits. The permitted activities of a representative office include data collection, market investigation, providing introductory services to potential clients, and coordination with the parent company. A foreign company wanting to establish a representative office in China must submit an application to authority for review and approval. The regulatory authorities are:

- *Ministry of Foreign Trade and Commerce:* For applications in trade, commerce, manufacturing, and cargo transportation
- *People's Bank of China and China Banking Regulatory Commission:* For applications in banking
- *China Insurance Regulatory Commission:* For applications in life insurance, nonlife insurance, reinsurance, and insurance brokerage

- *China Securities Regulatory Commission:* For applications in securities and investment management businesses
- *Ministry of Communications:* For applications in maritime transportation and maritime transportation agencies
- *Civil Aviation Administration of China:* For applications in air transportation

The application documents for the establishment of a representative office include the following:

- Signed application, including the name and address of the representative office, information of senior executives, intended activities, and the planned time horizon
- Documents showing a good standing in financial status
- A license issued by the relevant authority
- Letters of appointment of the executives stationed at the representative office and their resumes

Once approved, the chief representative of the office has to submit in person the certificate of approval to the State Administration for Industry and Commerce for formal registration. The representative must also register with the local taxation bureau, the state taxation bureau, the customs service, and the public security bureau. The office should also open a bank account at Bank of China. According to China-Britain Business Council, the process takes about two to three months.

JOINT VENTURES

Joint ventures can take several forms. A Chinese-Foreign Equity Joint Venture is an enterprise jointly established within Chinese territory by a foreign party and a Chinese party. Both foreign and Chinese investors invest and operate jointly and share proportionally the profits and losses as well as risks. The equity joint venture is a Limited Liability Company. A Chinese-Foreign Contractual Joint Venture is an enterprise jointly established within Chinese territories by a foreign party and a Chinese party. Both parties to a contractual joint venture should prescribe in the contract their respective conditions, rights, obligations, incomes distribution, responsibilities for risks and debts, the company management and negotiations on the property transaction at the expiration.

Equity Joint Ventures

For a Chinese-foreign equity joint venture, the proportion of the investment contributed by the foreign party shall in general not be less than 25 percent of the total. The partner could offer cash or other kinds of things instead, such as building, workshop, machinery, industrial property right, special technique, and field utilization right. The profits and other legal interests that foreign investors have shared can be remitted out or reinvested in China.

To encourage foreign interests, the Chinese government has indicated that "The state will not nationalize or expropriate equity joint ventures . . ." The agreement between the Chinese and the foreign entities, contract, and articles of association shall be submitted to authority for examination and approval. Under the law, an equity joint venture takes the form of a limited liability company. Either party to the venture could make investments in cash, in kind, or proprietary rights. Employees of an equity joint venture have the right to establish labor union. The Chinese government grants preferential treatment in the form of tax reductions or exemption of taxation to the joint venture. The joint venture shall open a foreign exchange account to conduct its foreign exchange business. Appendix F lists China's law on Chinese-foreign equity joint ventures.

Contractual Joint Ventures

When establishing a contractual joint venture, the foreign party usually provides all or a major part of the capital, while the Chinese party provides land, factory buildings, certain usable machines and facilities, and in some cases a certain amount of capital as well. Appendix G lists details of China's regulation on Chinese-foreign contractual joint ventures.

WHOLLY FOREIGN-OWNED ENTERPRISES

For some foreign investors, the prospect of having to partner with a Chinese investor presents too great a hurdle to investing in a Chinese enterprise. Others hesitate to share technology or business strategies. Still others simply lack the necessary contacts. Establishing a wholly foreign-owned enterprise (WFOE) is an alternative.

A WFOE is a Chinese corporation that is 100 percent owned by a foreign party. Because no Chinese joint venture partner is required, most technology or specialized manufacturing companies choose this as their preferred entity. Regulated under special statutes, in addition to the protections offered under standard Chinese Company law, there are additional benefits that flow to a WFOE. Figure 6.1 compares a representative office, a joint venture, and a wholly foreign-owned enterprise.

A WFOE can sell into the domestic market, manufacture for export only, or both. Some technology and components can be imported duty free. There are substantial tax holidays in certain favored industries. Virtually any technology company can qualify for these additional tax breaks.

Setting Up a WFOE

The most important factors that a company needs to take into consideration are as follows.[2] First, selecting a location needs to consider proximity to customer base and

FIGURE 6.1   Forms and Investment and Control Tradeoff

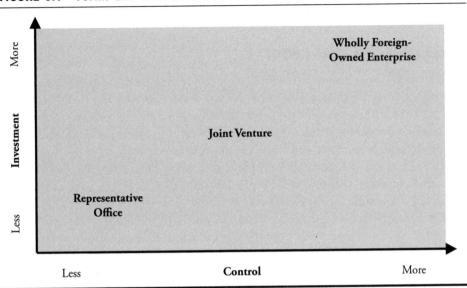

major cities, local availability of service industries and quality of infrastructure, human resource availability, quality of communications and living conditions, and availability of development zone with financial incentives.

Having selected the location for the enterprise, the next step is registration, for which it is necessary to draw up a detailed business plan. Among other points the business plan must cover:

- Reason for investing in China
- Predicted market growth
- Opportunities resulting from establishment of WFOE
- Costs of establishing and operating the WFOE
- Risk analysis
- Other key factors, including cash flows, predicted levels of imports and exports, and the commercial structure of the WFOE

The next consideration is business scope. According to WFOE regulations, "Foreign investors are permitted to set up a 100 percent foreign-invested enterprise in industries that are conducive to the development of China's economic benefits, and not prohibited or restricted by the state."

The location of the office is also important. Many factors impact the decision of where to house your operations. An analysis of whether to rent, buy, or build is helpful. If build is the choice, then it is prudent to appoint a local design bureau to ensure compliance with building regulations. In addition, you need to commission a construction company to build the facility if ready-built premises are not available. Once the building has been completed, it is time to staff the various positions in order to carry out the intended operations.

A Note on the Setup of a WFOE

Investment in China does not guarantee success, however, there is much evidence that an increased presence there will generate opportunities that may not have been originally envisaged. It is important to have a robust business plan that will stand scrutiny. Challenge statements that rules and regulations do not permit the establishment of your stated enterprise. Meet and lobby the mayor and every official in the municipality, so that everyone understands your plans and, more importantly, feels involved in your new and exciting enterprise. This should help to achieve the best terms and a condensed time frame for the establishment of your new enterprise.

During negotiations, the establishment of a WFOE should be made conditional on the selected development zone assisting in obtaining all the necessary permissions, licenses, and approvals. Such processes are quite tedious, however, and it is essential to secure the best terms available. Although a "fast track" is possible, the process will normally take around six months.

Meet officials informally before your application is submitted to explain your plans and expectations. Listen to their advice. They will be helpful and may be flexible if they can understand your overall plan. Convey enthusiasm to all. Ensure that officials understand the features of your enterprise and the benefits to their municipality through your investment.

Application Procedures

All documentation should be issued through the offices of your professional advisers who will be working with the selected development zone where you plan to create your enterprise:

Stage One: Submit initial report (usually takes around 30 days).

Stage Two: Submit feasibility study: investment details, level of employment, organizational structure, and expected profitability (allow 60 days for approval).

Stage Three: Submit formal application: name and address of WFOE, scale of production, plant required and technology to be imported, impact on environment, raw material requirements, names of directors, importation requirements, articles of association, and taxation of WFOE (additional 60 days).

Stage Four: Submit business proposal, feasibility study, list of equipment requirements, memorandum of understanding, legal documents of parent company, proof of company credit, names of directors, letter appointing directors to the board, recommendations for general manager and deputy general manager and their identification papers, notification of approval of WFOE, and name (another 30 days).

Stage Five: Application to foreign trade commission for business license.

Once your business license is approved, you may proceed with applications to the State Administration of Industry and Commerce. Having obtained approval from the tax and customs authorities, and the commodity inspection bureau, you are now legally entitled to open foreign exchange and renminbi accounts and can start to employ staff and commence the long processes that are needed when establishing any new facility. You are now in business in China.

HONG KONG CEPA

China and Hong Kong Special Administrative Region signed a Closer Economic Partnership Agreement (CEPA) on June 23, 2003. Under CEPA, Hong Kong companies enjoy zero tariffs for exports to China. China also granted preferential treatment to Hong Kong service suppliers for liberalization in market access to many service sectors.[3] The Hong Kong government has aggressively promoting CEPA as a way to attract more investments by companies from other countries that want to get access to China. CEPA provides business from overseas an attractive opportunity to leverage on the zero-tariff status of goods with a Hong Kong origin to compete favorably in fast-growing China. CEPA covers three areas: trade in goods, trade in services, and trade and investment facilitation. In 2004 and 2005, Beijing and Hong Kong expanded CEPA to CEPA II and CEPA III. CEPA II took effect on January 1, 2005, and CEPA III the year after, respectively. CEPA has been offering new business opportunities in the Mainland for Hong Kong businesses and service suppliers, enhancing the attractiveness of Hong Kong to overseas investors. The WTO-plus liberalization measures for services trade will give companies in Hong Kong a head-start over their competitors from other economies.

Trade in Goods

Starting from January 1, 2006, Beijing has given all products of Hong Kong origin (except prohibited articles) tariff-free treatment. This zero-tariff treatment requires manufacturers meeting the rules of origin (ROOs). The majority of products with agreed CEPA ROOs follow process-based rules of origin. The remaining products follow either a "Change in Tariff Heading" rule, a "value-added content" rule, or a rule having regard to the characteristics of products concerned. Change in Tariff Heading means that a product has been manufactured to the extent that its classification in the World Customs Organization Harmonized System falls in a different four-digit tariff heading from the classification of the constituent materials used. Value-added content rule refers to the total value of raw materials, component parts, labor costs, and product development costs incurred in Hong Kong being greater than or equal to 30 percent of the FOB value of the exporting goods.

Under the three phases of CEPA, the Mainland and Hong Kong have agreed on the CEPA ROOs for 1,370 products.[4] For products that have no agreed CEPA ROOs for the time being, both sides have agreed that Hong Kong manufacturers may apply and request to include them in subsequent phases of ROO discussions that will be held twice a year. This will provide greater flexibility to potential investors planning to manufacture products that are not currently produced in Hong Kong. The Trade and Industry Department (TID) of HK government has issued a circular to announce the timetable and procedures for local manufacturers to submit requests.

The Mainland has also agreed to relax the CEPA ROOs for watches by waiving the 30 percent value-adding requirement for watches of Hong Kong brand names. TID has issued a circular to announce the implementation details on the revised ROO for watches and registration procedures of Hong Kong brand watches.

To claim zero import tariff under CEPA, products being exported into the Mainland must be accompanied by a Certificate of Hong Kong Origin-CEPA (CO(CEPA)) issued by TID or one of the Government Approved Certification Organizations (GACOs). Before applying for CO(CEPA), manufacturers are required to apply for a Factory Registration (FR) with TID to demonstrate that their factories possess sufficient capacity to produce the goods for export.

Trade in Services

The Mainland has agreed to provide preferential treatment to Hong Kong service suppliers in 27 service areas:

1. Accounting
2. Advertising
3. Airport
4. Audiovisual
5. Banking
6. Cultural
7. Convention and exhibition
8. Distribution
9. Freight forwarding agency
10. Individually owned stores
11. Information technology
12. Insurance
13. Job referral agency
14. Job intermediary
15. Legal
16. Logistics
17. Management consulting
18. Medical and dental
19. Patent agency
20. Professional qualification examinations
21. Real estate and construction
22. Storage and warehousing
23. Securities and futures
24. Telecommunications

25. Tourism
26. Trade mark agency
27. Transport

CEPA permits earlier access for Hong Kong service suppliers to the Mainland market, ahead of China's World Trade Organization (WTO) timetable. In some sectors, like audiovisual services, transport services, and distribution services, the concessions go beyond China's WTO commitments.

Generally speaking, "juridical persons" as well as "natural persons" of Hong Kong will be able to enjoy preferential treatment granted by the Mainland, provided that they fulfill the definition and related requirements of Hong Kong service suppliers. Unless otherwise specified in CEPA, a natural person means a Hong Kong permanent resident, whereas a juridical person means any legal entity duly constituted or otherwise organized under the applicable laws of Hong Kong and which has engaged in substantive business operations in Hong Kong for three to five years.

Trade and Investment Facilitation

Both Beijing and Hong Kong agreed on enhancing cooperation in the following seven areas:

1. Trade and investment promotion
2. Customs clearance facilitation
3. Commodity inspection and quarantine, food safety and quality and standardization
4. Electronic business
5. Transparency in laws and regulations
6. Cooperation of small and medium enterprises
7. Cooperation in Chinese traditional medicine and medical products sector

Both have agreed that trade and investment facilitation plays a crucial role in the successful implementation of CEPA. Some of the measures under CEPA III have been worked out with the intention to enhance the flow of trade and investment between the two places. Major achievements include:

- Textiles and clothing products under Hong Kong's Outward Processing Arrangement (OPA) are exempt from the Mainland's export duty when they are reimported to Hong Kong; and
- Permission for certain types of Mainland securities and futures companies to come to establish in Hong Kong.

CEPA and WTO

Hong Kong is in close proximity to the dynamic Pearl River Delta Economic Zone, which covers Guangzhou, Shenzhen, Dongguan, Foshan, Zhongshan, Zuhai,

Jiangmen, and parts of Huizhou and Zhaoqing. Two of the special economic zones (SEZs) are in this region. Preferential policies in the SEZs included a number of features designed to attract foreign investment, such as a 15 percent tax rate, tax holidays of up to five years, and the ability to repatriate corporate profits and to repatriate capital investments after a contracted period. They also included duty-free treatment of imports of raw materials and intermediate goods destined for exported products, as well as exemption from export taxes.

China's accession to the WTO has sped up the openness of the Pearl River Delta region. Many multinational companies find it advantageous to extend their sales and distribution networks from Hong Kong into the rest of the region. The greater openness in services called for under the WTO accession agreement has opened China's markets to multinational service providers. In light industry, WTO entry allows the export-oriented firms of the Pearl River Delta region to expand their markets. By making it easier to import intermediate goods and capital equipment, greater openness allows Pearl River Delta region production facilities larger scope to leverage their competitive advantages in local and global markets.

With CEPA, the Greater Pearl River Delta region already exhibits a very high degree of integration between Hong Kong and the Pearl River Delta in light manufacturing. In many service sectors, CEPA lowered barriers of entry into the Chinese Mainland for Hong Kong service providers before China's WTO commitments take effect, allowing firms based in Hong Kong an early mover advantage.

Setting Up in Hong Kong

Setting up a presence in Hong Kong is simple and straightforward. The Hong Kong government has claimed that it takes six days and a fee of just a few hundred U.S. dollars. There are many types of structure to choose from, including private limited companies, branch office, representative office, partnership/sole proprietorship, and joint ventures. Each of those requires a business registration certificate. The certificate costs HK$2,600 and is renewable annually. The certificate is issued by the Inland Revenue Department. Alternatively, you can apply for a certificate that lasts three years for which a special rate applies.

To register a private limited company, check the availability of the company name, submit documents for registration, and then submit the application and fee for a business registration certificate. The submitted documents include a signed copy of the company's Memorandum and Articles of Association and a Statement of Compliance on Incorporation. Alternatively, a foreign company may consider buying a company off the shelf or purchase of an existing business.

Another option is to establish a branch in Hong Kong. Unlike a subsidiary, a branch leverages off the credit rating of the foreign company. One key difference between a branch and a subsidiary is the operating scope and tax treatment. The overseas company must submit to the Registrar of Companies the completed Form F1 (lists particulars of the company) and certified copies of incorporation, company's constitution, and account statements. The normal process takes 22 business days to process and issue a certificate of registration.

A representative office in Hong Kong is another option. For a representative office, the registration is simple but it may only collect information or maintain contacts with customers, so-called promotional and liaison work. A representative office cannot enter into contracts, except for renting office space and for utilities. A representative office is prohibited from carrying on any business in Hong Kong. If it does, it is required to register as a branch.

Partnerships/sole proprietorships do not have a separate legal entity, therefore the sole proprietor or partners are personally liable for the debts and liabilities of the business. The number of partners is limited to 20. Ongoing requirements are less onerous for partnerships/sole proprietorships than for a corporate structure. Finally, a joint venture is created when two or more partners want to undertake business together. Once the joint venture has been established, all partners have entered an agreement on the terms of the venture and they can establish the company.

CONCLUSION

For many large multinationals, entering China is an important strategic move. Understanding of Beijing's policy in terms of foreign entry makes a difference between success and failure. The chapter reviewed the areas where China favors foreign investments. The chapter also discussed the regulatory requirements for establishing a presence in various sectors of the financial services industry. In addition, some companies, especially export oriented, may benefit from the special access through Hong Kong under CEPA.

II

CHINA'S FINANCIAL MARKETS AND INVESTMENT BANKING

7

Opportunities and Challenges for Foreign Firms in China's Financial System

China's financial system is highly regulated and relatively underdeveloped. The high economic growth rate and the entry into the World Trade Organization (WTO) have led to reform of the financial sector in order to comply with WTO commitments and support economic growth. The reform and opening of the market provide foreign financial institutions access into this huge underdeveloped market. Large global financial institutions from all over the world have taken strategic positions in China to operate in retail banking, corporate banking, asset management, securities brokerage, investment banking, and other financial services.

THE FINANCIAL SYSTEM

There was only one bank in China's financial system from 1950 to 1978. The People's Bank of China (PBC) served as the central bank for the country as well as a commercial bank. After 1979, PBC's commercial business was transferred to state-owned commercial banks. The Bank of China (BOC) specialized in transactions relating to foreign trade and investment. People's Construction Bank of China (PCBC) aimed at transactions in fixed investment in manufacturing. The Agricultural Bank of China (ABC) took over business in rural area. In 1984, the Industrial and Commercial Bank of China (ICBC) was established to assume the remainder of the commercial banking business from the PBC. In 2003, China Banking Regulatory Commission (CBRC) was established to assume the regulatory and supervision functions of the banking sector. The PBC has since focused on the monetary policy and the liquidity of the financial system. Additionally, there are policy lending banks, city banks, joint-stock commercial banks, and foreign banks.

There are also nonbank financial institutions. Trust and investment corporations (TICs) support the development of the private sector and provide financing outside of the credit quotas imposed on commercial banks. To better manage the huge amount of nonperforming loans, the Chinese government set up asset management companies (AMCs) in 1999 to assume nonperforming loans from the state-owned commercial banks. Disposal of at least a portion of these loans has resulted in better coverage ratios and better return on equity. Three state-owned banks have successfully listed their shares in Hong Kong and in Shanghai.

Securities companies have played an important role in the development of China's financial system in the 1990s. The establishment of the Shanghai Stock Exchange and the Shenzhen Stock Exchange has facilitated the issuance of shares to privatize the state-owned enterprises. More than 1,300 Chinese companies have listed their shares in Shanghai and Shenzhen. Many now also list their shares in Hong Kong, London, New York, and other exchanges as well. The bond market is underdeveloped. The government securities market operates under tight policy guidance, not driven by market forces. The corporate bond market is insignificant. The derivatives markets are in an early stage of development.

The insurance market is dominated by the state-owned insurance companies as well. There are many joint ventures that have shifted their focus from market share to profitability. In the insurance market, the life insurance industry dates back to the establishment of the People's Insurance Company of China (PICC), which was established by the People's Republic of China (PRC) in 1949. PICC achieved monopoly status in China's insurance market by the mid-1950s. However, the Chinese government suspended virtually all of PICC's domestic insurance business in 1958, until the advent of economic reform in 1979, when PICC's domestic property and casualty insurance business was resuscitated. PICC's life insurance business resumed operations in 1982, with PICC being the only life insurance provider in China. Initially, the life insurance market focused principally on the group insurance sector, and life insurance products lacked diversity. In the late 1980s, more life insurance companies started to enter the market, with the establishment of two Chinese companies, Ping An Insurance Company of China and China Pacific Insurance Company, and the entry of foreign insurance companies. Distribution channels for individual life insurance products began to emerge and agency salesforces began to develop. Recently, a popular life insurance product is participating a 10- to 15-year endowment policy with guaranteed rates of return set by the government. These products often include additional coverage for health and personal accident. Private pension schemes and other investment products are not popular but the influx of foreign companies is likely to bring development to this area of the market. From 2007, foreign firms will also be allowed to offer all health coverage to domestic and foreign clients, and group, pension, and annuities policies by 2008.

The official Chinese currency is the renminbi (RMB) or the yuan. RMB is the only legal tender in China; foreign currency can be exchanged in banks, but is not allowed to circulate. China has an extensive array of regulations governing the inflow and outflow of capital. Residents borrowing abroad are subject to stringent controls.

The loans must be approved by and registered with the State Administration of Foreign Exchange (SAFE). Since 1996, the government has relaxed its foreign exchange controls and permitted limited convertibility of RMB in order to promote economic development, attract foreign investments, and encourage overseas investments by Chinese companies. Such deregulation has led to several high-profile U.S. acquisitions by Chinese companies. In May 2005, China's largest computer maker purchased IBM's PC business for $1.8 billion. In June 2005, China's Haier Group announced a $1.3 billion offer to buy Maytag and China National Offshore Oil Corporation launched an $18.5 billion unsolicited bid for Unocal. These bids were not successful, but signified China's financial power and its visibility in the global capital markets.

PEOPLE'S BANK OF CHINA

The PBC was established on December 1, 1948, based on the consolidation of the former Huabei Bank, Beihai Bank, and Xibei Farmer Bank. In September 1983, the State Council delegated the PBC as China's central bank. On December 27, 2003, the Standing Committee of the Tenth National People's Congress approved at its Sixth Meeting the amendment to the Law of the People's Republic of China on the People's Bank of China, which has strengthened the role of the PBC in the making and implementation of monetary policy and safeguarding the overall financial stability.

Under the guidance of the State Council, the PBC formulates and implements monetary policy, prevents and resolves financial risks, and safeguards financial stability.

The Law of the People's Republic of China on the People's Bank of China provides that the PBC performs the following major functions:

- Issuing and enforcing relevant orders and regulations
- Formulating and implementing monetary policy
- Issuing RMB and administering its circulation
- Regulating interbank lending market and interbank bond market
- Administering foreign exchange and regulating interbank foreign exchange market
- Regulating gold market, holding, and managing official foreign exchange and gold reserves
- Managing the State Treasury
- Maintaining normal operation of the payment and settlement system
- Guiding and organizing the antimoney laundering work of the financial sector and monitoring relevant fund flows
- Conducting financial statistics, surveys, analysis, and forecasts
- Participating in international financial activities
- Performing other functions specified by the State Council

The objective of the monetary policy is to maintain the stability of the value of the currency and thereby promote economic growth.

In China, monetary policy instruments include reserve requirement ratio, central bank base interest rate, rediscounting, central bank lending, open market operation, and other policy instruments specified by the State Council.

The Monetary Policy Committee (MPC) plays an important role in the making of monetary policy and in macroeconomic management. This committee is similar to the Federal Open Market Committee (FOMC) in the United States. However, the FOMC is independent of political influence while the MPC's recommendations are subject to the State Council's approval. The committee's responsibility is to advise on the formulation and adjustment of monetary policy and policy targets for a certain period, application of monetary policy instrument, major monetary policy measures, and the coordination between monetary policy and other macroeconomic policies. The committee plays its advisory role on the basis of comprehensive research on economy and the macrotargets set by the government.

Membership of the MPC includes the PBC's Governor and two Deputy Governors, a Deputy Secretary-General of the State Council, a Vice Minister of the State Development and Reform Commission, a Vice Finance Minister, the Administrator of the State Administration of Foreign Exchange, the Chairman of China Banking Regulatory Commission, the Chairman of China Securities Regulatory Commission, the Chairman of China Insurance Regulatory Commission, the Commissioner of National Bureau of Statistics, the President of the China Association of Banks, and an expert from academia.

The MPC performs its functions through its regular quarterly meeting. A special meeting may be held if called by the Chairman or endorsed by more than one-third of the MPC members. The meeting minutes, if approved by more than two-thirds of the members, are attached as an annex to the proposed recommendations by the PBC on money supply, interest rates, exchange rates, or other important monetary policy issues reported to the State Council for approval.

Recent Changes in Interest Rates

The People's Bank of China raised benchmark interest rates for RMB deposits and lending for financial institutions on August 19, 2006. The benchmark rate for one-year deposits was increased by 27 basis points from 2.25 percent to 2.52 percent. The one-year benchmark lending rate was raised by 27 basis points from 5.85 percent to 6.12 percent. Rates on deposits and lending for other maturity segments are presented in Table 7.1. To prevent the economy from overheating, the PBC in March 2007 raised interest rate on deposits and loans again by another 27 basis points.

For commercial mortgage loans, the lower limit of lending rates was lifted from 90 percent to 85 percent of the benchmark rate, while that of other commercial loans remain unchanged. Commercial banks have the discretion to set their interest rates of commercial mortgage loans above the announced lower limit according to relevant state policies and risk profiles of loans.

On another front, China raised the reserve requirement ratio of deposit-taking institutions by 0.5 percent on August 15, 2006. The reserve requirement ratio of rural

TABLE 7.1   Changes in Interest Rates in 2006

	Interest Rates	
Items	Before Adjustment	After Adjustment
Household and corporate deposits		
Demand deposit	0.72	0.72
Time deposit for deposit and withdraw both in lump sum		
3-month	1.71	1.80
6-month	2.07	2.25
1-year	2.25	2.52
2-year	2.70	3.06
3-year	3.24	3.69
5-year	3.60	4.14
Loans		
6-month	5.40	5.58
1-Year	5.85	6.12
1–3 year (inclusive)	6.03	6.30
3–5 year (inclusive)	6.12	6.48
Over 5 years	6.39	6.84

Source: People's Bank of China.

credit cooperatives (including rural cooperative banks) remains unchanged. The interest rate increases and the higher reserve requirements were implemented to slow down the rate of growth in fixed assets investment, fast expansion of money and credit, and widening trade surplus. Table 7.2 lists the changes in reserve requirements in recent years.

BANKING MARKETS

China's commercial banking industry consists of four large state-owned commercial banks (SOCBs) that dominate market shares in loans and deposits. Lending to poor performing state-owned enterprises (SOEs) has led to high nonperforming loans. China established four asset management companies (AMCs) in 1999 to buy nonperforming loans from commercial banks. The four state-run AMCs are China Orient, Great Wall, Huarong, and Cinda. As of late 2005, those four AMCs have acquired about $325 billion of nonperforming loans from China's five largest commercial banks. Those loans were sold mostly to domestic investors and local governments buying back the debt of SOEs in their jurisdictions. Foreign purchases of nonperforming loans remain relatively insignificant.

TABLE 7.2   History of Interest Rate Changes

Date	Reserve Requirements (%)	Lending Rate of One-Year Term (%)	Deposit Rate for One-Year Term (%)
July 1996	13.0	10.08	7.47
March 1998		8.64	5.67
March 1998	8.0	7.92	5.22
December 1998		6.69	3.78
July 1999	6.0	5.85	2.25
February 2002		5.31	1.98
August 2003	7.0		
April 2004	7.5		
October 2004		5.58	2.25
April 28, 2006		5.85	
July 5, 2006	8.0		
August 15, 2006	8.5		
August 19, 2006		6.12	2.52

Sources: People's Bank of China and various news items.

China made major commitments to reform its banking industry with respect to foreign banks. Over time, foreign banks were given permission to accept deposits and extend credits. The geographic coverage of their banking operations extended from Shanghai and Guangzhou to other cities in China. By the end of 2006, the geographical restrictions were lifted.

The Big Four

In 1995, the Chinese government introduced the Commercial Bank Law to commercialize the operations of the four state-owned banks, the Bank of China (BOC), the China Construction Bank (CCB), the Agricultural Bank of China (ABC), and the Industrial and Commercial Bank of China (ICBC). Those four state-owned commercial banks are called the Big Four.

ICBC is the largest bank in China by total assets, total employees, and total customers. BOC specializes in foreign-exchange transactions and trade finance. CCB specializes in medium to long-term credit for long-term specialized projects, such as infrastructure projects and urban housing development. ABC specializes in providing financing to China's agricultural sector and offers wholesale and retail banking services to farmers, township, village enterprises, and other rural institutions.

In 2002, BOC Hong Kong (Holdings) was successfully listed on the Hong Kong Stock Exchange. Furthermore, BOC also successfully completed its IPO by listing on the Hong Kong Stock Exchange in 2005, raising almost $10 billion.[1] ICBC's IPO in 2006 raising more than $19 billion is the largest in history.

Policy Banks

Three new policy banks, the Agricultural Development Bank of China (ADBC), China Development Bank (CDB), and the Export-Import Bank of China (Chexim), were established in 1994 to take over the government-directed spending functions of the four state-owned commercial banks. These banks are responsible for financing economic and trade development and state-invested projects. ADBC provides funds for agricultural development projects in rural areas, the CDB specializes in infrastructure financing, and Chexim specializes in trade financing.

Second-Tier Commercial Banks

In addition to the Big Four and policy banks, there are smaller commercial banks. The largest ones in this group include the Bank of Communication, CITIC Industrial Bank, China Everbright Bank, Hua Xia Bank, China Minsheng Bank, Guangdong Development Bank, Shenzhen Development Bank, China Merchants Bank, Shanghai Pudong Development Bank, and Fujian Industrial Bank. The second-tier banks are generally healthier in terms of asset quality and profitability and have much lower nonperforming loan ratios than the Big Four. The exception was Guangdong Development Bank, which was taken over by a consortium led by Citigroup after its severe distress.

Trust and Investment Corporations

During the early reform era of the 1980s, the government established several investment companies to engage in investment activities. However, many of those trust and investment corporations experienced severe liquidity problems after the bankruptcy of the Guangdong International Trust and Investment Corporation (GITIC) in late 1998. The largest surviving entity is China International Trust and Investment Corporation (CITIC), which has a banking subsidiary known as CITIC Industrial Bank.

Reforms in the Banking Industry

Years of government-directed lending has presented Chinese banks with large amounts of nonperforming loans. In 1999, four asset management companies were established to assume the nonperforming assets from the banks. The AMCs repackage the nonperforming loans and sell them off to investors.

The central government has allowed several small banks to raise capital through bonds or stock issues. Following the listing of Shenzhen Development Bank and Pudong Development Bank, China Minsheng Bank, the only private bank in China then, was listed on the Shanghai (A shares) Stock Exchange in December 2000.

After Beijing selected the Bank of China and China Construction Bank to pilot shareholding restructuring reform in late 2003, the similar reform of ICBC was kicked off in April 2005. By June 2005, ICBC had completed its financial reorganization. On October 27, 2005, China Construction Bank made a successful IPO in Hong Kong, issuing 26.49 billion H shares at a price of HK$2.35.[2] As indicated earlier, BOC and ICBC have also listed their shares, and they together raised almost $30 billion.

As foreign entry has intensified and the banking markets have become more competitive, Chinese banks need to continuously improve their services and operating efficiency. After listing their shares, they are subject to additional requirements.

Entry by Foreign Financial Institutions

The allure of the largest consumer market and the opening of the banking sector have created a mad rush by foreign banks to become shareholders in China's banks. In recent years, many foreign banks have invested in strategic stakes in Chinese banks. International Finance Corporation and HSBC started to acquire stakes in Nanjing City Commercial Bank and Bank of Shanghai in 1999 and 2001. Citibank followed with a 4.62 percent investment in Shanghai Pudong Development in 2003. Barclays started to offer a wide range of banking services to the Chinese public when it opened its first branch office in Shanghai in December 2005. In 2006, a Citigroup-led consortium won the right to buy 85 percent of China's Guangdong Development Bank for $3.2 billion, beating rival groups led by ABN AMRO and Societe Generale. The majority of foreign investments in Chinese banks took place during 2004 and 2006, to position themselves to take advantage of the WTO 2006 market-opening schedule.

SECURITIES MARKETS

A unique feature in China's stock markets is that companies may issue A shares and B shares. A shares are reserved for Chinese residents and are denominated in RMB. B shares were exclusively for foreign investors, but in February 2001, the PRC government allowed Chinese residents to purchase B shares. B shares are not convertible to A shares, but both types of shares give their owners the same rights with one exception: dividends for B shares are in foreign currencies. Indications from China have signaled most market observers to expect the convergence of A and B shares in the near future.

The special characteristics of B shares are:

- B shares are denominated in RMB, but are traded in foreign currency (in U.S. dollars in the Shanghai bourse and Hong Kong dollars in Shenzhen).
- Dividends and other payments are calculated and declared in RMB, but paid in foreign currency.
- B shares were only issued to foreign investors before 2001. After 2001, domestic individual investors can open B shares account and trade B shares.

- Dividends and capital gains from B shares can be sent abroad despite China's strict foreign exchange control.
- Foreign securities houses can serve as dealers of B shares and, if they are designated as qualified foreign institutional investors (QFIIs), they are allowed to engage in the business of A shares.[3]

B shares provide foreign investors with access to China's equity market. B shares trade on both exchanges. Before entering the WTO, foreign brokerage firms were only able to trade B shares through local brokers.

In addition to B share transactions, foreign investors can participate in China's stock markets through several other alternatives, including shares listed in Hong Kong (H shares), New York (N shares), and London (L shares). H shares are listed on the Hong Kong exchange to tap offshore financing. They are traded in Hong Kong dollars and can only be traded by Hong Kong residents or overseas investors. In Hong Kong, there are also Red Chip stocks, which are issued by Hong Kong companies that either are controlled by Chinese corporations or derive considerable revenues from operations in China. N shares are listed in New York in ADRs. Dividends are declared in RMB but paid in U.S. dollars. L shares are listed in London in accordance with a memorandum of understanding signed between the United Kingdom and China in 1996. As of February 2007, 86 companies issued both A and B shares while 34 companies floated A and H shares.

Market for B Shares

The face value of B shares is denominated in RMB, but B shares are traded in U.S. dollars on the Shanghai Stock Exchange and in Hong Kong (H.K.) dollars on the Shenzhen Stock Exchange. B shares allow Chinese companies to raise funds in U.S. or H.K. dollars without listing abroad. B share issuers are expected to meet the following requirements:

- The capital raised by issuing B shares shall be used in a manner consistent with state industrial policy.
- Compliance with regulations regarding fixed-asset investments and foreign investments.
- The joint-stock company shall be set up with at least five promoters, with more than half of them being located in China. The promoters must hold at least 35 percent of the issued shares at the time when the company is set up.
- The capital contributions by promoters shall not be less than RMB 150 million.
- The company must maintain a public float in excess of 25 percent of the company's total shares; however, if the company's total share capital exceeds RMB 400 million, the public float may be reduced to not less than 15 percent of the company's total shares.

- Neither (a) any predecessor entity (entities) of which the joint-stock company was part of; nor (b) any major promoter who is also a state-owned enterprise, had committed any significant breaches against the law over the past three years.
- Both (a) and (b) in the previous item have been continuously profitable for the past three years.
- Other requirements as stipulated by the CSRC from time to time.

Trading Characteristics of A and B Shares

The number of A shares is more than 10 times the number of B shares. Prior to 2002 QFII initiative, only Chinese citizens were allowed to own A shares. Similarly, only foreign investors were allowed to trade B shares prior to 2001. Now, QFIIs can trade and invest in A shares and Chinese residents can trade B shares. Thus, the convergence of A and B shares is expected. Table 7.3 lists the various indexes, including the A and B share indexes, from the Shanghai Stock Exchange.

Investment Management

Investment management industry started in China in 1998 when the CSRC approved 10 fund management companies for the first time. Unlike the United States, where the number of open-end funds dominates that of closed-end funds, there were no open-end funds in China until 2001. The lure of the Chinese markets lies in the country's high savings rate and low mutual fund penetration. In addition, the rising pension liabilities will also drive the growth of the fund management industry.

TABLE 7.3   Market Indexes on Shanghai Stock Exchange

Indexes	Previous Closing	Last	High	Low	Change (%)
SSE 180	3134.97	3175.10	3179.34	3128.78	1.28
SSE 50	1088.75	1101.97	1102.61	1085.76	1.21
SSE Composite	1725.04	1736.96	1740.79	1722.22	0.69
SSE New Composite	1440.76	1452.21	1455.99	1437.81	0.80
SSE Dividend	1153.58	1159.44	1162.18	1151.20	0.51
SSE A Share	1812.31	1824.46	1828.62	1809.29	0.67
SSE B Share	102.03	104.74	104.78	101.94	2.66
SSE Fund	1215.47	1229.65	1230.20	1214.20	1.17
SSE Government Bond	110.81	110.96	110.96	110.80	0.13
SSE Corporate Bond	120.05	119.98	120.05	119.93	−0.06

Source: Shanghai Stock Exchange, at close of September 28, 2006.

U.S. fund managers have entered the Chinese markets. Merrill Lynch established a joint venture with Bank of China International (investment banking arm of Bank of China). It began to sell the first fund in late 2004, listed on the Shenzhen Stock Exchange in the first quarter of 2005. Despite it being the second listed open-end fund, the fund raised only $130 million, less than half the amount hoped for. Investors can either trade listed open-end funds like regular stocks on an exchange, or redeem invested cash as with a regular mutual fund. American International Group, UBS, ING, Societe Generale, and Allianz have also established a presence to tap into the $1.5 trillion savings market.

As discussed earlier, QFIIs could invest in A shares starting December 2002. Foreign investors are also allowed to buy domestic Treasury and corporate bonds. Since the government owns a substantial amount of the nonfloating A shares, QFII allows the government to sell its stocks without turning to the stock market. The significance is that government has a new way of selling its shares and that foreign investors have access to the Chinese stock markets. QFIIs will also bring in professional asset management expertise to manage the assets of the growing retirement and pension programs. The pension reform from a pay-as-you-go system to a paid reserve system increases the long-term flows of capital to the stock market and drives the growth of the fund management business. Corporations and local government will also outsource the management of pension to fund managers. The high savings rate and the low mutual fund penetration provide a boost as well.

Bond Market

The bond markets include interbank, over-the-counter market, and exchange-traded bond market. Treasury bonds and financial bonds dominate the market. Financial bonds are issued by the Import and Export Bank of China, China Development Bank, and other policy banks. Corporate bond markets are small.

The interbank OTC market is mainly for block trading among financial institutions. The People's Bank of China (PBC) uses it to implement its monetary policies. The exchange-traded bond markets are on the two stock exchanges. Participants are securities firms, insurance companies, investment trusts, and institutional and individual investors. The PBC and commercial banks do not trade in this market. Instruments traded in this market are Treasury bonds, corporate bonds, and convertible bonds. This market is relatively small.

Treasury Bonds

The public sector dominates the issuance of domestic debt. Treasury bonds and policy financial bonds account for almost all of the debt issuance. In the United States, Treasury securities trade over the counter. In China, Chinese government securities trade over the counter as well as over the exchanges. The Ministry of Finance (MOF) issues Treasury bonds (the largest portion of the bond market), construction bonds, fiscal bonds, and special bonds. Government bonds can also be divided into two categories: book entry or bearer.

Financial Bonds

Policy banks, such as China Development Bank and Export-Import Bank, issue a significant amount of domestic debt. These bonds are known as financial bonds and are generally considered quasi-government paper. Proceeds from financial bonds are used to support infrastructure projects and develop strategic industries. Both government bonds and financial bonds play an important role in central bank's open market operations as well as in the repurchase agreement market. A repurchase agreement transaction is a financing arrangement in which a party puts up fixed-income securities as collateral to borrow cash and simultaneously agrees to repurchase the same securities in the future.

Corporate Bonds

The smallest segment of the market is corporate bonds. There are three types of corporate bonds, including central corporate bonds, local corporate bonds, and corporate short-term bonds. For issues larger than RMB 100 million, issuers can seek approval from CSRC to list on exchanges. Both Shanghai and Shenzhen stock exchanges require at least an A rating by domestic credit rating agencies. The interest rate on corporate bonds used to be capped at 1.4 times comparable bank deposit rate, regardless of credit rating. The reason is that many believe the risk is ultimately born by the government in a central planning economy where the state virtually owns all companies. Table 7.4 lists the total amount of issuance and trading summary of various instruments during 2006 as of August 1, 2006.

INSURANCE MARKETS

China's insurance market is small and has a limited variety of insurance products. The penetration rate is extremely low. As such, there is a great potential for the market to grow. Another factor limits the growth of the insurance industry is that China's undeveloped financial markets limit investment vehicles for insurance premiums. The financial market is not well developed and deep enough to accommodate a range of investment options. The Chinese insurance market traditionally focuses on savings products rather than risk products. In order to make the savings product attractive, they have to be priced at high interest rates. The available investment assets are deposit and some short-term bonds. These assets may not cover the interest rate guarantee in the policy. Furthermore, these assets are much shorter term than the liabilities sold by the insurer, thus creating an asset liability mismatch issue.

TABLE 7.4 Outstanding and Average Trading Summary Statistics for Year 2006

Yearly	Total	A-Share	B-Share	Securities Investment Fund	T-Bond Spot	T-Bond Repo	Financial and Corporate Bond	Convertible Bond
No. of listings	1113	826	54	24	49	9	60	17
No. of new listings	66	5	0	0	12	0	14	3
Issued volume	231422957	71805225	1074421	3930000	139725500		12255000	2283412
Market value	529891314	365281452	3524160	3571820	141379319		12979293	2755543
Tradable volume	177847831	18998754	1074421	3894100	139725500		12255000	418138
Market value of tradable volume	269196483	105871697	3524160	3538833	141379319		12979293	473305
Turnover in volume	150900654.2	57926666.01	865589.18	4223783.06	11126.67	73774.14	405.65	1171.24
Daily average	943129.09	362041.66	5409.93	26398.64	69.54	461.09	2.54	7.32
Daily high	2301943.12	870189.32	31196.68	116352.95	218.86	1428.99	20.27	62.62
Daily Low	316801.8	133986.41	1291.62	7268.5	10.36	139.87	0.17	0.08
No. of transactions	32563.88	2562.47	298.98	244.63	61.42	26.15	3.83	13.72
Daily average	203.52	166.02	1.87	1.53	0.38	0.16	0.02	0.09
Daily high	449.16	377.29	8.02	6.73	0.86	0.52	0.14	0.47
Daily low	79.15	60.31	0.51	0.45	0.15	0.05	0	0.01
Turnover in value	532508147.8	317867723.3	3036971.18	3312304.59	1117906.66	73774140	433060.93	1350671.69
Daily average	3328175.92	1986673.27	18981.07	20701.9	69868.79	461088.38	2706.63	8441.7
Daily high	7071320.66	5295333.35	100178.84	100771.99	219395.26	1428990	22954.16	72687.48
Daily low	1479879.13	661294.68	5292.82	4828.46	10349.63	139870	172.45	91.53

Source: Shanghai Stock Exchange.

China's insurance sector is facing adjustment under the WTO. Life insurance companies have paid out obligations that are greater than their current return on investments. One of the imminent consequences is that some domestic companies have sold large quantities of fixed-interest-rate insurance policies at the peak of business operations. The risk is that the rate those insurance companies earn might not be sufficient to cover payouts.

Another problem is that a few companies dominate the sector. Shortages of actuaries and professional insurance management staff have contributed to poor business practices by insurance companies. In quality of service and business skills, the country's insurance companies lag behind the international ones. Domestic insurance companies will have to make serious efforts at adopting international business and prudential practices so that they can adjust to international competition.

Market Potential for Foreign Insurers

China's insurance sector has registered 10 percent to 15 percent growth in premium income for the past several years. Many foreign insurance companies have been granted permission to operate some form of insurance business in China. The market, if developed in a planned and efficient way, is big enough to accommodate a whole array of companies.

The China Insurance Regulatory Commission estimated that in the near term the annual growth rate of the Chinese insurance industry will be sustained at about 12 percent. In the face of growing competition, near stagnant market share, and precarious bottom line, North American insurance companies are clamoring for new business and are increasingly looking for greener pastures outside their conventional geographical boundary. Asia, with its burgeoning economy, lion's share of world population, and increasingly open financial sector, seems to be the logical destination for these companies.

China, with its purchasing prowess of 1.3 billion people, leapfrogging economic growth, and slow-but-steadfast economic reforms, is attracting the investors most. The sleeping giant of Asia—China—is awakening and is well-poised to take on the mightiest of economic superpowers in the coming decades. China implemented land reforms across the country to ensure even distribution of wealth and increased purchasing power in the economy. Under its regimented centralized leadership, it has implemented a controversial but successful population policy, deemed critical to its survival and sustenance. It has achieved commendable success in the spread of literacy and education that has resulted in a vast knowledgeable workforce. After putting all the ingredients of success into place, it opened up its door for infusion of the scarce resource: capital formation.

China leveraged its enormous market potential to bring in foreign direct investment (FDI) in a somewhat discreet and selective manner. It opened up its market, yet at the same time kept a tight leash on the control and extent of reform in the hands of the government to ensure that its economy did not fall prey to the vagaries of market forces. This policy was successful because China was the only economy in East Asia that was not hurt during the great fall of crony capitalism in Asia during the 1990s.

China's average growth rate of around 10 percent during the past decade was spectacular, and it is poised to become the economic superpower in the near future, second only to the United States. Western economies rightly perceived the need to integrate the Chinese economy with the rest of the world, and it is now just a matter of time to complete the measures required under WTO agreement and other multilateral economic forums.

Brief History

In 1984, the State Council separated the state-run PICC from the PBC and offered standard insurance products such as life, property, and reinsurance services. To create a more competitive domestic insurance market environment, China permitted more than 10 smaller Chinese domestic insurance companies to set up operations during 1984 to 1998. Even with these newly established companies, by the mid-1990s PICC still controlled roughly 70 percent of China's insurance market. In 1996, to further stimulate and develop China's domestic insurance market, PICC was divided into three independent insurance companies: China Life Insurance, China Property Insurance, and China Reinsurance Co. In 1998, PICC was abolished, leaving the three companies to operate independently.

The rapid growth of the insurance industry required the establishment of a much-needed legal framework. In 1995, the National People's Congress promulgated a formal insurance law. Another major step was the establishment of the China Insurance Regulatory Commission (CIRC) in November 1998 which assumed insurance regulation responsibilities from the PBC. CIRC's responsibilities are:

- Formulates and enforces related laws and regulations
- Oversees insurance business operations
- Protects the interests of policy holders
- Develops the insurance market, maintains order in it, and ensures fair competition
- Facilitates insurance industry reform and restructuring
- Sets up a risk evaluation and advance warning system to minimize insurance risk

The establishment of the CIRC stabilized and strengthened the domestic insurance market and gradually improved the conditions for broader international involvement.

The Commission also declared that while property insurance firms can be wholly foreign-funded because of the short-term nature of property insurance, life insurance, which is fixed and long term, must take the form of joint ventures. The CIRC set about regulating management and claims settlement procedures, and reining in the approval of new firms.

New rules prohibited the representative offices of foreign insurers and risk management consulting agencies from getting involved in unauthorized intermediary business or recruiting sales agents in China. The objective of these rules was to give coverage to the domestic insurers and to stop the flight of premium income out of the country and to reduce domestic insurers' risk. The CIRC also aimed to increase the number of domestic reinsurers to break the existing reinsurance market monopoly.

Since domestic stock markets were perceived to be immature, inefficient, and shallow, the state banned insurers from participating in the stock market. The insurers were thus limited to investing in bank accounts or state bonds. But poor loan performance and repeated interest rates cuts led to insurers' insolvency. Hence, the CIRC allowed insurers to buy certain state-backed corporate bonds. As the stock market developed and with the enactment of the Securities Law, the CIRC, in 1999, allowed insurers either to trade in existing securities investment funds on the secondary market or to use five percent of their assets to purchase newly issued stocks through mutual funds in the primary market.

In 2000, the CIRC ruled that approved local finance companies were allowed to invest in insurance businesses. But they prohibited banks, securities institutions, the military, social groups, and state institutions from entering into the insurance business. Any registered firm with legal status could invest in an insurer as long as it had sound operations, made a profit, and had net assets constituting more than 30 percent of total assets. The shares of any single foreign shareholder was limited to 5 percent of an insurer's total share value. Also, the total ownership of foreign investors in an insurer was capped at 25 percent.

Inadequacy of business volume, strained profitability, limited product variation and coverage, nonprudent risk management, and dated technology are hindering the sector's global competitiveness. The CIRC has proposed that firms strive to lower the nominal rate of life insurance products, continue to develop new products, improve the quality of service, call back nonperforming assets, minimize risk through reinsurance, and adopt new tools to expand business and reduce operating costs.

Foreign Insurers in China

As part of the financial reforms and opening up of the market, China began to allow limited foreign access to its emerging insurance sector. In 1992, foreign insurance companies were invited to assist China in developing its domestic insurance market by imparting training to Chinese personnel, hosting symposiums on insurance issues, and supporting insurance education in China. Insurance companies were also encouraged to invest in China. But at the same time, the PBC required foreign insurance companies to meet various criteria in order to obtain permission to operate. Each local government also imposed specific requirements to receive a business license. By these procedures, the Chinese government was able to control the speed at which the insurance sector opened.

In practice, even companies with licenses faced many restrictions and limitations. Foreign insurance operations were limited to two cities. While most licenses were issued only for Shanghai, a few additional licenses were issued also for Guangzhou and Shenzhen. Since 1997, any foreign insurer wanting to write life insurance policies had to form a joint venture with a Chinese insurance partner. Life insurance policies could be sold only to individuals, not groups; property insurance could only be sold to foreign-invested businesses.

Because of these myriad problems, as well as the slow rate of approval of foreign business licenses, insurance was one of the major issues in the WTO entrance negotiations. As a result of the WTO, Chinese authorities have begun to restructure the domestic industry. Some of the steps taken include:

- Establishing more domestic insurance companies and permitting existing domestic insurance companies to operate in more cities
- Setting up alliances between domestic insurance companies and Chinese banks, starting with the largest insurance company, China Property Insurance, and the largest domestic state-owned bank, Industrial and Commercial Bank of China
- Providing training programs to enable Chinese insurance companies to compete with foreigners, to provide additional capable personnel for the insurance sector, and to hire foreign insurance professionals as advisers
- Increasing the percentage of Chinese insurance companies holding stock-based investment funds
- Enforcing regulations on both Chinese and foreign insurers to create a more fair and transparent insurance market environment

Changes under WTO

Under WTO commitments, several changes have taken place in the insurance industry, including:

- China permits foreign property and casualty firms to insure large-scale risks nationwide immediately upon accession.
- China expands the scope of activities for foreign insurers to include group health and pension lines of insurance, phased in over five years after joining the WTO.
- China allows 50 percent foreign ownership and phase out internal branching restrictions.

- For nonlife insurance, China allows 51 percent foreign ownership upon accession to WTO.
- China awards licenses for insurance business solely on the basis of prudential criteria, with no economic needs test or quantitative limits on the number of licenses issued.

Additional WTO commitments include:

- Internal branching is permitted consistent with the phase-out of geographic restrictions.
- Reinsurance, master policy insurance, and large-scale commercial risk insurance can be provided nationwide upon accession.
- Health, pension, and group products can be sold two and three years from accession, respectively; and brokerage services will be permitted.

China lifted nearly all geographic and business scope restrictions on foreign insurers near the end of 2004, fulfilling commitments made upon entry into the WTO. In 2005, negotiations were on the removal of remaining restrictions on foreign insurers, including the right to offer motor vehicle third-party liability insurance and set up wholly owned foreign life insurance businesses. By 2005, 37 foreign insurers entered the hugely promising Chinese market.

FOREIGN EXCHANGE MARKETS

Foreign companies operating in China are required to open a current account and a capital account with a designated foreign exchange bank. The current account is used for daily recurring transactions in the ordinary course of business. Current account transactions do not require SAFE's approval. The capital account is used for import and export capital, direct foreign investment and loans, and securities transactions. Prior approval of SAFE is required for all capital account transactions. The government permits current account items, including dividend payments and profits, to be freely converted into foreign currencies. Removing those funds from the country (repatriation), however, is a capital account activity and thus requires SAFE's approval.

The exchange rate was fixed at US\$1 = RMB 8.276. The United States has been pressing China to allow its currency to float. With \$1.2 trillion foreign exchange reserves and an increasing trade surplus, a freely trading Chinese RMB would rise in value against the dollar. That would make Chinese exports less competitive, make imports cheaper, and give a relief to U.S. manufacturers. If China let its currency rise against the dollar, other Asian countries would also permit their currencies to appreciate because their exporters would no longer fear being undercut by China.

On April 29, 2005, the RMB rose to 8.270 from the pegged value of 8.276 to the U.S. dollar. It lasted for 20 minutes. A rise of 0.006 might not seem much of a change. But, it came at a time of intense speculation that a Chinese revaluation might be imminent. The brief appreciation led to some speculation that China's financial system and currency regime were ready for its currency to float. Whatever caused the brief spike in the RMB value, the pressure to appreciate RMB is both internal and external. Many economists believe that China risks serious inflation if it continues printing RMB and exchanging them for the dollar in an effort to hold down the RMB value in the currency markets. On July 21, 2005, China finally appreciated RMB by 2 percent and changed its policy to tie its currency to a basket of currencies instead of U.S. dollars. The Chinese currency has continued to appreciate to 7.72 yuan per U.S. dollar by April 2007, as listed in Table 7.5. Many observers expect convergence of H.K. dollar and the RMB soon. The exchange rate of H.K. dollar to U.S. dollar is HK$7.79 = US$1.

TABLE 7.5 Renminbi Exchanges Rates with Major Currencies (RMB per 100 Unit of Quoted Currency)

Date	U.S. Dollar	Euro	Yen	H.K. Dollar
2007-04-20	771.8	1048.9	6.505	98.78
2006-09-26	791.5	1009.7	6.8004	101.684
2006-09-25	791.96	1012.35	6.7921	101.747
2006-09-01	795.9	1019.73	6.7823	102.328
2006-08-01	797.3	1016.83	6.956	102.601
2006-07-03	799.24	1021.65	6.9851	102.906
2006-06-01	802.1	1025.97	7.1222	103.39
2006-05-08	800.9	1018.96	7.1611	103.313
2006-04-03	802.1	970.13	6.7871	103.366
2006-03-01	803.9	959.54	6.9344	103.63
2006-02-06	805.6	969.67	6.7851	103.85
2006-01-04	807.02	970.91	6.9535	104.08
2005-12-01	808.04	952.25	6.7673	104.17
2005-11-01	808.45	974.69	6.9826	104.25
2005-10-08	809.2	973.88	7.1529	104.27
2005-09-01	809.98	986.74	7.2654	104.17
2005-08-01	810.56	982.21	7.2327	104.23
2005-07-29	810.8	977.78	7.198	104.22
2005-07-28	811.28	974.31	7.1954	104.23
2005-07-27	810.99	977.09	7.2496	104.25
2005-07-26	810.97	988.22	7.2421	104.25
2005-07-25	811.11	1001.41	7.3059	104.78
2005-07-22	811			
2005-07-21	827.65	999.14	7.3133	106.37
2005-07-20	827.65	994.81	7.3777	106.4

FINANCIAL MARKET REFORMS

China has taken steps to open its economy and to reform its financial markets. The financial market reforms have been successful, though not as fast as many have anticipated.

The measures that China has taken to open and reform its markets in recent years are beneficial to both China and foreign investors. In the financial markets, consistent with WTO commitments, China will continue to deregulate the markets in insurance, banking, asset management, foreign exchange, and securities. Previous sections in this chapter and earlier chapters have discussed the development of the financial markets, deregulatory process, and the expected upcoming changes. This section highlights some of the important reforms and extends the coverage to include recent observations in the foreign exchange market.

Major financial sector reforms starting in 2003 until recently are summarized in Table 7.6, highlighting the key changes implemented in participation by foreign banks in the domestic market, conversion of nontradable shares into tradable shares and other measures.

In reforming the foreign exchange market, China introduced advanced trading systems, new foreign exchange products, and widened the band that its currency can float. Those are summarized in Table 7.7.

Furthermore, China has also taken steps to boost its domestic demand and to focus on rural economic development and expand social and educational services.

TABLE 7.6   Financial Sector Reform

2003	2004	2005	2006
$45 billion recapitalization of two state-owned banks	Tighter capital adequacy requirements and stricter loan classification	$15 billion recapitalization of ICBC	Central bank launched nationwide consumer credit bureau
Foreign banks allowed greater RMB business and larger stakes in JVs	Lower barriers on foreign bank entry and branching	Program to convert nontradable shares to tradable	Expansion of QFII program
	Ceiling on bank lending lifted giving banks greater flexibility in loan pricing	Asian Development Bank and IFC received approval to issue Yuan denominated bond	Anticipated convergence of A and B shares
		Allowed limited foreign strategic investments in listed domestic companies	Successful IPO of ICBC
		Successful IPOs of two large state-owned banks	

Source: Newspaper reports and U.S. Department of Treasury.

TABLE 7.7 Foreign Exchange Market

2004	2005	2006
Allowed foreign banks to offer foreign exchange products	Allowed banks to trade non-RMB spot currency pairs in China on Reuters system and Chinese banks are allowed to act as market makers	Introduced OTC interbank trading in RMB spot delivery and allowed banks to act as FX market makers
Plan to introduce FX futures		First RMB interest rate swap
Introduced Reuters-based onshore, non-RMB FX trading platform	Abandoned fixed exchange rate (against U.S. dollars) and adopted managed float	China and CME agreed to allow electronic trading of CME FX and interest rate products
	Introduced interbank forward FX market	Expected to widen daily band for RMB spot against U.S. dollars
	Allowed institutions expanded ability to trade and hedge FX risk	
	Widened daily band to 3% for RMB spot against non-U.S. dollar currencies	
	Central bank did FX swap with local banks	

Source: Newspaper reports and U.S. Department of Treasury.

First, China has doubled the amount of exemption for personal income tax and eliminated the agricultural tax. Second, it established a minimum wage system to raise income of lower income urban households. The third major step taken was to enhance development of the rural areas. Beijing increased central government funding to finance infrastructure to supply drinking water, electricity, hydropower, and road construction. In addition, China moved to establish a consumer credit system to increase consumer finance, such as mortgage and automobile loans.

CONCLUSION

This chapter reviewed China's financial market reforms and the opportunities for foreign financial services companies. The reforms are expected to continue and will result in a financial market environment where financial institutions compete for business in terms of services, pricing, and management. In addition, the Chinese currency has appreciated and will continue to appreciate against the U.S. dollar. In the long term, some researchers believe an appreciation of 40 percent is appropriate. In the shorter term, the market has expected the convergence of the yuan and the H.K. dollar.

8

Private Equity Fund Management and Investing

An increasing number of private equity investors are investing in companies with significant presence in China. This reflects China's rising importance as one of the world's most important manufacturing bases and markets. This chapter provides a discussion on private equity including venture capital and buyout investing, in general and in China. We first review private equity investing in China and then examine general issues in fund raising, sourcing, due diligence, investing, risk factors, management fees, profit-loss allocations, and exit strategies. To be successful, it is essential to have local partnerships and to plan exits in advance.

OVERVIEW

Private equity (PE) refers to equity investment in a company in which the equity does not trade on a public stock market. Private equity covers a wide range of deals, including seed, expansion, turnaround, and buyout. Venture capital funding provides growing companies early stage financing. There are many failures for every successful investment. Buyouts are aimed at improving corporate performance and financial status to enhance value, and then take profits.

China has a large mass-manufacturing base, engineering and entrepreneurial talent, and large domestic markets. Those are favorable to a venture opportunity. China is an established low-cost manufacturing center for many industries, including electronics, automobile parts, textiles, semiconductors, and communications. Such capabilities are supported by a deep pool of educated talent that can be employed at a fraction of the cost of U.S. or European equivalents. The National Science Foundation reported that, in 2000, China graduated 195,000 bachelor-level engineers compared to 61,000 for the United States. Availability of low-cost engineering expertise makes China an attractive site for technology development that would be substantially more expensive if located in the West. With a growth rate around 10 percent, many multinationals see China's 1.3 billion people as an attractive consumer market. On top of those advantages, capital is flowing into China. Beijing encourages innovation and has implemented a program to develop Chinese technology standards in a number of strategic industries. Chinese companies are developing products and services to their own standards, especially in communications. Foreign companies are also setting up local engineering and development centers to take advantage of low-cost local talent.

In recent years, PE funds from all over the world are increasingly looking to China for investment opportunities. One big driver is the privatization of state-owned enterprises (SOEs). Another force behind such rising interests was the Chinese government's revision of rules governing foreign invested venture capital funds. Under the revised rules, it is easier to establish a fund in China and realize an exit. Until a few years ago, the biggest problem with investment in China was getting shares or capital out of China. Now many investments in China are being flipped. There is also momentum building because of listings in Hong Kong and/or the United States. One good example is Shanghai-based Semiconductor Manufacturing International, raising $1.8 billion in its Hong Kong listing. Private equity investors in this company included H&Q Asia Pacific, Goldman Sachs, Toshiba Corporation, Walden International, Vertex Venture Capital, and Oak Investment Partners. For SOEs, they provide PE firms attractive public market exit opportunities after introducing right corporate governance and sound management practices.

There is also an emergence of privately owned enterprises in China that are targets for PE funds to evaluate, though many privately owned enterprises are not very approachable targets as the owners do not generally want to cash out or give up control. Among them, hundreds of thousands would qualify to list on NASDAQ. But still, some PE managers believe there is too much money flowing into China chasing any deals without proper due diligence that will eventually hurt PE returns. Thus, some PE investors are very selective and some invest only in firms with management that operates under U.S. accounting standards.

Success Factors

Most foreign venture capital (VC) funds investing in Chinese companies are based offshore to take advantage of tax benefits and the more convenient exits these structures offer. Those offshore VC firms register in the Caymans, Bermuda, or the Virgin Islands. They then establish units in China to carry out day-to-day operations. Foreign venture capitalists also use onshore investment vehicles to carry out their businesses. They may directly invest in domestic companies, joint ventures, foreign wholly owned companies, and other opportunities. Most of these funds base their operations in Hong Kong, but some have representative offices on the Mainland.

To be successful, it is important to establish a good local network or a local partner who can bring a range of local contacts to the table. In addition, it is helpful to combine the European and U.S. experiences with China's situation. Some observers have suggested that for a non-Asian investor seeking to enter the Chinese market, a partnership with a Taiwanese, Hong Kong, or foreign VC firm with a Chinese office may be an ideal entry strategy because understanding the language and the culture is crucial to success. Such a partnership will shorten the learning curve and limit the risk. Some of the successful VCs in China today are those with local executives on their team who have been in the United States doing deals and then returned to the Mainland. There are also a number of U.S. businesspeople who have lived and worked in China who now broker deals between foreign companies and Chinese companies.

Another factor is discipline and prudent due diligence. This means that you have to know how to prioritize investment opportunities. One target may take three months to close, while the other may take nine months. Being good at setting realistic timelines for deals and devoting the appropriate level of resources to them is necessary. Once an investment is made, the challenges are to find the right management team. The best candidates are Chinese nationals who received their education and industry experience overseas. They understand the culture and language from both sides but also have the scope of experience and understanding of business processes, communications, and marketing required to run a successful business in China.

Private Equity Investors in China

One of the first Chinese private equity firms was China New Technology Venture Investment Co., founded in 1985. Foreign firms soon followed. International Data Group (IDG) established the first foreign fund to operate in China in the early 1990s. More PE firms followed over subsequent years. Table 8.1 lists leading PE funds in China. Table 8.2 lists the most top VC-backed entrepreneurs/companies in China.

U.S. Investment Banks

In the United States, investment banks are involved with PE investments, from raising capital for the funds to taking the portfolio company public or selling out to other businesses. An investment bank may simply raise money for external PE funds. An investment bank, alternatively, can manage the fund itself. Even though many PE investments prove less than successful, others are quite profitable with attractive overall annual returns.

Private equity includes venture capital and buyouts. The company in which the PE fund has made an investment is called the portfolio company. In addition to the many independent funds, major Wall Street houses all have PE operations. PE is of interest to investment banks because it has several benefits including management fee, capital gains, and contributing to underwriting and merger and acquisition business.

Many PE funds focus on specific industries such as software, biotechnology, real estate, or retail. Some pursue investments across a broad range of industries and geographic regions. PE funds that invest in the world markets need to have professionals knowledgeable in the cultural and regulatory complexities of each region. While each fund has its own unique objectives and returns, the PE industry on average has

TABLE 8.1 Top Venture Capital Funds in 2006

Rank	Fund	Rank	Fund
1	IDG Technology Venture Investment	26	Gobi Partners Ltd.
2	SAIF Partners	27	Redpoint Ventures
3	Sequoia Capital China	28	NewMargin Ventures
4	Legend Capital	29	Shenzhen Capital Group Co., Ltd.
5	Granite Global Ventures	30	Pacific Venture Partners
6	Softbank China Venture Capital	31	JAIC
7	Walden International	32	UCI
8	JAFCO Asia	33	Infotech Ventures Co., Ltd.
9	Intel Capital China	34	Shenzhen Fortune Venture Capital Co., Ltd.
10	CDH Ventures	35	Shandong High-Tech Investment Corporation
11	iD TechVentures Ltd.	36	Qualcomm Ventures
12	WI Harper	37	China-Singapore Suzhou Industrial Park Ventures Co., Ltd.
13	Doll Capital Management	38	Shenzhen Tsinghua Leaguer Venture Capital Co., Ltd.
14	Qiming Venture Partners	39	AsiaVest Partners
15	DT Capital Partners	40	Heilongjiang Chenergy-HIT Hi-tech Venture Capital Co., Ltd.
16	Venture TDF China LP	41	Bessemer Venture Partners
17	Capital Today Group	42	Chengwei Ventures
18	Orchid Asia Group Management Co., Ltd.	43	BlueRun Ventures
19	CEYUAN Ventures	44	Milestone Capital Management Ltd.
20	GSR Ventures	45	Tsinghua Venture Capital Management Co., Ltd.
21	NEA	46	Hunan High-Tech Venture Capital Co., Ltd.
22	Draper Fisher Jurvetson ePlanet	47	Zhejiang Venture Capital Co., Ltd.
23	Lightspeed Venture Partners	48	Tianjin Venture Capital Co., Ltd.
24	Northern Light	49	China Merchants Technology Holdings Co., Ltd.
25	Fidelity International Ventures	50	Wuhan Huagong Venture Capital Co., Ltd.

Source: Zero2ipo-China Venture Capital Annual Report 2006.

TABLE 8.2   Top Venture Backed Entrepreneurs/Companies of the Year 2006

Rank	Entrepreneur	Position	Enterprise	Investor
1	David Sun	CEO	Home Inns & Hotels Management Inc.	IDG Technology Venture Investment, etc.
2	Minhong Yu	Chairman and President	New Oriental Education & Technology Group	Tiger Fund
3	Hang Xu	Chairman	Shenzhen Mindray Bio-Medical Electronics Co., Ltd	Walden International
4	Vincent Mo	Chairman and CEO	www.soufun.com	IDG Technology Venture Investment, etc.
5	Ping Wu	CEO and President	Spreadtrum Communications Corp.	NEA, Legend Capital Limited, ePlanet Ventures, etc.
6	Yongqi Zhang	Principal	Global IELTS School	SAIF Partners
7	Light DK Peng	Chairman	LDK Solar Hi-Tech Co., Ltd.	Natexis Private Equity Asia, CDH Investments, JAFCO Asia, etc.
8	Congwu Cheng	President	AutoNavi Holdings Ltd.	Walden International, Sequoia Capital China, etc.
9	Chris Chen	CEO	Worksoft Creative Software Technology Ltd.	Legend Capital Limited, Doll Capital Management, Sequoia Capital China, etc.
10	Xiaochuan Zhang	President and CEO	Chinacars	Granite Global Ventures

Source: Zero2ipo-China Venture Capital Annual Report 2006.

provided good returns to investors in recent years. As discussed later, the management fee of 1.5 percent, on average, and incentive fees of 20 percent attract many top talents.

PRACTICAL CONSIDERATIONS

High-profile PE stories are attracting more investors from the United States and Europe to China. They hope to discover China's next Microsoft, Google, FedEx, and Bidu.com. Each PE fund has its own strategy (e.g., to target firms such as technology, infrastructure, biotech, or consumer staples). Despite the allure, there are challenges. This section outlines some of the important considerations a PE fund needs to consider when operating in China.

Offshore Holding Company

Foreign investors enjoy favorable tax treatment and other benefits if they own at least 25 percent in a Chinese company. This can take the form of a joint venture or wholly foreign-owned enterprise (WFOE). By regulation, a WFOE is wholly foreign owned and may not have any ownership by Chinese domestic residents. The tax benefits granted to a foreign invested enterprise (FIE) include a corporate tax holiday for the first two years of profitable operation and a 50-percent tax holiday for the next three years. Another benefit to the FIE is the ability to import manufacturing equipment duty-free. Of course, it is helpful to check with appropriate agencies for updates as there might be changes to current regulations.

One of the simple forms of FIE is direct ownership of the enterprise by the foreign investor. There are several advantages in making the investment in the FIE through an offshore holding company. The first advantage is that, when there are coinvestors, the business relationship is not governed by the law of China. Thus, the enforceability of each party's rights and obligations is more certain. Second, there is a great flexibility in follow-on financing at the holding company. In addition, it is easier to transfer ownership without Chinese governmental involvement.

SAFE Circular 75

State Administration of Foreign Exchange (SAFE) issued Circular 75 on October 21, 2005, to ease restriction on PE investing. Prior regulation required any Chinese domestic resident who directly or indirectly gained control of an offshore holding company to first obtain SAFE's approval. A prior approval by the SAFE was also required for any Chinese domestic resident to exchange domestic assets or equity interests for the stock or assets of a foreign company. Under SAFE Circular 75, Chinese domestic residents are required to register with SAFE rather than obtain approval.

Due Diligence

The importance of due diligence in any investment, anywhere, cannot be overstated. Investing in China must go through careful business and legal diligence at every stage. This includes background investigations of the key personnel and confirmation that the proposed deal is permitted under the law. It is also prudent to examine ownership and title issues, labor and social obligations, and real estate and environmental compliance. A typical due diligence involves the following:[1]

- *Presigning:* Nondisclosure agreement, letter of intent outlining the proposed deal and providing for a period of exclusivity, and documents needed for forming the FIE or special purpose vehicle
- *At signing:* Execution and delivery of agreements and related documents to effect the transaction

- *Prior to closing:* Formation of the FIE or the special purpose vehicle, and application for Chinese government approvals
- *At closing:* Contribution of capital into the formed entity, and use of such offshore capital to fund the Chinese domestic enterprise

During the process, many important factors are worth special consideration because there are differences between due diligence in the United States or Europe and China. The differences range from level of transparency, related party transactions, to enforceability of indemnification.[2] In financial reporting, the U.S. GAAP is more restrictive than the China GAAP. The conversion of financial statement from the China GAAP to U.S. GAAP can result in lower reported revenues, unexpected charges related to business combinations, and reduced profit due to stock option accounting. Understanding the impact of the conversion will help foreign PE funds to calibrate their expectations correctly and better evaluate their targets. In addition, PE funds have experienced a low success rate in closing the deal, normally at 20 to 30 percent. The reasons are quality of earnings issues, lack of transparency, and a time line from letter of intent to closing stretching from 6 months to 18 months. Table 8.3 outlines some of those important areas.

Exit Strategies

Main exit strategies are an initial public offering (IPO) or a sale. Exit via an IPO requires careful planning at the time of the investment. For example, Hong Kong Stock Exchange (Main Board) requires that the listed company have had the same owners for the full year immediately preceding the listing and that management has been substantially the same for the past three years.[3] Therefore, PE investors may want to con-

TABLE 8.3   Differences in Due Diligence

	China	*United States/Europe*
Transparency in financial information	Low, if any	High
Duration of due diligence	3–12 weeks	1–8 weeks
Preparation time by target before due diligence	May need extensive assistance	Minimal
Basis of financial statements	PRC GAAP, at best	US GAAP or IFRS
Audited financial statements	Not as reliable	Reliable
Related party transactions	Usually extensive, inadequate disclosure	Varies, fully disclosed
Disclosure of contingent liabilities	Rarely disclosed	Usually transparent
Reliability of representations and warranties	Untested	Normally reliable
Enforceability of indemnification	Untested	Strong

Source: Ernst & Young. "Annual Venture Capital Insights Report: Focus China, 2003/2004."

TABLE 8.4   VC-Backed IPOs

Listed Company	Listing Date	Exchange
Ctrip	December 9, 2003	NASDAQ
Huicong	December 17, 2003	HK GEM
Linktone	March 4, 2004	NASDAQ
SMICS	March 16, 2004	NYSE and HK MAIN
Sinocom	April 30, 2004	HK MAIN
ChinaCast	May 4, 2004	Singapore MAIN
Shanda	May 13, 2004	NASDAQ
ChangCheng	May 18, 2004	HK MAIN
Minghuahan	July 7, 2004	HK MAIN
KongZhong	July 9, 2004	NASDAQ
51 Job	September 29, 2004	NASDAQ
JRJ.com	October 15, 2004	NASDAQ
elong	October 28, 2004	NASDAQ
Zhenzhen Jiedian	November 18, 2004	NASDAQ
Nine	December 3, 2004	HK MAIN
the 9th	December 15, 2004	NASDAQ
Vimicro	November 14, 2005	NASDAQ
Actions Semiconductor	November 29, 2005	NASDAQ
SunTech	December 13, 2005	NASDAQ
China GrenTech	March 29, 2006	NASDAQ
Himax Tech	March 30, 2006	NASDAQ
New Oriental	September 6, 2006	NASDAQ

Sources: Zero2ipo Venture Capital Research Center and corporate news releases.

sider convertible debt instead of common shares if they plan to take a substantial stake in a company followed by a quick IPO. To exit from an investment via a sale, it is efficient for the PE investor to include drag-along clauses in the investment agreement to make sure that, if the requisite percentage of shareholders decides to sell, the minority shareholders will not delay the transaction. Table 8.4 lists samples of IPOs of companies backed by private investors. Table 8.5 provides several examples of sale as exit strategy.

If a transaction involves a SOE, the investor needs to be aware that every purchase or sale decision the enterprise makes is subject to review and approval by the State-Owned Assets Supervision and Administration Commission. Thus, it is possible that a deal that the investor has agreed with the management of a SOE is later deemed invalid. When dealing with a SOE, PE investors must be prepared to deal with multiple layers of bureaucracy.

Strategies for Exiting Distressed Investments

There will be instances when the investments are not successful and an exit, rather than turnaround, is the preferred strategy. The primary objective in such instance is to

TABLE 8.5   Sale of VC-Backed Companies

Acquirer	Chinese Target
Amazon	Joyo
Tom Online	Treasure Base
Sohu	Goodfeel
Sina	Grillion
Sohu	17173
Sohu	Focus.com
Hurray	Nihon Enterprise
HK.com	New Palm
Sina	MeMeStar
eBay	EachNet
Tom	Leiting Wuji
Yahoo	3721
NHN	GlobalLink
Shanda	Digital Red

Source: Zero2ipo.

maximize the salvage value. At the same time, it is important to minimize the negative public relations. The tools available are limited and the success of an exit also in large part depends on the relationship with local, provincial, and central government authorities. In the case of a JV, relationship with the commercial partner has a direct influence on negotiations and outcomes.

There are several options to exit a distressed investment. They are: (1) sell on "as is" basis, (2) fix and sell, and (3) termination of the JV agreement. The first stage in planning the exit from a JV is to review the status of the venture and the obligations of the foreign partner. The foreign PE investors should review the following information and materials:[4]

- *Joint venture contract and related agreements:* It is necessary to understand the foreign investor's obligations and rights on termination. Compliance with terms and conditions will avoid difficulties with sale/termination of the JV. Any issues that may affect the sale of the foreign partner's interest need to be identified early. In addition, rules and guidelines governing foreign economic contracts and the JV should be updated and reviewed.
- *Shareholding structure:* The review and assessment is to determine whether it is preferable to sell at the JV or the holding company level.
- *Current financial and operational status:* The review focuses on the operational issues, cash position, outstanding liabilities, and compensation issues to the domestic partner in a termination scenario.
- *Attitude of the domestic partner:* The best scenario is that the domestic partner buys in the exit strategy. A productive and amicable relationship with the domestic partner will help with formulating and implementing the exit strategy.

- *Board of directors and management:* The numbers of board seats held by the foreign investor and by the domestic partner have an impact on the exit strategy. The management structure plays an important role as well. If the domestic board members and the partner/management agree on the same exit strategy, then both sides can join forces to work toward the same goal.
- *Dispute resolution mechanism:* The foreign investor might have to resort to arbitration if the JV contract or local regulations call for such a process. In such a case, the effectiveness and fairness of the local arbitration procedures need to be considered. It is helpful to avoid arbitration if the process favors the local partner or the process is too slow.

A careful review and consideration of those factors is helpful to the foreign investor to develop a successful exit strategy. Some of the unexpected surprises can be avoided as well. Once this is completed, the next step is to decide on and implement one of the following exit strategies:

- *Sell to a third party:* The distressed business can be sold as is. Alternatively, the business can be fixed and then sold to a third party. Early contact and discussion with potential buyers can provide valuable input in deciding whether to sell as is or to fix and sell. The administrative process and difficulty in transferring ownership in China vary widely, depending on the degree of cooperation from the local partner and related government agencies. Without local cooperation, the purchaser of the foreign investor's interest in the business will have difficulties getting recognized by the local partner and registering new directors and related matters.
- *Sell to the domestic partner:* It is possible that the local partner or the local government may be willing to buy the foreign partner out. If this is done, the domestic partner will become the sole shareholder of the venture and it would be converted from a JV to a Chinese enterprise. The change in nature of the firm may result in costly consequences to the domestic partner. For example, certain benefits granted to a FIE may be lost.
- *Termination of the joint venture agreement:* There are two approaches to terminating the JV agreement. First, it is surrender of foreign investor's interest in the partnership to the local partner. The foreign investor wants to surrender in exchange for release from current or future obligations. The success of this option depends on the value of the JV to the domestic partner against the foreign investor's obligations. The second termination possibility is that it is allowed by the agreement. If not, this availability of this option to the foreign investor is contingent upon approval by the Chinese partner and/or the local government.
- *Bankruptcy:* Where it is the major creditor as well as shareholder of the company, the foreign investor might want to start legal procedures to liquidate the company to collect the amount due to it and to exit. The foreign investor needs to be aware that a Chinese court might require an applicant place a deposit to the court close to the amount of its claims.

- *Abandonment:* In the rare desperate situations, the foreign investor may just want to abandon the joint venture or to cease funding the operation as an exit strategy. Before taking such a strategy, foreign investors have to consider the consequences of such an action, including adverse publicity, possible director's liability, and negative impacts on the investor's other existing or prospective investments in China.

In summary, exiting an investment in China can be more challenging than entering it. Knowledge of the agreement, laws, and regulations is essential. The experience of what has been achieved in similar circumstances is invaluable. The foreign partner's leverage, however, in the exit process is inherently low.

PRIVATE EQUITY FUND OF FUNDS

In recent years, there have been many funds of funds. These funds often work with investors to develop PE goals and objectives. The primary aim of the managers of these funds of funds is to construct diversified portfolios of limited partnerships among venture capital and buyout opportunities. Each investment opportunity is considered for its potential to add diversification to investor portfolios. Factors considered before investing in a specific fund include identifiable track records, experience in institutional capital, well-defined strategies, discipline in dealing with short-term ups and downs and long-term value, and ability to realize profits with successful exits. Most often the fund of funds conducts reference checks and visits some of its portfolio companies.

Once the fund of funds has determined to invest in a PE fund, it negotiates business and legal issues before closing. After closing, the fund of funds closely monitors the activities and investments of the portfolio fund relative to its stated strategies and prior experience. Such a hands-on approach also covers attending annual meetings, participation on advisory and valuation committees, visits to partnership offices and selected portfolio companies. Another essential element in the fund of funds process is the consideration and judgment regarding the sale or retention of public securities distributed by the partnerships.

PRIVATE EQUITY VALUATION METHODS

Data on private companies are limited. Early stage companies generally experience a period of negative cash flows and negative earnings before they produce positive net income. The timing and the amount of future profits are highly uncertain. Thus, valuing private companies is subjective and difficult. In this section, we discuss several valuation approaches including comparables, net present value, option valuation, and venture capital methods.

The comparables approach compares the target with comparable transactions or comparable companies. Comparable transaction analysis evaluates transactions involving companies in the target's industry or similar industries over the past several years. Acquisition multiples are calculated for the universe of the comparable transactions. These multiples are then applied to the target's financial results to estimate the value at which the target would likely trade. This technique is most effective when data on truly comparable transactions are available. Similarly, the comparable company approach makes assessment of how the value of the potential acquisition candidate compares with the market prices of publicly traded companies with similar characteristics. This method is similar to the comparable transaction approach in that it identifies a pricing relationship and applies it to the candidate's earnings, cash flows, or book value. A change of control premium should be added to the value identified by this method to arrive at the estimated valuation range for the target. One weakness of this technique is that it works well only when there are good comparables for the target. Another weakness is that accounting policies often differ from one company to another, which could result in material differences in reported earnings or balance sheet amounts.

Another widely used technique is the discounted cash flow (DCF). The DCF method determines the value of the private concern by evaluating the cash flow projections of the target and discounting those projections to the present value. The DCF approach is future oriented, it begins with a projection of sales and operating profits. The usefulness of this technique depends on several assumptions. These assumptions include the impact on the company's other areas of business, length of projection period, additional working or fixed capital required, discount rate, and residual value. The value of the DCF should be estimated under different scenarios.

The option valuation method assigns a value to the flexibility that the PE has on making follow-on investments. This right is similar to a call option on a company stock, which is a right, not an obligation, to acquire an asset at a certain price on or before a particular date. Options pricing theory captures this "option" to either invest or not invest in the project at a later date. This valuable option is not accounted for by the DCF approach. The Black-Scholes model was the first widely accepted method to value European options using five variables: (1) exercise price, (2) stock price, (3) time to expiration, (4) standard deviation of stock returns, and (5) time value of money. To value a firm, the five variables used are (1) the present value of expenditures required to undertake the project, (2) the present value of the expected cash flows generated by the project, (3) the length of time that the PE can defer the investment decision, (4) the riskiness of the underlying assets, and (5) the risk-free rate. The value is then obtained once those input variables have been estimated. This approach is useful because it specifically incorporates the flexibility to wait, to learn more, and then to make the investment decision. The options valuation has its drawbacks, too. Many businesspeople are not aware of this "real option" concept. Furthermore, the real-world problems are often too complicated to be captured in the model.

The venture capital method takes into account negative cash flows and uncertain high future profits. It considers cash flow profile by valuing the target company at a time in the future when it expects to generate positive cash flows and earnings. The terminal value at that projected target date is discounted back to the present value by applying a discount rate, a target rate of return (TRR), instead of the cost of capital. The TRR is the rate of return that the venture capitalist requires when making an investment in the portfolio company. The terminal value is generally obtained using price-earnings ratio multiplied by the projected net income in the year. The amount of proposed investment is divided by the discounted terminal value to give the required final percentage ownership that the venture capitalist wants to own. The final step is to calculate the current percentage ownership taking into consideration the dilution effects when the portfolio company goes through several rounds of financing. This is done by calculating a retention ratio that factors in the dilutive effects of future rounds of financing on the venture capitalist's ownership. For example, assume that the portfolio company will sell 30 percent in the second round and then another 25 percent in the third round before it goes public. The retention ratio is 61.5 percent, meaning that 1 percent ownership in the initial investment is diluted to only 0.615 percent after two rounds of financing. If the venture capitalist invests $10 million and requires a final percentage ownership of 10 percent, she will require the current ownership percentage of

$$\frac{\text{Required final percentage ownership}}{\text{Retention ratio}} = \frac{10\%}{0.615} = 16.26\%$$

The 16.26 percent current percentage ownership is necessary for the venture capitalist to realize the target rate of return.

VENTURE CAPITAL

Venture capital firms make equity investments in entrepreneurial companies. The venture capitalists recoup their investments when the portfolio companies either go public or sell out to other corporations. The VC market includes the merchant banking subsidiaries of large institutions such as investment banks, bank holding companies, industrial companies, and insurance companies. The VC industry also has many independent, specialized investment entities.

Venture capitalists set up partnerships pooling funds from a variety of investors. They seek out fledgling companies to invest in and work with these companies as they expand and grow to become publicly traded companies. By going public or selling out to other businesses, the VC realizes its returns. VC-backed companies use venture capital for broad purposes such as seed capital, working capital, and acquisition capital. Seed capital is used to cover expenses during the setting up, development, and testing stages of a new product, process, or business. Working capital is raised to pay for outlays during the finalization of the development stage when the product is near market potential. Acquisition capital is to fund the purchase of a business.

Seed stage venture capital and leveraged buyouts are two investment strategies that can be viewed as the two end-points of a continuous investment spectrum in VC investing. It is common to view the private equity market as a broad umbrella consisting of seed, startup, growth, mezzanine, buyout, turn-around, and industry consolidation investing. The shift from one strategy to the next is subtle. It is a natural step to move from seed to start-up and then to expansion financing. At some point during the growth phase, an add-on acquisition is likely to present itself. Turn-around investing is called for when a business has run into operational or financial difficulties. Furthermore, consolidating a fragmented industry is another opportunity for VC investing.

VC Life Cycle

A private VC fund typically raises its capital from a limited number of sophisticated investors in a private placement and has a life of about 10 to 12 years. The investor base consists of wealthy individuals, pension plans, endowments, insurance companies, bank holding companies, and foreign investors. VC firms receive income from two sources: the annual management fee and profit allocation of the fund. The fund's main source of income is a capital gain from sale of stock of the portfolio companies. The general partner (venture capitalist) typically receives 20 percent of the profits and the limited partners (investors) receive 80 percent.

A VC fund passes through four stages. The first stage is fund-raising. It takes the general partner usually several months to a year to obtain capital commitment from VC investors. The second stage is investment. After sourcing a perspective deal, satisfactory due diligence leads to an investment. This phase typically lasts for about three to seven years. The next stage, which lasts until the closing of the fund, is to help portfolio companies grow. The final stage in the life of a VC fund is its closing. The VC fund should have liquidated its position in all of its portfolio companies by the expiration date of the fund. Liquidation takes one of the three forms: an initial public offering (IPO), a sale of the company, or bankruptcy.

Characteristics of VC Investing

Compared with other types of investing, VC investing has several unique features. The first is the venture capitalist's active involvement in sourcing portfolio company candidates, negotiating and structuring the transaction, and monitoring the portfolio company. Often the VC professionals serve as board members and/or financial advisers to the portfolio company.

Second, VC investing is generally intended for a period of several years, typically three to seven years, with the expectation of high returns when the portfolio company is successful and its securities soar in value. VC generally invests in common stock, stock plus debt unit, convertible debt, stock warrant, and preferred stock. Venture capitalists generally expect a target rate of return in the 30 percent to 50 percent range. Empirically, annual returns on VC investments are quite volatile.

The third difference from other types of investing is that when a VC fund finances a new business startup or a growth company, the company often is privately held. If the venture fund makes an investment in a buyout of a public company, the company is typically privately held after the buyout. Even in the rare cases when venture capitalists invest in public companies, they hold nonpublic securities.

Another important aspect is that VC funds will often take interest in a target only if the company has superior management. There are two basic reasons why venture capitalists avoid companies with weak management. First, it will be necessary after the investment to seek management replacements that can lead to significant business disruption. Second, seeking new management for the portfolio company requires a significant amount of time and effort from the VC professionals. Thus, it diverts them from other portfolio companies.

Finally, venture capitalists frequently seek board level representation or control. They do not necessarily demand a majority on the board. It depends on how mature the business is and what fraction of the business they own. Regardless of whether venture capitalists demand a majority, they seldom are silent investors. Frequently, VC professionals and the management of the portfolio company work in partnership. Venture capitalist's judgment and contacts are helpful as the portfolio company grows. This is because VC professionals do not view the investment as supplying capital alone, but rather as also providing advice on strategic and financial planning and management oversight in order to enhance value.

Setting Up Venture Capital Operations

Investment banks and banks are active in VC business. In addition, professionals experienced in private equity investing will set up their own shops as well. They often raise money from a limited number of sophisticated investors.

A VC fund is often set up in partnership form, mainly because of tax advantages granted to a "flow-through" entity. Each partner is required to report on his or her own federal tax return, if applicable, such partner's distributive share of the partnership's income, gains, losses, deductions, and credits for the tax year. There is no tax at partner level for a tax-exempt organization provided that the investments producing long-term capital loss are not debt financed and that the VC fund is engaged only in a passive investment activity rather than an active business.

Profit and Loss Allocations

A VC fund splits profits on a prenegotiated basis. A fund's profits are generally split with 20 percent of net profits going to the fund general partner as a carried interest and the remaining 80 percent to the limited partners in proportion to their contributed capital.

For loss allocation, the practice is that losses are allocated in the same manner as profits until such losses have offset all prior allocated profits and the general partner's capital contribution. Then losses exceeding this amount (excess losses) are allocated 100 percent to limited partners, but subsequent profits are allocated to the limited partners until the excess losses are recovered.

Distributions are subject to heavy negotiations. The general partner frequently has a certain degree of discretion on the timing of distributions.

Management Fee

Most charge 1.5 percent to 2.5 percent of capital commitments per year, payable to the general partner every quarter. In the 1980s, management fee was higher, in the range of 1.5 percent to 3.0 percent of asset fair value plus uncalled capital commitments. However, this approach created a conflict of interests in asset valuation and the timing of distributions.

Sometimes the agreement calls for stopping management fee or paying on a declining schedule after a specified period. For example, the management fee declines 10 percent each year after six years. When a venture fund is specializing in buyouts, the regular management fee is payable for a period of typically four to six years and then a lower monitoring fee thereafter. The booming PE market has given the fund management power to charge the so-called transaction fee, in addition to other fees. For example, Blackstone partners took in almost $200 million transaction fee in the buyout of Office Equity of about $39 billion in February 2007.

Other Issues

Limited partners are the passive investors contributing the major share of capital but have no direct involvement in running the fund. All limited partners must be individually indemnified against liabilities arising from the venture operations. The partnership agreement also provides for admission of additional partners and specifies the new allocation of profits and losses based on the contributed capital or other yardsticks.

The partnership agreement provides for a definite life of the partnership. It also contains provisions that stipulate the dissolution date. If needed, a majority vote by all partners can reset the date to a later period. Additionally, provisions must be set for raising additional capital as business grows. Ideally, further equity investment will be spread proportionally among all partners.

VC INVESTMENT STRATEGIES

Venture capital is high-risk, high-return investing. In pursuit of high returns while managing risk, VC professionals need to understand that many deals fail due to poor strategic planning and a lack of vision. Too often VC fund managers get bogged down in details, ignoring the big picture. Venture capitalists need to define their goals and source the myriad of prospects in order to find a good match with the best financial and strategic edge, before engaging in costly and time-consuming evaluation process. Once this phase is completed, many VC firms evaluate potential investments based on four fundamental criteria: management, marketing, products, and financial opportunity.

VC Investing Evaluations

Management experience is a major consideration in evaluating financing prospects. VC funds usually prefer to invest in a company with superior management. A strong management team is comprised of individuals who have successful track records in relevant industries and have gained a superior understanding of their market. It is likely that the team will work well together and have extraordinary drive to grow the company. An A Team with a B Product is more likely to get VC financing than a B Team with an A Product.

The ideal market is one that is growing rapidly and has the potential to become enormous. Popular industries include biotechnology, telecommunications, computer, Internet, and other specialty niche areas.

The ideal product has many proprietary features that differentiate it from others offered by competing companies. A commodity product has no unique features, can be manufactured by new entrants easily, and hence is not attractive. In addition, the product should achieve above average gross margins, offer repeat sales opportunities, and require only a limited amount of additional capital. Because the fate of the company should not be riding on a single product, plans for a full product line are important.

Once the VC fund managers identify a company that has superior management, an attractive market opportunity, and an excellent product, they seek to acquire stakes at as low a price as possible. An entrepreneur, alternatively, wants to have as high a price as possible. The price of the deal is the outcome of a complex negotiation process. Liquidity is the final goal. Thus, an assessment of likely exit opportunities is made before money is invested.

Risk Factors

Venture capital investing is subject to a high degree of risk. First, an early stage company has a limited history of revenue-producing activities. Its operations are subject to the difficulties associated with the growth of a new business and the competitive environment in which the company operates. Furthermore, the new business generally needs strong strategic-alliance partners. In addition to other benefits, strategic alliance will also help create name recognition that is an important factor in marketing any product or service. Without such partners, the growth of the company may not proceed as planned.

New products and technological changes present a big uncertainty. This is especially true when investing in a high-tech or a biotech company. The market evolves with rapid and frequent changes in technology and customer preferences. The company's growth and future financial performance depends on its ability to develop and introduce new products. Failure to anticipate or respond to the changing market environment will adversely affect the company's potential. There is no assurance that any new product will be successfully developed or achieve market acceptance, or that competitors will not develop and market products that render the company's products obsolete.

A new startup's success is critically dependent on a few key personnel. Retention and recruitment of a quality team is essential to the success of the company. Long-term employment contracts that defer a portion of compensation over time and contain noncompete provisions, stock options, and other profit-sharing schemes have been used with some success.

Before long, the company may need additional financing. The required additional investment will have substantial dilution effect. Venture capital usually has to accept the dilution, because there is no public market for the company's securities yet. Also, stop transfer instructions will be noted in the company's records with respect to these shares. Venture capital investors need to be prepared to accept the liquidity risk.

Venture Capital Transactions

Venture capital investing covers a wide range of the investment spectrum. Seed money is provided to the entrepreneur to establish the feasibility of the innovative concept or product. The next step is start-up financing, which involves financing for product development and the initial phase of marketing. After that, comes first-stage financing. At this stage of corporate development, the firm has developed a prototype that appears marketable. The firm begins its growth with second-stage financing. During the growth stage, funds are provided for working capital to finance goods in process, inventories, and shipping. The company is growing and the hopes for profitable operations are reflected in the progressively lower losses. Gradually, this development process leads directly to third-stage financing. In this phase, funds are needed for major expansion when sales begin to take off and the company is moving from "in the red" to "in the black." At a certain point in the process of corporate development, the company will be ready to go public or become a target of an acquisition. This marks the exit of the VC financing cycle.

Venture capital funds are also frequently involved with buyouts, troubled companies, and special situation investing. The following discussion groups the private equity investment spectrum into the start-up phase, growth stage, buyout financing, and special purpose investing. The exit strategies are covered in a later section.

Start-Up Phase Transactions

An entrepreneur, whether a scientist, corporate executive, or business professor, who has a new high-tech invention or a new improvement on an existing production or marketing process, may wish to start a business. The concept may require substantial research or other activities before the actual sales take place. So the entrepreneur approaches VC firms seeking financing for the proposed new business. If the entrepreneur convinces the venture capitalist that this is a solid and realistic business plan, that he is capable of executing the plan, and that the business will prosper, both parties will begin to negotiate and structure the transaction.

A typical transaction involves the entrepreneur contributing services, ideas and a small amount of capital, and the VC firm contributing a relatively large amount of money. Both parties would share the corporate ownership. The venture capitalist will generally insist on investing most of the funds in the form of convertible debt and/or preferred stock and only a small amount in common stock. The venture capitalist would also prefer to have the entrepreneur put up an amount of money in good faith. Venture capital professionals prefer to invest in convertible instruments, because it wants to recover most of its invested capital and wants only the profits to be shared. The arrangement would enable VC funds to receive most of the residual value if the business is not successful. When the company is successful, the VC fund recoups its invested capital and shares only profits with the entrepreneur. In addition, the interest expense is tax deductible to the portfolio company.

The entrepreneur is frequently asked to make an investment and to show his "good faith" in the project. To ensure that the entrepreneur will stay and make best efforts to grow the business, some of his shares will "time vest" based solely on his continued employment and some will "performance vest" based on achieving specified goals.

Control of the board can be split according to proportional equity ownership, or they can agree on allocation of directors different from the equity split. The venture capitalist will also seek provisions in the shareholder's agreement that set forth certain parameters for the sale of the company or for going public after a stated time period.

Growth Stage Transactions

Suppose a company is successful and needs more money to expand its business. The need sometimes arises from the desire of existing shareholders to redeem for the purpose of estate planning and/or liquidity (a recapitalization). At this stage, the business is not yet ready for a public offering. Hence, the company approaches venture capitalists for growth stage financing. A VC fund makes the investment because it believes that the value will rise once the company has the necessary funds for expansion. The infusion of new capital further enhances the existing borrowing base.

Growth stage investing is more complex than the early start-up stage. There are several major differences. In a growth-equity transaction, there are more shareholders with divergent interests with whom to negotiate. The company would have more assets, contingent liabilities, and operating history. A substantial due diligence research and a more extensive investment agreement are required.

In preparation for the investment, the venture capitalist conducts legal and business due diligence. The investigation examines contingent liabilities, material contracts, debt agreements, insurance, prior acquisition agreements and joint ventures, capital structure, and outstanding securities. A fair value is estimated after the due diligence. The ownership percentage for the VC financing is negotiated and determined.

VC Investing in a Buyout

There are three types of buyout targets: a corporate subsidiary, a private company, or a public company. In any case, VC fund managers need to be convinced that with additional capital and necessary improvements at the company, the target will increase in value.

The key acquisition issues involving buyout of a corporate subsidiary include purchase price, debt financing, and equity financing. The purchase price is the outcome of a comprehensive negotiation process. The currency used could be cash, subordinated notes, or preferred stock. The acquirer will seek representations and warranties from the target for several reasons. Information disclosure is crucial in evaluating the target. They can be used to call off the deal prior to closing if the target fails to conform to the representations and warranties. They are also used to recover money or to rescind the transaction if there is misrepresentation in representations and warranties. The VC firm will typically seek the right to terminate the transaction if any of the closing conditions such as successful completion of financing, satisfactory completion of due diligence, antitrust clearance, or necessary third-party consent, is not satisfied.

Buyout of a private company is, in many respects, similar to that of a corporate subsidiary, except that an individual or a group now owns the target. Buyout of a public company is more complex. The VC firm generally will seek protection against competing bids and/or compensation if another bidder ultimately triumphs. Typical protective devices include no-shop clause, breakup fees, lock options to buy un-issued target's shares, and a crown-jewel option to buy a key asset. Ideally, these protective devices are negotiated and signed before announcement. Another complexity involving a public company buyout is the federal and state securities laws.

Special Purpose Investing

VC funds also make an investment in industry consolidation and company turn-around. When a venture capitalist identifies a fragmented industry in which there are many small firms and no or few market leaders, the VC firm will recruit top-notch management to establish a leadership presence in the industry. When the venture capitalist identifies a company experiencing significant problems, it will seek to arrange an infusion of new turnaround capital as part of the shared-pain debt restructuring or workout for the troubled company.

Under a turnaround investment situation, the troubled company renegotiates its old debt by stretching out principal maturities, reducing interest rates, delaying interest payments, and also canceling a portion of its debt. To induce creditors to participate in the restructuring, the company needs to issue shares to creditors. The venture capitalist would want to invest new turnaround capital provided that he believes the business is basically sound and that creditors accept the restructuring. Other than this "shared-pain" restructuring, there are alternative debt workout transactions such as partial payments to creditors in cash and new debt, or partial payments in cash, new debt, and common stock. In addition, because the debt restructuring or workout involves issuance of stock or new debt instruments, the SEC and other disclosure rules should be followed unless the company can find an applicable exemption.

Investment Securities

The securities commonly used in venture investing include common stock, stock plus debt unit, convertible debt, stock warrant, and preferred stock. The simplest, but not necessarily the best, is to invest in common stock. Most venture capitalists would prefer to invest in a senior security that carries the rights to purchase common stock. In a stock plus debt structure, the debt component provides modest interest for a reasonably long term with minimum or no principal amortization. In a convertible debt transaction, the debt can be converted into equity at a predetermined conversion ratio. A preferred stock transaction is typically tailored to contain a variety of debt and equity features. Purchase of a stock warrant is generally made in combination with some other security. A package of straight debt plus a warrant is similar to a convertible debt. However, this type of combination may be more flexible than convertible debt, because the debt and warrant can trade separately.

Exit Strategies

Exit strategies are planned when the venture capital is making the front-end investments. This is important because the actual exit strategy may require cooperation from some shareholders who may not be in agreement with the exit pricing or timing. Therefore, it is important for the venture capitalist to have obtained certain contractual rights to control its exit. For this purpose, the venture capitalist will want to insist initially that the portfolio company and its other shareholders sign an agreement that gives the VC fund control over issues such as the timing of IPO, selection of underwriter, and right to demand additional SEC registrations subsequent to the IPO. When the VC fund is the majority shareholder, it will insist on having drag-along agreements that give it the right to find buyers for all or part of the portfolio company's stock. However, if the VC fund is a minority investor, it will often want take-along rights to sell alongside management and other shareholders.

The VC's exit strategy includes taking the portfolio company public or selling the portfolio company to another company. Selling out to another company can be structured as exchange for the acquirer's stock, cash, or a combination of cash and debt instruments.

If the VC's exit is through a public offering, there are several methods for reselling the restricted securities. Restricted securities can be sold via a subsequent private sale or a public offering registered with SEC. After the IPO, the portfolio company is a 1934 Act reporting company and hence may qualify for short-form registration statements that allow the portfolio company or its shareholders to sell securities with less delay and less expense than a full-blown S-1 registration statement. Once the portfolio company has completed its IPO, the VC and other holders can sell their restricted securities without filing an SEC registration statement if all SEC Rule 144 requirements, such as volume limitation, holding period, and SEC notification, are met. The holding period requirement for the resale of a limited amount of restricted securities is one year.

BUYOUT FUNDS

Buyout funds are investment firms that invest in leveraged buyouts (LBOs), which use borrowed money for a substantial portion of the purchase price of the buyout company. If the purchasers are management, the acquisition is sometimes called a management buyout. An LBO firm has several basic characteristics. The first is that it uses other people's money, meaning that the LBO firm acquires companies with as little of its own money as possible. The bulk of the purchase price is borrowed from banks and other lenders. The assets and future cash flows of the selling company typically secure the debt. Consequently, LBOs often involve low-tech businesses with a history of consistent profitability and lots of tangible assets. To support acquisition debt, the selling company needs to have low leverage in the first place. By using a large amount of leverage, the buyout firm enhances its investment returns because the lenders share little or none of the upside. Second, LBO firms generally look for distressed companies in out-of-fashion industries to avoid paying top dollar. After acquiring the company, the buyout firm seeks to enhance its operating performance. Managers are provided with equity participation to achieve this objective. The annual amounts of buyouts and mezzanine are on the rise in recent years. A mezzanine financing is debt capital granting the lender the right to convert it to equity interest.

Typical Buyout Financing Structure

Virtually all LBOs are financed with a combination of senior debt, subordinated debt, and equity. The amount of equity required in a transaction is determined in part by the amount of debt that can be borrowed. The following discussion describes the various components of financing in a typical LBO.

First, and probably the most important component of financing, is senior debt. Typically 50 percent to 70 percent of an LBO's funding takes the form of senior financing. A senior loan is collateralized by a first lien on the assets of the company. Senior financing is generally obtained from banks, although privately placed notes to institutional investors are also possible. Occasionally, a public issue of bonds may be the source of senior debt.

The senior debt almost always includes a revolving line of credit, which is based on a certain percentage of the appraised liquidation value of the eligible accounts receivables and inventory. A revolving line of credit is the bank line of credit on which the company pays a commitment fee and can take and repay the loan at will.

Another component of senior debt is a senior term loan. This loan is based on a certain percentage of the appraised fair market value of the land and buildings and the liquidation value of the machinery and equipment. Such loans are also limited by the predictability of cash flows to service senior debt. The term for senior term debt is usually five to eight years and, in the event of bankruptcy, holders will be paid before subordinated debt receives any payment.

Typically, 15 percent to 30 percent of an LBO is in the form of subordinated financing. It is raised from insurance companies or subordinated debt funds. Alternatively, it is raised with a public offering of high-yield or noninvestment-grade bonds to institutional investors. The term of such financing is typically 6 to 10 years, and principal payments are commonly deferred until after the senior debt is retired.

Equity financing accounts for the remaining 10 percent to 20 percent of the funds needed to finance an LBO. This portion of financing comes from LBO funds and other investors. Often, there is leverage here as well. They borrow money to invest in LBO funds or to participate in the equity investment. These funds make up the difference between the financing required and the financing available in the form of debt. Management usually invests in the equity of an LBO company together with an LBO fund, a corporate investor, or a group of institutional investors. The seller and subordinated lenders sometimes receive equity in the new company.

U.S. Leveraged Buyout Firms

The best-known buyout firms are Kohlberg Kravis Roberts & Co., the Carlyle Group, and Blackstone. Other well-known firms include Clayton, Dubillier, & Rice; Hicks, Muse, Tate, & Furst; Advent International; Brera Capital Partners; Welsh, Carson, Anderson, & Stowe; Apollo Advisors; Hellman & Friedman; Leonard Green & Partners; Fenway Partners; Thomas H. Lee Co.; and Forstmann Little & Co.

The buyout industry is global. Many U.S. shops are establishing or expanding operations overseas. For example, KKR, Clayton, Dubillier, & Rice and Hicks, Muse, Tate, & Furst began setting up buyout funds for continental Europe before the advent of the European Monetary Union in 1999. Examples of funds targeted at buyout opportunities in Asia include Unison Capital, Patricof & Co. Ventures, and the Carlyle Group. New Bridge is also active in Asia. At the same time, foreign firms such as London-based Doughty Hanson & Co. are targeting the U.S. markets for potential acquisitions.

Leveraged Buyouts and Economic Benefits

Leveraged buyouts have been blamed for many things, from the federal budget deficit to unemployment. It is true that many LBOs have resulted in corporate restructuring and massive layoffs. The high leverage gives corporations huge tax savings, which reduce the government's tax revenues. Some commentators have also criticized the huge premium paid in LBOs and the large profits and fees earned by those who engineer the transactions.

In reality, LBOs are merely tools of economic organization. Most U.S. corporations fared poorly in the 1970s; many lost market share and profits to Japanese, German, and other overseas rivals. Management's mind-set at that time was simply to hang on and not to take risks. But risk taking is as important to economic growth as technology, globalization, and productivity. Without risk taking, even the most promising technology would gather dust in the university laboratory. Michael Milken's junk bond finance and KKR's LBOs gave ambitious risk-takers the opportunity to establish a new entrepreneurial economy. In addition, with every LBO, more corporate senior managers got the message: Take actions to improve performance or lose your job. Thus, the LBOs and hostile takeovers have positive contributions to the economy.

CONCLUSION

Private equity funds are actively investing in many sectors of the Chinese economy, ranging from technology, finance, to real estate. China is like a magnet sucking in large sums of money because it is a low-cost manufacturing base and a huge market. In recent years, China's government has taken steps to ease restrictions to encourage foreign investments. In this chapter, we discussed China's private equity market, venture capital operations, and buyout structure. The next chapter covers mergers and acquisitions.

9

The Growing Market for Mergers and Acquisitions

Corporate restructure and privatization of state owned enterprises continue to drive the merger and acquisition (M&A) activity in China. The market has observed strong activity in consolidating industries and continued pre-initial public offering (IPO) investment in the banking sector. The Chinese government has also simplified approval procedures for overseas acquisitions by domestic corporations. Another emerging trend is the rapid increase in private equity activity, as Chapter 8 has discussed. Hostile takeovers are not common, but will emerge.

OVERVIEW

Some foreigners are enthusiastic while others are gloomy about China's mergers and acquisitions market. The top reasons for acquisitions are potential return on investments, synergies with core business, low-cost manufacturing, and improving position in China market. Those gnashing their teeth are folks who are on the ground actually doing the work. Regardless of their views or expectations, the M&A market has set records every year since 2002 for four years. In 2005, the inbound and domestic deals were valued at $46 billion, a 34 percent increase from $34 billion in 2004. In the absence of large deals in financial services, the total M&A volume declined in 2006 to $12.7 billion. M&A activities are expected to rise as privatization trend and emergence of private enterprises continue.

An additional favorable development came when the Chinese government clarified and simplified regulations. Though many government agencies continue to exercise jurisdiction over M&As, this is changing. Beijing also put many state-owned enterprises (SOEs) under the control of the State Assets Supervision and Administration Commission (SASAC), which has continued to simplify guidelines for sale of the SOE assets under its management. Beijing sees the M&A activity as a key driver of its industry restructure and privatization process. As such, the government has continued to expand the number of industries open to foreign acquisitions. This is to shunt SOEs into the private sector while retaining only the companies deemed crucial for national defense, energy, or national strategic interests. The second regulatory piece relating to the M&A market is the uncertainty created by the A share reforms. The government moved quickly to put in place measures granting foreign investors greater access to the A share market.

Another factor contributing to the active M&A market is that the economy is booming and many industries are fragmented. M&As help consolidate small operations to achieve economies of scale. For example, Nokia's plan to merge its four joint ventures (JVs) in China has been approved by the government. Two of China's largest consolidating acquisitions are: Midea acquired a controlling interest in Hualing and Kelon took control of Weili. In the automotive industry, Dongfeng Auto purchased CITIC Group's stake in Zhengzhou Nissan. Because China is regarded as one of the low-cost manufacturing bases with a huge consumer market, foreign firms use acquisition as a fast way to grab market share in China.

Outbound M&A

Armed with $1.2 trillion foreign exchange reserves, China has money to pursue foreign acquisitions. There is pressure from the United States and other countries to float (or appreciate) its currency at a faster pace to reduce its trade surpluses. The huge foreign exchange reserves have in part contributed to the overheating economy. In addition, it is to China's strategic interests to globalize some of its large SOEs. Outbound investments or acquisitions support this strategic direction. One example of a large cross-border deal was China National Petroleum Corporation's (CNPC) acquisition of Canadian-owned Petrokazakhstan in 2005. In the computer sector, China's largest computer maker Lenovo purchased IBM's PC business in 2005. This activity is expected to continue as ambitious companies seek value-added acquisitions to help them gain access to technology, brand, and distribution networks.

Hostile Takeover

The concept of a hostile takeover bid was relatively new in China. The first attempt at a hostile takeover was in the financial services industry. In September 2004, CITIC Securities offered $217 million unsolicited bid for 51 percent of Guangfa Securities. Concerns about job losses and benefit cuts prompted several groups of employees and shareholders to oppose the deal and increase their shareholding to fend off the bid. CITIC eventually withdrew the offer.

Caution

Despite the great potentials, caution is needed. About three-quarters of the prospects in China fall apart during the negotiation stage, compared to over 50 percent success rate in the United States. Common reasons for deals not to proceed as anticipated are high asking price, unpleasant due diligence surprises, and employment issues. Completion of the acquisition does not mean success. Post deal risk is significant. Many tough issues emerge after deal closing. In the United States, more than half of the mergers destroy shareholder value.[1] In China, when a foreign multinational tries to restructure an SOE, sometimes it is difficult to convince employees to buy in to performance incentives. For many employees, profit is not viewed as the primary objective.

CHINA PRESENCE AND SECTOR RESTRICTIONS

There are several ways that foreign investors usually establish a presence in China, including representative office, Sino-foreign joint venture, wholly foreign-owned enterprise (WFOE), and foreign-invested joint stock limited company (FISC).[2] These three—JVs, WFOEs, and FISC—are collectively the so-called foreign invested enterprises (FIEs). Those FIEs enjoy various policy incentives. Establishing a presence via one of those means is subject to China's foreign investment guidelines and restrictions.

China Presence

Many multinationals use a representative office in China as a first step into the market and as a way of maintaining a presence. A representative office is allowed to conduct local promotional and marketing activities. However, it is not allowed to engage in direct business operations in China (e.g., a representative office cannot sell products in China, personnel at the office are not permitted to sign contracts for the parent company, or to issue sales invoices).

A JV can take the form of an equity JV or a cooperative JV. Most foreign investors seeking to establish JVs have chosen equity JV. A foreign investor would prefer a cooperative JV if it desires to adopt a nonlegal person structure, needs flexibility in configuring profit distribution ratio, or wants to recover its investments early under certain circumstances. Joint ventures are popular vehicles for those who are not familiar with the local environment and prefer a Chinese partner with connections to help handle domestic issues. In some cases, Chinese law does not permit a WFOE setup in banking or communications industries.

A WFOE is 100 percent owned by the foreign investor. In recent years, WFOEs have become popular investment vehicles. A WFOE gives the foreign investor greater flexibility in terms of management and control. The foreign company does not have to face the complexity of dealing with the Chinese local partner. However, this type of entity may be subject to more stringent investment restrictions.

A FISC is in the form of issued shares, different from a JV or WFOE (nonshare-issuing limited liability company). Thus, a FISC is the only form of FIEs that can list shares on China stock exchanges. Other forms of FIEs would have to convert to FISC first before listing. With the listing advantage, it comes with a more restrictive requirement. The sponsors of the FISCs have to meet additional requirements and the foreign investor has to hold at least 25 percent of the equity. The minimum registered capital is RMB 30 million and the approval procedure is more burdensome.

Sector Restrictions

Foreign investment in domestic industries is guided by the Regulations for Guiding the Direction of Foreign Investment and the Catalog for Guiding Foreign Investment in Industries. Under these regulations, China has classified industries for foreign investment into four categories: encouraged, permitted, restricted, and prohibited.

An FIE in the encouraged business may be qualified for the local and simplified approval process. An enterprise in the restricted industries will be subject to additional scrutiny in the approval process and in some cases the Chinese local partner is required to hold more than 50 percent of the shares. For example, there are equity restrictions on foreign investments in telecommunications and financial services. On the other hand, foreign investors now can have operations in wholesale, retail, and franchise without geographic restrictions. Some restrictions will be phased out gradually. With the implementation of World Trade Organizations (WTO) commitments, foreign investors have gained greater access to these and other sectors.

China has taken measures such as the Closer Economic Partnership Arrangement (CEPA) with Hong Kong and Macau. This special arrangement provides investment and trade access to qualified Hong Kong and Macau enterprises on more favorable terms than the terms stipulated in WTO commitments. Foreign companies with a significant presence in Hong Kong or Macau benefit from CEPA, as these arrangements provide additional options to multinational corporations wanting to invest in certain industries in China.

TYPES OF M&A TRANSACTION

The previous section discussed the various types of structure that foreign investors use to establish a presence in China. The foreign investor wanting to make an acquisition or increase equity interest commonly carries out direct acquisition, indirect acquisition, asset acquisition, or special types of acquisition.

In a direct acquisition, the foreign investor purchases part or all of the nonlisted equity interest from the Chinese investors who own equity interest in the target company. Alternatively, the foreign investor can subscribe to the increased capital of the target company. This type of acquisition is subject to the full approval requirements. One of the advantages of direct acquisition is that it is the only option available if the Chinese target is purely domestic with no foreign parent company. Compared to an asset acquisition, a direct acquisition of the whole target company is generally simpler and administratively easier because the foreign investor does not have to pick and choose assets or employees. However, the process for a direct acquisition is more time consuming and is subject to the Chinese government's approval.

Another choice the foreign investor may use is indirect acquisition, in which the foreign investor acquires the Chinese company via offshore purchase from the Chinese company's foreign parent company. This approach is available only if the Chinese target has foreign investors and those foreign investors wish to sell. The offshore acquisition is conducted in the jurisdiction where the company is incorporated, not China. But, if the ultimate shareholders are Chinese nationals, certain filings must be made with the foreign exchange authorities. One advantage is that the transaction can be completed offshore and therefore is not subject to the approval of Chinese authorities. If the target is a listed company, the foreign investor can acquire interests through a foreign stock exchange. Thus, this is often the simplest and least administratively burdensome form of acquisition structure. However, this is not an option if the target company does not have foreign shareholders. The foreign investor also has to assume all claims against the invested company, either existing or contingent liabilities.

Another option the foreign investor has is to acquire the business or assets of the Chinese company. Similar to direct acquisition, such asset acquisition is subject to China jurisdiction and full approval requirements. Under Chinese law, a foreign investor is required to establish a foreign-invested entity (FIE) in order to purchase assets or businesses of a company. The biggest advantage is that the purchaser can select and acquire the preferred parts of the target company. In general, the liabilities and obligations of the target company remain with the target. If this involves creating a new FIE, tax holidays and other incentives may be available. Also, most asset acquisitions do not require approval by Chinese authorities. On the other hand, establishing a new FIE involves approval by Chinese authorities. In addition, an asset sale is taxable.

The Chinese government has issued special regulations governing the acquisition of SOEs by foreign investors. One of the special means is that the foreign investor can acquire domestic creditors' rights in the target. If the creditors own convertible debt, the foreign investor now has the opportunity to later convert such debts into equity in the target. With SOEs, there could be additional issues relating to state asset valuations and employee resettlement.

Although mergers are not common in China, Chinese regulations provide for two means of mergers: merger by absorption or merger by new establishment. In a merger by absorption, one company absorbs another. The absorbed is dissolved and its registered capital and assets merge into the surviving company. In a merger by new establishment, both companies are dissolved and a new company is set up to hold the aggregate of the two companies' registered capital and assets. The newly established company assumes all rights and liabilities of its predecessors.

REGULATIONS AND FOREIGN EXCHANGE CONTROL

Investing in China is subject to several layers of regulations. In addition to the approvals required of the various structures and acquisition means, the foreign investor is required to clear foreign exchange compliance as well. The Chinese government has introduced a new system for registration of FIEs and has adopted policies to allow capital movement and a wider band of its currency movement.

New Registration System

In 2004, China introduced new procedures for its enterprise establishment process. The objective is to move from a project approval system to a registration system. Under the new system, examination and approval will no longer be required for projects that do not involve government investment. Instead, the new system requires verification and examination or registration. The new verification system applies to major projects and restricted projects aimed to safeguarding public interest. The registration system applies to other projects.

In conjunction with introducing the new system, China also issued a List of Investment Projects to be Confirmed by the Government. This list sets out the major and restricted projects invested in and established by enterprises without using government funding. Any project on the list is subject to the verification system, and the applicant needs to submit an application to the government. It is not necessary to go through the procedures for examination and approval of project proposals or feasibility studies. All projects not on the list need only complete registration. Except where other regulations apply, registration is to be carried out with local authorities.

All foreign-invested projects are subject to the new verification system. The National Development and Reform Commission (NDRC) has authorities over the following foreign-invested projects:

- Encouraged projects and permitted projects with a total investment of $100 million or more
- Restricted projects with a total investment of $50 million or more

The NDRC verification does not replace the existing Ministry of Commerce's approval requirements. The following foreign-invested projects must be examined and approved by the Ministry of Commerce:

- Projects with a total investment above the prescribed limit
- Restricted projects
- Projects subject to quota and licensing restrictions

Furthermore, the Ministry of Commerce must approve: (1) the contract and articles of association of large foreign-invested projects and (2) major changes in capital, equity transfer, or mergers. All other projects not covered by these guidelines are to be approved by local government in accordance with relevant regulations.

Foreign Exchange

The State Administration of Foreign Exchange (SAFE) regulates foreign exchange transactions in China.[3] Four types of transactions involving the movement or conversion of foreign exchange are subject to strict regulatory control. There are:

1. *Inward remittance:* Remittance of foreign exchange into China from a foreign party.
2. *Settlement:* Conversion of foreign exchange to RMB.
3. *Sale:* Conversion of RMB into foreign exchange.
4. *Outward remittance:* Remittance of foreign exchange to a foreign party.

In regulating foreign exchange transactions, the SAFE distinguishes between current account items and capital account items.[4] The SAFE allows current account convertibility. Companies are only required to submit documents of the underlying transactions to the designated foreign exchange bank for verification. Prior approval by the SAFE is not required.

Foreign exchange transactions with regard to capital account items are heavily regulated. The Chinese government has planned to gradually move toward full capital account convertibility of its currency. For large cross-border transactions, prior approval by the SAFE would be necessary.

MERGER AND ACQUISITION AGREEMENTS

It is common to have a letter of intent (LOI) or memorandum of understanding (MOU) for M&As. An LOI or MOU is an important tool that can be used to reach agreement to begin the process. Though terms in the LOI or MOU are not legally binding, most parties in China expect them to be honored should the transaction proceed. An LOI or MOU generally includes the following key terms:

- Identities of the parties
- Total purchase price and method of payment
- Registered capital and business scope of the target company
- Investors' equity percentage or form of capital contribution
- New management arrangement
- Arrangement for labor and land
- Trademark and technology licensing
- Conditions necessary for the transaction to proceed

- Confidentiality and exclusivity
- Purchaser's right to due diligence and seller's undertaking to cooperate
- Other steps helpful for both parties to proceed with the deal

Due Diligence

Dues diligence is a must for M&As anywhere. Due diligence investigations afford the prospective acquirer an opportunity to assess the legal and financial status of the target company. Due diligence also facilitates consideration of structuring issues in the proposed deal based on the results of the investigation. However, many observers have noticed that the concept of due diligence is relatively new in China. Many Chinese companies do not keep proper records or accounting books, and Chinese often conclude transactions without detailed due diligence. Therefore, foreign investors may still find some Chinese companies are not willing to fully disclose information and grant full access to company records and books. Document forgery can also be an issue at times. Foreign investors need patience, experience, and diplomacy to perform proper due diligence.

Due Diligence Process

The due diligence process begins with the foreign investor and its adviser determining the nature and scope of the investigation. The prospective purchaser then sends to the target company a checklist of the items it intends to investigate. Upon receipt, the seller will provide answers to these questions and provide copies of the documents requested. The purchaser and its adviser will also visit the target company and interview the target's management and staff members to obtain information it desires to have. More and more sophisticated Chinese sellers hire advisers to prepare the relevant materials for due diligence. But, difficulties still remain. A Mercer survey indicated that the obstacles when conducting M&As in China include a lack of transparency at the target company and differences in corporate culture.[5] A typical due diligence covers the following items:

- Constitutional documents, government approvals, and operating licenses
- Company structure
- Assets
- Accounting
- Loans and guarantees, creditors, and debtors
- Land buildings
- Material contracts
- Labor- and social insurance-related issues
- Environmental matters
- Intellectual property matters
- Disputes, litigation, or arbitration

Representation and Warranties

If the due diligence is satisfactory, the purchaser will want to have definitive legal documentation prepared. The exact documentation required depends on the nature and structure of the transaction. Regardless of the type of transaction, the foreign investor would want to ensure that the acquisition documents include comprehensive representations, warranties, and undertakings. It is advisable for the acquisition document to contain full and comprehensive representations and warranties with specific compensation provisions to cover any issues that may not have been disclosed or discovered in the due diligence process.

Closing

Closing is governed by the acquisition contract. The objective is to permit buyers, sellers, lenders, and others to complete the transactions in a coordinated manner. Some of required closing documents include:

- Certificates of incorporation
- By-laws
- Letter evidencing listing of securities (if applicable)
- Approval or clearance by government agencies
- Comfort letters from accountants
- Legal and fairness opinions
- Instructions for securities and/or funds transfer
- Escrow agreements

The closing documents are carefully reviewed and then signed. When everyone is satisfied with the documents, they are exchanged and funds and/or securities are transferred in payment. The deal is closed.

Postmerger Integration

The period shortly after closing is the time when critical steps are taken to integrate the acquired business with the buyer organization. During the same period, a variety of legal, accounting, tax, insurance, employee benefits, and other steps take place to ensure a successful transition.

Many acquirers form transition teams composed of executives of both companies to coordinate the postmerger integration process. This includes developing recommendations for combining a wide range of functions and proposing the configuration of the new organization. It is better to organize a small team around postmerger projects in order to stabilize the organization and build early momentum.

Early management placement is critical in stabilizing the company. The crucial task is in deciding whom to retain, whom to redeploy, whom to dismiss, and at what price. It is also a difficult issue when the compensation schedule at the acquired company is out of line with acquirer's. Moreover, recruiters often attempt to lure away the best and brightest managers and technical stuff to competing organizations. The acquiring company then has to offer bonuses to retain these employees.

The changes in benefits, particularly changes in pensions, have highly complex ramifications. Important items in benefits are pensions, health insurance, life insurance and disability plans, and labor agreements. Health insurance is among the major cost items for a company. Life insurance and disability plans are two other benefits that require analysis to determine whether they match the buyer's objectives. Furthermore, collectively bargained labor agreements present a unique set of issues.

Manufacturing units and back office operations are also to be integrated after the merger. Another related issue is that every attempt should be made to prevent the rise of such feelings as "us versus them." Human resource issues in China are among the most challenging issues to deal with. A Mercer survey indicated that the most three important human resource issues in China are:[6]

1. Managing cultural integration
2. Retaining and focusing on key talent
3. Maintaining relationships after the deal

ACQUISITION MOTIVATIONS

Corporate acquisitions are capital investments. The decision to acquire is determined by whether acquisition will make a net contribution to shareholder wealth. The sources of gains include synergies, strategic planning, tax considerations, undervalued shares, agency problems, and diversification. From the seller's perspective, the decision to sell involves reasons such as founder's retirement, estate planning, eliminating personal liabilities, divesture, and venture capital exit strategies.

Buyer's Motivations

The most common argument put forth by acquirers in the merger market has been synergies. Cost-saving synergy is the one most frequently mentioned.[7] There are sometimes revenue synergies, which are the additional sales the parties involved would not have been able to obtain if they were operating independently. Another related potential benefit is financial synergy.[8] The cost of capital may be lowered as a result of a merger. If the streams of cash flows of the two companies are not perfectly correlated, a merger that reduces the instability of revenue streams can reduce the potential costs of financial stress. In addition, there might be economies of scale in flotation and transactions costs.

M&As frequently are a part of corporate strategic planning in a changing market environment as well. One aspect is to increase market power so that the firm has the ability to set prices or to compete more aggressively. Furthermore, the combined company may be better positioned to take advantage of further industry consolidation or marketing channels.

Another argument for acquisition is undervalued shares. This refers to the revaluation of shares because of new information generated during the merger negotiations or the tender offer process. There are two aspects to this argument:

1. The kick-in-the-pants explanation in which management is stimulated to adopt a higher-valued operating strategy.
2. The sitting-on-a-gold-mine hypothesis: the market revalues previously undervalued shares because of the dissemination of new information or the perception that bidders have superior information.

Agency problems are a result of the separation of ownership and management. If compensation to management is a function of firm size, then managers are motivated to expand regardless of returns to shareholders. Alternatively, if a profitable firm is in a mature industry but lacks attractive investment opportunities, the firm should distribute the surplus cash to stockholders by raising dividends or repurchasing shares. However, managers sometimes prefer to use it for acquisition or to retain the surplus cash, in the latter case, the firm often finds itself a takeover target.

Diversification for shareholders or reducing systematic risk has been regarded as a dubious reason for mergers. However, the perception is not necessarily correct and it has been possible to reduce risk for shareholders through mergers when economies of scope exist.[9] For horizontal mergers, the risk can be lowered if the market is imperfectly competitive. In the case of conglomerate mergers, the risk will be reduced if economies of scope exist.

Seller's Motivations

Turning to the selling business, owners and managers sell for many reasons. One major motivation is that founders and other individual owners sell as part of their retirement and estate planning, or as a strategy to other business ambitions. Another reason for sale is the recurring need for expansion capital when the public markets are either not desirable or unavailable. For a private company, another powerful stimulant to sell is the elimination of personal liabilities such as personal guarantees on corporate debt. Such guarantees may risk a family's entire wealth. Eliminating personal guarantees and liabilities is a strong motive.

Large companies sometimes divest businesses that do not fit into their strategic plans. Some business sales are forced by venture capitalists as an exit strategy. Also some sales are caused by financial distress.

Personal Issues

In practice, ego and pride such as who gets to run the show affects many merger deals. These social issues are among the most difficult aspects of negotiating multibillion-dollar deals. Often, a big factor in the success of a merger negotiation is an aging chief executive. Many megadeals tend to take place when a chief executive is nearing retirement and looking to go out with a bang.

Another practical issue involving the sale of private companies is related to nonfinancial concerns. By way of example, a seller entrepreneur's continuing involvement in the business may be a condition of sale. The nonfinancial factors sometimes involve the employees as well. It is also important for the seller entrepreneur to feel comfortable with the new management and owners.

Takeover Defenses

Takeover defenses generally fall into three categories. The first involves corporate charter and by-law amendments, which require shareholder approval. Another involves financial techniques that can be installed by directors without shareholder approval. Also, structural and strategic actions have been occasionally used to fend off unwanted takeover attempts.

Charter and by-law amendments include the following possibilities: The staggered board, in which directors serve a term of three years and only one-third are up for election every year. The aim is to prevent hostile acquirer from taking control of the board in one blow. The company may set a minimum acceptable price or a super-majority vote in an event of a takeover. Another possibility is to allow directors to make decision in a wide range of issues beyond the purchase price. Also, some companies reincorporate in a state with stiff anti-takeover laws.

Certain financial techniques or changes in capitalization are measures costly to the raiders. A "poison pill" is a right distributed to shareholders that allows them to buy additional shares triggered by certain events. Similarly, poison securities take on deterring character when the company is under siege. Poison shares are preferred stock with super-voting right, triggered by unwanted takeover attack. Poison puts are attachments to debt securities, triggered by a change of control, making it less attractive for a takeover. Capitalization changes include multiple classes of common stocks, with one class superior to the other in voting rights. Also, financial engineering techniques may produce temporary changes in capital structure. The techniques include leveraged recapitalization, self-tenders (large-scale repurchase), employee stock ownership plans (ESOPs), pension parachutes, and severance parachutes (golden parachutes).[10]

Strategic and structural defenses involve a wide range of initiatives. One common technique is to seek a "white knight," a more compatible buyer who will pay a higher price than the hostile bidder. A management buyout, in which management becomes its own white knight, is another tactic. Another defense is for the target to sell its crown jewel to keep a hostile acquirer away. At the other end of the spectrum the besieged company can use acquisitions as defensive tactics, either by purchasing a poor performing company to make it worse or by buying a business that competes with the acquirer to set up a possible antitrust conflict. The most extreme of this type of defense is the pac-man strategy, the counterattack by the target to tender the acquirer's shares.

STRATEGIC PLANNING AND INTERMEDIARY

Growth is vital to a business. Acquisitions are only one of the many alternatives; each should be evaluated carefully. The incentive to acquire exists when acquisition is more beneficial than other alternatives, including joint ventures, strategic alliance, minority investment, venture capital, licensing, technology sharing, franchising, and marketing and distribution agreements.

If acquisition is determined to be the best course of action, a team consisting of internal and external professionals plans and implement strategies during the acquisition process. Companies rely on in-house personnel or hire investment bankers to complete the acquisition. Lower expenses, reasons of confidentiality, staff transaction experience, and speed frequently motivate completing transactions in house. Alternatively, the advantages of negotiating through a third-party banker can tap into information flow in sales and trading and thus can obtain better terms regarding the pricing of securities and company assets. As an example, targets with bankers from 1993 to September 1996 received a median premium of 31.6 percent, while those without bankers received a 26.1 percent. For acquirers, those who used bankers paid a median premium of 30.3 percent, compared to a 32.3 percent premium for acquirers without bankers.

A successful acquisition program is often an integral part of a company's overall strategic plan. The strategic needs and preferences of management determine the initial selection criterion of targets. One way of finding the candidates is to hire an intermediary, broker, or finder. Each selected candidate should be evaluated. The key to evaluating an acquisition candidate is an understanding of the acquirer's business strategy and of reactions to the deal among shareholders. Then the evaluation process proceeds to perform a segmentation analysis to determine the segments in which the target operates. The competitive position and operating strategies of the target are analyzed as well.

The period shortly after closing is the time when critical steps are taken to integrate the acquired business with the buyer organization. During the same period, a variety of legal, accounting, tax, insurance, employee benefits, and other steps take place to ensure a successful transition.

INVESTMENT BANKING FEES AND VALUATION

Fees are usually negotiable and contingent upon the success of a deal. The old fee scale years ago was the Lehman 5-4-3-2-1 formula. Under this formula, 5 percent is paid on the first $1 million of sale price, 4 percent on the next $1 million, 3 percent on the next $1 million, 2 percent on the next $1 million, and 1 percent on the amount in excess of $4 million. For a large transaction, the fees are less than 1 percent of the deal's value. In China, fees are usually much lower than those in the United States. Many investment bankers seek an upfront retainer before they begin M&A work with a company, especially a private company where owners have been known to change their minds halfway through the process. Regardless of the transaction outcome, out-of-pocket expenses are billed to the client.

Another important contract is the confidentiality agreement. The basic function of the agreement is to protect sellers against the misuse of confidential information provided to potential buyers. The agreement typically contains: (1) confidentiality provisions to protect the seller against the business risks of disclosure or misuse of information by competitors and (2) standstill provisions to protect the seller against unsolicited takeover attempts by bidders. Other goals of the agreement include complying with securities law, governing the sale process, blocking the raiding of target personnel, and timing announcement.

The types of information bidders require include financial, technical, and human resource materials. At times, potential buyers may request that confidential technical information be excluded from the material provided to avoid any possible future claim that it has misused the target's proprietary information. Also, it is a good practice to require that all personnel contacts be made through the target's investment banker who must be properly briefed.

The agreement may prohibit the disclosure of negotiations by either buyer or seller. The selling company will try to control a bidder's ability to discuss the possible transaction with other potential acquirers. If the target is a public company, the contract typically contains standstill provisions setting the terms under which the bidder may acquire, vote, or dispose of target stock. A potential buyer with separate trading and investment functions, such as a securities dealer, may request that some of its units be permitted to continue trading in target stock without violating the standstill provided that trading and merchant banking divisions are separated by an information barrier between them (or a Chinese Wall).

The target may, through its investment banker and legal counsel, provide bidding guidelines that govern the substance, timing, and manner of submission of acquisition offers. The restrictions on proposals are most effective when coupled with a provision in which the bidder agrees not to request any waivers or amendments of the standstill. Typically, the bidder is subject to the time restrictions of the standstill and nonsolicitation provisions. Other provisions, such as technological know-how, may be perpetual or may expire after a stated number of years or a stated event.

Valuation and Financing

The valuation process involves a self-evaluation by the acquiring firm and the valuation of the acquisition candidate. The self-evaluation phase estimates the value of the acquiring firm and examines how it is affected by each of the various scenarios. The acquirer might overpay the target if its shares are undervalued. Alternatively, the target will be underpaid if the acquirer's shares are overpriced.

The valuation of the merger candidate is to determine what price to offer. The valuation techniques, as discussed next, are used only in determining the price range reference for the target company. Each acquirer uses the technique that fits its objective. Equally important, a risk analysis such as a scenario analysis or sensitivity analysis should be performed. The valuation is not complete until the impact of the acquisition on the acquirer is also carefully examined.

Several techniques are available to estimate the value of a business. They include:

- The discounted cash flow (DCF) technique is widely used in evaluating acquisitions. The DCF method determines the value by projecting future cash flows of the target and discounting those projections to the present value. The DCF approach is future oriented, it begins with a projection of sales and operating profit, based on the assessment of historical performance as well as certain assumptions regarding the future. The usefulness of this technique depends on several assumptions including the impact on the company's other areas of business, length of projection period, additional working or fixed capital required, discount rate, and residual value. The value of the DCF should be estimated under different scenarios. When the target is a startup and is expected to experience negative cash flows and negative earnings for a number of years, the venture capital valuation method can be used. As discussed in private equity chapter, the venture capital method takes into account negative cash flows and uncertain high future profits. It considers cash flow profile by valuing the target company at a time in the future when it expects to generate positive cash flows and earnings. The terminal value at that projected target date is discounted back to the present value by applying the target rate of return (TRR) as the discount rate.

- Comparable transaction analysis is undertaken to analyze transactions involving companies in the target's industry or similar industries over the past several years. Acquisition multiples are calculated for the universe of the comparable transactions. These multiples are then applied to the target's financial results to estimate the value at which the target would likely trade. This technique is effective when data on truly comparable transactions are available.

- The comparable company approach makes an assessment of how the value of the potential acquisition candidate compares with the market prices of publicly traded companies with similar characteristics. A change of control premium is added to arrive at the estimated valuation range for the target. One weakness of this technique is that it works well only when there are good comparables for the target. Another weakness is that accounting policies can differ substantially from one company to another, which could result in material differences in reported earnings or balance sheet amounts.

- The breakup valuation technique involves analyzing each of the target's business lines and summing these individual values to arrive at a value for the entire company. Breakup analysis is best conducted from the perspective of a raider. The process initially determines the value of the target in his hands. The acquisition cost is estimated in the next step. If value exceeds cost, the raider computes the rate of return. This technique provides the required guidance under a hostile bid.

- Target stock price history analysis examines the stock trading range of the target over some time period. The target price performance is analyzed against a broad market index and comparable-company performances. The offering price is based on the price index plus some premium. Similar analysis is performed on the acquiring firm if the transaction is a stock-for-stock exchange. The purpose is to determine the exchange ratio. This approach fails to account for future prospects of the company. Nevertheless, it does provide historical information many find useful in framing valuation thoughts.

- The M&A multiples technique analyzes the current and past broad acquisition multiples and the change of control premium. This technique is used when comparable transactions or comparable company are not available. The limitation is that a broad market average may not be applicable to a single transaction.

- Leveraged buyout analysis is performed when the target is a potential candidate for LBO. The objective is to determine the highest price a LBO group would pay. This is often the floor price for the target. On the other hand, it may set the upper value for the target company if a corporate buyer cannot be identified. The LBO analysis includes cash flow projections, rates of returns to capital providers, and tax effects. The primary difference between the LBO analysis and DCF technique is that LBO approach incorporates financing for the LBO. The availability of financing is dependent on the timing of cash flows, particularly in the first two years after the deal is completed. Clearly, the value derived by the LBO approach can be materially affected by temporary changes in financing conditions.

- Leveraged recapitalization method is aimed at identifying the maximum value that a public company can deliver to its shareholders today. In general, the analysis is performed in the context of a probable or pending hostile offer for the target. The value in a recapitalization is delivered to the shareholders through stock repurchase, cash dividends, and a continuing equity interest in a highly leveraged company. This technique focuses on the target's capital structure, and is largely affected by the availability of debt financing at a particular time.

- Price-to-sales ratio assumes that the value is some multiple of the sales the target generates. The method implicitly assumes that there is some relatively consistent relationship between sales and profits for the business. Obviously, the usefulness of the technique depends on the revenue-profit relationship. In practice, this method may be quite useful when acquiring a private company where gross sales are the only reliable data available.

- The book value approach is an accounting-based concept and may not represent the earnings power. Also, the value of intangible assets may not be reflected in the balance sheet. However, it will help provide an initial estimate of goodwill in a transaction.

- The multiple of earnings per share method (P/E ratio) involves taking the past or future income per share and multiplying that figure by an earnings multiplier, derived from publicly traded companies in the same industry. One difficulty is that the known multipliers do not reflect control premiums, as evidenced by the rise in the multiplier in the event of an acquisition. Another problem is that income does not necessarily represent cash flow from operations.
- Liquidation analysis could be used to establish a floor for valuation. This approach is relevant if a business is being acquired for its underlying assets rather than for its going concern.

Financing

In structuring an acquisition financing, financial positions and expectations of both parties must be considered simultaneously. The flexibility available through various means of payment (called acquisition currency) and the ability to balance the requirements of both parties are among the key ingredients of the negotiated outcomes. Taxable or tax-free transactions are important considerations in the choice of financing methods as well; buyers were more willing to pay a higher premium in tax-free transactions. For example, buyers between 1993 and September 1996 paid a median premium of 30 percent in tax-free acquisitions, compared to a 21.5 percent premium when pooling was not used.[11] The forms of payment include cash, common stock, preferred stock or debt, convertible securities, and contingent payments.

All-cash transactions can be closed faster than any other currency. Stock for stock transaction is another possibility. The most common appeal is that it substitutes stock for a large outlay of cash or a heavy accumulation of debt. The exchange of shares is a tax-free transaction. The recipients do not pay taxes on the stock received until they sell the stock. There is, however, a potentially negative consequence on dilution.

The issuance of preferred stock or debt in financing an acquisition is often necessary when the deal is large. The preference of deferring tax liability of the selling entity is another reason. It is possible to structure a note so that the sellers are not taxed until the principal payments are made. This method is easier to structure and is frequently used in the sales of closely held companies.

Payment by issuing convertible securities offers a means of issuing common stock in an M&A without immediate dilution. This also allows the acquirer to issue fewer shares than if financed entirely with common stock, because the conversion price is typically set at a level higher than the current market value. It does require payment of interest or preferred dividends for a period of time.

Earnout-contingent payments are structured so that part of the purchase price is contingent on target's post acquisition achievement of certain goals. The formula for additional compensation is often based on financial performance. Experienced M&A bankers representing a private company seller would typically recommend operating-based contingency instead of profit-based since the profit can be manipulated by the new owner. This approach helps bridge the gap when there is a large difference between the bid price and the asking price in a private transaction. It also provides a means to retain and motivate the former owners of a business after the sale.

Bridge loans are used to fund the transaction before other forms of financing are in place to secure closing a deal. Proceeds from debt issues, bank loans, and selling off assets are used to pay off bridge loans. Bridge loans are more expensive than other credit products. Structuring and underwriting fees can range from 1 percent to 5 percent. Closing fees and interest rates are higher than the borrower would normally incur. Bridge loans may also involve escalating interest costs or equity kicker or a penalty fee if the loan is not refinanced by a set date.

RISK ARBITRAGE

Risk arbitrage is an important part of the M&A market. The arbitrageurs help make the M&A market liquid and provide shareholders a way to sell stock at a price near the tender price right after the announcement. The arbitrageurs are in essence taking risk over from shareholders and hence expecting a high return.

A transaction can involve a cash exchange, an exchange of securities, or a combination of both. First consider the case of a cash offer. Suppose an acquirer is offering to buy the target's stock at a price of $50 per share at a time when it is trading at $40 per share, a 25 percent premium. The target's stock can be expected to rise to about $50. There is a chance that the acquirer might withdraw or change the offer, however. It is likely that the target's stock may rise to, say, $46 rather then $50. An arbitrageur purchasing the target at $46 will realize a profit of $4 per share if the acquisition takes place at $50. The arbitrageur will lose $6 or more per share if the deal does not go through and the target's share declines back to $40 or lower.

When the transaction involves an exchange of securities, the arbitrageur would long the securities of the target (expecting them to rise in price) and short the securities of the acquiring company (expecting them to decline). There are two risks involved, either the acquisition would not be consummated or the length of time it would take is longer than anticipated. As an example, assume that the stock of an acquirer is trading at $50 per share. The company offers to exchange one share of its stock for one share of the target, which trades at $40. The transaction is expected to be completed in three months. Suppose that the arbitrageur offers the target stock $46 per share. The target's shareholders can immediately take a $6 profit from the proposed deal by selling now to the arbitrageur. Alternatively, these shareholders can wait three months and receive one share of the acquirer's stock. This gives an extra $4 per share profit, but only if the acquisition is completed and only if the shares of the acquirer still trade at $50 per share.

Suppose the target's shareholder decides to sell to the arbitrageur and take a profit of $6 per share. The arbitrageur will have a profit of $4 per share if the deal is closed as proposed. The same outcome remains even if the shares of the acquirer trade at a level lower than $50. For example, the acquirer's shares trade at $48, instead of $50. The arbitrageur has a $2 profit from the short position (acquirer) and another $2 profit from the long position (target).

The primary risk is that the deal will not go through and the prices of both companies go back to their levels before the announcement. The arbitrageur is losing $6 per share. The secondary risk is that the time horizon involved might be longer than anticipated.

The level of complexity in risk arbitrage varies depending on the structure of the transaction. To reduce risk, the arbitrageurs must perform comprehensive research to examine the likelihood of the proposed transaction and the structure of the deal.

CONCLUSION

M&A activities are on the rise in China. Some foreign companies use acquisition to gain a presence in China. Some investors use M&A as a financial strategy, to buy low and sell high. This chapter described the market in China and discussed several of the recent changes in regulations. The chapter further reviewed the motivations for M&A for buyers and sellers, and examined issues relating to deal structure and financing.

10

Underwriting Stocks

I n the United States, investment banks earn billions of dollars each year through
underwriting equity and debt securities. The underwriting fees for initial public
offerings (IPOs) in the United States have averaged 7 percent of the proceeds
raised by the issuer. In China, the fees are much lower. The total expenses average at
3.4 percent. To make a profit, underwriters sometimes have to be creative and take a
position because the underwriting spread is zero. Despite the competitive pressure on
fees, China presents tremendous opportunities. Thousands of companies will issue
stocks in the years to come. Many U.S. and European banks have entered China.
This chapter discusses the market, A and B shares, overseas listing, regulations, and
opportunities.

MARKET OVERVIEW

China's biggest bank, the Industrial and Commercial Bank of China (ICBC), floated
a $19 billion share offering in Hong Kong and Shanghai which was the world's
biggest initial stock listing in history.[1] The new shares started trading on October 27,
2007. And judging by the overwhelming investor responses to China's share offerings,
it is clear that international investors have confidence in China's long-term economic
prosperity, reformation, and open market.[2] This is just one of the many examples that
foreign and Chinese investors are eager to buy a share of the fast-growing China.
Goldman Sachs, German insurer Allianz, and American Express have collectively
spent $3.8 billion for an 8.5 percent stake in the bank ahead of ICBC's offering.
Global players such as HSBC, Bank of America, UBS, Royal Bank of Scotland, Standard Chartered, and others have plowed more than $20 billion into strategic equity
stakes in Chinese banks in recent years.

IPO Trends in Greater China

The term Greater China includes China, Hong Kong, and Taiwan.[3] The number
of IPOs in Greater China was 185, 203, and 98 each year from 2003 to 2005

TABLE 10.1   IPOs in Greater China

	2003		2004		2005	
	Number of IPOs	Funds Raised ($ Billion)	Number of IPOs	Funds Raised ($ Billion)	Number of IPOs	Funds Raised ($ Billion)
HK Main	46	7.35	49	12.15	60	24.6
HK GEM	27	0.26	21	0.35	10	0.09
Shanghai A	67	5.71	61	2.96	3	0.35
Shanghai B	0	0	0	0	0	0
Shenzhen A	0	0	0	0	0	0
Shenzhen B	0	0	1	0.3	0	0
Shenzhen SME	0	0	38	1.1	12	0.36
Taiwan	45	0.61	38	0.3	13	0.17
Total	185	13.93	208	17.16	98	25.57

Source: PricewaterhouseCoopers. "Greater China IPO Watch," 2006; and China Securities Regulatory Commission.

(Table 10.1). In 2006, the number jumped to 140, raising $62 billion. The number of new H shares was 23 in 2006. In Shanghai, there was a decline, from 67 in 2003 to 61 in 2004 and dropped to 3 in 2005. In A shares listing, the number of IPOs was 70 in 2006. There were no IPOs on Shanghai B.[4] The number of B shares actually declined from 114 in 2000 to 109 in 2006.

Many of the IPOs are from five sectors. They are Industrials, Energy & Utilities, Financials, IT & Telecommunications, and Retailing. The largest 10 IPOs in Hong Kong in 2005 reflect concentration in those sectors (Table 10.2). In addition, Bank of

TABLE 10.2   Largest IPOs in Hong Kong in 2005

Company	Amount Raised ($ Millions)
China Construction Bank	9,230
China Shenzhua Energy	3,280
The Link Real Estate Investment Trust	2,790
Bank of Communications	2,170
China COSCO Holdings	1,230
Shanghai Electric Group	650
Dongfeng Motor	590
Foxconn International Holdings	480
Agile Property Holdings	470
Guangzhou R&F Properties	290

Source: PricewaterhouseCoopers. "Greater China IPO Watch," 2006; *Asian Wall Street Journal,* various issues; and Hong Kong Stock Exchange.

China raised $9.7 billion in May 2006 and ICBC collected more than $19 billion in October 2006 in their record-breaking listings.

CHINA STOCK MARKET

The Shanghai Stock Exchange and Shenzhen Stock Exchange were established in 1990. Shenzhen Shekou Anda Industry was the first company to list A shares on the Shenzhen Stock Exchange on December 1, 1990, marking the start of the A share market in China. To attract foreign investments in domestic companies, China launched B shares in 1991. As of February 2007, there were 1,453 listed companies in China, among them 109 companies issued B shares.

Institutional players in the stock market include securities companies, securities investment fund management companies, Qualified Foreign Institutional Investors (QFIIs), insurance companies, corporate annuities, and the Social Security Fund. QFIIs are foreign financial institutions that meet certain requirements and are permitted to carry out certain financial operations in China. The Chinese authorities also encourage Chinese companies to raise capital in the foreign markets. In 1993, Tsingtao Brewery became the first Chinese company to list in Hong Kong (H shares). As of year end 2006, 143 Chinese companies issued H shares. Many Chinese companies also list shares in the United States and London.

Meanwhile, China's securities market is opening to the outside world. International investors have been allowed to invest into B shares market since 1992. In 2002, foreign institutions were allowed to invest directly into China's A shares market via the QFII scheme. Furthermore, starting in 2001, eligible foreign companies can offer and list A shares in China's market. Since 2002, foreign companies have been allowed to acquire Chinese listed companies.

In 2005, the China Securities Regulatory Commission (CSRC) adopted measures to protect investors; in particular, the Securities Investor Protection Fund (SIPF) was established in the second half of 2005. The reform of nontradable shares was also launched. Before the reform, the A shares were divided into tradable and nontradable shares based on their tradability at stock exchanges. Majority of the nontradable shares are state-owned shares. By the end of 2004, the nontradable shares accounted for 64 percent of the total shares (among which the state owned 74 percent). The negative impacts of such a share division include distorting the pricing mechanism of shares, failing to align the common interests of shareholders, and hindering the preservation, appreciation, and transfer of state-owned assets as well as the restructuring of state assets management system.

Thus, these problems call for an action for changes. During the process when a listed company is undergoing the nontradable shares reform, a goodwill price is paid to the holders of tradable shares by holders of nontradable shares in return for the right to trade. The pricing of trading right is determined by negotiations between and among holders of tradable and nontradable shares. A pilot program was introduced in late April 2005, followed by a full-swing reform on all listed companies with nontradable shares. By March 2006, 768 listed companies had completed or engaged in the reform, accounting for 57 percent of the 1,349 listed companies eligible for the nontradable shares reform, or 63 percent of the whole market capitalization. The nontradable shares reform was completed at the end of 2006.

Unique Features of Chinese Initial Public Offerings

The involvement of investment banks and mutual funds can be used as the measurement of political connections in Chinese securities markets for several reasons. First, most investment banks are state-owned and only a few of them can be bookrunners in new securities issuance. Second, the government decides on who may go public, when, and the size. Investment banks are the underwriters as well as the intermediary between the authority and the issuing firm. Third, the allocation of new shares to mutual funds in IPOs makes investment banks more influential than before because they manage and/or control many mutual funds.

Underpricing IPOs is a common practice in China. Private enterprise IPOs are significantly underpriced compared to those of state-owned enterprises (SOEs). The differential in the degrees of underpricing exists because SOEs are larger in size and have favorable conditions in the process of going public, such as priority and they are subject to less rigorous standards.

Allocation of IPO shares is different in China. In the United States, investment banks decide who gets how many shares based on their business relationships. In Chinese A share markets, all domestic investors can register to buy a certain amount of new shares. The most popular method is to register online. If the number of shares subscribed is exactly equal to the amount of shares issued to the public, everyone gets the number of shares he or she has subscribed. If the total subscription is less than the amount of issuing shares, the underwriters have to buy the balance. If the total subscription exceeds the total issuing shares, the computers at the listing exchange will generate a random number for each 1,000 shares and draw winning numbers randomly.[5]

Investment banking fees are much lower in China. The 7 percent rule in the United States is unheard of in China.[6] The average issuing cost as a percentage of the proceeds is 3.4 percent in Chinese domestic stock market. The fees paid by nonstate firms are significantly higher than those by SOEs. The contributing factor to the difference is size; SOEs that go public tend to be larger companies. Private enterprises are smaller and thus pay a higher percentage in fees.

This is one example of costs for going public. Yun Tian Hua paid RMB14 million in issuing costs: 8.52 million (60 percent) is paid to the underwriting syndicate, 0.58 million (4 percent) to CPA firms, 0.55 million (3.9 percent) to asset evaluation firms, 0.4 million (2.9 percent) to law firms, 0.6 million (4.3 percent) to the sponsor of going public, 0.2 million (1.4 percent) to financial consultants, 0.32 million (2.3 percent) to registration office, 0.8 million (5.7 percent) travel expenses, and 2 million (14.3 percent) other fees.

Rationale for Going Public

Successful firms often need additional funds for expansion. There are alternatives to satisfy the needs, including public offering, private placement, venture capital funding, or debt financing. The entrepreneur needs to evaluate each alternative carefully when searching for new capital.

Advantages

An IPO provides a source for ongoing financing, which will enhance the chances for successful growth and thereby increase company value. If needed, a public company with a broader equity base has ready access to the capital markets for future financing. Another advantage is a greater public exposure and the improvement of corporate image. There is also a higher degree of public confidence because of the disclosures required of public companies. This allows for a greater borrowing capability.

Beyond the gain to the company coffer, the greatest financial advantage of going public falls to the founders of the company. The benefits are distributed to the founder-manager, passive founding investors, venture capitalists, and members of the management team who own shares. An IPO provides founding insiders with opportunity to diversify their wealth and to facilitate an exit from the business. With shares traded in the market, it provides for liquidity as well as better estate planning flexibility for insiders. In addition, if the founding stockholder wishes to take a personal loan from a financial institution, the marketable shares offer a more acceptable form of collateral. An IPO also provides an exit for venture capitalists. In essence, an IPO provides liquidity for shareholders.

Furthermore, there are added benefits for management and employees working for a public company. In a public company, stock option plans provide an attractive employment inducement. In addition to recruiting quality employees, the plan often leads to improvement in productivity and long-term loyalty by the employee-shareholders.

Because the company is now subject to scrutiny by the public, corporate governance is improved. First, shareholders will demand better governance. The best practice in the marketplace will influence the company as well. The listing exchange and regulations require better governance, too.

Disadvantages

Going public entails certain costs, risks, restrictions, and duties that prospective issuers should examine carefully. First of all, there is a lack of certain operating confidentiality resulting from the filing of the registration statement and meeting the subsequent reporting requirements. Some particularly sensitive areas of disclosure are remuneration packages (for the top five employees) and extensive company financial information.

Once the company becomes publicly owned, the management is under constant pressure to enhance short-term performance. The requirement that the board of directors or shareholders approve on certain management decisions could cause delays or missed opportunities. As a public company, shareholders may demand that the company establish a dividend policy. Furthermore, if a substantial portion of shares is sold to the public, the original owners could lose control of the company.

Another area of concern is the possible changes in accounting practices and reductions in management perquisites. Owner-managers are typically more concerned with tax savings than with earnings per share. Furthermore, the company's financial statements may not have been audited. Certain compensation packages and related-party transactions (such as a contract between the firm and a major shareholder) that were acceptable for a private company may appear imprudent in a public company.

One important but frequently ignored negative impact is the possible damage to the thriving entrepreneurial culture as a result of tighter legal constraints or public exposure. Moreover, the diffusion of corporate ownership could increase the possibility of a hostile takeover. Finally, the process of going public is expensive and time consuming. The expenses include underwriting spread, counsel fees, printing costs, and other incidental costs. Preparation of the registration documents and financial statements is a complicated process that demands a substantial amount of time from management. After going public, the company must meet the requirements of periodical reporting, disclosure of material information, and the Sarbanes-Oxley Act of 2002 (if listed in the United States). These add significantly to the cost of operations.

Process and Listing Requirements

Going public is a significant event at the company. The stock market, the listing exchange, and the regulators demand certain disclosure and best practices when a company goes public. Many of those requirements did not exist for a private company. The following discusses the various process and preparations that the issuer undertakes to become a public company.

The Process

Once a decision is reached to go public, the process begins. The first step is to take accounting, legal, and other due diligence. Next, it is necessary to obtain regulatory approvals. The process ends with successful marketing of the shares.

During the prelisting period, the company needs expert advice and assistance. The company will approach sponsors and underwriters. Also, the company has to perform an evaluation of the company's readiness to go public and decides what steps necessary to be ready. Organizational structure is worth evaluating. Many privately held businesses operate under common ownership. To go public, the corporation should combine all businesses and subsidiaries. At the same time, some of the assets or liabilities are better taken off the company's books. The owners/founders might want to review their personal tax planning arrangements, including income tax, capital gains tax, and estate planning. Once the structure of the listing company is decided, companies in the group should have annual audits of their financials.

Other advisers needed include sponsors and legal counsel. The sponsor deals with regulators and guides the company through the IPO process. Legal counsel with flotation experience is helpful in ensuring that the offering documents do not omit critical facts or contain misleading or false information.

The next essential step is due diligence. During the due diligence process, major activities cover preparation of prospectus, filing of listing application, response to comments from regulatory agencies, and issuance of prospectus to the investing public. A prospectus is a document the company prepares for the purpose of going public. It should contain full and true disclosure about the company, including business and industry description, product information, personnel information, financial status, and risk factors. The IPO team members will go through a process of due diligence to ensure there is no misleading or missing information in the prospectus. After filing, regulators will comment and pose questions, if not satisfied with the submitted materials. The company will revise the prospectus and send to prospective investors to market the new securities.

Everything does not end with the sale of the new shares. After listing, the company has to file regular reports with regulatory agencies and make timely disclosure of material events. For example, a listing company in China has to file financial status and operating results with the CSRC within the specified schedule: quarterly results in 30 days of quarter end, semi-annual results in 60 days, and annual reports in 120 days. In addition, corporate governance is increasingly complex and demanding. The listing exchange, regulators, and shareholders are demanding good corporate governance.

Requirements

A company applying for a public offering of A shares is required to submit an application to the CSRC and to meet the requirements stipulated in the Company Law, Securities Law, Provisional Regulations on the Administration of Issuing and Trading of Stocks, and other relevant laws and regulations. Methods of making a public offering include:

- A public offering of securities to unspecified investors
- A public offering of securities to more than 200 specified investors
- A public offering as prescribed by any law or administrative regulation

The public offering of stocks may be used to initiate a joint stock limited company, to make an IPO of an established company, or follow-on offerings of the listed company. To initiate a joint stock limited company, you must establish such a company via a public issuance of stocks. The promoter subscribes a significant portion of the shares while the rest are offered to the public. Such a public offering shall meet the following requirements:

- There shall be no less than 2 but no more than 200 promoters, of whom half or more shall have domiciles in China.
- The subscription by the promoters shall be no less than 35 percent of the total shares.

According to the Securities Law, an IPO of a company shall meet the following additional requirements as well:

- Has a complete and well-functioning organizational structure.
- Is capable of making profits continuously in a sound financial condition.
- There is no record of false financial statements over the past three years, and no record of other wrongdoings.
- Has met other requirements as prescribed by the CSRC.

Listed companies can issue additional shares to the public via a rights offering by placing shares to their existing shareholders or by offering a follow-on offering to the public.

Once the application is filed with the CSRC, it will review the application and issue its approval or disapproval. The CRSC has adopted the following procedures to review all applications:

- The issuers are required to make public their application documents after being accepted by the CSRC.
- The Public Offering Supervision Department of the CSRC conducts preliminary reviews of the application.
- The application documents are also subject to the review and examination of the Public Offering Review Committee.
- Taking into consideration the recommendation of the Review Committee, the CSRC decides whether to approve a public offering.

Unlike practices in the past, market forces now determine the pricing for a public offering. This new Inquiry Pricing System was introduced on a trial basis on January 1, 2005. It is a book-building pricing system that involves two stages. In the first stage, the issuer and its sponsor propose an initial price range to solicit price offers from institutional investors. After receiving the first round of feedback, the issuer and the lead underwriter adjust the price range and offer it to the institutional investors for a second-round feedback.

A company wanting to issue B shares has to meet similar, but different, requirements. Like A shares, B shares are also issued by joint-stock companies registered in China and listed on either Shanghai or Shenzhen stock exchange. The B shares are denominated in Chinese currency, but subscribed and traded in foreign currencies. Since 1992, the B shares have been issued and traded on both Shanghai (in U.S. dollars) and Shenzhen (in H.K. dollars) Stock Exchanges. Therefore, the B share market enables Chinese companies to raise foreign currencies from both Chinese and international investors. The requirements for B share issuers are:

- Capital raised by issuing B shares shall be used in a manner consistent with state industrial policy.
- Compliance with regulations regarding fixed-asset investments.

- Compliance with regulations on foreign investments.
- The promoters hold at least 35 percent of the issued shares at the time when the company is set up and the capital contributions by promoters are at least RMB 150 million.
- The company floats at least 25 percent of the total shares, or 15 percent if a company's total share capital exceeds RMB 400 million.
- Any related entity has not committed any significant breaches against laws over the past three years.

As of year-end 2005, 109 companies had issued a total of 19.47 billion B shares (total funds raised was RMB 38.08 billion). There was no new B share issued in 2006. Table 10.3 shows the summary statistics of the B share market.

Shanghai Stock Exchange Requirements

To go public in China, a company has to obtain approval from the CSRC and also meet the requirements of the listing exchange. The following discussion describes the requirements of the Shanghai Stock Exchange. Companies applying for the listing of shares must meet the following conditions:

- The shares have been publicly issued following approval of the State Council Securities Management Department.
- The company's total share capital is at least RMB 50 million.
- The company has been in business for more than three years and has made profits over the last three consecutive years. The number of shareholders with holdings of more than RMB 1,000 is not less than 1,000 persons. Publicly offered shares are more than 25 percent of the company's total share capital. For companies whose total share capital exceeds RMB 400 million, the minimum is 15 percent.
- The company has not been found guilty of any major illegal activities or false accounting records in the last three years.

TABLE 10.3   Summary Statistics of B Share Market

	2000	2001	2002	2003	2004	2005
Number of B Share Companies	114	112	111	111	110	109
Market Capitalization of B Share Companies (RMB 100 Million)	635.19	1276.65	802.57	937.23	746.22	619.73
Market Capitalization of Tradable B Shares (RMB 100 Million)	563.31	1118.28	765.81	872.60	690.17	602.08
Trading Volume of B Shares (100 Million Shares)	200.36	688.88	156.70	170.80	154.82	152.86
Turnover of B Shares (RMB 100 Million)	547.97	5063.13	848.42	845.30	642.64	564.94

Source: China Securities Regulatory Commission.

With the understanding of the requirements, the steps to follow are as follows:

1. CSRC approval: The applications for listing are subject to the approval of the CSRC.
2. Submission of listing application documents: After receiving the approval of the CSRC, the company files an application for listing to the SSE.
3. Share custody: Before a company's shares list and trade on the exchange, it must entrust its full register of shareholders to the Shanghai Branch of the China Securities Registration and Clearing Co.
4. Determination of the listing date.
5. Publication of listing notice: Following examination and verification of the SSE, the company must publish a listing notice five days prior to the listing and trading of its shares.
6. Listing and trading.

When filing an application for listing with the SSE, the application package must include various document required by the exchange. These include:

- Listing announcement
- General meeting of shareholders resolution to apply for listing
- Company ordinance
- Company business license
- Financial and accounting materials for the last three years or since the founding of the company
- Legal opinions in writing and a letter of recommendation from a securities company
- The most recent prospectus
- Listing application
- Documents evidencing approval from the CSRC
- Newly added financial materials as required following issue of the shares
- Photocopy of its business license
- Personal particulars of the secretary of the board of directors and contact details of the secretary of the board of directors, securities representative, and legal representative
- Report regarding the shareholdings of the company directors, supervisors, and senior management of the company
- Circular determining the listing abbreviation of the company's stock
- Documentation showing the full custody of the company's stock
- A written pledge of the company's largest shareholder pledging not to sell or repurchase its shareholding for a period of 12 months
- Other required documents

We have outlined the requirements imposed by the CSRC and SSE. Before the new stock lists and trades on the exchange, the company and the SSE sign an agreement. This Listing Agreement includes the following:

- The stock exchange provides trading facilities and service for the trading of the company's securities.
- Listed company undertakes to abide by relevant state securities laws, rules and regulations, and related rules of the exchange.
- The listed company and its directors, supervisors, and officers accept the supervision of the stock exchange and are subject to sanctions by the stock exchange for any violations.
- Listing fee, as Table 10.4 shows, and its method of payment.
- The SSE can cease the trading of listed securities in accordance with the law. If the SSE determines that a company's securities no longer meet the conditions for listing, it can temporarily suspend or cease the listing of such securities.

Shenzhen Stock Exchange

A Chinese company may choose to list on the Shenzhen Stock Exchange. The exchange has two sections, the Main Board and the Small and Medium Enterprise Board (SME). The listing requirements are:

- IPO approval granted by the CSRC
- Minimum 25 percent public holding
- Corporate size of at least RMB 30 million
- Good credit records in the past three years

In 1995, the exchange received CSRC's approval to set up the SME Board. The SME Board accommodates high-growth small and medium enterprises with greater high-tech contents. It has a separate management system including "operating under separate trading system, separate regulatory system, separate stock coding, and separate stock price index." The SME started in 2004 and as of April 2007 it had 130 listed companies.

Hong Kong Exchange

Similar to the Shenzhen Stock Exchange, the Hong Kong Exchange also has two sections, the Main Board and the Growth Enterprise Market (GEM). The company

TABLE 10.4 Listing Fee Schedule at Shanghai Stock Exchange

	A Shares	B Shares
Initial fees	0.03% of the total share capital, capped at 30,000 yuan	0.1% of the par value of listed shares capped at 5,000 U.S. dollars
Monthly fees	0.001% of the par value of listed shares, capped at 500 yuan	50 U.S. dollars

Source: Shanghai Stock Exchange.

wanting to list in Hong Kong has to submit completed Form A1 and other related materials. According to the exchange's requirements, the following is the time schedule for various submissions:[7]

- *At least 20 business days before the expected hearing date:*
  —Two copies of the advanced drafts of the accounts of the companies which comprise or will comprise the group of the listed issuer for the balance of the financial years or financial periods that make up the track record period
  —Where the listing document contains an accountant's report, two copies of a draft of any statement of adjustments relating to the accountant's report
  —Three drafts or copies of the memorandum and articles of association or equivalent document, unless previously supplied in the case of a listed issuer
- *At least 15 business days before the expected hearing date:*
  —In the case of a new applicant, a formal declaration relating to any other business activities and undertaking duly signed by each director/supervisor and proposed director/supervisor
  —Where the listing document contains a profit forecast, two copies of a draft of the board's profit forecast memorandum with principal assumptions, accounting policies, and calculations for the forecast
- *At least 10 business days before the expected hearing date:*
  —A copy of every contract required by the listing requirements or a memorandum giving full particular if there is no written contract
  —Two copies of a draft of the formal notice
  —Five drafts or proof prints of any application form to subscribe or purchase the securities for which listing is sought
  —In the case of a listed issuer, six drafts or proofs of the listing document
  —Five drafts or proof prints of any temporary document of title proposed to be issued
  —Two drafts or proof prints of the definitive certificate or other document of title proposed to be issued, unless previously supplied in the case of a listed issuer
  —In the case of a listed issuer, two copies of all resolutions which have been passed by the issuer and which are required to be registered under the Companies Ordinance

The exchange reviews all the submissions and will, if satisfied, grant an approval to the listing application. The new stock starts trading on the exchange.

QUALIFIED FOREIGN INSTITUTIONAL INVESTORS

China introduced the Qualified Foreign Institutional Investor (QFII) scheme in 2002 to link Chinese with global capital markets. The QFII scheme includes eligibility criteria, investment quotas, and foreign exchange controls, based on the condition of the stock market and reform schedule of its capital market. QFII scheme allows qualified foreign institutional investors to remit into China a certain quota of foreign capital and convert the capital to RMB to invest in China's securities market. Capital gains and dividends may be converted into foreign exchange and repatriated offshore.

Foreign institutions use QFII designation to carry out their investment objectives in China, including securities listed on China's stock exchanges (excluding B shares) such as A shares, government securities, convertible bonds and enterprise bonds, and other financial instruments as approved by CSRC. In order to gain such designation, they have to meet certain requirements:

- *Asset managers*
  - —Having operated fund business for over five years
  - —Total asset under management of at least $10 billion[8]
- *Securities/Insurance Companies*
  - —At least 30 years of experience
  - —Paid-in capital of no less than $1 billion
  - —Managing securities assets of no less than $10 billion
- *Commercial banks*
  - —Ranking among the top 100 in the world in total assets
  - —Assets of no less than $10 billion

To encourage more QFIIs, China lowered the qualification threshold in August 2006. For example, the securities asset requirement was reduced from $10 billion to $5 billion. The investment quota requirements are:

- Investment quota shall be approved by State Administration of Foreign Exchange (SAFE).
- The investment quota are between $50 million and $800 million.
- Approved investment quota shall be remitted into China within three months.
- A QFII may apply again for the cancelled quota or apply for an extra quota.
- A QFII that has remitted in principal for more than three months but less than one year may transfer its investment quota to other QFIIs or other applicants.

QFIIs are subject to a lockup period. The length of the lockup depends on the type of institution. For a closed-end fund company, the lockup is three years. The amount of repatriation each time, at most once a month, cannot exceed 20 percent of the total principal. Other QFIIs are subject to a one-year lockup. The amount of repatriation each time, at most once every three months, should not exceed 20 percent of the total principal. The lookup restrictions have been eased and the lookup repatriation periods shortened.

DEPOSITARY RECEIPTS

Many Chinese companies have listed on overseas exchanges, including Hong Kong, London, and United States. Listings in Hong Kong are often called the H shares, in

London L shares, and in New York N shares. The form of the listing is by way of depositary receipts, meaning the receipts that represent ownership of the underlying shares trade in the foreign markets and the underlying shares are held at a custodian in the local market.

Introduction to Depositary Receipts

Depositary receipts that list and trade in the United States are called American Depositary Receipts (ADRs). Some depositary receipts list and trade in London. Each ADR represents a specific number of underlying shares deposited at a local custodian in the issuer's home market. A variety of depositary instruments have been issued. Global depositary receipts (GDRs) differ from ADRs in that they are offered in two or more markets outside the issuer's home country.

Issuance and Cancellation

To establish a sponsored ADR program, the foreign company together with its underwriter and other members of the team work closely to ensure a successful launch. The issuer also selects a depositary bank to implement and manage the ADR program on an ongoing basis. Major depositary banks are Deutsche Bank, Citibank, JPMorgan Chase, and Bank of New York. Among them, Bank of New York has the largest market share. The issuer works with the depositary bank to select a custodian to safe keep the underlying shares in the issuer's home market.

Once the underlying shares are deposited with the custodian in the issuer's home market, the depositary then issues depositary receipts to investors. The broker delivers ADRs to the customer's account and the ADRs are created. The structure of ADRs typically includes a ratio called bundling, corresponding to the number of underlying shares per ADR, to align the trading price of the ADR to the customary price levels.

To cancel the ADR program, the steps are reversed. The broker receives ADRs from customers and delivers them to the depositary for cancellation. The depositary instructs the local custodian to release the underlying shares to the local broker who purchased the shares.

Types of Depositary Receipts Facilities

There are two types of ADR programs: unsponsored and sponsored. An unsponsored program is not supported by the foreign company, while a sponsored program is established by the foreign company. Sponsored and unsponsored programs for the same security cannot exist simultaneously because these ADRs for the same foreign security might trade at different prices, creating confusion.

An unsponsored ADR program is often initiated by a bank in response to investor demand. The issuer has no control over the program because there is typically no deposit agreement between the issuer and the depositary bank.

Sponsored ADRs include Level I, Level II, Level III, and Rule 144A. Level I ADRs are the easiest and least expensive way for a foreign company to gauge international interest in its securities and to begin building a presence in the United States.

Level I ADRs only trade in the over-the-counter market. Level II ADRs must comply with the SEC's full registration and reporting requirements. Companies that want to raise capital use a sponsored Level III facility. Level III ADRs are similar to those issued under Level II. In both programs, the issuer initiates the program, signs a deposit agreement with one depositary bank, and lists on one of the U.S. exchanges. The major difference is that a Level III program allows the issuer to make a public offering. To do so, the issuer must file a Form F-1 to register the shares underlying the Level III ADRs. The reporting requirements are more onerous for Level III than for Level I or Level II programs. Financial statements must be fully reconciled to the U.S. GAAP. The costs can be substantial; they include listing, legal, accounting, investor relations, and roadshows.

As an alternative to Level III programs, foreign companies can access the U.S. capital market by issuing ADRs under Rule 144A, called Rule 144A ADRs, to accredited investors. Rule 144A ADRs offer both advantages and disadvantages to issuers. Rule 144A ADRs do not have to conform to full reporting and registration requirements. They can be launched on their own or as part of a global offering. There are two disadvantages, however. First, Rule 144As cannot be created for a class of shares already listed on a U.S. exchange. In addition, they can only trade among qualified institutional investors; consequently, the market certainly is not as liquid as the public equity market.

Global Depositary Receipts

A global depositary receipt (GDR) allows an issuer to raise capital through a global offering in two or more markets at the same time. GDRs can be issued in either the public or private market in the United States and other countries. Most GDRs include a U.S. tranche that is structured as either a Level III ADR or as a private placement under Rule 144A and an international tranche that is placed outside the United States pursuant to Regulation S.

LISTING IN THE UNITED STATES AND LONDON

In the United States, similar to United Kingdom or other markets, the lead manager of the new issue begins by conducting due diligence research and then coordinates the preparation of detailed information about the firm and financial status (the registration statement) to be filed with the Securities and Exchange Commission (SEC). This is done in close coordination with the company, accountant, and counsel. The filing date is the day the investment bank turns in the registration statement to the SEC. Amendments to the registration statement are submitted to the SEC again. If there are no further changes, registration becomes effective.

There are two different types of agreements between the issuing company and the investment bank. The first type is the firm commitment, in which the investment bank agrees to purchase the entire issue and distribute it to both institutional and retail investors. The second type is known as a best efforts agreement. With this type of agreement, the investment bank agrees to sell the securities but does not guarantee the price.

There are other steps taking place during the registration process. The offering document, called the red herring or preliminary prospectus, is printed and distributed. The stock certificates are printed, and the listing exchange and the transfer agent are selected. The lead manager forms the underwriting group and promotes the issue in a roadshow.

After the issue goes public, the lead manager assures sufficient liquidity in the aftermarket by making market after the underwriting period. A public company is subject to the SEC disclosure requirements, including regular filings of financial data and timely disclosure of material information. The company is also required to send quarterly and annual financial statements to shareholders.

Sarbanes-Oxley Act of 2002

The collapse of Enron and the bankruptcies of several major telecommunications firms prompted intense congressional scrutiny of required corporate disclosures. As a result, on July 30, 2002, President Bush signed into law the Sarbanes-Oxley Act of 2002. The act mandates a number of reforms to enhance corporate responsibility, enhance financial disclosures and combat corporate and accounting fraud, and created the Public Company Accounting Oversight Board (PCAOB) to oversee the activities of the auditing profession.

The act imposes the most intense scrutiny of corporate behavior since the passage of the Securities Exchange Act of 1934. The act applies to all U.S. public traded companies, investment companies, and foreign issuers. First, the act requires two separate chief executive officer (CEO)/chief financial officer (CFO) certification requirements. Under the act, the CEO/CFO must state in each annual and quarterly report to the SEC that they have reviewed the report, the report is accurate, and that the CEO/CFO have established effective internal controls.

The second major feature of the act is that it prohibits registered public accounting firms from providing auditing clients with non-auditing services. Those non-auditing services include bookkeeping, design and implementation of financial information systems, appraisal or valuation services, actuarial services, internal audit outsourcing, management functions or human resources, broker-dealer or investment services, and legal services. The third main requirement of the act is that it sets standards for independence of directors on audit committee. Audit committees are empowered to engage independent counsel. Audit committees are required to establish procedures for receiving and dealing with complaints received by the issuer regarding accounting and controls.

The fourth requirement the act imposes is the enhanced disclosure of off-balance sheet transaction, especially of special purpose entities. Filings by directors and officers of forms under the Exchange Act are due within two days of a change in holdings. The issuer must disclose whether or not it has at least one financial expert on its audit committee.

Exchange Listing Requirements

The choice of exchange listing is part of the IPO process. The main U.S. securities trading markets are the New York Stock Exchange (NYSE), The American Stock Exchange (AMEX), the regional markets, and the over-the-counter markets (OTC). A brief description of the listing requirements follows.

The listing requirements on the NYSE are extensive.[9] The form for listing is very similar to a full S-1 registration statement. The minimum listing requirements are: 2,000 shareholders, 1.1 million publicly held shares, and market value of public shares of $60 million.

The AMEX is an alternative to NYSE listing. There are four listing standards for U.S. companies. Those standards deal with pretax income, number of public shareholders, and number of shares publicly held.

The National Association of Securities Dealers Automated Quotations (NASDAQ) is a computer-based quotation/trading system with terminals in broker/dealer offices all over the country. The minimum listing requirements for smallcaps are 300 shareholders, 1 million shares of public float valued at $5 million, a bid price of $4, and three market makers.

Aftermarket Trading and Research

Immediately following an IPO, an aftermarket develops for the shares of the company's stock. Once the shares are in public hands, their price may go up or down on the basis of many factors including ongoing demand for the stock, general market conditions, and, most importantly, the company's performance. But, in general, the offering price is lower than the aftermarket value.

Though an investment bank cannot make a stock price go up or down, it can write and disseminate research reports and sponsor investor meetings. Such research can have a major impact on the stock price. It is common to see a strong demand when research coverage on a stock is initiated. Consequently, research capability is one of the key factors companies consider when selecting an underwriter.

In the early 2000s, however, many questioned Wall Street analysts' credibility. For example, Eliot L. Spitzer's investigation (when he was New York State Attorney General) revealed that even as Merrill Lynch's analysts were advising investors to buy shares of certain companies, they were privately calling these same companies' prospects doubtful. Many observers have pointed out that the fundamental problem is that many securities firms compensated their investment research analysts based on a formulaic percentage of investment banking revenues. To assure the independence and integrity of investment research, the SEC approved new ethics rules in May 2002. The rules require the securities firms to provide more detailed disclosure of conflicts and give lawyers and ethics officers at the firm a leading role in acting as gatekeepers between analysts and investment bankers. The rules also require analysts to disclose whether they or their firms hold stock in the companies under review and to list the percentage of all ratings that they have assigned to buy, hold, and sell categories. In addition, they must provide a chart that plots the historical price movements of a security and indicates the points at which the analyst began and changed ratings and price targets. Finally, the rules impose blackout periods that prohibit analysts from trading in the companies that they cover for 30 days before and five days after their research report is published. Sarbanes-Oxley act also imposes Chinese Walls between analysts and other personnel.

London Stock Exchange

The London Stock Exchange (LSE) is home to hundreds of international companies from more than 50 countries. London's position at the heart of the global financial community is part of the reason many international companies choose to list in London.

The LSE also offers trading services specifically designed for international companies. International trading systems are accessed in real-time by over 91,000 trading terminals across the world, giving an unequalled range of professional investors direct visibility of the listed company. International companies can list a number of products in London, including shares, depositary receipts, and debt offering.

Internationally companies can apply for a primary listing in London; or if already listed on their own domestic market, can apply for a dual primary or secondary listing. Shares can be traded in over 20 global currencies. An alternative is to list DRs.

PRICING AND RISKS FOR UNDERWRITERS

The issuer often believes the stock is worth much more than the suggested price. But the underwriter wants to create a demand for the new issue so as to sell it quickly. The best way to do that is to offer the stock at a price attractive enough to encourage prospective purchasers to buy it. When the share does well, he also realizes a huge profit. This is because the entrepreneur retains a big portion of ownership. What has been sold to the public is just a fraction of his potential wealth.

Valuation and pricing are related but they deal with different issues. Valuation is estimating the value of the company. The underwriter typically conducts a survey of comparable public companies, which will help provide a preliminary valuation. The underwriter also looks into the following factors: efficiency, leverage, profit margins, use of proceeds, operating history, operating base, management, and product differentiation. Furthermore, it is important for the underwriter to take into account whether this is a single-product or a multiple-product company.

Pricing refers to setting the offering price. The main concern is how much the market will bear. Most underwriters follow historical traditions in pricing a new issue. The price should not be too high or too low in order to appeal to potential investors. For example, a price of $10 or less might be considered too risky, and a price of $50 or more might be considered too high unless for a prestigious company. It is common to see an IPO price range from $20 to $50 per share.

Underwriters price a new issue a certain percentage below what they consider a fair value. Thus, there is a difference between the price of an IPO and the price when those shares start trading in the secondary market. This creates an incentive for investors to put money into the new issue. This discounting practice is evidenced by the observations that a new issue typically trades at a much higher price by the end of the first trading day. The pricing disparities widen when an IPO is hot. While it is not easy for retail investors to get allocation of IPO shares in the United States, more and more brokerage firms offer IPO shares to individual investors. Before selling IPO shares to individuals, some brokerage firms might require a minimum balance, a subscription of premium services, or active trading. In addition, some also impose restrictions on investors who flip or sell the IPO shares after the first day of trading to make a quick profit. In China, retail investors get allocation of IPO shares through a "lottery" system in which an investor gets shares if his or her registered number is selected in the random drawing.

There are reasons for discounting. First, institutional investors demand a discount because they have been receiving allocations that jumped in the aftermarket. Second, it reduces underwriting risks and protects the underwriter's reputation. Third, it decreases the possibility of lawsuits by investors if they lose money purchasing the shares.

Timing is also critical. The offering price is adjusted upward when the underwriter has received a higher over-subscription in indications of interest. The offering price needs to be lowered or the issue may be postponed if indications of interest are weak.

Underwriting Risks and Compensation

It is customary for the lead underwriter to form a distribution syndicate consisting of the underwriting syndicate and a selling group. Each member in the underwriting syndicate is committed to buying a portion of the IPO shares, while members of the selling group accept no risk. The lead underwriter's decision to distribute shares outside of its own organization has its positives and negatives. The lead underwriter benefits because each underwriter shares a portion of the underwriting risk. Second, the syndicate manager has the responsibility to ensure liquidity in the aftermarket. A broad participation by the street provides incentives for other firms to make a market in the stock and provides research coverage. In addition, the lead manager has to make some economic concessions in sharing the underwriting spread. Another risk is that one of the syndicate members might outshine the lead manager and hence gain an edge in competing for future offerings. In general, the selection of underwriting syndicate and the selling group are based on a solid distribution of shares and the ability of market making.

Underwriting Risks

In underwriting, investment bankers sell risk services to the issuers by assuming at least part of the floating risk when they underwrite an offering by firm commitment.

A firm commitment becomes absolutely firm only on the offering day or the night before, when the underwriting agreement is signed. The signing typically occurs just before the issue becomes effective. By then, all the marketing has been done, the roadshows have been conducted, and the underwriter knows the indications of interest. Risk or uncertainty can occur when the market shifts after a firm commitment on price has been made.

Floating risk consists of waiting risk, pricing risk, and marketing risk. During the period after the filing of the registration statement, but before it is declared effective by the SEC, changes in market environment affect the offering price. Such waiting risk is mainly borne by the issuer. However, the pricing risk and marketing risk are exclusively borne by the underwriters. The pricing risk occurs when the market conditions worsen after the underwriting agreement has been signed. Marketing reduces flotation risk by building a "book of interest" before the effective date and by after-market trading. Forming a syndicate in which each member is taking only a portion of the deal also lessens the risk. Institutional sales help bankers place large pieces of new issues.

Compensation

The underwriting spread is the difference between the price to the public and the price the corporate issuer receives. The amount of the spread is determined through negotiation between the managing underwriter and the corporate issuer. All members of the syndicate are paid out of the spread. The varying amount of risk accepted by the members of the distribution syndicate is reflected in the compensation schedule. The manager's fee is compensation to the managing underwriter for preparing the offering. Participating in a thorough due diligence review and putting the deal together are the primary basis for the compensation.

The underwriting or syndicate allowance covers expenses incurred by the underwriting syndicate, including advertising, legal expenses, and other out-of-pocket expenses. Finally, the selling concession is allocated among all firms based on the amount of securities they sell. Therefore, the syndicate manager will have all three, the manager's fee, the underwriting allowance, and the selling concession. The underwriting dealers will get the underwriting allowance and the selling commission. The selling group is allocated a portion of the total selling concession.

COSTS OF GOING PUBLIC

The costs of a public offering are substantial. There are no hard and fast numbers. Total costs vary depending on the size of the offering and the company's ability to market the offering smoothly and efficiently. As an example, for an issue around $150 million, the total costs can be as high as 10 percent in the United States. Going public demands a great deal of time from top management, resulting in internal costs that may be difficult to quantify. Furthermore, there are costs of underpricing.

Direct Costs

Direct costs include direct expenses plus the underwriting spread. The company pays the direct expenses whether or not the offering is completed. The underwriter's commission is contingent on the completion. The first big item is the underwriting spread. This is negotiable and depends on factors such as the size of the offering, the type of underwriting commitment, and the type of security offered. There is also reimbursement for some of the banker's direct expenses. Additional compensation is in the form of warrants, stock issued to the underwriter before the public offering at a price below the offering, or a right of first refusal for future offerings.

Legal fees are usually the second largest item of expenses. They vary depending on the complexity of the company, the orderliness of its records, and the amount of time necessary to draft and file the registration statement.

Accounting fees are substantial as well. The accountant reviews and verifies the data in the registration statement and issues the comfort letter. These fees do not include audits of the financial statements, which vary depending on the size of the company and the number of years audited.

Printing costs are determined by the length, number of changes, and the number of photographs. Registration fees, registrar and transfer agent fees, and miscellaneous fees are significant.

Underpricing

A public offering is costly in yet another way. Since the offering price is typically less than the aftermarket value investors who bought the issue get a bargain at the expense of the firm's original shareholders. The original shareholders typically retain a large portion of the company's shares on which they made enormous profits.

When a company goes public, it is very difficult for the underwriter to judge how much investors will be willing to pay for the stock. Hence, underpricing is a means of soliciting investor interest. Many have observed the IPO shares soar 20 percent to 30 percent in price during the first day of trading. The underpricing was much higher during the Internet bubble years in the late 1990s.

Underpricing helps the underwriter because it reduces the risk of underwriting and gains them the gratitude of investors who buy the IPO issues. The true cost of underpricing is difficult to judge. If the business is sufficiently competitive, underwriters will probably take all these hidden benefits into account when negotiating the spread.

Hidden and Future Costs

During the lengthy process of preparing the listing of the company, unanticipated costs will crop up. These include extra transportation costs to and from consultants, counsels, accountants, and underwriter; meals and entertainment; postage; and phone calls, faxes, and messenger deliveries. Another important item is promotions. Thousands of dollars may be required to make the brokerage community and investors aware of the company. Another cost is director's and officer's liability insurance.

Although management has considerable control over the amount and extent of some of these hidden costs, the costs invariably exceed what is anticipated. In addition, the one cost that is difficult to put a dollar value on is the management time it takes to complete the offering.

A further consequence is the expense of being a public company. First, the SEC requires the company to file periodic reports, including annual Form 10-K, quarterly Form 10-Q, Form 8-K for report of significant events, and proxy and information statements. Significant costs and executive time are incurred in preparing and filing these reports. Compliance with the Sarbanes-Oxley of 2002 adds substantial costs.

CONCLUSION

The IPO of China's ICBC was the largest in the world in history. Multinational financial firms have invested tens of billions of dollars to take strategic stakes in China's banks and securities firms. Many companies will issue stocks in China or in foreign markets in the years to come. There are tremendous opportunities for investment banks to profit from China's growth to a powerhouse. This chapter described the IPO process and regulatory and listing requirements. Other issues such as pricing, risks, and after market are covered as well.

11

Underwriting Fixed-Income Securities

China's bond market falls far behind the stock market in terms of development. This is similar to most developing countries. To develop an efficient and sound financial market, Beijing has taken steps to reform the fixed-income market. Reform measures include trading system, market interest rate, rating, and various derivatives related to fixed-income instruments. This chapter reviews China's fixed-income market environment, partial deregulation of interest rate, trading mechanisms, and related issues. The chapter also describes the U.S. fixed-income market, which serves as the model for future development in China.

OVERVIEW

China's bond market is the third largest in the region, with government and quasi-government bonds dominating issuance and trading. There are five major types of instruments: (1) China government bonds issued by Ministry of Finance, (2) central bank paper issued by People's Bank of China, (3) financial bonds issued by government-backed policy banks and financial institutions, (4) corporate bonds issued by domestic corporations, and (5) commercial paper issued by either securities firms or private corporations. There are two main bond markets: the interbank bond market and the exchange markets (Shanghai Stock Exchange and Shenzhen Stock Exchange). The interbank bond market is China's over-the-counter (OTC) market.

The interbank OTC market is mainly for block trading among financial institutions. The People's Bank of China (PBC) uses it to implement its monetary policies. The Ministry of Finance and the PBC are the primary issuers of government bonds. China's policy banks, commercial banks, and other financial institutions issue financial bonds. The China Development Bank, Export and Import Bank of China, and the Agricultural Development Bank are China's policy banks.

Corporations such as China Mobile, Three Gorges, State Grid Corporation, and Shanghai Baosteel Group are some of the major domestic corporate bond issuers listed on both the Shanghai and Shengzhen stock exchanges. Supranational banks such as the Asian Development Bank, International Finance Corporation, and Japan Bank for International Cooperation have gained approval to issue renmimbi (RMB) denominated bonds subject to strict compliance to government rules and regulation.

Interbank Market

The interbank bond market is a quote-driven OTC market. It is the platform from which the China government sells bonds. Financial institutions use it to adjust their liquidity. PBC performs its open market operations to achieve its monetary policy goals in the interbank market. Trading on the interbank bond market is mainly in repurchase agreement and spot. A repurchase agreement (repo) transaction is a sale of the government security with a promise to repurchase the same at a later date. The repurchase date determines the term of the repo transaction. If the repurchase is on the next business day, it is an overnight repo. If the repurchase date is more than one business day, it is a term repo. The interest rate applied to the repo transaction is the repo rate.

Transactions between members of the Central T-bond Registration and Settlement Co. are matched in the China National Interbank Funding Center (CNIFC) by asking price, or made in the form of OTC trading by their own agreement. Open market operations are by agreement between the PBC and primary dealers. This is similar to the U.S. open market operations in that the Fed trades with primary dealers to influence market interest rate.

Trading System

An electronic trading system (ET03) was developed to facilitate bond issuance, trading, and data collection. In addition, the F-system was developed to analyze trading data within the interbank system. The ET03 has three subsystems for trading, brokering, and floor management. The new system provides quoting, trading, and information services for interbank credit lending, repo, bond trade, and distribution. It also provides same-city overnight lending for the jurisdiction areas of some PBC branches.

The system integrates the trading system, information system, and F-system into one. Quotation and trading on the ET03 are anonymous. After a transaction is completed, the identities of the counterparties are revealed. The system also allows trading members to download their quotations and transaction data in real time or afterward for further processing.

In the trading process, all quotations and market situations are accessible simultaneously on www.chinamoney.com.cn. The quotation, trading, and market data are embodied into the F-system, serving as the basis for bond analysis. The F-system is composed of five modules. The market situation module offers real-time and historical market analysis as well as an inquiry function. The inquiry function allows users to access information about the latest transactions and quotations. The bond yield module provides users with yield analysis in real-time, historical, and hypothetical circumstances. The position management module presents a user with its trading records as well as its total in the system. The counterparty management module facilitates users' inquiries into their own internal information, counterparty transactions and public information, and helps set a credit line by monitoring the counterparty's creditworthiness and inquiring into their trading record. The term structure module is designed to estimate the interest rate term structure. This helps users price bonds correctly.

Exchange Trading of Bonds

Treasury bonds, corporate bonds, and convertible bonds trade on both the Shanghai Stock Exchange (SSE) and the Shenzhen Stock Exchange (SZSE). Secondary market transactions for government bonds, including spot trading and repos, also take place on these exchanges. Deals are done based on tender prices. Trading on both the SSE and the SZSE follows the principle of price and time precedence. As Table 11.1 shows, there are 49 T-bond spot, 9 T-bond repo, 60 financial and corporate bonds, and 17 convertible bonds on the SSE.[1] The turnover volume for each is relatively small.

TABLE 11.1   Bond Trading on Shanghai Stock Exchange (in RMB)

Yearly	T-Bond Spot	T-Bond Repo	Financial & Corporate Bond	Convertible Bond
No. of listings	49	9	60	17
No. of new listings	12	0	14	3
Issued volume	139725500		12255000	2283412
Market value	141379319		12979293	2755543
Tradable volume	139725500		12255000	418138
Market value of tradable volume	141379319		12979293	473305
Turnover in volume	11126.67	73774.14	405.65	1171.24
Daily average	69.54	461.09	2.54	7.32
Daily high	218.86	1428.99	20.27	62.62
Daily low	10.36	139.87	0.17	0.08
No. of transactions	61.42	26.15	3.83	13.72
Daily average	0.38	0.16	0.02	0.09
Daily high	0.86	0.52	0.14	0.47
Daily low	0.15	0.05	0	0.01
Turnover in value	11179006.66	73774140	433060.93	1350671.69
Daily average	69868.79	461088.38	2706.63	8441.7
Daily high	219395.26	1428990	22954.16	72687.48
Daily low	10349.63	139870	172.45	91.53

Source: Shanghai Stock Exchange.
Note: Data are for January to August 2006. Volume and value are in RMB 1,000.

TABLE 11.2 China Treasury Yields

Government Bonds	Latest Yield
1-Year government bond	2.015
2-Year government bond	2.159
7-Year government bond	2.749
12-Year government bond	3.092
14-Year government bond	3.408
28-Year government bond	3.842

Note: Data are as of closing on October 5, 2006.

Treasury Bonds

The public sector dominates the issuance of domestic debt. Treasury bonds and policy financial bonds account for almost all of the debt issuance. In the United States, Treasury securities trade over the counter. In China, Chinese government securities trade over the counter as well as on the exchanges. The Ministry of Finance (MOF) issues Treasury bonds (the largest portion of the bond market), construction bonds, fiscal bonds, and special bonds. Government bonds can also be divided into two categories: book entry or bearer. Though government bonds are effectively risk free, they still trade at a high premium relative to bank deposits. The main reason is low liquidity. Table 11.2 lists the yields on China's government securities. Yields in China are lower than those in the United States, as Table 11.3 shows.

Financial Bonds

Policy banks, China Development Bank and Export-Import Bank, issue a significant amount of domestic debt. These bonds are known as financial bonds and are generally

TABLE 11.3 Yields of U.S. Government Securities

Maturity	Yield (%)
3 months	4.81
6 months	5.05
2 year	4.78
3 year	4.71
5 year	4.68
10 year	4.73
30 year	4.87

Source: Bloomberg, market close on October 5, 2006.

considered quasi-government paper. Proceeds from financial bonds are used to support infrastructure projects and develop strategic industries. Both government bonds and financial bonds play an important role in the central bank's open market operations as well as in the repo market.

Corporate Bonds

The smallest segment of the market is corporate bonds. There are three types of corporate bonds, including central corporate bonds, local corporate bonds, and corporate short-term bonds. For issues larger than RMB 100 million, issuers can seek approval from China Securities Regulatory Commission (CSRC) to list on exchanges. Both Shanghai and Shenzhen stock exchanges require at least an A rating by domestic credit rating agencies. The interest rate on corporate bonds used to be capped at 1.4 times comparable bank deposit rate, regardless of credit rating. The reason was that many believe the risk is ultimately born by the government, because the state virtually owns all companies in a central planning economy.

Convertible Bonds

Convertible bonds are corporate bonds that can be converted into shares under pre-agreed conditions. The issuance of convertible bonds should meet the requirements for new public offering as prescribed in the Securities Law. The issuer has to meet the following requirements as well:

- The net asset of a joint-stock limited company is at least RMB 30 million and the net asset of a limited-liability company is at least RMB 60 million.
- The accumulated outstanding bonds cannot exceed 40 percent of the net assets of a company.
- The average annual distributable profits over the latest three years are sufficient to pay one-year interests on the bonds.
- The raised funds are to be invested in a manner consistent with China's industrial policies.
- The interest rate of bonds does not exceed the band of interest rates as set by the State Council.

Bonds Issued by Securities Companies

The issuance of bonds by securities companies is subject to review and approval of the CSRC. In addition to requirements prescribed in the Securities Law, the issuing securities company should also comply with the following requirements:

- The latest unaudited assets shall be no less than RMB 1 billion.
- The company made profits in the preceding year.
- All risk control indicators have met the requirements by the CSRC.

- No material violation of laws or wrongdoing has been committed during the past two years.
- Internal control systems are effective with proper business firewalls and internal control of technical support.
- Assets of the company have not been misappropriated by any controlling natural person, legal person, other organization, or related party.
- Other requirements as prescribed by the CSRC.

Securities companies that apply to issue bonds via private placement should comply with not only the requirements specified in the Securities Law, but also have latest unaudited net assets of no less than RMB 500 million. Private placement can only be offered to qualified investors who understand the potential risks, and must meet the following requirements:

- It is a legal person or investment entity.
- It can invest in bonds according to related regulations and its articles of association.
- It has more than RMB 10 million of registered capital and over RMB 20 million of unaudited net assets.

Listing of Corporate Bonds

A company applying for a listing of corporate bonds shall meet the following requirements:

- The maturity of the corporate bonds shall be more than one year.
- The minimum size of issuance is RMB 50 million.
- It meets the issuing requirements.

The listing of convertible bonds, in addition to the previous requirements, shall meet the requirements for public offering of stocks as well. After the listing, the exchange may suspend the listing if any of the following occurs:

- The company has committed any wrongdoing.
- A major change takes place in the company so it fails to meet the listing requirements.
- Funds raised through the issuance of corporate bonds are used for other than the specified purposes.
- The company fails to fulfill its obligations according to the covenant of corporate bonds.
- The company has been operating at a loss for the latest two consecutive years.

Credit Rating Agencies

Credit rating in China started in 1987 and is still underdeveloped. Credit rating is fundamental to the development of the fixed-income market, but the small size of the corporate sector is not sufficient to support an active credit ratings market. There are four dominant credit rating agencies in China:

1. China Chengxin International Credit Rating Co. (a joint-venture with Fitch Ratings and the International Finance Corporation)
2. China Lianhe Credit Rating Co.
3. Dagong Global Credit Rating Co. (in partnership with Moody's)
4. Shanghai Far East Credit Rating Co.

Clearance and Settlement

In the money market, trades are settled T+0 for instruments maturing within seven days and T+1 for longer maturity. For bonds listed on exchanges, settlement is T+1.

BOND MARKET REFORMS

Bond market is an important foundation of the financial system. The credit rating and the monitoring of the financial status by rating agencies and analysts provide transparency of corporate financial well-being. Such monitoring is essential in early warning if there is any deterioration of a company's financial affairs. The market's re-action and the pressure on the management of the company will lead to corrective measures that lead to improvement of the corporate operations or reorganization or liquidation. It is healthy to be transparent and to take appropriate steps. Furthermore, a well-developed fixed-income market provides an important source of funding for parties in need of financing and an important asset class for investors to invest their money. In summary, fixed income is a big component of the financial system. It is a must to develop the fixed-income market in order to have a sound and efficient finan-cial system. China has taken steps to reform the bond market.

Market-Based Interest Rate Reform

PBC is taking steps to advance market-based interest rate reform. Among its priorities are to widen the floating band on lending rates. The interest rate in the corporate bond market will also be allowed to move within a wider range.

Market-based interest rate reform is significant to the formation of an effective benchmark yield curve. To achieve this, the government will issue more types of bonds to ensure a sufficient array of instruments at various maturities. A government securities yield curve is the basis for pricing corporate fixed-income securities and many derivative securities.

Ease Rules on Bond Issuance

In September 2003, the government allowed securities companies with net assets of RMB 1 billion and a record of profits in the previous year to issue bonds to the pub-lic or to qualified investors. The government has also planned to expand the scale and type of corporate bonds companies can issue. One of the initiatives was to allow small- and medium-sized enterprises to jointly issue domestic bonds.

Hong Kong Closer Economic Partnership Agreement

China and Hong Kong agreed to mutually recognize each other's securities and futures qualifications for practitioners, pursuant to their commitments under the Closer Economic Partnership Agreement (CEPA). This agreement aims to facilitate the flow of qualified personnel and expertise between PRC and Hong Kong.[2] The CEPA became effective in January 2004.

The PBC and the Hong Kong Monetary Authority have also signed a Memorandum of Cooperation that allows banks in Hong Kong to conduct RMB businesses such as deposit taking, RMB-HK dollars exchange, cash remittance, and credit card services.

China's commitments for banking and other financial services under the WTO included the removal of "all non-prudential measures restricting ownership, operation, and juridical form of foreign financial institutions, including on internal branching and licenses geographic restrictions." Areas of market opening and opportunities for foreign institutions are discussed throughout the book.

THE INTERBANK MARKETS

The national interbank bond market provides a market for the bond transactions and repos for commercial banks, rural credit cooperatives, insurance companies, securities firms, and other financial institutions. After several years of fast development, the interbank bond market has become the primary Chinese bond market. Most T-bonds and policy financial bonds are issued and traded in this market.

Bond Transactions in the Interbank Bond Market

Bond transactions in the interbank bond market include repos and spot transaction. In a typical repo transaction, a dealer puts up liquid securities as collateral against a cash loan while agreeing to repurchase the same securities at a future date at a higher price that reflects the financing costs. The sale is the start leg, and the repurchase is the close leg. The party that lends securities in exchange for cash is often referred to as the collateral seller. The counterparty that takes in securities and lends out funds is called the collateral buyer.

Spot transaction is a type of transaction in which both parties of transaction transfer the ownership of bonds according to an agreed price. The participants of the interbank bond market conclude each transaction with the counterparty in bidding modes, different from the trading mode of the Shanghai or Shenzhen Stock Exchange. At the stock exchanges, similar to stock transactions, bond transactions are completed after the computer systems process the bids of investors.

Service Providers

Central T-bond Registration and Settlement Co. offers market participants with bond custodian, settlement, and information services. National Interbank Funding Center provides intermediary and information services for the quotations and transactions. After authorized by PBC, the Inter-Bank Funding Center and the Central T-bond Registration and Settlement Co. can disclose relevant market information.

FUNDING AND HEDGING

This section briefly discusses several of the funding and hedging activities related to the fixed-income market,[3] including interest rate swaps, repurchase agreement, and currency swaps.

Interest Rate Swap

In January 2006, the PBC allowed interest rate swap transactions among companies and institutions on a trial basis. Interbank bond market rates and the one-year bank deposit rate serve as reference rates for interest rate swaps.

    An interest rate swap is a contract between two parties in which each party agrees to make a series of interest payments to the other on scheduled dates in the future. In most interest rate swaps, there are two legs; one counterparty pays a floating rate of interest such as LIBOR and the other pays a fixed rate or a different floating interest rate. For example, Company A borrows in the floating rate market by issuing a five-year floater at six-month LIBOR + 0.50 percent. Company B has issued a five-year fixed-rate bond at 1.50 percent over five-year Treasury. They then enter into an interest rate swap transaction with an AAA swap dealer. Under the swap agreement, counterparty A receives six-month LIBOR from the swap dealer and will pay a fixed rate of five-year Treasury plus 0.50 percent. The cost to Company A is then 1.00 percent over five-year Treasury, and A has converted floating rate obligation to fixed rate. Counterparty B pays a rate of six-month LIBOR and receives from the dealer the five-year Treasury plus 0.30 percent. Company B has changed the interest payments to floating at a cost of LIBOR + 1.20 percent. The swap dealer profits 20 basis points from the transactions.

Repurchase Agreement

PBC supervises the interbank bond repo market. There are several Treasury bonds listed on the SSE eligible for repo trade. The CSRC publishes monthly turnover statistics on Treasury bond repo transactions.

    In a typical repo transaction, a dealer puts up liquid securities as collateral against a cash loan while agreeing to repurchase the securities at a future date. The start leg is usually settled on the same day. The close leg, repurchase, is a forward transaction. A repo is in format a securities transaction, but is in essence a collateralized loan to finance the purchase of the underlying security. The repo markets are therefore often called financing markets.

Securities market participants enter into repo transactions because they have cash and want a short-term investment or because they have securities and need funding. Repo rates in part depend on the collateral used. The second factor is the term of the repo, which is usually for a maturity between one day and one year. Most of the repo transactions have maturities of three months or less. One-day transactions are called overnight repos, longer maturities are called term repos. An open repo is an overnight repo that rolls over automatically until terminated by either party.

Currency Swaps

A number of commercial banks in the PRC provide cross-currency swap services. The Bank of China and China Construction Bank are among these banks. In a straight currency swap, a borrower issues a foreign currency debt (such as euro) and immediately exchanges euro for its chosen currency (such as RMB). The counterparty of the exchange is typically a swap dealer. The borrower periodically pays the dealer RMB coupon interest and the dealer pays the interest to creditor in euro. When the loan comes due, the borrower reverses the transaction with the swap dealer, swapping RMB to get back euro needed to pay off the euro debt. The borrower has received RMB at the beginning of the loan and experiences a RMB outflow when the loan is paid off. The currency swap has facilitated the borrower's ability to borrow RMB from a foreign market, possibly at a lower cost, without currency risk. A currency swap involves three sets of cash flows rather than one cash flow as in an interest rate swap. The first cash flow entails an exchange of cash, for example, RMB for euros. The second set of cash flows is the exchange of periodic interest payments denominated in the appropriate currency. Finally, the principal that was exchanged in the first set of cash flows is exchanged.

U.S. TREASURY SECURITIES MARKET

Four types of government securities trade in the U.S. securities markets:

1. Treasury bills are short-term securities with a maturity period of up to one year. Currently, the Treasury Department issues 4-week, 13-week, and 26-week bills. These bills are discount instruments; they do not pay coupon interest. Holders of the bills receive the face amount at maturity.
2. Treasury notes are medium-term securities that have a maturity of between 2 and 10 years. Currently, the Treasury issues notes with a maturity period of 2, 3, 5, or 10 years. The 10-year note is the current interest rate benchmark.
3. Treasury bonds are long-term securities with a maturity period of 30 years. The Treasury suspended issuance of the 30-year bond in October 2001. Notes and bonds pay coupons every six months; hence, they are also called coupon

Treasury securities (or coupon Treasuries). The Department of Treasury reissued the long bond in 2006.

4. Treasury Inflation Protection Securities (TIPS) are inflation-indexed notes and bonds; the interest rate is fixed but the principal is adjusted for inflation. At maturity, holders will receive the greater of the par amount at original issue or the inflation-adjusted principal.

Coupon Stripping

In February 1985, the Treasury introduced a coupon-stripping program called Separate Trading of Registered Interest and Principal of Securities (STRIPS). For coupon Treasury securities, Coupon-stripping strips the interest payment and treats the component coupons and the principal as separate securities. In the marketplace, these STRIPS are frequently referred to as Treasury zeros or Treasury zero coupons. Each coupon strip entitles the owner to a specified amount of cash (coupon) on a specific date (coupon date), while the owner of the principal strip receives the principal amount at maturity. For example, suppose that a 10-year note with a face value of $1 million and a 4 percent coupon rate is stripped into its principal and 20 semiannual interest payments. The result is 21 Treasury zeros, with each coupon strip paying $20,000 and the principal strip paying $1 million. Each of the 21 strips becomes a security, and each can trade separately. As such, the program provides investors an additional option to buy just one of the coupon components or the principal component that was previously not available.

The U.S. Department of Treasury allows the reconstitution of stripped securities. To reconstitute a stripped security, a financial institution or a government securities broker-dealer must obtain the appropriate principal component and all related coupon strips for the security. The principal and interest components must be in the appropriate minimum or multiple amounts for the particular security being reconstituted. Once the components have been acquired, the institution forwards them to a Federal Reserve Bank and requests that they be reassembled into a fully constituted Treasury security. The ability to reconstitute a stripped security improves market efficiency, because there will be arbitrage opportunities if the price of the security is different from the value of its components.

Treasury Inflation-Indexed Securities

The first auction of TIPS, a 10-year note, was held in January 1997. Since then, the Treasury has also issued TIPS with maturities of 5, 10, 20, and 30 years. Differences between the yield on a regular Treasury security and that on a TIPS can be used to gauge market's expectations about future inflation. When TIPS are issued, the coupon rate set at auction remains fixed throughout the term of the security. The principal amount is adjusted for inflation, but the inflation-adjusted principal will not be paid until maturity. The principal amount will not drop below the par, even though deflation could cause the principal to decline. The index for measuring the inflation rate is the nonseasonally adjusted U.S. City Average All Items Consumer Price Index for All Urban Consumers (CPI-U).

Interest on TIPS is based on a fixed coupon rate applied to the inflation-adjusted principal, so investors are guaranteed a real rate of return above inflation. The real yield is typically lower than the nominal yield. For example, at the close of markets on October 5, 2006, the yield on the 10-year TIPS was 2.38 percent while that on the 10-year fixed-principal note was 4.71 percent. The yield differential of 2.33 percent reflected inflation expectations.

Because of the safety of Treasury securities and the political stability of the United States, foreigners often purchase U.S. Treasury securities whenever there is a financial or political crisis overseas. This phenomenon is known as a flight to quality. As we discuss later, the demand for the newest Treasury security in any maturity segment is generally higher than for older securities. The higher level of liquidity means that it is easy to trade large volumes. Consequently, the foreign money that flows into the United States as a result of a flight to quality is often used to purchase the on-the-run Treasury securities. This phenomenon is called a flight to liquidity.

Market Quotations

The *Wall Street Journal* and the business sections of most newspapers publish closing quotes (the last bid and offer prices at the close of the previous trading session) on all Treasuries, under the heading "Treasury Bonds, Notes & Bills." Data vendors such as Bloomberg and GovPX publish real-time quotes on their proprietary networks and websites. For Treasury bills, quotes include the maturity date, the number of days to maturity, bid, asked, changes, and asked yield. The bid and asked are quoted in terms of a rate discount. The bid rate is generally lower than the asked rate, because the price and interest rate are inversely related. The asked yield is the investment yield or bond equivalent yield based on the asked discount rate quoted.

Quotes on notes and bonds include the coupon rate, maturity, bid price, asked price, change in price, and asked yield. The price quotes are based on the percentage of par value. For example, a bid of 99:04 means that the dealer is bidding a price of 99 4/32, or 99.125 percent of the face value, and an asked of 99:06 means that the dealer is offering to sell at 99 6/32, or 99.1875 percent of the par amount. The difference of 2/32 between the bid and asked is referred to as the bid-asked spread. Changes are in 32nds. For example, a change of "+5" means that the asked price went up 5/32 over the prior day. The asked yield represents the yield to maturity based on the asked price plus accrued interest. Yield to maturity is the rate that discounts all future periodic coupons and principal at maturity to the asked price. When the yield to maturity is plotted against term to maturity, the result is a yield curve.

Treasury strips are also quoted in terms of price. The type of strip is indicated by abbreviations: "ci" indicates a coupon strip, "np" represents a note principal strip, and "bp" denotes a bond principal strip. TIPS are quoted on a price basis as well, but the yield is the real yield. It represents the yield investors receive in excess of and above inflation.

Treasury Issuing Process and Auctions

The Department of Treasury sells government securities at regularly scheduled auctions. Most Treasuries offered at an auction are bought by the primary dealers, which are financial institutions that are active in trading government securities and have established business relationships with the Federal Reserve Bank of New York. Individual investors purchase on a much smaller scale. The minimum amount that may be purchased at an auction is $1,000, and any bid in excess of $1,000 must be in multiples of $1,000.

The auction process begins with a public announcement by the Treasury. The announcement typically includes the following information:

- The offering amount
- A description of the offering, including the term and type of security, CUSIP number, auction date, issue date, dated date, maturity date, and interest payment dates
- Whether the security is eligible for STRIPS
- Procedures for submitting bids, the maximum bid amount, and payment terms

Auction Process

After the Treasury announces an auction, bids are accepted up to 30 days before the auction and may be submitted electronically via the Treasury Automated Auction Processing System (TAAPS), Treasury Direct website, by mail, or in person. Two types of bids can be submitted: noncompetitive and competitive. Small investors and individuals generally submit noncompetitive bids, in which the investor indicates the amount she wants to purchase without specifying a purchase price. The investor will receive the dollar amount submitted in the bid. In a noncompetitive tender, a bidder may not bid for more than $1 million in a bill auction or more than $5 million in a note or bond auction. The price is unknown until the auction results are announced. Primary dealers acting for their own accounts or on behalf of clients usually submit sealed competitive bids specifying both the amount and the price they are willing to pay. The bid is accepted if the bid yield is not higher than the stop yield. Otherwise, it is rejected.

A dealer is prohibited from bidding both competitively and noncompetitively for its own account in the same auction. Bids are submitted in terms of discount rate for bills, stated in three decimal places in 0.005 percent increments. The Treasury requires that competitive bids in note and bond auctions be expressed in yields using three decimals in 0.001 percent increments. These bids are accepted until 1:00 P.M. EST on the day of the auction. Ordinarily, primary dealers submit their competitive bids through TAAPS at the last possible moment, sometimes literally seconds before the deadline. The deadline for noncompetitive tenders is 12:00 noon EST on the auction date.

Competitive bidders are permitted to submit more than one bid. But no bidder may bid more than 35 percent of the total amount of the security being sold. Specifically, under the 35 percent rule, the bidder's net long position in the auction may not exceed 35 percent of the amount of the security in the auction.

The bids submitted through TAAPS are consolidated at the Federal Reserve Banks in New York, Chicago, and San Francisco. These bids are then sorted and reviewed electronically by the U.S. Treasury in Washington, DC. The Treasury nets out the total amount of noncompetitive tenders and allocates the balance to competitive bidders with bids at or below the high yield (the highest yield accepted at an auction), also known as the stop yield. The auction is a single-price or Dutch auction, meaning that both competitive and noncompetitive bidders are awarded securities at the price that results from the high yield (or high discount rate, for bills). All tenders at lower yields are accepted in full. All competitive bids at higher yields are rejected. The coupon rate is the high yield rounded down to the nearest one-eighth.

Example of a Treasury Auction

Suppose that the Treasury has received $1 billion in noncompetitive tenders in an $11 billion auction for five-year notes. In that case, $10 billion in securities will be awarded to competitive bidders. For this auction, there are six competitive bidders, A, B, C, D, E, and F. Table 11.4 shows the yield and the amount by each bidder, ranked from the lowest yield to the highest. The highest yield at which the $10 billion of securities can be sold is 4.250 percent. Under the Dutch auction system, all accepted bidders (A, B, C, D, and E) will pay a price that reflects a yield of 4.250 percent. In this example, D and E each bid $2 billion at 4.250 percent. After the security is awarded to A, B, and C, the remaining amount is $2 billion, so bidders D and E will each receive a $1 billion allocation.

The ratio of the bids received to the amount awarded is known as the bid-to-cover ratio. A high bid-to-cover ratio implies strength in the auction. Another mea-

TABLE 11.4   Yield and Quantity of Competitive Bids

Bidder	Bid Yield (%)	Bid Amount ($ Billions)
A	4.245	2
B	4.246	3
C	4.248	3
D	4.250	2
E	4.250	2
F	4.252	1

sure known as the tail of the auction is the difference between the average yield of all accepted bids and the high yield. When traders form trading strategies after the auction, they use the tail as a measure of the auction's success. The interpretation of a tail is more art than science, however. Generally, a short tail signals strength, so traders will trade more aggressively. A long tail indicates weakness in market demand, and hence traders will be cautious on the downside. At times, however, a long tail has a different implication. In an uncertain market environment, some bidders who need to have a specific security will be extremely aggressive. This will lead to a long tail. A short tail indicates a lack of such aggressiveness.

The auction results are released to the public within two hours of the auction, frequently by 1:30 or 2:00 P.M. EST. The announcement includes the amount of bids received, the total accepted, and the bid-to-cover ratio, as well as the high, low, and median bids, and the issuing price. For a coupon Treasury, the announcement includes a coupon rate as well.

When-Issued Trading and Dealer Bidding Strategies

A major feature of Treasury auctions is the "when, as, and if issued" trading, known as when issued trading. The when-issued (WI) trading begins immediately after the Treasury announcement and lasts until the settlement date, the date on which payment is made to settle a trade. Prior to the auction date, dealers and investors actively participate in the WI market. They may take either a long position or a short position in the security for a future settlement on the issue date. Thus, WI trades are forward contracts to be settled on the new issue settlement date.

Before the auction, WI trading is in terms of yields. The Treasury announces the coupon after the auction. After the coupon is announced, WI trading is on a price basis rather than a yield basis. Generally, the securities are issued several days after the auction. WI trading ends when the new security settles. Prior to the settlement of the note, the buyer does not have to pay for the purchase. The process of issuance is depicted in Figure 11.1.

WI trading affects the strategies bidders use in the auction because it affects their positions going into the auction. Bidders who buy a security in the WI market before the auction go into the auction with long positions. Those who have sold the security

FIGURE 11.1 Auction Process of U.S. Treasury Securities

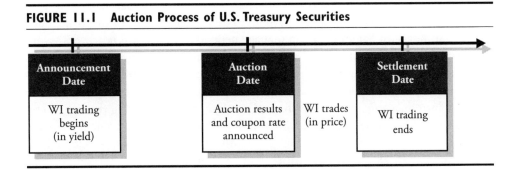

go into the auction with short positions. The WI market also serves in a price discovery role; trading in this market provides vital information on the strength of demand for the security and on the disparity of bidders' views about the market. Such information is useful in preparing bids. Alternatively, dealers who believe they have very valuable private information such as future interest rates may refrain from WI trading so that they can use that information in their bids.

Short Squeeze

Dealers typically enter the auction with significant short positions, because they have sold the security before the auction to clients who prefer to own the new issue. This presents significant risks, however. A dealer who is short and is unable to obtain a sufficient quantity of the security at the auction must either cover the short position before the issue date by buying in the WI market or must borrow the security on the issue date to make good on delivery. The most common mechanism used to borrow Treasury securities is the reverse repurchase agreement, in which the dealer lends money to the security holder in exchange for use of the security. In such a reverse repurchase transaction, however, the dealer is still short in the security and is exposed to the possibility of being unable to purchase it at the anticipated price. In other words, the dealer is caught in a short squeeze. A short squeeze occurs when an auction participant, or a group of participants, gains control of the security and withholds the supply from the cash or repurchase agreement markets.

A well-known short squeeze occurred in 1991. Salomon Brothers admitted to having controlled 94 percent of the two-year notes auctioned on May 22, 1991, in violation of the Treasury regulation that prohibits a bidder's long position from exceeding 35 percent of the issue in any single auction. Salomon acquired 44 percent of the notes at the auction and allegedly prearranged significant trades with big investors to give the firm a dominant position in the security. The two-year notes are generally in high demand because they have the shortest maturity of coupon Treasury securities. Many investors around the world buy them at auction and hold them to maturity, but the price sometimes declines modestly immediately after the auction, when interest in the note fades. Consequently, a common trading strategy is for traders and arbitrageurs to short ahead of the auction and cover the short after the price declines. Opposite to what was expected, the price of this particular two-year note jumped sharply after the auction. The two-year notes became so scarce that the collateral-specific repurchase agreement rates were about 75 to 200 basis points special. That is, holders of this particular note were able to borrow in the repo market at a favorable rate substantially below the market rate.

The scandal cost Salomon its top management, and it was fined nearly $300 million. The firm lost its credibility in the marketplace and might not have survived had not Warren Buffett, a major shareholder, provided a capital infusion and astute management to restore credibility. More importantly, in response to these problems, the Treasury introduced major changes in the Treasury market, including the right to reopen an issue. It also experimented for the first time with a Dutch auction for the two-year and five-year notes. As noted previously, the Treasury has now adopted the Dutch auction for all Treasury securities. Note that at the time of the Salomon scandal, the Treasury used multiple-price auctions to sell Treasury securities. Each accepted bid would pay a price that reflected the yield in the bid submitted. Thus, different dealers would pay different prices for the same security.

Coupon Rolls

Treasury coupon rolls play an important part in the process of distributing new Treasury coupon securities. In a coupon roll trade, a dealer purchases an on-the-run, or most recently issued, Treasury security from a customer for next-day settlement and simultaneously sells to that customer the same amount of the recently announced new security for forward settlement. In a reverse roll, a dealer sells an outstanding issue and buys a new security. The forward in a roll trade, a WI sale, settles on the new issue settlement date. The roll is the spread between the yield on the new security and that on the outstanding issue in the same maturity segment. A "give" in rolls indicates that the WI security provides a higher yield than the outstanding issue. A "take" in rolls implies the opposite—that the new issue has a lower yield.

Dealers use rolls to accommodate customers who have a preference for liquidity and tend to trade rolls to maintain positions in the current issues. Dealers also use rolls to position themselves for bidding at upcoming auctions. A dealer will seek to execute a roll if he is short in the outstanding issue because he anticipates a market decline or has to accommodate customers. By executing a roll, a dealer closes the short position on the outstanding issue and creates a short position on the new security. Hence, the dealer has an incentive to bid more aggressively at the upcoming auction.

Trading and Clearing of Treasury Securities

Once a Treasury security is issued, trading mainly occurs over-the-counter, with dealers, brokers, and other investors making trades by phone. In recent years, some dealers have set up electronic trading systems. The most active trading is generally in the on-the-run issues.

Treasury bills trade on a basis of discount rate and typically settle on the same day. The discount, the difference between the security's purchase price and its face value, is the investor's return. The following formula is used to determine the purchase price for short-term bills:

$$p = FV - d \times \left(\frac{M}{360} \right) \times FV,$$

where $p =$ The purchase price
$FV =$ The face value
$d =$ The discount rate
$M =$ The number of days from settlement to maturity.

As an example, suppose a bill with a current maturity of 175 days is quoted at a bid of 4.12 percent and an offer of 4.11 percent. The purchase price per $1 million for the bill is:

$$p = \$1,000,000 - 4.11\% \times \left(\frac{175}{360}\right) \times \$1,000,000 = \$980,020.83.$$

Coupon Treasuries trade on a price basis. The typical transaction size is $1 million to $100 million for institutions. Trades on coupon Treasuries generally settle on the next market day (called T+1 where T is the trade day), but cash or corporate settlements (T+3) can be arranged. The invoice price (also called the dirty price) of a coupon security consists of the quoted price (also called the clean price) plus the accrued interest. The accrued interest is calculated based on the actual number of days from last coupon payment to trade settlement and the actual number of days in the coupon period (or an actual/actual basis). For example, suppose that a 5 percent, 10-year note is quoted at a bid of 98:20 and an offer of 98:22. Assume that the number of days between the last coupon date and settlement is 136 days and the number of days in the coupon period is 183. If an investor purchases $1 million at par, the total invoice price is

$$p = \left(\$1,000,000 \times \left(98 + \frac{22}{32}\right)\%\right) + \left(\$1,000,000 \times \frac{5.00\%}{2} \times \frac{136}{183}\right) = \$1,005,454.23.$$

The total invoice price reflects the quoted price ($986,875, the first term on the right side of the equation) plus the accrued interest ($18,579.23, the second term on the right). The buyer has to pay the offer price plus the accrued interest to the dealer. Note that the Treasury pays interest every six months. Hence, the accrued interest calculation uses half of the annual coupon rate.

Dealer Trading

Every morning, dealers distribute to the traders information about each issue such as the price, yield, dollar value of a basis point or dollar value of an 01 (DV01), and the yield value of a 32nd. The DV01 is the change in the price of a bond resulting from a one-basis-point change in its yield. Frequently, the DV01 is expressed in dollars per million. The yield value of a 32nd is estimated by calculating the yield to maturity if the bond price changes by one 32nd. The difference between the initial yield and the new yield is the yield value of a 32nd. As an example, a 5 percent, 10-year note trading at par and yielding 5 percent has a value of a basis point (V01) of 0.07798 points, or a DV01 of $779.8 per $1 million dollars of par. This is calculated by taking the difference between the price at a yield of 5.00 percent (par) and the price at a yield of 4.99 percent (100.07798 percent of par). The formula for the yield value of a 32nd is

$1/(32 \times V01)$, which gives a yield value of a 32nd of 0.401 basis point. In the bills market, the DV01 is 0.01 percent of $FV \times (M/360)$. Therefore, the DV01 of a 90-day bill is $25.

A dealer makes money from several sources. First, the bid-asked spread; the price spread varies from 1/128 to 4/32, depending on liquidity, volatility, and remaining maturity. Second, a dealer may profit from a favorable market movement such as appreciation in the securities that the dealer is long and depreciation in the securities in which the dealer has a short position. Another source is carry, or the difference between the interest earned on the securities held in inventory and the financing costs. A positive carry, meaning that interest income is more than interest expense, is a source of profit. Conversely, when interest expense is greater than interest income, the dealer has a negative carry. For example, the carry is −12 basis points if the financing rate is 4.72 percent and the accrued interest is 4.60 percent.

Dealers frequently trade with each other through government interdealer brokers because of the speed and efficiency these brokers provide. Dealers give bids and offers to the brokers, who display the highest bid and lowest offer in a computer network linked to each trading desk. Traders responding to a bid or an offer, by "hitting" or "taking," pay a commission to the broker. Brokers keep the names of the dealers confidential. The quotes provided by the brokers represent prices in the interdealer market, also called the inside market.

In addition to interdealer brokers, GovPX provides real-time information on transactions by the primary dealers. Specifically, it publishes the best bid and best offer, the size, yields, the last trade side (hit/take), and the last trade size. GovPX has a distribution network that includes Bloomberg, Reuters, Bridge, Telerate, and MoneyLine.

MUNICIPAL SECURITIES MARKET

China does not have a municipal market, as local governments do not raise funds in the capital markets. In the United States, municipal bonds are an important means for local governments and municipalities to raise needed funds to finance projects for public goods. There are two basic types of municipal security structures: general obligation bonds (GOs) and revenue bonds. A variety of municipal securities are issued. The most basic types are general obligation bonds and revenue bonds, but several variations are issued as well. They differ mainly in the source of the revenues to pay the principal and interest.

General obligation bonds are municipal securities whose scheduled payments of principal and interest are backed by the full faith and credit of the issuer. Most GOs also have the added security that municipalities can raise property taxes to assure payment. These bonds, which must be approved by voters, are regarded as very safe.

Revenue bonds are municipal securities whose payments are secured by revenues derived from certain revenue-producing agencies or enterprises. Examples include water and sewage treatment facilities, hospitals, schools, and airports. Many of these bonds are issued by special authorities created for the purpose. The agency or authority often has the ability to levy charges and fees for its services. Usually, the yield is higher on a revenue bond than a general obligation bond because revenues are considered less secure than taxes.

In addition to these two basic types, a variety of other municipal securities have been issued. Several of them are special types of revenue bonds. Limited and special tax bonds are revenue bonds payable from the proceeds of a specific tax, such as a gasoline tax, a special assessment, or an ad valorem tax levied at a fixed rate (tax amount is in proportion to the value). Unlike GOs, these bonds are limited to the specific source of revenue.

Industrial revenue bonds are issued by a government agency to raise funds to develop industrial or commercial property for the benefit of private users. The money raised from this type of bond issue is used to pay for the construction of the new facilities. The facilities are then leased to the corporate guarantor. Hence, the safety of an industrial revenue bond depends on the creditworthiness of the corporate guarantor.

Housing bonds are a type of revenue bonds that are secured by mortgage payments on single-family homes. These bonds have the added protection that comes from federal subsidies for low-income families, Veteran Authority (VA) guarantees, and private mortgage insurance.

Moral obligation bonds are revenue bonds that, in addition to their primary source of revenues, are structured so that, in the event of a revenue shortfall, the state would make up the difference. The state is not legally obligated to do so, but the market perception is that failure to honor the moral pledge would have negative consequences for the state's own creditworthiness.

State and local authorities also issue municipal notes, which are short-term debt instruments with maturities ranging from about 60 days to one year. They are usually available in denominations of about $25,000. Municipalities use this type of financing as an interim step when they are expecting future revenue. For example, a municipality might issue tax anticipation notes while it waits for tax revenues to be paid. The safety of the issue depends on the security and the amount of the tax revenue the municipality expects to receive. Bond anticipation notes are issued when a municipality anticipates funds from a bond issue. For example, an issuer might delay a bond issue because of poor market conditions or because it wants to combine several projects into one larger issue. To tide it over while it waits, the municipality might issue BANs. Revenue anticipation notes are similar and are issued in anticipation of revenue coming in from the state or federal government.

Underwriting Process

The issuance of municipals is either by competitive bidding among several syndicates or negotiated with a dealer or syndicate. Most are done through negotiated deals. A municipality that chooses a competitive bidding process essentially will be selling its bonds at a public auction. After bids are solicited from various underwriters, the bonds are sold to the highest bidder, that is, the bid that produces the lowest financing costs for the municipality. To handle the bond sale and provide advice, the municipality usually hires a financial adviser. The financial adviser's responsibilities include preparing the preliminary and final official statements, recommending the structure of the issue, proposing a sale date, and evaluating the bids that are submitted. An official statement for a municipal bond issue is the equivalent of a prospectus for a stock or a corporate bond issue. It provides detailed financial information about the terms of the proposed issue, the issuer's financial status, and its operating data.

After the financial adviser designs the bond issue and the municipality approves it, notice of the bond sale is published. The notice includes such information as the specific date and time for submitting sealed bids, bidding by telephone or fax, minimum bids, and whether the security is book-entry. Underwriters or syndicates of underwriters review the specifications of the proposed bond issue and, if interested, submit sealed bids to the financial adviser. After the bidding closes, the financial adviser analyzes and compares the various bids to select the lowest-cost option.

In contrast to the competitive bidding approach, in a negotiated deal, there is no open bidding. Instead, the first step for the municipality is the selection of the underwriter or underwriting syndicate. If an underwriter has successfully handled prior bond issues for the issuer, the municipality may simply use that underwriter again without soliciting other proposals. Otherwise, the municipality requests proposals from several underwriters to make its selection. In a negotiated deal, the underwriter handles most of the activities associated with the bond issue on behalf of the municipality. Usually, the issuer does not hire an independent financial adviser. The issuer and the underwriter then negotiate the costs and terms of the bond issue including the interest rates, the underwriter's fees and charges, the original issue discount, and the issue date.

Required Disclosure

Like issuers of corporate stock and bonds, issuers of municipal securities are required by the Securities and Exchange Commission (SEC) to provide certain information to investors. SEC Rule 15c2-12 requires issuers to:

- Prepare official statements meeting the content requirements of the rule.
- File certain financial information and operating data with national and state repositories each year.
- Disclose any material events on a timely basis.

As explained earlier, the final official statement sets forth information about the term of the issue, the financial status of the issuer, its operating data, and annual updating and event disclosure. The rule also requires the underwriters to review the preliminary official statement.

By requiring issuers to provide continuing disclosure throughout the life of each of their bond issues, the rule addressed investors' complaints that they could not obtain information about municipal securities in the secondary market. In addition to the obvious benefits to investors, continuing disclosure is beneficial to municipal issuers as well. To the extent that continuing disclosure enhances the liquidity of a security in the secondary market, investors may accept a lower yield at issuance that saves issuers interest costs. Reliable continuing disclosure can also help an issuer avoid potential liability due to incomplete information.

To satisfy the continuing disclosure requirements, the issuer's financial information must be filed with each Nationally Recognized Municipal Securities Information Repository (NRMSIR) such as Bloomberg Municipal Repositories, DPC Data, J. J. Kenny Repository, and Thomson NRMSIR. The states also have information repositories.

In addition, the rule also requires the issuer to disclose any material event. An event or fact is material if it is likely to be significant to the deliberations of a reasonable investor. The event disclosure must be filed with each NRMSIR or the Municipal Securities Rulemaking Board and with the appropriate state information repository in a timely manner.

U.S. CORPORATE DEBT MARKETS

Various types of corporate debt securities are available to allow corporations to match their financing requirements with investor needs. This section reviews the major types of corporate debt instruments: commercial paper, medium-term notes, and various types of corporate bonds.

Commercial paper is a money market product and is a short-term unsecured promissory note. Corporations use it as an alternative to borrowing from banks. Although, the maturity of commercial paper ranges from 1 day to 270 days, the most common range is 30 days or less. Because the maturity does not exceed 270 days, commercial paper is exempt from registration with the SEC. Commercial paper rates are quoted on a discount basis. The purchaser pays a discount price and receives the face amount when the paper matures. The return to the investor is the difference between the purchase price and the face amount. Interest rates on commercial paper are often lower than bank lending rates, and the savings, when large enough, provide an advantage over bank credit.

Commercial paper is a cost-effective form of short-term funding, giving borrowers visibility in the institutional investor market and thereby facilitating future capital market activities. Commercial paper programs raise floating-rate funds, although derivatives may be used to fix rates for a fixed term. The minimum borrowing amount is typically $50 million, and program sizes can range into the billions.

For commercial paper, the convention is to assume a 360-day year. For example, the amount of discount for 7-day paper with $100,000 face value can be calculated:

$$d = F \times r \times \frac{M}{360} = \$100,000 \times 0.0545 \times \frac{7}{360} = \$105.97,$$

where d = The dollar amount of discount
 F = The face value
 r = The discount rate
 M = The number of days until maturity.

It is assumed that the discount rate is 5.45 percent. As shown, the paper can be purchased at a discount of $105.97. That is, the purchaser pays $99,894.03 and receives $100,000 from the issuer after seven days.

Medium-term notes (MTNs) are corporate debt instruments with a maturity ranging from 9 months to 30 years. Securities firms distribute MTNs for the issuers on a best efforts basis. In this case, the securities firms act as brokers helping to place the notes through their vast network of clients. The securities firms do not guarantee a price to the issuer. Unlike a typical bond issue where bonds are sold in large, discrete offerings, MTNs are sold in relatively smaller amounts on a continuous basis. Because the note offerings are ongoing, they are typically registered with the SEC under Rule 415 (shelf registration), which allows a corporation to issue securities up to an approved amount over a period of two years.

A corporate bond is a loan; it reflects a promise by the company to pay the bondholder a fixed amount of interest (the coupon payment) periodically and to repay the money borrowed—the principal or redemption value—at a specific date in the future, the maturity date. Securities firms handle the underwriting, or distribution of bonds in the primary markets, for the issuer. Once the bonds have been issued, dealers bid for bonds that investors wish to sell and offer bonds from their inventory to investors wanting to buy.

Bonds are long-term debt instruments; that is, they have maturities of longer than one year. Some bonds have very long-term maturities. During the mid-1990s, various institutions including Coca-Cola, Walt Disney, IBM, and Yale University issued bonds with maturities as long as a hundred years.

Corporations issue a number of different types of bonds. Convertible bonds have a feature that gives the bondholder the right to convert the par amount of the bond into a certain number of shares of the issuer's common stock. The ratio at which the par value is converted is known as the conversion ratio. Suppose that a conversion provision gives the holder the right to convert $1,000 par amount into the issuer's common stock at $40 per share, the conversion price. The conversion ratio is hence 25 to 1. The stock price substantially affects the value of a convertible. For example, if the shares of the issuer are trading at $35 and the market price of the bond is $1,000, there would be no reason for an investor to convert. A convertible bond with a conversion price far higher than the market price of the stock generally trades at or close to its bond value, because the bond is not likely to be converted. Conversely, when the share price is sufficiently higher than the conversion price, the convertible begins to trade more like equity, because the bondholder will convert it into shares of common stock.

Callable bonds grant the issuer the right to pay off the debt before maturity. Exercising the call provision becomes attractive to the issuer when the yield drops sufficiently to make up for the cost of calling the bonds. The cost to call includes a call premium, administrative expenses, and the expenditures arising from floating a new issue to refund the retired debt. Most call provisions provide for a call premium of one-half of the coupon rate. That means the issuer has the right to pay the bondholders the par amount plus one-half of the annual coupon payment to retire the bond. For example, the issuer has to pay $1,020 per bond if it calls the bond with a 4 percent coupon. The call feature is a disadvantage to investors who must give up the higher-yielding bonds. Therefore, investors generally demand a higher yield from callable bonds.

In contrast, puttable bonds contain a put provision, granting investors the right to put the bonds back to the issuer at par. Investors will choose to exercise the right to put back the bond when the yield is rising (the price is falling). Clearly, a puttable bond protects investors from downside risk. Therefore, investors are willing to accept a lower yield when purchasing a puttable bond.

Junk bonds, also called high-yield bonds, have credit ratings of BB (by Standard and Poor's) or lower. They are regarded as noninvestment grade or speculative grade.

Shelf Registration (Rule 415)

Shelf registration, Rule 415, allows a firm to register all the securities it expects to issue over a subsequent two-year period through one filing. Shelf registration provides flexibility in timing an offer and is less costly for issuing new securities. In essence securities can be viewed as sitting on a shelf so that they can be offered as soon as funds are needed or market conditions are favorable, without the need to prepare and file a new prospectus and registration for each sale. A Rule 415 registration statement can be updated after its original effective date by filing a post effective amendment, incorporating by reference of subsequently filed materials, or adding a supplemental prospectus.

Once the issuer's nonprice terms are decided and the issue's effectiveness nears its close, the issue could be placed on the market immediately or overnight. The price risk of a firm offer now shifts to the underwriter and the syndicate. Investment banks step up to bid to retain the prestige associated with being a leader firm in the syndicate game. In effect, the shortened new issue process has helped the issuers to reduce risk. This also leads to, at least in part, the shift of long-term professional relationship between a corporation and a specific investment banker to transactional finance, whoever offers better terms gets the business.

The lead manager runs the book during the selling period of the new issue. Prior to the final price setting, the lead manager keeps a record of indications of interest. Once the issue is declared effective, the lead manager maintains a record of actual sales by members of the syndicate and by the selling group. If a portion of the issue remains unsold because of rising interest rate, the syndicate manager can stabilize the market by offering to buy at or above the offering price.

The greatest risks are encountered when the inventory of unsold bonds grows due to unfavorable interest rate movement. The financing costs move up with the rise in rates. The risk-adjusted returns of new underwriting would now be less even if the underwriting spreads did not change.

Underwriting Spreads

The underwriting spread or gross spread is the difference between the price paid by the buyers and the proceeds to the company. The gross spread is generally less than 1 percent for high-quality issues. The underwriting spreads on junk bonds are as much as 3 percent. To that sum, the underwriter adds some out-of-pocket expenses for legal fees, due-diligence meetings, and so on. The average spreads during the 1970 to 2000 period were 1.15 percent. Bankers enjoyed lucrative spreads in the 1980s, more than 1.4 percent and over 2 percent in 1983 and 1988. In the 1990s, the spreads declined. By 2000, the spreads declined to 55.9 basis points.

Out of the gross spread, the lead underwriter typically collects a management fee of 20 percent. Syndicate members and selling dealers get the remaining 80 percent of the gross spread. Dealers who are not syndicate members but are part of the selling group get the selling commission of about 50 percent to 55 percent of the gross spread. As an example, the management fee comes to $200,000 for a $100 million bond issue at 1 percent spread. The underwriter discount for syndicate members is a quarter of the gross spread, $250,000, and the sales commission amounts to $550,000 for the issue. The lead underwriter collects the management fee, splits the underwriter discount proportionally with the syndicate members, and also receives sales commission for his own share of the distribution. The selling group is not committing its own capital to risk taking. If the bond price drops, the losses from stabilization and the added expenses will be shared on the preagreed ratio between the lead underwriter and the underwriting syndicate.

Members of the syndicate or the selling group receive reallowance if their sales of bonds are over and above those acquired from the manager. A reallowance is paid to the firm that actually makes the sale, but the member who agreed to release the bonds retains the balance of the spread.

Risk Management

If the issue rises in price after it is priced but before the syndicate's distribution is complete, the syndicate members will be able to sell out their share of the commitment more quickly but they cannot make sales at prices higher than the price stated on the prospectus. If the manager took a short position before the unanticipated price surge, he has to cover the short by either taking a higher market price resulting in a loss or by exercising the Green Shoe option.

Alternatively, the issue price might move down during this period. The flotation process now slows down. The syndicate members now face a greater inventory price risk on a larger inventory. Furthermore, investment bankers incur a higher financing cost due to the rising interest rates. Therefore, it is vital for investment bankers to correctly price the issue such that the downside risk is minimized.

Private Placements

Private placements differ structurally from the registered public deals because they are highly negotiated in covenants and pricing and they do not go through the SEC registration process. A private issue can save substantial amounts of legal and registration expenses against a comparable public issue. These expenses amount to several hundred thousand dollars prior to underwriter discount and commissions. Additional benefits are a high degree of flexibility in the amount of financing, investors are often more patient than venture capitalists, lower costs than approaching venture capitalists, and a quicker form of raising funds than venture capital markets.

The private placement of debt market is rapidly growing and accounts for a significant portion of the debt market. The resemblance of 144As to traditional private placements ends with the fact that they are not registered with SEC. Rule 144A deals generally are $100 million or more in size to provide liquidity for resale. Rule 144As look like public offerings, but can only be sold to qualified institutional buyers. These deals are usually underwritten and have two credit ratings.

Most Rule 144A issues carry registration rights. That means that noninvestment-grade borrowers can rush out 144A deals quickly and reap the benefits of hitting a strong market and go through the hoops of SEC registration later. Once SEC reporting requirements are satisfied, the Rule 144A securities are upgraded.

Privately placed debt tends to have a shorter maturity. Insurance companies, pension funds, and finance companies are big lenders in this market. Regulatory pressures to improve capital position forces some insurers to cut investments in this market. Seeking higher yields, pension funds and endowments are best positioned to fill the void left by the insurers.

CONCLUSION

Fixed-income market is an important foundation for the financial system. The fixed-income market in China is small, and the corporate debt market is insignificant. This chapter reviewed the several types of bonds issued and traded in China. Trading in the interbank OTC market and on exchanges was discussed. The chapter also presented, for a comparison, the U.S. Treasury, municipal, and corporate bond markets.

12

Derivatives Markets and Risk Management

China's derivative market is limited to several basic but important instruments. Until July 2005, the policy of fixed exchange rate with the U.S. dollar eliminated the need for managing currency risk. Since July 2005, China has allowed its currency to float within a narrow band against a basket of currencies. There has also been partial deregulation of interest rates. Gradually corporations and investors will need to manage both foreign exchange and interest rate risks. Stock market volatility and speculation and credit risk present promising potentials for new financial instruments. This chapter discusses several derivatives that trade in China's capital market and reviews some of the products that are coming soon.

OVERVIEW

The derivative market in China is relatively new and quite limited. The Interim Rules on Derivative Business of Financial Institutions took effect in March 2004. The rules define derivatives and provide guidance as to who may apply to conduct such business in China. The rules also specify approval requirements, risk management, and internal control framework. Financial institutions that qualify to apply to engage in derivative business include: foreign banks' mainland branches, Chinese banks, trust and investment companies, financing companies, financial leasing companies, and auto financing companies. There are two types of derivative businesses that an approved financial institution may engage in:

1. Proprietary derivatives trading for hedging purposes or for profits, and
2. Trading services to clients as a dealer or market maker.

The derivative market is limited to currency and interest rate futures, futures and forwards market for commodities, and interest rate and currency swaps. In 2005, the

People's Bank of China (PBC) issued administrative rules for trading bond forwards in the interbank market. Bond forward transactions are limited to government bonds, bank bonds, financial bonds, or other bonds authorized by the PBC.

In the next three sections, we describe the derivative instruments that are available in China, including repurchase agreements, forwards and futures, and swaps. Later sections discuss the structure, benefits, and applications of asset securitization; and credit derivatives that will see great potentials in China in the near future. The final section reviews several interesting instruments that were developed in the West.

REPURCHASE AGREEMENTS

In China, several government securities that list on the exchange are eligible for repurchase agreement trades. In a typical repo transaction, a dealer puts up liquid securities as collateral (in China, the listed bonds) against a cash loan while agreeing to repurchase the same securities by paying back the amount of the loan plus the repo interest. A typical transaction is depicted in Figure 12.1.

Market participants use repos to invest cash or to borrow money. For example, a securities dealer purchases and plans to hold overnight $100 million of 4.00 percent March 2010 Treasury notes. Typically, however, the dealer uses the repo market to obtain financing, as it is generally the cheapest funding source. Suppose a customer, a municipality, a mutual fund, or an insurance company, has excess funds of $100 million to invest. The overnight repo rate is 2.75 percent. On the start date, the dealer delivers these notes to the customer for cash. In leg two of the repo trade, the dealer buys back the same notes at $100 million plus one day interest of $7,638.89. The result is that the customer has invested $100 million and the dealer has financed the position overnight at an interest of 2.75 percent.

FIGURE 12.1   Structure of a Typical Deliverable Repo

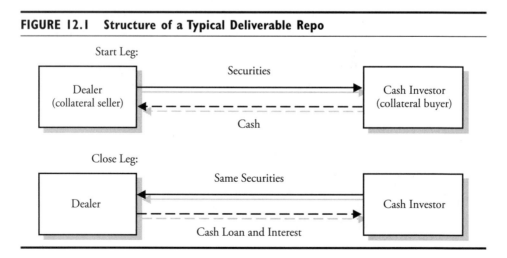

One-day transactions are called overnight repos. Longer maturities are called term repos. Repos may be arranged on an open basis and terminated when either party chooses to do so. The interest rate the collateral buyer demands for such a loan is called a repo rate. The overnight repo rate in the United States is generally at or below the federal funds rate, reflecting the security the cash lender enjoys in a collateralized repo transaction. At times, some securities, such as the most recently issued (called on-the-run) Treasury notes, trade at a lower rate. Collateral that commands a lower repo rate is said to be on special.

Once the repo rate is determined, the dollar amount of interest earned on the invested funds is calculated as follows:

$$I = F \times rr \times \frac{M}{360},$$

where $I =$ The dollar amount of interest
$F =$ The amount of funds invested
$rr =$ The repo rate
$M =$ The term of the repo transaction.

For example, a $50 million overnight repo investment at a rate of 4.70 percent would yield interest of $6,527.78:

$$\$6,527.78 = \$50,000,000 \times 4.70\% \times \frac{1}{360}.$$

Repo transactions also have several other important features. The collateral seller commonly has a right of substitution, that is, the right to take back the security and substitute other collateral of equal value and quality for it. Also, the market practice is that the coupon interest coming due on the collateral is passed through from the collateral buyer back to the collateral seller. This is referred to as coupon pass-through.

Both parties to a repo transaction are exposed to credit risk due to the possibility that the market value of the collateral might change. To obtain an added cushion against a fall in the value of the collateral during the term of the repo, collateral buyers typically demand a margin or haircut, which is a percentage of the collateral value in excess of the loan.

Triparty Repos

In a deliverable repo, the underlying securities are delivered against payment. At maturity, the collateral is returned and the loan plus interest is paid, as shown in Figure 12.1. The associated transaction costs include clearing fees, wire transfer charges, custodial fees, and account maintenance expenses. To avoid some of those costs and increase the cash investor's return, U.S. dealers offer alternatives that do not require the actual delivery of the collateral. The most popular choice is the triparty repo in which

FIGURE 12.2   A Triparty Repurchase Agreement Structure

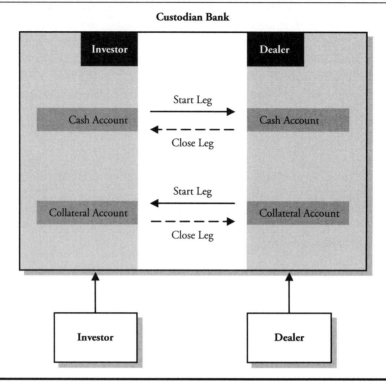

Note: Movements of funds and collateral take place within the same Custodian Bank. During the term of the repo, substitution, withdraw, or addition of collateral also are done within the same Custodian Bank.

a custodial bank stands between the two counterparties (Figure 12.2). The custodial bank maintains the cash account and the collateral account for both parties, so the actual delivery of the collateral and cash can be reduced to credit and debit transfers within the same bank. Hence, the Fedwire charges are eliminated.

During the term of a triparty repo, the collateral is marked to market daily. Additional securities are delivered to the collateral buyer's account when a deficit exists; excess securities are returned to the dealer's account when excess exists. On the termination date, the custodian transfers the principal and repo interest from the collateral seller's cash account to the investor's designated account. Simultaneously, the custodian returns the collateral from the investor's collateral account to the seller's collateral account.

Mechanics of Repos and Market Practices

Suppose an investor purchases $100 million of a 4.00 percent March 2010 Treasury notes from dealer X at an offer of 99 4/32. Suppose that the last coupon was paid 60 days ago and the next coupon date is 123 days away. This customer pays the dealer the clean price plus the accrued interest the next day against delivery. The total payment next day is:

$$\$100,000,000 \times \left(99\frac{4}{32}\% + 2.00\% \times \frac{61}{183} \right) = \$98,791,666.70.$$

Suppose the investor finances the purchase the next day with an overnight repo, same day settlement, with dealer Y. Assume the next morning the dealer quotes the customer a repo rate of 2.70 percent and a bid price of 98 6/32 for these notes. The dealer requires a 1 percent haircut. The amount of dealer financing is:

$$\$100,000,000 \times \frac{1}{1.01} \times \left(98\frac{6}{32}\% + 2.00\% \times \frac{61}{183} \right) = \$97,875,412.54.$$

The overnight repo could be rolled over or terminated by either party. Suppose it is terminated the next day. The customer is to pay dealer Y:

$$\$97,875,412.54 \times \left(1 + \frac{0.027}{360} \right) = \$97,882,753.20$$

via clearing house to dealer Y in return for the same $100 million notes. The one-day interest is $7,340.66.

In practice, however, it is not unusual for them to roll over the open repo for another day. In this case the base price for repo purposes would often remain at the same original price, 98 6/32. If the repo is rolled at a rate of 2.6 percent, the amount payable the next day will be

$$\$97,875,412.54 \times \left(1 + \frac{0.027}{360} + \frac{0.026}{360} \right) = \$97,889,821.98.$$

Note that the interest is not compounded. This open arrangement eliminates the need to repeatedly transfer the collateral for cash on a daily basis.

The customer could do a term repo if it needs a term financing instead of overnight. The calculation is similar to the previous example. For example, if the customer did a two-day term repo instead of rolling the open repo over. For the two-day financing at a rate of 2.7 percent, the customer would have to repay the following amount in return for getting back the collateral:

$$\$97,875,412.54 \times \left(1 + \frac{0.027}{360} \times 2 \right) = \$97,890,093.85.$$

The previous example assumes a haircut of 1 percent. The margin is an added cushion against a fall in the value of the collateral.

Specials

Most government securities are generic and trade at the same rates, often at a level close to the federal funds rate. These issues are referred to as the general collateral. At the same time, on-the-run coupon Treasuries often trade at lower repo rates, called specials. The on-the-run Treasuries have the greatest liquidity of all issues with similar maturities. They are frequently used for hedging or speculative trading. It is also common for traders and money managers, who prefer as much liquidity as possible, to maintain positions in the most recently issued security by regularly rolling into the on-the-run issues. The process of trading rolls by clients leads dealers to short the when-issued securities and buy the recently off-the-run issues. This tends to relieve repo market pressure in the newly off-the-run security and begin building pressure in the new on-the-run issue.

The spread between the special repo rate and the general collateral rate, or specialness, reflects the relative scarcity of the security involved. The collateral buyer demands the specific security to cover short and hence is willing to accept a lower rate in return for the use of that specific collateral. The spread between the special and the general collateral repo rates can be highly volatile. The on-the-run 10-year notes have consistently gone on special. The main reason is that mortgage-backed and corporate bond trading desks routinely short the 10-year to hedge their inventories against interest rate. Proprietary trading desks deploying global bond arbitrages also often require shorts in the 10-year to capture yield spread.

The status of a bond in the repo market is important in assessing the relative values of the bond in cash and futures markets. The status is one of the reasons why a bond may trade at a yield different from that implied by a smooth yield curve. If a trader is considering shorting a particular bond that looks rich compared with the yield curve, he needs to know the bond's status in the repo market. This is because the cost of borrowing that issue may be large enough to erode or even eliminate the potential profits. In the futures market, a cash-and-carry trade is when a trader buys a bond that is deliverable into a futures contract and shorts the correctly weighted number of contracts. This is similar to a repo trade. At the beginning, the trader pays a cash amount and receives a bond. At the expiry of the contract, the trader receives cash and delivers the bond. The implied repo rate can be calculated accordingly. The bond with the lowest implied repo rate is the cheapest to deliver. The net basis, the difference between actual and implied repo rate, is the value the market has assigned to the delivery option.

FORWARDS AND FUTURES

Forwards and futures are all trades for future settlement, meaning a trade takes place today but payment and delivery of the underlying security occur on the agreed date in the future. The key difference is that forwards are an over the counter type of trade while futures are standardized exchange trades. The following discusses spot trading first and then covers forwards and futures.

Spot Market Trading

A currency spot transaction is an exchange of one currency for another in the cash market. The spot rate is the current market price. The price quotes come in two forms, a direct quotation is the amount of domestic currency per unit of foreign currency and an indirect quotation is the amount of foreign currency per unit of domestic currency. American terms means a direct quote from the viewpoint of someone located in the United States. European terms means a direct quote from the viewpoint of someone located in Europe. In the over-the-counter market, U.S. dollars are quoted in European terms against most other currencies. Hence, the dollar is often the base currency. For example, the exchange rate between the U.S. dollar and the Chinese renminbi (RMB) was U.S.$1 = RMB 7.90 on October 13, 2006.

In the spot market, cross exchange rates are exchange rates in which the dollar is neither the base currency nor the terms currency. For example, sterling-yen is a cross rate, in which the sterling is the base currency and the yen is the terms currency. In the interbank market, most trading goes through the dollar. Suppose a bank customer wants to trade out of British pound into Chinese yuan. The bank can handle this trade for its customer by selling British pounds for U.S. dollars and then selling U.S. dollars for Chinese yuan. The cross rate for sterling-renminbi can therefore be derived from sterling-dollar and dollar-renminbi. The exchange rate on October 13, 2006, for sterling-dollar was 1.8635 and dollar-renminbi was 7.90. The derived cross rate for sterling-yuan would be 14.722.

Some banks specialize in making a direct market between nondollar currencies. Their direct quotes are generally consistent with cross exchange rates. If not, a triangular arbitrage is possible. Triangular arbitrage is the process of trading out of the U.S. dollar into a second currency, then trading it for a third currency, which is in turn traded for U.S. dollars. The purpose is to earn an arbitrage profit via trading from the second to the third currency when the direct exchange rate between the pair is not in alignment with the cross exchange rate.

Forwards

A forward transaction is a single purchase or sale of one currency for another for settlement in the future. For example, assume that ABC Company has located a new foreign supplier of fiber optics. On October 13, 2006, the company receives a quote of 400,000 Swiss francs (CHF) for a shipment. The price looks attractive given the current spot rate of 1.2670 CHF per dollar, or a cost of $315,706.9. Because the foreign supplier will need a few weeks to complete the manufacturing of optics, and there must be an additional time allowance for shipment, ABC Company believes that a payment date of December 13, 2006 is reasonable. The chief financial officer is aware that the current exchange rate is some of the best in recent memory, and he is concerned that the rate may change before payment is due. Any depreciation of the dollar before payment can be initiated would increase the ultimate cost of this material. To avoid this potential for a price hike, the company contacts its bank's foreign exchange desk to book a forward contract.

An outright forward transaction will be settled on a pre-agreed date, often three or more business days after the trade date.[1] The specific forward exchange rate may be different from the spot rate. Though the exchange rate at which the forward transaction is fixed at the outset, no money necessarily changes hands until the transaction takes place. The ABC Company would book a forward contract for settlement on December 13, 2006 to eliminate the uncertainty in the exchange rate.

The forward contracts can be tailored to meet the specific needs of a customer with respect to maturity, size, and currency. Because they are not standardized, they tend to be less liquid and more difficult to reverse. The standard contract periods are one, two, three, six, and twelve months (called straight dates). Customers can obtain odd-date or broken-date contracts for periods falling between standard dates.

If the foreign exchange market is efficient, the forward rate will move toward an equilibrium point at which the interest rate differential between the two currencies will be offset by a premium or discount in the forward rate. Because money can flow quickly and in large volume from one Eurocurrency to another, the Eurodeposit rates, spot exchange rates, and forward exchange rates are interdependent in which yields are identical across currencies. This condition is known as the interest rate parity. It can be expressed as:

$$F = S \frac{\left(1 + r_f\right)}{\left(1 + r_\$\right)},$$

where F is the forward rate expressed as units of foreign currency per dollar, S is the spot exchange rate expressed as units of foreign currency per dollar, $r_\$$ is the Eurodollar deposit rate, and r_f is the other Eurocurrency deposit rate.[2]

If the interest rate parity condition is violated, a covered interest arbitrage opportunity will present itself. For example, if the six-month Eurodollar deposits pay interest of 5.00 percent per year and six-month Euroyen deposits pay an interest of 2.00 percent a year, and there is no premium or discount on the forward yen against the dollar, there would be an arbitrage opportunity. It would pay to borrow yen at 2.00 percent, sell the yen spot for dollars and simultaneously resell dollars forward for yen six months. At the same time, the dollars are invested at a rate of 5.00 percent for six months. This arbitrage process will result in an appreciation of the yen relative to the dollar until equilibrium is reached.

Forward rates are quoted usually in premiums or discounts from the spot rate. The premium or discount is measured in points, which are the amount of foreign exchange that will neutralize the interest rate differential between two currencies for the applicable period. For any currency pair, if the base currency earns a lower interest rate than the terms currency, the base currency will trade at a forward premium, or above the spot rate. Conversely, if the base currency earns a higher interest rate, the base currency will trade at a forward discount, that is, below the spot rate. The formula for calculating the points is:

$$\text{points} = \left(\text{spot rate}\right) \times \left[\frac{1 + r_t \times \dfrac{\text{forward days}}{360}}{1 + r_b \times \dfrac{\text{forward days}}{360}} - 1 \right],$$

where r_t denotes the terms currency interest rate and r_b denotes the base currency interest rate. Thus, if we want to calculate the forward premium or discount points for a 181-day dollar-yen forward. The Eurodollar interest rate is assumed at 5 percent and the Euroyen interest rate at 3 percent. Assume also the spot rate is 106.00. The points are hence:

$$\text{points} = \left(106.00\right) \times \left[\frac{1 + 3\% \times \dfrac{181}{360}}{1 + 5\% \times \dfrac{181}{360}} - 1 \right] = -1.04.$$

The six-month outright forward discount for dollar-yen would be 1.04 yen per dollar. Hence, the six-month outright forward rate would be JPY 104.96 per dollar.

Exchange-Traded Currency Futures

A foreign exchange futures contract is an agreement to buy or sell a specific quantity of a particular foreign currency at a specified price on a specific future date. A futures contract month, also called delivery month, identifies the month and year in which the futures contract reaches maturity. A foreign exchange futures contract is hence similar to a forward contract. However, there are several important differences. First, futures contracts are traded on exchanges, but forward contracts are traded over-the-counter. Second, futures contracts are standardized in terms of contract size and maturity, and they are subject to trading rules of the exchange. Forward contracts, on the other hand, can be customized between parties. Third, futures contracts are marked to market daily at the settlement price. The settlement price is a price representative of futures transaction price at the close of the daily trading on the exchange. The buyer of a futures contract in which the settlement price is higher (lower) than the previous day's level has a positive (negative) settlement for the day. This is because the contract holder is entitled to purchase the underlying asset; a higher (lower) settlement price means the futures price of the underlying asset has increased (decreased). As a result, a long position is worth more (less). On the other side, the seller of the futures contract will have his margin decreased (or increased) exactly the amount the long's margin account is increased (decreased). Thus, the sum of the long and short's daily settlement is zero. This is known as a zero-sum game. Unlike futures contracts, forward contracts do not require initial margin or maintenance margin. Forwards require cash payments only at maturity. Fourth, futures contracts are made directly between two parties. In futures trading, the clearinghouse becomes the buyer to every seller and the seller to every buyer. In this way, the exchange drastically reduces counterparty risk.

These differences are significant. The fact that there is a clearinghouse and daily mark-to-market means credit risk is reduced. In the futures market, a contract can be cancelled simply by making a reverse transaction that nets out the position. In a forward contract, if a holder wants to close a position, there would be a second contract. If the second contract is arranged with a different counterparty, there would be two contracts and two counterparties, with credit risk on both.

SWAPS CONTRACTS

In China, currently there are interest rate swaps and currency swaps. This section covers both of them as well as other types of transaction such as commodity price swaps and real estate swaps.

A swap is an agreement between two parties to exchange payments based on identical notional principal. Swaps are popular financial transactions that have come to be the most widely used derivatives. The efficacy and flexibility of swaps are best in managing financial risk or making an arbitrage play in a volatile interest rate, exchange rate, commodity price, or equity return environment.

The notional principal amount outstanding of interest rate derivatives, which included interest rate swaps and options, and cross-currency interest rate swaps, was $285.7 trillion in 2006.[3] Credit default swaps grew 33 percent from $26.0 trillion in 2005 to $34.5 trillion. Finally, notional amount outstanding of equity derivatives, consisting of equity swaps, options, and forwards, grew from $5.6 trillion to $7.2 trillion.

Interest Rate Swaps

An interest rate swap is a contract between two parties in which each agrees to make a series of interest payments, based on a certain notional principal, to the other on scheduled dates in the future (Figure 12.3). In most interest rate swaps, there are two

---

FIGURE 12.3   An Interest Rate Swap

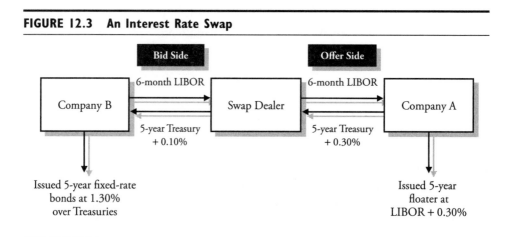

legs; one counterparty pays a floating rate of interest such as LIBOR and the other pays a fixed rate or a different floating interest rate. For example, Company A borrows in the floating rate market by issuing a five-year floater at six-month LIBOR + 30 basis points. Company B has issued a five-year fixed-rate bond at 130 basis points over five-year Treasury. They then enter into an interest rate swap transaction with an AAA swap dealer. Under the swap agreement, Company A receives six-month LIBOR from the swap dealer and pays a fixed rate of five-year Treasury plus 30 basis points percent. The final cost to Company A is then 0.6 percent over five-year Treasury. By way of a swap contracting, Company A has converted floating rate obligation to fixed-rate. Company B pays a rate of six-month LIBOR and receives from the dealer the five-year Treasury plus 10 basis points. Company B has changed the interest payments to floating at a cost of LIBOR + 1.20 percent. The swap dealer profits 20 basis points from the transactions.

Swaps can also be arranged to manage the risk of a specific asset or liability exposure. An asset swap combines an existing asset such as a bond with an interest rate swap to create a different return profile. The investor might use the fixed coupon to swap for a floating rate income, or vice versa. If the asset is a mortgage-backed security, index-amortizing swaps can be used to mirror the asset's remaining principal amount. Some swaps have a clean up call whereby the swap can be called away if the remaining notional principal drops to about 5 percent of the original amount. A mortgage swap falls into this type. The notional principal amortizes over the life of the swap and the tenor of the swap is shorter than the final maturity of the mortgage pool.

Currency Swaps

Before July 2005, RMB's exchange rate with the U.S. dollar was fixed. Thus, there was no need to hedge or manage currency risk because there was no risk. Since then, China has allowed its currency to float within a specified band against a basket of currencies. Now, RMB is "floating" and hence currency swap is a helpful transaction.[4]

Under a currency swap, two parties exchange the equivalent amounts of two different currencies (Figure 12.4). For example, a borrower issues a foreign currency debt (such as RMB) and immediately exchanges RMB for its chosen currency (such as dollar). The counterparty of the exchange is typically a swap dealer. The borrower periodically pays the dealer dollar coupon interest and the dealer pays the interest to creditor in RMB. When the loan comes due, the borrower reverses the transaction with the swap dealer, swapping dollar to get back RMB needed to pay off the RMB debt. The borrower has received dollars at the beginning of the loan and experiences a dollar outflow when the loan is paid off. The currency swap has facilitated the borrower's ability to borrow dollars from a foreign market without currency risk. The swap involves three sets of cash flows rather than one cash flow as in an interest rate swap. The first cash flow entails an exchange of cash, for example, dollars for RMB. The second set of cash flows is the exchange of periodic interest payments denominated in the appropriate currency. Finally, the principal that was exchanged in the first set of cash flows is exchanged. For example, suppose the spot exchange rate between RMB and U.S. dollars is 7.90 yuan per dollar. If the interest rate is 5 percent in China and

FIGURE 12.4   A Currency Swap

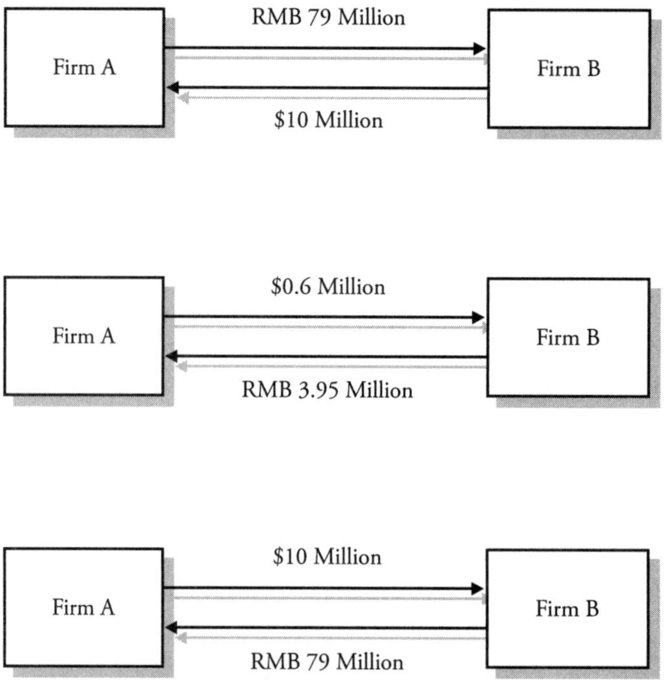

Note: This assumes an exchange rate of U.S. $1 = RMB 7.90.

6 percent in the United States, Firm A, which holds RMB 79 million and would like to exchange them for dollars, could enter into a currency swap agreement with Firm B, as shown in Figure 12.4. The annual interest payments in Figure 12.4 represent the amount of money in dollars (RMB) times the U.S. (RMB) interest rate.

Commodity Price Swaps

Volatility in commodity prices presents uncertainty in the earnings of corporations that spend a significant amount on commodities or energy. Companies that derive revenues from sales of commodities also are subject to the ups and downs in prices. Commodity price swaps can be used to stabilize part of the operating expenses or revenues. In a commodity swap agreement, each counterparty promises to make a series of payments to the other, and of which a commodity price or index determines at least one set of payments. Commodity swaps are becoming increasing common in energy and agriculture areas. The user of a particular commodity who does not want to risk price uncertainty for the long term may agree to pay a financial institution a fixed price, in return for receiving payments based on the market price for the commodity involved. A producer, however, who wishes to fix his income, may agree to pay the market price to a financial institution, in return for receiving a fixed payment stream. Both counterparties now have obtained their preferred structures.

The vast majority of commodity swaps involve oil. Airlines, for example, will often use commodity swaps in which they agree to make fixed payments for a number of years, and receive payments from the swap dealer on the same dates determined by an oil price index. The high oil prices in 2005 and 2006 substantially increased the percentage of fuel costs, both in absolute level and in percentage of total revenues. For example, an airlines company in Asia indicated that jet fuel accounted 40 percent of its total revenues in 2005. For oil swaps, it is common to base the variable payment on the average value of the oil index over a defined period of time. As such, the airlines substantially lower their exposure to just the basis risk.

Equity Swaps

The volatilities in different equity markets are not perfectly correlated, creating trading opportunities to hedge one market against another or to reallocate investments from one to the other. In an equity swap, an investor receives the return on some type of market index and in exchange pays to the swap dealer LIBOR (or a fixed rate or another market index). This was developed primarily to deal with the problems in cross-country investing. For example, a portfolio manager in the United States wanting to diversify 30 percent of his portfolio into the Japanese market may agree to pay the S&P 500 return to the swap dealer based on a notional principal equal to 30 percent of his portfolio and in exchange the dealer will pay him the return on the Nikkei index.

An equity swap agreement is also one of the most efficient ways of gaining exposure to emerging markets. The structure saves investors commissions, stamp duties, clearing fees, and spreads. This is especially useful for investors who, for legal or regulatory reasons, cannot invest directly in a particular country but would like to have exposure to that market.

There are many ways to structure an equity swap. The notional principal can be fixed or variable. It can be structured so that the party either absorbs or hedged against the currency risk.

Real Estate Swaps

Real estate market presents another opportunity for swaps. Morgan Stanley and Bankers Trust were the first to be in the real estate swaps market in 1993. In such a swap, the property owner agrees to pay the counterparty that wants to get into the real estate market a rate of return linked to the performance of the real estate market such as Russell-NCRREF Property Index. In exchange, the counterparty agrees to pay the property owner another type of return, such as floating interest rate. Banks, pension funds, and insurance companies that are strapped with too much real estate might find this market attractive. Because if they sell properties they not only would incur heavy transactions costs, time consuming selling process, but could also suffer a loss. In addition, they risk missing out if the market later takes off. The swaps provide investors, who have money to invest and think real estate promises big gains, exposures to the real estate market without the headaches of being a landlord.

ASSET BACKED SECURITIES

This market is relatively new in China. Asset securitization is the issuance of securities using a pool of similar assets as collateral.[5] There are mortgage-backed securities and asset-backed securities. Asset-backed securities (ABS) are backed by receivables other than mortgage loans. Securitized financing is one of the ways the global marketplace has grown and has played an important role in the development of the derivatives market. Securitization generates fee income for bankers and provides them with additional trading opportunities. Asset types used in securitization can include mortgages, automobile loans, credit card receivables, equipment leases, high-yield bonds, tax liens, and tobacco settlements.

Securitization Structure

A standardized structure and contract gives all participants confidence that the collateral exists in a form that provides a well-defined and legally enforceable manner to meet contractual obligations. The second element is the underwriter's due diligence research that presents potential risks and a proper valuation. A database of historical statistics enables participants to determine how the securities would perform under various scenarios. Standards specifying the quality of servicers are critical to successful securitization as well. The bankruptcy of the servicer or the sale of servicing rights cannot expose investors to loss. The sixth factor is a reliable supply of credit enhancements. Finally, computer modeling to track cash flows and transactions data is fundamental to the growth in volume.

Securitization involves several key elements (Figure 12.5). The loan originator makes the loan to the borrower and may service the newly created ABS as well. Ratings are an important element for all nonagency issues. Credit enhancements are used to assure that the cash flows from the pool are of sufficient quality to meet the scheduled payments. Investment banks underwrite and market the securities to investors. Investors play a vital role in the success of the process. The securities offered must meet their objectives.

Originator and Collateral

The originator may be a bank, a finance company, a credit card issuer, or a securities firm. In structuring a securitization program, it is essential that the originator achieve a true sale in the transfer of assets to the trust holding the collateral, called special purpose vehicle (SPV). In other words, the originator cannot retain any interest in the assets and must transfer the full title.

FIGURE 12.5   Securitization Structure

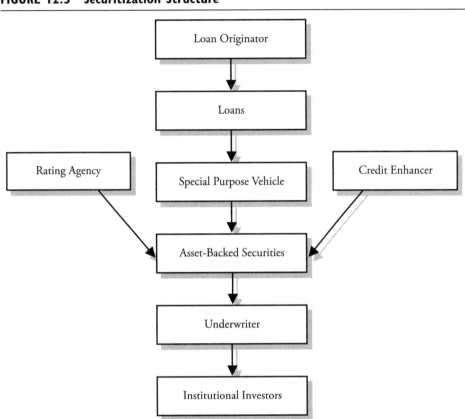

The collateral held in the SPV can be either existing or future income-producing assets. In an ABS, the originator sells an existing pool of assets, such as mortgages, to the SPV. In this case, investors who purchase the securities do not assume any originator performance risk, or the risk that the originator will fail to remain in business and produce the assets. Nevertheless, the originator's creditworthiness may still be a concern for investors if, as often happens, the originator is retained to service the collateral. If so, the originator's bankruptcy would likely affect the quality of its service. In contrast, under a future cash-flow securitization, the originator sells assets to the SPV before the assets have come into existence. The SPV then issues the securities and uses the proceeds to make a prepayment to the originator. In this case, investors assume the originator performance risk because the interest and principal on the securities will be paid only if the originator stays in business and creates the assets.

Servicing

The servicer collects money from debtors and distributes the funds, net of fees, to the SPV and to investors. Many securitization programs retain the originator as the servicer. To ensure that the originator's retention of some control over the assets will not prevent the transfer from being a true sale, the originator's role must be clearly limited to that of a collection agent for the trust, and the originator must be paid a reasonable servicing fee.

Special Purpose Vehicle

Another key element in any successful program is the establishment of a bankruptcy remote entity, the SPV. A primary factor that mitigates the risk of a securitization transaction is that the trust that serves as SPV is generally shielded from bankruptcy. Constraints in the documents setting up the transaction restrict the business activities of the SPV to those associated with the securitization. These documents also prohibit the SPV from incurring additional debt or otherwise transferring or encumbering the assets.

Credit Enhancement

The purpose of credit enhancement is to advance sale of the ABS. Under a securitization program, the credit risk of the issuer is not a concern to investors because the originator has transferred ownership of the assets to the SPV in a true sale. Securities backed by assets in the pool usually have several levels of credit enhancement to mitigate the potential loss arising from the credit risk of the underlying assets. The amount and type of credit enhancement depend on the historical loss experience of similar loans and the rating sought by the issuer. Internal credit enhancements include overcollateralization, excess spread, or a reserve account. External credit enhancement may be in the form of a bank letter of credit, a surety bond, or a financial guarantee from a bond insurance company. Major bond insurers are AMBAC and MBIA, and they carry a global triple-A rating. In general, the party providing this enhancement must be an entity with a rating at least as high as the desired transaction rating.

Credit Rating

It is common to have a tranche structure in which the ABS are separated into several tranches with differing credit ratings. Credit ratings provide investors with an indication of the likelihood that they will be repaid on time and in full. In analyzing a securitization program, rating agencies examine the legal and structural protections provided to investors.

Benefits and Costs

With securitization, the originator/issuer is able to tap into a new source of funding at a lower all-in cost of capital because the resulting securities present a better credit quality than the originator itself. To the extent that the originator continues to service the underlying assets, a steady stream of servicing fees is generated. As assets are removed from its balance sheet, the originator's exposure to interest rate risk is reduced. In addition, the credit risk associated with those assets is passed on to investors. The transfer of title to the assets to the SPV is of particular value to banks as originators, because it frees up capital for the bank to make new loans. As such, it permits the bank to lend additional funds to its customers. Furthermore, if the originator is at or near the debt/equity ratio permitted under financial covenants in outstanding indentures, securitization will allow the originator to raise needed capital without incurring balance sheet debt and triggering a breach of these financial covenants. A securitization is also an effective way to divest excess or nonessential assets.

Additionally, pricing efficiency and transparency resulting from the underwriting process and secondary market trading are only obtainable through asset-backed securities. Without securitization, there is at best infrequent and subjective valuation of the underlying asset. Moreover, by packaging individual illiquid loans into marketable securities, the issuer increases the liquidity of its assets. Table 12.1 summarizes the advantages of securitization as compared with individual loans.

However, issuers and originators also face some disadvantages. The up-front expenses and effort required for a first-time securitization are likely to exceed the expenses and effort associated with a bank borrowing or other debt offering. Another disadvantage is the required disclosure of asset data. Investors and rating agencies in particular will require the disclosure of a significant amount of information concerning the assets, which the originator may be reluctant to provide. In addition, detailed servicing reports monitoring the performance of the assets are typically required on a

TABLE 12.1   Value Added through Securitization

Individual Loans	Asset-Backed Securities
Illiquid	Liquid, active secondary markets for most.
Periodic valuation	Pricing efficiency and transparency.
Originator assesses risk	Rating agencies and credit enhancers assess risk.
Local investor base	National/global markets.
Higher cost of funding	Lower costs.
No servicing fee generated	Additional fee income if the originator acts as servicer.
Assets remain on the originator's balance sheet; additional loan origination requires additional capital	Assets are removed from the originator's balance sheet; additional funds are available to support more loan origination.
Unwanted assets remain on the originator's balance sheet	The originator can sell unwanted assets and use the proceeds to expand its core business.
Subject to debt/equity ratio constraints	Provide access to needed capital without incurring balance sheet debt.

regular basis. There are costs to issuers for securitizing assets. The actual costs depend on the size and type of assets as well. The average cost to issuer is about 1 percent.

Nonetheless, the securitization process benefits Wall Street. The securities created generate profits to bankers; they gain underwriting spreads and potential trading profits. For investors, they now have available asset classes that were not available before securitization. Securitization offers new investment opportunities. Some investors might find the new asset class and its yield attractive. For most investors, the benefit comes from portfolio diversification because correlation between asset classes is not perfect.

CREDIT DERIVATIVES

Credit derivatives are not yet available in China's domestic market. But, increasing use of credit derivatives in various applications will certainly soon find a market and gain regulation approval in China. Credit derivatives can help banks, financial companies, and investors manage the credit risk of their investment by insuring against adverse movements in the credit quality of the issuer. Specific applications include:

- Commercial banks to change the risk profile of loan books
- Investment banks to manage bond and derivatives portfolio
- Manufacturers to manage the exposure to a single customer
- Equity investors in project finance to deal with unacceptable sovereign risk
- Institutional investors or hedge funds to enhance yield or to speculate
- Employees to secure deferred remuneration

There are four broad types of credit derivatives: credit default swaps, credit-spread options, total return swaps, and credit-linked notes. The first deals were done in 1993 when Bankers Trust and Credit Suisse Financial Products in Japan sold notes whose redemption value depended on specified default events. The market got a slow start because of the disasters in financial derivatives. But, by 1997, the market had approached some $200 billion and was rapidly expanding. The total credit default swaps outstanding rose to $26 trillion in mid-2006.

Credit Default Swaps

A credit default swap is a contract in which one counterparty pays a premium in return for a contingent payment triggered by the default of one or more third-party reference credits. The premium is expressed in basis points of the notional amount, while the contingent payment is determined by the decrease in the price of the security below par after the reference credit has defaulted. For example, in June 1997, an international bank that already had a basket of 20 loans totaling more than $500 million to mostly investment-grade companies wanted to lend more money to the same companies. JPMorgan sold the bank the right to require Morgan to pay off any

FIGURE 12.6   A Credit Default Swap

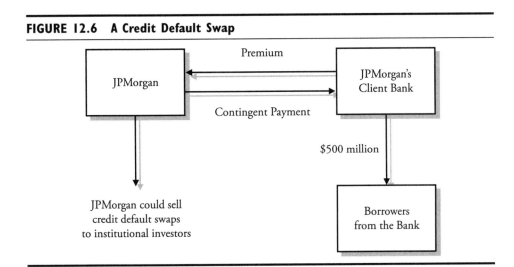

of the loans if a borrower went bankrupt. JPMorgan could retain the default risks in its portfolio and collect the premium, or sell them to institutional investors such as insurance companies, hedge funds, or other banks. Meanwhile, Morgan's client retained the actual loans and the customer relationship (Figure 12.6).

This transaction is actually a put option on a portfolio of loans or bonds. The client bank receives a payoff if a borrower goes bankrupt, that is, it has the right to sell the default loans to Morgan at par. In a similar manner, bond investors can use this type of credit option to hedge against a decline in the price of a bond. As an example, an institutional investor has a portfolio of five-year Italian government bonds. The investor pays the counterparty a premium of, say, 20 basis points a year. The counterparty is obligated to make a payment if Italy defaults on its debt, in which case the contingent payment is par less the final price. Of course, the notional principal and maturity can be tailored to provide the exact amount and tenor of protection required.

Corporates and investors in projects stand to benefit as well. Take an engineering company, all of its heavy drilling equipment in the next several years may be sold to just a few customers. If a customer goes bust, the equipment will be idled in inventory with no one else to sell to. To hedge against this risk, the engineering company can buy a credit swap on a notional principal that compensates for the loss of the sale. In project finance, an equity sponsor to a large project may want to hedge the portion of sovereign risk not guaranteed by an export credit agency-backed facility. It could enter into a credit default swap with a notional principal equal to the amount not covered by the sovereign guarantee.

Credit Spread Options

Credit spread plays focus on the yield differential between credit-sensitive instruments and the reference security. Credit spread options can be used by bond issuers to hedge against a rise in the average credit risk premium. As an illustration, suppose a Baa-company is planning to issue $50 million of two-year bonds in three months. The interest rate the company anticipates paying is the current spread of 80 basis points over the two-year Treasury notes. If there is an increase in the average risk premium for Baa companies before the bond's issuance, the interest payments will rise.

To hedge against the widening of the spread, the company could purchase a put option with a strike at the current level of spread. If the average risk premium rises above the strike in three months, the higher interest payments will be offset by gains from the option. Because the payments from the put option offsets the increased borrowing costs, purchasing the put option provides a hedge against increases in the credit premium. Alternatively, suppose that the credit risk premium falls. The put option has no payoff, but the company saves financing costs at the lower spread. Thus, purchasing the put option allows the corporate user to insure against increases in the credit risk premium while maintaining the benefits of lower funding costs if the spread declines.

Credit spread contracts have also been successfully used in emerging markets. In emerging markets, a credit spread is generally expressed as the yield spread of an emerging market instrument over the yield of a "risk-free" bond. Many structures are available that allow investors to bet on a specific credit spread or a basket of credit spreads. For example, when the sovereign Brazil 2027 global bond was offered at a spread of 525 basis points over the U.S. Treasury long bond, an institutional investor of Lehman Brothers' "locked in" a spread of 575 over the settlement in one year. The net settlement on the end date is determined by the credit spread of Brazil 2027 bond at that time. In this trade, the notional size is $10,000 per basis points of spread tightening or widening. The investor will receive $10,000 at the end date for each basis point by which the Brazil credit spread is below 575, but will pay $10,000 for every basis point the spread is greater than 575.

Total Return Swaps

In a total return swap, the market risk of the underlying asset is stripped out and transferred without actually transferring the asset. For example, a bank originates a loan and then collects and passes along the loan payments (total returns) to the swap dealer. In return, the dealer pays the bank a floating rate of interest such as a spread over three-month LIBOR. Periodically the swap is settled on the market value of the loan. The bank pays the swap dealer any positive change in value. Conversely, the dealer pays any negative change to the bank. The effect of this swap for the bank is to trade the total return from its loan portfolio for a guaranteed return of a spread over three-month LIBOR. Because the swap dealer now guarantees the return, the bank has eliminated the credit risk on this loan.

Total return swaps offer two advantages. First, they allow banks to diversify loan credit risk while maintaining confidentiality of their client's financial records. Second, the administrative costs of the swap transaction are lower than for a loan sale.

Credit-Linked Notes

A credit-linked note is a structured note in which the bond has an embedded option that allows the issuer to reduce the note's payments if a key financial variable specified deteriorates. For example, an automobile financing company may use debt to fund a portfolio of automobile loans. To reduce the credit risk, the company's credit-linked note promises to pay lenders higher coupon rate and the principal if the delinquency is below, say, 5 percent. However, if default exceeds 5 percent, investors accept a formula with potential loss of interest and principal. Some banks market a product known as zero-one structure. Instead of some coupon or principal loss, investors lose their entire principal if there is a higher default rate.

An automobile financing company would issue a credit-linked note because it provides a convenient mechanism to reduce the company's credit exposure. If default rates are high, the earnings are reduced, but the company pays a lower interest. Investors would consider buying such a security because they earn a higher expected rate of return than a comparable bond.

STRUCTURED NOTES

Structured notes are debt securities with interest and at times principal payments determined by formulas relating to the direction of interest rates, the range of volatility, the shape of the yield curve, the performance of equity market, commodity prices, or embedded options such as caps, floors, or call features. Customized complex features are difficult to evaluate, and hence, this reduces their liquidity.

Government agencies, banks, and corporations have participated in the structured markets as issuers. These institutions achieve low-cost, variable-rate financing. Institutional investors and money managers receive high-grade customized bonds designed to fit their preferences. For investment bankers, they earn underwriting fees while generating additional derivatives business.

Floaters

One of the earliest structured notes is a floater. The most basic type has the interest rate tied to LIBOR or T-bill rate. After a coupon reset, a floater trades at par and will make its next coupon payment on the next reset date. Between reset dates the price of the floater fluctuates depending on the market environment and credit quality of the issuer. Therefore, a floater is equivalent to a bond with one coupon remaining and with maturity equal to the time until next reset date. The Macaulay duration of a floater, regardless of maturity, is hence the time until its next coupon reset date.

A floater might have its interest rate tied to an index or a commodity price. For example, consider an oil refinery with a poor credit rating wanting to borrow money. It could issue a note with interest rate payment increases with oil price. If oil prices rise, the refinery has more cash flow to pay for the higher interests. When oil prices decline, its interest burden is lower. There are also deleveraged floaters. These notes generally give investors above-market initial yield and tie subsequent coupon adjustments to a formula on the changes in an index. Furthermore, some types of structured notes pay a promised fixed rate and additional payments based on the movement of a commodity price or stock index, in the latter case it is like a market indexed certificate of deposits.

Inverse Floaters

An inverse floater is a floating-rate security whose interest rate moves inversely with market rates. The coupon on an inverse floater is the difference between the fixed rate on the underlying bond and the rate on the floater. The interests on the floater and inverse floater must total the fixed rate paid by the underlying bond from which they are created. The value of an inverse floater varies inversely with the market interest rates. As rates increase, the inverse floater loses value from a higher discount rate and lower cash flows. The inverse floater gains from a lower discount rate and from an increase in cash flows when rates decline. A floor, typically at zero, is usually established for the inverse floater. As a result, a cap is imposed on the floater.

The duration of an inverse floater is longer than its maturity. This has often caught investors off guard. The duration of an inverse floater exceeds the duration of the underlying fixed-rate coupon bond. This is because the duration of the fixed-rate coupon bond is the weighted average of the duration of the floater and inverse floater. The duration of a floater is quite short, equal to the time until the next coupon reset date. Hence, the duration of the inverse floater exceeds the duration of the underlying fixed-rate bond.

Step-Ups

These securities pay an initial yield higher than a comparable government security and have coupons step-up at a prespecified date if the issue is not called. If the coupon has more than one adjustment period, it is called multistep-up. The higher initial yield compensates the investor for implicitly having sold a call option to the issuer.

Index-Amortizing Notes

Index-Amortizing Notes (IANs) amortize the outstanding principal according to a schedule linked to the level of a designated index such as LIBOR or constant maturity treasury index (CMT). The final principal repayment date is fixed. The future cash flows, average life, and the yield to maturity are all subject to uncertainty. IANs are generally issued at par and have a final maturity of 5 to 10 years.

Dual Index Notes

Dual index notes are also known as yield curve anticipation notes. The coupon rate is determined by the spread between two market indexes such as the prime rate, LIBOR, CMT yields of different maturities. Yield curve anticipation notes are among the most risky of various structures. One of the investments by Orange County was on yield curve anticipation notes. The notes would pay higher (lower) interest rates when the yield curve steepens (flattens). Orange County financed the purchase with open repos. In 1994, the Fed raised the Fed funds rate seven times. The yield curve flattened and financing costs moved up, resulting in a negative carry and a capital loss. Investment strategies like this and borrow-short-lend-long at a time of rising interest rates brought about the financial debacles of Orange County and others.

Range Notes

Range notes accrue interest periodically at a coupon tied to an index. Most range notes have two interest levels, a higher accrual rate during periods when the index remains within a designated range and a lower rate or no interest at all if the index moves outside of the range. These notes generally perform poorly in a volatile interest rate environment. The direction of the interest rate is not important, but rather the volatility matters. These notes are most risky when they are of a barrier nature, in which purchasers would lose all once the index breaks out of the range.

CONCLUSION

China has taken steps to gradually allow various types of derivatives instruments in the domestic market. Several basic, important derivatives already trade in China, including forwards, futures, repos, and interest rate and currency swaps. Other instruments such as credit derivatives will see huge volume when the market is open. This chapter reviewed several new financial products that already trade in China as well as some that will enjoy great success when China opens the gate to them.

13

Asset Management Business

China's asset management market is continuing to grow. Asset management is an important segment of the capital markets and has become an integral part of the investment banking business. Wall Street firms are buying into China's fund management because it is one of the most attractive segments of the financial services industry. This chapter describes the fund management business in China. This chapter also discusses the market trends and describes the structure and organization of a mutual fund. Furthermore, this chapter explains the structure of a hedge fund and the typical ranges of management fees and incentive fees.

OVERVIEW

China's stockpile of about 1.7 trillion U.S. dollars in personal savings has made it an ideal place for the fund management industry. Assets under management in the country ballooned to about $60 billion by 2005 from virtually zero just a few years ago.

A securities investment fund (SIF), or a mutual fund, is an investment intermediary that gathers money from investors and invests in a portfolio of publicly traded stocks and bonds.[1] Through the collective investments of the SIF, each investor shares in the returns from the fund's portfolio while benefiting from professional investment management, diversification, and liquidity. There are two types of SIFs:

1. *Closed-end funds:* Listed and traded on the stock exchange with a fixed number of shares
2. *Open-end funds:* Unlisted shares open to investors for purchase or redemption at net asset value

Closed-end funds started first and dominated the market until 2003. Starting in 2004, open-end mutual funds outnumbered closed end. The trend will continue because market participants expect China's fund industry to mimic the West in the future.

Development of the China Fund Industry

At year-end 2005, China had 54 closed-end and 164 open-end funds under the management of 53 (including 20 joint ventures) fund management companies (Table 13.1).[2] The total assets of these funds were RMB 469.1 billion in 2005. Securities investment funds have enjoyed tremendous growth in recent years, but the asset bases of mutual funds still remain a small part of China's financial system.

The fund industry was largely unregulated with significant operational problems until the promulgation of the Investment Fund Law in December 1997. The fund is not permitted to invest more than 10 percent in any one company and the fund cannot own more than 10 percent of a company's shares. Furthermore, 80 percent of assets held by the funds must be invested in stocks and bonds, and at least 20 percent must be invested in government bonds.

The China Securities Regulatory Commission (CSRC) introduced rules for open-end funds in 2000. Under the rules, fund management firms can charge investors a front-end load up to 5 percent of the investment and a back-end load up to 3 percent of the amount withdrawn. In September 2001, Hua An Fund Management became the first Chinese money management firm to launch an open-end fund, called Innovation Fund.[3] Hua An was also one of the first to obtain regulatory approval to issue an exchange-traded fund. Other examples of fund management companies are AIG-Huatai Fund Management, Yinhua Fund Management, and Fortune SGAM Fund Management.

Chinese Fund Categories and Regulations

There are varieties of funds in China, covering equity funds, bond funds, index funds, money market funds, umbrella funds, principal guaranteed funds, exchange traded funds, and listed open-ended funds. The offerings are certainly not as extensive as those in the United States. The size is still limited, and thus there is great potential.

TABLE 13.1   Mutual Funds in China

Year	Number of Closed-End Funds	Number of Open-End Funds	Net Asset Value (RMB 100 Million)
1998	5	0	104
1999	22	0	575
2000	34	0	847
2001	48	3	809
2002	54	17	1,186
2003	59	51	1,699
2004	54	107	3,238
2005	54	164	4,691

Source: China Securities Regulatory Commission.

In the fund industry, some relevant regulatory requirements are as follows:

- *Fund manager and custodian:* Fund management and custodianship should be separated. Fund managers manage the pooled assets while qualified commercial banks serve as custodians to safe keep the invested securities. A fund manager is required to be licensed by the CSRC, while a custodian is regulated by the CSRC and the China Banking Regulatory Commission. According to Article 13 of Securities Investment Fund Law, the following conditions shall be met in order to establish a fund management company:
  —A registered capital of no less than RMB 100 million.
  —Principal shareholders demonstrating a good track record and public reputation in securities business, securities investment consultation, trust assets management, or other financial assets management, committing no violation of law within the preceding three years.
  —Number of licensed fund professionals meeting the statutory requirement.
- *Placement of fund:* A fund company is required to, before its fund placement, submit its application and relevant documents to the CSRC. The fund placement shall start within six months from the date of receiving the ratification.
- *Fund operation:* In managing the assets, a fund manager shall apply portfolio investment technique to trade listed stocks, bonds, and other instruments permitted by the CSRC.

According to Article 59 of the Securities Investment Fund Law, a mutual fund is not permitted to engage in the following investments or activities:

- Underwriting of securities
- Providing loans or guarantees to others
- Engaging in investment with unlimited liability
- Trading other fund units, unless otherwise approved by the State Council
- Making capital contribution to the fund manager and custodian, or trading the stocks or bonds issued by the aforesaid manager and custodian
- Trading the securities issued or underwritten by the shareholders controlling the fund manager or custodian, or by the companies with other significant interests with the aforesaid manager or custodian
- Insider dealing, market manipulation, or other wrongdoings

Various Types of Investment Management

As discussed, open-end mutual funds are a recent development in China. It will take years to develop a market like the United States. Foreign financial institutions see high growth opportunities as Chinese people have huge savings and there are few investment vehicles to allocate money to earn competitive returns. In the West, there are many types of investment management, including mutual funds, unit investment trusts, hedge funds, closed-end funds, private client services business, leveraged buyout funds, and venture capital funds.

This chapter provides coverage on mutual funds, exchanged traded funds, hedge funds, and real investment trusts. The coverage on venture capital and buyout funds has been included in Chapter 8. The remainder of this section briefly describes each type of fund and provides a summary of China's mutual fund business.

A unit investment trust (UIT) is an investment company that purchases and holds a relatively fixed portfolio of securities. Units in the trust are sold to investors who receive a pro rata share of principal and interest or dividends. Unit investment trusts generally have a stated date for termination. When the trusts are dissolved, all proceeds are paid to unit-holders. Many types of UITs are available to meet various investment objectives and levels of risk tolerance, including corporate bond UITs, equity UITs, international bond UITs, mortgage-backed UITs, municipal bond UITs, and government securities UITs.

A closed-end investment company issues a fixed number of shares that list on a stock exchange or trade over the counter. After the shares are issued, investors wanting to buy or sell are trading with other investors. There are four main types of closed-end funds: international and global bond funds, international and global equity funds, domestic bond funds, and domestic equity funds. Demand and supply in the marketplace determine the price of a closed-end fund. The market price could be, and frequently is, different from the value per share. Many funds consistently trade at or around a particular level of discount or premium. Such a deviation from share value can occur for many reasons. For example, a closed-end fund that consistently outperforms others or offers a unique opportunity tends to trade at a premium. Alternatively, investor demand will be weak if a fund offers inferior returns or holds securities that are risky and difficult to evaluate.

Venture capital (VC) funds make equity investments in entrepreneurial companies. A private VC fund typically raises its capital from a limited number of sophisticated investors in a private placement. VC firms earn income from two sources: the annual management fee and the profit allocation of the fund.

Buyout funds are investment firms that invest in leveraged buyouts (LBOs). Three factors generally are considered essential in conducting a successful LBO: the ability to borrow large sums of money against the company's assets, the ability to retain or attract a strong management team, and the potential for the investment to increase in value. The ability of a company to support significant leverage depends on whether it can service the debt obligations. This, in turn, requires a company that is capable of generating large sums of cash on a regular basis or has substantial assets that can be sold to pay off the debt.

A mutual fund is an investment management company that pools money from investors who share similar investment objectives, such as obtaining current income, maximizing long-term capital growth, or a combination of both. A professional manager manages the fund to achieve its objective. Each share represents a proportional ownership in the fund's entire portfolio.

Exchanged-traded funds (ETFs) are designed to track the performance of the underlying index. ETFs are basically index mutual funds, that are listed and traded on an exchange. Investors trade during the trading hours at the real-time market prices, just like any listed security. There are hundreds of ETFs listed on the exchanges in the United States. In China, there are very few.

A hedge fund is an unregistered, private investment pool bound by the investment agreement investors have signed with the sponsors of the fund. A hedge fund generally is not subject to any limitations in portfolio selection. It is also not required to disclose information about its holdings and performance. In recent years, several hedge funds have listed shares on the exchange. Thus, now you do not have to be rich to invest in hedge funds.

Another type of investment company covered in this chapter is the real estate investment trust (REIT), a trust that pools capital from investors to acquire or to provide financing for real estate. It is similar to a closed-end fund for real estate in that retail investors can trade shares on a stock exchange. Investing in REITs gives an investor a practical and efficient way to include professionally managed real estate in an investment portfolio.

OPPORTUNITIES FOR FOREIGN INSTITUTIONS

Chinese have a high savings rate. More than $1.7 trillion in personal savings are in Chinese bank accounts earning a paltry interest. Fund managers are also eyeing the billions in China's national social security fund. Beijing has indicated it wants that money invested in low-risk products such as bond and money market funds. Also, huge growth is expected in private pension schemes and fund management for cash-rich Chinese corporations.

For foreign institutions, they enter by way of qualified foreign institutional investors scheme. In December 2002, China Securities Regulatory Commission (CSRC) and People's Bank of China (PBC) jointly issued the Provisional Measures on Administration of Domestic Securities Investments of Qualified Foreign Institutional Investors (QFIIs). The regulation for the first time allowed foreign investors to invest and trade in the domestic securities market. QFIIs are permitted to invest in the domestic A shares market as well as the debt market in the range of U.S.$50 million to $800 million. Many foreign financial institutions have obtained QFII designations. QFII qualifications requirements are:

- *Sound credit status:* Meet the requirements set by the CSRC on asset size and other factors.
- *Professional qualifications:* Employees have to meet professional qualifications in their home country.
- *Sound management structure and internal control:* Company should be in compliance with relevant regulations and have not received substantial penalties over the past three years.
- *Sound regulatory and legal system:* The applicant's home country has a sound legal and regulatory system and has signed a Memorandum of Understanding with the CSRC.

The asset size requirements vary depending on the type of financial services. For fund management companies, assets under management are $5 billion or more, with an operating history of at least five years. For insurance companies, the requirements are $1 billion of paid-in capital and assets of $5 billion. The requirements for securities firms are similar to insurance companies. To be a QFII in China, a bank has to be ranked in the top 100 in the world and has to have assets of at least $10 billion.

QFII are permitted to invest in: (1) publicly listed shares listed on the Shanghai or Shenzhen Stock Exchange other than B shares; (2) publicly traded Treasury bonds, convertible bonds, and corporate bonds; (3) other financial instruments approved by CSRC. However, a QFII may not purchase more than 10 percent of the total outstanding shares of any single listed company. Furthermore, for any listed company, the total combined shares held by all QFIIs may not exceed 20 percent of the total outstanding shares.

A qualified Chinese commercial bank and a foreign bank's Chinese branch can act as a custodian. After selecting a custodian, a QFII needs to open a special RMB account with the custodian bank, and only remit foreign capital, which then converts, to RMB to that account. As of December 2006, there are 14 banks in China that are qualified for the custodian business (Table 13.2).

A custodian bank's main business scope is to:

- Safeguard all the assets that the QFII puts under its custody.
- Conduct all QFII related foreign exchange settlement, sales, receipt, payment, and RMB settlement businesses.
- Monitor investment activities of QFII and report to CSRC and SAFE for any noncompliance.
- Compile an annual financial report on QFII's domestic securities investment activities in the previous year.

TABLE 13.2 QFII Custodian Banks

Domestic Banks	Foreign Banks
Agricultural Bank of China	Citibank
Bank of China	Deutsche Bank
Bank of Communications	HSBC
China Construction Bank	The Standard & Chartered Bank
China Merchants Bank	DBS Bank
China Everbright Bank	
The Industrial and	
Commercial Bank of China	
China Citic Bank	

Source: China Securities Regulatory Commission.

CSRC and SAFE are the regulators of the securities investment activities conducted by QFIIs. They are responsible for overseeing all transactions and conducting annual inspections on QFIIs. CSRC is the approval authority for QFII status. It interprets the rules regarding QFII and acts the role of a general regulator. SAFE takes charge of overseeing business tied with foreign exchange operations, such as the approval of the QFII investment quotas, issuance of the foreign exchange certificate, supervision of account management, and foreign exchange settlements.

There were 34 foreign financial institutions had been licensed as QFIIs with a total investment quota of $5.6 billion in 2005. The securities assets of the QFIIs amounted to RMB 34.7 billion, accounting for 90 percent of their investment quota. Of their investment portfolios, RMB 22.3 billion (64 percent) was invested in A shares, RMB 6.0 billion (17 percent) in funds, RMB 2.6 billion (7 percent) in convertible bonds, and RMB 3.7 billion (11 percent) in Treasury bonds. By 2006, QFIIs increased to 52.

OPEN-END MUTUAL FUNDS

A mutual fund offers investors a simple and convenient method of investing in a portfolio of securities.[4] The size of a mutual fund portfolio changes as new money comes in or investors redeem and as the value of the securities held by the fund rises or falls. Each mutual fund share represents ownership in all of the securities in the fund portfolio. Capital gains and dividends or interest income from these securities are paid out in proportion to the number of shares investors own. Therefore, an investor who invests $1,000 will get the same investment return per dollar invested as a fund shareholder investing $1,000,000.

There are several advantages to investing in mutual funds. First, an investor buying shares of a mutual fund is buying an ownership interest in all of the securities the fund owns. Fund managers generally invest in a variety of securities, affording portfolio diversification. A diversified portfolio helps reduce risk because losses from some securities will be offset by gains in others. Thus, investors can blunt the effect of a decline in value of any particular security. It is not cost effective for an average investor to construct a portfolio as diversified as a mutual fund.

The second advantage is professional management. Professional money managers select securities that best match the fund's objectives as described in the prospectus. These managers are experienced in interpreting the complexities of the financial markets and are backed by talented analysts who conduct extensive research on individual companies as well as the entire industry. Mutual funds provide an economical way for the individual investor to obtain the same kind of professional money management and diversification as is available to large institutions and wealthy investors.

The third advantage is that there are many types of mutual funds to choose from. There are thousands of mutual funds representing a wide variety of investment objectives, from conservative to aggressive and from sector to global. Table 13.3 lists various fund objectives as classified by the Investment Company Institute in the United States. Investors need to analyze their investment time horizon and risk tolerance level to determine what type of funds to choose. Additionally, it is easy to invest in mutual funds. Most mutual funds, whether managed by Fidelity

TABLE 13.3   Types of Mutual Funds

Equity Funds

Aggressive growth
Growth
Sector
Growth and income
Income equity
Emerging markets
Global equity
International equity
Regional equity

Hybrid Funds

Asset allocation
Balanced
Flexible portfolio
Income mixed

Taxable Bond Funds

Corporate bond
High yield
Global bond
Government bond
Mortgage backed
Strategic income

Tax-Free Bond Funds

State municipal bond
National municipal bond

Money Market Funds

Taxable money market
Tax-exempt money market—national
Tax-exempt money market—state

Source: *Mutual Fund Fact Book 2003*, Investment Company Institute, 2004.

or Vanguard, can be purchased through the fund companies directly or via brokerage firms.

Another benefit is that mutual funds issue both full and fractional shares. This allows investors to purchase shares based on an even dollar investment. Additionally, mutual funds, unless closed to new investments, continuously issue new shares to or buy back shares from investors. Finally, mutual funds are liquid. Investors can redeem shares on any business day at the net asset value. Many mutual funds also offer check-writing and online payment privileges.

Mutual Fund Share Pricing and Performance

A fund's net asset value (NAV) is the value of all the fund's assets, minus liabilities, divided by the total number of shares outstanding. For example, suppose a mutual fund owns a portfolio of stocks worth $200 million at the end of the business day; its liabilities are $20 million; and it has 2.4 million shares of the fund outstanding. The NAV is calculated as:

$$NAV = \frac{\$200,000,000 - \$20,000,000}{2,400,000} = \$75.00.$$

A fund's offering price is its NAV plus the applicable sales charge. The redemption price is its NAV minus the applicable redemption fee, or back-end load. In addition to the NAV, mutual fund quotes typically include performance data such as returns year-to-date, 3-year, 5-year, 10-year, and since inception.

Mutual Fund Fees and Expenses

Investors in mutual funds pay several types of fees and expenses. Investors may purchase mutual fund shares directly from the fund or through a broker, a bank representative, an insurance agent, or a financial planner. They are generally compensated through sales commissions or through 12b-1 fees. The 12b-1 fees are deducted from fund assets to pay for marketing and advertising expenses or to compensate sales professionals. By law, 12b-1 fees cannot exceed 1 percent of the fund's average NAV per year. In addition to 12b-1 fees, a fund's annual operating expenses include management fees, which are ongoing fees charged by the fund's investment adviser for managing the fund. These fees typically range from 0.50 to 1.5 percent of assets under management. Funds specializing in small capitalization or certain niche areas charge a higher fee. Index funds buy and hold securities selected to represent a target index or benchmark such as the S&P 500 Index. Their management fees could be as low as 10 basis points. In the long run, the impact of fee differentials on returns is significant. For example, suppose that two funds produce the same annual rate of return of 10 percent, before management fees, to investors during a 30-year investment horizon. One fund charges 0.20 percent in management fees, while the other charges 1.20 percent. For an initial investment of $1,000, the fund with a lower fee will return investors $16,522. The higher fees charged by the other fund will decrease the terminal value of the same amount of initial investment to $12,556. The additional 1 percent fee has lowered the terminal value by $3,966; almost four times the amount of initial investments.

Additionally, a shareholder may incur transaction expenses such as purchase, redemption, or exchange fees. Load funds charge a front-end load, a back-end load, or both. A front-end load, or sales charge, may be charged for the purchase of mutual fund shares. By law, this charge may not exceed 8.5 percent of the investment, although most fund families charge less than the maximum. A back-end load, sometimes referred to as a redemption or exit fee, is charged at the time of redemption. This fee typically applies for the first few years on a declining schedule and then disappears. A no-load fund does not have any front-end or back-end charge. An exchange fee may be charged when the shareholder transfers money from one fund to another within the same fund family. Finally, some funds charge an account maintenance fee to maintain low-balance accounts.

Growth of Mutual Funds in the United States

Mutual fund investing began to grow in popularity in the 1940s and 1950s, but the explosive growth did not occur until the 1980s. In 1960, there were 160 funds with $17 billion in assets. Ten years later, there were 361 funds with total assets of $47.6 billion. By 1980, the number of funds had reached 564, and the total assets under management had crossed the $100 billion mark to $134.8 billion. Another milestone was reached in 1990 when the 3,105 funds managed more than $1 trillion in assets. By the end of 1996, total industry assets had increased to $3.5 trillion. Total net assets increased by about $1 trillion in each of the subsequent two years, 1997 and 1998. By the end of 2005, total net assets of mutual funds were $8.9 trillion. By August 2006, the total amount grew to $9.5 trillion.[5]

Today's mutual fund menu runs the gamut from aggressive growth to global bonds to niche funds, which specialize in one segment of the securities markets. Nevertheless, funds can still be grouped into three general types: money market funds, bond funds, and stock funds. Money market funds invest in short-term securities that are highly liquid and low risk. These funds seek to maintain a stable NAV of $1, while providing a current level of income to shareholders. Bond mutual funds invest in fixed-income securities such as Treasury, agency, corporate, and municipal securities. Stock mutual funds primarily invest in common stocks.

Mutual fund management styles are either active management or indexing. An active management strategy seeks to outperform the market by applying informed and independent investment management. Most managers employ this strategy. Major active management firms include Fidelity, Putnam, Scudder, Oppenheimer, Alliance Capital, Morgan Stanley, Merrill Lynch, and John Hancock. The opposite is passive management, or indexing, in which the fund buys securities to replicate the performance of the overall market. The best-known index fund company is Vanguard. Many of the ETFs are also index types of funds.

Mutual Fund Selection and Asset Allocation

An investor's tolerance for risk and his or her investment horizon determine the type of mutual fund he or she selects. Table 13.4 provides a sample matrix of investment strategies. A capital preservation strategy is appropriate for investors who want income, a fair amount of stability, and some increase in the value of the investment. A strategy focused on moderate growth is for investors who primarily want a balance of moderate growth and moderate income with a fair amount of stability. For investors who want the potential for growth and capital appreciation, but also want some protection from stock market volatility, a wealth-building strategy is suitable. Aggressive growth is for investors who want the potential for substantial growth and capital appreciation.

In selecting a portfolio of mutual funds, an investor may also want to engage in asset allocation. Asset allocation is the process of strategically diversifying investments between stock, bond, and cash in order to achieve a return that is consistent with the investor's financial goals, investment horizon, and risk tolerance. A strategic asset allocation is a value-oriented technique that seeks to increase exposure to the market when recent market performance has been poor and to reduce exposure when recent market performance has been good. In contrast, a dynamic asset allocation strategy uses a strategy to ensure that the value of the portfolio does not fall below a certain level (portfolio insurance) to avoid large losses and to secure any favorable market move.

The benefit of risk reduction from diversification is well understood. In addition, allocating money into various asset classes can improve overall returns. For example, suppose an investor has a two-year investment horizon and is faced with two types of funds in two different asset classes. Fund A provides a return of 40 percent in the first year and 0 percent in the second year. Fund B returns investors 0 percent and 40 percent during the same two-year period. Thus, investing in either Fund A or Fund B gives a total return of 40 percent. If the investor allocates funds into these two classes 50/50, the total return is 44 percent. An allocation mix of 50/50 between Fund A and Fund B produces an additional return of 4 percent. Note that if the investor has

TABLE 13.4 Mutual Fund Investment Strategy Matrix

Risk Tolerance	Investment Horizon		
	0–3 Years	4–6 Years	7+ Years
High	Moderate growth	Wealth building	Aggressive growth
Moderate	Moderate growth	Moderate growth	Wealth building
Low	Capital preservation	Capital preservation	Moderate growth

Source: Fidelity Investments.

perfect timing and invests in Fund A in the first year and switches to Fund B in the second year, the total return will be 96 percent. Most investors do not have a crystal ball, however, so they are better off diversifying their investments.

Asset allocation has a profound effect on the performance investors can expect from their investment portfolios over time. To develop an asset allocation program, investors should first determine their financial goals and investment horizon. They should also evaluate their level of risk tolerance. The next step is to develop a detailed asset allocation strategy using assets that complement each other. Once the blueprint for asset allocation has been formulated, it is time to implement the strategy. The performance of the portfolio is reviewed periodically and compared to the investor's objectives. By periodically rebalancing the portfolio, the investor sells those assets that have appreciated and purchases those investments that have gone down in value. Such rebalancing helps maintain a constant portfolio risk level and prevents the asset allocation percentages from deviating from the plan.

EXCHANGED-TRADED FUNDS

An ETF is an index fund or trust that is listed on an exchange and can trade like a listed stock during trading hours.[6] Investors can trade shares in ETFs as a single security. The American Stock Exchange listed the first ETF, the Standard & Poor's depositary receipt (SPDR), in 1993. Since the first listing, the ETF market has experienced a tremendous growth. The number of ETFs increased from just 7 in 1997 to 190 in August 2005 and to 298 by August 2006. The total assets in ETFs were $19 billion in 1997, and increased to $227 billion in 2004 and to $358 billion by August 2006.[7]

There are a wide variety of mutual funds, with investment objectives ranging from sector to country to index. Many are actively managed, while some are passive, index type of funds. ETFs are mostly index type covering broad stock market, industry sector, international stock, and U.S. bond indexes. These ETFs add the ease and liquidity of trading to the benefits of traditional index investing. Examples of ETFs include Nasdaq-100 Index Tracking Stock, S&P 500 Index, Fortune 500 Tracking Stock, iShares Russell 2000, iShares MSCI-Brazil, iShares MSCI Emerging Markets, and iShares Lehman 1-3 Year Treasury Bond Fund. What ETFs do not yet offer are the actively managed funds that have been widely available in mutual funds. Thus, investors wanting the growth potential of an actively managed fund have to invest money in traditional mutual funds. It is worth noting that several ETF professionals have indicated that the introduction of ETFs with a certain degree of "active management" is under way.

Investing or trading ETFs has several advantages. As noted earlier, ETFs trade like a stock during trading hours. ETFs trade at intraday market prices, not the end of the day net asset value for a typical mutual fund purchase or redemption. The second advantage is the ability to purchase on margin and sell short, even on a downtick. This is significant, as investors cannot sell mutual funds short or purchase them on margin. Investors can also place stop loss and limit orders on ETFs.

Tax efficiency is another advantage that ETFs offers. An ETF trade is between investors, there is neither new money nor redemption. Low portfolio turnover generates fewer capital gains than mutual funds, especially actively managed ones. An ETF generally sells securities to reflect changes in the composition of the corresponding index. As such, ETFs incur lower turnover costs and lower operational costs.

Compared with actively managed funds, ETFs provide a high degree of transparency. ETFs are designed to track the performance similar to the underlying index. Thus, the securities and their weightings in the portfolio are readily available.

For institutional investors, ETFs provide several additional advantages. Many institutional investors often use futures to buy or sell exposure to an index. However, to gain long-term exposure, institutions have to roll those positions, usually on a quarterly basis. Trading ETFs is simpler and costs can be lower. For certain institutions that are not permitted to use futures, ETFs serve as an efficient alternative. Furthermore, ETFs offer exposure to sectors or indexes that might not be available with futures.

HEDGE FUNDS

A hedge fund is a private investment fund that employs investment strategies involving various types of securities in various markets. The defining characteristic of a hedge fund is that it can take both long and short positions, and use leverage and derivatives. These private investment partnerships suffered a setback in the late 1990s when they produced poor performance and several went bankrupt. In recent years, hedge funds' strong performance has found them many fans among pension plans, charities, school endowments, and rich individuals. Wall Street houses have established or bought into hedge funds to take advantage of the rising demand for such alternative investments. For example, JPMorgan Chase purchased Highbridge Capital Management in 2004 to ride such trends. There are over 8,000 hedge funds managing about $1.5 trillion by 2007.

Hedge funds now operate in currency, government securities, derivatives, and commodities transactions as well as merger and acquisition activities. Some use complex computer models to place huge bets on movements in financial markets. In the late 1990s, hedge funds received significant attention from the news media and government regulators. The Long Term Capital Management (LTCM) crisis in 1998 raised concern about whether greater regulatory oversight in the hedge fund industry was needed. As a result, the SEC has proposed rules to require registration of hedge fund managers.

Hedge Fund Structure

Hedge funds are structured as limited partnership to avoid the application of most securities laws (Figure 13.1). Offshore hedge funds are organized in locations outside of the United States and offered to non-U.S. residents. There are two types of partners in a hedge fund, a general partner (GP) and limited partners (LPs). The GP is the entity

FIGURE 13.1   Hedge Fund Structure

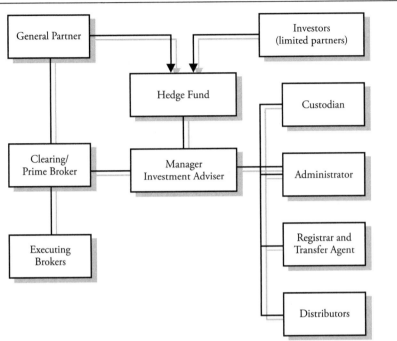

Note: Investors (limited partners) and the general partner invest money in the hedge fund. The general partner manages the fund ("Manager"). Other parties provide services necessary to carry out the fund's investment strategies and service investors.

who started the hedge fund. The GP handles all trading and day-to-day operations. The LPs contribute most of the capital but are not involved in trading or day-to-day operations. Note that individual investors now have access to hedge fund investing. They can buy shares of a hedge fund company that has listed shares on the exchange. For example, Fortress Investment Group LLC went public and listed its shares on the NYSE. Investors trade this hedge fund company stock just like any other listed stocks.

The typical entity of a GP is the limited liability partnership (LLP). The LLP is preferred because the GP of a limited partnership is not liable beyond the extent of his investment in a limited partnership. The GP often serves as the fund manager. Sometimes the GP relies on advice by an investment adviser to identify investment opportunities.

The GP and LPs typically sign a partnership agreement. The partnership agreement covers some of the following items:

- Investment objectives, strategies, and risk factors
- When limited partners can invest, increase investments, and withdraw from the fund
- Details of management fee and incentive fees
- Details of how full withdraws will be handled

The majority of U.S. hedge funds charge the standard 1 percent management fee and 20 percent incentive fees. The 1 percent fee is usually charged in 0.25 percent increments quarterly, in advance. However, some charge higher fees.

Most funds observe a "high-water mark." If in a given performance fee period a fund loses money, the investors will not be charged in later periods until the losses have been recovered. Another variation is the "preferred return" where a fund will not collect an incentive fee until a certain set rate of return has been achieved. Furthermore, most funds require a minimum duration of investments into the funds, known as the lockup period. The common lockup period is one year, even though a three-year lockup is not unheard of.

Prime brokerage is a suite of services providing hedge funds with custody, clearance, financing, and securities lending. These services make it possible for the hedge fund to have multiple brokers while maintaining one brokerage account. A prime broker acts as the back office for the fund by providing the operational services necessary for the money manager to effectively manage his business. This enables the GP to focus on investment strategies rather than on operational issues. The services a good prime broker provides include:

- Centralized custody
- Clearance
- Securities lending
- Competitive financing rates
- One debit balance/one credit balance
- Real time, daily, monthly, and annual portfolio accounting
- Position and balance validation
- Electronic trade download
- Wash sale reports
- Office facilities in selected markets

Management Style

Hedge fund managers use many different management styles and pursue various trading strategies. The risk to investors depends on the specific strategy pursued by the fund. As indicated in Table 13.5, a market-neutral strategy has low risk while emerging markets and macro styles post very high risks. Very few funds use only one strategy, and some change their investment styles over time. Even with the same investment style, the risks sometimes vary considerably. This can be largely explained by the differing liquidity of the fund's assets. For example, David Askin's funds (Granite Partners, Granite Corp, and Quartz Hedge Fund) were classified as market neutral. Nevertheless, Askin's investments proved to be extremely risky, as the market for mortgage-backed securities became very thin and eventually caused the collapse of his highly leveraged hedge funds in 1994. Another good example is Long Term Capital Management, which was also classified as market neutral. When Russia's default on its debt obligations in 1998 triggered a flight-to-quality and a flight-to-liquidity, liquidity in the global financial system dried up, and LTCM nearly collapsed. Another fund

TABLE 13.5 Hedge Fund Investment Styles

Style	Definition	Holding Period	Expected Volatility
Emerging markets	Invest in emerging markets; shorting is not permitted in some markets, so managers must resort to other alternatives to hedge	Short/ medium term	Very high
Short only	Go only short on securities	Medium	Very high
Macro	Strategies designed to profit from major currency or interest rate shifts	Medium	Very high
Sector play	Invest in a specific sector of the market	Medium	High
Distressed	Invest primarily in securities of companies in bankruptcy or reorganization	Medium/ long	Moderate
Growth	Dominant theme involves high-growth firms	Medium/ long	Moderate
Risk arbitrage	Simultaneously long the target and short the acquirer	Medium	Moderate
Convertible arbitrage	Long convertible securities and short the underlying equities	Medium	Low
High yield	Invest mainly in noninvestment-grade securities	Medium	Moderate
Event driven	Play on anticipated event	Medium	Moderate
Value	Dominant theme is intrinsic value: asset, cash flow, book value, and out-of-favor stock	Long	Low/ moderate
Opportunistic	Momentum trading with short-term horizon	Short	Low/ moderate
Market neutral	Combine positions to create a zero-beta portfolio	Short/ medium	Low
Convergence	Exploit temporary out-of-line relationships; take profits when relationships among various securities return to historical norm	Short/ medium	Low

Sources: Hennessee Hedge Fund Advisory Group and Van Hedge Fund Advisors, 2004.

betting on convergence plays went bust in 2006. Amaranth Advisors, based in Greenwich, Connecticut, made a convergence bet on the spread between two futures contracts. On September 18, 2006, the fund told its investors that it had lost more than $3 billion in the downturn of natural gas. By April of 2007, it had stopped operations.

Hedge Fund Performance

Hedge funds are extremely flexible in their investment options because they use financial instruments that are generally beyond the reach of mutual funds. This flexibility, which includes the use of hedging strategies to protect downside risk, gives hedge funds the ability to better manage investment risks. Studies have shown that hedge funds usually provide excellent returns to investors. Sources of such information include Hennessee Hedge Fund Advisory Group, Van Hedge Fund Advisors, and the Hedge Fund Association.

The strong performance results of hedge funds can be linked to their performance incentives, in addition to their investment flexibility. The hedge fund GP is usually heavily invested in a significant portion of the fund and shares the rewards as well as the risks. The incentive fee remunerates the hedge fund managers in accordance with their performance. In contrast, mutual funds generally pay managers a fixed percentage of the amount of money attracted, regardless of performance. This incentive fee structure tends to attract many of Wall Street's best practitioners to the hedge fund industry.

Nevertheless, the collapse of LTCM and the failures of several other hedge funds in 1998 suggested that the hedge fund industry was becoming the victim of its own success. First of all, the star managers were attracting too much money so it was difficult to find similar investment opportunities to get top returns. At the same time, talent was being diluted, meaning that some managers lacked the necessary skills to succeed. And with more and more funds pursuing similar trading strategies, the markets were becoming more efficient and less profitable. Under pressure to produce, some funds were using more leverage and/or changing management styles. Furthermore, many star traders could not do as well on their own as they did when with a Wall Street house. Once independent, they lost the support a big firm provides in risk monitoring, advanced technology, and multiple levels of management and governance.

In recent years, hedge funds have made a comeback. Many produced above average market returns to investors. As a result, these private investment partnerships have raised management fees and upped the incentive fees as well.

REAL ESTATE INVESTMENT TRUSTS

Real estate has been an exceptional asset class in recent years. Its performance topped most other asset classes. Even if it does not produce high returns, real estate still deserves a place in a portfolio in the long run. A real estate investment trust (REIT) is an investment company that pools funds from investors and invests in income-producing residential and commercial properties. The REITs differ from stocks in that they are engaged exclusively in the real estate business. Otherwise, they pay dividends and may be listed on an exchange. As large blocks of real estate become equitized, investment opportunities in REITs will expand.

The REIT market has grown from 75 REITs with a market capitalization of $2.3 billion in 1980 to 183 REITs with a capitalization of $438.0 billion by the end of 2006. This growth is attributable to several factors. First, REITs are liquid investments. Many REITs, like closed-end funds, are listed and traded on exchanges. Thus, investors can buy and sell interests in diversified portfolios of properties easily. Second, REITs have a unique corporate structure that requires them to distribute at least 95 percent of their income to shareholders. Hence, they pay high dividends to investors. They are also free from taxation at the corporate level. Third, returns on REITs are competitive. During the period 1981 to 2000, the average annual return for equity REITs was 12.43 percent. During that time, the average returns for U.S. small stocks and the S&P 500 Index were 13.33 percent and 15.68 percent, respectively. In 2004, REITs returned investors 30.4 percent, topping most other stock market benchmarks. Furthermore, REITs represent a good source of diversification for investment portfolios. During the period 1993 to 2000, the correlation of REIT returns with that of small stocks was 0.26; with the S&P 500, it was 0.25; and with long-term bonds, it was 0.16.

There are three types of REITs. An equity REIT is a corporation that purchases, owns, and manages real estate properties. The revenues come from rent. A mortgage REIT is a corporation that purchases, owns, and manages real estate loans. Its revenues come from interest from the mortgage loans. The third type is a hybrid REIT that combines the investment strategies of both equity REITs and mortgage REITs. Among these three types, equity REITs account for the biggest share of the total market by far. In 2006, for example, equity REITs accounted for $400.7 billion of the $438.0 billion total market capitalization of REITs.

CONCLUSION

China's high savings rate and low mutual fund penetration present a high growth opportunity for investment management. China's venture capital and private equity business is booming. Real estate investment trusts and hedge funds are the next wave. This chapter reviewed those important investment vehicles and discussed how foreign institutions participate in China's domestic markets.

III

PROFITABLE
INVESTMENTS IN CHINA

14

Profit from Investment Opportunities in China

It is important for an investor, either individual or institutional, to create a portfolio that reflects the objectives and constraints laid out in the investment policy. Asset allocation deals with how the funds in the portfolio will be divided among the various asset classes, including Chinese securities. Asset allocation is an important component in determining not only the risk and return of the portfolio, but also the composition of those returns. Allocating a certain portion of funds in Chinese securities is prudent as it provides for a better diversification and a higher return potential. This chapter discusses the various industries in China and explains asset allocation and the investing mechanics. In the next several chapters, we cover growth investing, value investing, and U.S. instruments that investors can use to profit from China's growth without going to China to make a direct investment.

OVERVIEW

Many Chinese companies have listed their shares overseas on exchanges such as NYSE, NASDAQ, or London. Those securities are available for investors outside China to purchase. In addition, some mutual funds, open-end or closed-end, invest in those securities or acquire shares in China directly. This section briefly reviews the various industries in China, some present opportunities for investments though some do not, yet. Selecting securities in different industries helps investors achieve diversification. Which Chinese securities to add depends on the investor's objectives, investment horizon, risk tolerance, and the holdings in the current portfolio. The brief description in this section is meant to provide an indication of which industries might have promising potentials.[1]

Aerospace and Aircraft

China's air transportation passenger volume is expected to grow annually by 8.5 percent. It is becoming the world's second largest aviation market and will need to acquire an additional large number of aircraft to handle the volume. For example, Shanghai Pudong International Airport was completed just several years ago and now is very crowded. It is not unusual for a visitor to wait for customs clearance for a long time. Expansion of the airport infrastructure is necessary. The increasing demand for airplanes benefits Boeing and Air Bus Industries. Furthermore, a new system of regional control centers and full conversion from program to radar-based air traffic control will be phased in over the next 10 to 15 years.

Agricultural Chemicals

China is one of the biggest agrochemical markets and a large agrochemical importer. Potash Corporation of Saskatchewan, Inc. (Potash Corp), engages in the production and sale of fertilizer, has seen its stock price surge because of its export to China. Agrochemical exports to China rank as the top destination among U.S. fertilizer exports. China's goal is to rely less on fertilizer imports in the future. However, the country lacks potassium resources and its phosphate is difficult to recover. Domestic output of fertilizer still cannot meet the total market demand, forcing China to import high-concentration and compound fertilizers.

China's accession to the WTO provides benefits to U.S. fertilizer exporters. WTO commitments stipulate that all quotas must be fully allocated, forbidding the past practice of limiting imports by only allocating a certain portion of the quota each year. Most significantly, foreign firms gained the right to import and distribute fertilizers, gradually dismantling the state-controlled trading monopoly. The stage is set for greater market access for U.S. suppliers; however, the appearance of nontariff barriers and a lack of transparency in the allocation process remain a problem.

Architecture Construction Engineering

The Beijing 2008 Olympics, the Western Development Strategy, and National Housing Reform all provide enormous opportunities for foreign companies to gain from China's architecture construction engineering (ACE) market. China's construction industry has experienced consistent growth over the past several years. Infrastructure investment was a key element of China's Tenth Five Year Plan (2001–2005), which focused on roads, rail systems, bridges, ports, and airports. This has led to an increasing number of foreign ACE firms involved in China. The exchange of design concepts, project management experience, and construction techniques has been invaluable to both foreign and local ACE firms. Several infrastructure funds from the United States invest in China's infrastructure.

The construction industry has contributed to the sustainable development of China's economy. According to statistics from the State Statistics Bureau, the construction industry accounts for 6.6 percent of the national GDP, making it the fourth biggest industry over the past five years. China's entry to the WTO stimulated demand for ACE services in projects such as hotels, high-rise buildings, and housing. Foreign investment has also been stimulated by this growth.

Financial Services

China's banking system has undergone significant changes in the past two decades. China's accession to WTO has led to a significant opening of this industry to foreign participation.

China's entry into the WTO has also created opportunities for foreign banks. To honor its WTO commitments, China released the Rules for Implementing the Regulations Governing Foreign Financial Institutions in the People's Republic of China in January 2002. The rules provide detailed regulations for implementing the administration of the establishment, registration, scope of business, qualification, supervision, dissolution, and liquidation of foreign financial institutions. Since then, several U.S. firms have acquired stakes in Chinese financial institutions. A Citigroup-led consortium has gained control of Guangdong Development Bank, well beyond the equity percentage limit set by the Chinese government. Several Chinese banks, including Bank of China and ICBC, have floated shares.

Computers and Telecommunications

Computing has entered a network era and related information technology sectors have witnessed rapid growth and many new digital products are entering the China market. Though domestic firms make competitive products, foreign involvement in technology and new ventures are expanding.

The rapid expansion of the Internet infrastructure in China attracts a growing number of new business ventures. For computing and network companies, the provision of personal computers, information appliances, routers, broadband switches, fiber optic networks, and digital wireless devices means new business. The China Internet Network Information Center (CNNIC) foresees high growth of these networks. As prices and demand adjusts in the Chinese market, American firms must aim to meet the challenges and opportunities.

Education

U.S. colleges, universities, and other training services are in a strong position to fulfill China's training needs. Short-term training programs or workshops in specialized fields as well as business education are particularly sought after. U.S. educational organizations can also sell teaching materials and equipment, convey the latest methodologies, lend or exchange faculty, and provide educational consulting services.

According to market surveys, Chinese consumers would spend 10 percent of their savings on education, meaning that the education market from a consumer perspective is worth at least $80 billion. In cities with populations of 10 million or more, at least 5 percent of families could and would pay for education costing more than $14,500. The Chinese government also plans to increase spending on education dramatically, from its budget allocation of 2.5 percent of gross domestic product to 4 percent, to meet China's education needs for the future. More and more middle-class

Chinese are borrowing to send their only child abroad to receive an international degree that would give them an advantage in China's increasingly competitive marketplace.[2] Chinese professionals are also attending vocational classes and using e-learning to upgrade their skills to increase their earning power.

Environmental Technologies

China's environmental problems stem from a deteriorating natural resource base, dense population, heavy reliance on soft coal, underpriced water and energy, and unprecedented industrial growth. The World Bank estimated that air and water pollution cost the Chinese economy up to 8 percent of GDP. In response, Beijing has unleashed a burst of environmental legislation to reduce its total pollution discharge.

However, local enforcement of environmental laws is spotty, investment in pollution control infrastructure inadequate, and competition from domestic firms increasingly strong. Products enjoying the best sales prospects include low-cost flue gas desulfurization systems, air and water monitoring instruments, drinking water purification products, vehicle emissions control and inspection devices, industrial wastewater treatment equipment, and resource recovery technologies.

Food Packaging Equipment

China's rapid economic growth means people's lifestyles change and standards of living rise. Under China's economic reform policies, most industries including the food, printing, plastics, pharmaceutical, and chemical industries, have developed rapidly. This has resulted in increasing demand for packaging and therefore packaging machinery.

Health Care Products and Services

China's medical device market is the largest in Asia outside Japan, and is one of the fastest growing in the world. The instability of the regulatory environment still negatively effects profit expectations. Over the next 10 to 12 years, however, China should deliver the type of returns it is very much capable of.

Energy

China's overall energy consumption ranks second in the world. Gasoline is a big component of the overall demand. There exists great potential in the domestic natural gas market. The consumption demand for natural gas in the power sector, chemical and fertilizer industries, and city gas grids will grow rapidly. If this trend continues through 2010, demand for gas is expected to reach 120 billion cubic meters and by 2020 to 220 billion cubic meters, or 10 percent of primary energy consumption.

China's growing demand for energy has caused this traditionally off-limits sector to gradually open up to increasingly larger scale foreign participation. Moreover, offshore industries with high technology components are in high demand. The best opportunities for U.S. participation are in natural gas infrastructure development and offshore oil exploration and production. Onshore oil projects are not as attractive due to lack of access to satisfactory leverage and geological data and a greater tendency to source equipment, services, and technology domestically. The offshore sector is more promising, where the technical challenges are greater and thus the value of foreign technical services more easily recognized by Chinese operators.

Plastic Materials and Resins

During the 10th five-year plan, the annual growth rate of general synthetic resins was about 6.8 percent and engineering plastics materials was 10 percent. However, the local output of plastics materials and resins can only satisfy 50 percent of market demand. As a result, China must import large quantities of plastics materials each year. The local market requires imports of general-purpose thermoplastic resins, including polyethylene (LDPE and HDPE), polypropylene, polystyrene, acrylonitrile butadiene styrene, and polyvinyl chloride. This market is subject to fluctuation of upstream supply and downstream market demand.

Power Generation

Investment in China's power industry is gaining momentum. Official statistics show power consumption growth in China averaging 7.8 percent annually throughout the 1990s. Starting from the second half of 2002, China's electricity supply was far short of demand because of dry spells that deceased hydroelectric supply, a generator shortage, and increased demand from energy-intensive industries. During this period, 21 provinces, municipalities, and autonomous regions in China suffered large-scale electricity shortages. Some had to implement blackouts to limit electricity consumption.

According to the International Energy Agency, to meet rapidly growing electricity demand, China will invest a total of nearly $2 trillion in electricity generation, transmission, and distribution in the next 30 years. Half of the amount will be invested in power generation; the other half will go to transmission and distribution.

Retail

As one of the first few sectors opened to foreign investment after China's WTO accession, the country's retail sector has witnessed booming growth with the influx of foreign retail giants. More than half of the world's top 50 retailers have entered China. Most of them have opened stores in Beijing, Shanghai, and other coastal cities. Competition in the retail sector is intense, as the growth in supply outpaces demand, leading to a decline in prices. Although the retail market is still dominated by domestic brands, foreign brands have made significant inroads. Foreign brands are particularly popular with the younger generations and the newly rich.

Security and Fire Prevention

China's safety and security market demand is growing rapidly. The market has expanded from its traditional base in the financial, insurance, custom, police, airport, and IT sectors to the construction, transportation, and education fields. In 2003, the Chinese safety and security equipment market was $7 billion. Industry experts estimated that by 2020 China's safety and security market will reach $30 billion.

By 2010 China will have 240 airports. With 100 new airports to be constructed in the next few years, airport security has become a critical safety issue for the Chinese government. Increasing tourism and a rise in air cargo volume will also necessitate an upgrade of security technology at existing airports to improve safety and efficiency.

Much of the safety and security demand will focus on high-tech equipment, such as digital technology, entrance guard communication systems, network technology for inspection control systems, and warning systems.

Machine Tools

One of the main drivers for increased demand in China for U.S. machinery products is the expansion of China's manufacturing capacity and increased competition among Chinese manufacturers. The automotive industry accounts for over half of China's machine tool industry and has been driving growth in this sector for the past few years.

In order to deal with the increased market opportunities and competition resulting from entry into the WTO, China has placed high emphasis on upgrading its conventional industries with more advanced high-tech machinery and equipment. China is also moving rapidly to restructure the state-owned enterprises. These two initiatives, along with the start up of numerous major national projects, are stimulating rapid growth in the demand for machine tool and tooling products in China. As a result, market opportunities exist for machine tool builders, as China is expected to continue to import advanced equipment and technology valued in the tens of billions of dollars.

Travel and Tourism

China has become one of the world's most-watched and hottest outbound tourist markets. With average growth of 10 percent and the rising income, a significant number of Chinese now have sufficient resources to spend on travel. According to the World Tourism Organization, China is projected to supply 100 million travelers by 2020, making it the number one supplier of outbound tourists.

There is clearly huge growth potential for the U.S. travel industry in China. In terms of total travel spending, China is currently ranked seventh and is expected to be the second-fastest growing in the world from 2006 to 2015, jumping into the number two slot for total travel spend by 2015.

Automotive

Under the protectionist policies, China's automotive industry has witnessed rapid growth since the country opened up to the outside world and adopted economic reforms. Now China is capable of manufacturing a complete line of automobile products and large automotive enterprises, such as the China First Automobile Group Corp. (FAW), Dongfeng Motor Corp. (DMC) and Shanghai Automotive Industry Corp. (SAIC), have flourished. Currently, domestic motor vehicles have more than 95 percent market share. Furthermore, Chery is now exporting automobile to the United States.

Since 1998, 50 percent of motor vehicles (cars and Trucks) in China have been purchased by individuals. As economic development continues, this percentage will steadily grow and they will become the dominant force bringing growth in China's automobile market. As incomes increase the high annual growth rate of private ownership is expected to accelerate.

China's accession to the WTO has helped facilitate the development of the automobile market by encouraging an open, rational market structure. However, membership in the WTO also means reduction of tariffs, abolition of nontariff barriers, and the opening up of the country's service sector. China's domestic auto industry will face increasing competition as the market becomes internationalized.

ALLOCATION TO CHINESE ASSETS

In recent years, many investors place some portion of their wealth in international securities, developed and emerging markets. China is the most important emerging market, and thus, many have decided to invest in China. The discussions in this chapter and the next chapters focus on Chinese securities listed in the United States and funds that invest in China. All those instruments trade in the United States.

Studies have found that there is a relatively low correlation between U.S. and overseas securities. It means that investors will receive a higher return for a given level of risk than by simply investing domestically. When investing internationally, investors need to consider several factors:

- Security performance in other countries
- Possible changes in the exchange rate
- Whether to hedge the exchange rate or not
- The degree of correlation between the foreign country's securities and U.S. securities

- The political risks
- Differing monetary policies, which can impact inflation and interest rates
- The higher transactions costs that are likely to occur from overseas investing
- Difficulties in obtaining data
- Different accounting standards
- Differing settlement procedures

When considering investments overseas in countries such as China, it is essential to consider possible changes in the exchange rate. For now, most anticipate Chinese currency to appreciate. But, in general, an appreciation of the dollar relative to the foreign currency will lead to a lower dollar denominated return because the investor will receive fewer dollars when converting the foreign currency back to dollars. Likewise, a depreciating dollar can enhance dollar returns as an investor receives more dollars when converting the foreign currency back to dollars.

Interest rate parity is an important factor that drives the decision to hedge or not. Interest rate parity states that the forward return is effectively equal to the difference between interest rates in the two countries. Therefore, the cash rates in the two countries will play an important part in determining the hedging decision.

There are several differing views regarding the currency decision. Some believe that the expected return to a portfolio of currencies should in the long run be equal to zero, making hedging unnecessary. Others believe that the low degree of correlation between currency returns and foreign market returns make hedging detrimental because it reduces some of the diversification benefits of holding the foreign currency. Still others argue that while foreign currency exposure leads to diversification benefits, it also introduces risk into the picture.[3] Money manager and author, Mark Kritzman, argued that the decision depends on the degree of correlation between the foreign asset returns and the exchange rate return. When the correlation is zero, he showed that the optimal strategy is to remain unhedged and when the correlation is 75 percent, then the optimal strategy is to be fully hedged. Kritzman's analysis shows that when there is a high degree of correlation between the foreign asset's returns and the exchange rate, there are no diversification benefits from remaining unhedged. Therefore, hedging should be employed. However, when the degree of correlation is relatively low, investors receive greater diversification benefits by remaining unhedged.

Market selection and currency decision are related. When there is no forward exchange market, then the two decisions need to be considered jointly. However, when a forward exchange market does exist, the foreign investment decision should be separated into the market decision and the currency decision.[4] The decision to invest in a foreign country is based on the risk premium offered in that country regardless of the country of the investor. Once the market decision has been made (such as investing in China), the decision to hedge or not, is determined by a simple comparison of the forward return compared to the expected percentage change in exchange rates. If the forward return is greater than the expected change in exchange rates, then it is advantageous to hedge. If the forward return is less than the expected change in exchange rates, then the investor will receive a higher return by remaining unhedged.

Investors will choose to invest in the country that offers the greatest risk premium. The currency decision is then based on hedging into the currency that offers the greatest potential. In the case of international bond management, the decision to hedge or not becomes even more critical. The higher degree of correlation between interest rates and exchange rates makes the currency decision much more important in the case of bonds.

Emerging Markets

When considering diversification into international markets (such as China), investors usually treat investments in developed nations differently from those in developing or emerging markets. Emerging markets can represent excellent opportunities for investing and can add diversification to an investor's portfolio. For a country to attract the capital of foreign investors, it must be investable.

There are several things that make emerging markets investing attractive. The first is the growth potential offered by industries in these countries. Second, emerging markets tend to exhibit a low degree of correlation with developed nations, thus they provide diversification benefits in addition to growth opportunities. Third, emerging market countries tend to exhibit a low degree of correlation with other emerging market countries, thus a well diversified portfolio of emerging markets securities may not be as inherently risky as one would believe.

There are several factors that make investments in emerging markets more risky than developed nations. First, because of the immaturity of these types of markets we can expect greater volatility. In addition, many investors tend to incorrectly link all emerging markets together, thus a crisis in one emerging country can spread quickly to another even when the crisis tends to be a local problem. A second risk with investing in emerging markets deals with liquidity. Many of these markets are not highly liquid and therefore buying and selling significant numbers of shares can be difficult and costly. Third, clearing and settlement procedures may not be well established in these markets. Fourth, there may be political risks involved in these countries. Finally, currency fluctuations can add additional risks to emerging market investments. As discussed in the previous section, if no practical forward exchange market exists, then the market and currency decisions need to be made jointly.

Strategic and Tactical Asset Allocation

Asset allocation is the most important decision an investor will make. How an investor's assets are allocated among the various classes of investment vehicles will not only determine the risks the investor takes, but the composition of returns (income versus capital gains), which in turn can affect tax liabilities.

The issue in asset allocation is how the pie should be divided among the different asset classes. Establishing the objectives and constraints of the investment is the first step in the portfolio management process. Once the policy statement has been established, an asset allocation can be made. The asset allocation decision can be broken into two parts. The long-run decision is determined by the investment policy statement and is referred to as the strategic asset allocation decision. The strategic decision determines the allocation of the policy portfolio. The short-run decision is referred to as tactical asset allocation. Tactical asset allocation refers to deviations from the policy portfolio. Good asset allocation requires that the investor continues to monitor conditions and adjust both the strategic and tactical asset allocation decisions.

Dynamic Asset Allocation and Portfolio Insurance

Dynamic asset allocation seeks to adjust the mix of assets in an effort to improve the return on the portfolio. There are three methods for portfolio asset allocation.[5] In a buy and hold strategy, the investor decides on an allocation for the portfolio and maintains that allocation regardless of what happens in the market. For example, an investor may choose a 60 percent stock, 40 percent bond allocation for his portfolio. As stock prices change relative to bond prices, the allocation will move away from the original 60/40 mix. This strategy is sometimes referred to as a drifting mix strategy, because the investor does not rebalance the portfolio to return to the designated allocation.

There are a number of advantages of the buy and hold strategy. First, because an investor does not choose to trade often, he reduces his transactions costs and possible capital gains tax liability. Second, by leaving the portfolio intact, he eliminates the mistakes that would be made by buying and selling securities at the wrong times. One disadvantage of the buy and hold strategy is that the investor's portfolio allocation may become overly weighted in stocks if the market is rising or under weighted in stocks if the market is falling. This "do nothing" strategy may cause the investor to move away from his original risk/return objectives.

In a constant mix strategy, the investor decides on an allocation for the portfolio and rebalances the portfolio periodically to maintain these proportions. For example, if the investor chooses to place 60 percent in stocks and 40 percent in bonds (a 60/40 mix), he will sell stocks if stock prices rise and use the proceeds to purchase bonds in order to maintain the 60/40 mix. Likewise, he will sell bonds and use the proceeds to purchase stocks if stock prices fall. The constant mix strategy has an investor selling as stock prices rise and buying as stock prices fall.

The advantage of a constant mix strategy is that it imposes a discipline on the investor to sell stocks as the market rises and buy stocks as the market falls. One disadvantage of this strategy is that it can lead to increased transactions costs and tax liabilities in volatile markets.

In a constant proportion strategy, the investor determines the amount to invest in stocks based on the following formula:

Dollars in stocks = m(Assets − Floor)

To implement the strategy, the investor sets the multiplier, m, and the floor. Strategies with a multiplier greater than one are referred to as constant proportion portfolio insurance strategies (CPPI). In this strategy, as stock prices fall and the value of assets gets smaller, the investor will reduce his holding in stocks and increase his holdings in bonds. Similarly, as stock prices rise and the value of assets increases, the investor will increase his holdings of stocks. Therefore, CPPI has investors buying into a rising market and selling as the market falls.

The purposes of CPPI is to protect the portfolio on the downside by reducing stock exposure as stock prices fall, while still maintaining upside potential by forcing the investor to add to his stock position as the market rises. In essence, the CPPI strategy creates a synthetic call option, that is, a strategy that has limited downside risk but still retains the opportunity to profit if price rises.[6]

Which strategy performs the best will depend on the direction and volatility of the market.[7] In a flat but oscillating market (one that goes up and down but finishes near its starting point), a constant mix strategy will prevail because it forces the investor to sell stocks when they are high and to buy them back as stock prices fall. However, this type of market can be devastating to the CPPI strategy because it forces the investor to sell stocks when they are low and repurchase them after they have rebounded. The buy and hold strategy will perform somewhere in between the constant mix and CPPI strategies.

In a bull market where reversals are uncommon, the constant mix strategy will have the worst performance because it forces the investor to sell stocks as the market is rising, only to see stocks rise further. The CPPI strategy will perform the best because it forces the investor to increase the amount of stocks held in the portfolio as the market rises. Once again, the performance of the buy and hold strategy will lie somewhere between the other two strategies.

Finally, if the market continues in a downward spiral, CPPI will perform the best because it forces the investor to bail out of stocks as stock prices fall. The constant mix strategy will have the worst performance because it will force the investor to buy stocks as prices are falling, only to see the prices fall even further.

Investing Styles

Investment styles can be grouped into three broad categories. Growth investors seek the stocks of companies that generate consistent increases in sales and income from one year to the next. The rate of sales and earnings growth among these stocks is generally greater than the majority of their peers. These types of stocks usually offer little or no dividend payment to investors since most earnings are retained and reinvested in a firm's business. Growth stocks typically have a high P/E ratio because investors are willing to pay a premium for growth. Google is a good example of a growth stock. Its revenues have grown fast in recent years. Its stock price has also posted dramatic gains throughout this time period.

Value investors search for stocks that are selling at a bargain price. They tend to look at the total value of a company's assets and compare it to the stock price. A stock that trades below the value of assets could be a bargain. Another method that value investors use is to compare a stock's P/E ratio with stocks of similar businesses. If the P/E of a company's stock is less than the P/E of its industry peers, the stock could be selling at a discount. A value investor would typically purchase this stock with the notion that its price will eventually rise to bring its P/E in line with its peers.

Momentum investors look for rising stock prices that appear to have enough inertia to rise even higher. These types of investors usually own a stock for a short period of time—hoping to generate some quick profits before the stock price peaks.

TRADING MECHANICS

Chapters 17 through 19 describe how U.S. investors can invest in various Chinese stocks, mutual funds, or exchange-traded funds in the United States. Thus, the following description focuses on trading mechanics in the United States.

Specialists versus Market Makers

In order for a market to function smoothly, an individual or institution needs to facilitate the transactions in a market by ensuring that a buyer exists for those who wish to sell and a seller exists for those who wish to buy. This facilitator is known as a market maker. Market makers exist in both auction markets such as the New York Stock Exchange (NYSE) and in the over-the-counter markets such as NASDAQ. These market makers use their own capital to purchase an inventory of securities where they are market makers. With this inventory of securities, the market maker is in a position to provide liquidity to the market by purchasing from sellers and selling to buyers.

On exchanges such as the NYSE and AMEX, market makers also serve as specialists. Specialist responsibilities differ from the market maker because they are responsible for maintaining a fair and orderly market. Unlike market makers, who are not required to undertake a transaction, specialists are obligated to maintain an orderly market by buying from sellers when other buyers cannot be found and selling to buyers when there is a shortage of sellers. It is essential that the specialist performs this job well because of a rating system that is used by the NYSE. This rating system plays an important role in determining new stock allocations by the NYSE.

One valuable piece of information the specialist has is the limit-order book, which contains limit orders placed by brokers. This information is valuable to the specialist in allowing him to know what traders are thinking. Even though this information may give the specialist an advantage over other market participants, he cannot use this information to trade ahead of clients, an activity that is known as front running.

Specialists earn their income by providing both the broker and dealer functions. In an actively traded stock, the specialist has little need to act as a dealer and therefore derives most of his income from the broker function. In stocks that have low trading volume and high price volatility, the specialist will need to provide more of the functions of a dealer and therefore earn most of his income from the bid-asked spread. A specialist can deal in more than one stock, however, there will only be one specialist per stock. In general, specialists balance the risks of market making by specializing in some high volume, low risk stocks and some higher risk securities.

Brokers

Without a middle person, it can be extremely costly for a market participant to find another investor who will take the other half of the transaction. For example, a buyer may have difficulty locating a seller and a seller may have difficulty locating a buyer. Therefore, this type of market allows a broker to serve as a middleman between buyers and sellers. There are several types of brokers. Commission brokers are employees of a firm that has membership on the exchange. These brokers buy and sell for customers of the firm. When an order is placed with a firm, the firm may contact its commission broker on the floor of the exchange, who will then go to the appropriate post on the floor and buy or sell shares as instructed. Floor brokers are independent members of an exchange who act as brokers for other members. During busy times, a member firm may need the services of a floor broker in order to handle all of its orders. Floor brokers were once referred to as $2 brokers because that was what they were paid for each order.

The difference between brokers and market makers is that brokers do not put their own capital at risk by holding an inventory of securities. They simply receive a commission for helping others complete the transaction.

Dealers

Trading begins with the investor's decision with regard to the security he wishes to trade and the type of order he wishes to place. The security that the investor wishes to purchase determines where the security will be purchased. For example, some securities trade on listed exchanges such as the NYSE and others trade in the over-the-counter market. Stocks and bonds that trade in the over-the-counter market must be purchased from a dealer or market maker in that security. In a dealer market, the dealer holds an inventory of the security and is willing to sell at offer price and willing to buy at the bid price. The difference between the sell and buy price is referred to as the bid-asked spread and represents what the dealer earns. The spread is determined by a number of factors including the stock's price volatility and trading volume. Because of the reduced price risk to the dealer, more liquid, less volatile stocks will tend to have narrower spreads. In an exchange-listed security, buyers and sellers come together to negotiate price directly in what is referred to as an auction market. However, even in auction markets like the NYSE, the specialist exists to ensure sufficient liquidity of the security.

Types of Accounts

Investors may open any of several types of accounts at a brokerage house. The most basic type of account is the cash account. With a cash account, the customer pays the brokerage house the full transaction value for any securities purchased and does not borrow any funds from the brokerage firm. Alternatively, investors may open a margin account that allows them to borrow money from the brokerage firm to purchase securities. Margin accounts are subject to various rules and regulations. Before engaging in margin transactions, the investor has to deposit cash or eligible securities, known as initial margin, with the broker. The Fed requires investors to deposit an initial margin of 50 percent of the trade value before purchasing eligible stocks or convertible bonds. After the transaction is completed, the individual exchanges and the brokerage firm will require that the investor maintain a certain equity level in the margin account, called maintenance margin. The New York Stock Exchange and the National Association of Securities Dealers require customers to keep a maintenance margin of 25 percent. Brokerage firms often require a higher percentage, as firms rate their customers and require a lower margin from their best customers and a higher margin from riskier customers.

Asset management accounts require a minimum balance to open and charge an annual fee. All offer automatic reinvestment of the account's cash balances in money market funds. Typically, account holders are issued a credit card and can also write checks against the account's assets. In addition, loans based on the marginable securities in the account can be obtained anytime.

In wrapped accounts, the broker serves as a consultant who gives a full range of financial advice and executes the transactions, including the purchase of mutual funds managed by other companies. All costs are wrapped in one fee. Many large full-service brokerage houses such as Merrill Lynch and Smith Barney offer these accounts.

Types of Orders

Customers can place three basic types of orders: market orders, limit orders, and stop orders. A market order instructs the broker to buy or sell the securities immediately at the best price available at that time. A market order ensures that the transaction will be completed, but the price of the trade is not known until it is executed.

A limit order specifies a particular price for the trade. In the case of a buy order, the customer specifies the maximum price that he is willing to pay; usually this price is lower than the current market price. In the case of a sell order, the customer specifies a minimum price that she is willing to accept to sell the security. A limit order can be effective for one day or good until canceled, which means that the order will remain in effect for 60 days unless it is canceled or renewed. There is no guarantee that the order will be filled. Limit orders can be specified as all or none (fill the whole order or nothing), immediate or cancel (fill any part of the order immediately or cancel the order), or fill or kill (fill the entire order or kill it).

A stop order can be used to purchase or sell a security after the price reaches a certain level. A buy stop order is placed above the current market price, and a sell stop order is placed below the current market price. A stop limit order becomes a limit order once the limit price is reached. For example, a buy stop order of 500 shares of Cisco Systems at $22 per share means that the order will be executed at the best market price once Cisco reaches $22 per share. A stop limit order for the same amount means that once Cisco reaches $22 the order becomes a limit order to sell at a limit price of $22.

Margin Transactions

When an investor undertakes an order, he can pay for the securities in cash or can borrow a portion of the cost. Buying on margin means that the investor borrowed some of the cost of the security and used the security as collateral for the loan. Not all securities can be purchased on margin. In general, all securities listed on national exchanges and OTC securities that have been approved by the Fed are marginable. Even though the Fed determines which securities can be purchased on margin, a brokerage house may choose not to allow an investor to purchase a marginable security on margin. Buying on margin has the effect of leveraging the purchase, that is, rate of return (both positive and negative) on the margin transaction will be greater than a cash purchase. For example, current margin requirements are 50 percent, which means that an investor can borrow up to 50 percent of the value of the stock. If an investor wishes to purchase $10,000 of stock, he only needs $5,000 in cash and can borrow the rest. The effect of borrowing $5,000 to purchase $10,000 in stock is that the rate of return on the investor's money will be twice that of a cash purchase. For example, if the stock price rises by 5 percent, then the investor will realize a 10 percent return. If the stock price falls by 5 percent the investor will realize a 10 percent loss. This effect is known as leverage. In this case, the leverage factor is 2, that is, returns are twice that of a cash purchase.[8]

An important concept that relates to margin is the investor's equity. The margin requirement previously discussed refers to initial margin, which is the amount an investor must put up in cash to purchase a security. However, if the price of the security falls in value, the investor's equity will fall and the investor may receive a margin call, which will require the customer to place additional funds in his account. If the customer elects not to place the necessary funds into the account, the brokerage house can sell some of the security until the margin requirement is met. In order to keep brokerage houses from requiring investors to put additional funds into their accounts every time the stock price falls, investors will not receive a margin call until the price drops sufficiently so that the proportion of equity to the total value of the stock falls to a level referred to as maintenance margin. When an investor's equity falls to the maintenance margin level, the investor will receive a margin call and be required to put cash into the account to raise the equity to the initial margin requirement. The amount that the investor must place in his account is referred to as variation margin.

TRADING AND TRADING COSTS

Successful trading requires both the ability to select securities that will outperform the market and the ability to implement these strategies in an effective manner. The difference between paper portfolios and actual portfolio returns has come to be known as the implementation shortfall. This shortfall occurs because money managers face hidden costs when implementing their portfolio strategy.

The costs of implementing a portfolio strategy have made execution techniques and trading costs an important part of a trading decision. Changes in technology have opened up a wide variety of tactics that the trader can use to implement a trade. The decision of whether or not to trade is determined by the benefits of trading relative to the costs incurred.

Direct Costs of Trading

Trading securities incurs a number of costs. When an investor desires to buy or sell a security, she incurs one of two direct costs. The type of cost that is incurred depends on the market where the security is purchased. In an auction market, buyers and sellers meet to negotiate a price. In order to reduce the costs of searching for the other end of the transaction, investors use brokers to help complete the transaction. Brokers do not hold an inventory and are simply paid a commission for finding the other end of the transaction.

In a dealer market, an individual known as a dealer or market maker stands ready to buy or sell securities from his own account. The dealer profits from the bid-asked spread. The size of this spread is determined by a number of factors including, the volume of trading in the security, the security's price volatility, and the number of other dealers trading this security. The greater the trading volume in a security the narrower the bid-asked spread should be because dealers will have an easier time managing their inventories. Likewise, lower price volatility should lead to lower inventory risk and hence should narrow the spread.

Hidden Costs

Most people view the costs of trading as simply the commissions charged on a transaction. However, the hidden costs of trading are often much more significant than the commissions paid. These costs are related to the cost of liquidity, and the cost that is paid by the trader is determined by whether the trader is buying liquidity or selling liquidity in the market place.

There are four major components to trading costs:[9]

1. Commissions represent the administrative costs of executing a trade and are incurred on every transaction.
2. Impact cost represents the cost of buying liquidity. Impact cost can be measured by looking at the change in price between the time an order is presented to a broker and the actual execution price.
3. Timing cost represents the costs that are incurred by not executing the entire order at the same time. Timing can be thought of as the cost of seeking liquidity. Timing costs occur because an order is too large to be presented to the mar-

ket for a single execution. Smaller orders are parceled out over time and it may take a number of days to complete the transaction. During this time, the price may have moved away from the target price.

4. Opportunity cost represents the cost of not executing the trade. These costs can occur for a number of reasons, including movements in price away from the target range. Opportunity costs are especially hard to measure because the securities that are not purchased are never reflected in the fund's actual performance.

With the exception of commissions, these types of costs are not directly observable to the investor and are difficult to measure. In addition, there is a tradeoff between impact and timing costs. A trader can reduce impact costs on large orders by doling out the trade into smaller trades. However, this technique can increase the timing costs.

There is a tradeoff between the different types of trading costs. The importance of these costs is determined by the type of trader. Information traders attempt to profit by trading on information that is not yet known by the market. For information traders, time is extremely important, as they attempt to trade before the market incorporates the information into the security's price. Therefore, impact costs are relatively unimportant to the information trader who is trying to acquire a position in the security before the information reaches the market. Information traders will choose to buy the security as long as the costs of executing the trade are less than the expected price movement due to the information. Because information traders may need to seek liquidity in the market, their costs of transacting should be high relative to other types of investors.

Value traders trade because they believe there is a discrepancy between the trade price and the equilibrium value. Value traders supply liquidity to the market place because they generally buy as price is falling and sell when price is rising so they tend to have low hidden transactions costs.

Passive managers, who track some market indices, are somewhere in between momentum and value traders. Because passive managers buy and sell securities simply to maintain the relationship between their portfolio and the index, they neither supply nor buy liquidity from the market.

In general, information traders would be expected to have the highest costs of transactions because of the necessity of executing the trade quickly. These costs can reduce the returns to an information strategy. Value investors, on the other hand, tend to buy out of favor securities and tend to have lower impact costs for their trades. Finally, the cost of passive management tends to fall somewhere between information investing and value investing.

EXECUTION TECHNIQUES

The costs of implementing a real portfolio make it crucial to consider execution strategies in the portfolio management process. The implementation shortfall occurs because paper portfolios do not face bid-asked spreads, impact, timing, or opportunity costs. In order to reduce these costs, a careful analysis of trading costs needs to be considered. The use of a number of different trading methods may be necessary to provide the best possible execution.

There are several trading alternatives that can be used to improve the opportunity of getting the best execution. Traders can use either a single-stock approach or a portfolio approach.[10] In the single-stock approach, trading takes place with one stock at a time. In the portfolio approach, trading a large number of securities is done simultaneously as one unit.

Single-Stock Trading

There are several alternatives that can be used in the single-stock approach. The upstairs block market can reduce costs relative to other trading alternatives because trades can be executed at or near the bid-offer spread. The upstairs block market gets its name because the market takes place upstairs off the floor of the exchange and these transactions are for large blocks of securities. This market consists of block houses—investment firms that help institutions locate other institutions that are interested in buying or selling blocks of stocks. There are several disadvantages to this approach. First, it is not suitable for all transactions. Second, large capitalization securities are generally more appropriate than small capitalization securities. Third, it can be difficult to find the other half of the trade. Finally, the exposure of the order to the market place can result in market impact.

The use of a call market is another method. One problem with continuous markets is that order flow arrives at different points in time during the day. This can lead to inefficient pricing of stocks. In a call market, trading takes place at specified times. The purpose of call markets is to gather all bid and asked prices for a stock and attempt to find the price that will clear the market.

The use of a dealer market entails using a broker/dealer to execute the transaction. Immediacy and certainty of execution are advantages of this approach. One disadvantage to this approach is that the dealer market usually has high costs.

Crossing networks are another method that can be used. A crossing network allows institutions to trade a portfolio of stocks rather than individual securities with one another. Crossing networks give buyers and sellers an opportunity to meet and negotiate a price directly, which allows them to trade inside the bid-asked spread. Crossing networks have a number of advantages, including confidentiality, fair pricing, and low commissions. One major disadvantage of crossing networks is their lack of liquidity.

Portfolio Trading

Portfolio transactions entail trading large numbers of securities as a single indivisible unit. Principal trades can be divided into two categories: cash only and derivatives related. Two types of derivatives transactions are basis trades and exchange for physicals. In a basis trade, a broker trades stock index futures in the broker's account during the course of a day and then crosses the client's portfolio into the broker's account at the end of the day at a basis or spread to the average futures price. At completion, the client has the desired cash portfolio and the broker has the offsetting cash position hedged with futures. In an exchange of physicals, the client starts off with futures and exchanges them with a broker for a cash position. Likewise, the client can start off with a cash position and exchange it for futures. One difference between the exchange of physicals and the basis approach is that exchange of physicals transactions must be posted on the relevant futures exchange.

Another method for trading a portfolio of securities is to use a substitution order. For example, suppose you are trying to create a portfolio that tracks the Russell 2000 using 400 stocks. Because a number of stocks will track the Russell 2000 well, it may not be necessary to specify the exact 400 stocks to purchase.

Strategies for International Trading

International investing offers a number of opportunities and challenges for the investment professional. Trading across borders allows an investor to take advantage of growth opportunities in emerging markets, and to reduce portfolio risk through international diversification in a way that would not be possible using only domestic investments. This risk reduction results from the low degree of correlation between U.S. and foreign markets.

The opportunities in international investing do not come without costs. First, limitations in data in other parts of the world may make it difficult for the investor to make fully informed decisions. Second, investments in foreign countries expose the portfolio to a number of different risks including, exchange rate risk and political risk. Also, overseas markets may be less liquid and subject to higher transactions costs.

The Process Begins

The first step for the investor is to determine the appropriate allocation to overseas markets. The examination can begin with a look at the historical returns and correlations between each market and the U.S. market. Once the investment manager determines how much to allocate to foreign investments, he must decide how to allocate these funds among the different countries. Finally, the allocation decision ends with the decision of how much to invest in each industry and company in each country.

The second issue that the investment manager needs to deal with is fluctuations in exchange rates. Foreign exchange rate risk can be left unhedged, can be partially hedged, or can be fully hedged. To hedge foreign exchange rate risk, the manager has a number of tools available including futures or forward contracts, options, and swaps.

Trade Analysis

Once the manager has decided which countries and which industries to invest in, a trading strategy must be established. A trading strategy begins by examining the liquidity and volatility for each security. By examining the liquidity in a market, the broker can devise a strategy to control market impact costs.

Morgan Stanley uses a trade liquidity report for each security to identify any problems that may occur in trading a security.[11] The list includes the following:

- The percentage of principal each name represents within its country
- The quantity the customer has requested to buy or sell
- The price
- The average daily volume (30-day moving average)
- The percentage the trade represents of average daily volume
- The 20-day volatility
- The bid and offer
- The percentage spread

This information allows the investor to determine which stocks are feasible for the portfolio. Stocks with very low volume may offer great potential to the "paper portfolio," however, purchasing the requisite amount may be impossible. When there are problems purchasing a desired security, the manager needs to consider the possibility of substitution.

Transition Trading

One method for implementing a global investment strategy is to handle transactions simultaneously across multiple markets. This method is referred to as transition trading or global program trading. In transition trading, the process is simplified so that the task is reduced to one execution list, one broker, one confirmation, and one settlement network. Another advantage of transition trading is that it allows quick reallocation of assets and effective management of cash flows. For example, different settlement dates in different countries allow a tailoring of the strategy so cash flows match the need for settlement money. One concern about transition trading is that the quick execution may lead to higher market impact costs.

Using Futures

Futures contracts can provide a method for a money manager to invest in foreign stocks. Futures offer a number of advantages over the direct purchase of equities. Futures have low transaction costs and can be purchased and sold quickly. Another major advantage to the use of futures is the limited currency risk. In a futures transaction, only the margin deposit is subject to currency fluctuations.

BROKERAGE SERVICES

On May 1, 1975 (May Day), the SEC allowed commissions paid to brokers on all transactions to be fully negotiable. Allowing brokers to lower rates charged to customers led to an entirely new industry, the discount broker. Prior to May 1975, brokers provided full service to customers in the form of security recommendations. The change in government regulations led to a new class of broker, the discount broker, who executed the trade at much lower costs than full service brokers. This class of broker was designed for individuals who wished to conduct their own research and only needed an outlet for executing the trade.

Changes in the fee structure used by brokers have not deterred brokerage firms from charging fees in excess of the pure costs of transactions. These costs are referred to as soft dollars. Soft dollars are the fees charged in excess of the pure costs of transaction and can be paid when they benefit the client. A 1975 amendment to the Securities Exchange Act provides a safe harbor for investment managers using soft-dollar arrangements.[12] Soft dollars can be paid to brokerage firms for research services or superior execution. One major concern with the use of soft dollars is that they are sometimes used to court business from an investment management firm. In cases where the investment management firm receives services from the broker that do not benefit the client, a breach of fiduciary duty has occurred.

The proliferation of the Internet has brought a new type of discount broker, the online broker, into the picture. Online brokers such as Etrade and Ameritrade allow investors to trade from their home computers for very low commission rates. There are several concerns regarding online trading. First, the question always arises about the quality of the execution. Are traders receiving the best possible price? Another concern that government regulators have is the rash of day traders who use low commission online brokers to conduct their transactions. Once, day trading was reserved for the market professional. However, the Internet and online trading have led to a proliferation of online day traders. Many of these traders have little or no investment knowledge and many have seen their life savings wiped out in a matter of days or weeks. A final issue regarding online brokerage firms is whether they are subject to the same "suitability" requirements that full service brokers must adhere to. That is, brokers are required by law to make sure that the investments they recommend are suitable for the individual client.

The trading of securities online by individual investors appears to only be the beginning of the Internet revolution. Currently, many firms have offered online trading for corporate finance chiefs. These firms allow companies to trade more sophisticated financial instruments such as foreign exchange options, interest rate derivatives, and swaps online.[13]

Electronic Communications Networks

Electronic communications networks (ECNs) are computerized trading systems that match buyers and sellers of securities. Instead of people executing trades over the computer, which is how the NASDAQ works, or through a specialist on an exchange floor, ECNs basically operate like giant eBays for securities. ECNs let buyers and sellers of stock meet without the use of intermediaries.

Since 1997, ECNs have been stealing market share from the established exchanges. Both regulatory forces and technology contributed to the emergence of ECNs as a force on Wall Street. In January 1997, as part of its settlement of a 1996 antitrust investigation into collusion among market makers, the NASD issued new rules to govern how market makers handle customers' limit orders. Under the rules, a market maker must post limit orders on the NASDAQ or send them to an ECN that will post them where everyone can see them. Before the guidelines went into effect, market makers could ignore a limit order they did not like. In 1997, the only ECN of any consequence was Instinet, which maintained a network where institutional investors could trade in secret with each other and with market makers. Suspicious of this private party, the SEC effectively forced ECNs to post their quotes on NASDAQ's comprehensive trading bulletin board, known as a Level II screen. The screen displays the best prices and quantities of all market makers' and ECNs'. In an instant, these networks can match buy orders with any corresponding sell orders.

Operating the Trading Desk

The work day for the trader begins long before the markets and exchanges open. Traders begin their day by examining the positions they hold and what new buy and sell orders have come from the foreign and branch offices. Examining his position and the incoming buy and sell orders gives the trader an idea of what deals need to be made and how to negotiate these deals. In addition to this information, the traders may attend a morning research meeting in order to gather the latest research information from the firm's analysts. This information may impact price and order flow. Once this information is gathered and examined, the trader begins communicating with his customers.

Successful implementation of the trading strategy requires that the portfolio manager communicate the goals of the strategy to the trader. Different portfolio strategies will necessitate different goals of trading. For example, a momentum or information-based manager may be more willing to accept higher market impact costs in order to have the order executed in a timely manner. On the other hand, a value based-manager may be willing to accept greater timing costs to reduce the market impact cost. In either case, if the trading strategy is communicated to the trader, the trader will be in a better position to achieve the goals set out by the portfolio manager.

Organizing and operating a trading desk can be a complicated task. A typical equity trading room may handle trades in equities, convertible bonds, foreign stocks, and options and futures.[14] Trades may be conducted for a number of mutual funds, pension funds, and other funds managed by the firm. Because of the differences in time zones, trading will take place around the clock.

After Hours Trading

As the world financial markets become more integrated, expanded trading hours recognize that different time zones allow for trading around the world 24 hours a day. Investors can trade equities after the exchanges close on a number of ECNs.

After hours trading is not without its problems. First, when the exchanges are closed, the number of buyers and sellers of a security tends to be small. The low volume generated by the relatively few buyers and sellers may mean that investors will not receive the best possible price for the trade. In addition, the low volume often leads to wider bid-asked spreads. Unlike normal trading hours, when the prices for securities are linked together, the prices on securities trading after hours may differ from ECN to ECN. Therefore, investors are not assured of receiving the best available price on their transaction.

CONCLUSION

Many vehicles are available to invest in China's growth without going to China. This chapter discussed diversification of portfolio to include securities issued by Chinese companies, trading, and related issues. U.S. investors can purchase Chinese stocks listed on U.S. exchanges like any other stock. Currency risk is not a concern in the short term, as most anticipate the Chinese RMB to appreciate. The next two chapters discuss investing in growth and value companies.

15

Investing in Growth Sectors

Growth investing has attracted many investors who believe growth companies have a higher growth in revenues or profits. Some have not taken into account the price they pay to participate in that growth. This is similar for Chinese stocks; some will return investors handsomely while others will disappoint. This chapter discusses the basics of growth investing, valuation approaches, and technical analysis to take advantage of the growth momentum.

GROWTH VERSUS VALUE INVESTING

Investment professionals commonly classify stocks as growth or value. Value investing focuses on a company's ability to generate stable earnings and growth style places emphasis on above average growth in revenues or earnings. Value and growth styles have outperformed each other at various times. Empirical observations do not conclude which will outperform the other all the time. It is difficult to predict when the market is going to shift toward favoring the growth or value style. Experienced professionals have difficulties timing the market.

Investors in growth stocks expect that the long-term earnings potential of those companies will outpace the market's expectations. This could be accomplished by new product innovations, gains in market share, or other situations that cause revenue growth to accelerate. In other words, growth companies are projected to grow faster than the average company. Google, Bidu.com, and Starbucks are in this category but there is no guarantee they will continue their rate of growth. However, fast-paced growth does not come cheap; investors usually pay a higher price for growth stocks and accept more price fluctuations. Furthermore, today's growth company will be a mature company in the future. No one has a crystal ball that predicts when that change will occur. Often, the market penalizes the price of a growth company severely if the earnings or revenues growth falls short of expectations by the smallest margin.

In mutual funds, some are classified as growth funds. These funds have diversified investments across many industries in the market, but tend to focus on companies with faster earnings growth rates. Among those growth funds, there are different targets in investing. Some specialize in large-cap companies; others invest in mid-cap or small-cap. For example, Fidelity Blue Chip Growth Fund invests in large capitalization, above-average growth potential companies similar to those that make up the S&P 500 or Russell 1000 indexes. There are also so-called mid-cap growth funds that focus on mid-cap stocks with above average growth. Finally, most people associate growth with small-cap stocks. Small-cap funds invest in common stocks of small-cap companies that exhibit above average growth characteristics.

The concept is the same when investing in Chinese stocks. Large, mature companies will not be the targets of growth investing. Many companies in information technology, semiconductor, biotechnology, or manufacturing industries are growth stocks at some point in their corporate development history.

GROWTH STOCKS

It is a universal belief that there is trade off between return and risk. These two characteristics are joined at the hip—you simply do not get one without the other. That is, there is no free lunch. Thus, some people conclude growth stocks in the long term provide a higher rate of returns because they are riskier. Is this logical? Let's look at data on returns and risks (as represented by standard deviation) from 1963 to 2002. For the S&P 500 Index, the average return was 11.04 percent and the standard deviation was 14.88 percent. Large growth stock produced an average return of 10.25 percent and a standard deviation of 16.65 percent. The results for small growth were not as impressive, the standard deviation was 24.6 percent and average return was 9.68 percent. In the value spectrum, large value returned investors 13.71 percent with a standard deviation of 15.39 percent. The small-cap value produced the best annual return with a higher risk, returns averaged at 17.59 percent with 19.20 percent standard deviation. Small-cap growth generated high rate of return and came with a higher risk.

The Shenzhen Stock Exchange has established a separate section for small growth companies (SME Board). The priority of the SME is to list enterprises with well-defined core business, high growth, and greater high-tech contents. The first listing came on board on June 25, 2004. As of April 20, 2007, 130 small to medium-sized companies are listed on the SME Board (Table 15.1). Larger companies are listed on the Main Board or the Shanghai Stock Exchange.

VALUATION OF INTERNET OR HIGH-GROWTH STOCKS

Growth investors place emphasis on the earnings growth relative to the market price. That is, growth investors are willing to pay more for a company that they believe has superior growth prospects that are not already reflected in the stock's price. Simply put, growth stocks command a higher stock price/earnings per share (P/E) ratio.

TABLE 15.1   Shenzhen Stock Exchange SME Listed Companies

Stock Code	Name	Listing Date	Issued Capital (RMB)	Industry
002001	NHU	6/25/2004	342,060,000	Petrochemicals
002002	JSQH	6/25/2004	91,700,000	Petrochemicals
002003	WEIXING	6/25/2004	89,783,433	
002004	HUAPONT PHARM	6/25/2004	132,000,000	Pharmaceuticals
002005	ETI	6/25/2004	161,600,000	Machinery
002006	JINGGONG SCIENCE	6/25/2004	96,000,000	Machinery
002007	HUALAN BIO.	6/25/2004	150,750,000	Pharmaceuticals
002008	HAN'S LASER	6/25/2004	240,786,000	Electronics
002009	MIRACLE LOGISTICS	6/29/2004	92,087,843	Machinery
002010	ZJ TRANSFAR	6/29/2004	120,000,000	Petrochemicals
002011	DUN AN ENVIRONMENTAL	7/5/2004	71,181,865	Machinery
002012	KAN	7/5/2004	194,789,298	Paper & Printing
002013	APM	7/5/2004	60,000,000	Machinery
002014	NOVEL	7/8/2004	102,740,000	Petrochemicals
002015	XIAKE	7/8/2004	100,640,000	Textiles & Apparel
002016	WEIER	7/8/2004	63,290,367	Machinery
002017	EASTCOMPEACE	7/13/2004	118,040,000	
002018	HUAXING CHEMICAL	7/13/2004	96,600,000	Petrochemicals
002019	XINFU PHARM	7/13/2004	68,250,000	Petrochemicals
002020	JINGXIN	7/15/2004	101,550,000	Pharmaceuticals
002021	ZOJE	7/15/2004	178,880,000	Machinery
002022	KHB	7/21/2004	210,375,000	Pharmaceuticals
002023	HAITE	7/21/2004	117,587,226	Transportation
002024	SUNING APPLIANCE	7/21/2004	1,441,504,000	Wholesale & Retail
002025	SACO	7/26/2004	165,000,000	Electronics
002026	SHANDONG WEIDA	7/27/2004	135,000,000	Metals & Non-metals
002027	HEDY	8/4/2004	302,335,116	IT
002028	SIEYUAN	8/5/2004	106,000,000	Machinery
002029	SEPTWOLVES	8/6/2004	110,500,000	Textiles & Apparel
002030	DAJY	8/9/2004	125,400,000	Pharmaceuticals
002031	GREATOO	8/16/2004	183,300,000	Machinery
002032	SUPOR	8/17/2004	176,020,000	Metals & Non-metals
002033	LIJIANG TOURISM	8/25/2004	99,323,048	Social Services
002034	MIZUDA	8/26/2004	81,120,000	Textiles & Apparel
002035	VANTAGE	9/1/2004	132,132,000	Metals & Non-metals
002036	YAK	9/3/2004	134,832,600	Textiles & Apparel
002037	JIULIAN DEVELOPMENT	9/8/2004	110,000,000	Petrochemicals
002038	SL PHARM	9/9/2004	124,200,000	Pharmaceuticals
002039	QIANYUAN POWER	3/3/2005	140,256,000	Utilities
002040	NANJING PORT	3/25/2005	245,872,000	Transportation
002041	DENGHAI SEEDS	4/18/2005	176,000,000	Agriculture
002042	FEIYA	4/27/2005	100,000,000	Textiles & Apparel
002043	DEHUA TB	5/10/2005	122,000,000	Timber & Furnishings
002044	JIANGSU SANYOU	5/18/2005	125,000,000	Textiles & Apparel
002045	GGEC	5/23/2005	160,000,000	Electronics
002046	BEARING-SCI&TECH.	5/26/2005	78,000,000	Machinery
002047	SHENZHEN GLOBE UNION	5/31/2005	224,142,702	Metals & Non-metals
002048	NBHX	6/3/2005	274,300,000	Machinery
002049	JINGYUAN ELECTRONICS	6/6/2005	90,000,000	Electronics
002050	SANHUA	6/7/2005	113,000,000	Machinery
002051	CAMCE	6/19/2006	190,000,000	Social Services

TABLE 15.1 (Continued)

Stock Code	Name	Listing Date	Issued Capital (RMB)	Industry
002052	COSHIP	6/27/2006	112,965,326	IT
002053	YSCC	6/27/2006	185,851,103	Food & Beverage
002054	DYMATIC CHEM	7/25/2006	134,000,000	Petrochemicals
002055	DEREN	7/25/2006	61,127,835	Electronics
002056	DMEGC	8/2/2006	180,000,000	Electronics
002057	Tianyuan Technology	8/2/2006	70,000,000	Petrochemicals
002058	WELLTECH	8/2/2006	62,368,840	Machinery
002059	KUNMING EXPO GARDEN	8/10/2006	215,000,000	Social Services
002060	GHEC	8/10/2006	220,000,000	Construction
002061	Jianshan Chemical	8/16/2006	139,980,000	Petrochemicals
002062	HONGRUN	8/16/2006	110,820,000	Construction
002063	YGSOFT	8/23/2006	109,820,000	IT
002064	Huafeng Spandex	8/23/2006	184,600,000	Petrochemicals
002065	DHCC	8/23/2006	86,236,687	IT
002066	Ruitai Technology	8/23/2006	60,000,000	Metals & Non-metals
002067	JING XING PAPER	9/15/2006	230,000,000	Paper & Printing
002068	BCCB	9/15/2006	89,000,000	Petrochemicals
002069	DZF	9/28/2006	113,100,000	Agriculture
002070	ZHONGHE	10/12/2006	108,000,000	Textiles & Apparel
002071	Jiangsu Hongbao	10/12/2006	122,680,000	Metals & Non-metals
002072	Demian	10/18/2006	160,000,000	Textiles & Apparel
002073	MESNAC	10/18/2006	71,235,000	Machinery
002074	DYDQ	10/18/2006	69,000,000	Machinery
002075	GAOXINZHANGTONG	10/25/2006	198,000,000	Metals & Non-metals
002076	CNLIGHT	10/25/2006	184,270,676	Electronics
002077	JIANGSU DAGANG	11/16/2006	180,000,000	Conglomerates
002078	SUN PAPER	11/16/2006	276,046,812	Paper & Printing
002079	SUZHOU GOOD-ARK	11/16/2006	138,000,000	Electronics
002080	sinomatech	11/20/2006	150,000,000	Metals & Non-metals
002081	Gold Mantis	11/20/2006	94,000,000	Construction
002082	DLXC	11/20/2006	83,200,000	Metals & Non-metals
002083	SUNVIM	11/24/2006	404,350,246	Textiles & Apparel
002084	Seagull	11/24/2006	176,548,464	Metals & Non-metals
002085	WANFENG AUTO WHEEL	11/28/2006	258,500,000	Machinery
002086	ORIENTAL OCEAN	11/28/2006	86,300,000	Agriculture
002087	XINYE TEXTILE	11/30/2006	234,380,000	Textiles & Apparel
002088	LYGF	11/30/2006	103,254,342	Metals & Non-metals
002089	nsu	11/30/2006	70,800,000	IT
002090	WISCOM	12/8/2006	102,000,000	IT
002091	JSGT	12/8/2006	128,000,000	Wholesale & Retail
002092	ZHONGTAI CHEMICAL	12/8/2006	236,000,000	Petrochemicals
002093	Gmtech	12/15/2006	66,750,000	IT
002094	Kingking	12/15/2006	107,305,540	
002095	NetSun	12/15/2006	60,000,000	IT
002096	HNNL IEMC	12/22/2006	58,755,600	Petrochemicals
002097	SUNWARD INTELLIGENT	12/22/2006	132,575,000	Machinery
002098	SBS	12/22/2006	155,000,000	
002099	Hisoar	12/25/2006	107,000,000	Pharmaceuticals
002100	TCSW	12/26/2006	96,000,000	Food & Beverage
002101	GUANGDONG HONGTU	12/29/2006	67,000,000	Machinery

(continued)

TABLE 15.1   (Continued)

Stock Code	Name	Listing Date	Issued Capital (RMB)	Industry
002102	Guanfu Household	12/29/2006	113,673,158	Metals & Non-metals
002103	Guangbo Shares	1/10/2007	189,940,000	Paper & Printing
002104	HengBao Co., LTD	1/10/2007	115,200,000	
002105	XLSY	1/12/2007	268,000,000	Paper & Printing
002106	LAIBAO HI-TECH	1/12/2007	195,200,000	Electronics
002107	WHYY	1/24/2007	69,990,000	Pharmaceuticals
002108	Cangzhou Mingzhu	1/24/2007	68,750,000	Petrochemicals
002109	XINGHUA CHEMISTRY	1/26/2007	160,000,000	Petrochemicals
002110	Sansteel MinGuang	1/26/2007	534,700,000	Metals & Non-metals
002111	Guangtai	1/26/2007	84,700,000	Machinery
002112	SCI-TECH	2/8/2007	80,000,000	Machinery
002113	TRFZ	2/8/2007	74,000,000	Petrochemicals
002114	LPXD	2/15/2007	102,140,000	Metals & Non-metals
002115	SUNWAVE	2/15/2007	80,000,000	IT
002116	Haisum	2/15/2007	114,000,000	Social Services
002117	TungKong	3/2/2007	110,000,000	Paper & Printing
002118	JLZX	3/2/2007	67,523,000	Pharmaceuticals
002119	Ningbo Kangqiang	3/2/2007	97,100,000	Electronics
002120	XINHAI	3/6/2007	68,000,000	
002121	SZCLOU	3/6/2007	60,000,000	Electronics
002122	TianMa Co., Ltd.	3/28/2007	136,000,000	Machinery
002123	RXPE	3/28/2007	64,000,000	Machinery
002124	TBGF	4/3/2007	68,500,000	Food & Beverage
002125	XTEMD	4/3/2007	75,400,000	Petrochemicals
002126	YINLUN	4/18/2007	100,000,000	Machinery
002127	XINMIN	4/18/2007	108,787,000	Textiles & Apparel
002128	OPENCUT COAL	4/18/2007	654,184,500	Mining
002129	TJSemi	4/20/2007	362,663,687	Electronics
002130	WOER	4/20/2007	54,350,000	

Source: Shenzhen Stock Exchange.

The rapid growth of the Internet and the success of Internet-based stocks such as Google, eBay, and Bidu.com have spurred interest in the future of stocks in this area. Analysis of many of these companies precludes the use of traditional valuation methods. Also, the short time span of these businesses makes it extremely difficult to forecast future revenues and earnings.[1] The analysis of companies in new industries is not new. In the 1980s personal computer companies represented a new area for analysis, as did companies conducting genetic engineering research. Projections for the future earnings of these companies in the 1980s were just as difficult as they were for Internet firms in the 1990s and the 2000s.

Some possible techniques for analyzing companies in emerging industries include:

- Adapting the traditional present value approach is one possibility. If the analyst can determine some reasonable future cash flows that will be generated by the firm, a present value method can be used. The risk associated with a new company in a new industry can be dealt with by incorporating a higher discount rate into the present value calculation.

- The analyst can look at venture capital mark ups to determine a reasonable starting point for the analysis. This is relevant because venture capitalists are analyzing new, growth companies at early stages.
- Determine the number of years it will take the firm to reach a target P/E ratio. For example, the analyst may determine that a P/E ratio of 25 is reasonable for this firm over the long haul. If the firm can attain this within, say, five years or less, the stock would be recommended.
- Consider the performance that the firm must sustain in order to justify the current market price. For example, suppose the current selling price of a firm has a 10-year earnings growth rate of 50 percent embedded in the price. The analyst must determine if the 50 percent growth rate is sustainable. A scenario analysis where the analyst determines the value of the stock for different growth rates may provide some insight on the stock's current valuation.
- Consider the company's cost of acquiring customers. Firms with the lowest cost would be valued the highest.
- For Internet stocks, a commonly used approach is the use of the number of people that "hit" the website on a regular basis, which is sometimes referred to as "eyeball count." The logic behind this method is that many Internet companies earn the majority of their money from advertising, and therefore a valuation of Internet stocks is akin to valuing other types of media companies such as television stations or newspapers.
- Consider how a new firm or technology is likely to change society or how the way business is conducted.[2]
- Consider the market cap of a firm and determine if the fundamentals can justify the valuation. For example, several years ago, Amazon.com was priced at a level that required a long-term high growth rate. The question the analyst must ask is "can this valuation be justified?" Its price inevitably dropped, as the company could not consistently meet the growth target assumed by the market.
- An approach that incorporates scenario analysis and the value of the stock under each scenario and then attempts to determine the probabilities of each scenario can be helpful in putting the stock's current valuation in perspective. For example, if a high probability exists that the best-case scenario will occur and the current value of the stock is below the projection in this scenario, the analyst would recommend purchasing this stock.

There are several other factors that an analyst should consider when evaluating start-up, emerging firms. First, successful investment in emerging firms (such as Internet companies) requires analyzing the firm. Firms that succeed are likely to be the first mover to establish a dominant position in their industry. For example, in the online auction business, eBay quickly established a dominant position. Even with other Internet powerhouses such as Amazon.com and Yahoo entering the online auction arena, eBay continues to be the preferred site for collectors and antique dealers.

A second consideration is that the expected returns to emerging companies are not likely to be normally distributed, but are more likely to have a bimodal distribution. This means that many emerging or Internet companies hit it big or go bust, so the analyst's expectation is not likely to be the most likely outcome.

Finally, an analyst should view investment in emerging or Internet companies in the same manner as venture capitalists. In this case, the analyst recognizes that only a handful of firms will succeed, but that the few that do succeed will more than offset the losses from a number of firms. Therefore, investing in a diversified basket of companies may be the best approach.

TRADING TECHNIQUES

Investing in growth is riskier than in value. Effective risk management is essential in successful investment and trading. The first step to successful trading is to ensure survival by making risk management a top priority. Many losers are washed out while trading their way out of a hole. Many of them have difficulties taking a loss and they hang on to money-losing securities. It is essential to understand that a 10 percent loss requires a gain of more than 11 percent just to break even, and that a 50 percent loss will require a gain of 100 percent to get back in the game.[3] Typically, a trader would place a stop right after he got into a position. The level of stop is chosen in such a way that any loss from a single position will be limited to a small percentage of the account.

Likewise, taking profits is sometimes emotionally hard. When the market moves in the anticipated direction, a trader needs to decide whether to stay put, take profits, or add to the position. A successful trader sets certain objectives for each position, once the objective is accomplished, he takes profits. Or if he decides to adjust his objective up, the stop needs to be adjusted in the same direction. The worst mistake for a trader is to cash out too quickly, then decide to hang on the next time and consequently lose a great deal of money.

There are three basic approaches to valuing stocks. The first is fundamental analysis that bases a security price on corporate and economic fundamentals. The fundamental approach for a security involves the analysis of the economy, industry, and company. This applies to equities and fixed-income securities. In commodities, fundamentalists study factors that affect market demand and supply. Currencies are affected by economic fundamentals such as production and inflation, and by political factors as well. In futures, expectations of interest rate and cash market conditions are important. Volatility and expected direction of price movements are key in determining the options valuation.

The second approach is the market efficiency hypothesis, in which securities prices are based on all available information so as to offer an expected rate of return consistent with their level of risk. There are three different degrees of informational efficiency. The least restrictive form is the weak form efficiency, which states that any information contained in the past is already included in the current price and that its future price cannot be predicted by analyzing past prices. This is because many market participants have access to past price information, and hence any free lunches would have been consumed. The second form of informational efficiency, semi-strong form efficiency, states that security prices fully reflect all relevant publicly available information. Information available to the public includes past prices, trading volumes, economic reports, brokerage recommendations, advisory newsletters, and other news articles. Finally, the strong form of informational efficiency takes the information set a step further and includes all public and private information. This version implies that even insiders who have access to nonpublic material information cannot make abnormal profits. Most studies support the notion of the semi-strong form of market efficiency, but do not support the strong form version of efficient market hypothesis. In other words, insiders can trade profitable on their knowledge of nonpublic material information. This advantage is unfair and hence insider trading is illegal.

Finally, technical analysis attempts to use information on past price and volume to predict future price movement. It also attempts to time the markets. For its purposes, technical analysis is based on several key assumptions including:

- Demand and supply determine market price.
- Securities prices tend to move in trends that persist for long periods.
- Reversals of trends are caused by shifts in demand and supply, which can be detected in charts.
- Many chart patterns tend to repeat themselves.

Technicians have developed numerous techniques that attempt to predict changes in demand (bulls) and supply (bears).

Market Making and Day Trading

Market making is an integral part of a dealer's business and is necessary for the underwriting business. In addition, the information on market flow the dealer obtains through market making is valuable. Dealers stand ready to buy at bid and sell at offer (asked). The bid-asked spread is largely determined by the dealer's perception of risks such as price uncertainty and carry in making the market. During volatile periods, market makers widen the spread to protect themselves. If the trader is making a market but feels that the market is going against him, he will hedge with other highly correlated securities.

In day trading, traders make money by buying securities or currencies and then selling them again in a short period, hoping to gain a small fraction of a point on the sale. Day trading is not investing, however. Day trading is a tough profession that is not for the faint of heart. It is a risk-versus-reward scenario that may allow the astute and disciplined trader to make profits greater than what he or she would make in most other professions. On the downside, day trading offers an exceptional opportunity to lose money fast.

Convertible Arbitrage

A growth stock presents a wonderful opportunity to invest in the company's convertible securities. The expectation is that the future market price will be higher, sometimes much higher, than the stated exercised price. If the investor is conservative, a convertible arbitrage is a safer alternative. A simple convertible arbitrage involves the purchase of convertible bonds or preferred stocks and then hedging that position by selling short the underlying equity. The resulting position generates income from the accrued interest or preferred dividends and interest earned on the short-sale proceeds. The short sale is to protect the investment from adverse stock market movements so that the overall position, if correctly hedged, will be nondirectional. The objective is to correctly position trades that produce certain current income and preserve principal regardless of stock market conditions.

As an example, suppose a convertible debenture that matures in one year trading at $1,050 is convertible into 100 shares of nondividend paying common. The common stock is trading at $10 a share. There is a $50 premium over the conversion value of $1,000. Assume that a bond of similar characteristics without the conversion feature is trading at $920. The $920 is the investment value.

Assume the common stock has an even chance of going to $7.5 or $12.50 over the next year. The conversion value is hence $750 or $1,250 one year later. The convertible arbitrageur could take advantage of this expected relationship by being long one bond at $1,050 and short 60 shares of common at $10. At a price of $7.50 the short position would be in the money for $150 while the bond would trade at a $130 loss, for a gross profit of $20 per bond.[4] If the price goes up to $12.50, the bond will be converted and result in a gain of $200 while the short position would lose $150. The net profit is $50.

Another type of convertible arbitrage involves the purchase of a convertible bond while simultaneously entering into contracts to hedge interest rate and credit risk and selling an options contract on the underlying equity to lock in arbitrage profits. The investor finances the purchase of the convertible bonds by way of a repurchase agreement in which the investor uses the bond as collateral to borrow funds. The long position on a convertible bond consists of two risks, one is interest rate risk and the other is credit risk. Suppose the convertible bond pays a fixed interest rate and is convertible into X shares of the issuer stock. The interest rate swap contract is hence structured to pay out a fixed rate and to receive a floating rate. The investor then enters into a credit default swap contract in which it pays the dealer a premium in exchange for a lump-sum payment to protect the value of the bond in case a credit event occurs. Now the investor is left with the option to convert and bears a certain cost. The investor will sell an options contract to receive premium income and lock in the arbitrage profits if the costs are less than the premium. Alternatively, the investor will not purchase the convertible bond and executes the related transactions if the costs are higher than the options premium.

These are just two examples of convertible arbitrage. In practice, the convertible bet is more complex and the strategies are constantly changing.

TECHNICAL ANALYSIS

Growth investing is more influenced by market momentum than value. Technical analysis suits the purpose. Technical analysis assumes that prices move in trends that persist for a certain period and that these trends can be detected by charts. This approach is a dramatic departure from the fundamental analysis or efficient market hypothesis. Many academicians equate technical analysis with mystics. Technicians often criticize fundamentalists and the market efficiency theorists for being divorced from the reality of the markets.

Charting is at the heart of technical analysis. Chartists often use support or resistance to describe whether it is a trading or a trending market. Prices generally move within the support-resistance range (trading range). Traders buy at support and sell at resistance. A breakout above a resistance point signals an upward trending market, while a breakout below a support indicates that the market is trending downward. Volume is an essential factor. A new high on a heavy volume is considered bullish, while a new high on a light trading volume may indicate a temporary move that is not likely to be sustainable.

There is no single magic for identifying trends and trading ranges. Technicians generally combine several methods. When they confirm one another, the signal is considered valid. When they contradict one another, it is better to pass up the trade. This section provides a brief description of several indicators frequently used by technicians. Figure 15.1 shows the point of resistance, support, and trading range. At point A, if the price continues to move upward, it is a bull market. But, if the price

FIGURE 15.1   Support and Resistance

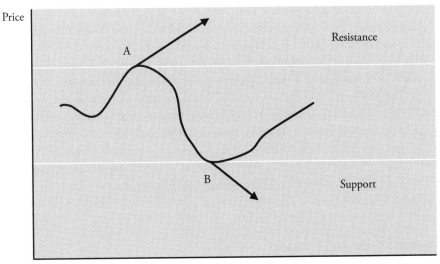

moves below the support at point B, then it is a bear market. When the price fluctuates between the support and the resistance, it is in a trading range.

Moving Average

One of the most commonly used technical techniques is the moving average (MA). Reporters and market commentators talk about it all the time. A moving average is the arithmetic average price of a security or an index over the past predetermined number of days:

$$MA = \frac{\sum_{t-(N-1)}^{t} P_t}{N},$$

where P = the security price or index value
N = the chosen time span
t = the most recent trading date.

As each day passes, the earliest day is dropped and the most recent one is included. Connecting each day's MA produces an MA line. When it falls, it shows bearish sentiment. When it rises, it signals a bull market. When the market is bullish, prices rise above an MA. When the bears dominate, prices fall below an MA. Hence a buy signal is given when the security price crosses above the MA and the MA is directed upward. A sell signal is given when the security price crosses below the MA and the MA is trending downward. There are no valid signals when the MA changes direction but the price does not cross over the MA. When price fluctuates in a broad sideways pattern, MA at times gives false signals. Technicians hence always use other indicators to confirm the direction of price.

Alternatively, a more complicated scheme involves the use of several MAs. For example, a technician might plot 4-week, 13-week, and 50-week MAs on the same graph. A buy signal is generated when the 4-week and 13-week averages cross over the 50-week MA from below. A sell signal is given when the shorter two averages fall through the 50-week MA. The two shorter MAs are used to filter false signals.

A weighted MA favors the most recent observations. A frequently used method is described as follows. For simplicity, assume the time span chosen is 7 days. Multiply the first price by 1, the second price by 2, . . . , and the seventh price by 7. Then divide the sum of these multiplications by the sum of the weights. The divisor is $1 + 2 + . . . + 7 = 28$. With a weighted MA, a buy or sell signal is given when the weighted MA changes direction.

Exponential Moving Average

A modified moving average that incorporates adaptive expectation concept is the exponential moving average (EMA). The basic principle is that recent prices have more impact on future changes. An EMA is another form of weighted MA. Technicians believe that an EMA is a better trend-following tool because it assigns a greater weight to the latest data and responds faster to changes than a simple MA. This is because the influence of the distant past prices on the future trend fades away as time goes by. The mathematical expression of EMA is:

$$EMA = P_{t+1} \times H + EMA_t \times (1 - H),$$

where $H = 2/(N + 1)$,
 $P =$ security price,
 $t =$ time point, and
 $N =$ the chosen time span.

The very first EMA is proxied by a simple MA. Then the line connecting all EMA points obtained from repeating the calculating process gives the EMA line. The trading rule is to trade from the long side when EMA rises, and to trade that security from the short side when the EMA falls. When the EMA moves repeatedly from side to side or remains flat, it is a trendless market.

Moving Average Convergence-Divergence

Another refinement of moving average techniques is the moving average convergence-divergence (MACD) that consists of two statistics: a difference in short-term and long-term EMAs, and the smoothing of this difference. The smoothing is used to generate signals of buys and sells. Hence MACD consists of three EMAs. The first is the shorter EMA (e.g., a 12-day EMA).[5] The second is a longer EMA (e.g., a 26-day EMA). Then the difference is calculated by subtracting the longer EMA from the shorter EMA. This is the so-called fast MACD line. The final step is to calculate a 9-day EMA of the fast line, which results in the slow signal line. A buy signal is given when the fast MACD line crosses above the slow signal line. A sell signal is given when the fast line crosses below the slow line.

Many MACD systems also use histograms. Some technicians believe histograms offer more insight into the balance of power between bulls and bears. It shows not only whether the market is bullish or bearish but also whether it is growing stronger or weaker. The MACD-histogram plots as a histogram the difference between the MACD fast line and the slow signal line. The histogram is positive when the fast line is above the slow line. Conversely, the histogram is negative. Hence when the MACD-histogram stops falling and ticks up it gives a buy signal. When the MACD-histogram stops rising and ticks down, it gives a signal to trade on the short side.

Filter Trading Rule

Technicians use filter rules to get in on a trend as the trend is starting and to get out as it begins to reverse. Typically, the rule specifies that when a security price moves up by

X percent above a previous low, the momentum will continue and thus buy and hold until price falls by Y percent below a previous high, at which time trade on the short side because the downside momentum is expected to continue. A trader using this rule would believe that in a positive breakout, the security price would continue to rise if the security rises X percent from some base. In contrast, a Y percent decline from some peak would be considered a breakout on the downside. The trader would hence expect a downward trend and would sell any holdings and might even sell short.

The specification of X percent and Y percent will determine the frequency of trading. A small percentage specification will result in a large number of transactions. A large percentage specification might miss certain market movements. Studies have found that filter rules may be effective when the filter is small, in the range of 1 to 5 percent.

Directional Movement Indicator

The directional movement indicator (DMI) is used to determine if a security is trending. The directional movement is the portion of today's trading range that is outside of the previous day's trading range. The process of calculating the DMI is briefly described next.

If today's range extends above yesterday's, the directional movement is positive (+DM). In contrast, if today's range extends below yesterday's range, the directional movement is negative (−DM). If today's range is inside yesterday's trading range or extends above and below it by an equal amount, there is no directional movement. If today's trading range extends both above and below yesterday's, the directional movement is either positive or negative, depending on which outside range is larger.

The next step is to identify the true range (TR) of the market. The TR is the largest of: (1) today's trading range, (2) the distance from today's high to yesterday's low, or (3) the distance from today's low to yesterday's close. Then the directional indicator (DI) is defined as +DI = +DM/TR and −DI = −DM/TR. Once the DIs are calculated, they are moving averaged to get smoothed directional lines. The relationship between positive and negative lines identifies the trend. When the smoothed +DI line is on top of the smoothed DI line, the trend is up. When the smoothed −DI line is on top of the smoothed +DI line, the trend is down. The crossover of +DI and −DI lines give buy and sell signals.

Many technicians also calculate the average directional indicator (ADI). ADI measures the spread between the smoothed +DI and smoothed −DI lines. It is calculated in two steps. The daily directional indicator (DDI) is calculated as:

$$DDI = \frac{\text{smoothed}\left(+DI\right) - \text{smoothed}\left(-DI\right)}{\text{smoothed}\left(+DI\right) + \text{smoothed}\left(-DI\right)} \times 100.$$

Then use EMA on DDI to obtain the ADI. In an upward trending market, the DDI rises and the spread between +DI and −DI lines increases. When DDI declines, it signals the reversal of trend.

Relative Strength Index

Relative strength index (RSI) is an index based on the momentum concept. It measures the strength of a security or an index by monitoring changes in its closing prices. It is based on the assumption that higher closes indicate strong markets and lower closes indicate weaker markets. The RSI is defined by the following formula:

$$RSI = \frac{AU}{AU + AD} \times 100.$$

AU is the average of net up closing changes for a selected number of days. Traders first choose a time span, for example, 10 days, then find all days when the security closed higher than the day before and add up the amounts of increases. The AU is equal to the sum divided by 10. AD is the average net down closing changes for the same number of days. Traders need to find all days when the security closed lower than the day before and add up the amounts of declines. AD is equal to the sum divided by 10. RSI is obtained by inputting the values of AU and AD into the formula. As is clear from the formula, RSI fluctuates between 0 and 100. If the ratio is 50, the ups and downs are equally divided. As the ratio goes up above 50, more closes are ups than downs, indicating an upward trend. Technicians would state that when the RSI passes 70 the market has reached its top. Conversely, if the RSI falls below 30, the market is near its bottom and a reversal is in sight. Many analysts have widened the band to 20 and 80.

Stochastic Oscillator

Stochastic oscillator (SO) compares a security closing price relative to its trading range over a certain period of time. There have been observations that in an upward trending market, prices tend to close near their highs, and in a downward trending market, they close near their lows. Further, as an upward trend matures, price tends to close further away from its highs; and as a downward trend matures, price tends to close away from its lows.

The SO is plotted as two lines: one fast line called %K and a slow line called %D. First, %K of fast stochastic is defined as:

$$\% K = \frac{P_t - P_L}{P_H - P_L} \times 100,$$

where P_t = today's closing price
P_L = lowest price traded during the selected number of days
P_H = highest point during the selected time span.

Then %D is obtained by smoothing the %K over a three-day period. The %D is smoothed once again to obtain %D of slow stochastic. The slow stochastic does a better job in filtering out market noise. The stochastic is plotted on a chart with value ranging from 0 to 100. References lines are drawn at 20 and 80 to mark overbought and oversold. Readings above 80 are strong and indicate that price is closing near its high. This means the market is overbought and is ready to turn down. Readings below 20 indicate that price is closing near its low. This implies the market is oversold and is ready to turn up.

Breadth of Market

Business reporters use the term breadth of market often. This technique measures the strength of advances over declines. The advance/decline (A/D) line shows each day the difference between the number of advancing issues and the declining issues, ignoring the unchanged. For example, if 1,234 stocks were traded higher for the day and 891 stocks declined, the A/D is +343. A cumulative A/D line is created by adding each day's A/D to the previous day's total. The cumulative A/D is then compared with the DJIA. An uprising cumulative A/D line supported by a higher DJIA signals a strengthening market. Conversely, a declining line coupled with a lower DJIA signals market weakness. Additionally, if a new high in the Dow index is accompanied by a new high in the A/D line, then the rally has broad support. When the DJIA reaches a new high but the cumulative A/D line only ups to a lower peak than the previous run, it shows that fewer stocks are participating and the bull run may come to an end. Similar analysis applies on a down market.

A variation of the technique is breadth advance decline (BAD). Data on NYSE listed stocks are generally used to construct the BAD. The BAD index is the simple moving average of the ratio of advances over the sum of advances and declines. Technicians believe that when the reading reaches 0.66, significant bull gains can be expected. When the ratio is 0.367 or lower, it is a bearish signal.

For an individual security, there is a technique called on balance volume (OBV) that creates a volume line along with a price chart at the bottom. If the stock closed higher, that day's volume is added. If the day closed lower, the volume is subtracted from the starting number. So volume is added on up days and subtracted on down days. The OBV often rises or falls before prices do, hence technicians believe that the OBV is a leading indicator of market trend.

Momentum and Rate of Change

Momentum and rate of change (RoC) show when the trend speeds up or slows down. Momentum subtracts a past price from today's price, while RoC divides today's price by a past price. They can be expressed as:

$$\text{Momentum} = P_t - P_{t-N}, \ \text{RoC} = \frac{P_t}{P_{t-N}}.$$

In this expressions, P_t is today's closing price and P_{t-N} is the close N days ago. For example, a 10-day momentum equals today's closing price minus the closing price 10 trading days ago. A 10-day RoC divides today's price by the closing price 10 days ago. The time window is kept short to detect short-term market changes. A long time window is for trend following.

When momentum or RoC rises to a new high, it signals that the prices are likely to rally higher. Conversely, when momentum or RoC falls to a new low, lower prices are expected. When prices rise but momentum or RoC declines, the market is near its top and it is time to take profits or consider shorting. Reverse this approach during downtrends.

Head and Shoulder

Head and shoulder (HS) tops indicate the market has reached it top. The head is a price peak surrounded by two lower tops (called shoulders). Volume is often higher on the left shoulder than on the head. An uptrend continues as long as each rally keeps on reaching a new high. Rising volume serves as a confirmation. Volume falls when the market is near its top. The decline from the head to the right shoulder is the beginning of a downtrend. Trading strategies on the existing long position include sell, tighten stop level, or sell some and hold the rest. Another strategy is to short the security and place a protective stop.

In an inverse HS, the head is at the lowest point surrounded by two shoulders. An inverse HS develops when a downtrend is near an end and an upturn is likely. In a downtrend, each new low falls lower than the previous low and each rally fails to reach a higher level. High volume confirms all declines. The decline to head usually comes with low volume. The rally out of the head breaks out of the downtrend and signals a likely bull market. During the right shoulder, there is usually a low volume. An increasing volume associated with each new high confirms that an uptrend has developed.

Elliot Waves

Under Elliot wave theory, the upward and downward moves of stock prices show repetitive patterns (waves). There are five waves in the direction of the main trend that is followed by three corrective waves (called "5–3" move). Elliot labeled the main direction of prices as impulsive waves and the correction as corrective waves. The "5–3" impulsive and corrective waves complete a cycle. Figure 15.2 shows the Elliot waves. Waves 1 to 5 are the impulsive waves and A, B, and C are the corrective waves.

Mutual Fund Cash Ratio

Mutual funds hold cash for several reasons. One obvious reason is for possible shareholder redemption. Second, the money from new purchases of funds may not have been invested. Third, a fund manager might buildup its cash position if he has a bearish outlook. Some technicians interpret the mutual fund cash ratio (cash/assets) as a contrarian indicator. They consider mutual funds to be a proxy for the institutional investor group and mutual funds are generally wrong at market timing. Therefore, a

FIGURE 15.2   Elliot Waves

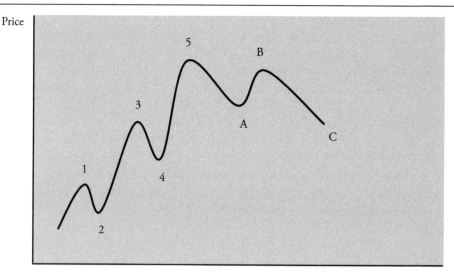

bullish sign is given when the cash ratio rises and a bearish signal is given when the cash ratio declines.

Additionally, a high cash ratio can be considered a bullish sign because of potential buying power, as the funds have to be and will be invested. Alternatively, a low cash ratio would mean that institutions have bought heavily and are left with little potential buying power.

Short Sales by Specialists

Short sales by exchange specialists are closely watched statistics. This is because specialist operations consistently generate high returns. Investors who want to follow smart money watch the specialists. Specialists regularly engage in short selling as part of their market making function, but they will be more aggressive in executing shorts when they feel strongly about the down trend.

The specialist short sale ratio is the ratio of short sales by specialists to the total short interest. Technicians view a decline of this ratio below 30 percent as a bullish sign because it means that specialists are attempting to minimize their participation in short selling. In contrast a reading of 50 percent or higher is a bearish sign.

Short Interest Ratio

Short interest is the total number of shares that have been shorted and not covered. Technicians compute a short interest ratio (SIR) as the outstanding short interest divided by the average daily trading volume on the exchange. As an example, suppose the short interest totaled 750 million shares and the average daily trading volume is 500 million shares, the SIR is 1.50. This means the short interest equals about 1.5 day's trading volume. The SIR can also be computed based on an individual stock.

Technicians interpret the SIR contrary to short-seller's belief. Traders selling short expect stock prices to decline, so an increase in SIR could be a bearish sign. On the contrary, technicians consider a high SRI bullish because it indicates potential demand for the security by those who have sold short and have not covered the sales.

Options Ratio

Traders and investors use options contracts for speculation or hedging. A call options contract is used to bet on the upside, while a put is on the downside. In technical analysis, the put/call ratio is used as a contrarian indicator. Technicians reason that a higher put/call ratio indicates a more pervasive bearish attitude, which to them is a bullish indicator. The ratio is typically less than one because investors tend to be relatively more bullish than bearish and avoid selling shorts or buying puts. A buy signal is given when the ratio is approaching 0.70. In contrast, a put/call ratio of 0.40 or lower is considered a bearish sign. A put/call reading of between 0.40 and 0.70 is neutral.

Odd-Lot Theory

In the United States, a round lot is the multiple of 100 shares. In some emerging markets, it is multiple of 1,000 shares. An odd lot is less than a round lot. The assumption is that only small investors trade odd lot. Thus, the odd-lot technique focuses on the trading activities of small investors. Most small investors do not engage in short selling except when they feel especially bearish. Technical analysts interpret heavy short selling by individuals as a signal that the market is close to trough because small investors only get pessimistic after a long decline in prices, just when the market is about to turn around. A buy signal is given when the ratio of odd-lot short sales as a percentage of total odd-lot sales is rising above 3 percent. A sell signal is given when the ratio declines to 1 percent or lower.

Another interpretation of the odd-lot behavior is based on a similar belief that small investors are unsophisticated and frequently make mistakes in market reversals. Small investors often do all right but frequently miss on key market turns. Specifically, the odd-lot investors are generally in the money as the market is going up. However, as the market continues upward, small investors get greedy and buy strongly just before the market reverses direction. Similarly, small investors are also assumed to be strong sellers right before the market bottoms out.

Investment Advisory Opinions

Technicians practicing this approach reason that most investment advisory services tend to be trend followers. Technicians develop a trading rule from the ratio of the number of advisory services that are bearish as a percentage of the number of services expressing an opinion. A bearish sentiment index of 60 percent indicates a pervasive bearish attitude by advisory services; contrarians would consider this a bullish sign. Conversely, a decline of the bearish sentiment index to below 20 percent indicates a sell signal.

CONCLUSION

Growth companies are expected to produce a higher growth rate than the average in the industry. Thus, many investors are willing to pay a higher price and expect the high growth rate to continue for sometime. Some of the companies continue to grow at a rate as expected. But, some growth companies disappoint investors. This chapter discussed the cautions investors should take when investing in growth companies. The chapter also reviewed some of the factors important in valuing such companies.

16

Investing in Value Sectors

Food, beverage, and retail stocks in many developed markets are considered value play. Those companies are able to maintain stable businesses and generate decent cash flows, but there are no substantial growth opportunities. In China or other developing economies, the concept is quite different. Those types of business present tremendous potential. As the overall income level rises, they spend more on necessities. Thus, companies serving those segments will enjoy a burst of demand and an increasing growth rate. After some years, those companies will mature and become value stocks. The strategic consideration is to invest in value stocks when they are classified as value. Investors often suffer when they believe they are buying value but in fact they are paying growth price.

VALUE OR GROWTH

Many companies in their corporate development process experience a growth stage. During that time period, their businesses are growing at an above average rate. The stocks of those companies are the target of growth investing. If an investor can identify that specific period and exit before growth slows down, she will enjoy a high rate of return on the investment. However, it is helpful to diversify the portfolio, even if growth stocks were able to generate higher returns during certain phase. Diversification in different asset classes (growth, value, real estate, or commodities) reduces risks and enhances returns. Thus, it is prudent to allocate a portion of the funds in value stocks as well.

Some of the growth stocks, after the period of above average growth, plateau to become value stocks. Very few are able to reengineer themselves to be in the growth category for a long time. Many eventually fade away or become mediocre. China will be no different. The companies that provide services or produce products where demands are growing fast experience high growth. Companies that have stable businesses and pay good dividends are the target of value investors. The objective of the SSE Dividend Index is to reflect the complete picture of high and steady dividend-paying companies on the Shanghai Stock Exchange. Table 16.1 lists those companies and agriculture, steel, and automotive companies are well represented.

As discussed in the previous chapter, growth stocks outperform value during certain periods while value does better during other periods. No one knows exactly when the switch from growth to value will occur. Thus, it is sensible to allocate funds in both (in addition to other asset classes for a diversified portfolio). The allocation of assets depends on many factors. It is helpful to establish an investment policy that lays out objectives and constraints.

Investment Policy and Guidelines

The very first step an investor needs to address is the objectives of the investment. An investment policy statement (IPS) can be indispensable in helping an individual or institution meet investment goals, serving several useful purposes:[1]

- The IPS provides record tracking policies and procedures for investment decisions.
- For an institutional investor, the IPS ensures continuity of the investment strategy when there is a high turnover of the investment policy board.
- The IPS can be valuable in reminding the investment committee or individuals of the investment strategy of the portfolio during turbulent market periods.
- The IPS provides a baseline to evaluate the performance of the overall portfolio.

In constructing the policy statement, it is helpful to get an understanding of a number of questions. Charles Ellis, a money manager, believes that answers to the following questions are beneficial in constructing the investment policy statement:

- What are the real risks of an adverse financial outcome, especially in the short run?
- What probable emotional reactions will I have to an adverse financial outcome?
- How knowledgeable am I about investments and markets?
- What other capital or income sources do I have? How important is this particular portfolio to my overall financial position?
- What, if any, legal restrictions may affect my investment needs?
- What, if any, unanticipated consequences of interim fluctuations in portfolio value might affect my investment policy?

Investment Objectives

The objectives of an investor are the starting point for preparing a sound financial plan. Objectives such as making as much money as possible are too broad to produce a sound financial plan. In fact, broad objectives like this may actually lead the investor or money manager to invest inappropriately. In addition, the objectives laid out in the policy statement need to be realistic. The goal of a recent college graduate to become

TABLE 16.1 High Dividend Stocks in Shanghai Exchange

Company Name	Code
Handan Iron & Steel Co., Ltd.	600001
Wuhan Iron and Steel Company Limited.	600005
Beijing Capital Co., Ltd.	600008
Huaneng Power International, INC.	600011
Hua Xia Bank Co., Limited	600015
Baoshan Iron & Steel Co., Ltd.	600019
Jinan Iron &Steel Co., Ltd.	600022
China Petroleum & Chemical Corporation	600028
Fujian Expressway Development Company Limited	600033
ZheJiang GuYueLongShan ShaoXing Wine Co. LTD.	600059
Nanjing Xingang High-Tech Co., Ltd.	600064
Zhengzhou Yutong Bus Co., Ltd.	600066
Nanjing Water Transport Industry Co., Ltd.	600087
Yunnan Yuntianhua Co., Ltd.	600096
Guangzhou Development Industry (Holdings) Co., Ltd.	600098
Shanghai Automotive Co., Ltd.	600104
HangZhou Iron & Steel Co., Ltd.	600126
Shanghai Aerospace Automobile Electromechanical Co., Ltd.	600151
Xiamen C&D Inc.	600153
Youngor Group Co., Ltd.	600177
Jilin Forest Industry Co., Ltd.	600189
Shanghai Zijiang Enterprise Group Co., Ltd.	600210
Lingyuan Iron & Steel Co., Ltd.	600231
Guangxi Guiguan Electric Power Co., Ltd.	600236
Nanjing Iron & Steel Co., Ltd.	600282
v v Food & Beverage Co., Ltd.	600300
Xian Typical Industries Co., Ltd.	600302
Liaoning Sg Automotive Group Co., Ltd.	600303
Gan Su Jiu Steel Group Hong Xing Iron & Steel Co., Ltd.	600307
Yingkou Port Liability Co., Ltd.	600317
Nanhai Development Co., Ltd.	600323
Wuxi Commercial Mansion Corp., Ltd.	600327
Gemdale Corporation	600383
Anhui Jianghuai Automobile Co., Ltd.	600418
Shanghai Datun Energy Resourses Co., Ltd.	600508
Black Peony (Group) Co., Ltd.	600510
Nanjing Chixia Development Co., Ltd.	600533
Shenzhen Expressway Co., Ltd.	600548
Xiamen Faratronic Co., Ltd.	600563
Anyang Iron & Steel Inc.	600569
Xinjiang Ba Yi Iron & Steel Co., Ltd.	600581
Heilongjiang Agriclture Company Limited	600598
Shanghai Jinling Co., Ltd.	600621
Shanghai Shenda Co., Ltd.	600626
Shenergy Company Limited	600642
China Enterprise Company Limited	600675
Shanghai Petrochemical Co., Ltd.	600688
Maanshan Iron & Steel Company Limited (Mas C.L.)	600808
Sdic Huajing Power Holdings Co., Ltd.	600886
Anhui Hengyuan Coal Industry and Electricity Power Co., Ltd.	600971

Source: Shanghai Stock Exchange, April 2007.

a millionaire by age 30 may be unrealistic given this person's $40,000 per year job. However, the goal of saving a million dollars and retiring at age 55 is attainable with a sound financial plan.

The return objectives are only the first part of the analysis. The risk that the investor is willing and able to assume must be taken into consideration. The risk tolerance of an investor depends on a number of factors, including the investor's age, current income and expenses, psychological makeup, level of wealth, time horizon, and liquidity needs.

A simple method advocated by the CFA Institute (formerly the Association for Investment Management Research, AIMR), lays out the objectives in the following manner:

- *Return requirements:* For individuals, this may include funding a new home, paying for a child's college education, or saving for retirement. The return objective should recognize the impact inflation will have on one's financial well being and therefore, the objective should seek returns that maintain the purchasing power of the investor.
- *Risk tolerance:* This is perhaps the most difficult to qualify because it is so closely tied to the constraints (discussed next) and can also be largely determined by an investor's psychological make up. Investing in China, or any other emerging markets, entails additional risks that need to be considered carefully.

Constraints

The objectives are largely determined by the constraints imposed on the investor. Liquidity needs should be directly addressed in the policy statement. There may be a number of needs that will require a portion of the investor's portfolio to remain in highly liquid assets. For example, parents of a college-bound child may require liquid assets to make tuition payments, or a young couple may wish to purchase a house in the next two years. If so, the portion of funds allocated to Chinese securities or mutual funds should not be large because volatility may cause losses in that time period. This is a time horizon constraint. The general rule is that the time horizon of the assets should match the time horizon of the investor's needs. That is, short-term needs require investment in highly liquid, short-term investment vehicles, whereas long-term investment needs permit investment in long-term assets. For example, the retirement investment for a 30-year-old has a long time horizon and should be invested using long-term, high return assets such as stocks. Investing in Chinese stocks may be appropriate in this case. A short-term goal of making a down payment on a house in six months should use short-term, highly liquid investments such as money market accounts or bank certificates of deposit.

The second constraint that needs to be considered is taxes. An institution such as an educational endowment that enjoys tax-exemption can ignore the tax consequences of an investment. In addition, money in an individual's 401(k) or other qualified retirement plan is tax deferred, so once again, taxes are not an issue in the investment allocation. However, for an individual's taxable accounts, taxes can be an important constraint. Investors who are in high tax brackets may wish to use tax-exempt securities, tax-efficient mutual funds, or stock in companies that pay little or qualified dividends in order to reduce the tax liability.

Another factor is the presence of any unique preferences or circumstances that the investor may face. For example, a person might wish to have sufficient funds to gift $300,000 to a grandchild or favorite charity. Another individual might have a trust fund that will distribute $100,000 per year when that person reaches the age of 35. These special circumstances will once again play a part in shaping the investment allocation.

Given the constraints, an investment policy statement can be completed in the following manner.

- *Liquidity:* Depends on the unexpected need for cash in excess of what can be covered by income. For an individual, liquidity will depend on the person's income relative to expenses. If income significantly exceeds expenses, then the individual will likely be able to cover unexpected needs for cash from current income. In this case, liquidity needs would be relatively low. For an institution, liquidity would depend on the possibility of unexpected cash outflows.
- *Time horizon:* This is important in asset allocation because individuals and institutions should match the duration of their assets and liabilities.
- *Taxes:* For individuals, taxes play an important role in defining the appropriate investment strategy. Individuals in high tax brackets may realize higher after-tax returns by investing in tax-free municipal bonds and tax efficient mutual funds to maximize after tax returns.
- *Laws and regulations:* Institutions may be governed by federal laws such as ERISA in the case of pension funds or by corporate charters as is the case for endowment funds.
- *Unique preferences and circumstances:* Each individual or institution may be guided by unique circumstances that needs to be incorporated into the IPS.

The objectives and constraints differ depending on the needs and circumstances of the investor. A sound IPS should also satisfactorily address the following questions:[2]

- Is the IPS carefully designed to meet the specific needs, risk constraints, and objectives of this particular investor?
- Is the IPS written clearly and explicitly that a competent stranger could manage the portfolio in compliance with the investor's needs?
- Would the client have been able to remain committed to the IPS during the capital market experiences of the past 10 years?
- Would the portfolio manager have been able to follow the IPS over the same period?
- Would the IPS, if implemented, have achieved the investor's objectives?

In addition to these objectives and constraints, the IPS should include how money managers are selected and evaluated and provide guidelines on the types and amount of various securities that are eligible for inclusion in the portfolio. For example, the portfolio might specify that equities should constitute from 50 percent to 60 percent, with 10 percent to 15 percent allocated to international stocks. Bonds and real estate investment trusts might make up the remaining part of the allocation, with 20 percent to 40 percent allocated to bonds and 5 percent to 10 percent devoted to REITs. Finally, the IPS should state how often a review of the investor's needs and constraints will be completed. In most instances, a review of the client's IPS should be conducted on an annual basis. If a significant unexpected change in an investor's circumstances occurs, a reevaluation may be necessary before the usual review.

INDIVIDUAL INVESTORS

Defining the objectives and constraints of an individual investor can be more difficult than for institutional investors. Institutional investors are governed by laws and by charters. Individual investors, on the other hand, have an almost limitless combination of needs and constraints. Individual investors also differ from institutional investors in how they view risk. There are four differences between individuals and institutions:[3]

1. *Risk:* Institutions generally view risk as the volatility of returns as measured by the standard deviation or beta. Individuals tend to view risk as the possibility of losing money.
2. *Traits:* Individuals can be categorized by their psychographics or personality traits, whereas institutions are categorized by who has a beneficial interest in their portfolio.
3. *Assets and goals:* Individuals can be classified financially by their assets and goals, whereas institutions have a more precise package of assets and liabilities.
4. *Tax structure:* Individuals have to deal with taxes, whereas institutions are sometimes free of taxes as long as they comply with certain regulations.

Individuals generally view three types of investments as risky.[4] First, unfamiliar instruments tend to be considered risky by the individual because of his fear of the unknown. Second, investors view previous losses in familiar instruments as more risky. Finally, contrary investing tends to be viewed as risky because individuals often have a difficult time going against the prevailing sentiment. In order to forge a long-lasting relationship with clients, the investment professional must not only understand how an investor views risk, but must have a sound understanding of the financial products in the marketplace that will be used to construct the client's portfolio. Even when dealing with experienced investors, it will be necessary for the investment adviser to educate clients about the merits of different investment vehicles and strategies.

Many of the objectives and constraints used in forming the IPS can be established by examining the investor's life cycle. This approach breaks investors' spending and savings patterns into four phases:

1. *Accumulation phase:* Occurs in the early years of an investor's life. Here the investor's net worth is usually small relative to liabilities. Usually the investor has limited diversification, with the majority of his or her net worth tied up in a home.
2. *Consolidation phase:* Occurs in mid- to late-career stage and is characterized by income that exceeds expenses. The investor may have accumulated a significant amount of wealth in a company retirement plan and may be past many of the expenses that younger investors face such as the purchase of a home or financing a child's education. This investor will be looking to balance the growth and risk of the portfolio.
3. *Spending phase:* Occurs when the investor is financially independent and living expenses are covered by accumulated assets rather than earned income. In this case, the investor will have no need to work in order to support her life style. This person may have retired or may be considering retirement. If the investor chooses to retire, the portfolio will need to be structured to generate sufficient income and growth to meet the investor's needs.
4. *Gifting phase:* Occurs in the final stage of the life cycle when the individual realizes that she has more assets than will ever be needed for financial security. In this phase, the investor may wish to begin gifting assets in an effort to reduce the size of his estate.

Each phase of the investor's life cycle plays an important part in determining an appropriate investment strategy. During each phase of the investor's life cycle, there are various objectives and constraints. For example, a 20-year-old may wish to save a sufficient amount of money to meet a goal of retiring at age 55. This individual may also have short-term goals such as saving for the purchase of a house or paying for a wedding. In order to make it easier to prepare the IPS, two policy statements could be used, one for the long-term retirement portfolio and one for the shorter-term financial goals. Investors who are in the consolidation, spending, or gifting phases may have goals that can be easily handled with one IPS.

Investor Behavior

There are two approaches for examining investor behavior. Classical decision-making theory uses three assumptions to determine the appropriate decisions under risk. First, investors are assumed to look at their investments in a portfolio context. This assumption, known as asset integration, implies that investors take a systematic look at all their investments as a whole. Decisions to buy or sell securities are not viewed on an individual basis, but are viewed in terms of how the transaction will affect the entire portfolio. Second, investors are assumed to be risk averse.[5] Finally, decisions are assumed to be based on rational expectations, which mean that individuals are coherent, accurate, and unbiased forecasters. This assumption requires that investors have the ability to process large amounts of complicated information in order to make their investment decisions.

An alternative to classical decision-making theory is behavioral decision research. This approach blends psychology and observations of human behavior to help determine how an individual will behave under uncertainty. Much of the research in this area casts doubts on the validity of the classical assumptions. Researchers have found that individual's decision making may be hindered by their lack of understanding of the situation. The classical and behavioral approaches can be contrasted by comparing the following:

- *Risk aversion versus loss aversion:* When an investor is risk averse, the pain of a loss is greater than the joy of a gain, so investors will always choose the safe alternative unless the risky outcome has a very high expected return.
- *Reference dependence:* In behavioral decision making, an investor's decision will also depend on where they are now, their reference point.
- *Asset segregation:* In classical theory, investors view assets in a portfolio context, however in behavioral decision making, they tend to view each asset individually. Therefore, they often make mistakes by choosing an incorrect combination of securities.
- *Mental accounting:* In classical theory, preferences do not depend on how the decision is framed. However, because behavioral researchers have found that individuals tend to place items in specific "mental accounts," the framing of the problem does matter. For example, many individuals tend to have separate mental accounts for entertainment and living expenses. When people are asked whether they will buy a $50 ticket to a show after losing the ticket, they tend to respond differently than when they find they have lost a $50 bill on the way to the show. The reason for this is that in the first case, the person has spent his "show account" money, whereas in the second case, he believes the "show account" money has not been spent and the loss comes from some other account. In each case, the cost is the same, an additional $50 to attend the show. From an investing perspective, individuals may have separate mental accounts, for example, one for vacations, one for their child's education, and so on. As another example, individuals may have separate mental accounts for the income and principal of their investments. These individuals may have no difficulty spending funds from the income account, but will not withdraw funds from the principal account. Many behavioral researchers believe that mental accounting is used to impose discipline on the investor. For example, parents are less likely to spend their children's college fund when the assets are segregated from other household funds.
- *Biased expectations:* In classical theory, people make unbiased, rational decisions. However, in real life, researchers have found that people are overconfident in their abilities to predict unknown future events.

VALUE AND GROWTH IN A PORTFOLIO

In an uncertain world, we need to be able to quantify the degree of uncertainty of our guesses. In standard financial theory, we use the variance or standard deviation of the returns. The variance measures how spread out the values are around the average or mean value. The larger the spread, the greater the risk is. The standard deviation, which is sometimes used in place of the variance, is simply the square root of the variance and is used because it is in the same units as the return.

One problem with the use of the variance or standard deviation as a measure of risk is that it treats values above the mean the same way it treats values below the mean. In finance, returns above the mean are a good thing and should not be treated in the measurement of risk.

Once the risk and returns for the individual securities are computed, we are interested in finding the risk and return for a portfolio of securities. One of the most important concepts of portfolio management is the concept of diversification. Diversification allows an investor to reduce risk without sacrificing return. Diversification is sometimes stated as not putting all your eggs in one basket, or spreading the risks of the portfolio over a number of different assets. This concept, although correct in principle, is too simplistic to really understand how diversification reduces risk. An investor can own numerous stocks, however, if they are all in the same industry, the investor is likely to see very little diversification benefit. For example, if an investor only owns Dell, HP, and Acer, he or she is likely to receive less diversification benefit than if the investment had been spread over companies in different industries. Why? Because these three companies are all in the personal computer industry and their respective successes are determined in large part by the market demand for personal computers. A dip in demand will affect all three negatively and a rise in demand will benefit all three. Because the prices of those three stocks tend to move closely together, there will be only limited benefits of diversifying into these three stocks. However, if this investor chose to buy Dell, Toyota, and General Electric, he or she would likely receive greater diversification benefits because only the fortunes of Dell are tied to the personal computer industry. Similarly, Toyota's success is determined by the demand for automobiles, a factor that probably has little effect on Dell or GE. In this case, we can say that movements in these stocks are not closely related.

Portfolio Risk and Return

Once the expected return and variance for the individual securities have been computed, the issue is how to find the risk and return for a portfolio of securities. The expected return for a portfolio of assets is simply the weighted average of the expected returns of the securities held in the portfolio. The weights used in the calculation are simply the percentages invested in each security.

Given that the expected return for a portfolio is computed as the weighted-average of the expected returns of the securities in the portfolio, does this intuition extend to the computation of the variance of the portfolio? Unfortunately, the answer is no. When computing the risk of a portfolio we need to consider both the risk of each individual asset as well as the relationship between each pair of assets. This relationship can be measured by looking at the covariance or correlation between each pair of assets. The relationship is important because two risky assets may in fact have no risk when combined together into a portfolio if they move in opposite directions. This negative correlation will reduce or eliminate the risk of the portfolio because loses in one asset will be offset by gains in the other. Even when securities exhibit positive correlations, there will still be benefits from diversification if the relationship between the two securities is not perfect.

To estimate the relationship between two assets, we can calculate their correlation, or correlation coefficient, indicating the strength and direction of a linear relationship between two random variables. When one variable moves in the same direction by the same percentage as the other, those two variables are said to be perfectly correlated. In other words, the correlation coefficient is 1. If they move by the same percentage but in opposite directions, then the correlation coefficient is −1. In the real world, it is rare to find two securities that exhibit perfect correlation. In fact, in most cases, the correlation between pairs of assets tends to be positive. Even so, there will still be benefits from diversifying into both assets. However, the lower the degree of correlation between two assets, the greater the diversification benefit is.

In examining the risk/return relationship for different possible portfolios, we are able to eliminate many of the possible combinations because they are inefficient. When we speak of efficient portfolios, we are looking at portfolios that meet one of the following criteria:

1. The highest expected return for a given level of risk or
2. The lowest risk for a given level of return.

The efficient portfolios can be graphed in risk-return space to create what is known as the efficient frontier (Figure 16.1). All portfolios above point K on the curve are efficient, while portfolios on the curve but below K are inefficient because they are dominated by portfolios on the upper portion of the curve. Thus, the real efficient frontier is from K and to the right of the curve.

The efficient frontier indicates what portfolios we should consider when investing, but not which portfolio is optimal. Each point on the efficient frontier represents the highest return possible at a given risk. Put another way, any point on the efficient frontier is the minimum risk that investors take at a given return level. The choice of a best portfolio depends on an investor's risk and return preferences. However, when a riskless (or risk-free) interest rate is introduced at which investors can borrow and lend, the optimal portfolio is the one where a line from the riskless interest rate is tangent to the efficient frontier.[6] This portfolio has come to be known as the market portfolio because it consists of all risky assets available to the market, held in their market value proportions. The line that is tangent to the efficient frontier is known as the capital market line (Figure 16.2 on p. 324). The capital market line shows the

FIGURE 16.1   Efficient Frontier

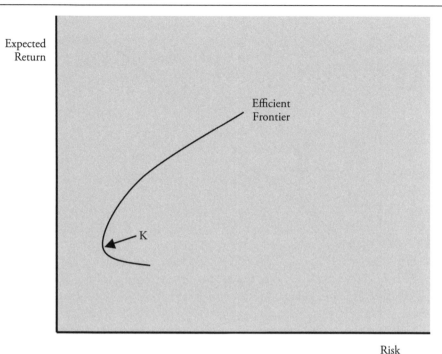

tradeoff between expected return and total risk for a portfolio consisting of money in the riskless asset and risky portfolio M.

An interesting insight that can be drawn from the capital market line is that there is only one best portfolio. Investors who are more conservative will place a portion of their wealth in the risk-free asset and purchase some of risky portfolio M. More aggressive investors will place 100 percent of their wealth in risky portfolio M or may actually choose to borrow so they can invest additional funds in M. The conclusion of the theoretical model presented here also has a real world implication, simply that the best portfolio will be a broad-based index fund like the S&P 500 or Wilshire 5000. Investors can then adjust the amount of risk they wish to take by lending some of their funds (purchasing Treasury securities) or borrowing additional funds (purchasing on margin). The more funds are invested in Treasuries, the lower the expected rate of return will be. If the investor invests all his money in the market portfolio M, the return will be the same as the overall market. On the other hand, if the investor is more aggressive and borrows funds to buy M, then the expected returns will be higher than the market index.

The key to successful portfolio management is to combine these theoretical issues of portfolio optimization with an investor's objectives and constraints and current economic forecasts to create an appropriate asset allocation for the investor.

FIGURE 16.2 **Capital Market Line**

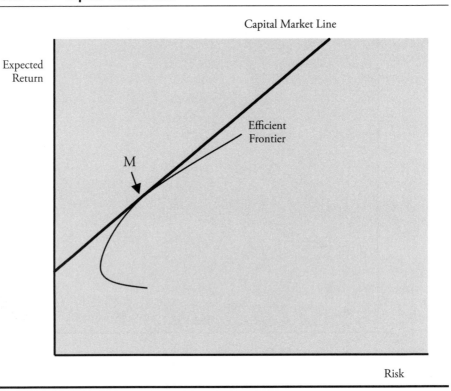

STOCK TRADING STYLES

There are many investment styles and trading tactics for value or growth investing. The most basic approach to defining management style is active management versus passive management. Passive managers seek to replicate the returns of some index, like the S&P 500. Active managers seek to add value to a portfolio by selecting securities that will outperform the market, or by adjusting the composition of the portfolio based on their forecasts of the overall direction of the market. In general, active managers can be classified by the type of analysis they perform. Fundamental analysis deals with the analysis of financial statements and analysis of economic fundamentals in order to determine the value of a security and its growth prospects. Many value investors use this approach. Technical analysis is the art of identifying patterns in securities prices and volume. Technical analysts believe that trends can be identified and that these trends will tend to persist. A third investment approach is arbitrage trading. Arbitrage can take several forms, from profiting from price differences between securities in different markets to betting on the probability that a merger will be completed. Both arbitrage and technical analysis have been covered in a previous chapter. Thus, we focus on fundamental analysis here.

Fundamental Analysis

There are several ways to classify analysts that use fundamental analysis. First, the analyst can take a top down investment approach. The top down approach begins with an analysis of the aggregate economy. This information is used to determine which industries will prosper given the general economic outlook. Finally, an analysis of which companies will be the top performers in the best industries is determined by evaluating the financial statements of these companies in order to determine the overall financial health, growth prospects, and value of a company's security. The second approach that can be used is a bottom up approach. In this case, the analyst begins the analysis at the company level and works his way up to the aggregate economy to make sure that outlook for the economy will support the company and its industry.

Whether the analyst uses a top down or bottom up approach, they are usually placed in one of two camps, value investors or growth investors. Value investors seek out companies that they believe the market has incorrectly undervalued. Growth investors by contrast are less concerned about value and more concerned about the growth rate of earnings. Growth investors are not only looking for companies with accelerating earnings growth, but firms whose growth exceeds expectations of other investors.

A third type of analyst is a hybrid that looks for growth at a reasonable price. Keep in mind that all three types of analysts care about both the price of a security and the rate at which earnings will grow. The difference lies in the emphasis that is paid to each component. Value investors place greater emphasis on the price paid relative to the firm's earnings. That is, they are not looking for firms with superior growth prospects, but rather firms that are inexpensive relative to their current level of earnings. Growth investors, on the other hand, place a great deal of emphasis on the earnings growth relative to the market price. That is, growth investors are willing to pay more for a company that they believe has superior growth prospects that are not already reflected in the stock's price. Growth-at-a-reasonable-price investors would tend to take a more balanced view on the importance of earnings growth and price.

A fourth style of investing is referred to as sector rotation. Analysts that follow a sector rotation strategy rotate the portfolio into different industry sectors in order to prosper from perceived mispricing. In addition to shifting between sectors, managers may shift between value and growth stocks, or between small and large cap stocks.

Finally, there are analysts that attempt to outperform the market through the use of market timing. Market timing is a strategy where the manager adjusts the stock/bond mix or the risk of the portfolio based on market forecasts. When the market is expected to rise, the manager increases the portfolio's percentage in stocks or shifts the portfolio into higher risk stocks, which are likely to rise faster than the market. If the market is expected to fall, the manager will reduce the percentage of stocks or decrease the risk of the portfolio. If the analyst is correct, the portfolio will suffer smaller losses. Market timing is an unreliable method for attempting to beat the market because of the difficulty in predicting the overall movement in the market.

Economic Analysis

Top-down investing begins with an analysis of the overall economy. Some successful investors such as Warren Buffett and Peter Lynch regard economic analysis as fruitless because of the difficulty in forecasting overall movements in the economy and because great companies thrive regardless of the overall movements in the economy. Other investors, such as John Neff, view economic analysis as fundamental to their investment decision making. Some of the economic information that can be used includes:

- *Interest rate forecasts:* Interest rates determine the cost of raising funds for firms, therefore interest rates can be important in determining profitability. In addition, interest rates determine the return on assets such as bonds, which serve as substitutes for stocks. Therefore, an increase in interest rates makes bonds more attractive relative to stocks.
- *Shifts in the yield curve:* The yield curve represents a plot of the yield to maturity and the term to maturity for Treasury securities. Shifts in the yield curve are often indicators of future economic activity and corporate profitability. For example, a flat or inverted yield curve puts a downward pressure on banks' net interest margin.
- *GDP forecasts:* Gross domestic product represents the income of the aggregate economy and so can be important in determining demand growth for products.
- *Leading economic indicators:* May provide some indication of the future direction of the economy in the coming months.
- *Demographic shifts:* Changes in the size and age of the population can have profound implications for investing. For example, an aging population may benefit businesses such as pharmaceutical companies.

Industry Analysis

Once an analyst has determined the overall outlook for the economy, the focus then shifts to the industry. Industry analysis looks at the profitability and future growth prospects of an industry in order to determine which industries will offer the greatest investment opportunities. Michael Porter in his book *Competitive Advantage: Creating and Sustaining Superior Performance* (1988) provided a framework for analyzing the profitability of an industry, listing five factors that determine industry competitiveness:

1. Bargaining power of buyers
2. Bargaining power of suppliers
3. Threat of new entrants

4. Threat of substitutes
5. Rivalry among existing competitors

Industries will be more profitable when these factors are in the industry's favor. For example, industries that have products with few substitutes and where entry into the industry is difficult will tend to be more profitable than industries that face less favorable conditions.

Another method for analyzing the future profitability of an industry is to look at the industry life cycle. The industry life cycle model looks at the different phases an industry passes through over its lifetime:

1. Pioneering and development
2. Rapid accelerating growth
3. Mature growth
4. Stabilization and market maturity
5. Deceleration of growth and decline

Industries in the first or second stage of the industry life cycle will tend to see improving profitability whereas industries in the fourth or fifth stage will tend to see stable or even declining profitability. The industry life cycle can be difficult to use these days because many firms are in a number of lines of business, all of which may be in different phases of the product life cycle.

Generic Competitive Strategies

In addition to his work on industry competitiveness, Michael Porter also looks at the generic strategies that a firm can pursue. Firms can choose to be a cost leader, a differentiator, or follow a focus strategy. According to Porter (1988), a firm's success depends on how well it pursues its strategy. Firms that try to be all things to all people wind up in what Porter refers to as "stuck in the middle," a position that tends to be least profitable. Firms that follow a cost strategy hope to attain greater profitability by having cost savings in excess of the discount offered to customers. Similarly, firms that follow a differentiation strategy hope to attain greater profitability charging a price in excess of the added costs of differentiating their product. The final strategy deals with the breadth of the market that the firm chooses to target using the first two strategies. A firm can try to focus on a narrow segment of the market or target a broader segment of the market. Figure 16.3 is a grid of the generic competitive strategies a firm can pursue.

A firm can choose to take a cost leadership role in a very broad market, such as Wal-Mart, or it can choose to take a broad differentiation strategy such as Coca Cola. A firm can also choose to use cost leadership or differentiation in a fairly narrow market. A good example of a firm that follows a cost focus strategy would be GEICO, the direct marketer of automobile insurance. Rather than target all drivers, GEICO chooses to focus only on "good drivers."

FIGURE 16.3

Porter's Generic Strategies

Competitive Advantage

	Cost Leadership	Differentiation
	Cost Focus	Differentiation Focus

(left axis label: **Competitive Scope**)

VALUATION TECHNIQUES

In deciding whether to recommend the purchase of a security, the analyst needs to determine the value of the asset. There are several different methods that can be used. Discounted cash flow models look at the present value of future cash flows such as dividends, earnings, or free cash flow to determine the value of a firm's equity. Relative valuation approaches compare the relative value of a security against comparable stocks in the same industry or against the industry average.

Discounted Cash Flow

Discounted cash flow models are based on the principle of present value. Value is found by taking the present value of the expected future cash flows:

$$\text{Value} = \sum_{t=1}^{n} \frac{CF_t}{\left(1+r\right)^t}$$

Where CF_t denotes the expected cash flow in period t, n denotes the life of the asset, and r denotes the discount rate that reflects the riskiness of the cash flow. For stocks, the cash flow will be dividends. The discount rate will be determined by the riskiness of the projected cash flows, with lower rates for safer assets and higher rates for riskier ones.

Once the analyst has determined the appropriate cash flow to use in the valuation model, a discount rate needs to be determined. In general, discount rates are based on the general level of interest rates, the expected inflation rate, and the uncertainty of the future cash flows. Estimation of the discount rate usually entails adding a risk premium and the expected inflation rate to the risk-free rate of interest. The risk premium can be determined using historical data or a theoretical model such as the capital asset pricing model.

The basic discounted cash flow model assumes that the cash flows from the asset terminates at some given date. This makes the basic model perfectly suited for valuing fixed-income assets that have a terminal life. However, when valuing the stock of a firm, there is no maturity date and the cash flows (dividends, earnings) from the stock can change over time. Two variations to the basic discounted cash flow model can be used. The two models differ in the assumption they make about the growth of the cash flow stream. The constant growth model assumes that the cash flow stream will grow at a constant rate indefinitely. The multistage growth model assumes that the cash flow will grow at an above normal growth rate for a short, definable period of time, and then slow to its normal growth rate.

If the growth rate is assumed constant indefinitely, the present value of the stock is:

$$P_0 = \frac{D_0\left(1+g\right)}{k-g} = \frac{D_1}{k-g}.$$

In this equation, P_0 is the value of the stock, D_0 is the current dividend, D_1 is the dividend to be paid next year, g is the expected dividend growth rate, and k is the discount rate. This model assumes that the company pays dividends, the dividend growth rate is constant, and the discount rate is larger than the dividend growth rate. For example, suppose that a company just paid a dividend of $0.60 per share, that the dividend payments are expected to grow at an annual rate of 12 percent indefinitely, and that the discount rate is 16 percent. The value of the stock is therefore:

$$P_0 = \frac{\$0.60\left(1+12\%\right)}{16\%-12\%} = \$16.80.$$

For a mature company with stable growth, the constant growth model is appropriate. Note that it is difficult for a company to reengineer itself again and again to sustain a growth rate higher than overall economic growth rate. Small firms often show initially high growth that is not sustainable forever. In such a case, a two-stage or more growth model is appropriate. Suppose a firm currently pays $0.60 dividends per share that are expected to grow by 30 percent for the next two years, and then slow to

10 percent thereafter. If the discount rate is 15 percent, the market will value the stock at $18.31 per share:

$$P_0 = \frac{D_1}{(1+k)} + \frac{D_2}{(1+k)^2} + \frac{\dfrac{D_2(1+g)}{(k-g)}}{(1+k)^2}$$

$$P_0 = \frac{\$0.60(1+30\%)}{(1+15\%)} + \frac{\$0.60(1+30\%)^2}{(1+15\%)^2} + \frac{\dfrac{\$0.60(1+30\%)^2(1+10\%)}{15\%-10\%}}{(1+15\%)^2} = \$18.31.$$

The present value of the future dividends is $18.31. This means that the current stock value is $18.31 per share. If the stock trades at a level lower than the calculated value, the stock is said to be undervalued. Conversely, the stock is overpriced if it trades at a level higher than the value. The stock is correctly priced if the current market price is $18.31 per share.

Capital Asset Pricing Model

The discount rates used in the dividend growth models come from the capital asset pricing model (CAPM), which provides a linkage between the risk of a stock and the required rate of return that investors demand. Under the CAPM, the total risk of a stock consists of two components. The first is nondiversifiable, which is a measure of the stock's risk relative to an average stock. This is called the systematic risk. The second component is the risk that is company specific and is diversifiable. Thus, the required rate of return for a stock is:

$$E(R) = R_f + \beta(R_m - R_f).$$

In the equation, $E(R)$ denotes the required rate of return, R_f denotes the risk free rate, R_m denotes the return on the market portfolio, and β (beta) is the systematic risk of the stock. It is common to use the return on the 90-day Treasury bills as the risk-free rate and to use the S&P 500 return as a proxy for market return. The graphic representation of the relationship between risk and return identified in the equation is called the security market line. As shown in Figure 16.4, the required rate of return increases with the systematic risk of the stock. The security market line begins at R_f on the vertical axis, meaning investors can expect to earn the risk-free rate if the stock has a beta of zero. Every point on the security market line implies that the rate of return in-

FIGURE 16.4 Security Market Line

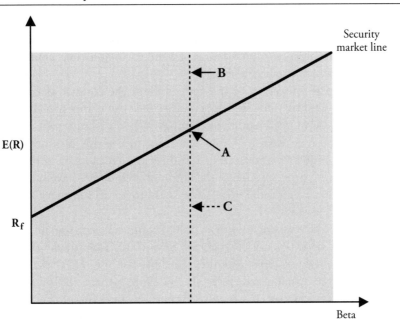

vestors expect to earn is the same as the required rate of return determined by the riskiness of the stock and market conditions. In other words, every security represented by a point (point A) on the security market line is correctly priced. Any point (point B) that lies above the security market line implies that the stock is underpriced because investors expect to earn a rate that is higher than the required rate of return. Conversely, any point (point C) below the security market line means the stock is overpriced because the rate of return investors expect to receive is lower than the required rate of return.

For example, suppose that the 90-day Treasury bills yield 5.00 percent and the S&P 500 index returns investors 11.00 percent annually. Assume that the beta of a stock is 1.2. The rate of returns investors demand on this stock will be:

$$E(R) = 5.00\% + 1.2(11.00\% - 5.00\%) = 12.2\%.$$

This 12.2 percent is the discount rate that can be used to calculate the present value of future dividends in the dividend growth model.

Relative Valuation

The relative valuation approach compares the security with other similar securities. The assumption is that other firms in the industry will have similar valuations. Valuation methods such as the price-to-earnings ratio (P/E), price-to-book ratio, or price-to-sales ratio represent relative valuation measures. For example, if the average firm in the industry has a P/E of 25, then a firm with earnings of $4 per share will have a projected price of $100 per share. As an example, Google traded at $466.02 per share on December 27, 2006, with a market capitalization of $142.67 billion. The implied P/E ratio was 59.18. Is this a reasonable valuation?

The P/E ratio is a measure of the cost of $1 of the company's earnings. This measure is widely used by value investors, as they seek out companies that are selling for prices that are cheap relative to their earnings. When a relative valuation measure such as the P/E ratio is used, it is important not to use this measure to compare firms in different industries. For example, industries that use a great deal of capital in the manufacturing process, such as the automobile industry have historically had lower P/E ratios than other industries. Table 16.2 provides a summary of the various relative valuation measures.

In cases where companies are not making profits, analysts use alternative measures such as book value (B), sales (S), or cash flows (CF). The value of the stock is assumed to be a multiple of those measures. Analysts also use other relative valuation measures to analyze specific industries. In industries where the number of subscribers/users can play a crucial part in determining the value of the firm, such as cable television, Internet service providers, and telephone companies, a value can be placed on each subscriber. Table 16.3 presents some of these valuation measures.

TABLE 16.2   Summary of Relative Valuation Methods

Method	Advantages	Disadvantages
Price to earnings	Widely reported and easy to compute.	Cannot be used when a firm does not report earnings. Most P/E ratios use historical earnings rather than future earnings.
Price to book value	Can be used even if the firm does not report earnings.	Influenced by accounting methods. Cannot be used when a company records negative book value.
Price to sales	Can be computed for even the most troubled company.	Fails to recognize the cost side. It does not provide a measure of profitability.
Price to cash flow	Can be used for firms that have negative earnings but positive cash flows.	Fails to recognize amortization and depreciation.

TABLE 16.3   Alternative Relative Valuation Methods

Type of Business	Valuation Ratio	Comments
Restaurants	Enterprise Value to Number of Restaurants	Measures the value per restaurant in operation
Hotels	Enterprise Value to Number of Rooms	Measures the value per room
Cable television/internet service provider	Enterprise Value to Number of Subscribers	Measures the value per subscriber
Cellular telephone	Enterprise Value to Number of Persons in Coverage Area	Measures the value per potential customer

CONCLUSION

Value investing targets companies with stable earnings and dividend payment. Those companies are often in the more mature stage of their corporate development. This chapter reviewed the approaches to value investing. The chapter also presented several valuation techniques.

17

Investing in Chinese Companies Listed on U.S. Exchanges

Many Chinese companies list their shares on U.S. exchanges in the form of American depositary receipts (ADRs) to raise capital and gain liquidity and prestige. American investors use ADRs to diversify their portfolios globally and reduce risk. ADRs allow investors who do not or cannot invest directly in non-U.S. dollar-denominated securities overseas to do so. ADRs overcome the mechanical difficulty of making trades in countries whose market hours do not correspond to those in the United States. Market hours in China do not overlap at all. As a result, Chinese ADRs present an efficient, cost-effective, and liquid way to make specific investments in Chinese companies.

CHINESE COMPANIES LISTED IN THE UNITED STATES

An ADR of a Chinese company is a negotiable certificate that trades in the United States and represents ownership of shares in a Chinese corporation. Each ADR represents a specific number of underlying shares deposited at a local custodian in China. Table 17.1, 17.2, and 17.3 lists samples of Chinese ADRs on the New York Stock Exchange, American Stock Exchange, and NASDAQ.

In the United States, the growth of ADRs in recent years is a testament to their popularity. The total number of sponsored ADRs has increased from 352 in 1990 to 1,858 in 2004 and 1,984 by 2006. In 2000, the dollar value of transactions in exchange-traded ADRs exceeded $1 trillion for the first time. Trading activities slowed down in the subsequent years, but climbed to $1.5 trillion in 2006, a record high. Table 17.4 lists both the amount of capital raised through ADRs and the dollar value of trading in recent years. One of the most significant growth areas of the ADR market in 2005 was in capital raising transactions. During 2006,

TABLE 17.1   Chinese Companies Listed On New York Stock Exchange

Company	Symbol	Sector/Industry
Aluminum Corp. of China Ltd.	ACH	Aluminum
China Eastern Airlines Corporation Limited	CEA	Airlines
China Life Insurance Company Limited	LFC	Life Insurance
China Mobile Limited	CHL	Mobile Telecommunications
China Netcom Group Corporation (Hong Kong) Limited	CN	Fixed Line Telecommunications
China Petroleum & Chemical Corporation	SNP	Integrated Oil & Gas
China Southern Airlines Company Limited	ZNH	Airlines
China Telecom Corporation Limited	CHA	Fixed Line Telecommunications
China Unicom	CHU	Mobile Telecommunications
Guangshen Railway Co. Ltd.	GSH	Travel & Tourism
Huaneng Power International Inc.	HNP	Electricity
PetroChina Company Ltd.	PTR	Integrated Oil & Gas
Semiconductor Manufacturing International Corporation	SMI	Semiconductors
Sinopec Shanghai Petrochemical Company Limited	SHI	Commodity Chemicals
Suntech Power Holdings Co., Ltd.	STP	Electrical Components & Equipment
Yanzhou Coal Mining Co. Ltd.	YZC	Coal
American Dairy Inc.	ADY	Food Products
Nam Tai Electronics Inc.	NTE	Consumer Goods/Business Equipment
Sinopec Shanghai	SHI	Basic Materials/ Synthetics

49 new ADR offerings by non-U.S. companies and governments raised a record $45.1 billion, nearly tripling 2004's full-year total of $11.3 billion in 53 new ADR offerings.

ADRs account for a significant portion of U.S. investors' investments in foreign securities. In September 2006, the total value of U.S. holdings in non-U.S. equities was $3.5 trillion. Out of that amount, $1 trillion is held in the form of DRs.

In August 2005, Chinese Internet search engine company Baidu.com caused excitement when it completed its IPO and listed ADRs on NASDAQ. Baidu closed its

Table 17.2   Chinese Companies Listed On American Stock Exchange

Company	Symbol	Sector/Industry
Sinovac Biotech	SVA	Healthcare/Drug Manufacturers—Other
Tiens Biotech	TBV	Healthcare/Drug Related Products

TABLE 17.3   Chinese Companies Listed on NASDAQ

Company	Symbol	Sector/Industry
INTAC International	INTN	Diversified Communication Services
China Automotive Systems Inc.	CAAS	Consumer Goods/Auto Parts
China Techfaith Wireless	CNTF	Technology/Diversified Communication Services
Chinadotcom/CDC Corp.	CHINA	Technology/Internet Information Providers
AsiaInfo Holdings	ASIA	Internet Software & Services
China Medical Technology	CMED	Healthcare/Medical Instruments and Supplies
Chindex International Inc.	CHDX	Services/Medical Equipment Wholesale
Comtech Group Inc.	COGO	Technology/Diversified Communication Services
Ctrip.com International Ltd.	CTRP	Services/Resorts and Casinos
China Yuchai International Ltd.	CYD	Industrial Goods/Diversified Machinery
Deswell Industries Inc.	DSWL	Consumer Goods/Rubber and Plastics
Focus Media Holding Ltd.	FMCN	Services/Advertising Agencies
International Displayworks Inc.	IDWK	Technology/Diversified Electronics
51job Inc.	JOBS	Services/Staffing and Outsourcing Serivvces
China Finance Online Co. Ltd.	JRJC	Services/Business Services
Kongzhong Corp.	KONG	Services/Business Services
eLong Inc.	LONG	Services/Personal Services
Linktone Ltd.	LTON	Technology/Wireless Communications
The9 Ltd.	NCTY	Services/Gaming Activities
Ninetowns Digital World Trade Holdings Ltd.	NINE	Technology/Business Software
Qiao Xing Univ Tel	XING	Technology/Diversified Communication Services
Webzen	WZEN	Technology/Multimedia & Graphics software
UTStarcom	UTSI	Technology/Wireless Communications
Tom Online	TOMO	Technology/Wireless Communications
Sohu.com	SOHU	Technology/Internet Information Providers
Shanda Interactive	SNDA	Technology/Internet Software & Services
Sina Corp.	SINA	Technology/Internet Software & Services
Radica Games	RADA	Consumer Goods/ Toys & Games
Pacificnet Inc.	PACT	Technology/ Communication Equipment
Netease.com	NTES	Technology/Internet Information Providers
Baidu	BIDU	Internet Information Providers

first day of trading more than 350 percent higher, becoming the best-performing foreign or domestic IPO on all U.S. stock exchanges during the year.

Baidu's investment bankers Goldman Sachs and Credit Suisse First Boston priced the ADRs at $27 but they opened at $66 and then soared to $122.54 at the end of the first trading day. The driving force behind Baidu's spectacular market debut was its resemblance and ties to Google.

TABLE 17.4 Capital Raised through and Trading Value of ADRs ($ Billions)

Year	Capital Raised by Issuing ADRs	Value of ADR Trading
1997	18.6	503
1998	10.2	563
1999	22.0	667
2000	30.1	1,185
2001	8.5	752
2002	6.8	550
2003	10.3	630
2004	11.3	852
2005	32.5	1,200
2006	45.1	1,500

Source: Bank of New York.

ADR STRUCTURE AND ISSUANCE

To establish a sponsored ADR program (Figure 17.1), the Chinese company selects a team of accountants, lawyers, an investor relations firm, investment bankers, and a financial printer. The independent accountant offers expertise in international offering and U.S. capital markets. The legal counsel advises on U.S. securities regulations and related matters. In selecting an investor relations firm, it is wise to seek an international firm with experience in advising and assisting non-U.S. companies. The investor relations firm prepares publicity strategy for the listing event. The appointment of an investment bank with appropriate transaction experience, sector and industry knowledge, and distribution capabilities is essential to a successful program. Investment bank's aftermarket support is a key element as well. The financial printer plays an important role in the process because it manages the creation of the confidential document, SEC filings, printing, and distribution.

The issuer also selects a depositary bank to implement and manage the ADR program on an ongoing basis. Major depositary banks are Deutsche Bank, Citibank, JPMorgan Chase, and Bank of New York. Among them, Bank of New York has the largest market share, about 64 percent in 2006.[1] The issuer works with the depositary bank to select a custodian to safekeep the underlying shares in the issuer's home market. The issuer, the depositary bank, and, in most cases, the ADR holders enter into a deposit agreement that sets forth the terms of the depositary receipt program. Based on the contract, the depositary bank performs the specified services on behalf of the issuer and investors. In addition, if the ADR lists on the NYSE, the issuer has to file an application with the exchange for listing and select a specialist to be the trader of the stock.

Once the underlying shares are deposited with the depositary's custodian in the issuer's home market, the depositary then issues depositary receipts to investors. For example, an investor wishes to purchase a new ADR. To issue the new ADR, the U.S. broker contacts a foreign broker to purchase shares in the foreign corporation's local market.

FIGURE 17.1   ADR Structure

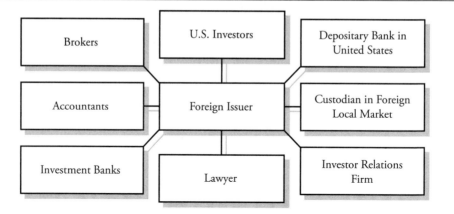

Foreign Issuer
- Determine its objectives.
- Appoint U.S. depositary bank, lawyers, investment bank, and investor relations firm.
- Determine program type.
- Obtain approval from Board of Directors, shareholders, and regulators.
- Provide financial information to accountants.
- Develop investor relations plan.

U.S. Depositary Bank
- Advise on ADR structure.
- Appoint custodian.
- Assist with ADR registration requirements.
- Coordinate with lawyers, accountants, and investment bankers to ensure all program implementation steps are completed.
- Prepare and issue depositary receipts.
- Enlist market makers.
- Send ADR program announcement to brokers and traders.

Brokers
- Execute and settle trades.

Custodian
- Receive and safe keep underlying shares.
- Confirm deposit of underlying shares.
- Communicate with U.S. depositary bank on corporate actions and related issues.
- Transmit dividend payments.

Investor Relations Firm
- Develop a plan to promote the ADR program.
- Help in roadshow.
- Place tombstone advertisement announcing program establishment.

Lawyers
- Advise on type of DR structure.
- Draft and negotiate deposit agreement.
- File appropriate registration statements or establish exemptions with SEC.
- File registration statements to list on U.S. exchanges (Levels II and III).

Investment Bankers
- Advise on type of ADR structure.
- Obtain CUSIP number.
- Obtain DTC, Euroclear, Cedel, and PORTAL eligibility as needed.
- Arrange and conduct roadshow.
- Line up market makers.
- Price and launch securities.

Accountants
- Prepare financial statements in accordance with (or reconciled to) U.S. Generally Accepted Accounting Principles (GAAP) for Exchange Act registered securities.

Investors
- Evaluate investment objectives and decide on asset allocation.
- Select an ADR if it meets his/her investment objectives.

Those shares are deposited with a local custodian. The custodian instructs the depositary bank to issue ADRs evidencing ownership of the deposited shares. The depositary bank delivers the ADRs to the broker who initiated the trade. The broker delivers ADRs to the customer's account and the ADRs are created. Once the ADR program is established, the depositary bank acts as the liaison between the foreign issuer and U.S. investors.

The structure of ADRs typically includes a ratio called bundling, corresponding to the number of underlying shares per ADR, to align the trading price of the ADR to the customary price levels. Several factors affect this ratio. First, the issuer will want to conform to the price range of industry peers in the United States. Second, each exchange has average price ranges for listed shares. In addition, some institutional and individual investors also have preference for shares traded in certain ranges. Once the ratio is set, the price of the ADRs should reflect the dollar equivalent price of the shares in the home market. For example, suppose the ratio has been set at 1 to 1. Assume the underlying shares in the home market are trading at $15.25, and the ADR is selling for $15.75. The arbitrageur will buy shares in the foreign market and issue ADRs until the arbitrage profits are driven away. In contrast, if the underlying shares trade at a higher level, the arbitrageur will buy the ADRs, cancel the ADRs, and sell the underlying shares in the foreign local market.

To cancel the ADR program, the steps are reversed. The broker receives ADRs from customers and delivers them to the depositary for cancellation. The depositary instructs the local custodian to release the underlying shares to the local broker who purchased the shares.

Arbitrage between ADRs and the underlying shares can result in on-going issuances and cancellations. For example, issuances and cancellations take place when, instead of finding a counterparty to the trade in the United States, the broker based on a client's buy order instructs the depositary bank to buy additional shares in the issuer's local market and issue new receipts. On the other hand, the broker receiving a sell order could instruct the depositary bank to release shares held in local custodian and cancel receipts. A massive cancellation of an ADR is called flow back because of the selling by U.S. investors and the displacement of trading activity to the home country.

LISTING REQUIREMENTS

There are two types of ADR programs: unsponsored and sponsored. An unsponsored program is not supported by the foreign company, while a sponsored program is established by the foreign company. Sponsored and unsponsored programs for the same security cannot exist simultaneously because these ADRs for the same foreign security might trade at different prices, creating confusion.

Unsponsored Programs

Some of the ADRs traded in the United States are not sponsored. An unsponsored ADR program is often initiated by a bank in response to investor demand. The issuer has no control over the program because there is typically no deposit agreement between the issuer and the depositary bank.

The ADRs must be registered with the Securities and Exchange Commission (SEC). The depositary bank and the issuer together submit an application to the SEC under Rule 12g3-2(b) seeking exemption from the full reporting requirements (eligibility for exemption is discussed in the next section).

Upon SEC approval, the unsponsored ADRs can trade only in the over-the-counter market. The SEC requires that material public information in the issuer's home country be supplied to the commission and made available to U.S. investors. The depositary will mail the issuer's annual reports and certain public information to U.S. investors upon request. The SEC does not require this material to be translated into English or to be adjusted for differences between the local accounting standards and U.S. generally accepted accounting principles (GAAP).

Though foreign companies cannot raise capital with an unsponsored ADR, they gain several advantages. This program provides an inexpensive and simple way of expanding the investor base in the United States. The SEC compliance and reporting requirements are minimal. Also, an unsponsored program can be converted to a sponsored facility. To do so, the issuer "buys out" the unsponsored facility by contacting the depositary bank of the unsponsored program, having it exchange its ADRs for the new sponsored ADRs.

Sponsored Programs

Sponsored ADRs include Level I, Level II, Level III, and Rule 144A. The choice depends on the needs and wishes of the issuer.

Level I ADRs

Level I ADRs are the easiest and least expensive way for a foreign company to gauge international interest in its securities and to begin building a presence in the United States. The issuer must obtain a Rule 12g3-2(b) exemption from the SEC and must also file a Form F-6 and sign a deposit agreement. The issuer has greater control over a Level I program than over an unsponsored program because a deposit agreement is executed between the issuer and one exclusive depositary bank. The agreement defines the responsibilities of the depositary, including responding to investor inquiries, maintaining stockholder records, and mailing annual reports and other materials to shareholders.

Level I ADRs only trade in the over-the-counter market. The main advantages of these ADRs are their low cost and their ability to coexist with a Rule 144A ADR facility (called a side-by-side program). A side-by-side program allows the foreign issuer to combine the benefits of a publicly traded program with the efficiency of a private offering as a capital-raising tool. Also, a Level I program is easy to set up; one can be established in as little as nine weeks. Furthermore, it is relatively inexpensive to upgrade the program to Level II or Level III.

Level II ADRs

Level II ADRs must comply with the SEC's full registration and reporting requirements. The issuer must file with the SEC a Form F-6 for registering the ADRs and a

TABLE 17.5   Trends of Sponsored and Listed ADRs

Year	Sponsored ADRs	Exchange-Listed ADRs
1997	1,527	458
1998	1,681	501
1999	1,729	520
2000	1,791	570
2001	1,819	563
2002	1,847	537
2003	1,817	504
2004	1,858	498
2005	1,912	523
2006	1,984	478

Source: Bank of New York.

Form 20-F to meet the reporting requirements. Such compliance allows the issuer to list its ADRs on the New York Stock Exchange (NYSE), the American Stock Exchange, or the NASDAQ; each of which has its own reporting and disclosure requirements. Table 17.5 shows how the numbers of sponsored and exchange-listed ADRs have grown in recent years.

Full registration and listing increase liquidity and marketability and enhance the issuer's name recognition in the United States. The issuer is also able to monitor the ownership of its shares in the United States. Because the issuer must comply with the rigorous SEC requirements, it is well positioned to upgrade and make a public offering in the U.S. market.

A Level II program is more expensive and time-consuming to set up and maintain, compared to a Level I facility. Another disadvantage is that a foreign company cannot use Level II to raise capital in the United States.

Level III ADRs

Companies that want to raise capital use a sponsored Level III facility. Level III ADRs are similar to those issued under Level II. In both programs, the issuer initiates the program, signs a deposit agreement with one depositary bank, lists on one of the U.S. exchanges, and files Forms F-6 and 20-F with the SEC. The major difference is that a Level III program allows the issuer to make a public offering. To do so, the issuer must file a Form F-1 (similar to Form S-1 for U.S. companies) to register the shares underlying the Level III ADRs. The reporting requirements are more onerous for Level III than for Level I or Level II programs. Financial statements must be fully reconciled to the U.S. GAAP. The costs can be substantial; they include listing, legal, accounting, investor relations, and road shows. Establishment of a Level II or Level III program usually takes 15 weeks or more, depending on individual program specifics. In addition, the issue must conform to the listing requirements of the exchange (Table 17.6).

In summary, a Level I facility allows a foreign issuer to enjoy the benefits of a publicly traded security. Companies wanting to list shares on a U.S. exchange use Level II programs, and companies wishing to raise capital use Level III. Each higher

TABLE 17.6 ADR Listing Requirements at NYSE

Criteria	Worldwide	Domestic May Satisfy Either A, B, or C
Distribution:		
Round-lots holders Total shareholders	5,000	A. 2,000 U.S. round lot shareholders B. 2,200 total shareholders and 100,000 shares monthly trading volume (most recent 6 months) C. 500 total shareholders and 1,000,000 shares monthly trading volume (most recent 12 months)
Public shares	2.5MM	1.1MM
Public market value	$100MM	
IPOs, carve outs and spin offs	N/A	$60MM
All other listings	N/A	$100MM
Financials:		
Earnings		
Aggregate pretax income for last three years	$100MM	$10MM
Minimum pretax income in each of two preceding years	$25MM	$2MM (all three years must be positive)
Valuation/revenue test may satisfy either A or B		
A. Valuation of cash flow test:		
Global market capitalization	$500MM	$500MM
Revenues (most recent 12 month period)	$100MM	$100MM
Aggregate cash flow for last three years	$100MM	$25MM (all three years must be positive)
Minimum cash flow in each of two preceding years	$25MM	N/A
B. Pure valuation test:		
Global market capitalization	$750MM	$750MM
Revenues (most recent fiscal year)	$75MM	$75MM

TABLE 17.6   (Continued)

Criteria	Worldwide	Domestic *May Satisfy Either A, B, or C*
Affiliated company for new entities with a parent or affiliated company listed on the NYSE:		
Global market capitalization	$500MM	$500MM
At least 12 months of operating history	Yes	Yes
Affiliated listed company is in good standing	Yes	Yes
Affiliated listed company retains control of the entity	Yes	Yes

Source: New York Stock Exchange

level of ADR program reflects additional SEC registration requirements and increases the visibility and attractiveness of the ADR to institutional and retail investors.

Rule 144A ADRs

As an alternative to Level III programs, foreign companies can access the U.S. capital market by issuing ADRs under Rule 144A, called Rule 144A ADRs, to accredited investors, thereby avoiding SEC registration and reporting requirements. Under Rule 144A, there is no holding period restriction if the resale is made to qualified institutional buyers (QIBs), an institution that owns and invests on a discretionary basis at least $100 million in securities of an unaffiliated entity. In the case of registered broker-dealers, the requirement is $10 million.

Through Rule 144A ADRs, foreign companies have access to the U.S. private placement market and may raise capital without conforming to the full burden of SEC registration and disclosure. Issuing Rule 144A ADRs is considerably less costly than initiating a Level III program. Establishment can take as little as seven weeks.

Rule 144A ADRs offer both advantages and disadvantages to issuers. Rule 144A ADRs do not have to conform to full reporting and registration requirements. They can be launched on their own or as part of a global offering. There are two disadvantages, however. First, Rule 144As cannot be created for a class of shares already listed on a U.S. exchange. In addition, they can only trade among QIBs; consequently, the market certainly is not as liquid as the public equity market. Table 17.7 provides a summary of the different SEC filings required of different ADR programs.

ADVANTAGES OF ADRs

The ADR market offers distinct benefits for investors, brokers, market makers, and issuers. ADRs greatly simplify the trading of foreign equities. Without ADRs, a U.S.

TABLE 17.7   ADR Filing Requirements and Trading

Type of ADRs	SEC Filing	Exchange Listing and Trading	Raising Capital
Unsponsored:			
	Form F-6 12g3-2(b)	Over the counter	No
Sponsored:			
Level-I	Form F-6 12g3-2(b)	Over the counter	No
Level-II	Form F-6 Form 20-F	NYSE/Amex/NASDAQ	No
Level-III	Form F-6 and Form F-1 Form 20-F	NYSE/Amex/NASDAQ	Yes
Rule 144A	N/A	Private placement market	Yes

Note: For reporting purposes, Level-II financial statements must be partially reconciled to U.S. GAAP, and Level-III financial reports must be fully reconciled to U.S. GAAP.

investor who wished to purchase a foreign security would have to find a broker with capabilities in the specific foreign market where the security trades. A single trade would involve multiple parties, currency concerns, and settlement delays.

Investors benefit in other ways as well. The depositary bank collects dividends, converts the currency, and issues payments in U.S. dollars. An ADR program also helps investors avoid the regulations of countries that prohibit physical delivery of shares overseas. The ADRs are registered in the United States, so records exist to protect ownership rights.

Many institutional investors are restricted from investing in securities that are not traded on a U.S. exchange. Listed ADRs represent a way for them to add international exposure to their portfolios. Similarly, institutions that invest only in the United States because they have no custodian facilities or arrangements abroad can invest in ADRs.

The Bank of New York publishes an ADR Composite Index that tracks the performance of ADRs in the United States. In addition, there are regional indexes representing Europe, Asia, and Latin America. For the purpose of tracking the performance of a particular country, the available country indexes include Argentina, Brazil, Sweden, Russia, China, India, Germany, Spain, Chile, and Taiwan. JPMorgan Chase also publishes detailed information about the ADR market, issuing company, and industry data.

Securities dealers and brokers find ADRs attractive as well. ADRs standardize widely varying securities practices. Because processing is simplified, settlement risk is reduced. Securities in ADR form are easily transferable, and automated book-entry systems for clearing are well established. The T+3 settlement cycle (now moving toward T+1) minimizes losses from fails.[2] The depositary can also prerelease ADRs to help bridge timing differences in settlement cycles in different nations. In a prerelease, the depositary with the knowledge that the trade of underlying shares has been executed issues an ADR before the underlying shares are physically deposited with an overseas custodian.

For Chinese companies, ADRs provide the most effective means of entering the U.S. market. An ADR program provides a simple means of diversifying the Chinese company's shareholder base. It enhances the company's visibility and name recognition in the United States. As a result of global demand and trading, the program may increase liquidity and local share price. An ADR program can also be used to help build a stronger financial presence in the United States. Features such as dividend reinvestment plans help ensure a continual stream of investment into an issuer's program. In addition, ADRs provide an easy way for U.S. employees of non-U.S. companies to invest in their companies' employee stock purchase programs. These benefits have motivated foreign companies to launch ADRs in the United States. During the 1997 to 2006 period, ADR offerings raised almost $200 billion in capital. Companies from many countries including the United Kingdom, Australia, Japan, Hong Kong, Mexico, Brazil, France, the Netherlands, Germany, Russia, Chile, China, and Taiwan have issued ADRs in the United States.

TRADING ADRs

The share price in the issuer's home market, exchange rates, and transaction costs will determine the ADR price. Additional factors to consider in the valuation process include consideration for differing accounting principles, effects of currency swings, liquidity, and character of the home market.

Many foreign companies supply U.S. GAAP-adjusted information in their financial data. Though the information is helpful in understanding the level of impact that differing accounting principles have on reported earnings, these adjustments should not be regarded as the same as what a company would have reported if it were a U.S. concern. Several reasons exist why investors should view these GAAP adjustments with caution. First, these numbers often are just estimates by company. Adjustments may also carry differing tax implications that are not applicable in the United States. In addition, managers of foreign companies plan and evaluate finances and performance within their own accounting principles, tax system, social, cultural, and political environment. They are not necessarily motivated to produce good earnings under U.S. GAAP.

ADRs trade in dollars; hence, the translated earnings provide a point of reference. However, the level and trend of exchange rates often cloud the picture. For example, the same amounts of revenues taken in or expenses paid out in local currency could be translated into volatile dollar amounts simply due to exchange rate fluctuations. Furthermore, in the area of emerging market ADRs, politics ranks higher than other factors when considering a stock. In emerging markets, political stability, regulation, and management are more important than GAAP accounting or disclosure.

Another important factor is liquidity, both as an ADR and as the underlying stock in its home market. The ADR market has been growing. But some ADRs are not as successful. For example, Bookham Technology of U.K. dropped its program in

December 2004 and Samson Exploration of Australia terminated its ADR in February 2005. Liquidity of the underlying security is also important. In countries such as Germany and Japan, cross-holdings decrease liquidity. In such situations, the companies can be less responsive to minority shareholders and their interests. Additionally, ADR and the underlying security should trade at "an equivalent price." Specifically, the ADR price is equal to the ordinary share converted to dollars at the prevailing exchange rate, adjusted for the appropriate ratio and any transactions costs. At times, split market pricing occurs due to either market inefficiencies or new information.

Once issued, ADRs trade the same way U.S. stocks trade. When an ADR is sold to another investor, the existing ADR is transferred from one ADR holder to the buyer according to U.S. clearing and settlement rules. The depositary receipt to depositary receipt trading is known as intramarket trading and accounts for roughly 95 percent of all ADR transactions in the United States. U.S. ADR investors enjoy the same type and range of services that investors would receive as if they owned U.S. shares.

ADR trading involves several factors that are not common in trading domestic equities. An ADR is not a U.S. domestic stock because the foreign company's local political, economic, and market valuations will significantly affect the local price. A trader must be keenly aware of local price and market movements, and not just concentrate on the U.S. market. Clearly, ADRs represent foreign stocks and apart from being affected by the local price, they are also affected by currency fluctuations. Local commissions are another cost factor in calculating ADR price.

In certain markets, local taxes are a factor when calculating an ADR price. Many ADR issuing countries such as China, Taiwan, Korea, and Australia have local or registration taxes. Depositary banks charge the ADR conversion fees, for issuance when buying and for cancellation when selling sponsored ADRs.

As an example, ABC stock is offered at £10.00/share in London. The cost factors when a U.S. trader is offering are listed in Table 17.8. The U.S. trader's offer

TABLE 17.8   ADR Offer and Bid Price Calculations

Offer Price	
Local Offer Price	£10.00
0.5% transfer tax	0.05
1.0% ADR tax	0.10
0.2% local commission	0.02
Subtotal	£10.17
In U.S.$ (U.S.$/£ exchange rate 1.700)	$17.289
ADR price (ADR ratio 2:1 + ADR creation fee 5 cents)	$34.628
Bid Price	£9.95
Local bid price − 0.2% local commission	0.02
Subtotal	£9.93
In U.S.$ (U.S.$/£ exchange rate 1.700)	$16.881
Bid price (ADR ratio 2:1 − ADR creation fee 5 cents)	$33.712

price should be $34.628. If only the local price of £10.00 had been used in the calculation without including the assumed transfer, local tax, and commission, then the equivalent U.S. price would have been $34.00. The costs have added $0.628 to the price. As Table 17.8 shows, on a mathematical basis, the bid and offer are $33.712 and $34.628. In practice, however, traders would quote a narrower spread because of competition and other factors such as their own position in the stock.

U.S. REGULATIONS

Publicly traded ADRs must be registered with the SEC. If the ADRs represent new shares, the registration must cover both the ADRs and the newly issued shares. For securities offered outside United States, Regulation S provides a safe harbor exemption.

Registration of ADRs for Outstanding Shares

When ADRs are issued for outstanding shares, Form F-6 is used to register the ADRs under the Securities Act of 1933. The simplified registration procedure is available only where the issuer of the deposited shares has obtained an exemption under Rule 12g3-2(a) or (b). The general eligibility requirements for an exemption are:

- The ADR holder is entitled to withdraw the deposited securities at any time subject only to the temporary delay caused by closing transfer books.
- The relevant fees, taxes, and similar charges have been paid.
- The issuer is reporting pursuant to requirements of Section 13(a) or 15(d) of the Securities Exchange Act of 1934, or the deposited shares are exempt by Rule 12g3-2(b) unless the issuer concurrently files a registration statement on another form for the deposited securities.

Under Rule 12g3-2(a), a foreign issuer is exempt from the reporting requirements of the Securities Exchange Act of 1934 if it does not have a class of equity securities held by at least 300 persons resident in the United States. This exemption is unlikely to be available if the ADR program is successful, however, so the issuer usually must satisfy the reporting requirements or qualify for an exemption under Rule 12g3-2(b). Under Rule 12g3-2(b), a foreign issuer is granted an exemption if it meets the following requirements:

- Its ADRs or underlying securities are not listed on a U.S. exchange or quoted on the NASDAQ.
- It submits to the SEC certain information that was made available to its shareholders or to foreign government authorities in the foreign local market.
- It provides the SEC the same information during each subsequent fiscal year.

Registration of ADRs for New Shares

When ADRs represent new shares (as in a Level III program) or shares distributed by a statutory underwriter, both the ADRs and the deposited shares must be registered with the SEC. As mentioned, Form F-6 is available only for the registration of ADRs. The underlying securities must be registered on Form F-1, F-2, or F-3. The forms differ primarily with respect to the amount of information that a foreign issuer does not have to disclose in full if the issuer has already provided the information or is providing it through other filings. Unless the foreign issuer has shares registered or is reporting under the 1934 act, Form F-1 must be used.

Regulation S

Regulation S, which applies to GDRs, provides two types of safe harbor exemptions for securities offered overseas without registration. One is the issuer safe harbor, which addresses offers and sales by issuers, their affiliates, and securities professionals involved in the initial offerings of securities. The second is the resale safe harbor, which addresses resales by securities professionals such as brokers. Two general conditions must be satisfied to take advantage of these safe harbors: (1) any offer or sale must be made in an offshore transaction, and (2) no direct selling efforts may be made in the United States.

Regulation S and Rule 144A are closely related. The SEC has maintained the position that foreign issuers may undertake private placements in the United States (Rule 144A) at the same time they are making an offshore Regulation S offering without violating that regulation's prohibition against U.S. direct selling efforts. Substantial care must nevertheless be taken to avoid spillover of such securities into the U.S. public markets.

CONCLUSION

For Chinese companies, ADRs are a cost-effective way to improve their visibility and raise capital in the United States. ADRs provide U.S. investors with an additional venue to make specific foreign investments without the problem of differing settlement processes and securities custody. There are several types of ADR programs. An unsponsored ADR facility is not initiated by the foreign issuer, and typically there is no deposit agreement between the issuer and the depositary bank. Sponsored facilities issue four types of ADRs: Level I, Level II, Level III, and Rule 144A ADRs. Issuers of ADRs must comply with U.S. securities laws, including the Securities Act of 1933 and the Securities Exchange Act of 1934. For ADR issuers, Regulation S, Rule 144A, and Rule 12g3-2(b) provide certain exemptions.

18

Investing in Chinese Mutual Funds

U.S. investors can benefit from China's growth by purchasing mutual funds that invest in the securities of Chinese companies. Many mutual fund companies offer funds that invest in securities traded in China while some purchase Chinese securities listed and traded in the United States. Investing in those funds adds additional risks such as currency risk and several other risks unique to developing countries. This chapter discusses advantages and disadvantages, fund structure, regulation, and listing samples of Chinese mutual funds.

CHINESE MUTUAL FUNDS

An easy way to start investing in the Chinese economy is to find a Chinese mutual fund, a mutual fund managed by an experienced fund manager with a focus on growing Chinese companies. Morningstar is a good place to start researching Chinese mutual funds that meet the investment objectives. Using their Fund Screener, the investor can search the database using the set criteria such as fund type, ratings/risk, and returns. In addition, the investor can read the prospectus to gain a better understanding of the fund that he or she is interested in investing.

Mutual Fund Prospectus

Before purchasing a mutual fund, it is prudent to read its prospectus. The prospectus is the fund's primary selling document and contains valuable information, such as the fund's investment objectives or goals, investment strategies, risks of investing in the fund, fees and expenses, and past performance. The prospectus also identifies the fund's managers and advisers and describes its organization and how to purchase and redeem shares. Major items included in a mutual fund prospectus are:

- *Date of issue:* Appears on the front cover. Mutual funds update their prospectuses at least once a year.
- *Risk/return bar chart and table:* Right after the fund's narrative description of its investment objectives or goals, strategies, and risks, a bar chart showing the fund's annual total returns for each of the past 10 years or for the life of the fund if it is less than 10 years old. All funds that have had annual returns for at least one calendar year must include this chart (see Table 18.1).
- *Fee table:* Describes the fund's fees and expenses. These include the shareholder fees and annual fund operating expenses. The fee table includes an example that helps investors compare costs among different funds by showing the costs associated with investing a hypothetical $10,000 over a 1-, 3-, 5-, and 10-year period.
- *Financial highlights:* Contains audited data concerning the fund's financial performance for each of the past several years, including net asset values, total returns, and various ratios.

Fees and expenses are an important consideration in selecting a mutual fund because these charges lower your returns. Many investors find it helpful to compare the fees and expenses of different mutual funds before they invest. Items listed under shareholder fees include sales loads, redemption fees, exchange fee, and account fee. Funds that use brokers to sell their shares must compensate the brokers. Funds may do this by imposing a sales load on investors. The SEC does not limit the size of sales load a fund may charge, but the National Association of Securities Dealers (NASD) does not permit mutual fund sales loads to exceed 8.5 percent. A redemption fee is another type of expense that some funds charge when the shareholders redeem their shares. How much the load of a fund impacts the returns to shareholders depends on

TABLE 18.1   Mutual Fund Performance Table

	1 Year	5 Year (or Life of Fund)	10 Year (or Life of Fund)
Return before taxes	_____%	_____%	_____%
Return after taxes on distributions	_____%	_____%	_____%
Return after taxes on distributions and sale of fund shares	_____%	_____%	_____%
Index (reflects no deductions for [fees or expenses])	_____%	_____%	_____%

Source: Securities and Exchange Commission.

TABLE 18.2 Effect of Load Fees on Holding Period Returns

Load	Shares Purchased	Annualized Holding Period Returns				
		1 Year	3 Years	5 Years	10 Years	20 Years
0.0%	100.0	10.00%	10.00%	10.00%	10.00%	10.00%
1.0%	99.0	8.90%	9.63%	9.78%	9.89%	9.94%
3.0%	97.0	6.70%	8.89%	9.33%	9.67%	9.83%
5.0%	95.0	4.50%	8.14%	8.88%	9.14%	9.72%
8.5%	91.5	0.65%	6.79%	8.06%	9.03%	9.51%

how long the fund is held. Because the load is a fixed percentage of the net asset value and is only paid when shares are purchased, the impact diminishes with time. Funds that are held for short periods of time will be affected more by the load than funds that are held for long periods of time. Table 18.2 provides an example of how the impact of loads diminishes over time. Table 18.2 assumes that the investor begins with an initial investment of $1,000 and that the fund grows at a compound rate of 10 percent per year.

As Table 18.2 shows, the greatest impact on the returns occurs for short holding periods. For example, for a fund charging a 1 percent load fee, the lost rate of return for the first year is 110 basis points.[1] However, if the investor holds the fund for 20 years, the impact of the load is only 6 basis points per year. The impact is even more obvious for the fund charging a load fee of 8.5 percent. For a one-year holding period, the fund loses 935 basis points, however, when the holding period is extended to 20 years, the fund loses only 49 basis points per year. Table 18.3 shows how these load fees affect the accumulation values of the funds for different holding periods.

A purchase fee is a fee that some funds charge when the shareholders purchase their shares. A purchase fee differs from, and is not considered to be, a front-end sales load because a purchase fee is paid to the fund (not to a broker) and is typically imposed to defray some of the fund's costs associated with the purchase. An exchange fee is a fee that some funds impose on shareholders if they exchange (transfer) to another

TABLE 18.3 Accumulation Values for Different Load Fees

Load	Shares Purchased	Accumulation Values				
		1 Year	3 Years	5 Years	10 Years	20 Years
0.0%	100.0	$1,100	$1,331	$1,611	$2,594	$6,727
1.0%	99.0	$1,089	$1,318	$1,594	$2,568	$6,660
3.0%	97.0	$1,067	$1,291	$1,562	$2,516	$6,526
5.0%	95.0	$1,045	$1,264	$1,530	$2,464	$6,391
8.5%	91.5	$1,007	$1,218	$1,474	$2,373	$6,156

fund within the same fund group. An account fee is a fee that some funds separately impose on investors in connection with the maintenance of their accounts.

In addition, there are annual fund operating expenses. The first item under this category is the management fee. Management fees are fees that are paid out of fund assets to the fund's investment adviser. There are also the so-called 12b-1 fees for distribution expenses. Under NASD rules, 12b-1 fees that are used to pay marketing and distribution expenses cannot exceed 0.75 percent of a fund's average net assets per year. Finally, there are other expenses such as custodial expenses, legal expenses, accounting expenses, transfer agent expenses, and other administrative expenses

Sample Mutual Funds

In the United States, investors have many mutual funds that invest in Chinese securities to choose from. Some of those funds focus on securities of Chinese companies listed in the United States. Others focus on securities issued and listed on exchanges in China or Hong Kong. The funds that invest directly in China's A share markets rely on the investment quota allocated under the designation of Qualified Foreign Institutional Investor (QFII). Under Chinese regulation, a QFII may invest in stocks listed and traded on a stock exchange, securities investment funds, warrants listed and traded on a stock exchange, and other financial instruments approved by the CSRC. Investors can buy or sell Chinese mutual funds just like they trade any other mutual funds. Table 18.4 lists samples of Chinese mutual funds.

Risks

Investments in Chinese companies through Chinese mutual funds involve certain risks that are not typically associated with the United States. These additional risk factors include greater government control over the economy, political and legal uncertainty, currency fluctuations and control, the risk that Beijing does not continue the economic reforms, and the risk of nationalization. In addition, the Chinese securities markets are emerging markets and information available about Chinese companies may not be as complete and timely as information about listed U.S. companies.

Political and economic factors in China present a risk. The laws and regulations in China may change with little or no advance notice. Uncertainty also includes the investment regulations allowing QFIIs to invest in China A shares. Any such change may adversely affect the market conditions and hence the value of securities in the fund portfolio.

Inflation and tax changes post another risk. Economic growth in China in the past was accompanied by periods of high run away inflation. In recent years, the Chinese government has implemented macro-policies to prevent the economy from over heating. If those measures fail, investments in China could be negatively impacted. Furthermore, changes in the Chinese tax system may have retroactive effects. If a fund's reserve is not sufficient to cover the retroactive withholding tax, it might have to liquidate a portion of the portfolio.

TABLE 18.4   Mutual Funds Investing in China

AIM China
The investment seeks long-term growth of capital. The fund normally invests at least 80 percent of assets in a diversified portfolio of equity and equity-related transferable securities, including warrants and convertible securities, and/or debt securities of companies with substantial exposure to China. It does not expect to invest more than 25 percent of assets in debt securities. The fund may invest in initial public offerings (IPOs) of securities. It may hold a portion of assets in cash or cash equivalents, including shares of affiliated money market funds.

AllianceBernstein Great China '97
The investment seeks capital appreciation. The fund normally invests at least 80 percent of assets in equity securities issued by Greater China companies. It may invest a significant portion of assets, which may be greater than 50 percent in Hong Kong companies. The fund may also invest up to 20 percent of assets in debt issued by Greater China companies, and in equity or debt issued by companies not included in the Greater China region. It may only invest in investment-grade debt. The fund is nondiversified.

Columbia Greater China
The investment seeks long-term growth of capital. The fund normally invests at least 80 percent of assets in equities of companies located in or that are related to the Greater China Region. It may invest in common and preferred stocks, warrants, convertible debt, ADRs, and GDRs. The fund is nondiversified.

Dreyfus Premier Greater China
The investment seeks long-term capital appreciation. The fund normally invests at least 80 percent of assets in stocks of companies traded in Greater China, consisting of China, Hong Kong and Taiwan. It may also invest in securities of companies that derive at least 50 percent of their revenues from Greater China or have at least 50 percent of their assets in Greater China. The fund may invest in common stocks, preferred stocks and convertible securities, including those purchased in initial public offerings. It is nondiversified.

Eaton Vance Greater China Growth
The investment seeks long-term capital appreciation. The fund normally invests at least 80 percent of assets in equity securities, including investment-grade convertible securities, issued in Hong Kong, China, Taiwan, South Korea, Singapore, Malaysia, Thailand, Indonesia, and the Philippines. It may invest 25 percent or more of assets in securities in any one country in the China region. The fund invests in companies with a broad range of market capitalizations, including smaller companies. At times, it may attempt to hedge foreign currency fluctuations by entering into forward currency exchange contracts. The fund is nondiversified.

Fidelity China Region
The investment seeks long-term growth of capital. The fund normally invests at least 80 percent of assets in securities of Hong Kong, Taiwanese, and Chinese issuers and other

(continued)

TABLE 18.4 (Continued)

investments that are tied economically to the China region. It usually invests primarily in common stocks. The fund may invest up to 35 percent of total assets in any industry that accounts for more than 20 percent of the Hong Kong, Taiwanese, and Chinese market.

Gartmore China Opportunities
The investment seeks long term capital appreciation. The fund invests at least 80 percent of its net assets in securities of companies located in China including Hong Kong. The fund will invest primarily in common stocks, initial public offerings (IPOs), as available, and depositary receipts. The fund may also invest in equity-linked notes.

ING Greater China
The investment seeks long-term capital appreciation. The fund normally invests at least 80 percent of assets in equity and equity-related securities of issuers that are located in, derive at least 50 percent of revenue from, have at least 50 percent of assets in, or are principally traded in the Great China region. The Greater China region consists of China, Hong Kong and Taiwan. The fund may invest up to 10 percent of assets in warrants, and up to 20 percent in fixed-income securities. It may invest in ADRs, IDRs and GDRs. The fund is nondiversified.

JHancock Greater China Opp
The investment seeks long-term capital appreciation. The fund invests at least 80 percent of assets in equities of companies located in China, Hong Kong, or Taiwan (Greater China). These companies have securities that are traded on stock exchanges in Greater China, are organized under the laws of and conduct business in a Greater China country, or derive more than half of their revenues from Greater China operations. It may invest 20 percent of assets in securities of companies located outside of Greater China, with an emphasis on companies that are positioned to benefit from economic growth in Greater China. The fund is nondiversified.

Matthews China
The investment seeks long-term capital appreciation. The fund normally invests at least 80 percent of total net assets in the common and preferred stocks of companies located in China. China includes its administrative and other districts, such as Hong Kong. It may invest up to 20 percent of total assets in equity and other securities of issuers located outside of the China region, and in non-convertible bonds and other debt securities issued by foreign issuers and foreign government entities.

Oberweis China Opportunities
The investment seeks to maximize long-term capital appreciation. The fund invests at least 80 percent of assets in the securities of Chinese companies that are organized under the laws of The People's Republic of China, Hong Kong, Taiwan or Singapore. It generally holds equities of small to mid-size companies.

Old Mutual Clay Finlay China
The investment seeks long-term capital appreciation. The fund normally invests at least 80 percent of net assets, plus any borrowings for investment purposes, in equity securities of companies that: are organized under the laws of China, Hong Kong, or Taiwan;

TABLE 18.4   (Continued)

are primarily traded on the China, Hong Kong, or Taiwan exchanges; or derive at least 50 percent of their revenues from business activities in China, Hong Kong, or Taiwan, but which are listed and traded elsewhere. It is nondiversified.

Templeton China World A
The investment seeks long-term capital appreciation. The fund normally invests at least 80 percent of assets in securities of "China companies." It may invest up to 20 percent of assets in securities that do not qualify as China company securities, but whose issuers, in the judgement of the manager, are expected to benefit from development in the economy of China. The fund may also invest up to 20 percent of net assets in debt obligations of China companies, which may be lower-rated or unrated, when consistent with the Fund's investment goal. It is nondiversified.

U.S. Global Investors China Reg Opp
The investment seeks long-term capital appreciation. The fund normally invests at least 80 percent of its net assets (plus any borrowings for investment purposes) in equity securities issued by China region companies. The China region consists of the People's Republic of China, Armenia, Azerbaijan, Bangladesh, Georgia, Hong Kong, India, Indonesia, Kazakhstan, Korea, Kyrgyzstan, Laos, Malaysia, Mongolia, Nepal, Pakistan, Philippines, Singapore, Taiwan, Tajikistan, Thailand, Turkmenistan, Uzbekistan, and Vietnam. This fund is nondiversified.

The third risk factor is nationalization and expropriation. It is difficult to predict if the Communist government will nationalize private assets, as it did back in 1949. If this takes place or if Beijing renounces its debt obligations, the investment could suffer a total loss. One additional significant risk is the issue of disclosure. Disclosure and regulatory standards in China are less stringent than the United States. Information about Chinese listed companies is not as readily available. Also, the assets or profits on the financial statements of a Chinese issuer many not reflect its financial position or operating results in the way that would be reflected had China adopted GAAP.

Chinese corporate and securities laws are another concern. China operates under a civil law system, in which court precedent is not binding. Thus, there is uncertainty regarding the interpretation of the law. Chinese laws providing investor protection are underdeveloped and will not provide investors with protection comparable to the United States.

Finally, investment and repatriation restrictions are a significant risk for funds that directly invest in China through QFII. The Chinese government may limit QFIIs in their investments in the securities of certain Chinese issuers entirely, if foreign investment is banned in that industry. These restrictions may affect the mutual fund's ability to achieve its investment objective. A related risk is foreign exchange control. The Chinese government heavily regulates the domestic exchange of foreign currencies. These restrictions may adversely affect the fund and its investment.

Exchange-Traded Funds

The other option is to use an exchange-traded fund (ETF). An ETF is a type of investment company whose investment objective is to achieve the same return as a particular market index. Thus, an ETF will primarily invest in the securities of companies that are included in a selected market index. Chapter 19 discusses ETFs in detail.

GROWTH OF MUTUAL FUNDS IN THE UNITED STATES

Mutual fund investing began to grow in popularity in the 1940s and 1950s, but the explosive growth did not occur until the 1980s. In 1960, there were 160 funds with $17 billion in assets. Ten years later, there were 361 funds with total assets of $47.6 billion. By 1980, the number of funds had reached 564, and the total assets under management were $134.8 billion. In 1990, U.S. mutual funds managed more than $1 trillion. By yearend 2006, more than $10 trillion was invested in mutual funds (Table 18.5).

The enormous growth and diversity of the mutual fund industry have led to the development of new fund categories with various investment objectives. Funds can still be grouped into three general types: money market funds, bond funds, and stock funds. Money market funds invest in short-term securities that are highly liquid and low risk. These funds seek to maintain a stable NAV of $1, while providing a current level of income to shareholders. Bond mutual funds invest in fixed-income securities such as Treasury, agency, corporate, and municipal securities. Stock mutual funds primarily invest in common stocks.

Mutual Fund Selection and Asset Allocation

The type of mutual funds appropriate for a given investor will depend on the individual's tolerance for risk and investment horizon, or the time until the money is needed. Table 18.6 provides a sample matrix of investment strategies. A capital preservation

TABLE 18.5 Mutual Fund Industry Statistics ($ Billions)

	Dec 2006	Dec 2005
Stock Funds	5,669.6	4,939.8
Hybrid Funds	633.1	567.3
Taxable Bond Funds	1,103.0	1,018.5
Municipal Bond Funds	360.9	338.8
Taxable Money Market Funds	1,895.2	1,706.5
Tax-Free Money Market Funds	351.7	334.0
Total	10,413.0	8,904.8

Source: Investment Company Institute.

TABLE 18.6 Mutual Fund Investment Strategy Matrix

	Investment Horizon		
Risk Tolerance	0–3 Years	4–6 Years	7+ Years
High	Moderate growth	Wealth building	Aggressive growth
Moderate	Moderate growth	Moderate growth	Wealth building
Low	Capital preservation	Capital preservation	Moderate growth

Source: Fidelity Investments.

strategy is appropriate for investors who want income, a fair amount of stability, and some increase in the value of the investment. A strategy focused on moderate growth is for investors who primarily want a balance of moderate growth and moderate income with a fair amount of stability. For investors who want the potential for growth and capital appreciation, but also want some protection from stock market volatility, a wealth-building strategy is suitable. Aggressive growth is for investors who want the potential for substantial growth and capital appreciation.

In selecting a portfolio of mutual funds, an investor may also want to engage in asset allocation. Asset allocation is the process of strategically diversifying investments in order to achieve a return that is consistent with the investor's financial goals, investment horizon, and risk tolerance. A strategic asset allocation is a value-oriented technique that seeks to increase exposure to the market when recent market performance has been poor and to reduce exposure when recent market performance has been good. In contrast, a dynamic asset allocation strategy uses portfolio insurance to avoid large losses and secure any favorable market move.

The benefit of risk reduction from diversification is well documented and understood. In addition, allocating money into various asset classes can improve overall returns. For example, suppose an investor has a two-year investment horizon and is faced with two types of funds in two different asset classes. Fund A provides a return of 40 percent in the first year and 0 percent in the second year. Fund B returns investors 0 percent and 40 percent during the same two-year period. Thus, investing in either Fund A or Fund B gives a total return of 40 percent. If the investor allocates funds into these two classes 50/50, the total return is 44 percent. An allocation mix of Fund A and Fund B will results in an additional return of 4 percent.[2] Note that if the investor has perfect timing and invests in Fund A in the first year and switches to Fund B in the second year, the total return will be 96 percent. Most investors do not have a crystal ball, however, so they are better off diversifying their investments.

Asset allocation has a profound effect on the performance investors can expect from their investment portfolios over time.[3] Market timing and selection of individual securities account for less than 10 percent of a portfolio's performance. To develop an asset allocation program, investors should first determine their financial goals and investment horizon. They should also evaluate their level of risk tolerance, which depends on each individual's investment horizon, psychological ability to withstand market downswings, and financial situation. The next step is to develop a detailed asset allocation strategy using assets that complement each other. Once the blueprint for asset allocation has been formulated, it is time to implement the strategy. The performance of the portfolio is reviewed periodically and compared to the investor's objectives. By periodically rebalancing the portfolio, the investor sells those that have appreciated and purchases those investments that have gone down in value. Such rebalancing helps maintain a constant portfolio risk level and prevents the asset allocation percentages from deviating from the plan.

BENEFITS OF INVESTING IN MUTUAL FUNDS

One of the most important benefits of investing in a mutual fund is the diversification it offers. There is an old credo "never put all your eggs in one basket." The same holds true when investing. It is foolhardy to assume that putting all money into one security would yield, in the long-term, the same or better results as a diversified portfolio. By investing in only one security, the investor is susceptible to both systematic and unsystematic risk. Systematic risk is the risk that cannot be diversified away, because it is a risk associated with the investing markets as a whole, nothing can be done to diversify it away.

Unsystematic risk, however, is the risk associated with a specific firm, and can be diversified away by purchasing many securities in different industries. If a person is invested in only one security, the chances of a loss increase greatly, since they would have to deal with the ups and downs of their specific company and the risks associated with the market. With a mutual fund, buying a share of a mutual fund is like buying a portion of a share in all of the underlying securities, which gives an investor diversification.

The second benefit is the research and knowledge put into the management of a mutual fund. Mutual fund managers are experienced professionals that have a much deeper knowledge base than the normal personal investor does. They have studied many different types of techniques for investing and have knowledge of the portfolio, mutual fund, and diversification theories. Those managers also have a research team supplying them with the latest and sophisticated research on the company, industry, and overall economy. By purchasing shares in a mutual fund, investors gain from the knowledge and the professional experience of the fund manager.

Furthermore, what makes this an added value is that the fund is managed by the manager continually (continuous monitoring). There is little need for the investor to worry about the day-to-day activities of the underlying securities. This is being taken care of by the fund manager, who will buy or sell securities, or change the investment strategy in any way that is needed to continually meet the funds objective.

Another benefit is that if an investor were to build his own portfolio, there would be transaction costs associated with every trade the investor would make. While some securities brokerages offer small fees, these could still add up over the lifetime of a portfolio to become quite substantial. In purchasing a mutual fund, these fees are greatly reduced.

Furthermore, in some cases, the mutual fund company will offer dividends that technically do not represent any earnings from the fund. These are called return of capital distributions in which the company gives some money back to the investors. The benefit of these is that they are completely nontaxable in almost every case. In the case of a company that invests internationally, the fact that the company must pay foreign taxes usually adds up to some sort of savings or deduction for the investors on their U.S. taxes as well.

Also, there is a particular tax advantage that comes with purchasing shares of a mutual fund right before the cut off date for receiving of dividends. If a person buys the mutual fund right before this date, it is almost a certainty that the shares will suffer a loss at face value. For example, suppose we purchase one share of ABC Municipal Bond Fund for $10.00 on the last possible day that shares can be purchased in order to receive the dividend (interest). Assume that the following week the fund pays $2.00 in dividends, which makes your share now worth $8.00. If the shares are sold, this allows for a write-off for a loss of $2.00 even though technically you have not lost any money. This allows for yet another tax advantage.[4]

Last, an added advantage of mutual funds is the fact that a person can purchase shares in the mutual fund for generally any amount due to the fact that mutual funds have percentages of shares. This enables an investor to put in the amount they wish to invest, not a set amount per share. Of course the amount sent in must at least cover whatever charges are incurred with buying the fund. Still, this is an advantage over purchasing separate securities.

In summary, the benefits of investing in a mutual fund as opposed to investing in a single security (or building your own portfolio) are:

- Mutual funds give an investor instant diversification.
- Mutual funds offer professional management and research.
- Buying shares in a mutual fund reduces the amount of brokerage fees.
- Mutual fund investors can purchase fractional shares.

DRAWBACKS OF INVESTING IN MUTUAL FUNDS

There are drawbacks to mutual fund investing. One potential drawback to mutual fund investing is that when a person invests in a mutual fund, he leaves the managerial decisions up to the fund manager. While this usually is a benefit, as most fund managers bring with them a level of professional expertise in research and investing that the investor normally does not possess, it can conversely become a drawback if the fund manager is incapable of making the right decisions.

Another drawback is that perhaps the fund manager is a capable manager, but his investment decisions are not the right fit for every investor. While this is not particularly the fund manager's fault, it is a drawback to someone who has not done his own research. Another possibility is that the manager is knowledgeable but employs an investment strategy that is not conducive to achieving the mutual fund objective.

There are savings by investing in a mutual fund over a single security or building your own portfolio. However, it is not a mandatory action that managers pass the savings on to the investor. While it is common that some savings are passed on, it is not law. This represents another drawback to mutual fund investing. Another problem with a fund manager not passing on the savings to the investor is that this may cause the fees associated with the mutual fund to become unreasonable. This can culminate in scaring away many potential investors, causing would-be investors to purchase a fund in which the costs are lower.

Similar to the aforementioned disadvantage is the fact that the fund manager may make so many changes (purchases, sales, reduction in shares, increase in shares, etc.) that the costs associated with the fund increase. This can be either an increase in the expense ratio or any other costs that are associated with the fund. What this could mean to the investors who own the fund or an investor who is interested in purchasing the fund is that the costs become much higher than what the investor was initially paying. This could potentially end up with the same results as the former disadvantage, in which both the investor and fund company are financially hurt. This is sometimes referred to as a chum-and-earn problem.

Another issue that could be associated with a fund manager being in control of the fund is that an investor many not feel as in control of her investments than if she owned one singular security or built a portfolio on her own. While this is not a problem with the fund manager per se, it does represent a disadvantage to the investor. If the investor does not feel comfortable with the fund manager's decisions, or if the investor feels that perhaps she would do a better job managing her investment than the manager could, it could cause her to not purchase shares of a particular fund.

Another drawback is the notion that there may be certain restrictions on how and when the investor can sell his shares of a mutual fund, as is the case with redemption fees, transactions fees, or contingent deferred sales charges. This can influence an investor's decision to sell shares of the fund, even against her instinctive judgments. If a fund is already losing money, or the costs associated with a fund become too high, this can cause the investor to lose even more.

Last, another disadvantage to mutual fund investing may be that fund shares can only be sold or purchased after the closing of the market each day. This could cause a major loss in value to the investor.

In summary, the primary disadvantages of mutual fund investing are:

- The investor must rely on the fund manager's knowledge.
- A fund manager may not pass on the savings to the investor, causing higher costs to be incurred.
- A fund manager can make too many transactions, resulting in higher fees and costs.
- Investors may feel a loss of control of their investments.
- Fund shares can only be bought or sold at the end of each day, no matter what time the sell or buy order is issued during a day.[5]

STRUCTURE AND REGULATION OF MUTUAL FUNDS

Mutual funds are highly regulated financial entities that must comply with securities laws and regulations. This section reviews the basic structure of mutual funds and the regulatory environment in which they operate.

Basic Structure of Mutual Funds

The structure of a typical mutual fund includes directors, investment adviser/management company, principal underwriter, custodian, independent public accountants, and transfer agent. The directors or trustees of an investment company must perform their responsibilities with the care expected of a prudent person. They are expected to evaluate the performance of the investment adviser, principal underwriter, and other parties that provide services to the fund. Independent directors serve as watchdogs for shareholder interests. Investment advisory and distribution contracts must be approved by a majority of a fund's independent directors.

The investment adviser is responsible for making portfolio selections in accordance with the objectives and policies set forth in the prospectus. As noted earlier, most advisory contracts provide for an annual fee based on a percentage of the fund's average net assets during the year, generally between 0.5 and 1.5 percent (higher for specialized funds, but can be as low as 10 basis points for index funds). The principal underwriter markets and distributes mutual fund shares to the investing public, and independent accountants must certify the financial statements in a fund's annual report.

Most funds use bank custodians. The SEC requires mutual fund custodians to protect the funds by segregating their portfolio securities from the rest of the bank's assets. Fund transfer agents maintain records of shareholder accounts. Transfer agents typically serve as dividend disbursing agents as well. They prepare and mail account statements, tax information, and other notices to shareholders. Some transfer agents also prepare and mail statements confirming shareholder transactions and maintain customer service departments to respond to shareholder inquiries.

Mutual fund shareholders are entitled to purchase or redeem shares based on the NAV on the request date. Shareholders also have certain voting rights. Although most mutual funds no longer have annual shareholder meetings, certain matters such as changes in investment objectives or policies deemed fundamental require shareholder approval.

Regulation of Mutual Funds

The mutual fund industry is highly regulated. Most of the federal securities laws that govern the industry were inacted by Congress in the wake of the stock market crash of 1929 and the Great Depression. These laws, which are intended to protect investors, include the Investment Company Act of 1940, the Investment Advisors Act of 1940, the Securities Act of 1933, and the Securities Exchange Act of 1934. Other important regulations are found in Internal Revenue Code of 1986, state notice filing requirements, and antifraud statutes.

Under the Investment Company Act of 1940 (ICA), a mutual fund's investment in each security is generally limited to an amount not greater than 5 percent of the fund's assets and not more than 10 percent of the outstanding voting securities of such issuer. The act also regulates the ability of mutual funds to employ certain investment techniques such as futures, options, and swaps. The act specifically prohibits certain transactions between a fund and its principal underwriter, investment adviser, or other affiliated persons.

The ICA requires all funds to safeguard their assets by placing them in the hands of a custodian and by providing fidelity bonding of officers and employees of the fund. Under the act, a mutual fund is required to determine its NAV each business day. Each mutual fund is required to maintain detailed books and records regarding the securities it owns and its outstanding shares, to file semiannual reports with the SEC, and to send such reports to shareholders.

The Investment Advisers Act of 1940 (IAA) regulates the activities of investment advisers, including advisers to investment companies and private money managers. The IAA regulation generally covers people who are engaging in the business of providing advice or issuing reports about securities to clients for compensation. Under the Investment Advisers Supervision Coordination Act of 1997 (IASCA), investment advisers must register with the SEC if they have more than $25 million in client assets under management or advise registered investment companies. Investment advisers who do not advise a registered investment company may rely on an existing exemption from SEC registration. This exemption applies to investment advisers who had fewer than fifteen clients during the past 12 months, do not hold themselves out to the public as investment adviser, and do not advise any registered investment company. Because the assets under management for some advisers may fluctuate above and below $25 million, causing needless SEC and state registrations and withdrawals, the SEC has raised the threshold for mandatory registration to $30 million. When assets under management dip below $25 million, withdrawal from SEC registration is required.

Even when investment advisers are not registered under the IAA because they manage less than $25 million and do not advise a registered investment company, they may still be required to register under state law. State-registered investment advisers whose assets under management grow to $30 million are required to register with the SEC.

The Securities Act of 1933 requires that all prospective mutual fund investors receive a current prospectus describing the fund and that the fund provides, upon request, a Statement of Additional Information. Mutual funds are subject to special SEC registration rules because they continuously offer new shares to the public. To facilitate the continuous offering of shares, the act permits a mutual fund to update its prospectus at regular intervals, and whenever material changes occur, and to register an indefinite number of shares. After the end of each fiscal year, mutual funds pay a registration fee to the SEC based on the shares actually sold. Mutual funds are permitted to net redemptions against sales when calculating their SEC registration fees.

The Securities Exchange Act of 1934 regulates broker-dealers, including principal underwriters and others who sell mutual fund shares, and requires them to register with the SEC. In addition, all sales and research personnel must demonstrate their qualifications by passing an examination administered by the NASD. A mutual fund's principal underwriter is required to have a Registered Principal. This officer must take special qualification examinations administered by the NASD.

The Internal Revenue Code of 1986 provides a mutual fund entity-level tax exemption if the fund distributes substantially all of its income to its shareholders. The mutual fund shareholders report the dividends received from the fund on their individual tax returns. Several types of income retain their character when they flow through a mutual fund to its shareholders. These include long-term capital gains (paid out as a capital gain dividend) and municipal bond income exempt from federal taxes (the exempt-interest dividend). In addition, all local governments recognize that the character of federal obligation interest, which is exempt from state and local taxation, can flow through a mutual fund to its shareholders.

TYPES OF MUTUAL FUNDS

Mutual funds can be classified in a number of different ways depending on how the fund is managed and what types of securities the fund purchases. One basic distinction between funds is whether they are actively or passively managed. An actively managed fund attempts to add value by pursuing a strategy of actively selecting securities in an attempt to beat the fund's benchmark. A passively managed fund, often times referred to as an index fund simply tries to match the performance of some index such as the S&P 500 or the Russell 2000 index. These funds have advantages over actively managed funds because they incur relatively low expenses and, because of their low portfolio turnover rate, tend to be tax efficient. Funds can also be classified based on the types of strategies they follow.

Aggressive Growth Funds

Aggressive growth funds are highly speculative because they pursue a strategy of purchasing the stocks of companies that have the greatest chance for capital appreciation. These types of companies tend to be small, unproven companies that have the potential to become the next Microsoft, Bidu.com, or Google but who face great risk in the market place. In many instances, these companies have little or no earnings and perhaps no viable product. The chances for success of these companies is relatively small, however those that do succeed are likely to see their stock prices rise many times.

Growth Funds

Growth funds seek capital appreciation through investment in well-established large or mid-cap companies with above average growth potential. Growth funds are less risky than aggressive growth funds because the majority of the fund's holdings are in established companies that already have earnings and a viable product. The goal for the manager of a growth fund is to find companies with earnings growth exceeding those expected by the market. These funds still face significant risk because earnings growth may not beat the expectations of the market.

Equity Income Funds

Equity income funds invest in stocks with high dividend yields. Equity income funds tend to emphasize the preservation of capital and tend to be much less risky than either growth or aggressive growth funds. Equity income funds tend to hold mature, blue chip companies that pay reasonable dividends as well as utilities and other high yielding stocks.

Growth and Income Funds

Growth and income funds seek to balance current income and long-term capital gains. Growth and income funds will tend to use high yielding stocks to generate the income component of the fund's returns, although they may opt to hold some bonds to enhance current income. These funds also tend to favor high quality blue chip stocks. The income component and the more conservative nature of these funds makes them much less risky than growth or aggressive growth funds.

Balanced Funds

Balanced funds hold a balanced portfolio of stocks and bonds in an attempt to generate both current income and long-term capital gains. Unlike growth and income funds, the balanced fund uses bonds to generate the current income component of its returns. Balanced funds generally set a range for their stock/bond asset mix. For example, a fund may hold between 25 and 50 percent of its assets in bonds. One advantage of balanced funds is the discipline that is imposed on the fund's managers. Because the fund will need to rebalance the portfolio to maintain the stock/bond mix, the manager is required to sell stocks when the price is high and use the proceeds to purchase bonds. Similarly, when the market falls, a manager will be forced to purchase stocks when their prices are low. Balanced funds tend to have lower risk than all equity funds.

Bond Funds

Bonds represent debt obligations of companies, state, local, federal, and foreign governments. Because the payments from the issuer to the bondholder represent a legal obligation, bond funds tend to be conservative in nature.[6] Each type of bond will have different interest rate risks, tax consequences, and cash flow characteristics.

Bond funds are classified by the types of bonds they purchase and the average maturity or duration of the bonds held in the portfolio. Some of the bond funds available to investors are:

- *Government bond funds:* Invest in U.S. Treasury and agency securities.
- *Mortgaged-backed bond funds:* Invest in various types of mortgage-backed securities such as GNMA issues.
- *High-grade bond funds:* Invest in highly rated corporate bonds.
- *High-yield corporate bond funds:* Invest in less creditworthy bonds for the higher yields they offer.
- *Municipal bond funds:* Invest in tax-exempt state and local bonds. Municipal bonds are exempt from federal tax and state tax in the issuing state. Single state funds tend to be advantageous for residents of that state because interest is also exempt from state income tax. Multistate funds are exempt from federal income tax, however, bondholders may be subject to state and local income tax on any interest from the bonds.

There are several issues that an investor should consider when deciding on the purchase of a bond mutual fund. First, when purchasing a bond fund, the maturity of the bond fund does not decrease over time as is the case with the direct purchase of a bond. Therefore, an investor who purchases a bond fund with average maturity of 7 to 10 years will not see the maturity diminish with the passage of time. The second consideration that a bond investor should consider is the expenses of the fund. In the case of stocks, an argument can be made that additional expenses on research allow the manager to improve performance. However, when considering a government bond fund, the homogeneity of the assets do not allow even the most brilliant fund manager to add much value. In addition, the lower historical returns of bonds relative to stocks make expenses much more important to the investor's realized return.

Index Funds

Index funds attempt to match the performance of some index like the S&P 500, Russell 2000, or Wilshire 5000 index. The appeal of index funds is their low cost, tax efficiency, and the fact that most actively managed funds fail to beat the market index on a consistent basis. There are several ways that a fund can construct a portfolio to match the performance of its index. The first method is simply to purchase all the securities held in the portfolio in the same proportions as they are held in the index. This is known as a full replication strategy. A second approach known as sampling, attempts to match the performance of the index without purchasing all the securities in the index. For example, a statistical sampling technique may be used to purchase 300 of the stocks in the S&P 500 index. The sampling approach may choose to hold all the industries in the index in their same proportions but not all the stocks. A third approach known as enhanced indexing uses an approach similar to the sampling approach except the portfolio is tilted to reflect the most promising stocks in the industry in an attempt to beat the index by a small percentage each year.[7]

Sector Funds

Sector funds focus on companies in specific sectors of the economy. Sector funds allow an investor to invest in a specific area of the economy such as health care or the Internet without having to search out individual stocks. For example, there are sector funds for technology, utilities, transportation, the Internet, health care, and precious metals. In general, these funds have a goal of capital appreciation. Because the portfolio is concentrated in a specific sector of the economy, these funds tend to be highly risky.

Socially Responsible Funds

Socially responsible funds invest in the stocks and bonds of companies that the fund views as socially responsible. These funds tend to invest in companies that are environmentally friendly, do not produce morally objectionable products such as cigarettes or alcoholic beverages, and behave responsibly towards its workers and society. These types of funds provide an outlet for investors who care more about social responsibility than corporate profits. Although most companies in these types of funds are not to be the high fliers in the market, many feel that socially responsible companies will tend to prosper over the long haul.

Asset Allocation Funds

Asset allocation deals with how a portfolio's assets are divided among the various investment vehicles, such as stocks, bonds, and cash equivalents. Asset allocation funds seek to adjust the composition of the funds holdings of stocks, bonds, and cash to reflect market conditions. For example, if the fund manager believes that the market is likely to have a downward correction, she may move funds from stocks to bonds or cash. If the manager is correct, the portfolio will suffer a smaller loss than a fund that is fully invested in equities. Once the correction has taken place, the manager can then move money back into the stock market and purchase stocks at more reasonable prices.

One selling point of asset allocation funds is that they allow investors to pass the asset allocation decision onto professional fund managers. One major drawback is that guessing the future direction of the market can be extremely difficult, with many investment professionals believing that it is impossible.

International Funds

International funds invest in the securities of non-U.S. stocks, and thus allow investors to participate in the success or failure of non-U.S. companies. There are numerous categories of international funds. Some funds can invest anywhere in the world, whereas other funds limit their investments to a particular country or region of the world. Other funds may invest in less-developed or emerging markets. Funds can also use an approach of indexing to some international benchmark or can choose to build a portfolio based on individual security selection.

One argument for international investing that is gaining popular acceptance is that investing abroad can reduce the overall risk of an investor's portfolio. The diversification benefit results from the lower degree of correlation between international stocks and U.S. equities. The lower the correlation between assets, the greater the benefits of diversification will be.

Global Funds

Global funds are similar to international funds except they allow the fund manager to purchase U.S. securities as well. This gives the fund manager more leeway in determining which securities to add to the portfolio. One drawback is that the portfolio may become more heavily weighted toward U.S. stocks than the investor desires.

Money Market Funds

Money market funds invest in short-term debt obligations of various borrowers such as the U.S. Treasury, state governments, or corporations. The short-term nature of the fund's assets make money market funds suitable for meeting an investor's short-term savings needs. Money market funds can be classified in a number of ways:

- *Government securities money market funds:* These types of funds invest in obligations of the U.S. Treasury or government agencies. This makes these types of funds virtually default free.
- *Tax-exempt money market funds:* These funds invest in short-term tax-exempt municipal securities.
- *General-purpose money market funds:* Invest in a variety of short-term instruments from Treasury bills to commercial paper to certificates of deposit.

CONCLUSION

One efficient approach to investing in China's growth opportunities is to buy Chinese mutual funds. Many of those funds invest in Chinese companies listed in the United States. Investors can purchase those securities here directly as well, but purchase of those funds offers many advantages. Some of the financial institutions have direct access to China's A share and B share markets by way of QFII designation. Chapter 19 discusses Chinese ETFs that investors can use to participate in China's securities markets.

19

Investing in Chinese Exchanged-Traded Funds Listed on U.S. Exchanges

A nother approach for U.S. investors to invest in China is to purchase U.S. exchange-traded funds (ETFs) tracking China indexes. Several ETFs are listed in the United States. Investing in those ETFs presents several advantages over mutual funds, including low costs, buying and selling flexibility during trading hours, tax efficiency, and a wide array of investment strategies. This chapter discusses ETFs, how they are created, advantages and disadvantages, arbitrage, and the market mechanics.

ETFs

An exchange-traded fund (ETF) is a type of investment company established to achieve the same return as a particular market index. Similar to index mutual funds, ETFs are created to track an index such as the S&P 500 or the DJIA, the market index of a specific country, a fixed basket of selected stocks, a fixed-income index, a currency, or commodity prices. ETFs are considered a passive investment strategy because there is no active management once the ETF is created. However, as indexes are reconstituted, the ETFs change their holdings to mirror the new composition of the index. Thus, an ETF is a basket of securities that trades as a whole on one of the stock exchanges such as AMEX, NYSE, NASDAQ, or foreign exchanges.

ETFs are created to deliver the return of a specific index, sector, or basket of securities. As there are differences in the indexes that track specific sectors, there are corresponding differences in the ETFs that mirror those indexes. For investors, one important factor in choosing one ETF over another is to decide on the specific investment objective as represented by the underlying index or sector. Another factor in evaluating an ETF is to determine how closely its return mirrors the performance of the underlying index, called the tracking error. The lower the tracking error, the greater the success of the ETF in delivering the return of its index is.

ETFs differ from open-end mutual funds in several ways. ETFs can be traded real time during the trading hours, while open-end mutual funds are purchased or sold at the end of day net asset value (NAV). Investors trade ETFs over the exchange, but they purchase open-end mutual funds directly from the fund company such as Fidelity or Bernstein. Open-end mutual funds cover indexes as well as many other actively managed objectives, which are not available through ETFs. On the other hand, investors can short sell ETFs and trade them on margin. Investors pay full amount when purchasing open-end mutual funds.

There are differences between ETFs and closed-end funds as well. A closed-end fund is a mutual fund created by an initial public offering with a fixed number of shares. Once created, investors buy and sell shares to each other on the secondary market. The supply and demand pressure can cause the fund to trade at a premium or discount to the net asset value of the underlying securities. But like ETFs, they have some of the same intraday trading flexibility as stocks in that they are trade continuously throughout the day and are marginable. Table 19.1 compares ETFs and other investment solutions.

An ETF, like any other type of investment company, will have a prospectus. All investors who purchase Creation Units (bundles of stock used to create an ETF) receive a prospectus. Some ETFs also deliver a prospectus to secondary market purchasers. ETFs that do not deliver a prospectus are required to give investors a document known as a Product Description, which summarizes key information about the ETF and explains how to obtain a prospectus. ETFs that are legally structured as open-end companies must also have statements of additional information. Open-end ETFs (but not UIT ETFs) must provide shareholders with annual and semi-annual reports.

An ETF trades like a stock. Just like an index fund, an ETF represents a basket of stocks that reflects an index. An ETF, however, is not a mutual fund. It trades just like

TABLE 19.1   Comparison between ETFs and Other Products

	ETFs	Common Stocks	Open-End Mutual Funds	Closed-End Mutual Funds
Intraday liquidity	V	V		V
Portfolio transparency	V			
Tax efficient	V			
Diversification	V		V	V
Low expenses	V			
Professional management	V		V	V
Fully invested	V			V
Marginable	V	V		
Short sell	V	V		

any other company on a stock exchange. Unlike a mutual fund that has its NAV calculated at the end of each trading day, an ETF's price changes throughout the day, fluctuating with supply and demand. It is important to remember that while ETFs attempt to replicate the return on indexes, there is no guarantee that they will accomplish it. This is because, for various reasons discussed later, most ETFs have tracking errors.

Types of ETFs

According to publications by Morgan Stanley and information from AMEX, ETF managers/trustees include Bank of New York (BLDRs and HOLDRs), Barclays Global Investors (iShares series), State Street Global Advisors (DIAMONDS, SPRDs, and streetTRACKS), PowerShares Capital Management (PowerShares), Fidelity, First Trust, ProShares, Rydex, Van Eck, Vanguard, Victoria Bay, and WisdomTree. Some of them offer ETFs that duplicate similar indexes.

The first ETF in the United States was Spiders (SPDR) designed to track the S&P 500 index fund, which started trading on the AMEX in 1993. Today, there are hundreds of ETFs tracking a wide variety of sector-specific, country-specific, and broad-market indexes. There are also ETFs that provide investors exposure to commodities and currencies. Investors can find an ETF for just about any sector of the market. All ETFs are passively managed. Some of the more popular ETFs are:

- *NASDAQ-100 Index Tracking Stock (QQQQ):* This ETF tracks 100 largest and most actively traded nonfinancial stocks on the NASDAQ. This largely tracks the technology sector. The diversification it offers can be a huge advantage when there is volatility in the markets.
- *SPDRs:* Bundle the benchmark S&P 500 and give investors ownership in the index, allowing individual investors to own the index's stocks in a cost-effective manner. Another nice feature of SPDRs is that they divide various sectors of the S&P 500 stocks and sell them as separate ETFs. They track performance in biotech, dividend, homebuilding, metals & mining, oil & gas, retail, pharmaceuticals, and semiconductor.
- *iShares:* Barclay's brand of ETFs. There are many iShares ETFs tracking various types of indexes, from S&P 500, S&P 400, Russell 2000, value, growth, to global. iShares ETFs also include fixed income, emerging markets, and many international markets based on MSCI indexes.
- *PowerShares:* Many PowerShares Dynamic ETFs trade on the AMEX. Similar to others, PowerShares Dynamic ETF series tracks markets in energy, financial, food and beverage, industrials, media, large cap, mid cap, and small cap.
- *streetTracks:* Offers ETFs for investors to take stakes in EURO STOXX 50, a variety of Wilshire indexes, capital markets, banks, and Japan.
- *VIPERs:* Vanguard's brand of the financial instrument. Vipers (Vanguard Index Participation Receipts) are structured as share classes of open-end funds. Vanguard also offers a variety of ETFs for many different areas of the market

including the financial, healthcare, utilities, large cap, mid cap, small cap, REIT, materials, information technology, and others.

- *DIAMONDs:* These ETF shares, Diamonds Trust Series I, track the Dow Jones Industrial Average. The fund is structured as a unit investment trust.

In addition to those listed, there are other ETFs from Claymore, First Trust, and Rydex that offer investors exposure to the market. For investors, ETFs today offer a complete menu of choices for them to invest in various segments of the markets in the United States and other countries.

Another way to classify the types of ETFs in the United States is to base the classification on the type of index the ETF is designed to replicate. Under this method, there are U.S. Major Market ETFs, U.S. Specialty Market ETFs, U.S. Sector and Industry ETFs, International ETFs, Global ETFs, U.S. Fixed Income ETFs, Commodity ETFs, and Currency ETFs.

Creation and Redemption of ETFs

The process to create and redeem ETF shares is different from that for mutual fund shares. When an investor buys shares of an open-end mutual fund, the investor pays cash to the fund company, which then uses that cash to purchase securities and in turn issue additional shares of the fund. When the investor redeems their mutual fund shares, the shares are returned to the mutual fund in exchange for cash. In the case of a closed-end mutual fund, the fund pools funds from investors and invest in its target securities. The size is fixed, while the portfolio value increases or decreases with the values of securities in the portfolio. If the fund was to liquidate, the funds would be returned to investors. The creation of an ETF, however, is quite different and does not involve cash.

Creation

The process begins when a prospective ETF manager (the sponsor) files a plan with the SEC to create an ETF. After the SEC has approved the application, the sponsor forms an agreement with an authorized participant who is empowered to create or redeem ETF shares. An authorized participant is generally a market maker, specialist, or large institutional investor.

The authorized participant borrows shares of stock and places those shares in a trust, and uses them to form creation units of the ETF. Creation units are bundles of stock varying from 10,000 to 600,000 shares, but 50,000 shares are commonly designated as one creation unit of a given ETF. Then, the trust provides shares of the ETF to the authorized participant. Because this transaction is in-kind, that is, securities are traded for securities and no cash changes hands, there are no tax implications. Once the authorized participant receives the ETF shares, the shares are then sold to the public on the open market just like shares of stock.

When ETF shares are bought and sold on the exchange, the underlying securities that were borrowed to form the creation units remain in the trust account. The trust generally has little activity beyond paying dividends from the stock held in the trust to the ETF owners and providing administrative oversight. The creation units are not impacted by the transactions that take place on the market when ETF shares are traded.

Redemption

When ETF shareholders want to sell their shares, they can do so by one of two methods. The first is to sell the ETF shares on the open market. Most individual investors use this option, as their shares are usually not large enough to form a creation unit. If the shares are sold at a higher price, there will be capital gains, and hence tax consequences. For institutional players in the ETF market, they often use the second option. They gather enough shares of the ETF to form a creation unit and then exchange the creation unit for the underlying securities. When these investors redeem, the creation unit is destroyed and the securities are turned over to them. The beauty of this option is in its tax implications for the portfolio.

We can see these tax implications best by comparing the ETF redemption to that of mutual fund redemption. When mutual fund investors redeem shares from a fund, all shareholders in the fund are affected by tax burden because to redeem the shares, the mutual fund may have to sell the securities it holds, realizing the capital gain, which is subject to tax. Every shareholder of this mutual fund takes a proportional burden of this sale. Also, mutual funds are required to pay out all dividends and capital gains on a yearly basis. So even if the portfolio has lost value that is unrealized, there is still a tax liability on the capital gains that had to be realized because of the regulatory requirement to pay out dividends and capital gains.

ETFs alleviate this problem by paying large redemptions, in creation units, with shares of stock. When such redemptions are made, the shares with the lowest cost basis in the trust are given to the investor. This increases the cost basis of the ETF's overall holdings, minimizing capital gains for the ETF. It does not matter to the redeemer that the shares it receives have the lowest cost basis because the redeemer's tax liability is based on the purchase price it paid for the ETF shares, not the fund's cost basis. When the investor sells the shares of stock on the open market, any gain or loss incurred has no impact on the ETF. In this manner, investors with smaller portfolios are protected from the tax consequences of trades made by investors with large portfolios.

Arbitrage

ETFs generally trade at a price close to the net asset value of the underlying stocks in the index. However, because the price of an ETF can also be influenced by investor demand, it can sometimes trade at a premium or discount to the NAV. For example, during the third quarter of 2006, the DIAMONDS price was on average equal to its NAV. But, detailed examination indicated that it traded at a small discount for 29 days and a premium for 33 days. During the same period, SPDRs traded at a discount for 38 days and a premium for 25 days. For PowerShares Halter USX China, the discount days were 20 and premium days were 41.

When the premium/discounts are very small and insignificant, investors continue to trade they way they do. When the premium/discounts are large enough, arbitrage comes in. If an ETF is trading at a discount, the authorized participant/arbitrageur can buy up ETF shares to form creation units, exchange them for the underlying stocks, and sell the stocks for a profit. On the other hand, if there is a lot of demand for an ETF and it starts to trade at a premium, the authorized participant can buy the underlying stocks, exchange them for ETF shares, and then sell the ETFs to generate a profit.

We will show the arbitrage by way of a numerical example. Assume a specialist, for example Kellogg, sets the offer price of an ETF share at $35, while the NAV of the underlying portfolio is $36. Another specialist, perhaps Bear Hunter, spots the opportunity and starts buying up as many shares as possible. Bear Hunter can then turn around and redeem the shares at $36. In the hypothetical example, let's assume 1,000,000 shares were purchased and subsequently redeemed. At a $1 profit per share, Bear Hunter is ahead by $1 million. Institutions can also reverse the process if the ETF trades at a premium to the NAV. The actions of the arbitragers set the supply and demand of the ETFs back into equilibrium to match the value of the underlying shares.

Benefits of ETFs

ETFs offer many advantages to investors. The first advantage of holding an ETF is cost. Index linked ETFs have some of the lowest expenses in the marketplace. Their expense ratios are lower than open-end mutual funds. For example, Vanguard Total Stock Market Index Fund (VTI) has an expense ratio of 7 basis points, while the average ratio is 1 percent to 1.50 percent for actively managed domestic equity open-end funds. Table 19.2 shows some of the expense ratios for ETFs and open-end mutual funds.

TABLE 19.2 Expense Ratios of ETFs and Mutual Funds

	Average
ETFs:	
U.S. Major Market ETFs	27 bps
U.S. Specialty Market ETFs	69 bps
U.S. Style ETFs	29 bps
U.S. Sector/Industry ETFs	43 bps
International Equity ETFs	52 bps
All Equity ETFs	40 bps
Fixed-Income ETFs	17 bps
Open-end Mutual Funds:	
Actively Managed Domestic Equity	150 bps
Actively Managed International Equity	170 bps
Passive/Indexed Domestic Equity	72 bps
Passive/Indexed International Equity	99 bps
Passive/Indexed Fixed-Income	43 bps

Source: Exchange-Traded Funds. Morgan Stanley, August 15, 2006.

The second advantage is the convenience that an ETF offers. A mutual fund can only be bought or sold at the net asset value at the end of each trading day. An ETF, however, trades exactly like an individual security would. ETFs can be bought and sold throughout the trading day, as well as can be sold short or on margin like an individual security. This can be quite useful in reacting to market information almost immediately, not being forced to wait until the end of the day, like a mutual fund.

The next advantage is that it offers more flexibility than even the most reasonable of mutual funds. While the abilities to trade like an individual security have already been previously discussed, it is fair to mention that an ETF can also be held for any amount of time that the investor feels they wish to hold. There are no redemption fees or any other type of charge that could feasibly prevent a person from purchasing an ETF and selling it five minutes later. For a mutual fund with a back-end load, investors sometimes postpone the sale in order to spread the load. With an ETF, an investor can buy or sell with the complete freedom of an individual security. It is in this respect that an ETF gives investors flexibility.

The fourth advantage is the instant diversification it offers. Like a mutual fund, an ETF actually holds many different securities as a basket. Being that a piece of the total basket is placed into every share purchased offers a level of diversification that an individual stock could never offer alone. With ETFs, the diversification is as complete, if not more complete than even the best of index-based mutual funds. In that respect, an ETF is potentially the investment which offers the highest amount of diversification per share, since its underlying investments can number into the thousands.

Another advantage is that ETFs tend to be more tax efficient. With actively managed mutual funds, a fund manager can accumulate a large amount in taxes through realized gains due to turnovers in the portfolio. This is passed on to the investor. ETFs, being similar in nature to passive mutual funds, are able to avoid this since very little turnover is needed on average, with changes to the index being the only changes that must be made to the ETF tracking that index. In this respect, ETFs can keep their taxes on realized gains to a relative minimum. Secondly, ETF holders do not have to pay capital gains taxes until they sell. This is in direct contrast to almost all mutual funds, which require that taxes be paid throughout the holding period. This is clearly evidenced by a research by Morgan Stanley, which indicates that the average gains distributions as a percentage of net asset value is 0.01 percent for SPDR and is 1.68 percent for open-end S&P 500 mutual funds during periods of 1993 through 2005.[1]

Yet another advantage of ETFs is the notion of transparency. An ETF offers transparency in two ways, through disclosure of their holdings and through the ETF's price. Exchanges calculate and disseminate estimated ETF underlying portfolio values throughout the trading day. This information keep investors informed of the approximate market price/NAV relationship when making a trade decision. For a large part of actively managed mutual funds, the investor is not entirely aware of what the fund holds. It is really only the fund manager that knows the full scoop on the fund's current holdings. With an ETF, due to its passive nature, the investor almost always knows what is being held because it hardly ever changes. Investors know the NAV of a mutual fund only after the end of the trading day.

As for the price, ETF holders can even decide what price to buy the ETF at through the use of a limit order. A limit order is a stock order (in this case a buy order) to purchase an investment at a price that the investor will specify. Now there is no need to worry if the price stays above the limit price, since then, the order will not execute. If the price drops to or below the limit price, then the order executes. With a mutual fund, the investor sends in a check for a certain amount, and gets their shares for whatever the price is at the end of that trading day.

The last advantage of holding an ETF is the notion of portability. A problem with holding a mutual fund is that competitors might not allow you to hold a fund of another fund company. For example, if I hold shares of a mutual fund with Oppenheimer, I might not be able to transfer my holdings in this fund to a Fidelity account without first liquidating my holdings (and vice versa). This means I would have to pay my capital gains tax on my Oppenheimer holdings just to be able to invest in a Fidelity fund, not to mention closing out my account in Oppenheimer. I could keep an account in both, but again, this causes inconvenience. A stipulation like this is likely to keep investors locked in to one fund family for quite some time. ETFs do not have this problem since they are traded on exchanges like any other individual security. In this respect, ETFs are very portable investments, as you can keep them with you no matter what brokerage you would use.

In summary, the main advantages of ETFs are:

- ETFs have lower expense ratios.
- ETFs are convenient, with ability to trade like an individual security.
- ETFs do not have a minimum holding period requirement. Investors tend to hold on to the load open-end mutual funds longer, because extending holding period lowers the average load per year.
- ETFs are more tax efficient.
- ETFs are transparent through disclosure of their holdings and through the ETF's price.
- ETFs are portable across any investment house or brokerage.

Disadvantages of ETFs

There are at least five major disadvantages to holding an ETF. The first major disadvantage is commissions. Since ETFs are bought and sold exactly like an individual security, they are purchased through exchanges rather than through the company offering a fund. While this can be as low as $5.00 for some online brokerages, it could be much higher with some of the full-service brokerage houses. In the case of a long-term buy-and-hold investor, these fees are not really a major issue. However, for investors who take a more active role in portfolio management, the transaction fees can actually become quite expensive over time. Imagine being charged even $100.00 per transaction to shift around your assets every two months. For a small investor who buys 100 shares at a time, it takes a lot more time for the increase in value of an investment to absorb such a cost every few months, or at the very least, makes it much harder to. In this respect, commissions can become quite cumbersome.

Similar to the commission disadvantage is the notions of the next two disadvantages. The first is the notion of dollar-cost averaging. Dollar-cost averaging is a technique used by "buy and hold" investors as a means of minimizing short-term risk. For example, let's assume that an investor wishes to purchase 10,000 shares of XYZ Company stock. Assume that this stock is trading for $10.00 per share. The investor has two options; they could either pay $100,000 and buy the shares all at once, or spread the purchase over a period of time. This period of time could be any time span really, but is usually done over a period of weeks or months. For this example, let's say the investor would purchase 1,000 shares every week for 10 weeks. Now to illustrate the use of dollar-cost averaging, let's look at the example in Table 19.3.

As the table shows, there is a difference. By the end of week 12, the value is the same for both, but the return overall is higher for the investor using the dollar-cost averaging method because their purchases were spread out over time, resulting in a cheaper overall cost. Now, notice also that the stock's price from weeks one through eight had fluctuated downwards. This enabled the dollar-cost investor to not assume as much loss as the investor who bought the stock all in one lump purchase. What if the stock had fluctuated upwards though? The example in Table 19.4 illustrates this. Looking at this example, we can see that just the opposite has happened.

The next disadvantage is the notion of over trading. During the 1990s, day trading came into prominence. Day trading is when an investor purchases a particular se-

TABLE 19.3 Dollar Cost Averaging

		XYZ STOCK	
Week	*XYZ Price*	*One Time Investment Value*	*DCA Investment Value*
1	$10.00	$100,000.00	$10,000.00
2	$ 8.00	$80,000.00	$18,000.00
3	$ 7.50	$75,000.00	$25,500.00
4	$ 9.00	$90,000.00	$34,500.00
5	$10.00	$100,000.00	$44,500.00
6	$11.00	$110,000.00	$55,500.00
7	$ 9.00	$90,000.00	$64,500.00
8	$ 8.00	$80,000.00	$72,500.00
9	$12.00	$120,000.00	$84,500.00
10	$14.00	$140,000.00	$98,500.00
11	$16.00	$160,000.00	$160,000.00
12	$18.00	$180,000.00	$180,000.00
	Total return	80.00%	82.74%
	Average share price	$10.00	$9.85

TABLE 19.4   Investment Value

		XYZ STOCK	
Week	XYZ Price	One Time Investment Value	DCA Investment Value
1	$10.00	$100,000.00	$10,000.00
2	$11.00	$110,000.00	$21,000.00
3	$13.00	$130,000.00	$34,000.00
4	$12.00	$120,000.00	$46,000.00
5	$11.00	$110,000.00	$57,000.00
6	$10.00	$100,000.00	$67,000.00
7	$ 9.00	$90,000.00	$76,000.00
8	$11.00	$110,000.00	$87,000.00
9	$12.00	$120,000.00	$99,000.00
10	$14.00	$140,000.00	$113,000.00
11	$16.00	$160,000.00	$160,000.00
12	$18.00	$180,000.00	$180,000.00
	Total return	80.00%	59.29%
	Average share price	$10.00	$11.30

curity and sells within a small period of time, to make a quick profit. A day trader can profit quite well from jumping in and out of positions all day so long as the securities they are purchasing are profiting. During a time like the late 1990s, when securities could have an upswing of 10 percent or more in a single day, this was quite profitable. But in the more recent markets, 10 percent down swings are also equally as common, making this approach very risky. With the advent of ETFs, and given their nature of trading like a single security, ETFs have also become the focus of day trading, only this time, it is the bet on a particular index rising during the course of a day. This exposes an ETF investor to the same exposure of risk that would be inherent for the day trading of an individual security as well.

Another disadvantage to holding an ETF is that while the ETF does give an investor instant diversification, holding one ETF is still not a wise choice as a means of being a complete portfolio. The investor still needs to build the rest of, and then manage their portfolio. In this respect, they will not receive the same professional management that is associated with the purchase of an actively managed mutual fund.

The last disadvantage to holding an ETF is the notion of liquidity. Liquidity, as a definition in regards to investments, is determined by the ease with which an investment can be converted into cash. While some ETFs, such as Spiders, have a high trading volume and are considered very liquid, a large amount of ETFs only have a trading volume numbering on average in the thousands. This can represent a problem when an investor wishes to unload some of his investments. Mutual fund owners again, do not have this problem.

In summary, the disadvantages are as follows:

- Commission fees can become quite expensive over time.
- Dollar-cost averaging can also become a significant cost over time, and exposes an investor to risks not associated with mutual funds.
- Over-trading exposes an ETF investor to the same exposure of risk that would be inherent for the day trading of an individual security.
- The lack of professional management for ETF investors exposes them to risks due to lack of the same level of knowledge as active fund managers.
- Some ETFs are illiquid.

ETF Tracking Errors

Just like index mutual funds, ETFs track the performance of specific indexes. The manager's primary objective is to minimize the difference between the index return and the ETF return (called tracking error). HOLDRS do not have tracking errors because they are based on static baskets of securities that are unmanaged. Differences in fund and benchmark returns arise for several reasons.

Observations on ETF Tracking Errors

A key difference between an ETF and the index it tracks is the expense ratio. Theoretically, the ETF gives investors a lower return by the expense ratio. In 2005, the average tracking error was higher than expense ratios. U.S. Major Market ETFs and Fixed Income ETFs had the lowest tracking error, 18 basis points that were one basis point higher than the expense ratio. U.S. Style ETFs had a tracking error totally offset by the expense ratio. The tracking error was 62 basis points for sector and industry ETFs, which were 22 basis points over its expense ratio. The highest tracking error was in the International ETF group, 103 basis points, 44 basis points higher than its expense ratio.

Reasons for Tracking Errors

As the observations have indicated, the tracking errors can not be explained by the expense ratios. The first source of error is SEC diversification requirement. Under the Investment Company Act of 1940, securities that have a weighting of 5 percent or more cannot not compose more than 50 percent of the total fund assets. When the weighting of some companies in some indexes exceed the SEC limit, the ETF managers are forced to deviate from a perfect replication of the index.

Another source of tracking errors, as mentioned above, is the expense ratio. Although expense ratios for ETFs are the lowest in the business, they still exist. ETF returns, or for that matter any fund's performance, are net of any fees.

The third reason relates to dividend reinvestment policy. Most ETFs use the management investment company (or open-ended) structure, which allows for immediate reinvestment of dividends. However, some of the earliest ETFs are unit investment trusts (UITs). UITs are less flexible than their management investment company cousins, but the UIT structure was chosen for the initial ETFs because it was inexpensive and did not require a board of directors. The bottom line is that UITs cannot immediately reinvest dividends. This type of structure distributes dividends to shareholders quarterly, which causes minor tracking error.

The next possible source is the existence of premium/discounts. Generic ETF returns are typically measured on a monthly or yearly basis. At the market close at the end of the month or year, an ETF may trade at a premium or discount to the NAV of the underlying securities. This will lead to discrepancies in index and ETF performance. From a practical standpoint, however, ETF tracking error within an investor portfolio depends on premiums and discounts at the time when the ETF was bought and sold.

Another source is rebalancing. When an index rebalances, an ETF is required to follow suit. However, the timing of the trades is at the discretion of the fund manager. The timing, market impact, and transactions costs of the changes can affect performance.

Finally, some international ETFs trade in the United States while the underlying markets are closed. Sometimes it appears that these ETFs are not trading close to NAV, but the reason is that there is a mismatch in the timing of calculating index return and ETF NAV. In other words, this tracking error is perceived, not actual.

CHINA ETFs

Three big plays in the China ETF arena are iShares FTSE/Xinhua 25 Index (FXI), PowerShares Golden Dragon Halter USX China (PGJ), and iShares MSCI Hong Kong Index (EWH). In addition, Morgan Stanley has issued several products for U.S. investors to bet on China. For example, Morgan Stanley in 2005 listed index-linked notes (CAX) that tracks the performance of AMEX China Index. Note that the index includes 15 of the Chinese stocks listed in the United States. Those 15 stocks are CNOOC, China Telecom, CDC Corporation, China Mobile, China Unicom, China Yuchai, Huaneng Power, Nam Tai Electronics, Netease.com, PetroChina, SINA Corporation, Shanda Interactive, China Petro & Chem, SOHU.com, and UTStarcom. The issue date was September 23, 2005, and the issuing price was $10. At maturity on December 20, 2009, the payment will be $10 plus the supplemental value. The supplemental redemption amount of this ETF will be equal to the product of $10 times the percentage, if any, by which the final average index value exceeds the initial index value. If the final average index value is greater than the initial index value, the supplemental redemption amount will be calculated as follows:

$$\text{Supplemental redemption amount} = \$10 \times \frac{\text{final index value} - \text{initial index value}}{\text{initial index value}},$$

Where initial index value = 112.05 (the closing value of the AMEX China Index on September 23, 2005, the day we priced the notes for initial sale to the public),

final average index value = the arithmetic average of the closing values of the AMEX China Index on each of the five determination dates, as calculated by the calculation agent on the final determination date.

If the final average index value is less than or equal to the initial index value, the supplemental redemption amount will be zero. In that case, investors will receive only the principal amount of $10 for each note that she holds and will not receive any supplemental redemption amount. Thus, the principal is 100 percent protected. If the final index value if higher than the initial value, then the investor will receive $10 plus the supplemental amount. For example, the investor will receive a total of $12.36 if the final index value is 138.50.

As another example, Morgan Stanley China A Share Fund is a closed-end fund with the objective to seek capital growth, by investing at least 80 percent of its assets in A shares of Chinese companies listed on the Shanghai and Shenzhen Stock Exchanges. The fund also might invest up to 15 percent in warrants, structured instruments, or other transactions. It is the first U.S. registered investment company that invests principally in China A shares.

iShares FTSE/Xinhua China 25 Index (FXI) consists of 25 of the largest and most liquid Chinese companies. FXI is well diversified, from holdings in Oil (PetroChina, Sinopec, and CNOOC), Technology (China Mobile), Financial Institutions (China Life Insurance and CITI Pacific), and Construction (China Construction Bank). Table 19.5 lists the top holdings of FXI.

PowerShares Golden Dragon Halter USX China (PGJ) seeks to replicate the Halter USX China Index, which is comprised of the U.S. listed securities of com-

TABLE 19.5   Top Holdings of iShares FTSE/Xinhua 25 Index

	Top Holdings as of December 6, 2006
9.25%	PetroChina Co., Ltd.-Class H
8.71%	China Mobile, Ltd.
8.06%	Industrial and Commercial Bank of China Asia, Ltd.-Class H
7.17%	China Life Insurance Co., Ltd.-Class H
6.00%	Bank of China, Ltd.
4.62%	China Telecom Corp., Ltd.-Class H
4.25%	China Petroleum & Chemical Corp.-Class H
4.22%	China Construction Bank-Class H, 144A
4.14%	China Shenhua Energy Co., Ltd.-Class H
4.12%	Bank of Communications Co., Ltd.-Class H

Source: Barclays Global Investors and Yahoo Finance.

TABLE 19.6 Top Holdings of PowerShares Golden Dragon

Top Holdings as of December 6, 2006

6.04%	PetroChina Co. Ltd. (ADS)
5.90%	China Mobile Ltd. (ADS)
5.19%	China Telecom Corp. Ltd. (ADS)
5.04%	China Petroleum & Chemical Corp. (ADS)
4.79%	Suntech Power Holdings Co. Ltd. (ADS)
4.71%	China Life Insurance Co. Ltd. (ADS)
4.64%	China Netcom Group Corp. (Hong Kong) Ltd. (ADS)
4.59%	Baidu.com Inc. (ADS)
4.57%	Aluminum Corp. of China Ltd. (ADS)
4.56%	China Unicom Ltd. (ADS)

Source: PowerShares Capital Management and Yahoo Finance.

panies that derive a majority of their revenue from the People's Republic of China. Table 19.6 lists its top 10 holdings.

iShares MSCI Hong Kong Index (EWH) seeks to provide investment results that correspond generally to the price and yield performance of publicly traded securities in the Hong Kong market, as measured by the MSCI Hong Kong Index. Table 19.7 lists its top 10 holdings.

There are also indirect approaches to investing in China. China's neighbors have been doing business in the country and are doing quite well. The top companies in iShares MSCI Singapore Index (EWS) do business with mainland China. The holdings include banks, oil rig builder, and telecommunications. Besides business with China, Singapore has a healthy economy. The other close neighbor, Taiwan, is represented with the iShares MSCI Taiwan (EWT) ETF. This ETF is devoted to large companies in Taiwan.

TABLE 19.7 Top Holding of iShares MSCI Hong Kong Index

Top Holdings as of October 31, 2006

9.40%	Hutchison Whampoa, Ltd.
8.13%	Cheung Kong Holdings, Ltd.
7.43%	Sun Hung Kai Properties, Ltd.
5.71%	CLP Holdings, Ltd.
4.89%	Hang Seng Bank, Ltd.
4.87%	Swire Pacific, Ltd.-Class A
4.66%	Esprit Holdings, Ltd.
4.19%	Hong Kong Exchanges and Clearing, Ltd.
4.09%	BOC Hong Kong Holdings, Ltd.
4.05%	Hong Kong & China Gas

Source: Barclays Global Investors and Yahoo Finance.

It tracks the Taiwan stock market well. Many of those large Taiwanese companies have significant operations in China. Unlike companies in Singapore or Hong Kong, though, Taiwanese government has limited investments of Taiwanese companies in China at 40 percent of the capital.

CONCLUSION

There are several ways to invest in China. Many investors, especially individuals and some small institutional investors do not have the resources or expertise to access the local Chinese market. For U.S. investors, they can purchase ADRs, China mutual funds, or China ETFs. This chapter provided a discussion of the U.S. ETF market and discussed several China ETFs. The chapter also discussed the benefits of using ETFs, tracking errors, and discussed the creation and redemption of ETFs.

Appendix A

Foreign Corrupt Practices Act: Antibribery Provisions

The 1988 Trade Act directed the Attorney General to provide guidance concerning the Department of Justice's enforcement policy with respect to the Foreign Corrupt Practices Act of 1977 (FCPA), 15 U.S.C. §§78dd-1, *et seq.,* to potential exporters and small businesses that are unable to obtain specialized counsel on issues related to the FCPA. The guidance is limited to responses to requests under the Department of Justice's Foreign Corrupt Practices Act Opinion Procedure (described below at p. 10) and to general explanations of compliance responsibilities and potential liabilities under the FCPA. This brochure constitutes the Department of Justice's general explanation of the FCPA.

U.S. firms seeking to do business in foreign markets must be familiar with the FCPA. In general, the FCPA prohibits corrupt payments to foreign officials for the purpose of obtaining or keeping business. In addition, other statutes such as the mail and wire fraud statutes, 18 U.S.C. §1341, 1343, and the Travel Act, 18 U.S.C. §1952, which provides for federal prosecution of violations of state commercial bribery statutes, may also apply to such conduct.

The Department of Justice is the chief enforcement agency, with a coordinate role played by the Securities and Exchange Commission (SEC). The Office of General Counsel of the Department of Commerce also answers general questions from U.S. exporters concerning the FCPA's basic requirements and constraints.

BACKGROUND

As a result of SEC investigations in the mid-1970s, over 400 U.S. companies admitted making questionable or illegal payments in excess of $300 million to foreign

Source: U.S. Department of Justice.

government officials, politicians, and political parties. The abuses ran the gamut from bribery of high foreign officials to secure some type of favorable action by a foreign government to so-called facilitating payments that allegedly were made to ensure that government functionaries discharged certain ministerial or clerical duties. Congress enacted the FCPA to bring a halt to the bribery of foreign officials and to restore public confidence in the integrity of the U.S. business system.

The FCPA was intended to have and has had an enormous impact on the way U.S. firms do business. Several firms that paid bribes to foreign officials have been the subject of criminal and civil enforcement actions, resulting in large fines and suspension and debarment from federal procurement contracting, and their employees and officers have gone to jail. To avoid such consequences, many firms have implemented detailed compliance programs intended to prevent and to detect any improper payments by employees and agents.

Following the passage of the FCPA, the Congress became concerned that U.S. companies were operating at a disadvantage compared to foreign companies who routinely paid bribes and, in some countries, were permitted to deduct the cost of such bribes as business expenses on their taxes. Accordingly, in 1988, the Congress directed the Executive Branch to commence negotiations in the Organization of Economic Cooperation and Development (OECD) to obtain the agreement of the United States' major trading partners to enact legislation similar to the FCPA. In 1997, almost 10 years later, the United States and 33 other countries signed the OECD Convention on Combating Bribery of Foreign Public Officials in International Business Transactions. The United States ratified this Convention and enacted implementing legislation in 1998.

The antibribery provisions of the FCPA make it unlawful for a U.S. person, and certain foreign issuers of securities, to make a corrupt payment to a foreign official for the purpose of obtaining or retaining business for or with, or directing business to, any person. Since 1998, they also apply to foreign firms and persons who take any act in furtherance of such a corrupt payment while in the United States.

The FCPA also requires companies whose securities are listed in the United States to meet its accounting provisions. See 15 U.S.C. §78m. These accounting provisions, which were designed to operate in tandem with the antibribery provisions of the FCPA, require corporations covered by the provisions to make and keep books and records that accurately and fairly reflect the transactions of the corporation and to devise and maintain an adequate system of internal accounting controls. This brochure discusses only the antibribery provisions.

ENFORCEMENT

The Department of Justice is responsible for all criminal enforcement and for civil enforcement of the antibribery provisions with respect to domestic concerns and foreign companies and nationals. The SEC is responsible for civil enforcement of the antibribery provisions with respect to issuers.

ANTIBRIBERY PROVISIONS

Basic Prohibition

The FCPA makes it unlawful to bribe foreign government officials to obtain or retain business. With respect to the basic prohibition, there are five elements which must be met to constitute a violation of the Act:

A. *Who*—The FCPA potentially applies to *any* individual, firm, officer, director, employee, or agent of a firm and any stockholder acting on behalf of a firm. Individuals and firms may also be penalized if they order, authorize, or assist someone else to violate the antibribery provisions or if they conspire to violate those provisions.

   Under the FCPA, U.S. jurisdiction over corrupt payments to foreign officials depends upon whether the violator is an "issuer," a "domestic concern," or a foreign national or business.

   An "issuer" is a corporation that has issued securities that have been registered in the United States or who is required to file periodic reports with the SEC. A "domestic concern" is any individual who is a citizen, national, or resident of the United States, or any corporation, partnership, association, joint-stock company, business trust, unincorporated organization, or sole proprietorship which has its principal place of business in the United States, or which is organized under the laws of a State of the United States, or a territory, possession, or commonwealth of the United States.

   Issuers and domestic concerns may be held liable under the FCPA under *either* territorial or nationality jurisdiction principles. For acts taken within the territory of the United States, issuers and domestic concerns are liable if they take an act in furtherance of a corrupt payment to a foreign official using the U.S. mails or other means or instrumentalities of interstate commerce. Such means or instrumentalities include telephone calls, facsimile transmissions, wire transfers, and interstate or international travel. In addition, issuers and domestic concerns may be held liable for any act in furtherance of a corrupt payment taken *outside* the United States. Thus, a U.S. company or national may be held liable for a corrupt payment authorized by employees or agents operating entirely outside the United States, using money from foreign bank accounts, and without any involvement by personnel located within the United States.

   Prior to 1998, foreign companies, with the exception of those who qualified as "issuers," and foreign nationals were not covered by the FCPA. The 1998 amendments expanded the FCPA to assert territorial jurisdiction over foreign companies and nationals. A foreign company or person is now subject to the FCPA if it causes, directly or through agents, an act in furtherance of the corrupt payment to take place within the territory of the United States. There is, however, no requirement that such act make use of the U.S. mails or other means or instrumentalities of interstate commerce.

Finally, U.S. parent corporations may be held liable for the acts of foreign subsidiaries where they authorized, directed, or controlled the activity in question, as can U.S. citizens or residents, themselves "domestic concerns," who were employed by or acting on behalf of such foreign-incorporated subsidiaries.

B. *Corrupt intent*—The person making or authorizing the payment must have a corrupt intent, and the payment must be intended to induce the recipient to misuse his official position to direct business wrongfully to the payer or to any other person. You should note that the FCPA does not require that a corrupt act succeed in its purpose. The *offer* or *promise* of a corrupt payment can constitute a violation of the statute. The FCPA prohibits any corrupt payment intended to *influence* any act or decision of a foreign official in his or her official capacity, to induce the official to do or omit to do any act in violation of his or her lawful duty, to *obtain* any improper advantage, or to *induce* a foreign official to use his or her influence improperly to affect or influence any act or decision.

C. *Payment*—The FCPA prohibits paying, offering, promising to pay (or authorizing to pay or offer) money or anything of value.

D. *Recipient*—The prohibition extends only to corrupt payments to a *foreign official,* a *foreign political party* or *party official,* or any *candidate* for foreign political office. A "foreign official" means any officer or employee of a foreign government, a public international organization, or any department or agency thereof, or any person acting in an official capacity. You should consider utilizing the Department of Justice's Foreign Corrupt Practices Act Opinion Procedure for particular questions as to the definition of a "foreign official," such as whether a member of a royal family, a member of a legislative body, or an official of a state-owned business enterprise would be considered a "foreign official."

The FCPA applies to payments to *any* public official, regardless of rank or position. The FCPA focuses on the *purpose* of the payment instead of the particular duties of the official receiving the payment, offer, or promise of payment, and there are exceptions to the antibribery provision for "facilitating payments for routine governmental action" (see below).

E. *Business Purpose Test*—The FCPA prohibits payments made in order to assist the firm in *obtaining* or *retaining business* for or with, or *directing business* to, any person. The Department of Justice interprets "obtaining or retaining business" broadly, such that the term encompasses more than the mere award or renewal of a contract. It should be noted that the business to be obtained or retained does *not* need to be with a foreign government or foreign government instrumentality.

Third-Party Payments

The FCPA prohibits corrupt payments through intermediaries. It is unlawful to make a payment to a third party, while knowing that all or a portion of the payment will go directly or indirectly to a foreign official. *The term "knowing" includes conscious disre-*

gard and deliberate ignorance. The elements of an offense are essentially the same as described above, except that in this case the "recipient" is the intermediary who is making the payment to the requisite "foreign official."

Intermediaries may include joint venture partners or agents. To avoid being held liable for corrupt third party payments, U.S. companies are encouraged to exercise due diligence and to take all necessary precautions to ensure that they have formed a business relationship with reputable and qualified partners and representatives. Such due diligence may include investigating potential foreign representatives and joint venture partners to determine if they are in fact qualified for the position, whether they have personal or professional ties to the government, the number and reputation of their clientele, and their reputation with the U.S. Embassy or Consulate and with local bankers, clients, and other business associates. In addition, in negotiating a business relationship, the U.S. firm should be aware of so-called "red flags," *i.e.,* unusual payment patterns or financial arrangements, a history of corruption in the country, a refusal by the foreign joint venture partner or representative to provide a certification that it will not take any action in furtherance of an unlawful offer, promise, or payment to a foreign public official and not take any act that would cause the U.S. firm to be in violation of the FCPA, unusually high commissions, lack of transparency in expenses and accounting records, apparent lack of qualifications or resources on the part of the joint venture partner or representative to perform the services offered, and whether the joint venture partner or representative has been recommended by an official of the potential governmental customer.

PERMISSIBLE PAYMENTS AND AFFIRMATIVE DEFENSES

The FCPA contains an explicit exception to the bribery prohibition for "facilitating payments" for "routine governmental action" and provides affirmative defenses which can be used to defend against alleged violations of the FCPA.

Facilitating Payments for Routine Governmental Actions

There is an exception to the antibribery prohibition for payments to facilitate or expedite performance of a "routine governmental action." The statute lists the following examples: obtaining permits, licenses, or other official documents; processing governmental papers, such as visas and work orders; providing police protection, mail pickup and delivery; providing phone service, power and water supply, loading and unloading cargo, or protecting perishable products; and scheduling inspections associated with contract performance or transit of goods across country.

Actions "similar" to these are also covered by this exception. If you have a question about whether a payment falls within the exception, you should consult with counsel. You should also consider whether to utilize the Justice Department's Foreign Corrupt Practices Opinion Procedure.

"Routine governmental action" does *not* include any decision by a foreign official to award new business or to continue business with a particular party.

Affirmative Defenses

A person charged with a violation of the FCPA's antibribery provisions may assert as a defense that the payment was lawful under the written laws of the foreign country or that the money was spent as part of demonstrating a product or performing a contractual obligation.

Whether a payment was lawful under the written laws of the foreign country may be difficult to determine. You should consider seeking the advice of counsel or utilizing the Department of Justice's Foreign Corrupt Practices Act Opinion Procedure when faced with an issue of the legality of such a payment.

Moreover, because these defenses are "affirmative defenses," the defendant is required to show in the first instance that the payment met these requirements. The prosecution does not bear the burden of demonstrating in the first instance that the payments did not constitute this type of payment.

SANCTIONS AGAINST BRIBERY

Criminal

The following criminal penalties may be imposed for violations of the FCPA's antibribery provisions: corporations and other business entities are subject to a fine of up to $2,000,000; officers, directors, stockholders, employees, and agents are subject to a fine of up to $100,000 and imprisonment for up to five years. Moreover, under the Alternative Fines Act, these fines may be actually quite higher—the actual fine may be up to twice the benefit that the defendant sought to obtain by making the corrupt payment. You should also be aware that fines imposed on individuals may *not* be paid by their employer or principal.

Civil

The Attorney General or the SEC, as appropriate, may bring a civil action for a fine of up to $10,000 against any firm *as well as* any officer, director, employee, or agent of a firm, or stockholder acting on behalf of the firm, who violates the antibribery provisions. In addition, in an SEC enforcement action, the court may impose an additional fine not to exceed the greater of (i) the gross amount of the pecuniary gain to the defendant as a result of the violation, or (ii) a specified dollar limitation. The specified dollar limitations are based on the egregiousness of the violation, ranging from $5,000 to $100,000 for a natural person and $50,000 to $500,000 for any other person.

The Attorney General or the SEC, as appropriate, may also bring a civil action to enjoin any act or practice of a firm whenever it appears that the firm (or an officer, director, employee, agent, or stockholder acting on behalf of the firm) is in violation (or about to be) of the antibribery provisions.

Other Governmental Action

Under guidelines issued by the Office of Management and Budget, a person or firm found in violation of the FCPA may be barred from doing business with the Federal government. *Indictment alone can lead to suspension of the right to do business with the government.* The President has directed that no executive agency shall allow any party to participate in any procurement or nonprocurement activity if any agency has debarred, suspended, or otherwise excluded that party from participation in a procurement or nonprocurement activity.

In addition, a person or firm found guilty of violating the FCPA may be ruled ineligible to receive export licenses; the SEC may suspend or bar persons from the securities business and impose civil penalties on persons in the securities business for violations of the FCPA; the Commodity Futures Trading Commission and the Overseas Private Investment Corporation both provide for possible suspension or debarment from agency programs for violation of the FCPA; and a payment made to a foreign government official that is unlawful under the FCPA cannot be deducted under the tax laws as a business expense.

Private Cause of Action

Conduct that violates the antibribery provisions of the FCPA may also give rise to a private cause of action for treble damages under the Racketeer Influenced and Corrupt Organizations Act (RICO), or to actions under other federal or state laws. For example, an action might be brought under RICO by a competitor who alleges that the bribery caused the defendant to win a foreign contract.

GUIDANCE FROM THE GOVERNMENT

The Department of Justice has established a Foreign Corrupt Practices Act Opinion Procedure by which any U.S. company or national may request a statement of the Justice Department's present enforcement intentions under the antibribery provisions of the FCPA regarding any proposed business conduct. The details of the opinion procedure may be found at 28 CFR Part 80. Under this procedure, the Attorney General will issue an opinion in response to a specific inquiry from a person or firm within thirty days of the request. (The thirty-day period does not run until the Department of Justice has received all the information it requires to issue the opinion.) Conduct for which the Department of Justice has issued an opinion stating that the conduct conforms with current enforcement policy will be entitled to a presumption, in any subsequent enforcement action, of conformity with the FCPA. Copies of releases issued regarding previous opinions are available on the Department of Justice's FCPA web site.

Appendix B

Law of the People's Republic of China on Banking Regulation and Supervision

CHAPTER I: GENERAL PROVISIONS

Article 1: This law is enacted for the purposes of improving banking regulation and supervision, standardizing banking supervisory process and procedures, preventing and mitigating financial risks in the banking industry, protecting the interests of depositors and other customers, as well as promoting a safe and sound banking industry in China.

Article 2: The banking regulatory authority under the State Council shall be responsible for the regulation and supervision of the banking institutions in China and their business operations.

For the purposes of this law, the term "banking institutions" means financial institutions established in the People's Republic of China that take deposits from the general public, including, among others, commercial banks, urban credit cooperatives and rural credit cooperatives, and policy banks.

The provisions of this law pertaining to the regulation and supervision of banking institutions are applicable to the regulation and supervision of asset management companies, trust and investment companies, finance companies, financial leasing companies and other financial institutions established in the People's Republic of China as authorized by the banking regulatory authority under the State Council.

The banking regulatory authority under the State Council shall, in accordance with the applicable provisions of this law, regulate and supervise the finan-

Source: China Banking Regulatory Commission.

cial institutions that, subject to its approval, are established outside the People's Republic of China, as well as the overseas business operations conducted by the financial institutions referred to in the preceding two paragraphs.

Article 3: The objectives of banking regulation and supervision are to promote the safety and soundness of the banking industry and maintain public confidence in the banking industry.

Towards these objectives, the banking regulation and supervision shall protect fair competition in the banking industry and promote the competitiveness of the banking industry.

Article 4: The banking regulatory authority shall exercise banking regulation and supervision in accordance with laws and regulations and in line with the principles of openness, fairness and efficiency.

Article 5: The banking regulatory authority and its supervisory staff shall be protected by law while performing supervisory responsibilities in accordance with laws and regulations. There shall be no interference by local governments, government departments at various levels, public organizations or individuals.

Article 6: The banking regulatory authority under the State Council shall establish supervisory information sharing mechanisms with the People's Bank of China and other regulatory authorities under the State Council.

Article 7: The banking regulatory authority under the State Council may establish supervisory cooperation mechanisms with the banking supervisory authorities in other countries and regions for the supervision of cross-border banking.

CHAPTER II: THE BANKING REGULATORY AUTHORITY

Article 8: The banking regulatory authority under the State Council may, if deemed necessary for performing its responsibilities, set up local offices, and shall exercise centralized oversight of its local offices.

The local offices of the banking regulatory authority under the State Council shall perform supervisory functions as authorized by the banking regulatory authority under the State Council.

Article 9: The supervisory staff of the banking regulatory authority shall have the professional skills and work experiences as required for performing their duties.

Article 10: The staff of the banking regulatory authority shall perform their duties with integrity and in accordance with laws and regulations. They shall not take advantage of their positions to seek inappropriate gains, or concurrently hold a position in enterprises including financial institutions.

Article 11: The staff of the banking regulatory authority shall preserve the confidentiality of information for the State according to applicable laws and regulations, and for the banking institutions subject to their supervision and other parties concerned.

The banking regulatory authority under the State Council shall make relevant arrangements for preserving the confidentiality of information while exchanging supervisory information with the banking supervisory authorities in other countries and regions.

Article 12: The banking regulatory authority under the State Council shall make public its supervisory process and procedures, and put in place a supervisory accountability system and an internal compliance monitoring mechanism.

Article 13: Local governments and relevant government departments at various levels shall cooperate and provide assistance for the banking regulatory authority to exercise its supervisory activities, such as resolving problem banking institutions, and investigating and taking enforcement actions against activities that violate laws and regulations.

Article 14: The banking regulatory authority under the State Council shall be subject to the oversight by relevant government agencies such as the audit institution and supervisory institution under the State Council.

CHAPTER III: REGULATORY AND SUPERVISORY RESPONSIBILITIES

Article 15: The banking regulatory authority under the State Council shall, in accordance with applicable laws and administrative regulations, formulate and promulgate supervisory rules and regulations for banking institutions.

Article 16: The banking regulatory authority under the State Council shall, in accordance with the criteria and procedures provided in applicable laws and administrative regulations, authorize the establishment, changes, termination and business scope of banking institutions.

Article 17: The banking regulatory authority under the State Council shall review and assess the source of capital, financial strength, ability to replenish capital and integrity of the shareholders while reviewing the applications for the establishment of a banking institution or changes in the shareholders that hold a certain percentage or more of the total capital or total shares as stipulated in applicable laws and regulations.

Article 18: Products and services offered by a banking institution within its business scope authorized by the banking regulatory authority under the State Council shall, in accordance with applicable regulations, be subject to prior approval of the banking regulatory authority under the State Council or the report for filing requirement. The banking regulatory authority under the State Council shall, in accordance with applicable laws and administrative regulations, make public the products and services that are subject to prior approval or report for filing requirement.

Article 19: Without the authorization of the banking regulatory authority under the State Council, no institution or individuals may establish a banking institution or engage in banking businesses.

Article 20: The banking regulatory authority under the State Council shall conduct fit and proper test for directors and senior managers of banking institutions. For this purpose, the banking regulatory authority under the State Council shall formulate specific rules and procedures on the fit and proper test.

Article 21: Prudential rules and regulations applied to banking institutions may be stipulated in laws or administrative regulations, or formulated by the banking regulatory authority under the State Council in accordance with applicable laws and administrative regulations.

"Prudential rules and regulations" referred to in the preceding paragraph shall cover, among others, risk management, internal controls, capital adequacy, asset quality, loan loss provisioning, risk concentrations, connected transactions and liquidity management.

The banking institutions shall observe these prudential rules and regulations.

Article 22: The banking regulatory authority under the State Council shall, within a prescribed period of time, make a decision of approval or rejection in writing in response to the following applications. If a decision of rejection is made, it shall specify the reasons for rejection:

(1) In the case of establishment of a banking institution, within six months from the date of receiving the application documents
(2) In the case of changes or termination of a banking institution or offering new products or services within the business scope authorized by the banking regulatory authority under the State Council, within three months from the date of receiving the application documents; and
(3) In the case of fit and proper test for directors and senior managers, within one month from the date of receiving the application documents.

Article 23: The banking regulatory authority shall conduct off-site surveillance of the business operations and risk profile of banking institutions. For this purpose, it shall establish a supervisory information system to analyze and assess the risk profile of banking institutions.

Article 24: The banking regulatory authority shall conduct on-site examination of the business operations and risk profile of banking institutions.

The banking regulatory authority shall formulate on-site examination procedures to standardize on-site examination activities.

Article 25: The banking regulatory authority under the State Council shall regulate and supervise banking institutions on a consolidated basis.

Article 26: The banking regulatory authority under the State Council shall respond to the proposals of the people's Bank of China for the examination of banking institutions within thirty days from the date of receiving the proposals.

Article 27: The banking regulatory authority under the State Council shall establish a rating system and an early warning system for the purpose of supervision of banking institutions, thus, based on the rating and risk profile of banking institutions, determining the frequency and scope of on-site examination as well as other supervisory measures that may be deemed necessary.

Article 28: The banking regulatory authority under the State Council shall establish a system to identify and report emergency situations in the banking sector.

The banking regulatory authority shall, as soon as identified any emergency situations that may result in systemic banking risks, hence causing severe social instability, report to the chief responsible person of the banking regulatory authority under the State Council. The chief responsible person of the banking regulatory authority under the State Council shall, when deemed necessary, report to the State Council while informing relevant government agencies including the People's Bank of China and Ministry of Finance.

Article 29: The banking regulatory authority under the State Council shall, in collaboration with relevant government agencies including the People's Bank of China and Ministry of Finance, establish mechanisms to address emergency situations in the banking sector, including formulating contingency plans, designating institutions and staff members, specifying their responsibilities, and stipulating resolution measures and procedures, hence ensuring timely and effective resolution of the emergency situations in the banking sector.

Article 30: The banking regulatory authority under the State Council shall compile and publish statistics and reports of banking institutions in accordance with applicable regulations of the State.

Article 31: The banking regulatory authority under the State Council shall guide and oversee the activities of the self-regulated organizations of the banking industry.

The self-regulated organizations of the banking industry shall submit their articles of association to the banking regulatory authority under the State Council for filing.

Article 32: The banking regulatory authority under the State Council may engage in the international activities related to banking regulation and supervision.

CHAPTER IV: SUPERVISORY METHODS AND PROCEDURES

Article 33: The banking regulatory authority shall, for the purpose of performing its responsibilities, have the authority to require banking institutions to submit, in accordance with applicable regulations, balance sheets, income statements, other financial and statistical reports, information concerning business operations and management, and the audit reports prepared by certified public accountants.

Article 34: The banking regulatory authority may take the following measures to conduct on-site examination for the purpose of exercising prudential supervision:

(1) to enter a banking institution for on-site examination
(2) to interview the staff of the banking institution and require them to provide explanations on examined matters

(3) to have full access to and make copies of the banking institution's documents and materials related to the on-site examination, and to seal up documents and materials that are likely to be removed, concealed or destroyed; and

(4) to examine the banking institution's information technology infrastructure for business operations and management.

The on-site examination shall be subject to prior approval of the chief responsible office of the banking regulatory authority. The on-site examination team shall comprise no less than two examiners, who shall produce their examiner' certificates and the examination notice upon examination. If the on-site examination team comprises less than two examiners, or the examiners fail to produce their examiner' certificates or the examination notice upon examination, the banking institutions shall have the right to refuse the examination.

Article 35: The banking regulatory authority may, for the purpose of performing its responsibilities, hold supervisory consultations with the directors and senior managers of a banking institution to inquire about the major activities concerning its business operations and risk management.

Article 36: The banking regulatory authority shall require banking institutions to disclose, in accordance with applicable regulations, to the public reliable information, including, among others, financial reports and statements, risk management policies and procedures, changes in the directors and senior managers and information on other significant matters.

Article 37: When a banking institution fails to meet prudential rules and regulations, the banking regulatory authority under the State Council or its provincial office shall require it to take remedial measures within a prescribed period of time. If the banking institution fails to correct the deficiencies within the prescribed period of time, or the safety and soundness of the banking institution is likely to be severely threatened and the interests of its depositors and other customers are likely to be jeopardized, the banking regulatory authority under the State Council or its provincial office may, subject to the approval of its chief responsible officer, take the following measures depending on the severity of the circumstances:

(1) to suspend part of the businesses of the banking institution and/or withhold approval of new products or services

(2) to restrict dividend or other payments to shareholders

(3) to restrict asset transfers

(4) to order the controlling shareholders to transfer shares or restrict the powers of relevant shareholders

(5) to order the banking institution to replace the directors and/or senior managers or restrict their powers; and

(6) to withhold approval of branching.

The banking institution shall report to the banking regulatory authority under the State Council or its provincial office once it is restored to meet the prudential rules and regulations after taking corrective measures. The banking regulatory authority under the State Council or its provincial office shall terminate the measures prescribed in the preceding paragraph within three days after the verification of compliance.

Article 38: When a banking institution is experiencing or likely to experience a credit crisis, thereby seriously jeopardizing the interests of depositors and other customers, the banking regulatory authority under the State Council may take over the banking institution or facilitate a restructuring. The take-over or restructuring shall be carried out in accordance with applicable laws and administrative regulations.

Article 39: When a banking institution has been found serious violation of laws and regulations, or significant unsafe or unsound practices, thereby seriously threatening financial order and public interests unless it is closed, the banking regulatory authority under the State Council shall have the authority to close the institution in accordance with applicable laws and regulations.

Article 40: In the case of the take-over, restructuring, or closure of a banking institution, the banking regulatory authority under the State Council shall have the authority to require the directors, senior managers and other staff of the banking institution to perform their duties according to the requirements of the banking regulatory authority under the State Council.

In the course of the take-over, restructuring or liquidation after the closure of a banking institution, the banking regulatory authority under the State Council shall have the authority, subject to the approval of its chief responsible person, to take the following measures against the directors and senior managers directly in charge and other staff directly held responsible:

(1) when the departure from the People's Republic of China of the directors and senior managers directly in charge and other staff directly held responsible is likely to jeopardize the national interests, the banking regulatory authority under the State Council may request the border control authority to prevent them from leaving the People's Republic of China; and

(2) to request the judicial authority to prohibit the directors and senior managers directly in charge and other staff directly held responsible from moving or transferring their properties, or establishing other rights on their properties.

Article 41: The banking regulatory authority or its provincial office shall have the authority, subject to the approval of its chief responsible person, to inspect the bank accounts of the banking institution suspected in violation of laws and regulations, and the bank accounts of its staff and connected parties, and may, subject to the approval of its chief responsible person, request the judicial authority to freeze the illegally obtained funds that are suspected to be transferred or concealed.

CHAPTER V: LEGAL LIABILITY

Article 42: When the supervisory staff of the banking regulatory authority commits any of the following acts, he or she shall be subject to administrative sanctions according to law. If the case constitutes a crime, he or she shall be investigated for criminal liability according to law:

(1) to authorize, in violation of regulations, a banking institution's establishment, changes, termination, business scope or offering of products or services within its business scope
(2) to conduct on-site examination of banking institutions in violation of regulations
(3) to fail to report emergency situations in the banking sector in accordance with Article 28 of this law
(4) to inspect bank accounts or request freezing of funds in violation of regulations
(5) to take enforcement actions against a banking institution in violation of regulations; and
(6) other acts such as abuse of power and/or neglect of duties.

The supervisory staff of the banking regulatory authority who commits embezzlement, bribery or divulgence of national or commercial confidential information shall, if the case constitutes a crime, be investigated for criminal liability according to law, and if the case does not constitute a crime, be subject to administrative sanctions according to law.

Article 43: When a banking institution is established, or banking businesses are conducted without the authorization of the banking regulatory authority under the State Council, the banking regulatory authority under the State Council shall have the authority to ban such institution or businesses. If the case constitutes a crime, criminal liability shall be pursued according to law. If the case does not constitute a crime, the banking regulatory authority under the State Council shall confiscate the illegal gains. If the amount of illegal gains exceeds 500,000 yuan, a fine ranging from one to five times the amount of illegal gains shall be imposed. If no illegal gains are involved or the amount of illegal gains is less than 500,000 yuan, a fine ranging from 500,000 yuan to 2,000,000 yuan shall be imposed.

Article 44: When a banking institution commits any of the following acts, the banking regulatory authority under the State Council shall order it to take corrective measures, and, if illegal gains are involved, shall confiscate the illegal gains. If the amount of illegal gains exceeds 500,000 yuan, a fine ranging from one to five times the amount of illegal gains shall be imposed. If no illegal gains are involved, or the amount of illegal gains is less than 500,000 yuan, a fine ranging from 500,000 yuan to 2,000,000 yuan shall be imposed. If the case is particularly serious, or the banking institution fails to make correction within the prescribed period of time, the banking regulatory authority under the State Council may order suspension of business for rectification or revocation of its banking license. If the case constitutes a crime, criminal liability shall be pursued according to law:

(1) to establish a branch without authorization
(2) to change or terminate business operations without authorization
(3) to offer a product or service without approval or filing with the banking regulatory authority under the State Council; and
(4) to raise or lower interest rates on deposits or loans in violation of regulations.

Article 45: When a banking institution commits any of the following acts, the banking regulatory authority under the State Council shall order it to take corrective measures, and concurrently impose a fine ranging from 200,000 yuan to 500,000 yuan. If the case is particularly serious, or the banking institution fails to make correction within the prescribed period of time, the banking regulatory authority under the State Council may order suspension of business for rectification or revocation of its banking license. If the case constitutes a crime, criminal liability shall be pursued according to law:

(1) to appoint directors or senior managers without the fit and proper test
(2) to refuse or obstruct the off-site surveillance or on-site examination
(3) to submit statements, reports, documents or materials that are false or conceal important facts
(4) to fail to disclose information to the public in accordance with regulations
(5) to fail to meet prudential rules and regulations with serious consequences; and
(6) to refuse to take measures as required by Article 37 of this law.

Article 46: When a banking institution fails to submit statements, reports, documents or materials in accordance with regulations, the banking regulatory authority under the State Council shall order it to take corrective measures. If the banking institution fails to make correction within the prescribed period of time, the banking regulatory authority may impose a fine ranging from 100,000 yuan to 300,000 yuan.

Article 47: When a banking institution violates laws, administrative regulations or other national regulations on banking regulation and supervision, the banking regulatory authority may, in addition to the enforcement actions prescribed in Article 43 to Article 46 of this law, take the following measures depending on the severity of the circumstance:

(1) to order the banking institution to impose disciplinary sanctions on the directors and senior mangers directly in charge and other staff directly held responsible
(2) if the case does not constitute a crime, to issue a disciplinary warning to the directors and senior managers directly in charge and other staff directly held

responsible and concurrently impose on them a fine ranging from 50,000 yuan to 500,000 yuan; and

(3) to disqualify the directors and senior mangers directly in charge as being unfit and improper for a specified period of time or for life, and/or to bar the directors and senior mangers directly in charge and other staff directly held responsible from banking for a specified period of time or for life.

CHAPTER VI: SUPPLEMENTARY PROVISIONS

Article 48: Where the laws and administrative regulations provide otherwise the regulation and supervision of policy banks and asset management companies, these provisions shall prevail.

Article 49: Where the laws and administrative regulations provide otherwise the regulation and supervision of the wholly foreign-funded banking institutions, Sino-foreign joint venture banking institutions and branches of foreign banking institutions that are established in the People's Republic of China, these provisions shall prevail.

Article 50: This law shall enter into effect as of February 1, 2004.

Appendix C

Securities Law of the People's Republic of China

CHAPTER I: GENERAL PROVISIONS

Article 1: The present Law is formulated for the purpose of regulating the issuance and transaction of securities, protecting the lawful rights and interests of investors, safeguarding the economic order and public interests of the society and promoting the growth of the socialist market economy.

Article 2: The present Law shall be applied to the issuance and transaction of stocks, corporate bonds as well as any other securities as lawfully recognized by the State Council within the territory of the People's Republic of China. Where there is no such provision in the present Law, the provisions of the Corporation Law of the People's Republic of China and other relevant laws and administrative regulations shall be applied. Any listed trading of government bonds and share of securities investment funds shall be governed by the present Law. Where there is any special provision in any other law or administrative regulation, the special provision shall prevail. The measures for the administration of issuance and transaction of securities derivatives shall be prescribed by the State Council according to the principles of the present Law.

Article 3: The issuance and transaction of securities shall adhere to the principles of openness, fairness and impartiality.

Article 4: The parties involved in any issuance or transaction of securities shall have equal legal status and shall persist in the principles of free will, compensation and integrity and creditworthy.

Article 5: The issuance and transaction of securities shall observe laws and administrative regulations. No fraud, insider trading or manipulation of the securities market may be permitted.

Source: China Securities Regulatory Commission.

Article 6: The divided operation and management shall be adopted by the industries of securities, banking, trust as well as insurance. The securities companies and the business organs of banks, trust and insurance shall be established separately, unless otherwise provided for by the state.

Article 7: The securities regulatory authority under the State Council shall adopt a centralized and unified supervision and administration of the national securities market. The securities regulatory authority under the State Council may, in light of the relevant requirements, establish dispatched offices, which shall perform their duties and functions of supervision and administration upon the authorization.

Article 8: Under the centralized and unified supervision and administration of the state regarding the issuance and transaction of securities, a securities industry association shall be lawfully established, which shall adopt the self-regulating administration.

Article 9: The auditing organ of the state shall carry out auditing supervision of stock exchanges, securities companies, securities registration and clearing institutions and securities regulatory bodies.

CHAPTER II: ISSUANCE OF SECURITIES

Article 10: A public issuance of securities shall satisfy the requirements of the relevant laws and administrative regulations and shall be reported to the securities regulatory authority under the State Council or a department upon authorization by the State Council for examination and approval according to law. Without any examination and approval according to law, no entity or individual may make a public issuance of any securities. It shall be deemed as a public issuance upon the occurrence of any of the following circumstances: (1) Making a public issuance of securities to non-specified objects; (2) Making a public issuance of securities to accumulatively more than 200 specified objects; or (3) Making a public issuance as prescribed by any law or administrative regulation. For any securities that are not issued in a public manner, the means of advertising, public inducement or public issuance in any disguised form may not be adopted thereto.

Article 11: An issuer that files an application for public issuance of stocks or convertible corporate bonds by means of underwriting according to law or for public issuance of any other securities, to which a recommendation system is applied, as is prescribed by laws and administrative regulations, shall employ an institution with the qualification of recommendation as its recommendation party. A recommendation party shall abide by operational rules and industrial norms and, on the basis of the principles of being honesty, creditworthy, diligent and accountable, carry out a prudent examination of application documents and information disclosure materials of its issuers as well as supervise and urge its issuers to operate in a regulative manner. The qualification of the recommendation party as well as the relevant measures for administration shall be formulated by the securities regulatory authority under the State Council.

Article 12: A public offer of stocks for establishing a stock-limited company shall satisfy the requirements as prescribed in the Corporation Law of the People's Republic of China as well as any other requirements as prescribed by the securities regulatory authority under the State Council, which have been approved by the State Council. An application for public offer of stocks as well as the following documents shall be reported to the securities regulatory authority under the State Council: (1) The constitution of the company; (2) The promoter's agreement; (3) The name or title of the promoter, the amount of shares as subscribed by the promoter, the category of contributed capital as well as the capital verification certification; (4) The prospectus; (5) The name and address of the bank that receives the funds as generated from the issuance of stocks on the behalf of the company; and (6) The name of the underwriting organization as well as the relevant agreements. In case a recommendation party shall be employed, as prescribed by the present Law, the Recommendation Letter of Issuance as produced by the recommendation party shall be submitted as well. In case the establishment of a company shall be reported for approval, as prescribed by laws and administrative regulations, the relevant approval documents shall be submitted as well.

Article 13: An initial public offer (IPO) of stocks of a company shall satisfy the following requirements:

(1) Having a complete and well-operated organization
(2) Having the capability of making profits successively and a sound financial status
(3) Having no false record in its financial statements over the latest 3 years and having no other major irregularity; and
(4) Meeting any other requirements as prescribed by the securities regulatory authority under the State Council, which has been approved by the State Council. A listed company that makes any initial non-public offer of stocks shall satisfy the requirements as prescribed by the securities regulatory authority under the State Council, which have been approved by the State Council and shall be reported to the securities regulatory authority under the State Council for examination and approval.

Article 14: A company that makes an IPO of stocks shall apply for public offer of stocks as well as the following documents to the securities regulatory authority under the State Council:

(1) The business license of the company
(2) The constitution of the company
(3) The resolution of the general assemble of shareholders
(4) The prospectus
(5) The financial statements
(6) The name and address of the bank that receives the funds as generated from the public offer of stocks on the behalf of the company; and
(7) The name of the underwriting institution as well as the relevant agreements. In case a recommendation party shall be employed, as prescribed by the pres-

ent Law, the Recommendation Letter of Issuance as produced by the recommendation party shall be submitted as well.

Article 15: The funds as raised through public offer of stocks as made by a company shall be used according to the purpose as prescribed in the prospectus. Any alteration of the use of funds as prescribed in the prospectus shall be subject to a resolution of the general assembly of shareholders. In case a company fails to correct any unlawful alteration of its use of funds or where any alteration of its use of funds fails to be adopted by the general assembly of shareholders, the relevant company may not make any IPO of stocks. In the foregoing circumstance, a listed company may not make any non-public offer of stocks.

Article 16: A public issuance of corporate bonds shall satisfy the following requirements:

(1) The net asset of a stock-limited company being no less than RMB 30 million yuan and the net asset of a limited-liability company being no less than RMB 60 million yuan

(2) The accumulated bond balance constituting no more than 40% of the net asset of a company

(3) The average distributable profits over the latest 3 years being sufficient to pay the 1-year interests of corporate bonds

(4) The investment of raised funds complying with the industrial policies of the state

(5) The yield rate of bonds not surpassing the level of interest rate as qualified by the State Council; and

(6) Meeting any other requirements as prescribed by the State Council.

The funds as raised through public issuance of corporate bonds shall be used for the purpose as verified and may not be used for covering any deficit or non-production expenditure. The public issuance of convertible corporate bonds as made by a listed company may not only meet the requirements as provided for in paragraph 1 herein but also meet the requirements of the present Law on public offer of stocks, and shall be reported to the securities regulatory authority under the State Council for examination and approval.

Article 17: With regard to an application for public issuance of corporate bonds, the following documents shall be reported to the department as authorized by the State Council or the securities regulatory authority under the State Council:

(1) The business license of the company

(2) The constitution of the company

(3) The procedures for issuing corporate bonds

(4) An assent appraisal report and an asset verification report; and

(5) Any other document as prescribed by the department as authorized by the State Council or by the securities regulatory authority under the State Council.

In case a recommendation party shall be employed, as prescribed by the present Law, the Recommendation Letter of Issuance as produced by the recommendation party shall be submitted as well.

Article 18: In any of the following circumstances, no more public issuance of corporate bonds may be carried out:

(1) Where the corporate bonds as issued in the previous public issuance have not been fully subscribed
(2) Where a company has any default on corporate bonds as publicly issued or on any other liabilities, or postpones the payment of the relevant principal plus interests, and such situation is still continuing; or
(3) Where a company violates the present Law by altering the use of funds as raised through public issuance of corporate bonds.

Article 19: The formats and reporting ways of application documents as reported by an issuer for examination and approval of securities issuance according to law shall be prescribed by the legally competent organ or department in charge of examination and approval.

Article 20: The application documents for securities issuance as reported by an issuer to the securities regulatory authority under the State Council or the department as authorized by the State Council shall be authentic, accurate and integrate. A securities trading service institution and its staff that produces the relevant documents for securities issuance shall strictly perform its/his statutory duties and functions and guarantee the authenticity, accuracy and integrity of the documents as produced thereby.

Article 21: Where an issuer files an application for an IPO of stocks, it shall, upon submitting the application documents, disclose the relevant application documents in advance according to the provisions of the securities regulatory authority under the State Council.

Article 22: The securities regulatory authority under the State Council shall establish an issuance examination committee, which shall examine the applications for stock issuance according to law. The issuance examination committee shall be composed of the professionals from the securities regulatory authority under the State Council and other relevant experts from outside the said authority, adopt the means of voting for the determination of applications for stock issuance and set forth the opinions on examination. The specific formulation measures, tenure of members as well as work procedures of the issuance examination committee shall be formulated by the securities regulatory authority under the State Council.

Article 23: The securities regulatory authority under the State Council shall take charge of the examination and approval of applications for stock issuance in light of the statutory requirements. The procedures for examination and approval shall be publicized and shall be subject to supervision according to law. The personnel participating in the examination and verification of stock issuance may not have any interest relationship with an issuance applicant, may not directly or indirectly accept any present of the issuance applicant, may not hold any stock as verified for issuance and may not have any private contact with an issuance applicant. The department as authorized by the State Council shall conduct the examination and approval of applications for issuance of corporate bonds by referring to the preceding 2 paragraphs herein.

Article 24: The securities regulatory authority under the State Council or the department as authorized by the State Council shall, within 3 months as of acceptance of an application for securities issuance, make an decision on approval or disapproval according to the statutory requirements and procedures, whereby the time for an issuer to supplement or correct its application documents for issuance according to the relevant requirements may not be calculated within the aforesaid term for examination and approval. In the event of disapproval, an explanation shall be given in writing.

Article 25: Where an application for securities issuance has been approved, the relevant issuer shall, in accordance with the provisions of the relevant laws and administrative regulations, announce the relevant financing documents of public issuance before publicly issuing any securities and shall make the aforesaid documents available for public reference in designated places. Before the information of securities issuance is publicized according to law, no insider may publicize or indulge the relevant information. An issuer may not issue any securities before an announcement of the relevant financial documents of public issuance.

Article 26: The securities regulatory authority under the State council or the department as authorized by the State Council shall, where finding any decision on approving securities issuance fails to comply with the relevant statutory requirements and procedures and if the relevant securities haven't been issued, revoke the decision on approval and terminate the issuance. As to any securities that have been issued but haven't been listed, the relevant decision on approval for issuance shall be revoked. The relevant issuer shall, according to the issuing price plus interests as calculated at the bank deposit rate for the corresponding period of time, return the funds to securities holders. A recommendation party shall bear the joint and several liabilities together with the relevant issuer, except for one who is able to prove his exemption of fault. Where any controlling shareholder or actual controller has any fault, he shall bear the joint and several liabilities together with the relevant issuer.

Article 27: After a legal offer of stocks, an issuer shall be liable for any alteration of its operation or its profits by itself. The investment risk as incurred therefrom shall be borne by investors by themselves.

Article 28: Where an issuer issues any securities to any non-specified object and if the said securities shall be underwritten by a securities company, as is provided for by laws and administrative regulations, the issuer shall conclude an underwriting agreement with a securities company. The forms of "sale by proxy" and "exclusive sale" shall be adopted for the underwriting operation of securities. The term "sale by proxy" refers to an underwriting form, whereby a securities company sells securities as a proxy of the relevant issuer and, upon the conclusion of the underwriting period, returns all the securities unsold to the relevant issuer. The term "exclusive sale" refers to an underwriting form, whereby a securities company purchases all of the securities of an issuer according to the agreement there between or purchases all of the residing unsold securities by itself upon the conclusion of the underwriting period.

Article 29: An issuer that makes public issuance of securities has the right to select a securities company for underwriting according to law at its own will. A securities company may not canvass any securities underwriting business by any unjust competition means.

Article 30: a securities company underwrites any securities, it shall reach an agreement with the relevant issuer on sale by proxy or exclusive sale, which shall indicate the following items:

(1) The name, domicile as well as the name of the legal representative of the parties concerned
(2) The classes, quantity, amount as well as issuing prices of the securities under sale by proxy or exclusive sale
(3) The term of sale by proxy or exclusive sale as well as the start-stop date
(4) The means and date of payment for sale by proxy or exclusive sale
(5) The expenses for and settlement methods of sale by proxy or exclusive sale
(6) The liabilities of breach; and
(7) Any other matter as prescribed by the securities regulatory authority under the State Council.

Article 31: A securities company that is engaged in the underwriting of securities shall carry out verification on the authenticity, accuracy and integrity of the financing documents of public issuance. Where any false record, misleading statement or major omission is found, no sales activity may be carried out. Where any securities have been sold out under the foregoing circumstances, the relevant sales activity shall be immediately terminated and measures for correction shall be taken.

Article 32: Where the total face value of securities as issued to non-specified objects is beyond RMB 50 million yuan, the said securities shall be underwritten by an underwriting syndicate. An underwriting syndicate shall be composed of securities companies acting as principal underwriters and participant underwriters.

Article 33: The term for sale by proxy or exclusive sale may not exceed 90 days at the most. A securities company shall, within the term of sale by proxy or exclusive sale, guarantee the priority of the relevant subscribers in purchasing securities under sale by proxy or exclusive sale. A securities company may not reserve in advance any securities under sale by proxy thereby or purchase in advance and sustain any securities under exclusive sale thereby.

Article 34: Where any stock is issued at a premium, the issuing price thereof shall be agreed on through negotiation of the relevant issuer and the securities company that is engaged in underwriting.

Article 35: As to a public offer of stocks through sale by proxy, when the term of sale by proxy expires and if the quantity of stocks fails to reach 70% of the planned quantity in a public offer, it shall be deemed as a failure. The relevant issuer shall return the issuing price plus interests as calculated at the bank deposit rate for the contemporary period of time to the subscribers of stocks.

Article 36: In a public offer of stocks, when the term for sale by proxy or exclusive sale expires, an issuer shall report the information on stock issuance to the securities regulatory authority under the State Council for archival purpose within the prescribed time.

CHAPTER III: TRANSACTION OF SECURITIES

Article 37: The securities as purchased and sold by any party who is involved in any securities transaction shall be the securities that have been legally issued and delivered. No securities that have been illegally issued may be purchased or sold.

Article 38: All stocks, corporate bonds or any other securities that have been legally issued, where there are any restrictive provisions of laws on the term of transfer thereof, may not be purchased or sold within the restrictive term.

Article 39: All stocks, corporate bonds or any other securities that have been publicly issued according to law shall be listed in a stock exchange as legally established or in any other places for securities transaction as approved by the State Council.

Article 40: The means of public and centralized transaction or any other means as approval by the securities regulatory authority under the State Council shall be adopted for listed trading of securities in stock exchanges.

Article 41: The securities as purchased or sold by the parties involved in securities transaction may be in paper form or in any other form as approved by the securities regulatory authority under the State Council.

Article 42: The securities transaction shall be carried out in the form of spot goods as well as any other form as prescribed by the State Council.

Article 43: The practitioners in stock exchanges, securities companies as well as securities registration and clearing institutions, the functionary of securities regulatory bodies as well as any other personnel who have been prohibited by laws and administrative regulations from engaging in any stock transaction shall, within their tenures or the relevant statutory term, not hold or purchase or sold any stock directly or in any assumed name or in a name of any other person, nor may they accept any stocks from any other person as a present. Anyone, when becoming any person as prescribed in the preceding paragraph herein, shall transfer the stocks he has held according to law.

Article 44: The stock exchanges, securities companies as well as securities registration and clearing institutions shall keep secret for the accounts as opened for their clients according to law.

Article 45: A securities trading service institution and the relevant personnel that produce such documents as auditing reports, asset appraisal reports or legal opinions for stock issuance may not purchase or sell any of the aforesaid stocks within the underwriting term of stocks or within 6 months as of the expiration of the underwriting term of stocks. Except for the provisions as prescribed in the preceding paragraph herein, a securities trading service institutions and the relevant personnel that produce such documents as auditing reports, asset appraisal reports or legal opinions for listed companies may not purchase or sell any of the aforesaid stocks within the period from the day when an entrustment of a listed company is accepted to the day when the aforesaid documents are publicized.

Article 46: The charge for securities transaction shall be reasonable. The charging items, standards as well as methods shall be publicized. The charging items, standards and administrative measures of securities transaction shall be uniformly formulated by the relevant administrative department under the State Council.

Article 47: Where any director, supervisor and senior manager of a listed company or any shareholder who holds more than 5% of the shares of a listed company, sells the stocks of the company as held within 6 months after purchase, or purchases any stock as sold within 6 months thereafter, the proceeds generated therefrom shall be incorporated into the profits of the relevant company. The board of directors of the company shall withdraw the proceeds. However, where a securities company holds more than 5% of the shares of a listed company, which are the residing stocks after sale by proxy as purchased thereby, the sale of the foregoing stocks may not be limited by a term of 6 months. Where the board of directors of a company fails to implement the provisions as prescribed in the preceding paragraph herein, the shareholders concerned have the right to require the board of directors to implement them within 30 days. Where the board of directors of a company fails to implement them within the aforesaid term, the shareholders have the right to directly file a litigation with the people's court in their own names for the interests of the company. Where the board of directors of a company fail to implement the provisions as prescribed in paragraph 1herein, the directors in charge shall bear the joint and several liabilities according to law.

CHAPTER IV: LISTING OF SECURITIES

Article 48: An application for the listing of any securities shall be filed with a stock exchange and shall be subject to the examination and approval of the stock exchange according to law and a listing agreement shall be reached by both parties. The stock exchanges shall, according to the decision of the department as authorized by the State Council, arrange the listing of government bonds.

Article 49: As for an application for the listing of any stocks, convertible corporate bonds or any other securities, to which a recommendation system is applied, as prescribed by laws and administrative regulations, an institution with the qualification of recommendation shall be employed as the recommendation party. The provisions of paragraphs 2 and 3 of Article 11 of the present Law shall be applied to the recommendation party of listing.

Article 50: A stock-limited company that files an application for the listing of its stocks shall satisfy the following requirements:

(1) The stocks shall have been subject to the examination and approval of the securities regulatory authority under the State Council and shall have been publicly issued
(2) The total amount of capital stock shall be no less than RMB 30 million yuan
(3) The shares as publicly issued shall reach more than 25% of the total amount of corporate shares; where the total amount of capital stock of a company exceeds RMB 0.4 billion yuan, the shares as publicly issued shall be no less than 10% thereof; and
(4) The company may not have any major irregularity over the latest years and there is no false record in its financial statements. A stock exchange may prescribe the requirements of listing that are more strict than those as prescribed in the preceding paragraph herein, which shall be reported to the securities regulatory authority under the State Council for approval.

Article 51: The state encourages the listing of corporate stocks that comply with the relevant industrial policies and fulfill the relevant requirements of listing.

Article 52: With regard to an application for the listing of stocks, the following documents shall be reported to a stock exchange:

(1) The listing report
(2) The resolution of the general assembly of shareholders regarding the application for the listing of stocks
(3) The constitution of the company
(4) The business license of the company
(5) The financial statements of the company for the latest years as audited by an accounting firm according to law
(6) The legal opinions as well as the Recommendation Letter of Listing
(7) The latest prospectus; and
(8) Any other document as prescribed by the listing rules of the stock exchange.

Article 53: Where an application for the listing of stocks has been subject to the examination and approval of a stock exchange, the relevant company that has reached a listing agreement thereon shall announce the relevant documents for stock listing within the prescribed period and shall make the said documents available for public reference in designated places.

Article 54: A company that has reached a listing agreement may not only announce the documents as prescribed in the preceding Article herein but also announce the following items:

(1) The date when the stocks have been approved to be listed in a stock exchange
(2) The name list of the top 10 shareholders who hold the largest number of shares in the company as well as the amount of stocks as held thereby
(3) The actual controller of the company; and
(4) The names of the directors, supervisors and senior managers of the company as well as the relevant information on the stocks and bonds of the company as held thereby.

Article 55: Where a listed company is in any of the following circumstances, the stock exchange shall decide to suspend the listing of its stocks:

(1) Where the total amount of capital stock or share distribution of the company changes and thus, fails to meet the requirements of listing
(2) Where the company fails to publicize its financial status according to the relevant provisions or has any false record in its financial statements, which may mislead the investors
(3) Where the company has any major irregularity
(4) Where the company has been operating at a loss for the latest 3 consecutive year; or
(5) Under any other circumstance as prescribed in the listing rules of the stock exchange.

Article 56: Where a listed company is in any of the following circumstances, the stock exchange shall decide to terminate the listing of its stocks:

(1) Where the total amount of capital stock or share distribution of the company changes and thus, fails to meet the requirements of listing, and where the company fails again to meet the requirements of listing within the period as prescribed by the stock exchange
(2) Where the company fails to publicize its financial status according to the relevant provisions or has any false record in its financial statements, and refuses to make any correction
(3) Where the company has been operating at a loss for the latest 3 consecutive years and fails to gain profits in the year thereafter
(4) Where the company is dissolved or is announce bankruptcy; or
(5) Under any other circumstance as prescribed in the listing rules of the stock exchange.

Article 57: A company shall, when applying for the listing of corporate bonds, fulfill the following requirements:

(1) The term of corporate bonds shall be more than 1 year
(2) The amount of corporate bonds to be actually issued shall be no less than RMB 50 million yuan; and
(3) The company shall meet the statutory requirements for the issuance of corporate bonds when applying for the listing of its bonds.

Article 58: A company shall, when filing an application for the listing of its corporate bonds, report the following documents to a stock exchange:

(1) The listing report
(2) The resolution as adopted by the board of directors regarding the application for listing
(3) The constitution of the company
(4) The business license of the company
(5) The measures for financing through the issuance of corporate bonds
(6) The amount of corporate bonds to be actually issued; and
(7) Any other document as prescribed in the listing rules of the stock exchange. With regard to an application for the listing of convertible corporate bonds, the Recommendation Letter of Listing as produced by the relevant recommendation party shall be reported.

Article 59: Where an application for the listing of corporate bonds has been subject to the examination and approval of the stock exchange, the company that has reached a listing agreement thereon shall, within the prescribed period, announce its report on the listing of its corporate bonds as well as the relevant documents and make its application documents available for public reference in designated places.

Article 60: After any corporate bonds are listed, where the relevant company is in any of the following circumstances, the stock exchange may decide to suspend the listing of its corporate bonds:

(1) Where the company has any major irregularity
(2) Where the company has any major change and thus fails to meet the requirements for the listing of corporate bonds
(3) Where the funds as raised through the issuance of corporate bonds fail to be used according to the purpose as verified
(4) Where the company fails to perform its obligations according to the measures for financing through the issuance of corporate bonds; or
(5) Where the company has been operating at a loss for the latest 2 consecutive years.

Article 61: Where a company is in any of the circumstances as described in item (1) or (4) of the preceding Article herein and the consequences as incurred therefrom have been verified to be serious, or where a company is under any of the circumstances as described in any of item (2), (3), or (5) of the preceding Article herein and fails to eliminate the relevant consequence within a specified time limit, the stock exchange shall decide to terminate the listing of corporate bonds of the company. In case a company is dissolved or declared bankrupt, the stock exchange shall terminate the listing of corporate bonds thereof.

Article 62: Any company, which is dissatisfied with a decision of a stock exchange on disapproving, suspending or terminating its listing, may file an application for a review with the review organ established by the stock exchange.

Section I: On-going Information Disclosure

Article 63: The information as disclosed by issuers and listed companies according to law shall be authentic, accurate and integrate and may not have any false record, misleading statement or major omission.

Article 64: As for the stocks that have been publicly issued upon the verification of the securities regulatory authority under the State Council or for the corporate bonds that have been publicly issued upon the verification of the department as authorized by the State Council according to law, the prospectus or the measures for financing through the issuance of corporate bonds shall be announced. In an IPO of stocks or corporate bonds, the relevant financial statements shall be announced as well.

Article 65: A company whose shares or bonds have been listed for trading shall, within two months as of the end of the first half of each accounting year, submit to the securities regulatory authority under the State Council and the stock exchange a midterm report indicating the following contents and announce it:

(1) The financial statements and business situation of the company
(2) The major litigation involving the company
(3) The particulars of any change concerning the shares or corporate bonds thereof as already issued
(4) The important matters as submitted to the general assembly of shareholders for deliberation; and
(5) Any other matter as prescribed by the securities regulatory authority under the State Council.

Article 66: A listed company whose shares or bonds have been listed for trading shall, within four months as of the end of each accounting year, submit to the securities regulatory authority under the State Council and the stock exchange an annual report indicating the following contents, and announce it:

(1) A brief account of the company's general situation
(2) The financial statement and business situation of the company
(3) A brief introduction to the directors, supervisors, and senior managers of the company well as the information regarding their shareholdings
(4) The information on shares and corporate bonds as already issued, including the name list of the top 10 shareholders who hold the largest numbers of shares in the company as well as the amount of shares as held thereby

(5) The actual controller of the company; and

(6) Any other matter as prescribed by the securities regulatory authority under the State Council.

Article 67: In the event of a major event that may considerably affect the trading price of a listed company's shares and that is not yet known to the investors, the listed company shall immediately submit a temporary report regarding the said major event to the securities regulatory authority under the State Council and the stock exchange and make an announcement to the general public as well, in which the cause, present situation and possible legal consequence of the event shall be indicated: The term "major event" as mentioned in the preceding paragraph herein refers to the following circumstances:

(1) A major change in the business guidelines or business scope of the company

(2) A decision of the company on any major investment or major asset purchase

(3) An important contract as concluded by the company, which may have an important effect on the assets, liabilities, rights, interests or business achievements of the company

(4) Any incurrence of a major debt in the company or default on an overdue major debt

(5) Any incurrence of a major deficit or a major loss in the company

(6) A major change in the external conditions for the business operation of the company

(7) A change concerning directors, no less than one-third of supervisors or managers of the company

(8) A considerable change in the holdings of shareholders or actual controllers who each hold or control no less than 5% of the company's shares

(9) A decision of the company on capital decrease, merger, division, dissolution, or application for bankruptcy

(10) Any major litigation involving the company, or where the resolution of the general assembly of shareholders or the board of directors have been cancelled or announced invalid

(11) Where the company is involved in any crime, which has been filed as a case as well as investigated into by the judicial organ or where any director, supervisor or senior manager of the company is subject to compulsory measures as rendered by the judicial organ; or

(12) Any other matter as prescribed by the securities regulatory authority under the State Council.

Article 68: The directors and senor managers of a listed company shall subscribe their opinions for recognition in the periodic report of their company in written form. The board of supervisors of a listed company shall carry out an examination on the periodic report of its company as formulated by the board of directors and produce the relevant examination opinions in writing. The directors, supervisors and senior managers of a listed company shall guarantee the authenticity, accuracy and integrity of the information as disclosed by their listed company.

Article 69: Where the prospectus, measures for financing through issuance of corporate bonds, financial statement, listing report, annual report, midterm report, temporary report or any information as disclosed that has been announced by an issuer or a listed company has any false record, misleading statement or major omission, and thus incurs losses to investors in the process of securities trading, the issuer or the listed company shall be subject to the liabilities of compensation. Any director, supervisor, senior manager, or any other person of the issuer or the listed company directly responsible shall be subject to the joint and several liabilities of compensation, except for anyone who is able to prove his exemption of any fault. Where any shareholder or actual controller of an issuer or a listed company has any fault, he shall be subject to the joint and several liabilities of compensation together with the relevant issuer or listed company.

Article 70: The information as prescribed by law to be disclosed shall be publicized through the media as designated by the securities regulatory authority under the State Council and shall, at the same time, be made available for public reference at the company's domicile and a stock exchange.

Article 71: The securities regulatory authority under the State Council shall carry out supervision over annual reports, midterm reports, temporary reports of listed companies as well as their announcements, over the distribution or rationing of new shares of such listed companies and over the controlling shareholders and any other obligor of information disclosure of listed companies. The securities regulatory body, stock exchange, recommendation party or securities company involving in underwriting as well as the relevant personnel thereof shall, before an announcement is made by a company according to the provisions of the relevant laws and administrative regulations, divulge any content concerned before the announcement.

Article 72: Where a stock exchange decides to suspend or terminate the listing of any securities, it shall announce the decision in a timely manner and report it to the securities regulatory authority under the State Council for archival purpose.

Section II: Prohibited Trading Acts

Article 73: Any insider who has access to any insider information of securities trading or who has unlawfully obtained any insider information is prohibited from taking advantage of the insider information as held thereby to engage in any securities trading.

Article 74: The insiders who have access to insider information of securities trading include:

(1) Directors, supervisors, and senior managers of an issuer
(2) Shareholders who hold no less than 5% of the shares in a company as well as the directors, supervisors, and senior managers thereof, or the actual con-

troller of a company as well as the directors, supervisors, and senior managers thereof

(3) The holding company of an issuer as well as the directors, supervisors, and senior managers thereof

(4) The personnel who may take advantage of their posts in their company to obtain any insider information of the company concerning the issuance and transaction of its securities

(5) The functionary of the securities regulatory body, and other personnel who administer the issuance and transaction of securities pursuant to their statutory functions and duties

(6) The relevant personnel of recommendation institutions, securities companies engaging in underwriting, stock exchanges, securities registration and clearing institutions and securities trading service organizations; and

(7) Any other person as prescribed by the securities regulatory authority under the State Council.

Article 75: For the purpose of the present Law, the term "insider information" refers to the information that concerns the business or finance of a company or may have a major effect on the market price of the securities thereof and that hasn't been publicized in securities trading. The following information all falls into the scope of insider information:

(1) The major events as prescribed in paragraph 2 of Article 62 of the present Law

(2) The plan of a company concerning any distribution of dividends or increase of capital

(3) Any major change in the company's equity structure

(4) Any major change in guaranty of the company's obligation

(5) Where the mortgaged, sold or discarded value of a major asset as involved in the business operation of the company exceeds 30% of the said asset in a one-off manner

(6) Where any act as conducted by any director, supervisor or senior manager of the company may be rendered liabilities of major damage and compensation

(7) The relevant plan of a listed company regarding acquisition; and

(8) Any other important information that has been recognized by the securities regulatory authority under the State Council as having a marked effect on the trading prices of securities.

Article 76: Any insider who has access to insider information or has unlawfully obtained any insider information on securities trading may not purchase or sell the securities of the relevant company, or divulge such information, or advise any other person to purchase or sell such securities. Where there is any other provision of the present Law on governing the purchase of shares of a listed company by a natural person, legal person or any other organization who holds or holds with any other person not less than 5% of the company's shares by means of an agreement or any other arrangement, it shall prevail. Where any insider trading incurs any loss to investors, the actor shall be subject to the liabilities of compensation according to law.

Article 77: Anyone is prohibited from manipulating the securities market by any of the following means:

(1) Whether anyone, independently or in collusion with others, manipulates the trading price of securities or trading quantity of securities by centralizing the advantage in respect of funds, shareholding advantage or utilizing information advantage to trade jointly or continuously

(2) Where anyone collaborates with any other person to trade securities pursuant to the time, price and method as agreed upon in advance, thereby affecting the price or quantity of the securities traded

(3) Where anyone trades securities between the accounts under self-control, thereby affecting the price or quantity of the securities traded; or

(4) Where anyone manipulates the securities market by any other means. Where anyone incurs any loss to investors by manipulating the securities market, the actor shall be subject to the liabilities of compensation according to law.

Article 78: It is prohibited for state functionaries, practitioners of the news media as well as other relevant personnel concerned to fabricate or disseminate any false information, thereby seriously disturbing the securities market. It is prohibited for stock exchanges, securities companies, securities registration and clearing institutions, securities trading service institutions and the practitioners thereof, as well as the securities industry association, the securities regulatory body and their functionaries to make any false statement or give any misleading information in the activities of securities trading. The securities market information as disseminated by any media shall be authentic and objective. Any dissemination of misleading information is prohibited.

Article 79: It is prohibited for securities companies as well as their practitioners to commit any of the following fraudulent acts in the process of securities trading, which may injure the interests of their clients:

(1) Violating the entrustment of its client by purchasing or selling any securities on the behalf

(2) Failing to provide a client with written confirmation of a transaction within the prescribed period of time

(3) Misappropriating the securities as entrusted by a client for purchase or sale, or the funds in a client's account

(4) Unlawfully purchasing or selling securities for its client without any authorization, or unlawfully purchasing or selling any securities in the name of a client

(5) Inveigling a client into making any unnecessary purchase or sale of securities in order to obtain commissions

(6) Making use of mass media or by any other means to provide or disseminate any false or misleading information to investors; or

(7) Having any other act that goes against the true intention as expressed by a client and damages the interests thereof. Where anyone practices any trickery

and thus incurs any loss to the relevant clients, the actor shall be subject to the liabilities of compensation according to law.

Article 80: It's prohibited for any legal person to unlawfully make use of any other person's account to undertake any securities trading. It's prohibited for any legal person to lend its or any other's securities account.

Article 81: The channel for capital to go into the stock market shall be broadened according to law. It's prohibited for any unqualified capital to go into the stock market.

Article 82: It's prohibited for any person to misappropriate any public fund to trade securities.

Article 83: The state-owned enterprises and state-holding enterprises that engage in any transaction of listed stocks shall observe the relevant provisions of the state.

Article 84: When stock exchanges, securities companies, securities registration and clearing institutions, securities trading service organizations as well as their functionaries discover any prohibited activities in securities trading, they shall report such activities to the securities regulation body in time.

Section III: Acquisition of Listed Companies

Article 85: An investor may purchase a listed company by means of tender offer or agreement as well as by any other legal means.

Article 86: Where an investor, through securities trading at a stock exchange, comes to hold or holds with any other person 5% of the shares as issued by a listed company by means of agreement or any other arrangement, the investor shall, within three days as of the date when such shareholding becomes a fact, submit a written report to the securities regulatory authority under the State Council and the stock exchange, notify the relevant listed company and announce the fact to the general public. Within the aforesaid prescribed period, the investor may not purchase or sell any more shares of the listed company. In case an investor holds or holds with any other person 5% of the shares as issued by a listed company by means of agreement or any other arrangement, he shall, pursuant to the provisions of the preceding paragraph herein, make report and announcement of each 5% increase or decrease in the proportion of the issued shares of the said company he holds through securities trading at a stock exchange. Within the reporting period as well as two days after the relevant report and announcement are made, the investor may not purchase or sell any more shares of the listed company.

Article 87: The written report and announcement as made according to the provisions of the preceding Article herein shall include the following contents: (1) The name and domicile of the shareholder; (2) The description and amount of the shares as held; and (3) The date on which the shareholding or any increase or decrease in the shareholding reaches the statutory percentage.

Article 88: Where an investor holds or holds with any other person 30% of the stocks as issued by a listed company by means of agreement or any other arrangement through securities trading at a stock exchange and if the purchase is continued, he shall issue a tender offer to all the shareholders of the said listed company to purchase all of or part of the shares of the listed company. It shall be stipulated in a tender offer as issued to a listed company that, where the share amount as promised to be sold by the shareholders of the target company exceeds the scheduled amount of stocks for purchase, the purchaser shall carry out the acquisition according to the relevant percentage.

Article 89: Before any tender offer is issued pursuant to the provisions in the preceding Article herein, the relevant purchaser shall submit a report on the acquisition of a listed company to the securities regulatory authority under the State Council beforehand, which shall indicate the following items:

(1) The name and domicile of the purchaser
(2) The decision of the purchaser on acquisition
(3) The name of the target listed company
(4) The purpose of acquisition
(5) The detailed description of the shares to be purchased and the amount of shares to be purchased in schedule
(6) The term and price of the acquisition
(7) The amount and warranty of the funds as required by the acquisition; and
(8) The proportion of the amount of shares of the target company as held by the purchaser in the total amount of shares of the target company as issued, when the report on the acquisition of the listed company is reported. A purchaser shall concurrently submit to the stock exchange a report on the acquisition of the relevant company.

Article 90: A purchaser shall, after 15 days as of the day when the report on the acquisition of a listed company is submitted pursuant to the preceding Article herein, announce its tender offer. Within the aforesaid term, where the securities regulatory authority under the State Council finds that any report in the acquisition of a listed company fails to satisfy the provisions of the relevant laws and administrative regulations, it shall notify the relevant purchaser in a timely manner. The relevant purchaser may not announce its tender offer. The term for acquisition as stipulated in a tender offer shall be not less than 30 days but not more than 60 days.

Article 91: Within the acceptance term as prescribed in a tender offer, no purchaser may revoke its tender offer. Where a purchaser requests for altering its tender offer, it shall submit a report to the securities regulatory authority under the State Council and the stock exchange in advance and announce the alteration upon the approval thereby.

Article 92: All the terms of acquisition as stipulated in a tender offer shall apply to all the shareholders of a target company.

Article 93: In the event of an acquisition by tender offer, a purchaser shall, within the term for acquisition, not sell any share of the target company, nor shall it buy any share of the target company by any other means that hasn't been stipulated by provisions of its tender offer or that oversteps the terms as stipulated in its tender offer.

Article 94: In the event of an acquisition by agreement, a purchaser may carry out share transfer with the shareholders of the target company by means of agreement according to the provisions of the relevant laws and administrative regulations. In the case of an acquisition of a listed company by agreement, a purchaser shall, within three days after the acquisition agreement is reached, submit a written report on the acquisition agreement to the securities regulatory authority under the State Council and the stock exchange as well as announce it to the general public. No acquisition agreement may be performed before the relevant announcement.

Article 95: In the event of an acquisition by agreement, both parties to the agreement may temporarily entrust a securities registration and clearing institution to keep the stocks as transferred and deposit the relevant funds in a designated bank.

Article 96: In the event of an acquisition by agreement, where a purchaser has purchased, held or held with any other person 30% of the shares as issued by a listed company through agreement or any other arrangement and if the acquisition is continued, the purchaser shall issue an offer to all of the shareholders of the target listed company for purchasing all of or part of the company's shares, unless a tender offer is been exempted from being issued by the securities regulatory authority under the State Council. A purchaser that purchases the shares of a listed company by means of tender offer according to the provisions of the preceding paragraph herein shall abide by the provisions of Articles 89~93 of the present Law.

Article 97: Upon the expiration of a term for acquisition, where the share distribution of an target company fails to fulfill the requirements of listing, the listing of stocks of the said listed company shall be terminated by the stock exchange according to law. The shareholders that still hold the shares of the target company have the right to sell their shares pursuant to the equal terms as stipulated in the relevant tender offer. The purchaser shall make the purchase. When an acquisition is concluded, if a target company fails to meet the requirements of being a stock-limited company any more, its form of enterprise shall be altered according to law.

Article 98: In an acquisition of a listed company, the stocks of the target company as held by a purchaser may not be transferred within 12 months after the acquisition is concluded.

Article 99: When an acquisition is concluded, if the purchaser merges with the target company by dissolving the target company, the original shares of the company as dissolved shall be changed by the purchaser according to law.

Article 100: Where an acquisition is concluded, a purchaser shall, within 15 days, report the acquisition to the securities regulatory authority under the State Council and the stock exchange as well as announce it.

Article 101: The purchase of the shares of a listed company as held by an organization that has been authorized by the state for investment shall be subject to the approval of the relevant administrative departments according to the provisions of the State Council. The securities regulatory authority under the State Council shall formulate the specific measures for acquisition of listed companies in light of the principles of the present Law.

CHAPTER V: STOCK EXCHANGES

Article 102: For the purpose of the present Law, the term "stock exchange" refers to a legal person that provides the relevant place and facilities for concentrated securities trading, organizes and supervises the securities trading and applies a self-regulating administration. The establishment and dissolution of a stock exchange shall be subject to the decision of the State Council.

Article 103: A constitution shall be formulated for the establishment of a stock exchange. The formulation and revision of the constitution of a stock exchange shall be subject to the approval of the securities regulatory authority under the State Council.

Article 104: The words "stock exchange" shall be indicated in the name of a stock exchange. No other entity or individual may use the name of "stock exchange" or an identical name.

Article 105: The income that is at the discretion of a stock exchange, as generated from various commissions, shall first be used to guarantee the normal operation of the place and facilities of the stock exchange as well as the gradual improvement thereof. The gains as accumulated by a stock exchange that adopts a membership system shall belong to its members. The rights and interests of a stock exchange shall be jointly shared by its members. No accumulated gains of a stock exchange may be distributed to any member within the holding term.

Article 106: A stock exchange shall have a council.

Article 107: There shall be a general manager in a stock exchange, who shall be subject to the appointment and dismissal of the securities regulatory authority under the State Council.

Article 108: Anyone, under the circumstance as prescribed in Article 147 of the Corporation Law of the People's Republic of China or under any of the following circumstances, may not assume the post of person-in-charge of a stock exchange:

(1) Where a person-in-charge of a stock exchange or securities registration and clearing institution or any director, supervisor or senior manager of a securities company who has been removed from his post for his irregularity or disciplinary breach and if it has been within 5 years as of the day when he is removed from his post; or

(2) Where a professional of a law firm, accounting firm or investment consulting organization, financial advising organization, credit rating institution, asset

appraisal institution or asset verification institution who has been disqualified for his irregularity or disciplinary breach and if it' has been within 5 years as of the day when he is removed from his post.

Article 109: A practitioner of a stock exchange, securities registration and clearing institution, securities trading service organization or securities company or any functionary of the state organ, who has been dismissed for his irregularity or disciplinary breach, may not be employed as a practitioner of a stock exchange.

Article 110: Only a member of a stock exchange may enter into a stock exchange to engage in the centralized trading of securities.

Article 111: An investor shall conclude an entrustment agreement with a securities company on securities trading, open an account of securities trading in a securities company and entrust the securities company to purchase or sell securities on the behalf in writing, by telephone or any other means.

Article 112: A securities company shall, based on the entrustment of its investors, declare orders and engage in the centralized trading at a stock exchange according to the rules of securities trading and shall, based on trading results, bear the relevant liabilities of settlement and delivery. A securities registration and clearing institution shall, on the basis of trading results and according to the rules of settlement and delivery, conduct settlement and delivery of securities and capital with the relevant securities company and handle the formalities of transfer registration of securities for clients of the relevant securities company.

Article 113: A stock exchange shall guarantee a fair centralized trading, announce up-to-the-minute quotations of securities trading, formulate the quotation tables of the securities market on the basis of trading days as well as announce it. Without permission of a stock exchange, no entity or individual may announce any up-to-the-minute quotations of securities trading.

Article 114: Where any normal trading of securities is disturbed by an emergency, a stock exchange may take the measures of a technical suspension of trading. In the event of an emergency of force majeure or with a view to preserving the normal order of securities trading, a stock exchange may decide a temporary speed bump. Where a stock exchange adopts the measure of a technical suspension of trading or decides a temporary speed bump, it shall report it to the securities regulatory authority under the State Council in a timely manner.

Article 115: A stock exchange shall exercise a real-time monitoring of securities trading and shall, according to the requirements of the securities regulatory authority under the State Council, report any abnormal trading thereto. A stock exchange shall carry out supervision over the information as disclosed by a listed company or the relevant obligor of information disclosure, supervise and urge it/him to disclose information in a timely and accurate manner according to law. A stock exchange may, when it requires so, restrict the trading through a securities account where there is any major abnormal trading and shall report it to the securities regulatory authority under the State Council for archival filing.

Article 116: A stock exchange shall withdraw a certain proportion of funds from the transaction fees, membership fees and seat fees as charged thereby to establish a risk fund. The risk fund shall be subject to the administration of the council of the stock exchange. The specific withdrawal proportion and use of risk fund shall be provided for by the securities regulatory authority under the State Council in collaboration with the fiscal department of the State Council.

Article 117: A stock exchange shall deposit its risk fund into a special account of its opening bank and may not unlawfully misuse it.

Article 118: A stock exchange shall, pursuant to laws and administrative regulations of securities, formulate the rules on listing, trading and membership administration as well as any other relevant rules, and shall report them to the securities regulatory authority under the State Council for approval.

Article 119: Any person-in-charge and any other practitioner of a stock exchange that has any interest relationship or any of his relatives has any interest relationship with the performance of his duties relating to securities trading shall withdraw.

Article 120: Any trading result of a transaction, which has been conducted in accordance with the trading rules as formulated according to law, may not be altered. A trader who has conducted any rule-breaking trading may not be exempted from civil liabilities. The proceeds as generated from any rule-breaking trading shall be dealt with pursuant to the relevant regulations.

Article 121: Where any staff of a stock exchange who is engaged in securities trading violates any trading rule of the stock exchange, the stock exchange shall impose him disciplinary sanctions. Under any serious circumstances, the qualification thereof shall be revoked and the violator shall be prohibited from entering into the stock exchange to engage in any securities trading.

CHAPTER VI: SECURITIES COMPANIES

Article 122: The establishment of a securities company shall be subject to the examination and approval of the securities regulatory under the State Council. No entity or individual may engage in any securities business without the approval of the securities regulatory under the State Council.

Article 123: For the purpose of the present Law, the term "securities company" as mentioned in the present Law refers to a limited-liability company or stock-limited company that has been established and engages in business operation of securities according to the Corporation Law of the People's Republic of China as well as the provisions of the present Law.

Article 124: The establishment of a securities company shall fulfill the following requirements:

(1) Having a corporation constitution that meets the relevant laws and administrative regulations

(2) The major shareholders having the ability to make profits successively, enjoying good credit standing and having no irregular or rule-breaking record over the latest 3 years, and its net asset being no less than 0.2 billion yuan.

(3) Having a registered capital that meets the provisions of the present Law

(4) The directors, supervisors and senior managers thereof having the post-holding qualification and its practitioners having the qualification to engage in securities business

(5) Having a complete risk management system as well as an internal control system

(6) Having a qualified business place and facilities for operation; and

(7) Meeting any other requirement as prescribed by laws and administrative regulations as well as the provisions of the securities regulatory authority under the State Council, which have been approved by the State Council.

Article 125: A securities company may undertake some of or all the following business operations upon the approval of the securities regulatory authority under the State Council:

(1) Securities brokerage

(2) Securities Investment consulting

(3) Financial advising relating to activities of securities trading or securities investment

(4) Underwriting and recommendation of securities

(5) Self-operation of securities

(6) Securities asset management; and

(7) Any other business operation concerning securities.

Article 126: A securities company shall indicate the words "limited-liability securities company" or "stock-limited securities company" in its name.

Article 127: Where a securities company engages in the business operation as prescribed in item (1), (2) or (3) of Article 125 of the present Law, its registered capital shall be RMB 50 million yuan at the least. Where a securities company engages in any of the business operations as prescribed in item (4), (5), (6) or (7), its registered capital shall be RMB 100 million yuan at the least; Where a securities company engages in two or more business operations as prescribed in item (4), (5), (6) or (7), its registered capital shall be 500 million yuan at the least. The registered capital of a securities company shall be the paid-in capital. The securities regulatory authority under the State Council may, according to the principals of prudent supervision and in light of the risk rating of all business operations, adjust the requirement of minimum amount of registered capital, which shall be no less than the minimum amount as prescribed in the preceding paragraph herein.

Article 128: The securities regulatory authority under the State Council shall, within 6 months as of accepting an application for establishing a securities company, carry out an examination according to the statutory requirements and procedures and on the basis of the principle of prudent supervision, make a decision on approval or disapproval and thereafter, notify the relevant applicant. In the case of disapproval, an explanation shall be given. Where an application for establishing a securities company has been approved, an applicant shall, within the prescribed period, apply for registration of establishment with the organ in charge of corporation registration and collect its business license therefrom. A securities company shall, within 15 days as of collecting its business license, file an application for the Securities Business Permit with the securities regulatory authority under the State Council. Without a Securities Business Permit, a securities company may not engage in any business operation of securities.

Article 129: Where a securities company establishes, purchases or cancels a branch, alters its business scope or registered capital, alters its shareholders or actual controllers who hold more than 5% of its stock rights, alters any important article of its constitution, has any merger or spilt-up, alters its form of corporation, suspends its business, goes through dissolution or bankruptcy, it shall be subject to the approval of the securities regulatory authority under the State Council. Where a securities company establishes, purchases a securities operation institution abroad or purchases the shares of any securities operational institution abroad, it shall be subject to the approval of the securities regulatory authority under the State Council.

Article 130: The securities regulatory authority under the State Council shall formulate provisions on the risk control indicators of a securities company such as net capital, the ratio between net capital and liabilities, the ratio between net capital and net assets, the ratio between net capital and operational scale of self-operation, underwriting and asset management, the ratio between liabilities and net asset as well as the ratio between current assets and current liabilities. A securities company may not provide any financing or guaranty for its shareholders or any related person thereof.

Article 131: The directors, supervisors and senior managers of a securities company shall be honest and integrate, have good moral grade, be familiar with the laws and administrative regulations on securities and have the ability of operation and management as required by the performance of their functions and duties, and shall have obtained the post-holding qualification as verified by the securities regulatory authority under the State Council before assuming his post. Anyone who is under any circumstance as prescribed in Article 147 of the Corporation Law of the People's Republic of China or is under any of the following circumstances may not hold the post of director, supervisor or senior manager of a securities company:

(1) Where a person-in-charge of a stock exchange or securities registration and clearing institution or a director, supervisor or senior manager of a securities company has been removed from his post for his irregularity or disciplinary

breach and if it has been within 5 years as of the day when he is removed from his post; and

(2) Where a professional of a law firm, accounting firm or investment consulting organization, financial advising organization, credit rating institution, asset appraisal institution or asset verification institution has been disqualified for his irregularity or disciplinary breach and if it has been within 5 years as of the day when he is removed from his post.

Article 132: A practitioner of a stock exchange, securities registration and clearing institution, securities trading service institution or securities company or any functionary of the state organ, who has been dismissed for his irregularity or disciplinary breach, may not be employed as a practitioner of a stock exchange.

Article 133: A functionary of the state organ and any other personnel as prohibited by laws and administrative regulations from taking any job in a company on a part-time basis may not take any job in a securities company on a part-time basis.

Article 134: The state shall establish the securities investor protection fund. The securities investor protection fund shall be composed of the capital as paid by securities companies and any other capital as lawfully raised. The specific measures for financing, administration and use of the foregoing fund shall be formulated by the State Council.

Article 135: A securities company shall withdraw a trading risk reserve from its annual after-tax profits to cover any loss from securities transaction. The specific proportion for withdrawal shall be prescribed by the securities regulatory authority under the State Council.

Article 136: A securities company shall establish and improve an internal control system, adopt an effective measure of separation so as to prevent any interest conflict between the company and its clients or between different clients thereof. A securities company shall undertake its operations of securities brokerage, underwriting, self-operation and asset management in a separate manner but not in a mixed manner.

Article 137: A securities company shall undertake its self-operation in its own name and may not make use of any other person's name or in an individual's name. A securities company shall undertake its self-operation by using its own capital and funds as lawfully raised. A securities company may not lend its self-operation account to any other person.

Article 138: A securities company may enjoy its right of independent management according to law and its legal operation may not be interfered.

Article 139: The trading settlement funds of the clients of a securities company shall be deposited in a commercial bank and be managed through accounts as separately opened in the name of each client. The specific measures and implementation procedures shall be formulated by the State Council. A securities company may not incorporate any trading settlement funds or securities of its clients into its own assets. Any entity or individual is prohibited from misusing any trading settlement funds or securities of its/his clients in any form. Where a securities company goes bankruptcy or goes through liquidation. The trading settlement funds or securities of its client may not be defined as its insolvent assets or liquidation assets. Under any other circumstance as irrelevant to the liabilities of its clients or under any other circumstance as prescribed by law, the trading settlement funds or securities of its clients may not be sealed-up, frozen, deducted or enforced compulsorily.

Article 140: Where a securities company engages in any brokerage business, it shall arrange a uniformly formulated the power of attorney of securities transactions for the entrusting party. Where any other means of entrustment is adopted, the relevant entrustment records shall be made. For an entrustment of securities transaction as made by a client, whether the transaction is concluded or not, the entrustment records shall be kept in the relevant securities company within the prescribed period.

Article 141: Upon accepting an entrustment of securities transaction, a securities company shall, on the basis of the description of the securities, trading volume, method of bidding, price band, etc. as indicated in the power of attorney, undertake securities trading as an agent according to the trading rules and make trading records in a faithful manner. After a transaction is concluded, a securities company shall, according to the relevant regulations, formulate a transaction report and deliver it to the relevant clients. The statements in a check sheet that confirms trading acts and results in securities trading shall be authentic. Such statements shall be subject to the examination of an examiner, other than the relevant transaction handler, on a transaction-by-transaction basis, so as to guarantee the consistency between the balance of securities in book account and the securities as actually held.

Article 142: Where a securities company provides any service of securities financing through securities transactions for its client, it shall meet the provisions of the State Council and shall be subject to the approval of the securities regulatory authority under the State Council.

Article 143: A securities company that engages in brokerage operation may not decide any purchase or sale of securities, class selection of securities, trading volume or trading price on the basis of full entrustment of its client.

Article 144: A securities company may not make a promise to its clients on the proceeds as generated from securities transactions or on compensating the loss as incurred from securities transactions by any means.

Article 145: A securities company and the practitioners thereof may not privately accept any entrustment of its client for securities transaction beyond its business place as established according to law.

Article 146: Where any practitioner of a securities company violates the trading rules by implementing the instructions of his securities company or taking advantage of his post in any securities trading, the relevant securities company shall bear all the liabilities as incurred therefrom.

Article 147 A securities company shall keep the materials of its clients regarding account opening, entrustment records, trading records and internal management as well as business operation in a proper manner. No one may conceal, forge, alter or damage the aforesaid materials. The term for keeping the aforesaid materials shall be no less than 20 years.

Article 148: A securities company shall, according to the relevant provisions, report the information and materials regarding operation and management such as its business operation and financial status to the securities regulatory authority under the State Council. The securities regulatory authority under the State Council has the right to require a securities company as well as the shareholders and actual controllers thereof to provide the relevant information and materials within a prescribed period. The information and materials as reported or provided by a securities company and the shareholders and actual controllers thereof to the securities regulatory authority under the State Council shall be authentic, accurate and complete.

Article 149: The securities regulatory authority under the State Council may, when believing it requires so, entrust an accounting firm or an asset appraisal institution to carry out an auditing or appraisal on the financial status, internal control as well as asset value of a securities company. The specific measures thereof shall be formulated by the securities regulatory authority under the State Council in collaboration with the relevant administrative departments.

Article 150: Where the net capital or any other indicator of risk control of a securities company fails to satisfy the relevant provisions, the securities regulatory authority under the State Council shall order it to correct in a prescribed period. Where a securities company fails to correct within the prescribed period or any act thereof has injured the sound operation of the securities company or has damaged the legitimate rights and interests of its clients, the securities regulatory authority under the State Council may take the following measures in light of different circumstances:

(1) Restricting its business operation, ordering it to suspend some business operations and stopping the approval of any new operation thereof
(2) Stopping the approval for establishing or taking over any business branch
(3) Restricting its distribution of dividends, restricting the payment of remunerations to or provision of welfare for its directors, supervisors or senior managers
(4) Restricting any transfer of property or the setting of any other right to its property
(5) Ordering it to alter its directors, supervisors and senior managers or restricting the right thereof

(6) Ordering the controlling shareholders to transfer their stock right or restricting its shareholders from exercising the shareholders' rights; and

(7) Revoking the relevant business license. A securities company shall, upon rectification, submit a report to the securities regulatory authority under the State Council. The securities regulatory authority under the State Council shall lift the relevant measures as prescribed in the preceding paragraph herein within 3 days as of concluding the relevant examination and acceptance of a securities company that has met the requirements of risk control indicators upon examination and acceptance.

Article 151: Where a shareholder of a securities company makes any fake capital contribution or spirits away registered capital, the securities regulatory authority under the State Council shall order him to correct within the prescribed period and may order him to transfer the stock rights of the securities company as held thereby. Before a shareholder as prescribed in the preceding paragraph herein corrects his irregularity and transfers the stock right of the securities company as held thereby according to the relevant requirements, the securities regulatory authority under the State Council may restrict the shareholders' rights thereof.

Article 152: Where any director, supervisor or senior manager of a securities company fails to fulfill his accountability in a diligent manner and thus incurs any major irregularity or rule-breaking act or major risk to his securities company, the securities regulatory authority under the State Council may revoke the post-holding qualification thereof and order his company to remove him from his post for alteration.

Article 153: Where any illegal operation of a securities company or any major risk thereof seriously disturbs the order of the securities market or injures the interests of the relevant investors, the securities regulatory authority under the State Council may take such supervisory measures as suspending its business for rectification, designating any other institution for trusteeship, take-over or cancellation.

Article 154: During a period when a securities company is ordered to suspend its business for rectification, or is designated for trusteeship, or is being taken over or liquidated, or where any major risk occurs, the following measures may be adopted to any director, supervisor, senior manager or any other person of the securities company directly responsible upon the approval of the securities regulatory authority under the State Council: (1) Notifying the export administrative organ to prevent him from exiting the Chinese territory; and (2) Requesting the judicial organ to prohibit him from moving, transferring his properties or disposing his properties by any other means, or setting any other right to his properties.

CHAPTER VII: SECURITIES REGISTRATION AND CLEARING INSTITUTIONS

Article 155: A securities registration and clearing institution is a non-profit legal person that provides centralized registration, custody and settlement services for securities transactions. The establishment of a securities registration and clearing institution shall be subject to the approval of the securities regulatory authority under the State Council.

Article 156: The establishment of a securities registration and clearing institution shall fulfill the following requirements:

(1) Its self-owned capital shall be no less than 0.2 billion yuan
(2) It shall have a place and facilities as required by the services of securities registration, custody and settlement
(3) Its major managers and practitioners shall have the securities practice qualification; and
(4) It shall meet any other requirement as prescribed by the securities regulatory authority under the State Council. The words "securities registration and clearing" shall be indicated in the name of a securities registration and clearing institution.

Article 157: A securities registration and clearing institution shall perform the following functions:

(1) The establishment of securities accounts and settlement accounts
(2) The custody and transfer of securities
(3) The registration of roster of securities holders
(4) The settlement and delivery for listed securities trading of a stock exchange
(5) The distribution of securities rights and interests on the basis of the entrustment of issuers
(6) The handling of any inquiry relating to the aforesaid business operation; and
(7) Any other business operation as approved by the securities regulatory authority under the State Council.

Article 158: A national centralized and unified operation shall be adopted for the registration and settlement of securities. The constitution and operational rules of a securities registration and clearing institution shall be formulated according to law and shall be subject to the approval of the securities regulatory authority under the State Council.

Article 159: The securities as held by the relevant holders shall be all put under the custody of a securities registration and clearing institution in a listed trading. A securities registration and clearing institution may not misuse any securities of its clients.

Article 160: A securities registration and clearing institution shall provide the roster of securities holders as well as the relevant materials to a securities issuer. A securities registration and clearing institution shall, according to the result of securities registration and settlement, affirm the fact that a securities holder holds the relevant securities and provide the relevant registration materials to a securities holder. A securities registration and clearing institution shall guarantee the authenticity, accuracy and integrity of the roster of securities holders as well as records of transfer registration and may not conceal, forge, alter or damage any of the aforesaid materials.

Article 161: A securities registration and clearing institution shall take the following measures to guarantee a sound operation of its business:

(1) Having the necessary service equipment and complete data protection measures

(2) Having established complete management systems concerning operation, finance and security protection; and

(3) Having established a complete risk management system.

Article 162: A securities registration and clearing institution shall keep the original voucher of registration, custody and settlement as well as the relevant documents and materials in a proper manner. The term for keeping the aforesaid materials shall be no less than 20 years.

Article 163: A securities registration and clearing institution shall establish a clearing risk fund so as to pay in advance or make up any loss of the securities registration and clearing institution as incurred from default delivery, technical malfunction, operational fault or force majeure. The securities clearing risk fund shall be withdrawn from the business incomes and proceeds of a securities registration and clearing institution and may be paid by clearing participants according to a specified percentage of securities trading volume. The measures for raising and managing the securities clearing risk fund shall be formulated by the securities regulatory authority under the State Council in collaboration with the fiscal department of the State Council.

Article 164: The securities clearing risk fund shall be deposited into a special account of a designated bank and shall be subject to special management. Where a securities registration and clearing institution makes any compensation by using the securities clearing risk fund, it may recourse the payment to the relevant person as held responsible.

Article 165: An application for dissolving a securities registration and clearing institution shall be subject to the approval of the securities regulatory authority under the State Council.

Article 166: An investor who entrusts a securities company to undertake any securities trading shall apply for opening a securities account. A securities registration and clearing institution shall, according to the relevant provisions, open a securities account for an investor in his own name. An investor who applies for opening an account shall hold the legitimate certificates certifying his identity of a Chinese citizen or its qualification of a Chinese legal person, unless it is otherwise provided for by the state.

Article 167: A securities registration and clearing institution shall, when providing the netting service for a stock exchange, require the relevant clearing participant to deliver securities and funds in full amount and provide the guaranty of delivery according to the principles of delivery versus payment (DVP). Before a delivery is concluded, nobody may use the securities, funds or collaterals as involved in the delivery. Where a clearing participant fails to perform the duty of delivery according to the schedule, a securities registration and clearing institution has the right to dispose the properties as prescribed in the preceding paragraph herein according to the operational rules.

Article 168: The clearing funds and securities as collected by a securities registration and clearing institution according to the operational rules shall be deposited into a special account for settlement and delivery. The settlement and delivery that can only be applied to the securities trading as concluded according to the operational rules may not be enforced compulsorily.

CHAPTER VIII: SECURITIES TRADING SERVICE INSTITUTIONS

Article 169: Where an investment consulting institution, financial advising institution, credit rating institution, asset appraisal institution or accounting firm engages in any securities trading service, it shall be subject to the approval of the securities regulatory authority under the State Council and the relevant administrative departments. The measures for the administration of examination and approval of the practice of securities trading services, in which an investment consulting institution, financial advising institution, credit rating institution, asset appraisal institution or accounting firm engages, shall be formulated by the securities regulatory authority under the State Council and the relevant administrative departments.

Article 170: The staff of an investment consulting institution, financial advising institution or credit rating institution who engage in securities trading service shall have the special knowledge of securities as well as work experience on securities business or securities trading service for more than 2 years. The standards for recognizing the securities practice qualification and the measures for administration thereof shall be formulated by the securities regulatory authority under the State Council.

Article 171: An investment consulting institution as well as its practitioners that engage in securities trading services may not have any of the following acts:

(1) Engaging in any securities investment as an agent on the behalf of its entrusting party
(2) Concluding any agreement with an entrusting party on sharing the gains of securities investment or bearing the loss of securities investment
(3) Purchasing or selling any stock of a listed company, for which the consulting institution provides services
(4) Providing or disseminating any false or misleading information to investors through media or by any other means; or
(5) Having any other act as prohibited by any law or administrative regulation. Any institution or person that has any of the acts as prescribed in the preceding

paragraph herein and thus incurs any loss to investors shall be subject to the liabilities of compensation.

Article 172: An investment consulting institution or credit rating institution that engages in securities trading services shall, according to the standards of or measures for charging as formulated by the relevant administrative department of the State Council, charge the relevant service commissions.

Article 173: Where a securities trading service institution formulates and generates any auditing report, asset appraisal report, financial advising report, credit rating report or legal opinions for the issuance, listing and trading of securities, it shall be diligent and responsible by carrying out examination and verification for the authenticity, accuracy and integrity of the contents of the documents as formulated and generated. In the case of any false record, misleading statement or major omission in the documents as formulated and generated, which incurs any loss to any other person, the relevant securities trading service institution shall bear the joint and several liabilities together with the relevant issuer and listed company, unless a securities trading service institution has the ability to prove its exemption of fault.

CHAPTER IX: SECURITIES INDUSTRY ASSOCIATION

Article 174: The securities industry association is a self-regulating organization for the securities industry and is a public organization with the status of a legal person. A securities company shall join the securities industrial association. The power organ of the securities industrial association is the general assembly of its members.

Article 175: The constitution of the securities industrial association shall be formulated by the general assembly of its members and shall be report to the securities regulatory authority under the State Council for archival purpose.

Article 176: The securities industrial association shall perform the following functions and duties:

(1) Educating and organizing its members to observe the laws and administrative regulations on securities
(2) Safeguarding the legitimate rights and interests of its members and reporting the suggestions and requirements of its members to the securities regulatory body
(3) Collecting and straightening out the securities information and providing services for its members
(4) Formulating the rules that shall be observed by its members, organizing the vocational training for the practitioners of its member entities and carrying out vocational exchange between its members
(5) Holding mediation over any dispute regarding securities operation between its members or between its members and clients

(6) Organizing its members to make research on the development, operation and the relevant contents of the securities industry

(7) Supervising and examining the acts of its members and, according to the relevant provisions, giving a disciplinary sanction to any member that violates any law or administrative regulation or the constitution of the association; and

(8) Performing any other function and duty as stipulated by the constitution of the industrial association.

Article 177: A council shall be established within the securities industrial association. The members of the council shall be selected through election according to the provisions of the constitution.

CHAPTER X: SECURITIES REGULATORY BODIES

Article 178: The securities regulatory authority under the State Council shall carry out supervision and administration of the securities market according to law so as to preserve the order of the securities market and guarantee the legitimate operation thereof.

Article 179: The securities regulatory authority under the State Council shall perform the following functions and duties regarding the supervision and administration of the securities market:

(1) Formulating the relevant rules and regulations on the supervision and administration of the securities market and exercising the power of examination or verification according to law

(2) Carrying out the supervision and administration of the issuance, listing, trading, registration, custody and settlement of securities according to law

(3) Carrying out the supervision and administration of the securities activities of a securities issuer, listed company, stock exchange, securities company, securities registration and clearing institution, securities investment fund management company or securities trading service institution according to law

(4) Formulating the standards for securities practice qualification and code of conduct and carrying out supervision and implementation according to law;

(5) Carrying out the supervision and examination of information disclosure regarding the issuance, listing and trading of securities

(6) Offering guidance for and carrying out supervision of the activities of the securities industrial association according to law

(7) Investigating into and punishing any violation of any law or administrative regulation on the supervision and administration of the securities market according to law; and

(8) Performing any other functions and duties as prescribed by any law or administrative regulation. The securities regulatory authority under the State council may establish a cooperative mechanism of supervision and administration

in collaboration with the securities regulatory bodies of any other country or region and apply a trans-border supervision and administration.

Article 180: Where the securities regulatory authority under the State Council performs its duties and functions, it has the right to take the following measures:

(1) Carrying an on-the-spot examination of a securities issuer, listing company, securities company, securities investment fund management company, securities trading service company, stock exchange or securities registration and clearing institution

(2) Making investigation and collecting evidence in a place where any suspected irregularity has happened

(3) Consulting the parties concerned or any entity or individual relating to a case under investigation and requiring the relevant entity or person to give explanations on the matters relating to a case under investigation

(4) Referring to and photocopying such materials as the registration of property right and the communication records relating to the case under investigation

(5) Referring to and photocopying the securities trading records, transfer registration records, financial statements as well as any other relevant documents and materials of any entity or individual relating to a case under investigation; sealing up any document or material that may be transferred, concealed or damaged

(6) Consulting the capital account, security account or bank account of any relevant party concerned in or any entity or individual relating to a case under investigation; in the case of any evidence certifying that any property as involved in a case such as illegal proceeds or securities has been or may be transferred or concealed or where any important evidence has been or may be concealed, forged or damaged, freezing or sealing up the foregoing properties or evidence upon the approval of the principal of the securities regulatory authority under the State Council

(7) When investigating into any major securities irregularity such as manipulation of the securities market or insider trading, upon the approval of the principal of the securities regulatory authority under the State Council, restricting the securities transactions of the parties concerned in a case under investigation, whereby the restriction term may not exceed 15 trading days; under any complicated circumstance, the restriction term may be extended for another 15 trading day.

Article 181: Where the securities regulatory authority under the State Council performs its functions and duties of supervision or examination or investigation, the personnel in charge of supervision and examination or investigators shall be no less than 2 and shall show their legitimate certificates and the notice of supervision and examination as well as investigation. Where the personnel in charge of supervision and examination or investigation are less than 2 or fail to show their legitimate certificates and the notice of supervision and examination or investigation, an entity under examination and investigation has the right to refuse.

Article 182: The functionary of the securities regulatory authority under the State Council shall be duteous, impartial and clean, and handle matters according to law, and may not take advantage of his post to seek any unjust interests or divulge any commercial secrete of the relevant entity or individual as accessible in his performance.

Article 183: Where the securities regulatory authority under the State Council performs its functions and duties according to law, the entity or individual under examination and investigation shall coordinate with it, provide the relevant documents and materials in a faithful manner and may not refuse any legitimate requirement, obstruct the performance of duties and functions or conceal any document or material concerned.

Article 184: The regulations, rules as well as the working system of supervision and administration as formulated by the securities regulatory authority under the State Council according to law shall be publicized to the general public. The securities regulatory authority under the State Council shall, according to the results of investigation, decide the punishment on any securities irregularity, which shall be publicized to the general public.

Article 185: The securities regulatory authority under the State Council shall establish an information pooling mechanism of supervision and administration in collaboration with any other financial regulatory authority under the State Council. Where the securities regulatory authority under the State Council performs its functions and duties of supervision and examination or investigation according to law, the relevant departments shall coordinate with it.

Article 186: Where the securities regulatory authority under the State Council founds any securities irregularity as involved in a suspected crime when performing its functions and duties according to law, it shall transfer the case to the judicial organ for handling.

Article 187: The functionary of the securities regulatory authority under the State Council may not hold any post in an organization under its supervision.

CHAPTER XI: LEGAL LIABILITIES

Article 188: Where any company unlawfully makes any public issuance of securities or does so in any disguised form without any examination and approval of the statutory organ, it shall be ordered to cease the issuance, return the funds as raised plus the deposit interests as calculated at the interest rate of the bank at the corresponding period of time and be imposed a fine of 1% up to 5% of the funds as illegally raised. A company that has been established through any unlawful public issuance of securities or through any unlawful public issuance of securities in a disguised form shall be revoked by the organ or department that performs the functions and duties of supervision and administration in collaboration with the local people's government at or above the county level. The person-in-charge or any other person directly responsible shall be given a warning and imposed a fine of 30,000 yuan up to 300,000 yuan.

Article 189: Where an issuer fails to meet the requirements of issuance and cheats for the verification for issuance by any fraudulent means, if the relevant securities haven't been issued, a fine of 300,000 yuan up to 600,000 yuan shall be imposed; if the relevant securities have been issued, a fine of 1% up to 5% of the illegal proceeds as unlawfully raised shall be imposed. The person-in-charge and any other person directly responsible shall be imposed a fine of 30,000 yuan up to 300,000 yuan. Any controlling shareholder or actual controller of an issuer that instigates any irregularity as prescribed in the preceding paragraph herein shall be subject to the punishments as prescribed in the preceding paragraph.

Article 190: Where a securities company underwrites or, as an agent, purchases or sells any securities, which have been unlawfully issued in a public manner without any examination and approval, it shall be ordered to stop its underwriting operation or purchase or sale on an agency basis. The illegal proceeds shall be confiscated and a fine of 1~5 times of its illegal proceeds shall be imposed. Where there is no illegal proceeds or its illegal proceeds is less than 300,000 yuan, a fine of 300,000 yuan up to 60,000 yuan shall be imposed. Where any loss has been incurred to an investor, the securities company shall bear the joint and several liabilities of compensation together with the issuer. The person-in-charge and any other person directly responsible shall be given a warning and imposed a fine of 30,000 yuan up to 300,000 yuan and the post-holding qualification or securities practice qualification thereof shall be revoked.

Article 191: Where a securities company that engages in securities underwriting is under any of the following circumstances, it shall be ordered to correct and given a warning. The illegal proceeds shall be confiscated and a fine of 30,000 yuan up to 600,000 yuan may be imposed concurrently. Under any serious circumstances, the relevant business licenses shall be suspended or revoked. Where any loss has been incurred to any other securities underwriting institution or investor, it shall be subject to the liabilities of compensation according to law. The person-in-charge and any other person directly responsible shall be given a warning and may be concurrently imposed a fine of 30,000 yuan up to 300,000 yuan. Under any serious circumstances, the post-holding qualification or securities practice qualification thereof shall be revoked:

(1) Conducting any advertising or any other publicity for recommendation, which is false or may mislead investors
(2) Canvassing any underwriting business by any means of unjust competition; or
(3) Having any other irregularity in violation of the relevant provisions on securities underwriting.

Article 192: Where a recommendation party produces a recommendation letter with any false record, misleading statement or major omission, or fails to perform any other statutory functions and duties, it shall be ordered to correct and given a warning. Its business income shall be confiscated and a fine of 1~5 times of its business income shall be imposed. Under any serious circumstances, the relevant business license shall be suspended or revoked. The person-in-charge and any other person directly responsible shall be given a warning and imposed a fine of 30,000 yuan up to 300,000 yuan. Under any serious circumstances, the post-holding qualification or securities practice qualification thereof shall be revoked.

Article 193: Where an issuer, a listed company or any other obligor of information disclosure fails to disclose information according to the relevant provisions or where there is any false record, misleading or major omission in the information as disclosed, the securities regulatory body shall order it to correct, give a warning and impose it a fine of 300,000 yuan up to 600,000 yuan. The person-in-charge and any other person directly responsible shall be given a warning and imposed a fine of 30,000 yuan up to 300,000 yuan. Where an issuer, a listed company or any other obligor of information disclosure fails to submit the relevant reports or where there is any false record, misleading or major omission in any report as submitted, the securities regulatory body shall order it to correct, give a warning and impose it a fine of 300,000 yuan up to 600,000 yuan. The person-in-charge and any other person-in-charge directly responsible shall be given a warning and imposed a fine of 30,000 yuan up to 300,000 yuan. Any controlling shareholder or actual controller of an issuer, a listed company or any other obligor of information disclosure insti-gates any irregularity as prescribed in the preceding 2 paragraphs herein shall be subject to the punishments as prescribed in the preceding 2 paragraphs.

Article 194: Where an issuer or a listed company unlawfully alters the use of funds as raised through public issuance of securities, it shall be ordered to correct. The person-in-charge and any other person directly responsible shall be given a warning and imposed a fine of 30,000 yuan up to 300,000 yuan. Any controlling shareholder or actual controller of an issuer or a listed company who instigates any irregularity as prescribed in the preceding paragraph herein shall be given a warning and imposed a fine of 300,000 yuan up to 600,000 yuan. The person-in-charge and any other person directly responsible shall be subject to the punish-ment according to the provisions of the preceding paragraph.

Article 195: Where a director, supervisor, senior manager of a listed company or a shareholder who holds more than 5% of the shares of a listed company violates the provisions of Article 47 of the present Law by buying or purchasing any stock of the listed company, he shall be given a warning and be concurrently imposed a fine of 30,000 yuan up to 100,000 yuan.

Article 196: Any stock exchange as illegally established shall be banned by the people's government above the county level. Its illegal proceeds shall be confis-cated and a fine of 1~5 times of its illegal proceeds shall be imposed. Where there is no illegal proceeds or the illegal proceeds is less than 100,000 yuan, a fine of 100,000 yuan up to 500,000 yuan shall be imposed, The person-in-charge and an other directly responsible shall be given a warning and imposed a fine of 30,000 yuan up to 300,000 yuan.

Article 197: Any securities company that is unlawfully established or that unlawfully undertakes any securities operation without an approval shall be banned by the securities regulatory body, the illegal proceeds shall be confiscated and a fine of 1~5 times of the illegal proceeds shall be imposed. Where there is no illegal proceeds or the illegal proceeds is less than 300,000 yuan, a fine of 300,000 yuan up to 600,000 yuan shall be imposed, The person-in-charge and any other person directly responsible shall be given a warning and imposed a fine of 30,000 yuan up to 300,000 yuan.

Article 198: Where any personnel without a post-holding qualification or securities practice qualification is unlawfully employed in violation of the provisions of the present Law, the securities regulatory body shall order it to correct, give a warning and impose it a fine of 100,000 yuan up to 300,000 yuan. The person-in-charge and any other person directly responsible shall be given a warning and imposed a fine of 30,000 yuan up to 300,000 yuan.

Article 199: Where any person who is prohibited by laws and administrative regulations from engaging in securities trading holds or purchases or sells any stock directly or in an assumed name or in a name of any other person, he shall be ordered to dispose the stocks as unlawfully held thereby according to law. The illegal proceeds shall be confiscated and a fine of no more than the equivalent value of stocks as traded shall be imposed. In the case of any functionary of the state, an administrative sanction shall be given according to law.

Article 200: Where any practitioner of a stock exchange, securities company, securities registration and clearing institution or any functionary of the securities industrial association provides any false material or conceals, forges, alters or damages any trading record for the purpose of inducing investors to purchase or sell securities, the securities practice qualification thereof shall be revoked and a fine of 30,000 yuan up to 100,000 yuan shall be imposed. In the case of any functionary of the state, an administrative sanction shall be given according to law.

Article 201: Where a securities trading service institution and its staffs that produce any auditing report, asset appraisal report or legal opinions for the issuance of stocks violate the provisions of Article 45 of the present Law by purchasing or selling any stock, it shall be ordered to dispose the stocks as illegally held thereby according to law. The illegal proceeds shall be confiscated and a fine of no more than the equivalent value of the stocks as traded shall be imposed.

Article 202: Where an insider who has access to insider information of securities trading or any person who has obtained any insider information purchases or sells the securities, divulges the relevant information or advises any other person to purchase or sell the securities before the information regarding the issuance or trading of securities or any other information that may have any big impact on the price of the securities is publicized, he shall be ordered to dispose the securities as illegally held thereby according to law. The illegal proceeds shall be confiscated and a fine of 1~5 times of the illegal proceeds shall be imposed. Where there is no illegal proceeds or the illegal proceeds is less than 30,000 yuan, a fine of 30,000 yuan up to 600,000 yuan shall be imposed. Where an entity is involved in any insider trading, the person-in-charge and any other person directly responsible shall be given a warning and imposed a fine of 30,000 yuan up to 300,000 yuan. Any functionary of the securities regulatory body that conducts any insider trading shall be given a heavier punishment.

Article 203: Where anyone violates the present Law by manipulating the securities market, he shall be ordered to dispose the securities as illegally held thereby according to law. The illegal proceeds shall be confiscated and a fine of a fine of 1~5 times of the illegal proceeds shall be imposed. Where there is no illegal proceeds or the illegal proceeds is less than 30,000 yuan, a fine of 30,000 yuan up to 300,000 yuan shall be imposed. Where an entity manipulates the securities market, the person-in-charge and any other person directly responsible shall be given a warning and imposed a fine of 100,000 yuan up to 600,000 yuan as well.

Article 204: Where anyone violates the relevant laws by purchasing or selling any securities during a period when any transfer of securities is prohibited, he shall be ordered to correct, given a warning and imposed a fine of no more than the equivalent value of the securities as illegally traded shall be imposed. The person-in-charge and any other person directly responsible shall be given a warning and imposed a fine of 30,000 yuan up to 300,000 yuan.

Article 205: Where a securities company violates the present Law by providing any securities financing, the illegal proceeds shall be confiscated, the relevant business license shall be suspended or revoked, and a fine of no more than the equivalent value of the funds as raised through securities financing shall be imposed. The person-in-charge and any other person directly responsible shall be given a warning and imposed a fine of 30,000 yuan up to 300,000 yuan and the relevant postholding qualification or securities practice qualification shall be revoked.

Article 206: Where anyone violates the provisions of paragraph 1 or 3 of Article 78 of the present Law by disturbing the securities market, the securities regulatory body shall order it to correct. The illegal proceeds shall be revoked and a fine of 1~5 times of the illegal proceeds shall be imposed. Where there is no illegal proceeds or the illegal proceeds is less than 30,000 yuan, a fine of 30,000 yuan up to 200,000 yuan shall be imposed.

Article 207: Where anyone violates the provisions of paragraph 2 of Article 78 by making any false statement or giving any misleading information in the activities of securities trading, the securities regulatory body shall order it to correct and a fine of not less than 30,000 yuan up to 200,000 yuan shall be imposed; in the case of any state functionary, an administrative sanction shall be given according to law.

Article 208: Where any legal person violates the present Law by opening any account in any other person's name or making use of any other person's account to purchase or sell any securities, it shall be ordered to correct and be imposed a fine of 1~5 times of the illegal proceeds. Where there is no illegal proceeds or the illegal proceeds is less than 30,000 yuan, a fine of 30,000 yuan up to 300,000 yuan shall be imposed. The person-in-charge and any other person directly responsible shall be given a warning and imposed a fine of 30,000 yuan up to 100,000 yuan. Where a securities company provides any securities trading account of its own or of any other person for any irregularity as prescribed in the preceding paragraph herein, not only the punishments as prescribed in the preceding paragraph shall be given accordingly, but also the post-holding qualification or securities practice qualification of the person-in-charge or any other person directly responsible shall be revoked.

Article 209: Where a securities company violates the present Law by engaging in the self-operation of securities by making use of any other's name or an individual's name, it shall be ordered to correct. The illegal proceeds shall be confiscated and a fine of 1~5 times of the illegal proceeds shall be imposed. Where there is no illegal proceeds or the illegal proceeds is less than 30,000 yuan, a fine of 30,000 yuan up to 200,000 yuan shall be imposed. Under any serious circumstances, the business license of securities self-operation shall be suspended or revoked. The person-in-charge and any other person directly responsible shall be given a warning and be imposed a fine of 30,000 yuan up to 100,000 yuan and the relevant post-holding qualification or securities practice qualification shall be revoked.

Article 210: Where a securities company purchases or sells any securities or handles any trading matter in violation of the entrustment of its clients or handles any other non-trading matter in violation of the true intension as expressed by its clients, it shall be ordered to correct and imposed a fine of 10,000 yuan up to 100,000 yuan. Where any loss has been incurred to its client, it shall be subject to the liabilities of compensation according to law.

Article 211: Where a securities company or securities registration and clearing institution misuses any fund or securities of its client, or unlawfully purchases or sells any securities for its client without any entrustment thereby, it shall be ordered to correct. The illegal proceeds shall be confiscated and a fine of 1~5 times of the illegal proceeds shall be imposed. Where there is no illegal proceeds or the illegal proceeds is less than 100,000 yuan, a fine of 100,000 yuan up to 300,000 yuan shall be imposed. Under any serious circumstances, it shall be ordered to close or the relevant business license thereof shall be revoked. The person-in-charge and any other person directly responsible shall be given a warning and imposed a fine of 30,000 yuan up to 100,000 yuan and the relevant post-holding qualification or securities practice qualification thereof shall be revoked.

Article 212: Where a securities company undertakes any brokerage business, accepts a full entrustment of its client to purchase or sell any securities or makes any promise on the proceeds as generated from securities trading or on the compensation of any loss as incurred from securities trading, it shall be ordered to correct. The illegal proceeds shall be confiscated and a fine of 50,000 yuan up to 200,000 yuan shall be imposed. The relevant business license may be suspended or revoked. The person-in-charge and any other person directly responsible shall be given a warning and imposed a fine of 30,000 yuan up to 100,000 yuan. The relevant post-holding qualification or securities practice qualification thereof may be revoked.

Article 213: Where a purchaser fails to perform its obligations such as announcing the acquisition of a listed company, issuing a tender offer or reporting the acquisition report of a listed company or unlawfully alters its tender offer according to the present Law, it shall be ordered to correct, given a warning and imposed a fine of 100,000 yuan up to 300,000 yuan. Before any correction, for the stocks that constitute more than 30% of shares of the target company as held thereby or held within any other person through an agreement or any other arrangement, the voting right thereof may not be exercised. The person-in-charge and any other person directly responsible shall be given a warning and imposed a fine of 30,000 yuan up to 300,000 yuan.

Article 214: Where a purchaser or any controlling shareholder of a purchaser takes advantage of the acquisition of a listed company to injure the legitimate rights and interests of the target company as well as the shareholders thereof, it shall be ordered to correct and given a warning. Under any serious circumstances, a fine of 100,000 yuan up to 600,000 yuan shall be imposed. Where any loss is incurred to the target company or the shareholders thereof, it shall be subject to the liabilities of compensation according to law. The person-in-charge and any other person directly responsible shall be given a warning and imposed a fine of 30,000 yuan up to 300,000 yuan.

Article 215: Where a securities company or any of its practitioners violates the present Law by privately accepting any entrustment of purchasing or selling securities from a client, it shall be ordered to correct and given a warning. The illegal proceeds shall be confiscated and a fine of 1~5 times of the illegal proceeds shall be imposed. Where there is no illegal proceeds or the illegal proceeds is less than 100,000 yuan, a fine of 100,000 yuan up to 300,000 yuan shall be imposed.

Article 216: Where a securities company violates the relevant provisions by undertaking any transaction of unlisted securities without an approval, it shall be ordered to correct. The illegal proceeds shall be confiscated and a fine of 1~5 times of the illegal proceeds shall be imposed.

Article 217: Where a securities company fails to start its business within 3 months after establishment without any justifiable reason, or suspends its business for a consecutive 3 months, the organ in charge of corporation registration shall revoke the business license of the company.

Article 218: Where a securities company violates the provisions of Article 129 of the present Law by unlawfully establishing, purchasing or revoking any branch, or unlawfully going through any merge, split-up, business suspension, dissolution or bankruptcy, or establishing, purchasing a securities operation institution abroad or purchasing the shares of a securities operation institution abroad, it shall be ordered to correct. The illegal proceeds shall be confiscated and a fine of 1~5 times of the illegal proceeds shall be imposed. Where there is no illegal proceeds or the illegal proceeds is less than 100,000 yuan, a fine of 100,000 yuan up to 600,000 yuan shall be imposed. The person-in-charge and any other person directly responsible shall be given a warning and imposed a fine of 30,000 yuan up to 100,000 yuan. Where a securities company violates the provisions of Article 129 of the present Law by altering the relevant items, it shall be ordered to correct and imposed a fine of 100,000 yuan up to 300,000 yuan. The person-in-charge and any other person directly responsible shall be given a warning and imposed a fine of no more than 50,000 yuan.

Article 219: Where a securities company violates the present Law by engaging in any securities operation beyond its business scope as permitted, it shall be ordered to correct. The illegal proceeds shall be confiscated and a fine of 1~5 times of the illegal proceeds shall be imposed. Where there is no illegal proceeds or the illegal proceeds is less than 300,000 yuan, a fine of 300,000 yuan up to 600,000 yuan shall be imposed. Under any serious circumstances, it shall be ordered to close down. The person-in-charge and any other person directly responsible shall be given a warning and imposed a fine of 30,000 yuan up to 100,000 yuan and the relevant post-holding qualification or securities practice qualification shall be revoked.

Article 220: Where a securities company fails to carry out its securities operation of brokerage, underwriting, self-operation or asset management in a separate manner according to law but carries out its securities operation in a mixed operation, it shall be ordered to correct. The illegal proceeds shall be confiscated and a fine of 300,000 yuan up to 600,000 yuan shall be imposed. Under any serious circumstances, the relevant business license shall be revoked. The person-in-charge and any other person directly responsible shall be given a warning and imposed a fine of 30,000 yuan up to 100,000 yuan. Under any serious circumstances, the relevant post-holding qualification or securities practice qualification shall be revoked.

Article 221: Where a securities company submits any false document of certification or adopts any other fraudulent means to conceal any major fact so as to cheat for the securities business license or a securities company has any severe irregularity in the securities trading and thus, fails to meet the requirements of business operation any more, the securities regulatory body shall revoke its securities business license.

Article 222: Where a securities company or its shareholder or actual controller violates the relevant provisions by refusing to report or provide information or materials regarding its business and management to the securities regulatory body or in the case of any false record, misleading statement or major omission in the aforesaid information or materials as reported or submitted, it shall be ordered to correct, given a warning and imposed a fine of 30,000 yuan up to 300,000 yuan. The relevant business license of the securities company may be suspended or revoked. The person-in-charge and any other person directly responsible shall be given a warning and imposed a fine of no more than 30,000 yuan and the relevant post-holding qualification or securities practice qualification shall be revoked. Where a securities company provides financing or guaranty for its shareholder or any person related to its shareholder, it shall be ordered to correct, given a warning and imposed a fine of 100,000 yuan up to 300,000. The person-in-charge and any other person directly responsible shall be imposed a fine of 30,000 yuan up to 100,000 yuan. Where a shareholder has any fault, the securities regulatory authority under the State Council may restrict his shareholders' right before he makes correction according to the relevant requirements. Where anyone refuses to correct, he may be ordered to transfer the stock right of the securities company as held thereby.

Article 223: Where a securities trading service institution fails to fulfill its accountability in a diligent manner so that any document as formulated or produced thereby has any false record, misleading statement or major omission, it shall be ordered to correct. The proceeds as generated from its business shall be confiscated. Its securities business license shall be suspended or revoked. A fine of 1~5 times of its business income shall be imposed. The person-in-charge and any other person directly responsible shall be given a warning and imposed a fine of 30,000 yuan up to 100,000 yuan and the relevant post-holding qualification or securities practice qualification shall be revoked.

Article 224: Where anyone violates the present Law by issuing or underwriting any corporate bond, he shall be given a punishment by the department as authorized by the State Council in accordance with the relevant provisions of the present Law.

Article 225: Where a listed company, securities company, stock exchange, securities registration and clearing institution, or securities trading service institution fails to keep the relevant documents and materials according to the relevant provisions, it shall be ordered to correct, given a warning and imposed a fine of 30,000 yuan up to 300,000 yuan. Where any relevant document or material is concealed, forged, altered or damaged, the violator shall be given a warning and imposed a fine of 300,000 yuan up to 600,000 yuan.

Article 226: Where a securities registration and clearing institution is unlawfully established without any approval of the State Council, it shall be cancelled by the securities regulatory body, the illegal proceeds shall be confiscated and a fine of 1~5 times of the illegal proceeds shall be imposed. Where an investment consulting institution, financial advising institution, credit rating institution, asset appraisal institution or accounting firm undertakes any securities trading service without the relevant approval, it shall be ordered to correct. The illegal proceeds shall be confiscated and a fine of 1~5 times of the illegal proceeds shall be imposed. In case a securities registration and clearing institution or a securities service trading institution violates the present Law or any operational rules as formulated according to law, the securities regulatory body shall order it to correct and confiscate the illegal proceeds and impose it a fine of 1~5 times of the illegal proceeds. Where there is no illegal proceeds or the illegal proceeds is less than 100,000 yuan, a fine of 100,000 yuan up to 300,000 yuan shall be imposed. Under any serious circumstances, it shall be ordered to close down or its securities business license shall be revoked.

Article 227: Where the securities regulatory authority under the State Council or the department as authorized by the State Council is in any of the following circumstances, the person-in-charge and any other person directly responsible shall be given an administrative sanction according to law:

(1) Verifying or approving an application for issuing securities or for establishing a securities company, which fails to comply with the present Law
(2) Violating the provisions of Article 180 of the present Law by taking such measures as on-the-spot examination, investigation and evidence collection, consultation, freeze-up or seal-up
(3) Violating the relevant provisions by giving any administrative sanction to the relevant institution or personnel; or
(4) Performing any other functions and duties in an unlawful manner.

Article 228: Where any functionary of the securities regulatory body or any member of the issuance examination committee fails to perform the duties and functions as prescribed in the present Law, misuses his power, neglects his duty, takes advantage of his post to seek any unjust interests or divulges any commercial secrete of the relevant entity or individual as accessible in his performance, he shall be subject to legal liabilities.

Article 229: A stock exchange that grants any approval to an application for securities listing that fail to meet the requirements as prescribed in the present Law shall be given a warning. Its business income shall be confiscated and a fine of 1~5 times of its business income shall be imposed. The person-in-charge and any other person directly responsible shall be imposed a fine of 30,000 yuan up to 300,000 yuan.

Article 230: Anyone that refuses or obstructs the performance of the securities regulatory body as well as its functionary on the functions and duties of supervision, examination and investigation by no means of violence or threat shall be given an administrative sanction of public security according to law.

Article 231: Where anyone violates the present Law and constitutes a crime, he shall be subject to criminal liabilities according to law.

Article 232: Where anyone violates the present Law and shall be subject to civil liabilities of compensation and payment of fines and penalties and if his properties are not sufficient to cover all the payment at the same time, he shall be first subject to civil liabilities.

Article 233: In case anyone violates the relevant laws and administrative regulations or the relevant provisions of the securities regulatory authority under the State Council and is under any serious circumstances, the securities regulatory authority under the State Council may take measures of prohibiting the relevant responsible persons from entering into the securities market. For the purpose of the present Law, the term of "prohibition from entering into the securities market" as mentioned in the preceding paragraph refers to a system, whereby a person may not undertake any securities practice or hold any post of director, supervisor or senior manager of a listed company within a prescribed term or for life.

Article 234: The fines as collected and the illegal proceeds as confiscated shall be all turned over into the State Treasury.

Article 235: Where any party concerned is dissatisfied with a decision of the securities regulatory body or a department as authorized by the State Council on punishment, it may file an application for an administrative review or file an litigation with the people's court.

CHAPTER XII: SUPPLEMENTARY ARTICLES

Article 236: The securities that have been approved for listed trading in a stock exchange according to the relevant administrative regulations before the present Law comes into force may continue to be traded according to law. The securities operation institution that has been approved for establishment in accordance with the relevant administrative regulations and the provisions of the administrative department of finance of the State Council before the present Law comes into force but fails to comply with the provisions of the present Law in a complete manner shall satisfy the requirements as prescribed by the present Law within the prescribed term. The specific measures for implementation shall be separately prescribed by the State Council.

Article 237: Where an issuer applies for verifying the public issuance of any stocks or corporate bonds, it shall pay the expenses for examination according to the relevant provisions.

Article 238: Any domestic enterprise that directly or indirectly issues any securities abroad or lists its securities abroad for trading shall be subject to the approval of the securities regulatory authority under the State Council according to the relevant provisions of the State Council.

Article 239: As for any subscription or trading of stocks of a domestic company in a foreign currency, the specific measures thereof shall be formulated by the State Council separately.

Article 240: The present Law shall be implemented as of January 1, 2006.

Appendix D

Insurance Law of the People's Republic of China

CHAPTER I: GENERAL PROVISIONS

Article 1: This law has been formulated with a view to standardizing the insurance activities, protecting the legitimate rights and interests of parties to insurance activities, strengthening the supervision and administration of the insurance business and promoting its healthy development.

Article 2: Insurance used in this law refers to the act of payment of premiums by the insurants to insurers and the responsibility of the insurers to give indemnity to the insurants in case of losses to property of the insurants caused by a specific contingency or perils of death, injury, sickness of the insured upon the stipulated age according to terms as set in the contracts.

Article 3: All insurance activities within the territory of the People's Republic of China shall be governed by this law.

Article 4: Insurance activities shall be subject to the rule of laws and administrative regulations, be in compliance with the social ethics and the principle of free will.

Article 5: The parties concerned in insurance activities shall abide by the principle of good faith in the exercise of rights and performance of obligations.

Article 6: Insurance companies shall be set up according to this law to engage in commercial insurance business. No other entity or individual is allowed to engage in such business.

Article 7: Legal persons and other organizations which want to be insured within the territory of the People's Republic of China shall enter into insurance policy documents with the insurance companies within the territory of the People's Republic of China.

Source: China Insurance Regulatory Commission.

Article 8: In carrying out business, insurance companies shall follow the principle of fair competition. Illicit competition is not allowed.

Article 9: Insurance supervisory and regulatory body under the State Council shall exercise supervision and administration of the insurance business according to the provisions of this law.

CHAPTER II: INSURANCE CONTRACT

Section 1: General Provisions

Article 10: An insurance contract is an agreement for defining insurance rights and obligations of the insurants and the insurers.

An insurant refers to a person who has signed insurance contract with an insurer and undertakes the obligation of paying insurance premiums according to the amount stipulated in the insurance contract.

An insurer refers to an insurance company which has signed insurance contracts with the insurant and undertakes the responsibility to pay indemnity or insurance money to the latter.

Article 11: In signing an insurance contract, the insurant and the insurer shall observe the principle of fairness, mutual benefit, reaching agreements through consultation and free will without harming the public interest.

Insurance companies or other entities are not allowed to sign insurance contracts with others by coercion except otherwise provided by law or administrative decrees or regulations.

Article 12: An insurant shall own the insurable interest in the objects of insurance.

If an insurant has no insurable interest in the objects of insurance, the insurance contract shall be invalid.

Insurable interest refers to the interest of the insurant in the objects of insurance recognized by law.

Objects of insurance refer to property or related interest insured or life and health of a person insured.

Article 13: An insurance contract shall hold after the insurant applies for insurance and the insurer agrees to underwrite the insurance and the two sides have reached agreement on the clauses of the contract.

The insurer shall issue insurance policies or other insurance certificates to the insurant in a timely manner and specify on the insurance policies or other insurance documents the contents of the contracts agreed by the two sides. The insurant and the insurer, upon agreement, may also conclude insurance contracts in the form of written agreement other than those provided for in the preceding paragraph.

Article 14: After an insurance contract is concluded, the insurant shall pay premium as agreed upon in the contract and the insurer shall start to undertake insurance liabilities at the time agreed upon.

Article 15: The insurant may terminate the insurance contract after the contract is signed except otherwise provided for by this law or by the insurance contract.

Article 16: The insurer is not allowed to terminate the insurance contract after the contract is signed except otherwise provided for by this law or by the insurance contract.

Article 17: In concluding an insurance contract, the insurer should explain the contents of the clauses of the insurance contract and may raise inquiries on matters concerning the objects of insurance or the insurant, and the insurant shall make true representations.

If the insurant conceals facts deliberately and refuses to perform the obligations of making true representations or fails to perform the obligations of making representations due to negligence that would be enough to affect the insurer from making the decision of whether or not to agree to accept the insurance or raise the insurance premium, the insurer has the right to terminate the insurance contract.

If the insurant deliberately refuses to perform the obligations of making true representations, the insurer shall not undertake to pay indemnity or insurance money for insured risks that occur before the contract is terminated and shall not return the insurance premium.

If the insurant fails to perform the obligations of making representations due to negligence, thereby seriously affecting the occurrence of insured risks, the insurer shall not undertake to pay indemnity or insurance money for contingency that occurs before the contract terminates but may return the insurance premium.

Insured risks refer to the contingencies or perils covered by the insurance as agreed upon in the insurance contract.

Article 18: If an insurance contract provides for the exemption of liabilities for the insurer, the insurer shall clearly state in before signing the insurance contract. If no clear statement is made about it, the clause shall not be binding.

Article 19: An insurance contract shall contain the following:

1. Name and domicile of the insurer
2. Names and residences of the insurant and the insured and the name and residence of the beneficiaries of life insurance
3. Objects of insurance
4. Insurance liability and liability exemption
5. Insurance term and the starting time of insurance liabilities
6. Insured value
7. Insured amount
8. Premium and the method of payment
9. The method of payment of insurance indemnity or insurance money
10. Liabilities for breach of contract and the handling of disputes
11. The year, month and date in which the contract is signed.

Article 20: The insurant and the insurer may reach agreement on related matters other than those stated in the preceding paragraph.

Article 21: The insurant and the insurer, after consultation, may alter the contents of the insurance contract within the valid period of the insurance contract.

In altering the contents of an insurance contract, the insurer shall take notes on the original insurance policies or other insurance documents or attach a rider or a written agreement on the alteration signed by the insurant and the insurer.

Article 22: The insurant, the insured or beneficiaries shall notify the insurer of the occurrence of the insured risks in time after they have learned about them.

The insured refers to a person who is protected by the property or life insurance contract and who enjoys the right to insurance claims. An insurant may be an insured.

A beneficiary refers to a person who has been designated by the insured or the insurant to enjoy the right to insurance claims. The insurant or the insured may be the beneficiary.

Article 23: In claiming for indemnity or payment according to an insurance contract after an insured risk occurs, the insurant, the insured or the beneficiaries are obliged to provide evidence or materials to prove the nature and causes of the contingency and losses caused by it.

If the insurer deems the evidence or materials provided incomplete according to the agreement in the insurance contract, the insurer shall notify the insurant, the insured or the beneficiaries and demand for additional evidence or materials.

Article 24: After receiving the claim by the insured or beneficiaries for compensation or payment of insurance money, the insurer shall make a timely verification and notify the insured or beneficiary of the verification results; perform the obligations of compensation or payment within ten days after reaching an agreement on the compensation or payment with the insured or beneficiaries if the case is of insured liability. The insurer shall make compensation or payment according to the insured amount and according to the time limit for compensation or payment as agreed in the insurance contract.

If an insurer has failed to perform the obligations provided for in the preceding paragraph, the insurer shall compensate for the losses arising therefrom in addition to the payment of insurance money.

No entity or individual is allowed to illegally interfere in the performance by the insurer of the liabilities to compensation or payment; nor shall it limit the right of the insured or beneficiaries from obtaining the insurance money.

The insured amount refers to the maximum amount for compensation or insurance money payment to be paid by the insurer.

Article 25: If the insurer does not deem a contingency as insured liability after receiving the claims for compensation or insurance money from the insured or beneficiaries, the insurer shall issue a notice to insured or beneficiaries of the refusal of the claim.

Article 26: The insurer shall pay in advance according to the minimum amount determined by the evidence or materials if the amount for compensation or payment cannot be determined within 60 days starting from the date of receiving the insurance claims and related evidence and materials. The differences shall be made up for after the insurer finally determines the amount of compensation or payment.

Article 27: The right to claims for compensation or insurance payment by the insured or beneficiaries covered by insurance other than life insurance shall cease to exist if it is not exercised within two years starting from the date when the insured risk is known.

The right to claims for compensation or insurance payment by the insured or beneficiaries covered by life insurance shall cease to exist if it is not exercised within five years starting from the date of the occurrence of the insured risks.

Article 28: If the insured or beneficiaries falsify the occurrence of insured risks which have not occurred and claim for compensation or insurance payment, the insurer has the right to terminate the insurance contract, with the insurance premiums not to be returned.

If the insurant, the insured or beneficiaries deliberately fabricate the occurrence of the insured risks, the insurer has the right to terminate the insurance contract and shall refuse to perform the obligations of compensation or insurance payment, except otherwise provided for in the first paragraph of Article 64 of this law, with the insurance premiums not to be returned.

If, after an insured contingency occurs, the insurant, the insured or beneficiaries are found to have forged or fabricated related certificates, materials or other evidence to prove the causes of the insured risks or for exaggerating the losses, the insurer shall not compensate or pay for the part falsified.

If the insurant, the insured or beneficiaries are found to have committed one of the acts listed in the preceding three paragraphs that have caused the insurer to pay the insurance money or other expenses, the payment shall be returned or compensated for.

Article 29: If an insurer transfers part of a liability assumed to another insurer, it is re-insurance.

At the request of the re-insurance underwriter, the re-insurer shall make representations of its own liabilities or the related information of the original insurance to the re-insurance underwriter.

Article 30: The re-insurance underwriter shall not claim for the payment of premium from the insurant of the original insurance contract.

The insured or beneficiaries of the original insurance contract shall not claim for compensation or insurance money from the re-insurance underwriters.

The re-insurer shall not refuse to perform or delay the performance of the originally insured liability on the pretext of non-performance of the re-insurance liability by the re-insurance underwriter.

Article 31: If the clauses of an insurance contract are in dispute among the insurer and the insurant, the insured or beneficiaries, the people's court or arbitration organizations shall make interpretations favorable to the insured and beneficiaries.

Article 32: The insurer or re-insurance underwriter shall be obliged to keep confidential the information about the operations and property as well as the privacy of the insurant, the insured, the beneficiary or the re-insurer it has got to know in handling the insurance business.

Section 2: Property Insurance Contract

Article 33: A property insurance contract is an insurance contract with the property or related interests as the object of insurance.

The property insurance contract that appears in this section is called "contract" for short, except otherwise specified.

Article 34: The insurer shall be notified of the transfer of the objects of insurance and the insurance contract shall be altered with the consent of the insurer to continue to underwrite the policy. But the transport insurance contracts and contracts with otherwise agreements are exceptions.

Article 35: When the insured liability starts for the transport insurance contract and the voyage insurance for means of transport, the parties to the contract may not terminate the contract.

Article 36: The insured shall observe the relevant regulations on fire, safety, production operations and labor protection and protect the objects insured.

According to the contract, the insurer may carry out safety checks of the objects insured and timely put forward written proposals to the insurant or the insured to eliminate unsafe factors or hidden dangers.

If the insurant or the insured has failed to perform its due obligations concerning the safety of the objects insured, the insurer has the right to demand additional insurance premiums or terminate the contract.

The insurer may, with the consent of the insured, adopt precautionary measures in order to safeguard the objects insured.

Article 37: If within the validity period of the contract, the risks of the objects of insurance have increased, the insured shall notify the insurer in good time according to the contract and the insurer has the right to claim for additional insurance premiums or terminate the contract.

If the insured fails to perform the obligation of notifying the insurer of the increased risks, the insurer shall not undertake to compensation for the occurrence of the insured contingencies that occur due to the increase in the risks of the objects insured.

Article 38: The insurer shall reduce insurance premiums and return the corresponding premiums on the daily basis if any of the following cases occurs, except otherwise provided for:

1. The circumstances on which the premium rating is based have changed and the risks concerning the objects insured have markedly been reduced.
2. The insured value of the objects of insurance has markedly been reduced.

Article 39: If, before the insured liability starts, the insurant demands termination of the contract, the insurant shall pay commissions to the insurer and the insurer shall return the premiums paid. If, after the insured liability starts, the insurant demands the termination of the contract, the insurer may collect the insurance premiums due for the period from the date when the insured liability starts to the date of the termination of the contract, with the remaining returned to the insurant.

Article 40: The insured value of the objects insured shall be agreed upon between the insurant and the insurer and specified in the contract or determined according to the actual value of the objects of insurance at the time when the insured risks occur.

The insured amount shall not exceed the insured value. If it exceeds the insured value, the part in excess shall be invalid.

If the insured amount is less than the insured value, except otherwise provided for, the insurer shall undertake to compensation according to the proportion between the insured amount and the insured value.

Article 41: The insurant of double insurance shall notify all the insurers of the double insurance.

If the insured amount of double insurance exceeds the insured value, the total amount of compensation made by all insurers shall not exceed the insured value. Except otherwise provided for in the contract, each insurer shall undertake to compensation according to the proportion of its insured amount in the total insured amount.

Double insurance refers to insurance contracts signed by an insurant with more than two insurers for the same objects of insurance, the same insurable interest and the same insured risks.

Article 42: When an insured risk occurs, the insured shall be obliged to adopt all necessary measures to prevent or mitigate losses.

After an insured risk occurs, all the necessary and reasonable cost paid by the insured to prevent or mitigate the losses of the objects insured shall be covered by the insurer. The amount undertaken by the insurer shall be calculated separately from the compensation for the losses of the objects insured, with the maximum amount not exceeding the insured amount.

Article 43: If part of the objects insured sustains losses, the insurant may terminate the contract within 30 days after the insurer pays the indemnities. Except otherwise provided for, the insurer may also terminate the contract. In the case in which the insurer terminates the contract, the insurer shall notify the insured 15 days in advance and return the premiums on the part not sustaining losses to the insured after deducting the part receivable from the date when the insured liability starts to the date when the contract is terminated.

Article 44: If, after an insured risk occurs, the insurer has paid up all the insured amount and the insured amount is equal to the insured value, all the rights of the objects insured sustaining losses shall be in the possession of the insurer. If the insured amount is less than the insured value, the insurer shall retain part of the rights according to the proportion between the insured amount and the insured value.

Article 45: If an insured risk occurs due to the damage of the objects insured by a third party, the insurer shall, starting from the date of paying the indemnities, subrogate the insured to exercise the right to indemnities from the liable third party.

If, after the insured risk occurs as provided for in the preceding paragraph, the insured has already obtained indemnities from the third party, the insurers may pay the indemnities in the amount after the indemnities paid by the third party to the insured are deducted.

The subrogation of the insurer to exercise the right to claim for indemnities according to the provisions of the first paragraph of this article shall not affect the right of the insured to claim for indemnity from the third party on the part not compensated for.

Article 46: If, after an insured risk occurs, the insured has forfeited the right to claim for indemnities from the third party before the insurer pays the insurance money, the insurer shall not undertake to indemnities.

If, after the insurer has paid indemnities to the insured, the insured forfeits the right to indemnities from the third party, without the insurer's consent, the act is invalid.

If, due to the fault of the insured, the insurer cannot subrogate the insured to exercise the right to claim for indemnities, the insurer shall reduce the payment of insurance money correspondingly.

Article 47: Except the family members or other members of the insured deliberately cause the insured risk to occur as provided for in the first paragraph of Article 44 of this law, the insurer shall not subrogate the family members or other members of the insured to exercise the right to indemnity claims.

Article 48: When the insurer exercises the right of subrogation to indemnity claims, the insured shall provide the insurer with necessary documents and the related information in its knowledge.

Article 49: The necessary and reasonable expenses paid by the insurer and the insured for investigating and establishing the nature and the causes of the insured risks and the losses of the objects of insurance shall be covered by the insurer.

Article 50: The insurer shall, according to the provisions of law or the agreement in the contract, directly pay insurance money to the third party if damages are caused by the insured covered by the liability insurance.

Liability insurance refers to insurance that makes the liability to indemnities of the insured to the third party as the object.

Article 51: If the insured risk that has caused harm to the third party due to the insured is brought for arbitration or before the court, the necessary and reasonable expenses as arbitration fees or the litigation expenses paid by the insured shall be covered by the insurer.

Section 3: Life Insurance Contract

Article 52: A life insurance contract is an insurance contract that takes the life and body of persons as the objects of insurance.

The life insurance contract is called "contract" for short except otherwise specified.

Article 53: An insurant shall have the insurable interest for the following people:

1. The insurant himself
2. Spouse, children and parents
3. Other members of the family or blood relatives other than those specified in the preceding paragraph for whom the insurant has or shares the obligations of support.

Except the provisions of the preceding paragraph, if the insured agrees to let the insurant to sign the contract for him, the case shall be regarded as the insurant having insurable interest in the insured.

Article 54: If the age of the insured stated by the insurant is not true and the true age does not conform to the age limit agreed in the contract, the insurer may void the contract and return the insurance premium after deducting the commissions, except when the time has exceeded two years starting from the date of the conclusion of the contract.

If the insurance premium paid by the insurant is less than what is payable due to the misstatement of age on the part of the insurant, the insurer has the right to correct and demand retroactive payment of premiums from the insured or pay the insurance money according to the proportion of the premiums actually paid and the premiums payable.

If the insurance premium paid by the insurant is more than what is payable due to the misstatement of age on the part of the insurant, the insurer shall return the premiums in excess of the due amount.

Article 55: The insurant is not allowed to take out the whole life policies for people incapable of civil acts; neither shall the insurer underwrite such policies.

But the cases in which parents take out life insurance policies for their children not coming of age are not limited by the preceding provisions. But the lump sum settlement upon the death of the insured shall not exceed the limit set by the insurance supervision and administration department.

Article 56: A contract that makes death as the conditions for payment of proceeds shall be invalid without the written approval of the insured for the contract and the insured amount.

The insurance policies issued according to the contract that makes death as the conditions for payment of proceeds shall not be transferred or used as mortgage without the written approval of the insured.

But the life insurance taken by parents for their children not coming of age is not limited by the provisions in the first paragraph of this article.

Article 57: After a contract comes into effect, the insurant may pay the insurance premium by a lump sum or by installments as agreed upon in the contract.

If a contract provides for the payment of premium in installments, the insurant shall pay the first payment of premiums at the time when the contract is signed and pay the rest according to the time limit set in the contract.

Article 58: After the insurant pays the first payment of premiums according to contract that provides for premium payment in installments, but the insurant fails to pay the premium of the period within 60 days of the prescribed period, the contract shall become void or the insurer shall reduce the insured amount according to the conditions provided for in the contract.

Article 59: In the case of the void of the contract as provided for in the preceding article, the effect of the contract may be restored after the insurer and the insured reach agreement through consultation and the insurant pays the premium retroactively. However, in the case when the two sides fail to reach agreement within two years after the termination of the contract, the insurer has the right to terminate the contract.

If the contract is terminated as provided for in the preceding paragraph, the insurer shall return the cash value of the insurance policies as agreed upon in the contract if the insurant has paid up insurance premium for more than two full years. If the insurant has not paid up the premium for two years, the insurer shall return the premium paid after deducting the commissions.

Article 60: The insurer shall not demand payment of premiums for life insurance by taking legal actions.

Article 61: The beneficiaries of life insurance shall be designated by the insured or the insurant.

In appointing beneficiaries, the insurant shall get the approval of the insured.

If the insured is a person incapable of civil acts or whose capability of civil acts is restricted, the guardian shall appoint the beneficiaries.

Article 62: The insured or the insurant may appoint one or several persons as beneficiaries.

In the case of several beneficiaries, the insured or the insurant may determine the order and shares of the benefit among them. If the share of benefit is not determined, the beneficiaries shall share the benefit equally.

Article 63: The insured or the insurant may change the beneficiaries and notify the insurer in writing.

The insurer shall take notes on the insurance policies after receiving the written notice on the change of the beneficiaries. In changing the beneficiaries, the insurant shall get the consent of the insured.

Article 64: After the death of the insured, the insurance money shall be treated as the legacy of the insured and the insurant shall perform the obligation of paying the insurance money to the inheritors of the insured if any of the following cases occurs:

1. Beneficiaries are not appointed
2. The beneficiaries die before the insured and there are no other appointed beneficiaries
3. The beneficiaries lose the right to the insurance benefit according to law or forfeit the right to benefit and there are no other beneficiaries.

Article 65: If the insurant or the beneficiaries deliberately cause the death, injury or sickness of the insured, the insurer shall not undertake to pay the insurance money.

If the insurant has paid up insurance premiums for more than two full years, the insurer shall, according to the provisions of the contract, return the cash value of the policies to the other beneficiaries enjoying the right to benefit. If a beneficiary deliberately causes the death or injury of the insured or deliberately and unsuccessfully murders the insured, the beneficiary shall lose the right to the benefit.

Article 66: If the insured to the contract that takes the death of the insured as the condition of payment commits suicide, the insurer shall not undertake to pay the insurance, except the cases provided for in the second paragraph of this article, but the insurer shall return the insurance premiums paid by the insurant according to the cash value of the policy.

If the insured commits suicide two years after the contract that takes death as the condition of payment is signed, the insurer shall pay the insurance according to contract.

Article 67: If the insured deliberately commits crimes that lead to its own injury or death, the insurer shall not undertake to insurance payment. If the insurance premium has been paid for more than two full years, the insurer may return the cash value according to the policy.

Article 68: If a person covered by life insurance dies, is injured or sick due to the acts of any third party, the insurer shall not be entitled to recover from the third party after paying insurance to the insured or beneficiaries. But the insured or the beneficiaries shall have the right to claim compensation against the third party.

Article 69: If a contract is terminated by the insurant, who has paid up premiums for more than two full years, the insurer shall return the cash value of the policies within 30 days starting from the date of receiving the notice of contract termination. If the premium has been paid for less than two full years, the insurer shall return the premium after deducting the commissions according to the provisions of the contract.

CHAPTER III: INSURANCE COMPANY

Article 70: Insurance companies shall adopt the following organizational forms:

1. Joint stock company
2. Wholly state-owned company.

Article 71: The opening of an insurance company shall get the approval of the insurance supervision and administration department.

Article 72: The opening of an insurance company shall meet the following requirements:

1. It shall have articles of association as provided for by this law and the company law
2. It shall have the minimum registered capital provided for in this law
3. It shall have senior management staff with professional knowledge and work experience
4. It shall have a sound organizational setup and management system
5. It shall have offices and other related facilities that are up to the requirements.

In examining and approving the applications for setting up insurance companies, the insurance supervision and administration department shall take into consideration the need of the development of the insurance business and fair competition.

Article 73: The minimum amount of registered capital for an insurance company shall be RMB 200 million.

The minimum amount of registered capital shall be the paid in money capital.

Insurance supervision and administration department may adjust the minimum amount of registered capital in the light of the business lines of an insurance company and its operational scale. But the amount shall not be less than the limit set in the first paragraph of this article.

Article 74: In applying for the establishment of an insurance company, the following documents and materials shall be submitted:

1. An application, which should specify the name, registered capital and business line of the insurance company to be set up
2. Feasibility study report
3. Other documents and materials required by the insurance supervision and administration department.

Article 75: An applicant may start preparations for the establishment of the insurance company according to the provisions of this law and the company law after the application passes the preliminary examination. If it has the conditions of establishment as provided for in Article 71 of this law, an official application shall be filed with the insurance supervision and administration department, together with the following documents and materials:

1. Articles of association of the insurance company
2. List of shareholders and their shares or investment contributors and the amount of investment each contributes
3. Certificates of credit rating and related materials for shareholders who hold over 10 percent of the shares of the company

4. Certificate for capital verification produced by the registered capital verification organizations
5. Resumes and qualification certificates of senior management personnel to be appointed
6. Operational principles and plans;
7. Materials about the operational sites and other facilities associated with the business operations; and
8. Other documents and materials as required by the insurance supervision and administration department.

Article 76: Insurance supervision and administration department shall take the decision of approval or disapproval within six months starting from the date of reception of the official applications for establishment of insurance companies.

Article 77: If the establishment of an insurance company is approved, the department of approval shall issue the permit for insurance operation, and the insurance company shall, on the strength of the operational permit, go through the registration procedures with the administrations for industry and commerce and draw the business license.

Article 78: If an insurance company fails to go through the registration procedures without justifiable reasons within six months starting from the date of the acquisition of the insurance operational permit, the permit shall cease to be valid automatically.

Article 79: After the establishment of an insurance company, it shall draw 20 percent of the registered capital as the guaranty funds and deposit them in the banks designated by the insurance supervision and administration department. The deposits shall not be used unless for liquidation purposes.

Article 80: In opening subsidiaries within the territory of the People's Republic of China, an insurance company shall get the approval from the insurance supervision and administration department and obtain insurance business permits for the subsidiaries.

The subsidiaries of an insurance company do not enjoy the status of legal persons, whose civil liabilities shall be borne by the head office.

Article 81: In opening representative offices within the territory of the People's Republic of China, an insurance company shall get the approval from the insurance supervision and administration department.

Article 82: An insurance company shall get the approval of the insurance supervision and administration department in one of the following alterations:

1. Change in name
2. Change in registered capital
3. Changes in the operational sites of the head office or its subsidiaries
4. Changes in the line of business
5. Separation or consolidation of the company

6. Revision of the articles of association
7. Changes in the investment contributors or the shareholders who hold at least 10 percent of the shares of the company; and
8. Other changes as provided for by insurance supervision and administration department.

In replacing board chairman and general manager, an insurance company shall submit it to the insurance supervision and administration department for examining the qualifications.

Article 83: The provisions of the Company Law shall apply with regard to the organizational setup of an insurance company.

Article 84: A wholly state-owned insurance company shall set up a board of supervisors which shall be made up of representatives from the insurance supervision and administration department, related experts and selected staff members of the insurance company. The board shall exercise supervision over the various reserve funds drawn by the company, the minimum ability of payment and the maintenance and increment of the values of state assets and the acts of senior management personnel in observing the laws, administrative degrees or regulations and the acts harmful to the interests of the company.

Article 85: In the cases of separation, consolidation or the occurrence of the causes for dissolution according to the articles of association, an insurance company shall be dissolved with the approval of the insurance supervision and administration department. The company shall set up a liquidation group according to law to conduct liquidation.

Insurance companies operating life insurance businesses are not allowed to be dissolved apart from separation or consolidation.

Article 86: If an insurance company has its insurance operational permit revoked by insurance supervision and administration department due to violations of law or administrative decrees, the insurance company shall be cancelled according to law. The insurance supervision and administration department shall undertake to form a liquidation group to carry out liquidation according to law.

Article 87: If an insurance company becomes insolvent, it shall be declared bankrupt by the People's Courts and with the approval of the insurance supervision and administration department. If an insurance company is declared bankrupt, the liquidation group shall be organized by the people's courts, insurance supervision and administration department and related personnel to carry out liquidation according to law.

Article 88: If an insurance company with life insurance operations is cancelled or declared bankrupt according to law, the life insurance contracts and reserve funds it holds shall be transferred to another insurance company undertaking life insurance. If the company fails to reach transfer agreement with another life insurance company, the insurance supervision and administration department shall designate a life insurance company to accept the business.

There any life insurance contract or reserve fund as provided for in the preceding paragraph is transferred or accepted upon the designation of the insurance supervision and administration department, the legitimate rights and interests of the insured and beneficiaries shall be retained.

Article 89: In the case when an insurance company is declared bankrupt, the property shall be liquidated according to the following order after giving priority to paying for the bankrupt expenses:

1. To pay the wages of the workers and labor insurance expenses
2. To pay indemnities or insurance money
3. To pay taxes in arrears; and
4. To pay debt owed by the company.

If the property is not enough for payment for items in the same order, it shall be paid out proportionately.

Article 90: If an insurance company terminates its business operations according to law, it shall cancel its insurance operational permit.

Article 91: The Company Law and other related laws and administrative decrees and regulations shall apply to items about the establishment, alteration, dissolution and liquidation of an insurance company that have not been provided for in this law.

CHAPTER IV: INSURANCE OPERATIONAL RULES

Article 92: The business scope of an insurance company:

1. Property insurance, including property loss insurance, liability insurance and credit insurance
2. Personal insurance, including life insurance, health insurance and accidental injury insurance.

No insurer is allowed to engage in property insurance and life insurance concurrently; however, an insurance company undertaking property insurance business may undertake short-term health insurance and accidental injury insurance businesses upon verification of the insurance supervision and administration department.

The business scope of an insurance company shall be verified by the insurance supervision and administration department. An insurance company shall operate within the business scope verified.

An insurance company may not concurrently operate any businesses other than those specified in this Law and other laws and administrative regulations.

Article 93: With the approval of the insurance supervision and administration department, an insurance company may undertake the following re-insurance businesses of the insurance operations provided for in the preceding article:

1. Outward re-insurance
2. Inward re-insurance.

Article 94: An insurance company shall draw various kinds of liability reserve funds in accordance with the principles of safeguarding the interests of the insured, and guaranteeing the payment capacity.

The specific measures for drawing and carrying down liability reserve funds by insurance companies shall be formulated by the insurance supervision and administration department.

Article 95: An insurance company shall, according to the insurance indemnities or payment claimed and the insurance indemnities or payment not yet claimed after the insured contingencies occur, draw reserve for outstanding losses.

Article 96: Apart from drawing reserves according to the provisions of the preceding two articles, an insurance company shall draw public accumulation funds according to the provisions of relevant laws, administrative decrees or regulations and the requirements of the state financial and accounting system.

Article 97: In order to protect the interests of the insured and support the steady and safe operations of insurance companies, an insurance company shall draw insurance guaranty fund according to the provisions by the insurance supervision and administration department.

The insurance guaranty fund shall be managed in a concentrated way and be used in a planned way.

The specific measures for management and use of the insurance guaranty fund shall be formulated by the insurance supervision and administration department.

Article 98: An insurance company shall have the minimum payment ability compatible with its size of business operations. The difference of the actual assets subtracting actual liabilities shall not be less than the amount stipulated by the insurance supervision and administration department. If the amount is less than the prescribed amount, capital funds shall be increased to make up for the deficit.

Article 99: The year's premiums retained by an insurance company undertaking property insurance shall not exceed four times that the total of the actual capital fund plus public accumulation fund.

Article 100: The liability undertaken by an insurance company for a risk unit, namely, the maximum loss caused by one insured risk, shall not exceed 10 percent of the total of the actual capital fund plus public accumulation fund. The part in excess of the amount shall be re-insured.

Article 101: The risk unit rating method and plan against huge risks of an insurance company shall be examined and approved by the insurance supervision and administration department.

Article 102: An insurance company shall make re-insurance according to the relevant regulations of the insurance supervision and administration department.

Article 103: An insurance company shall make re-insurance with insurance companies within the territory of the People's Republic of China by priority.

Article 104: Insurance supervision and administration department have the right to restrict or ban insurance companies from re-insuring out to insurance companies outside the territory of the People's Republic of China or accepting inward re-insurance business from outside the territory of the People's Republic of China.

Article 105: The operation of funds of an insurance company shall be steady and safe according to the principle of safety and ensure the property to maintain or increase its value.

The operation of funds of an insurance company is confined to bank deposits, purchasing of government bonds, financial bonds and other way of fund operation provided for by the State Council.

No insurance company may use its funds to set up any security operation organization or enterprise irrelevant to insurance.

The proportion of the fund operated by an insurance company or the funds for specific projects in the total amount of funds shall be provided for by the insurance supervision and administration department.

Article 106: An insurance company and its staff members are not allowed to commit the following acts:

1. To deceive insurants, the insured or beneficiaries
2. To conceal important information associated with insurance contracts
3. To obstruct the insured from performing the obligation of making faithful representations according to the provisions of this law or induce the insured not to perform the obligations of making faithful representations provided for by this law.
4. To promise rebates or other interests other than those provided for in the contracts to the insurant, the insured or beneficiaries.
5. To deliberately fabricate insurance risks that have never occurred to make false indemnities and cheat for insurance money.

CHAPTER V: SUPERVISION AND ADMINISTRATION OF THE INSURANCE BUSINESS

Article 107: The basic insurance clauses and insurance rates for the categories of insurance that concern public interest or the compulsory or newly developed categories of life insurance shall be submitted to insurance supervision and administration department for examination and approval. The insurance supervision and administration department shall abide by the principles of protection of public interest and prevention of unfair competition in the examination and approval. The scope of and specific measures for examination and approval shall be formulated by the insurance supervision and administration department.

The insurance clauses and insurance rates of other categories of insurance shall be submitted to insurance supervision and administration department for record.

Article 108: Insurance supervision and administration departments shall establish and perfect the regulatory index system for payment capacity to monitor the minimum payment capacity of insurance companies.

Article 109: An Insurance supervision and administration department shall have the right to check the operations, financial situation and operation of funds of insurance companies and have the right to demand for the supply of related written reports and materials within the prescribed time limit.

Insurance companies shall be subject to the supervision and check pursuant to law.

An insurance supervision and administration department shall have the right to check the deposits of insurance companies in financial institutions.

Article 110: If an insurance company fails to draw or carry down various reserves or fails to make re-insurance as provided for by this law or seriously violates the provisions of this law about fund operation, insurance supervision and administration department shall order the insurance company to adopt the following measures to correct within a prescribed time limit:

1. To draw or carry down various reserves according to law
2. To handle re-insurance according to law
3. To correct the acts of law-violating fund operation
4. To re-appoint leading members and related managing personnel.

Article 111: If insurance supervision and administration department have taken the decision demanding correction within a prescribed time limit according to the provisions of the preceding article and the insurance company has failed to correct within the prescribed time limit, the insurance supervision and administration department shall decide to send professional personnel or designate related personnel of the insurance company to form an organization to carry out overhaul of the insurance company.

The overhaul decision shall specify the name of the insurance company to be overhauled, causes for overhaul, overhaul organization and time limit for the overhaul and make an announcement.

Article 112: In the course of the overhaul, the overhaul organization has the right to supervise over the routine operations of the insurance company. The responsible members and related managing personnel of the insurance company shall perform their functions under the supervision of the overhaul organization.

Article 113: The original business operations shall continue while the company is being overhauled. But the insurance supervision and administration department have the right to stop it from underwriting new policies or suspend part of its original operations and adjust the operation of funds.

Article 114: If an insurance company subject to overhaul has corrected its law-violating acts and restored its normal operation, the overhaul organization shall file a report to the insurance supervision and administration department for approval before the overhaul is declared ended.

Article 115: If an insurance company has violated the provisions of this law and jeopardized the public interests and will possibly seriously threaten or has already threatened the payment ability of the company, the insurance supervision and administration department may take over the insurance company.

The purpose of the taking over is to adopt necessary measures against the insurance company taken over in order to protect the interests of the insured, restore the normal operation of the insurance company. The debts and liabilities of the company shall not change due to the take-over.

Article 116: The composition of the take-over organization and methods shall be determined by the insurance supervision and administration department, which shall make an announcement.

Article 117: Upon the expiry of the take-over period, the insurance supervision and administration department may decide to extend the period, but the maximum term of the take-over period shall not exceed two years.

Article 118: Upon the expiry of the take-over period, if the insurance company taken over has restored its ability of normal operation, the insurance supervision and administration department may decide to terminate the take-over.

If the take-over organization deems the property of the insurance company taken over not enough to clear all its debts, it may, with the approval of the insurance supervision and administration department, apply with the people's court for declaring the insurance company bankrupt.

Article 119: An insurance company shall, within three months after the end of each accounting year, submit the operations report, financial and accounting report and related statements to the insurance supervision and administration department and make an announcement according to law.

Article 120: An insurance company shall, at the end of each month, submit the operational statistics of the preceding month to the insurance supervision and administration department.

Article 121: The actuaries to be employed by an insurance company shall have been acknowledged by the insurance supervision and administration department and the insurance companies shall establish an actuarial report system.

Article 122: The business reports, accounting reports, actuarial reports and other related statements, documents and materials must faithfully record the insurance operations, and may not contain any false records, misleading statements or major omissions.

Article 123: An insurer or the insured may retain independent appraisal organizations or experts with legal qualifications to carry out appraisal and evaluation of the insured risks.

The appraisal organizations or experts legally retained to make appraisal and evaluation of the insured risks shall do so impartially pursuant to law. Those causing damages to the insurer or insured deliberately or by neglect shall be liable for compensation pursuant to law.

The appraisal organizations or experts legally retained to make appraisal and evaluation of the insured risks shall follow the laws and administrative regulations with respect to taking charges.

Article 124: An insurance company shall keep properly all the books about its business operations, original vouchers and related materials.

The books, original vouchers and related materials provided for in the preceding paragraph shall be kept for at least ten years starting from the date of the termination of insurance contracts.

CHAPTER VI: INSURANCE AGENTS AND INSURANCE BROKERS

Article 125: An insurance agent is an entity or individual who, entrusted by the insurer, collects commissions from the insurer and, on behalf of the insurer, handles insurance business within the scope authorized by the insurer.

Article 126: An insurance broker is an entity which, for the sake of the interests of the insurant, provides intermediary services in signing insurance contracts on behalf of the insurant with the insurer and collect commissions according to law.

Article 127: In entrusting an insurance agent to handle the insurance business, an insurer shall sign an agent agreement with the insurance agent to agree upon the rights and obligations as well as other agent matters pursuant to law.

Article 128: An insurance company shall be responsible for the acts of an insurance agent to handle insurance business as authorized by the insurer.

If an insurance agent conducts any acts beyond the authorized scope in handling insurance business for the insurer, and the insurant is justified to believe that it is authorized and has signed the insurance contract, the insurer shall bear the insurance liabilities; however, the insurer may claim damages against the insurance agent pursuant to law.

Article 129: In the handling of life insurance business, an individual insurance agent is not allowed to accept the trust of more than two insurers at the same time.

Article 130: If losses have been incurred on the insured due to the fault of an insurance broker, the insurance broker shall be liable to compensation.

Article 131: In handling insurance business, insurance agents and insurance brokers are not allowed to conduct any of the following acts:

1. To deceive the insurer, insurant, insured or beneficiary
2. To conceal any important information about the insurance contract
3. To frustrate the insurant from performing the obligation of faithful statement provided for in this Law, or to induce it not to perform such obligation

4. To promise the insurant, insured or beneficiary of any interest other than those stipulated in the insurance contract
5. To use their administrative power, position or the advantage of their profession or any other illicit means to force, induce or restrict the insured to sign insurance contracts.

Article 132: An insurance agent and an insurance broker shall acquire the qualifications provided for by insurance supervision and administration department and obtain the insurance agency business permit of insurance brokerage permit from the insurance supervision and administration department and go through the registration procedures with the administrations for industry and commerce, obtain business licenses and pay the guaranty money or take out professional liability insurance policies.

Article 133: An insurance agent and an insurance broker shall have their own operational sites, special books to record the receipts and expenditures of their agency operations or brokerage operations, and accept the supervision by the insurance supervision and administration department.

Article 134: Insurance agency commissions and broker commissions may only be paid to the insurance agents and insurance brokers with legal qualifications, and may not be paid to others.

Article 135: An insurance company shall set up a record of its own insurance agents.

Article 136: An insurance company shall strengthen the training and management of the insurance agents, enhance the professional ethics and quality of the insurance agents, and may not abet or mislead the insurance agents to do any activities against the obligation of good faith.

Article 137: The provisions of Article 109 and Article 119 of this Law shall apply to insurance agents and insurance brokers.

CHAPTER VII: LEGAL LIABILITY

Article 138: Where any insurant, insured or beneficiary commits any of the following acts for the purpose of deception and if the cases are serious enough to constitute a crime, he shall be subject to criminal liabilities:

1. The insurant deliberately fabricates the objects of insurance to deceive into getting insurance money
2. To defraud the insurer of insurance money by falsifying the occurrence of insured risks that have not actually happened
3. To defraud the insurer of insurance money by deliberately causing the occurrence of insured risks that have caused property losses.

4. To defraud the insurer of insurance money by deliberately causing the death, injury or sickness of the insured and other contingencies.
5. To defraud the insurer of insurance money by forging or altering certificates, materials and other evidence associated with insured contingencies or by instigating, inducing or buying over others to provide false evidence, materials or other evidence, or by fabricating the causes of contingencies or exaggerating losses.

If the case involving one of the acts listed in the preceding paragraph is not serious enough to constitute a crime, administrative punishments shall be meted out according to relevant state regulations.

Article 139: If an insurance company or any of its staff members conceals any important information about the insurance contract to deceive the insured or beneficiaries or refuses to perform the liabilities of indemnity or insurance payment as agreed upon in the contract and if the cases are serious enough to constitute a crime, the offender shall be subject to criminal liabilities. If the cases are not serious enough to constitute a crime, the insurance supervision and administrative departments shall impose a fine of more than RMB 50,000 and less than RMB 300,000 on the insurance company concerned; and impose a fine of more than RMB 20,000 but less than RMB 100,000 on the staff members who have violated the law; if the case is serious, the insurance company's business scope shall be restricted or the insurance company shall be ordered to accept new businesses.

If an insurance company or any of its staff members obstructs the insurant from performing its obligation of making true representations or promises any insurant, insured or beneficiary of illegal insurance premium rebates or other interests, and if the case is serious enough to constitute a crime, the offender shall be subject to criminal liabilities pursuant to law; if the case is not serious enough to constitute a crime, the insurance supervision and administration department shall order them to get right and impose a fine ranging from RMB 50,000 to RMB 300,000 on the insurance company concerned; the staff members who have violated the law shall imposed on a fine ranging from RMB 20,000 to RMB 100,000; if the case is serious, the insurance company's business scope shall be restricted or the insurance company shall be ordered to accept new businesses.

Article 140: If an insurance agent or insurance broker is found to have deceived any insurer, insurant, insured or beneficiaries, and if any crime is constituted, he shall be subject to criminal responsibilities pursuant to law; if the case is not serious enough to constitute a crime, the insurance supervision and administration department shall order the agent or broker to correct, concurrently with a fine ranging from more RMB 50,000 to RMB 300,000; if the case is serious enough, the insurance agency business permit or the insurance brokerage business permit shall be revoked.

Article 141: If any insurance company or its staff members is found to have fabricated the occurrence of insured risks to settle claims so as to gain by fraud any insurance money, and if the case is serious enough to constitute a crime, the offender shall be subject to criminal responsibilities pursuant to law.

Article 142: Those who establish insurance companies or engage in commercial insurance activities without authorization in violation of this Law shall be stopped by the insurance supervision and administration department; if a crime is constituted, the offender shall be subject to criminal liabilities pursuant to law; if the case is not serious to constitute a crime, the insurance supervision and administration department shall confiscate the illegal gains, and impose a fine ranging from 1 time to 5 times of the illegal gains, if there are no illegal gains or the illegal gains are less than RMB 200,000, a fine ranging from RMB 200,000 to RMB 1,000,000 shall be imposed.

Article 143: If an insurance company, in violation of this Law, operates beyond the business scope approved or concurrently operates any business other than those provided for by this Law or any other law and administrative regulation, the offender shall be subject to criminal liabilities pursuant to law if a crime is constituted; if the case is not serious enough to constitute a crime, the insurance supervision and administration department shall order it to correct, and to return the premiums collected, confiscate the illegal proceeds and impose a fine ranging from one time to five times the illegal proceeds; if there are no illegal proceeds or the illegal proceeds are less than RMB 100,000, a fine ranging from RMB 100,000 to RMB 500,000 shall be imposed; if the acts are not corrected within the prescribed time limit or have caused serious consequences, the insurance company shall be ordered to suspend operation for overhaul or its insurance business permit shall be revoked.

Article 144: If an insurance company is found to have changed the name, articles of association, registered capital or the operational sites of the company or its subsidiaries without approval and in violation of this Law, the insurance supervision and administration department shall order it to correct and impose a fine ranging from RMB 10,000 to RMB 100,000.

Article 145: If any of the following acts is committed in violation of the provisions of this law, the insurance supervision and administration department shall order the law violators to correct and concurrently impose a fine ranging from RMB 50,000 to RMB 300,000; if the case is serious, the business scope may be limited or handling of new operations shall be suspended or even the insurance operation permit shall be revoked:

1. To fail to draw and deposit guaranty funds or use guaranty funds in violation of the regulations
2. To fail to draw or carry down various kinds of liability reserves or fail to draw reserve for outstanding losses according to the provisions of this law.
3. To fail to draw insurance guarantee fund or public accumulation funds
4. To fail to handle re-insurance according to regulations
5. To operate the funds of an insurance company in violation of related provisions

6. To set up subsidiaries or representative offices without approval
7. To separate or consolidate without approval.
8. To fail to submit the insurance clauses or rates of the categories of insurance that shall be submitted for examination and approval pursuant to law.

Article 146: If any of the following acts is committed in violation of the provisions of this Law, the insurance supervision and administration department shall order correction, and for failure in the correction within the prescribed time limit, a fine ranging from RMB 10,000 to RMB 100,000 shall be imposed.

1. To fail to submit relevant reports, statements, documents and materials according to related provision
2. To fail to submit for the record the insurance clauses or rates of the categories of insurance that shall be submitted for record according to related provisions.

Article 147: If any of the following acts is committed in violation of the provisions of this law, the offender shall be subject to criminal liabilities pursuant to law if a crime is constituted; if the case is not serious enough to constitute a crime, the insurance supervision and administration department shall order the violator to correct and impose on a fine ranging from RMB 100,000 to RMB 500,000; if the case is serious, the business scope may be limited or handling of new operations shall be suspended or even the insurance operation permit shall be revoked:

1. To provide false reports, statements, documents or materials
2. To refuse or obstruct the checks and supervision according to law.

Article 148: If any of the following acts is committed in violation of the provision of this law, the insurance supervision and administration department shall order correction and impose a fine ranging from RMB 50,000 to RMB 300,000:

1. Serious cases of over-insurance
2. To underwrite insurance policies with death as the conditions for payment for people incapable of civil acts.

Article 149: Those who violate the provisions of this Law by illegally engaging in the insurance agency business or brokerage business without getting the insurance agency business permit or brokerage permit, the insurance supervision and administration department shall stop them; the offender shall be subject to criminal liabilities pursuant to law if a crime is constituted; if the case is not serious enough to constitute a crime, the insurance supervision and administration department shall confiscate their illegal proceeds and concurrently impose a fine more than one time and less than five times the illegal proceeds. If there are no illegal proceeds or the illegal proceeds are less than RMB 100,000, a fine ranging from RMB 100,000 to RMB 500,000 shall be imposed.

Article 150: Insurance supervision and administration department shall, regarding the different situations, give such punishments as a warning or replacement and the concurrent imposition of a fine ranging from RMB 20,000 and to RMB 100,000 to the senior management personnel or other people directly responsible for an act that violates the provisions of this Law and is not serious enough to constitute a crime.

Article 151: For an act that violates any provisions of this Law and has caused damages to others, the violators shall undertake the civil responsibility.

Article 152: For those who are found to have approved the application for the establishment of an insurance company not up to the required standards or approved an insurance agent or broker not up to the requirements, or those who abuse their power or neglect their duties, if the cases are serious enough to constitute a crime, the offender shall be subject to criminal liabilities pursuant to law; or administrative sanctions shall be given if the cases are not serious enough to constitute a crime.

CHAPTER VIII: SUPPLEMENTARY PROVISIONS

Article 153: For marine insurance the relevant provisions of the commercial maritime law shall be abided by. This law shall apply to matters not covered by the commercial maritime law.

Article 154: The provisions of this law are applicable to Chinese-foreign joint equity insurance companies, solely foreign-funded insurance companies and branches of foreign insurance companies; if there are separate provisions by other laws or administrative regulations, those laws and regulations shall apply.

Article 155: The state supports the development of insurance businesses in the service of agricultural production. Regulations on agricultural insurance shall be provided for by other laws and administrative regulations.

Article 156: There shall be separate provisions of laws or administrative regulations concerning insurance organizations other than those provided for in this law.

Article 157: The insurance companies approved before the law is promulgated shall continue to operate and those not up to the requirements provided by this law shall strive to measure up to the requirements within a prescribed time limit. Specific procedures shall be formulated separately by the State Council.

Promulgated by The Standing Committee of the National People's Congress on 2002-10-28. The revision has been in effect since January 1, 2003. Another revision is expected in 2007.

Appendix E

Encouraged, Restricted, and Prohibited Foreign Investment Industries

ENCOURAGED INDUSTRIES

I. Agriculture, Forestry, Husbandry, Fishing and Related Industries.

1. The reclamation and development of wastelands, barren hills and shoals (except where there are military installations) and transformation of medium and low-yield farmland and low-yield forests;
2. The development of new high-quality, high-yield strains of food grains, cotton, oil crops, sugar crops, vegetable, flowers and plants, and forage grass crops;
3. Serial non-soil cultivation and production of vegetables, flowers and plants;
4. Forest plantation and the introduction of improved varieties of forest trees;
5. Development of fine breeds of stud stock, birds, and aquatic products (excluding China's indigenous precious varieties);
6. Breeding of famous, special or fine aquatic products and deep-water fishing;
7. New lines of highly efficient and safe crude agricultural chemicals (which have a pest-killing and bacteria-killing rate of over 80 percent and do not harm human beings, animals and crops);
8. High-concentration chemical fertilizers (urea, synthetic ammonia and phosphamidon);
9. New production technology and new kinds of agricultural plastic film (fiber film, photolysis film and multi-function film and raw materials);
10. Veterinary antibiotics (special animal antibiotics, veterinary antibiotics against internal and external parasites, new forms of veterinary antibiotics), veterinary anthelmintics;
11. New products and new doses of anti-insect chemicals;

Source: Ministry of Commerce of the People's Republic of China.

471

12. All-valence compound fodder, additives and the development of fodder protein resources;
13. New technology and equipment for the storage, preservation and processing of vegetables, fruits, meat products and aquatic products;
14. Forestry chemical products and new technology for the comprehensive utilization of inferior, small and fuel forests;
15. The construction and management of comprehensive water control projects (Shareholding by the Chinese parties and with more than 300,000 tones of daily water supply or with installed capacity of more than 250MW);
16. The manufacturing of water-saving irrigation equipment;
17. The manufacturing of new agricultural machinery, agricultural tools and related spare parts.
18. Ecological and environment regulation projects.

II. Light Industry

1. Mold design, processing and manufacturing of non-metal products;
2. Commercial-grade paper pulp (with an annual output of wood pulp of more than 170,000 tones per year, plus the construction of raw material base);
3. Post dressing and processing of leather;
4. Mercury-free manganese-alkaline batteries, lithium batteries and hydronickelate batteries;
5. High-tech industrial sewing machines;
6. Polyimide wrap;
7. Production of new and high efficiency ferment.
8. Synthetic spices and single-ion spices;
9. Research and popularization of freon substitution technology;
10. Processing of conic-acetic acid cellulose and silk string for tobacco industry.

III. Textile Industry

1. Wood pulp of fabric (with an annual output of more than 100,000 tones, plus the construction of raw material base.);
2. Textile dyeing and after-treatment;
3. Dyeing and renovating of highly imitated fabric and high-grade fabric clothe;
4. Manufacturing of auxiliary, oil-seed and dye stuff.

IV. Transport, Post and Communications Industry

1. Railway transport technology and equipment: designing and manufacturing of locomotives and their major parts; rail-line design and construction; technology and equipment manufacturing for high-speed railways; manufacturing of communication signals and transport safety monitoring equipment; manufacturing of electric power railway installation and equipment;

2. Construction and management of local railways and associated bridges, tunnels and ferries (off limits to solely foreign-funded enterprises);
3. Road and port machinery and its designing and manufacturing technology;
4. Construction and management of urban subway and light-duty rail system (shareholding by the Chinese parties);
5. Construction and management of roads, bridges, tunnels and ports (shareholding by the Chinese parties in public ports projects);
6. Constructing and operating of public dock equipment in harbor (shareholding by the Chinese parties);
7. Construction and management of civil airports (shareholding by the Chinese parties);
8. Manufacturing of equipment for DCS/CDMA system.
9. Manufacturing of synchronous optical fiber of more than five time-groups, microwave communication systems at 2.5 GB/S or above;
10. Manufacturing of metric instruments for light communication, wireless communication and data communication at 2.5GB/S;
11. Manufacturing of asynchronous transfer mode (ATM) exchange equipment.

V. Coal Industry

1. Designing and manufacturing of coal mining, excavation and transportation machinery;
2. Coal mining and dressing (shareholding by the Chinese parties for special and rare coal);
3. Production of coal liquid and liquefied coal;
4. Comprehensive development and utilization of coal;
5. Comprehensive utilization and development of fuels with low calorific value and associated resources;
6. Manufacturing of transportation pipe for coal;
7. Exploitation and development of coal bed gas.

VI. Power Industry

1. Construction and management of power plants with single generator capacity of over 300,000 kw;
2. Construction and management of hydropower stations;
3. Construction and management of nuclear power stations (shareholding by the Chinese parties);
4. Construction and management of power stations utilizing anti-pollution coal-burning technology;
5. Construction and management of power stations utilizing new types of energy (including solar energy, wind energy, magnetic energy, geothermal energy and tidal energy);

VII. Ferrous Metallurgical Industry

1. Super-high power electrodes with the productivity of 50 tons and above (equipped with outer-furnace refining and casting), coke ovens with the productivity 50-ton and above;
2. Stainless steel smelting;
3. Manufacturing of cold-rolled silicon steel plates;
4. Manufacturing of hot-rolled and cold-rolled stainless steel plate;
5. Steel pipes for petroleum transportation;
6. Processing of waste steel;
7. Exploitation and selection of iron/manganese mines;
8. Manufacturing of direct reducing steel and smelt reducing steel;
9. Aluminium alumina, hard clay pit and grog;
10. Deep processing of tamping coke and coal tar;
11. Manufacturing of magnesium dust.

VIII. Non-Ferrous Metallurgical Industry

1. Single (more than 8 inches in diameter) and multi-crystal silicon;
2. Hard alloy, chemical tin compound and antimony compounds;
3. Compound materials of non-ferrous metals, new alloy materials;
4. Exploitation of copper, lead and zinc mines (off limits to solely foreign-funded enterprises);
5. Exploitation of aluminium mines (off limits to solely foreign-funded enterprises) and aluminium oxide (more than 300,000 tones);
6. Rare-earth minerals application;

IX. Petroleum, Petrochemical and Chemical Industry

1. Ionic membrane caustic soda and new organic chlorine product series;
2. Manufacturing of ethene with annual output over 600,000 tons (shareholding by the Chinese parties);
3. Manufacturing of PVC resin (shareholding by the Chinese parties);
4. Comprehensive utilization of ethene byproduct: C5-C9;
5. Engineering plastic products and plastic alloys;
6. Necessary raw materials for synthetic materials (bisphenol A, butadiene-styrene latex, pyridine, 4.4'diphenyl methane diisocyanic ester);
7. Raw materials of basic organic chemicals: comprehensive utilization of benzene, methylbenzene, para-xylol derivatives, ortho-xylol derivatives and meta-xylol derivatives;
8. Synthetic rubber (liquid styrene-butadiene rubber, butyl rubber, isoprene rubber, acetyl propionyl rubber, butadiene flange duprene rubber, lactoprene rubber, acrylic rubber and alcoholate fluoride rubber);

9. Fine chemical industry: dyes, intermediates, catalysts, auxiliaries and new color products and new technology; commercial processing technology of dyes and colors; high tech chemical products for electronics and paper-making; food additives, fodder additives, leather chemical products, oil field auxiliaries, surfactant, water treatment agents, glues, non-organic fibres, non-organic dust fillings and equipment;

10. Manufacturing of titanium whitening power through chlorination;

11. Chemical products that use coal as raw material;

12. Comprehensive recycling of waste gas, liquid and residue;

13. Manufacturing of clarifier, catalyzer and other auxiliary for automobile waste gas;

14. Development and utilization of the new exploitation technology for increasing oil utilization ratio (Shareholding by Chinese parties);

15. Construction and management of oil and gas pipes, oil depots and ports designated for oil transportation (Shareholding by the Chinese parties).

X. Machinery Industry

1. Manufacturing of welding robots and highly-efficient welding production lines;

2. Heat-resistant insulating materials (with the F and H insulating grades) and finished insulating products;

3. Manufacturing of trackless collection, loading and transport equipment for underground mines; motorized self loading and unloading mining vehicles that can handle more than 100 tones of load; mobile crushers; double-in double-out coal grinders; bucket-wheel excavators with speed higher than 3000 cubic meters per hour; mining loaders of more than 5 cubic meters; whole-section tunneling machines;

4. Manufacturing of paper reeling machines and single paper multi-color plastic printer;

5. Manufacturing of mechanical and electrical well-cleaning equipment and medicine production;

6. Manufacturing of complete sets of turbine compressors, aminomethane pumps and mixer-guarantors used in synthetic ammonia projects with annual production of more than 300,000 tones; in urea projects with annual production of more than 480,000 tones; in ethylene projects with annual production of more than 300,000 tones (the State shall command the majority of shares in the projects);

7. Manufacturing of complete sets of textile, new spinning machines and new papermaking (Including paper pulp) machines;

8. Development and manufacturing of online precision measurement equipment;

9. Manufacturing of monitoring equipments for safety and environmental protection purposes;

10. Components and parts of new types of instruments and materials (mainly intelligent instrument sensors, instrument socket connectors, flexible circuit boards, photoelectron switches, proximity switches and other new types of switches; instrument functional materials);

11. Research and development centers for the designing of essential machineries, fundamental components and important technical equipment;

12. Proportion and servo hydraulic pressure technology, low-power gas valve and vacuum filler;

13. Fine punching molds, precision hollow molds and standardized molds;

14. Manufacturing of urban sewage treatment equipment that can handle 250,000 tons of sewage per day; industrial liquid waste membrane treatment equipment; up-flowing anaerobic fluidized bed equipment and other organic liquid waste treatment equipment, coal ashes building blocks equipment (50,000ñ100,000 tons per year), waste plastics recycling equipment, industrial boiler desulphurization and identifications equipment, large heat-and acid-resistant bag-type collectors;

15. Manufacturing of large, precision and special bearings;

16. Manufacturing of major automobile components and parts: brake assembly, driving assembly, gearbox, steering gear, diesel engine fuel pump, piston (including piston ring), air valve, hydraulic tappet, axle pad, booster, clarifying filter (triple filter), aluminium radiator, diaphragm clutch, constant-velocity universal joint, shock absorber, car air conditioning system, safety air bag, seat angle adjusting device, car lock, rear-view mirror, glass lift, combined dashboard, engines, lamps and bulbs, special high-strength fasteners, special bearings;

17. Manufacturing of automobile molds (including punching molds, injection molds, pressed molds), clamping apparatus (including welding fixture and examination fixture);

18. Automobile casting and forging blanks;

19. Automobile technology research centers and automobile design and development institutions;

20. Highly-specialized vehicles such as those used in deserts in petroleum industry and other special industries;

21. Manufacturing of key components for motorcycles: carburetor, magnet engine, electric starter, lamp, and tray break;

22. Manufacturing of new technical equipment for online testing of water quality;

23. Manufacturing of special machines and facilities for flood prevention and rescue work in emergencies;

24. Manufacturing of silt cleaner;

25. Manufacturing of forage-processing sets (10 tons/hour) and relative main components;

26. Design and manufacturing of new-type instruments and equipment for oil exploitation and exploration.

XI. Electronic Industry

1. Manufacturing of LSI with 0.35-micron (and less) line width;
2. New types of electronic components and spare parts (including sectional components) and power electronic components and spare parts;
3. Manufacturing of photoelectric components, sensitive components and sensors;
4. Manufacturing of medium and large computers;
5. Manufacturing of compatible digital TV, high-definition TV (HDTV) and digital cassette recorders;
6. Development of special semiconductor and photoelectron materials;
7. Manufacturing of new types of display components (flat panel display devices);
8. Computer aided design (CAD), computer aided tests (CAT), and computer aided manufacturing (CAM), computer aided engineering (CAE) systems and other computer application systems;
9. Manufacturing of special electronic equipment, instruments, tools and molds;
10. Manufacturing of hydrologic data collection instruments and equipment;
11. Manufacturing of satellite communication equipment;
12. Manufacturing of data interconnection equipment;
13. Manufacturing of air traffic control system equipment (sole investment by foreign enterprises are not permitted);
14. Development and manufacturing of large capacity laser disk and magnetic disk storage and related components;
15. Development and manufacturing of new types of printing devices (laser printers, etc.)
16. Manufacturing of equipment for digital communication and multimedia systems;
17. Production of single-mould optical fiber;
18. Manufacturing of telecommunication equipment for network integration;
19. Manufacturing of new technical equipment supporting the telecommunication network;
20. Manufacturing of broadband integrated service digital network (ISDN) equipment

XII. Building Materials and Equipment and Other Non-Metallic Minerals Industries

1. High quality floating glass production lines with daily melting output of 500 tons and more;
2. High-grade sanitary ceramics production lines with annual output of 500,000 pieces and its necessary hardware and plastic ware;
3. New types of building materials: wall materials, decoration materials, waterproof materials and heat preservation materials;

4. New types of dry cement production line with 4,000 tons (and more) of daily output (only in mid-west regions);
5. Storage and transport facilities for bulk cement;
6. Kiln wire-drawing production line with annual output of 10,000 tons (and more) of glass Fiber and glass fiber reinforced plastic products;
   -Inorganic nonmetal materials and products (quartz glass and artificial crystal);
   -High grade fireproof materials special for glass, porcelain and glass fiber kiln;
   -Flat glass deep processing technology and equipment;
7. Manufacturing of tunnel excavators, urban subway drilling machines;
8. Manufacturing of special urban sanitary equipment;
9. Manufacturing of tree transplanting machinery;
10. Manufacturing of road milling and repairing machinery;

XIII. Pharmaceutical Industry

1. Raw chemical materials that are within the patented period under the protection of China's patent administration; special medical intermediates that need to be imported;
2. Production of fever-allaying medicine and antichloristic adopting new technology and equipment;
3. Vitamin: niacin;
4. New types of anti-cancer, cardio-and cerebral-vascular medicines;
5. Medicine agents: slow-releasing agents, release controlling agents, targeting agents, skin-penetrating and other new types of forms of medicines and related supplements;
6. Amino acids: serine, tryptophan proteinochromogen, histamine, etc.;
7. New types of medicine packaging materials, containers and advanced pharmaceutical equipment;
8. New types of highly efficient and economic contraceptive medicines and devices;
9. New technologies and equipment that can improve the quality and packaging of traditional Chinese medicine;
10. New techniques to analyze traditional Chinese medicine's active agents and extraction;
11. New types of medicine produced by biological engineering technology;
12. Exploitation and application of new adjuvant;
13. Production of diagnosis reagents for hepatitis, aids and radiation immunity

XIV. Manufacturing of Medical Equipment

1. X-ray machines of more than 800 milliamperes, featuring intermediate frequency, computer controlling, digital image processing technology and low radiation;
2. Electronic endoscopes;
3. Medical tubes.

XV. Aviation Industry

1. Design and manufacturing of civil aeroplane (Shareholding by the Chinese parties);
2. Manufacturing of civil aeroplane spare parts;
3. Design and manufacturing of aviation engine (Shareholding by the Chinese parties);
4. Manufacturing of aviation airborne equipment;
5. Manufacturing of light combustion turbine;
6. Design and manufacturing of civil satellite (Shareholding by the Chinese parties);
7. Manufacturing of civil satellite payloads (Shareholding by the Chinese parties);
8. Manufacturing of civil satellite spare parts;
9. Development of civil satellite application technology;
10. Design and manufacturing of civil carrier rocket (Shareholding by the Chinese parties).

XVI. Newly Emerged Industries

1. Microelectronics technology;
2. New material;
3. Bioengineering technology (excluding genetic engineering technology);
4. Information and communications networking technology;
5. Isotope radiation and laser technology;
6. Ocean development and oceanic energy development;
7. Technology of seawater desalting and utilization;
8. Energy-saving technology development;
9. Resources regeneration and comprehensive utilization technology;
10. Engineering and technology for the control of environmental pollution.

XVII. Service Industry

1. International economic and scientific and technological information consultation services;
2. Repairing and after-sale services of precision instrument and equipment;
3. Construction of high-tech and new product development centers, enterprise hatch

XVIII. Industries whose Products Are solely for Export with Permission

RESTRICTED INDUSTRIES

I. Light Industry

1. Production of washing machines, refrigerators, freezers
2. Production of synthetic emtrol, alcohol ether and alcohol ether sulfate
3. Manufacture of compressors with a shaft power of 2 kw or less which are specially used for air-conditioners and refrigerators.

II. Textile Industry

1. Chemical fiber drawn work of conventional chipper
2. Production of viscose staple fiber with an annual single thread output capacity of less than 20,000 tons

III. Petroleum, Petrochemical, Chemical Industries

1. Barium salt production
2. Refinery with an output capacity of less than 5 million tons a year
3. Cross-ply and old tire reconditions (not including radial tire)
4. Production of sapphire acid basic titanium white

IV. Machinery Industry

1. Manufacture of equipment for producing long Dacron thread and short fiber
2. Manufacture of power generating units of diesel engines
3. Production of all kinds of ordinary abrasives (containing boule and silicon-carbide), grindstone with a diameter of less than 400 mm and man-made diamond saw bit
4. Production of leectric drill and electric grinder
5. Ordinary carbon steel welding rod
6. Ordianry standard fasteners, small and medium sized ordinary bearings
7. Ordinary lead acid accumulator
8. Containers
9. Elevators
10. Alufer hub

V. Electronic Industry

1. Satellite television receiver and key parts
2. Exchange boards for the use of digital program-control bureau and for the use of private branch exchange

VI. Medicine Industry

1. Production of chloramphenicol, lincomycin, gentamicin, dihydrostreptomycin, amicacin, tetracycline hydrochloride, oxytetracycline, acetyl spiramycin, medemycin, kitasamycin, ilotycin, norfloxacinum, ciprofloxacin and ofloxacin
2. Production of Analgin, aspirin, paracetamol, Vitamin B1, Vitamin B2 and Vitamin B6

VII. Medical Apparatus and Instruments

  1. Production of low or medium class type-B ultrasonic displays

VIII. Transportation Service

  1. Taxi (The purchase of cars is restricted within China)
  2. Gas station (restricted to projects related to super highway)

(B)

I. Agriculture, Forestry, Animal Husbandry, Fishery and Related Industries

  1. Development and production of food, cotton and oil-seed (the Chinese party will be the holding party or play a leading role)
  2. Processing and export of the logs of precious varieties of trees (wholly foreign owned enterprises are not allowed)
  3. Inshore and continental-river fishing (wholly foreign owned enterprises are not allowed)
  4. Cultivation of traditional Chinese medicines (wholly foreign owned enterprises are not allowed)

II. Light Industry

  1. Product of table salt, and salt for industrial use
  2. Production of non-alcoholic beverage of foreign brand (including solid beverage)
  3. Production of millet wine and famous brands of poirits
  4. Tobacco processing and industries such as cigarettes and filter tips
  5. Processing and production of blue wet hide of pig, cow and sheep
  6. Production of natural spices
  7. Processing of fat or oil
  8. Paper and paper plate

III. Textile Industry

  1. Wool spinning, cotton spinning
  2. Raw silk, grey silk fabric
  3. Highly emulated chemical fiber and special kinds of fiber such as aromatic synthetic fiber, and carbon fiber (wholly foreign owned enterprises are not allowed)
  4. Fibre and polyester, acrylic fiber and spandex which are not used as fiber (wholly foreign owned enterprises are not allowed)

IV. Communication and Transportation, Post and Telecommunications Industries

1. Construction and management of main lines of railways (the Chinese party will be the holding party or take a leading role)
2. Transprotation by water (the Chinese party will be the holding party or take leading role)
3. Entry and exit automobile transportation (wholly foreign owned enterprises are not allowed)
4. Air freight (the Chinese party will be the holding party or take a leading role)
5. General aviation (the Chinese party will be the holding party or take a leading role)

V. Power Industry

1. Construction and management of conventional coal-fired power plants whose single-machine capacity is less than 300,000 kw (with the exception of small power grid, power plants in remote area and power plants of low-quality coal and coal refuses)

VI. Non-ferrous Metal Industry (wholly foreign owned enterprises are not allowed)

1. Copper and aluminum processing
2. Mining, dressing, smelting, and processing of precious metals (gold, silver, platinum families)
3. Mining of non-ferrous metals such as wolfram, tin and antimony
4. Exploration, mining, selection, smelting and separation of rare-earth mental

VII. Petroleum, Petrochemical Industry and Chemical Industry

1. Sensitive materials (cartridge, film, PS plate, and photographic paper)
2. Mining and processing of baron, magnesium, iron ores
3. Benzidine
4. Chemical industry products such as ionic membrane caustic soda and organo-chlorine serial products
5. Radial tire (the Chinese party will be the holding party or play a leading role)
6. Synthetic fiber raw materials: precision terephthalic acid, vinyl cyanide, capro-lactam and nylon 66 salt

VIII. Mechanical Industry

1. Complete automobiles (including limousines, trucks, passenger cars, and reequipped cars) and complete motorcycles (the Chinese party will be the holding party and take a leading role)
2. Engines of automobiles and motorcycles (the Chinese party will be the holding party or take a leading role)

3. Production of compressors of air conditioners for cars, electron-controlled fuel-oil injecting systems, electronic controlled brade and locking-prevention systems, safety aeocysts and other electronic equipment, power generating machines and aluminum radiating machines

4. Reconditiong and disassembling refitting of old cars and motorcycles

5. Fire power equipment: (power unit, turbine, boiler, supplementary machine and controlling equipment) manufacture of units of over 100,000 kw, gas turbine combined cycle power equipments, cyclic fluidized bed boiler, coal gasification combined cyclic technique and equipment (IGCC), pressure boost fluidized bed (PFBC), desulfrization and denitrification equipment (wholly foreign owned enterprises are not allowed)

6. Hydroelectric equipment: manufacture of hydropower generating units with a wheel diameter of over 5 meters (including hydropower supplementary machines and controlling units), large scale pump storage groups of over 50,000 kw, large scale tubular tubine units of 10,000 kw over (wholly foreign owned enterprises are not allowed)

7. Nuclear power group: manufacture of nuclear power groups of 600,000 kw or over (wholly foreign owned enterprises are not allowed)

8. Manufacture of power transmitting and transforming equipment: large scale transformers of 200 kilovolts or over high-voltage switches, mutual inductor, cable equipment (wholly foreign owned enterprises are not allowed)

9. Manufacture of crawler dozers of less than 320 horsepower, wheeled forklifts of less than 3 cubic meters, and cranes of less than 50 tons (wholly foreign owned enterprises are not allowed)

10. Manufacture of sheet continuous caster

IX. Electronic Industry

1. Color TV (including projection television), color kinescope and glass shielding

2. Video recorders and magnetic heads, magnetic drums and movement of video recorders

3. Analogue type mobile communications systems (honey-comb, colony, wireless beeper call, wireless telephone)

4. Receiving equipment of satellite navigation and key parts (wholly foreign owned enterprises are not allowed)

5. Manufacturing of the system of VSAT

6. Manufacturing of photo timing digital serial communication systems of less than 2.5 GB/S and microwave communication systems of 144MB/S and lower

X. Building Material Equipment and Other Non-metal

Products Industries Exploration, mining and processing of diamond and other natural gems (wholly foreign owned enterprises are not allowed)

XI. Medicine Industry

1. Traditional Chinese herb medicines, Chinese patent drug semis and finished products (with the exception of preparing technique of traditional Chinese patent drug semis and finished products (with the exception of preparing technique of traditional Chinese herb medicine in small pieces ready for decoction))
2. Precursor of narcotics: ephedrine, pscudoephedrine, ergotinine, ergotamine, lsergic acid and so on
3. Pennicillin G
4. Production of addiction marcotic and psychoactiove drug (the Chinese party will be the holding party or play a leading role)
5. Production of vaccinums that involve high tech: vaccinum against AIDS, vaccinum against type-C hepatitis, contraceptive vaccinum and so on (the Chinese party will be the holding party or play a leading role)
6. Immunity vaccinums included in the State's plan, bacterins, antitoxins and anatoxin (BCG vaccine, pliomyelitis, DPT vaccine, measles vaccine, Type-B encephalitis, epidemic cerebrospinal menignitis vaccine)
7. Production of Vitamin C
8. Production of blood products

XII. Medical Apparatus and Instruments Industry

1. Disposable injectors, transfusion systems, blood transfusion systems and blood bags
2. Manufacture of large medical treatment equipment such as CT, MRI and accelerators for medical use

XIII. Shipping Industry (the Chinese party will be the holding party or a leading role)

1. Repairing, design and manufacture of special ships, high performance ships and over 35,000-ton ships
2. Design and manufacture of diesel engines for ships, auxiliary machines, wireless communication, navigation equipment and parts

XIV. Domestic and Foreign Trade, Tourism, Real Estate and Service Industry (wholly foreign owned enterprises are not permitted)

1. Domestic commerce (the Chinese party will be the holding party or play a leading role)
2. Foreign trade (the Chinese party will be the holding party or play a leading role)
3. Travel agencies

4. Cooperation school-running (with the exception of elementary education)
5. Medical establishments (the Chinese party will be the holding party or play a leading role)
6. Accounting, audit and legal consultation services and agencies
7. Agent services (boats and ships, freight, futures, sales, advertisement, etc.)
8. High-class hotels, villas, high-class office buildings, and international exhibition centers
9. Golf links
10. Development of land
11. Large scale tourist, cultural and recreational parks and artificial landscapes
12. Construction and management of national tourist attractions

XV. Finance and Relevant Trades

1. Banks, finance companies and trust investment companies
2. Insurance companies, insurance brokerages and underwriting agent companies
3. Bond companies, insurance brokerages and underwriting agent companies
4. Financial lease
5. Foreign exchange brokerages
6. Financial, insurance and foreign exchange consultation
7. Production, processing, wholesales and retail of gold, silver, gems and jewelry

XVI. Miscellaneous

1. Printing, publishing and issuing business (the Chinese party will be the holding party or play a leading role)
2. Testing, appraising and attestation business of import and export goods (wholly foreign-owned enterprises are not permitted)
3. Production, publishing and issuing of audio and video products and electronic publication (the Chinese party will be the holding party or play a leading role)

PROHIBITED

I. Agriculture, Forestry, Animal Husbandry, Fishery and Related Industries

1. Wild animal and plant resources protected by the State
2. China's rare precious breeds (including fine genes in plants industry, husbandry and aquatic products industry)
3. Growing of green tea and special tea forests (famous tea, black tea, etc)

II. Light Industry

1. Ivory carving and tiger-bone processing
2. Hand-made carpet
3. Bodiless lacquerware
4. Enamel products
5. Blue and white porcelain
6. Xuan paper, and ingot-shaped tablets of Chinese ink

III. Power Industry and Urban Public Facility

1. Construction and management of electricity network
2. Construction and management of urban networks of water supply, water drainage, gas and heat power

IV. Exploration, Selection, or Processing of Mining Industry, Exploration, selection, smelting or processing of radioactive mineral products

V. Petroleum Industry, Petrochemical Industry and Chemical Industry

1. Mining and processing of szaibelyite
2. Mining and processing of Celestine

VI. Medicine Industry

1. Traditional Chinese medicines which have been listed as national protected resources (musk, licorice root, etc.)
2. Preparing technique of traditional Chinese medicine in small pieces ready for decoction and products of exclusive recipe of traditional Chinese medicine already prepared

VII. Transportation and Post & Telecommunications Service

1. Management of post and telecommunications business
2. Air traffic control

VIII. Trade and Finance

1. Commodity future, financial future and related finance business

IX. Broadcasting and Film Industries

1. Broadcasting stations, TV stations (networks) at various levels, launching stations and relay stations
2. Production, publishing, issuing or showing of films
3. Video tape showing

X. Journalism

XI. Manufacturing Industry of Weapons

XII. Miscellaneous

1. Projects that endanger the safety and performance of military facilities
2. Developing and processing of carcinogenic, teratogenic, and mutagenesis raw materials
3. Racecourse, gambling
4. Pornographic service

Appendix F

China's Law on Chinese-Foreign Equity Joint Ventures

Article 1: The People's Republic of China, in order to expand international economic cooperation and technological exchange, permits foreign companies, enterprises and other economic organizations or individuals(hereinafter referred to as the "foreign party") to jointly establish and operate equity joint ventures within the territory of the People's Republic of China with Chinese companies, enterprises or other economic organizations (hereinafter referred to as the "Chinese party") based on the principle of equality and mutual benefit, and upon the approval of the Chinese Government.

Article 2: The Chinese Government shall protect in accordance with the law the investments of the foreign party, the profits due to it and its other lawful rights and interests in an equity joint venture under the agreement, contract and articles of association approved by the Chinese Government. All the activities of an equity joint venture shall comply with the provisions of the laws and regulations of the People's Republic of China.

The state will not nationalize or expropriate equity joint ventures; under special circumstances, based on the requirements of social and public interests, equity joint ventures may be expropriated in accordance with legal procedures, and corresponding compensation shall be provided.

Article 3: The agreement, contract and articles of association of an equity joint venture signed by the parties to the venture shall be submitted to the state department in charge of foreign economic relations and trade (hereinafter referred to as "the examination and approval authority") for examination and approval. The examination and approval authority shall decide within three months to approve or

Source: Ministry of Commerce of the People's Republic of China.

disapprove. After an equity joint venture has been approved, it shall register with the state department in charge of administration of industry and commerce, obtain its business licence, and commence business operations.

Article 4: The form of an equity joint venture shall be a limited liability company. The proportion of the foreign party's contribution to the registered capital of an equity joint venture shall in general not be less than 25 percent.

The parties to the venture shall share profits and bear risks and losses in proportion to their respective contributions to the registered capital. The transfer of a party's contribution to the registered capital must be agreed upon by each party to the venture.

Article 5: The parties to an equity joint venture may make their investments in cash, in kind, in industrial property rights, etc. The technology and equipment contributed by a foreign party as its investment must be advanced technology and equipment which is truly suited to the needs of China. In case of losses caused by deception through the intentional provision of outdated technology and equipment, compensation shall be paid for such losses. The investment of a Chinese party may include providing the right to use a site during the term of operation of the equity joint venture. If the right to use a site is not a part of the investment by a Chinese party, the venture shall pay the Chinese Government a fee for its use.

The various investments mentioned above shall be specified in the contract and articles of association of the equity joint venture, and the value of each contribution (except for the site) shall be appraised and determined through discussions between the parties to the venture.

Article 6: An equity joint venture shall establish a board of directors with a size and composition stipulated in the contract and the articles of association after consultation between the parties to the venture; and each party to the venture shall appoint and replace its own director(s). The chairman and the vice-chairman of the board shall be determined through consultation between the parties to the venture or elected by the board. Where a director appointed by the Chinese party or the foreign party serves as chairman, a director appointed by the other party shall serve as vice-chairman. The board of directors shall decide important issues concerning the equity joint venture based on the principle of equality and mutual benefit. The function and powers of the board of directors shall be to discuss and decide, pursuant to the provisions of the articles of association of the equity joint venture, all important issues concerning the venture, namely: the development plan of the enterprise, production and business programs, the budget, distribution of profits, plans concerning labor and wages, the termination of business, and the appointment or hiring of the general manager, the deputy general manager(s), the chief engineer, the chief accountant and the auditor, as well as their functions and powers and their remuneration, etc. The positions of general manager and deputy general manager(s) (or the factory manager and deputy factory manager(s)) shall be assumed by nominees of the respective parties to the venture. The employment, dismissal, remuneration, welfare, labor protection and insurance of the employees of an equity joint venture shall be stipulated according to laws in the agreement or contract between employees and the venture.

Article 7: Employees of an equity joint venture, in accordance with laws to set up labor union to protect employees' lawful rights by conducting union's activities. An equity joint venture shall provide the labor union with necessary conditions.

Article 8: From the gross profit earned by an equity joint venture, after payment of the venture's income tax in accordance with the provisions of the tax laws of the People's Republic of China, deductions shall be made for the reserve fund, the bonus and welfare fund for staff and workers, and the enterprise development fund as stipulated in the articles of association of the venture and the net profit shall be distributed to the parties to the venture in proportion to their respective contributions to the registered capital.

An equity joint venture may enjoy preferential treatment in the form of tax reductions and exemptions in accordance with provisions of state laws and administrative regulations relating to taxation. When a foreign party uses its share of the net profit as reinvestment within the territory of China, it may apply for a refund of part of the income tax already paid.

Article 9: An equity joint venture shall, on the basis of its business license, open a foreign exchange account with a bank or another financial institution which is permitted by the state foreign exchange control authority to engage in foreign exchange business. Matters concerning the foreign exchange of an equity joint venture shall be handled in conformity with the foreign exchange control regulations of the People's Republic of China. An equity joint venture may, in the course of its business activities, raise funds directly from foreign banks. The various items of insurance of an equity joint venture shall be obtained from insurance companies in the territories of China.

Article 10: For the raw and processed materials, fuel, auxiliary equipment, etc. needed by an equity joint venture in the approved business scope thereof, shall be purchased in China or on the international market pursuant to the principle of fairness. An equity joint venture shall be encouraged to sell its products outside the territory of China. Export products may be sold on foreign markets by an equity joint venture directly or by entrusted institutions related to it, and they may also be sold through China's foreign trade institutions. The products of an equity joint venture may also be sold on the Chinese market. When necessary, an equity joint venture may set up branch institutions outside China.

Article 11: The net profit received by a foreign party after fulfillment of its obligations at law and under the provisions of agreements and contracts, the funds received by it upon the expiration or termination of an equity joint venture as well as other funds may be remitted abroad in accordance with foreign exchange control regulations in the currency stipulated in the joint venture contract. The foreign party shall be encouraged to deposit in the Bank of China the foreign exchange which may be remitted abroad.

Article 12: The wage income and other legitimate income of foreign staff and workers of an equity joint venture may be remitted abroad in accordance with foreign exchange control regulations after payment of individual income tax under the tax laws of the People's Republic of China.

Article 13: The term of operation of equity joint ventures may be agreed upon differently according to different lines of business and different circumstances. The term of operation of equity joint ventures engaged in some lines of business shall be fixed while the term of operation of equity joint ventures engaged in other lines of business may or may not be fixed. Where the parties to an equity joint venture with a fixed term of operation agree to extend the term of operation, they shall submit an application to the examination and approval authority not later than six months prior to the expiration of the operation term. The examination and approval authority shall decide, within one month of receipt of the application, to approve or disapprove.

Article 14: If serious losses are incurred by an equity joint venture, or one party fails to fulfill its obligations under the contract and the Articles of association, or an event of force majeure occurs, etc., the contract may be terminated after consultation and agreement between the parties to the venture, subject to approval by the examination and approval authority and to registration with the state department in charge of administration of industry and commerce. In case of losses caused by breach of contract, economic responsibility shall be borne by the breaching party.

Article 15: When a dispute arises between the parties to a venture and the board of directors is unable to resolve it through consultation, the dispute shall be settled through conciliation or arbitration conducted by an arbitral institution of China, or through arbitration by another arbitral institution agreed upon by the parties to the venture. The partied to a joint venture may submit the disputes to the People's court, if the parties neither stipulated any arbitrations clause in the joint venture contract nor reach such written arbitration clause after the occurrence of disputes.

Article 16: This law shall come into force on the date of its promulgation.

Appendix G

China's Law on Chinese-Foreign Contractual Joint Ventures

Article 1: This Law is formulated to expand economic cooperation and technological exchange with foreign countries and to promote the joint establishment, on the principle of equality and mutual benefit, by foreign enterprises and other economic organizations or individuals (hereinafter referred to as the foreign party) and Chinese enterprises or other economic organizations (hereinafter referred to as the Chinese party) of Chinese-foreign contractual joint ventures (hereinafter referred to as contractual joint ventures) within the territory of the People's Republic of China.

Article 2: In establishing a contractual joint venture, the Chinese and foreign parties shall, in accordance with the provisions of this Law, prescribe in their contractual joint venture contract such matters as the investment or conditions for cooperation, the distribution of earnings or products, the sharing of risks and losses, the manners of operation and management and the ownership of the property at the time of the termination of the contractual joint venture. A contractual joint venture, which meets the conditions for being considered a legal person under Chinese law, shall acquire the status of a Chinese legal person in accordance with law.

Article 3: The State shall, according to law, protect the lawful rights and interests of the contractual joint ventures and of the Chinese and foreign parties. A contractual joint venture must abide by Chinese laws and regulations and must not injure the public interests of China. The relevant State authorities shall exercise supervision over the contractual joint ventures according to law.

Article 4: The State shall encourage the establishment of productive contractual joint ventures that are export-oriented or technologically advanced.

Source: Ministry of Commerce of the People's Republic of China.

Article 5: For the purpose of applying for the establishment of a contractual joint venture, such documents as the agreement, the contract and the articles of association signed by the Chinese and foreign parties shall be submitted for examination and approval to the department in charge of foreign economic relations and trade under the State Council or to the department or local government authorized by the State Council (hereinafter referred to as the examination and approval authority). The examination and approval authority shall, within 45 days of receiving the application, decide whether or not to grant approval.

Article 6: When the application for the establishment of a contractual joint venture is approved, the parties shall, within 30 days of receiving the certificate of approval, apply to the administrative authorities for industry and commerce for registration and obtain a business license. The date of issuance of the business license of a contractual joint venture shall be the date of its establishment. A contractual joint venture shall, within 30 days of its establishment, carry out tax registration with the tax authorities.

Article 7: If the Chinese and foreign parties, during the period of operation of their contractual joint venture, agree through consultation to make major modifications to the contractual joint venture contract, they shall report to the examination and approval authority for approval, if the modifications include items involving statutory industry and commerce registration or tax registration, they shall register the modifications with the administrative authorities for industry and commerce and with the tax authorities.

Article 8: The investment or conditions for cooperation contributed by the Chinese and foreign parties may be provided in cash or in kind, or may include the right to the use of land, industrial property rights, non-patent technology or other property rights.

Article 9: The Chinese and foreign parties shall, in accordance with the provisions of the laws and regulations and the agreements in the contractual joint venture contract, duly fulfill their obligations of contributing full investment and providing the conditions for cooperation. In case of failure to do so within the prescribed time, the administrative authorities for industry and commerce shall set another time limit for the fulfillment of such obligations; if such obligations are still not fulfilled by the new time limit, the matter shall be handled by the examination and approval authority and the administrative authorities for industry and commerce according to relevant state provisions.

The investments or conditions for cooperation provided by the Chinese and foreign parties shall be verified by an accountant registered in China or the relevant authorities, who shall provide a certificate after verification.

Article 10: If a Chinese or foreign party wishes to make an assignment of all or part of its rights and obligations prescribed in the contractual joint venture contract, it must obtain the consent of the other party or parties and report to the examination and approval authority for approval.

Article 11: A contractual joint venture shall conduct its operational and managerial activities in accordance with the approved contract and articles of association for the contractual joint venture. The right of a contractual joint venture to make its own operational and managerial decisions shall not be interfered with.

Article 12: A contractual joint venture shall establish a board of directors or a joint managerial institution which shall, according to the contract or the Articles of association for the contractual joint venture, decide on the major issues concerning the venture.

If the Chinese or foreign party assumes the chairmanship of the board of directors or the directorship of the joint managerial institution, the other party shall assume the vice-chairmanship of the board or the deputy directorship of the joint managerial institution.

The board of directors or the joint managerial institution may decide on the appointment or employment of a general manager, who shall take charge of the daily operation and management of the contractual joint venture.

The general manager shall be accountable to the board of directors or the joint managerial institution. If a contractual joint venture, after its establishment, chooses to entrust a third party with its operation and management, it must obtain the unanimous consent of the board of directors or the joint managerial institution, report to the examination and approval authority for approval, and register the change with the administrative authorities for industry and commerce.

Article 13: The employment, dismissal, remuneration, welfare, labor protection and labor insurance, etc. of the staff members and workers of a contractual joint venture shall be specified in contracts concluded in accordance with law.

Article 14: The staff and workers of a contractual joint venture shall, in accordance with law, establish their trade union organization to carry out trade union activities and protect their lawful rights and interests.

A contractual joint venture shall provide the necessary conditions for the venture's trade union to carry out its activities.

Article 15: A contractual joint venture must establish its account books within the territory of China, file its accounting statements according to relevant provisions, and accept supervision by the financial and tax authorities.

If a contractual joint venture, in violation of the provisions prescribed in the preceding paragraph, does not establish its account books within the territory of China, the financial and tax authorities may impose a fine on it, and the administrative authorities for industry and commerce may order it to suspend its business operations or may revoke its business license.

Article 16: A contractual joint venture shall, by presenting its business license, open a foreign exchange account with a bank or any other financial institution which is permitted by the exchange control authorities of the State to conduct transactions in foreign exchange. A contractual joint venture shall handle its foreign exchange transactions in accordance with the provisions of the State on foreign exchange control.

Article 17: A contractual joint venture may obtain loans from financial institutions within the territory of China and may also obtain loans outside the territory of China.

Loans to be used by the Chinese and foreign parties as investment or conditions for cooperation, and their guarantees, shall be provided by each party on its own.

Article 18: The various kinds of insurance coverage of a contractual joint venture shall be furnished by insurance institutions within the territory of China.

Article 19: A contractual joint venture may, within its approved scope of operation, import materials it needs and export products it produces. A contractual joint venture may purchase, on both the domestic market and the world market, the raw and processed materials, fuels, etc. within its approved scope of operation.

Article 20: A contractual joint venture shall achieve on its own the balance of its foreign exchange receipts and expenditures. If a contractual joint venture is unable to achieve the balance of its foreign exchange receipts and expenditures on its own, it may, in accordance with State provisions, apply to the relevant authorities for assistance.

Article 21: A contractual joint venture shall, in accordance with State provisions on tax, pay taxes and may enjoy the preferential treatment of tax reduction or exemption.

Article 22: The Chinese and foreign parties shall share earnings or products, undertake risks and losses in accordance with the agreements prescribed in the contractual joint venture contract. If, upon the expiration of the period of a venture's operation, all the fixed assets of the contractual joint venture, as agreed upon by the Chinese and foreign parties in the contractual joint venture contract, are to belong to the Chinese party, the Chinese and foreign parties may prescribe in the contractual joint venture contract the ways for the foreign party to recover its investment ahead of time during the period of the venture's operation.

If the foreign party, as agreed upon in the contractual joint venture contract, is to recover its investment prior to the payment of income tax, it must apply to the financial and tax authorities, which shall examine and approve the application in accordance with State provisions concerning taxes. If, according to the provisions of the preceding paragraph, the foreign party is to recover its investment ahead of time during the period of the venture's operation, the Chinese and foreign parties shall, as stipulated by the relevant laws and agreed in the contractual joint venture contract, be liable for the debts of the venture.

Article 23: After the foreign party has fulfilled its obligations under the law and the contractual joint venture contract, the profits it receives as its share, its other legitimate income and the funds it receives as its share upon the termination of the venture, may be remitted abroad according to law.

The wages, salaries or other legitimate income earned by the foreign staff and workers of contractual joint ventures, after the payment of the individual income tax according to law, may be remitted abroad.

Article 24: Upon the expiration or termination in advance of the term of a contractual joint venture, its assets, claims and debts shall be liquidated according to legal procedures. The Chinese and foreign parties shall, in accordance with the agreement specified in the contractual joint venture contract, determine the ownership of the venture's property.

A contractual joint venture shall, upon the expiration or termination in advance of its term, cancel its registration with the administrative authorities for industry and commerce and the tax authorities.

Article 25: The period of operation of a contractual joint venture shall be determined through consultation by the Chinese and foreign parties and shall be clearly specified in the contractual joint venture contract. If the Chinese and foreign parties agree to extend the period of operation, they shall apply to the examination and approval authority 180 days prior to the expiration of the venture's term. The examination and approval authority shall decide whether or not to grant approval within 30 days of receiving the application.

Article 26: Any dispute between the Chinese and foreign parties arising from the execution of the contract or the articles of the association for a contractual joint venture shall be settled through consultation or mediation. In case of a dispute which the Chinese or the foreign party is unwilling to settle through consultation or mediation, or of a dispute which they have failed to settle through consultation or mediation, the Chinese and foreign parties may submit it to a Chinese arbitration agency or any other arbitration agency for arbitration in accordance with the arbitration clause in the contractual joint venture contract or written agreement on arbitration concluded afterwards.

The Chinese or foreign party may bring a suit in a Chinese court, if no arbitration clause is provided in the contractual joint venture contract and if no written agreement is concluded afterwards.

Article 27: The detailed rules for the implementation of this Law shall be formulated by the department in charge of foreign economic relations and trade under the State Council and reported to the State Council for approval before implementation.

Article 28: This Law shall come into force as of the date of its promulgation.

Appendix **H**

Provisional Administrative Rules Governing Derivatives Activities of Financial Institutions

CHAPTER I: GENERAL PROVISIONS

Article 1: The Provisional Administrative Rules Governing Derivatives Activities of Financial Institutions (hereinafter referred to as the Rules) is formulated in accordance with the "Law of the People's Republic of China on Banking Regulation and Supervision," the "Law of the People's Republic of China on Commercial Banks" and other applicable laws and regulations for the purpose of regulating and supervising the derivatives activities conducted by financial institutions, thereby effectively controlling the risks associated with the derivatives activities of financial institutions.

Article 2: The term "financial institutions" referred to in the Rules shall mean the financial institutions incorporated in the territory of the People's Republic of China, including banks, trust and investment companies, finance companies, financial leasing companies, auto financing companies, and branches opened by foreign banks in China (hereinafter referred to as foreign bank branches).

Article 3: The term "derivatives" referred to in the Rules shall mean the financial contracts that derive their values from the prices of one or a number of underlying assets or indices, and that are basically classified as forwards, futures, swaps and options. The term "derivatives" shall also mean the structured financial instruments with the characteristics of forwards, futures, swaps, and options, and various combinations thereof.

Source: China Banking Regulatory Commission.

Article 4: The derivatives activities referred to in the Rules may be classified into two types.

(1) The first type is the derivatives transactions conducted by a financial institution for the purpose of its own profit or hedging the risks arising from its own balance sheet positions. The financial institution engaging in this type of derivatives activities is considered as the end-user of derivatives.

(2) The second type is the derivatives services provided by a financial institution for its customers (including financial institutions). The financial institution engaging in this type of derivatives activities is considered as a derivatives dealer. Among the financial institutions acting as derivatives dealers, those further providing derivatives quotes and derivatives services for their customers or other dealers are considered as the derivatives market-makers.

Article 5: China Banking Regulatory Commission (hereinafter referred to as the CBRC) shall be in the position of regulating and supervising the derivatives activities of financial institutions. A financial institution seeking to conduct derivatives activities shall obtain a prior approval from the CBRC, and shall be subject to the oversight and examination by the CBRC.

Non-financial institutions shall not provide derivatives services for their customers.

Article 6: A financial institution engaging in derivatives activities that involve foreign exchange, stocks and commodities, or in the exchange-based derivatives activities shall comply with applicable rules and regulations including those on foreign exchange administration.

CHAPTER II: REGULATION OF MARKET ENTRY

Article 7: A financial institution applying to conduct derivatives activities shall meet the following conditions:

(1) It shall have in place complete and sound policies and procedures for risk management and internal controls of derivatives activities;

(2) It shall have in place a sound processing system for derivatives transactions that automatically connects the front, middle and back offices, and a real-time risk management system;

(3) The managerial personnel in charge of the derivatives activities shall have more than five years' experience of direct involvement in derivatives activities and risk management, and shall have a clean record;

(4) It shall have at least: (a) two professional traders who have more than two years' working experience in derivatives or related transactions and who have received professional training of more than six months on derivatives business skills; (b) one personnel responsible for risk management of derivatives activities; and (c) one personnel responsible for research and development of risk models or risk assessment related to derivatives activities. All

such personnel shall serve in full time, shall not act concurrently in each other's positions and shall have a clean record;

(5) It shall have proper premises and facilities for derivatives activities;

(6) Where the applicant is a foreign bank branch, its home country or region shall have in place a legal framework for the regulation and supervision of derivatives activities and its home country supervisor shall have relevant supervisory competence; and

(7) It shall meet other conditions set out by the CBRC.

Where the applicant is a foreign bank branch who does not meet the aforementioned conditions of (1) to (5), it shall meet the following conditions in addition to the aforementioned conditions of (6) and (7):

(1) It shall have a letter of authorization from its head office (or regional head office) to specify, among others, the types and size of the derivatives activities it is authorized to conduct; and

(2) Except as otherwise prescribed by its head office, its derivatives transactions shall be uniformly executed in a real time manner through the systems run by its head office (or regional head office), and the related transaction settlement, exposure management and risk controls shall be uniformly conducted at its head office (or regional head office) level.

Article 8: Where a policy bank, a Chinese commercial bank (excluding the city commercial bank, rural commercial bank and rural co-operative bank), a trust and investment company, a finance company, a financial leasing company or an auto financing company seeks to conduct derivatives business, the application shall be filed by the applicant as a legal entity and submitted to the CBRC's headquarters for approval.

Where a city commercial bank, a rural commercial bank or a rural co-operative bank seeks to conduct derivatives business, the application shall be filed by the applicant as a legal entity, and the application documents shall be submitted to the CBRC's local office in the location of the applicant, and, following the approval of the CBRC's local office, to the CBRC's headquarters for final approval.

Where a foreign-funded financial institution seeks to conduct derivatives business, the application documents shall be signed by the delegated person(s) and submitted to the CBRC's local office in the location of the applicant, and, following the approval of the CBRC's local office, to the CBRC's headquarters for final approval. Where the foreign-funded financial institution seeks to conduct derivatives in more than two of its branches in China, the application shall be filed by the applicant's head office if the applicant is a locally incorporated legal entity or the applicant's lead branch in China if the applicant is a foreign bank, and the application documents shall be submitted to the CBRC's local office in the location of the entity who files the application, and, following the approval of the CBRC's local office, to the CBRC's headquarters for final approval.

Article 9: A financial institution applying to conduct derivatives activities shall submit the following documents and information (in triplicate) to the CBRC's headquarters or local office:

(1) an application letter, a feasibility study and a business plan or business expansion strategies;

(2) internal management policies pertaining to derivatives activities

(3) accounting rules and procedures pertaining to derivatives activities

(4) names and biographical information of the managerial personnel in charge of derivatives activities and of the principal derivatives traders

(5) policies and procedures for the quantification of risk exposures and the management of risk limits

(6) a report of the safety test of the premises, facilities and systems for derivatives activities; and

(7) other documents and information deemed necessary by the CBRC.

Where the applicant is a foreign bank branch who does not meet the conditions of (1) to (5) provided in Article 7 of the Rules, it shall submit to the CBRC's local office the following documents or information in addition to those provided above:

(1) the letter of authorization issued by the applicant's head office (or regional head office) to authorize, among others, the types and size of derivatives activities conducted by the applicant; and

(2) except as otherwise prescribed by its head office, the document issued by the applicant's head office (or regional head office) to provide assurance that all derivatives transactions conducted by the applicant shall be executed in a real time manner through the systems run by its head office (or regional head office), and the related transaction settlement, exposure management and risk controls shall be conducted at its head office (or regional head office) level.

Article 10: The internal management policies and procedures of a financial institution pertaining to its derivatives activities shall at least contain the following:

(1) derivatives business guidelines, business operating processes and procedures the processes and procedures should reflect the segregation of duties among the front, middle and back offices, and the contingency plan for emergency situations

(2) parameters used for risk models and quantification

(3) types of derivatives activities and risk controls policies

(4) policies and procedures for risk reporting and internal audit

(5) policies and procedures for the management of derivatives activities research and development as well as for the ex post evaluation

(6) rules of conduct observed by derivatives traders

(7) a description of responsibilities and accountability of the managerial personnel at various levels in charge of derivatives activities and of the derivatives traders, and a description of the associated incentives mechanisms

(8) a description of the training programs provided for managerial personnel and employees in the front, middle and back offices; and

(9) other aspects required by the CBRC.

Article 11: Upon receiving from a financial institution a complete set of application documents and information specified in the Rules, the CBRC shall provide its decision of approval or denial within 60 days.

Article 12: Where a financial institution incorporated in the territory of the People's Republic of China authorizes its branch or subsidiary to conduct derivatives activities, it shall conduct stringent review of the branch or subsidiary's capability of relevant risk management and issue a letter of authorization to authorize, among others, the types and size of derivatives activities conducted by the branch or subsidiary. The branch or subsidiary shall conduct derivatives business transactions in a real time manner through the systems run by its head office, and the related transaction settlement, exposure management and risk controls shall be conducted uniformly at its head office level.

Upon receiving the letter of authorization from its head office to provide or change the authorization, the branch or subsidiary mentioned in the above paragraph shall present the letter of authorization to the corresponding CBRC's local office within 30 days.

CHAPTER III: RISK MANAGEMENT

Article 13: A financial institution shall determine whether it is positioned to conduct the derivatives business, and if it is, the appropriate types and size of its derivatives activities, by taking into account its business goals, financial strength, management competence and the risks inherent in the derivatives.

Article 14: A financial institution engaging in derivatives activities shall, in accordance with the classification of derivatives activities provided in Article 4 of the Rules, have in place risk management and internal controls policies and a transaction processing system that are consistent with the nature, scale and complexity of its derivatives activities.

Article 15: The senior management of a financial institution engaging in derivatives activities shall have adequate knowledge of the risks associated with the financial institution's derivatives activities; shall review, approve and appraise the policies, procedures, organization and delegation of powers in respect to the derivatives activities and risk management; and shall, by establishing an independent risk management unit and a sound examination reporting system, have adequate access to the information of the risks exposed in the financial institution's derivatives activities, and on this basis provide effective oversight and guidance on the derivatives activities.

Article 16: The senior management of a financial institution engaging in derivatives activities shall choose the parameters and methods for measuring the risk exposures in accordance with the nature and complexity of the financial institution's derivatives activities; shall stipulate and regularly update the relevant risk limits, stop loss limits, the contingency plan in consistency with the financial institution's overall strength, capital base, profit earning capacity and business principles as well as its projection of market risks; and shall put into place the relevant monitoring and processing procedures in accordance with the limits. The senior management in charge of derivatives activities shall be properly segregated from those in charge of risk management.

Article 17: A financial institution engaging in derivatives activities shall have in place specific requirements on the qualifications of the derivatives traders, analysts and other professional staff, and provide training for its employees involved in derivatives marketing and other related activities with the curricula designed to reflect the nature and complexity of the financial institution's derivatives activities and risk management and intended to help the employees acquire necessary professional skills and meet the qualification requirements.

Article 18: A financial institution engaging in derivatives business shall have in place policies and procedures for assessing the suitability of its counterparties, including, among others, assessing whether the counterparties are capable of understanding the terms of the contract and of fulfilling their obligations under the contract, identifying whether the proposed derivatives transaction meets the business objectives of its counterparties, and assessing the credit risks of its counterparties.

When dealing with derivatives activities that involve high risks, the financial institution shall have in place specific requirements on the qualifications and obligations of its counterparties.

When performing as required in this article, a financial institution may to some extent rely on the written documents provided by its counterparties in good faith.

Article 19: A financial institution providing derivatives services for domestic corporations and individuals shall fully disclose to the corporations and individuals the risks associated with its services, and shall obtain from the corporations and individuals a letter of confirmation to provide the assurance that they fully understand and are capable of accommodating the risks.

The information disclosed by the financial institution to the corporations and individuals shall contain at least the following:

(1) a description of the terms and inherent risks of the derivatives contract; and
(2) a description of the material factors that lead to the potential loss in the derivatives.

Article 20: A financial institution engaging in derivatives activities shall make appropriate use of such credit risk cushions as collateral to reduce the credit risks of its counterparties, and develop appropriate methods and models to assess the credit risks as well as effective measures to control the risks.

Article 21: A financial institution engaging in derivatives activities shall have in place appropriate methods or models to assess the market risks arising from derivatives activities, and follow the mark-to-market approach to manage the market risks and make adjustments to the scale, scope and risk exposures of derivatives activities.

Article 22: A financial institution engaging in derivative business activities shall have in place adequate liquidity arrangements that are consistent with the scale and scope of its derivatives activities, and that provide the assurance of its ability to perform contractual obligations under abnormal market conditions.

Article 23: A financial institution engaging in derivatives activities shall have in place sound mechanisms and policies to control the operational risks.

Article 24: A financial institution shall have in place sound mechanisms and policies to control the legal risks, and stringently examine the legal status and business qualifications of its counterparties. When entering into a derivatives contract with its counterparties, a financial institution shall make reference to the relevant legal documents that prevail in international derivatives market, give due consideration to such elements as the protection of interests through legal enforcement in case of defaults, and take proper measures to prevent the legal risks that may arise during the drafting, negotiation and signing of the derivatives business contract.

Article 25: A financial institution engaging in derivatives activities shall submit to the CBRC its financial statements, statistical reports and other statements in respect to its derivatives activities.

The financial institution shall, in accordance with the disclosure requirements specified by the CBRC, disclose to the public the risk exposures, losses, profit changes of its derivatives activities, and, if there is any, the extraordinary situation in its derivatives activities.

Article 26: The CBRC shall have the power to examine at any time the documents and statements of a financial institution's derivatives activities, and conduct regular examinations to check whether the financial institution's risk management policies and internal controls as well as transaction processing system are consistent with the nature of its derivatives activities.

Article 27: A financial institution engaging in derivatives activities shall promptly report to the CBRC any significant risks and material losses incurred in its derivatives activities, and submit to the CBRC its remedial proposals.

The financial institution shall promptly report to the CBRC any significant changes in its derivatives activities as well as its transaction processing and risk management systems.

Where the cases mentioned in the preceding two paragraphs involve foreign exchange administration and external payments, the cases shall be reported at the same time to the State Administration of Foreign Exchange.

Article 28: A financial institution engaging in derivatives activities shall properly maintain, among others, all derivatives business records and related documents, accounting books, original certificates, telephone tape-recording and other materials and information. For the purpose of review, the telephone tape-recording shall be maintained for no less than six months, and other documents or materials shall be maintained for three years starting from the expiry date of the derivatives contracts, unless otherwise required by the accounting rules.

CHAPTER IV: LEGAL LIABILITY

Article 29: Where a derivatives trader of a financial institution is found in the operation that violates the Rules or the financial institution's internal rules, and the case causes material economic loss to the financial institution or its customers, the financial institution shall impose a penalty on the senior management, the managerial personnel and the trader that are held directly responsible for the operation. The penalty shall range from recording the personnel's demerit to removing the personnel from the office depending on the severity of the offense. If the case constitutes a criminal offence, it shall be delivered to the judicial authority to pursue criminal liability.

Article 30: Where a financial institution is found in the unauthorized derivatives activities, it shall face a penalty imposed by the CBRC in accordance with the Rules on Penalty for Illegal Financial Activities.

Where a non-financial institution is found in violation of the Rules to provide derivatives services to its customers, the CBRC shall have the power to terminate such services and confiscate the illegal income if there is any. If the case constitutes a criminal offense, it shall be delivered to the judicial authority to pursue criminal liability.

Article 31: Where a financial institution is found in violation of the Rules to have failed to submit to the CBRC the required reports, statements and information, or to disclose the required information of its derivatives activities, it shall face a penalty imposed by the CBRC in accordance with the Law of the People's Republic of China on Banking Regulation and Supervision, the Law of the People's Republic of China on Commercial Banks, and the Regulation of the People's Republic of China on Foreign-funded Financial Institutions, as well as other applicable laws, regulations and financial rules.

Where a financial institution is found to have provided the derivatives activities information that is proved to be false or have concealed important facts, it shall face a penalty imposed by the CBRC in accordance with the Rules on Penalty for Illegal Financial Activities.

Article 32: Where a financial institution is found to have failed to implement the risk management and internal controls policies pertaining to its derivatives activities, the CBRC shall have the power to suspend or terminate the financial institution's derivatives activities.

CHAPTER V: SUPPLEMENTAL PROVISIONS

Article 33: The CBRC shall have the power of the interpretation of the Rules.

Article 34: The Rules shall enter into effect on March 1, 2004, and shall prevail where there is any discrepancy between the Rules and the formerly promulgated rules in respect to the derivatives activities of financial institutions.

Appendix I

ETFs on American Stock Exchange

Product Name	Symbol	Issuer
Claymore MACROshares Oil Down Tradeable Shares	DCR	Claymore MACROshares Oil Down Tradeable Trust
Claymore MACROshares Oil Up Tradeable Shares	UCR	Claymore MACROshares Oil Up Tradeable Trust
Claymore/BNY BRIC ETF	EEB	Claymore Exchange-Traded Fund Trust
Claymore/Sabrient Insider ETF	NFO	Claymore Exchange-Traded Fund Trust
Claymore/Sabrient Stealth ETF	STH	Claymore Exchange-Traded Fund Trust
Claymore/Zacks Sector Rotation ETF	XRO	Claymore Exchange-Traded Fund Trust
Claymore/Zacks Yield Hog ETF	CVY	Claymore Exchange-Traded Fund Trust
DIAMONDS	DIA	PDR Services LLC
First Trust Amex Biotechnology Index Fund	FBT	First Trust Exchange-Traded Fund
First Trust DB Strategic Value Index Fund	FDV	First Trust Exchange-Traded Fund
First Trust Dow Jones Internet Index Fund	FDN	First Trust Exchange-Traded Fund
First Trust Dow Jones Select MicroCap Index Fund	FDM	First Trust Exchange-Traded Fund
First Trust IPOX-100 Index Fund	FPX	First Trust Exchange-Traded Fund
First Trust Morningstar Dividend Leaders Index Fund	FDL	First Trust Exchange-Traded Fund
First Trust Value Line Equity Allocation Index Fund	FVI	First Trust Exchange-Traded Fund
Market Vectors Environmental Services Index Fund	EVX	Market Vectors ETF Trust
Market Vectors Gold Miners ETF	GDX	Market Vectors ETF Trust
Market Vectors Steel Index Fund	SLX	Market Vectors ETF Trust
MidCap SPDRs	MDY	PDR Services LLC
NASDAQ-100 Index Tracking Stock	QQQQ	NASDAQ Financial Products Services, Inc
PowerShares Aerospace & Defense Portfolio	PPA	PowerShares Exchange-Traded Fund Trust
PowerShares Cleantech Portfolio	PZD	PowerShares Exchange-Traded Fund Trust
PowerShares DB Commodity Index Tracking Fund	DBC	PowerShares DB Commodity Index Tracking Fund
PowerShares DB G10 Currency Harvest Fund	DBV	PowerShares DB G10 Currency Harvest Fund
PowerShares Dividend Achievers Portfolio	PFM	PowerShares Exchange-Traded Fund Trust
PowerShares Dynamic Banking Sector Portfolio	PJB	PowerShares Exchange-Traded Fund Trust
PowerShares Dynamic Basic Materials Sector Portfolio	PYZ	PowerShares Exchange-Traded Fund Trust
PowerShares Dynamic Biotechnology & Genome Portfolio	PBE	PowerShares Exchange-Traded Fund Trust
PowerShares Dynamic Building & Construction Portfolio	PKB	PowerShares Exchange-Traded Fund Trust

(continued)

Product Name	Symbol	Issuer
PowerShares Dynamic Consumer Discretionary Sector Portfolio	PEZ	PowerShares Exchange-Traded Fund Trust
PowerShares Dynamic Consumer Staples Sector Portfolio	PSL	PowerShares Exchange-Traded Fund Trust
PowerShares Dynamic Energy Exploration & Production Portfolio	PXE	PowerShares Exchange-Traded Fund Trust
PowerShares Dynamic Energy Sector Portfolio	PXI	PowerShares Exchange-Traded Fund Trust
PowerShares Dynamic Financial Sector Portfolio	PFI	PowerShares Exchange-Traded Fund Trust
PowerShares Dynamic Food & Beverage Portfolio	PBJ	PowerShares Exchange-Traded Fund Trust
PowerShares Dynamic Hardware & Consumer Electronics Portfolio	PHW	PowerShares Exchange-Traded Fund Trust
PowerShares Dynamic Healthcare Services Portfolio	PTJ	PowerShares Exchange-Traded Fund Trust
PowerShares Dynamic Heathcare Sector Portfolio	PTH	PowerShares Exchange-Traded Fund Trust
PowerShares Dynamic Industrials Sector Portfolio	PRN	PowerShares Exchange-Traded Fund Trust
PowerShares Dynamic Insurance Portfolio	PIC	PowerShares Exchange-Traded Fund Trust
PowerShares Dynamic Large Cap Growth Portfolio	PWB	PowerShares Exchange-Traded Fund Trust
PowerShares Dynamic Large Cap Portfolio	PJF	PowerShares Exchange-Traded Fund Trust
PowerShares Dynamic Large Cap Value Portfolio	PWV	PowerShares Exchange-Traded Fund Trust
PowerShares Dynamic Leisure & Entertainment Portfolio	PEJ	PowerShares Exchange-Traded Fund Trust
PowerShares Dynamic MagniQuant Portfolio	PIQ	PowerShares Exchange-Traded Fund Trust
PowerShares Dynamic Market Portfolio	PWC	PowerShares Exchange-Traded Fund Trust
PowerShares Dynamic Media Portfolio	PBS	PowerShares Exchange-Traded Fund Trust
PowerShares Dynamic Mid Cap Growth Portfolio	PWJ	PowerShares Exchange-Traded Fund Trust
PowerShares Dynamic Mid Cap Portfolio	PJG	PowerShares Exchange-Traded Fund Trust
PowerShares Dynamic Mid Cap Value Portfolio	PWP	PowerShares Exchange-Traded Fund Trust
PowerShares Dynamic Networking Portfolio	PXQ	PowerShares Exchange-Traded Fund Trust
PowerShares Dynamic OTC Portfolio	PWO	PowerShares Exchange-Traded Fund Trust
PowerShares Dynamic Oil Services Portfolio	PXJ	PowerShares Exchange-Traded Fund Trust
PowerShares Dynamic Pharmaceuticals Portfolio	PJP	PowerShares Exchange-Traded Fund Trust
PowerShares Dynamic Retail Portfolio	PMR	PowerShares Exchange-Traded Fund Trust
PowerShares Dynamic Semiconductors Portfolio	PSI	PowerShares Exchange-Traded Fund Trust
PowerShares Dynamic Small Cap Growth Portfolio	PWT	PowerShares Exchange-Traded Fund Trust
PowerShares Dynamic Small Cap Portfolio	PJM	PowerShares Exchange-Traded Fund Trust
PowerShares Dynamic Small Cap Value Portfolio	PWY	PowerShares Exchange-Traded Fund Trust
PowerShares Dynamic Software Portfolio	PSJ	PowerShares Exchange-Traded Fund Trust
PowerShares Dynamic Technology Sector Portfolio	PTF	PowerShares Exchange-Traded Fund Trust
PowerShares Dynamic Telecom & Wireless Portfolio	PTE	PowerShares Exchange-Traded Fund Trust
PowerShares Dynamic Utilities Portfolio	PUI	PowerShares Exchange-Traded Fund Trust
PowerShares Financial Preferred Portfolio	PGF	PowerShares Exchange-Traded Fund Trust
PowerShares Golden Dragon Halter USX China Portfolio	PGJ	PowerShares Exchange-Traded Fund Trust
PowerShares High Growth Rate Dividend Achievers Portfolio	PHJ	PowerShares Exchange-Traded Fund Trust
PowerShares High Yield Equity Dividend Achievers Portfolio	PEY	PowerShares Exchange-Traded Fund Trust
PowerShares International Dividend Achievers Portfolio	PID	PowerShares Exchange-Traded Fund Trust
PowerShares Listed Private Equity Portfolio	PSP	PowerShares Exchange-Traded Fund Trust
PowerShares Lux Nanotech Portfolio	PXN	PowerShares Exchange-Traded Fund Trust
PowerShares Value Line Industry Rotation Portfolio	PYH	PowerShares Exchange-Traded Fund Trust
PowerShares Value Line Timeliness Select Portfolio	PIV	PowerShares Exchange-Traded Fund Trust
PowerShares Water Resource Portfolio	PHO	PowerShares Exchange-Traded Fund Trust
PowerShares WilderHill Clean Energy Portfolio	PBW	PowerShares Exchange-Traded Fund Trust
PowerShares WilderHill Progressive Energy Portfolio	PUW	PowerShares Exchange-Traded Fund Trust

Product Name	Symbol	Issuer
PowerShares Zacks Micro Cap Portfolio	PZI	PowerShares Exchange-Traded Fund Trust
PowerShares Zacks Small Cap Portfolio	PZJ	PowerShares Exchange-Traded Fund Trust
Rydex Russell Top 50 ETF	XLG	Rydex ETF Trust
Rydex S&P Midcap 400 Pure Value ETF	RFV	Rydex ETF Trust
Rydex S&P 500 Pure Growth ETF	RPG	Rydex ETF Trust
Rydex S&P 500 Pure Value ETF	RPV	Rydex ETF Trust
Rydex S&P Equal Weight Consumer Discretionary ETF	RCD	Rydex ETF Trust
Rydex S&P Equal Weight Consumer Staples ETF	RHS	Rydex ETF Trust
Rydex S&P Equal Weight ETF	RSP	Rydex ETF Trust
Rydex S&P Equal Weight Energy ETF	RYE	Rydex ETF Trust
Rydex S&P Equal Weight Financial ETF	RYF	Rydex ETF Trust
Rydex S&P Equal Weight Health Care ETF	RYH	Rydex ETF Trust
Rydex S&P Equal Weight Industrials ETF	RGI	Rydex ETF Trust
Rydex S&P Equal Weight Materials ETF	RTM	Rydex ETF Trust
Rydex S&P Equal Weight Technology ETF	RYT	Rydex ETF Trust
Rydex S&P Equal Weight Utilities ETF	RYU	Rydex ETF Trust
Rydex S&P Midcap 400 Pure Growth ETF	RFG	Rydex ETF Trust
Rydex S&P Smallcap 600 Pure Growth ETF	RZG	Rydex ETF Trust
Rydex S&P Smallcap 600 Pure Value ETF	RZV	Rydex ETF Trust
SPDR Biotech ETF	XBI	streetTRACKS Series Trust
SPDR Dividend ETF	SDY	streetTRACKS Series Trust
SPDR Homebuilders ETF	XHB	streetTRACKS Series Trust
SPDR Metals & Mining ETF	XME	streetTRACKS Series Trust
SPDR Oil & Gas Equipment & Services ETF	XES	streetTRACKS Series Trust
SPDR Oil & Gas Exploration & Production ETF	XOP	streetTRACKS Series Trust
SPDR Pharmaceuticals ETF	XPH	streetTRACKS Series Trust
SPDR Retail ETF	XRT	streetTRACKS Series Trust
SPDR Semiconductor ETF	XSD	streetTRACKS Series Trust
SPDRs	SPY	PDR Services LLC
Select Sector SPDR-Consumer Discretionary	XLY	State Street
Select Sector SPDR-Consumer Staples	XLP	State Street
Select Sector SPDR-Energy	XLE	State Street
Select Sector SPDR-Financial	XLF	State Street
Select Sector SPDR-Health Care	XLV	State Street
Select Sector SPDR-Industrial	XLI	State Street
Select Sector SPDR-Materials	XLB	State Street
Select Sector SPDR-Technology	XLK	State Street
Select Sector SPDR-Utilities	XLU	State Street
Short Dow30 ProShares	DOG	ProShares Trust
Short MidCap400 ProShares	MYY	ProShares Trust
Short QQQ ProShares	PSQ	ProShares Trust
Short S&P500 ProShares	SH	ProShares Trust
Ultra Dow30 ProShares	DDM	ProShares Trust
Ultra MidCap400 ProShares	MVV	ProShares Trust
UltraShort QQQ ProShares	QID	ProShares Trust
UltraShort S&P500 ProShares	SDS	ProShares Trust
United States Oil Fund, LP	USO	United States Oil Fund, LP
Vanguard Consumer Discretionary ETF	VCR	Vanguard World Funds
Vanguard Consumer Staples ETF	VDC	Vanguard World Funds

(continued)

Product Name	Symbol	Issuer
Vanguard Dividend Appreciation ETF	VIG	Vanguard Specialized Funds
Vanguard Emerging Markets ETF	VWO	Vanguard International Equity Index Funds
Vanguard Energy ETF	VDE	Vanguard World Funds
Vanguard European ETF	VGK	Vanguard International Equity Index Funds
Vanguard Extended Market ETF	VXF	Vanguard Index Funds
Vanguard Financials ETF	VFH	Vanguard World Funds
Vanguard Growth ETF	VUG	Vanguard Index Funds
Vanguard Health Care ETF	VHT	Vanguard World Funds
Vanguard High Dividend Yield ETF	VYM	Vanguard Whitehall Funds
Vanguard Industrials ETF	VIS	Vanguard World Funds
Vanguard Information Technology ETF	VGT	Vanguard World Funds
Vanguard Large-Cap ETF	VV	Vanguard Index Funds
Vanguard Materials ETF	VAW	Vanguard World Funds
Vanguard Mid-Cap ETF	VO	Vanguard Index Funds
Vanguard Mid-Cap Growth ETF	VOT	Vanguard Index Funds
Vanguard Mid-Cap Value ETF	VOE	Vanguard Index Funds
Vanguard Pacific ETF	VPL	Vanguard International Equity Index Funds
Vanguard REIT ETF	VNQ	Vanguard Specialized Funds
Vanguard Small-Cap ETF	VB	Vanguard Index Funds
Vanguard Small-Cap Growth ETF	VBK	Vanguard Index Funds
Vanguard Small-Cap Value ETF	VBR	Vanguard Index Funds
Vanguard Telecommunication Services ETF	VOX	Vanguard World Funds
Vanguard Total Stock Market ETF	VTI	Vanguard Index Funds
Vanguard Utilities ETF	VPU	Vanguard World Funds
Vanguard Value ETF	VTV	Vanguard Index Funds
iShares COMEX Gold Trust	IAU	iShares COMEX Gold Trust
iShares Cohen & Steers Realty Majors	ICF	BGI
iShares Dow Jones Select Dividend Index Fund	DVY	BGI
iShares Dow Jones Transportation Average Index Fund	IYT	iShares Trust
iShares Dow Jones U.S. Basic Materials Sector Index Fund	IYM	iShares Trust
iShares Dow Jones U.S. Consumer Goods Sector Index Fund	IYK	iShares Trust
iShares Dow Jones U.S. Consumer Services Sector Index Fund	IYC	iShares Trust
iShares Dow Jones U.S. Energy Sector Index Fund	IYE	iShares Trust
iShares Dow Jones U.S. Financial Sector Index Fund	IYF	iShares Trust
iShares Dow Jones U.S. Financial Services Index Fund	IYG	iShares Trust
iShares Dow Jones U.S. Healthcare Sector Index Fund	IYH	iShares Trust
iShares Dow Jones U.S. Industrial Sector Index Fund	IYJ	iShares Trust
iShares Dow Jones U.S. Real Estate Index Fund	IYR	iShares Trust
iShares Dow Jones U.S. Technology Sector Index Fund	IYW	iShares Trust
iShares Dow Jones U.S. Telecommunications Sector Index Fund	IYZ	iShares Trust
iShares Dow Jones U.S. Total Market Index	IYY	iShares Trust
iShares Dow Jones U.S. Utilities Sector Index Fund	IDU	iShares Trust
iShares FTSE/Xinhua China 25 Index Fund	FXI	BGI
iShares Goldman Sachs Natural Resources	IGE	BGI
iShares Goldman Sachs Networking	IGN	BGI
iShares Goldman Sachs Semiconductor	IGW	BGI
iShares Goldman Sachs Software	IGV	BGI

Product Name	Symbol	Issuer
Shares Goldman Sachs Technology	IGM	BGI
iShares KLD 400 Social Index Fund	DSI	iShares Trust
iShares Lehman 1–3 Year Treasury Bond Fund	SHY	BGI
iShares Lehman 20+ Year Treasury Bond Fund	TLT	BGI
iShares Lehman 7–10 Year Treasury Bond Fund	IEF	BGI
iShares Lehman Aggregate Bond Fund	AGG	BGI
iShares MSCI Australia Index Fund	EWA	iShares, Inc.
iShares MSCI Austria Index Fund	EWO	iShares, Inc.
iShares MSCI Belgium Index Fund	EWK	iShares, Inc.
iShares MSCI Canada Index Fund	EWC	iShares, Inc.
iShares MSCI EAFE Growth Index Fund	EFG	BGI
iShares MSCI EAFE Value Index Fund	EFV	BGI
iShares MSCI EMU Index Fund	EZU	iShares, Inc.
iShares MSCI Emerging Markets	EEM	BGI
iShares MSCI France Index Fund	EWQ	iShares, Inc.
iShares MSCI Germany Index Fund	EWG	iShares, Inc.
iShares MSCI Hong Kong Index Fund	EWH	iShares, Inc.
iShares MSCI Italy Index Fund	EWI	iShares, Inc.
iShares MSCI Japan Index Fund	EWJ	iShares, Inc.
iShares MSCI Malaysia Index Fund	EWM	iShares, Inc.
iShares MSCI Mexico Index Fund	EWW	iShares, Inc.
iShares MSCI Netherlands Index Fund	EWN	iShares, Inc.
iShares MSCI Singapore (Free) Index Fund	EWS	iShares, Inc.
iShares MSCI Spain Index Fund	EWP	iShares, Inc.
iShares MSCI Sweden Index Fund	EWD	iShares, Inc.
iShares MSCI Switzerland Index Fund	EWL	iShares, Inc.
iShares MSCI Taiwan Index Fund	EWT	iShares, Inc.
iShares MSCI United Kingdom Index Fund	EWU	iShares, Inc.
iShares MSCI-Brazil Index Fund	EWZ	iShares, Inc.
iShares MSCI-EAFE	EFA	BGI
iShares MSCI-Pacific Ex-Japan	EPP	BGI
iShares MSCI-South Africa	EZA	BGI
iShares MSCI-South Korea Index Fund	EWY	iShares, Inc.
iShares NASDAQ Biotechnology	IBB	BGI
iShares Russell 1000 Growth Index Fund	IWF	iShares Trust
iShares Russell 1000 Index Fund	IWB	iShares Trust
iShares Russell 1000 Value Index Fund	IWD	iShares Trust
iShares Russell 2000 Growth Index Fund	IWO	iShares Trust
iShares Russell 2000 Index Fund	IWM	iShares Trust
iShares Russell 2000 Value Index Fund	IWN	iShares Trust
iShares Russell 3000 Growth Index Fund	IWZ	iShares Trust
iShares Russell 3000 Index Fund	IWV	iShares Trust
iShares Russell 3000 Value Index Fund	IWW	iShares Trust
iShares Russell Midcap Growth Index Fund	IWP	BGI
iShares Russell Midcap Index Fund	IWR	BGI
iShares Russell Midcap Value Index Fund	IWS	BGI
iShares S&P 100 Index Fund	OEF	BGI
iShares S&P 1500 Index Fund	ISI	iShares Trust
iShares S&P 500 Growth Index Fund	IVW	iShares Trust

(continued)

Product Name	Symbol	Issuer
Shares S&P 500 Index	IVV	iShares Trust
iShares S&P 500 Value Index Fund	IVE	iShares Trust
iShares S&P Europe 350 Index Fund	IEV	iShares Trust
iShares S&P Global Energy Sector	IXC	BGI
iShares S&P Global Financial Sector	IXG	BGI
iShares S&P Global Healthcare Sector	IXJ	BGI
iShares S&P Global Information Technology Sector	IXN	BGI
iShares S&P Global Telecommunications Sector	IXP	BGI
iShares S&P Latin America 40	ILF	BGI
iShares S&P MidCap 400 Growth Index Fund	IJK	iShares Trust
iShares S&P MidCap 400 Index Fund	IJH	iShares Trust
iShares S&P MidCap 400 Value Index Fund	IJJ	iShares Trust
iShares S&P SmallCap 600 Growth Index Fund	IJT	iShares Trust
iShares S&P SmallCap 600 Index Fund	IJR	iShares Trust
iShares S&P SmallCap 600 Value Index Fund	IJS	iShares Trust
iShares S&P/TOPIX 150	ITF	BGI
iShares Silver Trust	SLV	iShares Silver Trust
iShares iBoxx $ InvesTop Investment Grade Corporate Bond Fund	LQD	iShares Trust
streetTRACKS DJ Global Titans ETF	DGT	streetTRACKS Series Trust
streetTRACKS DJ Wilshire Large Cap ETF	ELR	streetTRACKS Series Trust
streetTRACKS DJ Wilshire Large Cap Growth ETF	ELG	streetTRACKS Series Trust
streetTRACKS DJ Wilshire Large Cap Value ETF	ELV	streetTRACKS Series Trust
streetTRACKS DJ Wilshire Mid Cap ETF	EMM	streetTRACKS Series Trust
streetTRACKS DJ Wilshire Mid Cap Growth ETF	EMG	streetTRACKS Series Trust
streetTRACKS DJ Wilshire Mid Cap Value ETF	EMV	streetTRACKS Series Trust
streetTRACKS DJ Wilshire REIT ETF	RWR	streetTRACKS Series Trust
streetTRACKS DJ Wilshire Small Cap ETF	DSC	streetTRACKS Series Trust
streetTRACKS DJ Wilshire Small Cap Growth ETF	DSG	streetTRACKS Series Trust
streetTRACKS DJ Wilshire Small Cap Value ETF	DSV	streetTRACKS Series Trust
streetTRACKS DJ Wilshire Total Market ETF	TMW	streetTRACKS Series Trust
streetTRACKS Dow Jones EURO STOXX 50 Index Fund	FEZ	streetTRACKS Series Trust
streetTRACKS Dow Jones STOXX 50 Index Fund	FEU	streetTRACKS Series Trust
streetTRACKS Gold Shares	GLD	streetTRACKS Gold Trust
streetTRACKS KBW Bank ETF	KBE	streetTRACKS Series Trust
streetTRACKS KBW Capital Markets ETF	KCE	streetTRACKS Series Trust
streetTRACKS KBW Insurance ETF	KIE	streetTRACKS Series Trust
streetTRACKS KBW Regional Banking ETF	KRE	streetTRACKS Series Trust
streetTRACKS Morgan Stanley Technology ETF	MTK	streetTRACKS Series Trust
streetTRACKS Russell/Nomura PRIME Japan ETF	JPP	streetTRACKS Index Shares Funds
streetTRACKS Russell/Nomura Small Cap Japan ETF	JSC	streetTRACKS Index Shares Funds

Source: American Stock Exchange.

Chapter Notes

CHAPTER 1: AN OVERVIEW OF CHINA'S POWERFUL AND GROWING ECONOMY

1. "China Reports Another Year of Strong (or Even Better) Growth," nytimes.com, January 26, 2006.
2. "Rising Mortgage Rates Seen if China Cuts Role," *Chicago Tribune,* January 14, 2006, p. 18.
3. "President Jiang on Special Economic Zones," *People's Daily,* online edition, November 15, 2000.
4. The export processing zones in Taiwan and Korea were very successful and helped the development of those economies.
5. WTO Press, "WTO Ministerial Conference Approves China's Accession," press no. 252, November 10, 2001.
6. Republican Policy Committee, "China and the WTO: Chinese Legal Commitments and Their Effects on the U.S.-China Economic Relationship," Washington, DC, December 2005.
7. U.S.-China Business Council.

CHAPTER 2: OPENING FINANCIAL MARKETS THROUGH WORLD TRADE ORGANIZATION MEMBERSHIP

1. "WTO Successfully Concludes Negotiations on China's Entry," WTO press release, September 17, 2001.
2. "Meeting of the Working Party on the Accession of China," WTO press release, September 17, 2001.
3. Deloitte & Touche, "Financial Services Foresight-Going for Growth in China," April 2005.
4. J. P. Bonin and H. Yiping, *Foreign Entry into Chinese Banking: Does WTO Membership Threaten Domestic Banks? World Economy,* vol. 25, no. 8 (Malden, MA: Blackwell Publishers, 2002), pp. 1077–1093.
5. Linklaters & Alliance, "Links to China: China's Accession to the WTO—Securities," *Legal Research Note,* February 2002, pp. 1–8.
6. S. M. Harner, "Financial Services and WTO: Opportunities Knock," *China Business Review,* vol. 27, no. 2 (March–April 2000), p. 10.

7. "Chinese Banks Urged to Prepare for Post-WTO Competition," *People's Daily,* May 10, 2001.

8. Hong Kong Trade Development Council, "Overview of Reform in China's Banking Industry in 2005," *Industrial Profile,* 16, 2006.

9. H-shares are stocks of Chinese companies listed in Hong Kong.

10. PricewaterhouseCoopers, "Foreign Banks in China," 2005.

11. Hong Kong Trade Development Council, "China's Commitment to Open Insurance Business," *Industrial Profile,* January 21, 2002.

12. KPMG, "Foreign Insurers in China: Opportunity and Risk," 2005.

CHAPTER 3: HUGE OPPORTUNITIES AND UNIQUE CHALLENGES OF INVESTING IN CHINA

1. KPMG, "Coming of Age: Multinational Companies in China," 2005.

2. FIEs are firms in which foreign ownership exceeds 20 percent.

3. Xinhuanet report (English), January 14, 2006.

4. G. Fairclough, "Made-in-China SUVs, Sedans for U.S. Market," *Newsday,* April 2, 2006, E11.

5. China Chain Store and Franchise Association, "Foreign Retailers Opening New Outlets," news release, February 27, 2006.

6. China Chain Store and Franchise Association, "Carrefour China to Add 20 Stores and 10,000 Employees in 2006," news release, February 24, 2006.

7. China Chain Store and Franchise Association, "B&Q to Open More than 100 Chain Store in China," news release, February 22, 2006.

8. The financial weakness of the domestic institutions makes them more willing to accept equity investment from foreign firms. In addition to money, they also want to learn the expertise of those foreign counterparts.

9. According to a report by the U.S.-China Business Council, January 12, 1998, China's media reported that in its five-year anti-corruption campaign 670,000 CCP members had been disciplined and more than 120,000 people expelled from the Party, including former Beijing Party chief Chen Xitong. China has also executed some officials found guilty of bribery.

10. M. Johannsen, "Understanding Eastern and Western Culture and Business Practice," http://www.legacee.com/Culture/CultureOverview.html.

CHAPTER 4: NAVIGATING CHINA'S BUSINESS CULTURE, POLITICAL RISKS, AND CORRUPTION

1. This is based on articles published in http://resources.alibaba.com/article/157/Business _Culture_throughout_China.htm.

2. C. S. Fan and H. I. Grossman, "Entrepreneurial Graft in China," *Providence Journal,* May 3, 2001, p. B5.

3. The FCPA's bribery provisions, however, contain an exception for so-called facilitating payments, as well as two affirmative defenses. The facilitating-payments exception permits companies to make payments for the purpose of expediting the performance of routine gov-

ernmental actions, such as clearing goods through customs and obtaining telephone service. The two affirmative defenses apply to payments that are legal in the foreign official's country and payments of expenses incurred by foreign officials (such as travel and lodging expenses) in connection with the promotion, demonstration, or explanation of products or services, or the performance of a contract.

4. Embassy of the People's Republic of China in the United States, "Party Enhances Internal Supervision," February 17, 2004.

5. Xinhua News Agency, "CPC Regulations Raise Confidence in Corruption Fight," February 21, 2004, http://www.china.org.cn/english/China/87995.htm.

6. Xinhua News Agency, "New Anti-Corruption Method Sparks Debate," May 20, 2005.

CHAPTER 5: CHINESE BUSINESS AND FINANCIAL LAW

1. Article 1 of the Law of the People's Republic of China on Banking Regulation and Supervision.

CHAPTER 6: GREASING THE WHEELS AND ENTERING THE CHINESE MARKETS

1. Ministry of Commerce of the People's Republic of China.

2. China-Britain Business Council, London, United Kingdom.

3. Invest Hong Kong, The Government of the Hong Kong Special Administrative Region, Hong Kong.

4. The lists of products and their CEPA ROOs can be found in the Trade and Industry Department (TID)'s CEPA website at http://www.tid.gov.hk/english/cepa/tradegoods/trade_goods .html.

CHAPTER 7: OPPORTUNITIES AND CHALLENGES FOR FOREIGN FIRMS IN CHINA'S FINANCIAL SYSTEM

1. Chinese regulators considered allowing BOC to list its stock in Shanghai and Shenzhen in addition to its listing in Hong Kong. This would mark the first local IPO since China closed the market for new offerings last year.

2. H shares are stocks of Chinese companies listed in Hong Kong.

3. QFIIs are modeled after Taiwan. The designation provides certain foreign investors access to the domestic markets.

CHAPTER 8: PRIVATE EQUITY FUND MANAGEMENT AND INVESTING

1. Benesch Frielander Coplan & Aronoff LLP, "China Insights," Columbus, OH, May/June 2006, pp. 1–7.

2. Ernst & Young, "Due Diligence Success Factors in China," *Conducting Successful Transactions in China,* Hong Kong, pp. 13–16.

3. Paul Hastings, "China Matters," Los Angeles, CA, 2005, pp. 1–2.

4. PricewaterhouseCoopers, "Industry Watch," Hong Kong, December 2003.

CHAPTER 9: THE GROWING MARKET FOR MERGERS AND ACQUISITIONS

1.   According to studies by McKinsey and Ernst & Young, as reported in "The New Face of Chinese M&A," by T. Levine and K. Woodard, April 1, 2006, http://tpwebapp.tdctrade.com.

2.   A representative office is prohibited from engaging in direct business operations in China.

3.   It is important to go through the approval process when investing in China. If the funds are channeled into China without the official approval, the investor in the future will have difficulties taking money out of the country.

4.   Current account items refer to funds for daily operations while capital account items are nontrade or nonrecurring expenses such as investment or real estate purchases.

5.   Mercer Human Resources Consulting, "The Great Buyout: M&A in China," 2006.

6.   See note 5.

7.   There are three types of synergies: economies of scale for horizontal merger, economies of scope for conglomerate merger, and economies of vertical integration for vertical integration.

8.   The financial synergy is subject to debate. Some argue that the lower probability of bankruptcy benefits bondholders at the expense of shareholders.

9.   C. F. Lee and K. T. Liaw, "Mergers Can Reduce Systematic Risk," *Advances in Financial Planning and Forecasting*, vol. 6 (November 1994), pp. 347–353.

10.   Those are used in the United States.

11.   This is based on a JPMorgan study, as reported in S. Lipin, "Takeover Premiums Lose Some Luster," *Wall Street Journal* (December 31, 1996), pp. 13–14.

CHAPTER 10: UNDERWRITING STOCKS

1.   China Securities Regulatory Commission approved the initial public offering on September 26, 2006.

2.   Goldman Sachs Group and UBS AG are underwriters of Bank of China's IPO.

3.   Hong Kong is a special administrative region of China. China claims Taiwan as part of its territory, but Taiwan claims it is an independent nation.

4.   A and B shares are two different type of shares issued by Chinese companies in China. Initially, A shares were for domestic citizens and B shares were for foreign investors. Recent financial market reforms have lifted the restrictions and now certain qualified foreign investors can trade A shares and domestic investors are allowed to trade B shares.

5.   There are another two kinds of issuing methods that are related bank deposit and the difference from Internet issuing is that each subscriber will be allocated with some shares according to the odds ratio.

6.   Of course, the underwriting spreads for larger deals are much lower, 3 to 4 percent at times.

7.   "Rules Governing the Listing of Securities on the Stock Exchange of Hong Kong Limited," 2006.

8.   In U.S. dollars, unless specified otherwise.

9.   Detailed listing requirements are available through the exchange's website.

CHAPTER 11: UNDERWRITING FIXED-INCOME SECURITIES

1. Repos in the United States are over-the-counter transactions.

2. Under CEPA, qualified Hong Kong companies also enjoy greater access to China's market in trade and services.

3. Detailed discussion of those and other derivative securities are provided in Chapter 12.

CHAPTER 12: DERIVATIVES MARKETS AND RISK MANAGEMENT

1. Note that spot trading is T+2.

2. In the case of Chinese currency, this may not apply. This is because the exchange rate is not freely floating.

3. ISDA Survey.

4. RMB is expected to appreciate for some time, as it is estimated to be undervalued against U.S. dollar for about 40 percent.

5. A market for ABS requires certain changes in accounting practice and regulatory act that allows the various elements of securitization.

CHAPTER 13: ASSET MANAGEMENT BUSINESS

1. We use "securities investment fund" and "mutual fund" to denote the same investment intermediary.

2. Fund management companies here are not the asset management companies that Chinese government set up to assume nonperforming loans from the state-owned commercial banks. The four asset management companies are: Great Wall AMC for the Agricultural Bank of China, Orient AMC for the Bank of China, Huarong AMC for the Industrial and Commercial Bank of China, and Xinda AMC for the China Construction Bank.

3. Hua An is China's first qualified domestic institutional investor (QDII).

4. The discussion in this section focuses on open-end mutual funds.

5. Investment Company Institute.

6. Chapter 19 provides a detailed discussion on ETFs and those tracking Chinese markets and list on U.S. exchanges.

7. Morgan Stanley.

CHAPTER 14: PROFIT FROM INVESTMENT OPPORTUNITIES IN CHINA

1. U.S. Department of Commerce.

2. Most families have only one child because of the one-child policy.

3. M. Kritzman, *The Portable Financial Analyst: What Practitioners Need to Know*, (New York: McGraw Hill, 1995), chapter 21.

4. B. D. Singer and D. S. Karnosky, "The General Framework for Global Investment Management and Performance Attribution," *Journal of Portfolio Management,* (Winter 1995), pp. 84–92.

5. A. F. Perold and W. F. Sharpe, "Dynamic Strategies for Asset Allocation," *Financial Analysts Journal* (January/February 1988), pp. 16–27.

6. This is exactly the profit opportunity of a long position in a call option.

7. This analysis assumes that there are no taxes or transactions costs.

8. The leverage factor = 1/percent margin requirement.

9. W. H. Wagner, "Defining and Measuring Trading Costs," in *Execution Techniques, True Trading Cost, and the Microstructure of Markets,* ed. Association for Investment Management Research (1993).

10. J. D. Rose and D. C. Cushing, "Making the Best Use of Trading Alternatives," in *Execution Techniques, True Trading Cost, and the Microstructure of Markets,* ed. Association for Investment Management Research (1993).

11. P. Micioni, "Strategies for International Trading," in *Execution Techniques, True Trading Cost, and the Microstructure of Markets,* ed. Association for Investment Management Research (1993).

12. Section 28(e) states that an investment manager has not breached a fiduciary duty by paying a price in excess of the best execution price "if such commission was reasonable in relation to the value of the brokerage and research services provided."

13. P. M. Sherer, "Online Trading for Corporate-Finance Chiefs Arrives," *Wall Street Journal* (October 13, 1999), pp. C1–C21.

14. B. C. Browchuk, "Organizing and Operating the Trading Desk: Part I," in *Execution Techniques, True Trading Cost, and the Microstructure of Markets,* ed. Association for Investment Management Research (1993).

CHAPTER 15: INVESTING IN GROWTH SECTORS

1. They were relatively new when they first floated shares and attracted large sums of money.

2. C. W. Smith refers to this as the "transformational idea" in *Success and Survival on Wall Street* (Lanham, MD: Rowman and Littlefield, 1999).

3. This is generally not understood. When you lose 50 percent of your equity, your capital base is only half of what you started with. You need to double in order to bring the equity back to the initial level. For example, you lose $50 on $100 equity. The new balance is $50. A 100 percent gain on the new capital base, $50, will bring the amount back to $100.

4. The short position of 60 shares will make a profit of $150 when the price drops from $10 to $7.5 per share. The bond loses retains its investment value of $920, a decline of $130 from its price of $1,050. The result is a net profit of $20.

5. The 12-day, 26-day, and 9-day EMAs are commonly used in MACD.

CHAPTER 16: INVESTING IN VALUE SECTORS

1. D. B. Trone, W. R. Albright, and P. R. Taylor, *The Management of Investment Decisions* (Homewood, IL: Irwin Professional Publishing, 1996), chapter 5.

2. C. D. Ellis, *Investment Policy: How to Win the Loser's Game* (Homewood, IL: Dow Jones Irwin, 1985), p. 62.

3. R. W. Kaiser, "Individual Investors," in *Managing Investment Portfolios: A Dynamic Process,* eds. J. L. Maginn and D. L. Tuttle (Boston: Warren, Gorham and Lamont, 1990).

4. See note 3.

5. The definition of risk aversion is sometimes misunderstood. Risk aversion does not imply that investors will always choose the safest investment. Risk aversion says that investors need to be rewarded for taking on risk and that as their level of risk increases, they must receive proportionately greater rewards for taking on another unit of risk.

6. The assumption is that investors will be able to borrow or lend unlimited amount at the risk free rate.

CHAPTER 17: INVESTING IN CHINESE COMPANIES LISTED ON U.S. EXCHANGES

1. Bank of New York, "The Depositary Receipt 2005," New York, 2006.

2. A fail occurs when a trade does not settle on settlement date.

CHAPTER 18: INVESTING IN CHINESE MUTUAL FUNDS

1. The 110 basis point loss is calculated as the 100 basis point cost of the load plus the 10 basis points that the portfolio loses by having 1 less share appreciating at 10 percent.

2. Note that, in order to maintain a 50/50 allocation mix, some funds will be shifted from Fund A to Fund B at the beginning of the second year.

3. A study found that more than 90 percent of a portfolio's total rate of return was attributable to its asset allocation policy.

4. But, the distribution of $2 is taxable.

5. This gives ETFs an advantage because ETFs can be purchased and sold any time during the trading hours.

6. The two exceptions would be funds that invest in emerging market debt and funds that seek out the bonds of distressed companies.

7. Technically, enhanced indexing doesn't represent the passive investment strategy that is associated with indexing.

CHAPTER 19: INVESTING IN CHINESE EXCHANGED-TRADED FUNDS LISTED ON U.S. EXCHANGES

1. Morgan Stanley, "Exchange-Traded Funds," August, 2006.

Glossary

Accrued interest The interest due on a fixed-income security since the last interest payment.

Active management strategy An investment management strategy that seeks to outperform the market by applying various research and techniques.

Aftermarket The public market for a security after the initial public offering.

American depositary receipt Certificate representing shares of a foreign company that trades in the United States.

A shares A class of Chinese stock that is reserved for Chinese residents and has denominations in Chinese local currency. Only certain qualified foreign investors can purchase A shares.

Asset allocation Diversification of investments in various asset classes to achieve a return that is consistent with the investor's financial goals.

Asset-backed security Securities backed by nonmortgage assets such as installment loans, leases, receivables, tax liens, revolving credit, commercial loans, and high-yield bonds.

Asset management company A type of company established by the Chinese government to assume and manage the nonperforming assets of state-owned commercial banks.

Asset securitization The issuance of securities using a pool of similar assets as collateral.

Basis point One one-hundredth of 1 percent.

Best efforts underwriting An underwriting arrangement in which underwriters agree to use their best efforts to sell the shares on the issuer's behalf.

Bid-asked spread The difference between the price at which a dealer sells a security and the price at which the dealer buys it.

Bid-to-cover ratio The ratio of the bids received to the amount awarded in a Treasury security auction.

Break fee Payments by the acquisition target to the first accepted bidder if the target accepted another offer.

Bulge bracket firm Major underwriter in a syndicate.

B shares Shares in Chinese stocks that were exclusively for foreign investors.

Buyout fund Investment firms that invest in leveraged buyouts (LBOs).

Callable bond Bonds that grant the issuer the right to pay off the debt before maturity.

Capital Asset Pricing Model (CAPM) Provides a linkage between the risk of a stock and the required rate of return investors demand.

Capital market line   Shows the trade off between expected return and total risk of a portfolio consisting of money in riskless asset and risky market portfolio.

Carry   The difference between interest income and interest expense.

China Banking Regulatory Commission (CBRC)   Chinese government entity responsible for regulating banks.

China Insurance Regulatory Commission (CIRC)   Chinese government body that regulates insurance companies.

China Securities Regulatory Commission (CSRC)   Chinese government body that regulates securities business.

Chinese wall   The safeguards, also called firewall, that ensure that various units of an investment banking firm do not receive any inappropriate or inside information.

Clearing   The processing of a trade and the establishment of what the parties to the trade owe to each other.

Closed-end mutual fund   One type of investment companies that offers a fixed number of shares and the shares trade on an exchange.

Closer Economic Partnership Agreement   An agreement between China and Hong Kong Special Administrative Region that grants companies in Hong Kong special access to China.

Collateral buyer   The counterparty that takes in securities and lends out funds in a repurchase agreement.

Collateralized bond obligation   Securities backed by high-yield bonds.

Collateralized loan obligation   Securities backed by commercial loans.

Collateralized mortgage obligation   A type of mortgage-backed securities that separates the securities into tranches.

Collateral seller   The party that lends securities in exchange for cash in a repurchase agreement transaction.

Comfort letter   A letter from accountant expressing assurance on any unaudited interim financial statements included in the prospectus.

Commercial paper   An unsecured promissory note with a maturity of no more than 270 days.

Commodity swap   In a commodity swap agreement, each counterparty promises to make a series of payments to the other, and of which a commodity price or index determines at least one set of the payments.

Competitive bid   Bid that specifies both the amount and the price the bidder is willing to pay.

Constant growth model   Assumes that the dividend growth rate is constant over time.

Convertible arbitrage   Trading involves the purchase of convertible bonds or preferred stocks and then hedging that investment by selling short the underlying equity. Another type of strategy involves additional trading of an interest rate swap, a credit default swap, and an options contract to hedge risks and lock in a certain spread.

Convertible bond   Bonds that grant the holder the right to convert the par amount of the bond into a certain number of shares of the issuer's common stock.

Cooling-off period   A period following the filing of the registration statement with the SEC, prior to the issue's offering.

Coupon pass-through   The collateral holder in a repurchase transaction has to pass over to the cash borrower any coupon received from the collateral.

Coupon roll A coupon roll trade combines two trades in which a dealer purchases from a customer an on-the-run coupon security for next day settlement and simultaneously sells to that customer the same amount of the recently announced new security for forward settlement.

Coupon stripping Strips interest payment coupons from a coupon Treasury and treats each of the component coupons and the principal as a separate security.

Credit default swap A synthetic instrument in which counterparty pays a premium in return for a contingent payment triggered by the default of the reference credits.

Credit derivative A derivative security with payoffs linked to a credit-related event.

Credit linked note A structured note in which the instrument has an embedded option that allows the issuer to reduce the security's payments if a specified credit variable deteriorates.

Credit spread contract The payoffs of the contract depend on the yield differential between a credit sensitive instrument and the reference security.

Currency swap In a currency swap contract, the two counterparties agree to exchange certain amounts of currencies on scheduled dates.

Daylight overdraft The amount a financial institution has overdrawn on the Fedwire during the day.

Deliverable repo A type of repurchase agreement under which the underlying securities are delivered against payment; at maturity, the collateral is returned and the loan plus interest is paid.

Delivery versus payment Funds and securities are transferred at the same time.

Deposit agreement An agreement that sets forth the terms of an American Depositary Receipt (ADR).

Depositary bank A custodian to safekeep underlying shares in an issuer's home market.

Depositary receipt A negotiable certificate that represents ownership of shares in a foreign corporation.

Derivative security A contract with its value derived from an asset of an index.

Discounted cash flow A valuation approach that uses a discount rate to calculate the present value of future cash flows from a company.

Due diligence Obligation of the underwriter to investigate and assure that there are no misstatements or omissions in the registration statement.

Dutch auction This is a single-price auction; both competitive and noncompetitive bidders are awarded securities at the price that results from the high yield.

DV01 The change in the price of a bond resulting from a one-basis point change in its yield.

Dynamic asset allocation A strategy used to ensure the value of the portfolio does not fall below a certain level to avoid large losses and to secure favorable market moves.

Effective When the registration statement has been approved by the Securities and Exchange Commission (SEC) and the security can be sold to investors.

Effective date Date when an offering is declared effective by the SEC. The issue can then be sold to the public.

Efficient frontier A portfolio on the efficient frontier is one that has the highest return for a given a mount of risk or the lowest risk for a given level of return.

Efficient market hypothesis A security price fully reflects all available information so as to offer a rate of return consistent with its level of risk.

Electronic communications network A computerized trading system that matches buyers and sellers of securities.

Emerging market The securities market of a developing country.

Equity swap An equity swap involves an investor receiving capital gains plus dividends in a target market and in turn paying to the swap dealer LIBOR and any decrease in the market index.

Exchange-traded fund An index fund or trust listed on an exchange and can trade like a listed stock during trading hours.

Exempt securities Securities that are exempt from SEC registration requirements.

Fail A trade fails to settle on the settlement date.

Federal funds market The market for bank reserves.

Federal funds rate The interest rate on federal funds.

Federal Open Market Committee (FOMC) A major component of the Federal Reserve Board (Fed); it consists of the seven members of the board and five of the 12 Federal Reserve Bank presidents.

Fedwire A Fed communications and settlement system that enables financial institutions to transfer funds and book-entry securities.

Feng shui A Chinese practice that configures office or home environment in ways that promote health, happiness, and prosperity.

Filing date The day the underwriter turns in the registration statement with the regulator.

Financial engineering The development of new financial instruments such as derivative contracts using sophisticated mathematical and statistical models and computer technology.

Firm commitment A type of underwriting agreement in which investment bankers risk their own capital by purchasing the whole block of new securities from the issuer and then re-sell them to the public.

First-price auction A Treasury auction technique in which each accepted bidder pays his bid price for the security awarded. This is no longer in use in the United States. The U.S. Treasury has changed the auction mechanism to Dutch auction.

Flight to liquidity When investors use the foreign money that flows into the United States, as a result of flight to quality, to purchase the most recently auctioned Treasury securities which generally provide a higher level of liquidity.

Flight to quality The purchase of U.S. Treasury securities by foreigners whenever there is a financial or political crisis overseas.

Floater A security with interest rate tied to LIBOR or T-bill rate.

Floating risk Consists of waiting risk, pricing risk, and marketing risk during the underwriting of a security.

Flotation cost The total costs of issuing securities.

Foreign direct investment A long-term investment by a foreign direct investor.

Foreign exchange reserve Foreign currency deposits, often as a result of international trade surplus, held by a central bank or a monetary authority.

Foreign invested enterprise A company that receives funds or capital from a foreign company.

Front-end load The amount that purchasers of mutual funds pay when they buy the fund shares.

Fundamental analysis A technique that bases a stock price on corporate and economic fundamentals.

General obligation bond   Municipal securities with the full faith and credit of the issuer backing the scheduled payments of principal and interest.

Glass-Steagall Act of 1933   Separates commercial and investment banking activities.

Global depositary receipt (GDR)   The underlying shares are held with a local custodian and the depositary issues certificates, GDRs, to foreign markets.

Gramm-Leach-Bliley Act of 1999   Removed restrictions that had been imposed on the financial services industry by the Glass-Steagall Act. The Gramm-Leach-Bliley Act permits affiliation of banks, investment banks, and insurance companies.

Green shoe option   An option allowing investment bankers to purchase up to a specified number of additional shares, typically 15 percent of the issue, from the issuer in the event they sell more than agreed in the underwriting agreement.

Gross settlement   Transactions are settled on a bilateral, trade-for-trade basis.

Gross spread   The difference between the price offered to the public and the price the underwriter pays to the issuer.

Growth investing   An investment style that focuses on companies with higher than average growth rate in the industry.

Guanxi   Relationship or connection.

Haipai   Shanghai style, meaning hospitality and generosity.

Haircut   A margin required when borrowing money in the repurchase agreement market.

Hedge fund   A private investment fund that employs investment strategies in various types of securities in various markets and whose offering memorandum allows for the fund to take both long and short positions, use leverage and derivatives.

H share   A Chinese company stock listed in Hong Kong.

Impact cost   The cost of buying liquidity.

Implied repo rate   The calculated return in a short sell in a fixed-income security.

Implied volatility   The variability in an underlying security implied by the current option premium.

Indenture   A bond contract that sets forth the legal obligations of the issuer and names a trustee representing the interests of the bondholders.

Indication of interest   Investor's interest in purchasing a new security that is still in registration. This is not a formal commitment to buy.

Indirect quotation   The amount of foreign currency per unit of domestic currency.

Initial public offering   A company's first equity issue in the public markets.

Interest rate swap   A contract between two parties in which each party agrees to make a series of interest payments to the other on scheduled dates.

Inverse floater   A floating rate security whose interest rate moves inversely with a specified reference rate. A fixed-rate bond can be separated into a floater and a reverse floater.

Investment adviser   A person who engages in the business of providing advice or issuing reports about securities to clients for compensation.

Investment Advisors Act of 1940   Requires registration of investment advisers and compliance with statutory standards.

Investment banking   Underwriting and distribution of new issues of securities, as well as financial advice and execution of mergers and acquisitions, divestures, and restructurings.

Investment Company Act of 1940 Governs the activities of investment companies.

Issuer safe harbor A safe harbor that addresses offers and sales by issuers, their affiliates, and securities professionals involved in the initial offerings of securities.

Junk bond High-yield debt instruments with credit ratings below investment grade.

Lead manager The investment bank that acts on behalf of the entire syndicate.

Level I ADR The easiest and least expensive way for a foreign company to gauge interest in its securities and to begin building a presence in the United States.

Level II ADR Listed on one of the national exchanges and must comply with the SEC's full registration and reporting requirements.

Level III ADR Similar to Level II ADRs except that the issuer is allowed to make a public offering.

Leveraged buyout A buyout of a company with a large portion of the purchase price financed by debt.

LIBOR London Interbank Offered Rate.

Limit order An order to trade at the specified price or better.

Managing underwriter Lead investment bank of an underwriting syndicate.

Market impact Market impact is the difference between the price at which a stock trade is executed and the average of that stock's high, low, opening, and closing of the day.

Market order An order to trade at the market price.

Merchant banking An investment bank commits its own capital on a long term basis by taking an equity interest or creditor position in companies.

Monetary Policy Committee (MPC) The main policy body in the making of monetary policy and macroeconomic management in China.

Mortgage pass-throughs Securities backed by pools of mortgage obligations in which payments of the underlying mortgages are passed over to the security holders.

Mutual fund An investment management company that pools funds from investors who have similar investment objectives.

Net asset value The total value of a fund portfolio divided by the number of shares issued to investors.

Official statement A document provides material information to investors on a new issue of municipal securities. An official statement describes the issue, the issuer, and the legal opinions.

Open-end mutual fund A type of mutual fund structure that continuously offers new shares to the public and accepts redemption based on the net asset value of the fund.

Open repo An arrangement in a repurchase transaction in which the repo is rolled over until terminated by either party.

Portfolio company After a venture capital sourcing a perspective deal, satisfactory due diligence leads to an investment, the invested company then becomes a portfolio company.

Preliminary prospectus The preliminary prospectus is filed with the SEC and provided by underwriters to prospective purchasers. It does not disclose the offering price, underwriting spread, or net proceeds. This is the red herring.

Primary dealers Banks and securities broker-dealers that bid at the auction and trade government securities with the Federal Reserve Bank of New York.

Prime brokerage A suit of services providing hedge funds with custody, clearance, financing, and securities lending.

Private equity fund A fund established to invest in private equity, including venture capital and buyouts.

Private placement The sale of new securities to a few qualified investors instead of through a public offering. Privately placed securities do not have to be registered with the SEC.

Prospectus Part I of the registration statement is the prospectus that contains detailed information on the issue and on the issuer's condition and prospects. This is distributed to the public as an offering document. Before the final prospectus is completed, securities firms generally distribute to perspective investors the preliminary prospectus.

Quiet period Begins with the signing of the letter of intent and ends 25 days after the effective date if the security is listed on an exchange or quoted on NASDAQ. During this period, the company is subject to SEC guidelines on publication of information outside of the prospectus.

Qualified foreign institutional investor A foreign financial institution that meets certain requirements and has received permission to invest and conduct permitted businesses in China.

Qualified institutional buyer An institution that has at met certain requirements to trade privately placed securities.

Real estate investment trust A trust that pools capital from investors to acquire or to provide financing for real estate.

Real estate swap The property owner agrees to pay the counterparty a rate of return linked to the performance of the real estate market. In exchange, the counterparty pays the property owner another type of return.

Red herring The preliminary prospectus.

Registration statement The document companies use to register with the SEC new issues of securities. Disclosed in the registration statement are various kinds of important information for investors when making investment decisions, including the business of the issuer, purpose of funds, description of the security, risk factors, and the background of the management.

Regulation S Provides two types of safe harbor exemptions for securities offered overseas without registration and it applies to global depositary receipts.

Renminbi (RMB) Chinese currency.

Renqing Personal favor.

Repo rate The interest rate the collateral buyer demands for this type of loan.

Repurchase agreement A financing tool in which a dealer sells the collateral for cash and simultaneously contracts to repurchase the same securities at a future date at a higher price that reflects the financing rate.

Resale safe harbor A safe harbor under Regulation S that addresses re-sales by securities professionals such as brokers.

Restricted securities Securities purchased in a private placement directly from an issuer are subject to a one-year holding period restriction. Restricted securities frequently will have a legend printed on the back of the certificate stating that the shares cannot be sold or disposed of without registration.

Right of substitution The rights of the collateral seller in a repo transaction to take back the security and substitute other collateral of equal value and quality for it.

Road show   The meetings in a various cities during an underwriting period for the purpose of increasing interest in the offering.

Rule 144   Governs the sale of restricted securities acquired in a private placement.

Rule 144A   Addresses private sales of restricted securities among qualified institutional buyers.

Rule 415   A shelf registration rule that allows an issuer to file a single registration document indicating that it intends to sell a certain amount of securities at one or more times within the next two years thus minimizing the floating risk.

Sarbanes-Oxley Act of 2002   Imposes duties and penalties for noncompliance on public companies. The act prohibits an auditor from performing specified nonaudit services contemporaneously with an audit. In corporate responsibility, the act requires the chief executive officer and the chief financial officer to certify various issues in periodic financial reports. The act also requires every public company to include in its annual report an internal control report. The issuer's auditor shall attest to and report on the assessment of such internal control structure and procedures. This is often referred to as the Section 404 certification.

Secondary offering   A public offering of shares owned by existing shareholders.

Second-price auction   A Dutch auction used by the Department of Treasury to sell its securities in which all accepted bids pay the same price, the lowest price (highest yield) accepted.

Securities Act of 1933   Requires registration of a new security issue unless an exemption is available, also known as "truth in securities" law.

Securities Exchange Act   This 1934 Act requires timely and accurate disclosure of material information, prohibits sales practice abuses and insider trading.

Securities investment fund   A mutual fund.

Settlement   The transfer of money and securities between parties to the trade so the transaction is completed.

Shelf registration   An issuer files a single registration document indicating that it intends to sell a certain amount of securities at one or more times within the next two years. This is Rule 415.

Short sale   The sale of securities not owned by the seller in the expectation of falling price or as part of an arbitrage.

Short squeeze   Traders and arbitrageurs who short ahead of the auction are forced to pay a sharply higher price to buy or accept a special repo rate to reverse in the security in order to make good delivery.

Special economic zone   A geographic area in China established to increase foreign investment and to bring in foreign management expertise and technology.

Special purpose vehicle   A bankruptcy remote legal entity established for a securitization program.

Specials   When government securities trade at a lower rate than the general collateral in the repo market, these securities are called specials.

State Administration of Foreign Exchange   Chinese government entity that regulates the foreign exchange market.

State-owned commercial bank   A bank owned by the Chinese government.

State-owned enterprise   A large corporation owned by the Chinese government.

Stop order   An order to trade when the price reaches the specified level to stop large losses.

Stop yield   The highest yield that is accepted at the Treasury securities auction.

Strategic asset allocation A value-oriented technique seeking to increase exposure to the market when recent market performance is poor and to reduce exposure when recent market performance has been strong.

Structured note Debt securities with interest and at times principal payments depending on formulas and terms specific to the security.

Sunshine policy Policy in China putting all major activities of government officials under the scrutiny of the public to curb corruption.

Systematic risk The component of risk of a security that moves with the market and cannot be diversified away.

Tail The tail of an auction is the difference between the average yield of all accepted bids and the stop yield.

Technical analysis Attempts to forecast a security price by using techniques analyzing past prices and trading volumes.

Total return swap The counterparty exchanges the returns of the underlying assets for a floating rate of interest.

Treasury auction This is the method used to issue government securities.

Triparty repo A custodian bank maintains accounts for both parties in a repo transaction and hence the actual delivery of securities and cash can be reduced to just credit and debit transfers within the bank.

Underwriter An investment banking firm that purchases securities directly from an issuer and resells them to investors.

Underwriter spread The difference between the price the underwriters pay to the issuer and the price they receive from resale of the securities.

Underwriting agreement The contract that establishes the relationship between the corporate issuer and the underwriting syndicate. It includes the type of underwriting, the underwriters' remuneration, the offering price, and the number of shares.

Underwriting discount The percentage of discount from the offering price that the underwriter obtains from the issuer.

Underwriting syndicate Each member in the underwriting syndicate is committed to buying a portion of the new security. There is also the selling group that helps sell the issue but accepts no risk.

Unit investment trust An investment company that purchases and holds a relatively fixed portfolio of securities.

Value investing An investment technique that focuses on a company's ability to generate stable earnings.

Venture capital A type of private equity that invests in new, growing businesses.

When-issued trading The when-issued trades of Treasury securities begin right after the auction announcement and until the new issue settlement date.

Wholly foreign-owned enterprise (WFOE) A company doing business in China that is wholly owned by a foreign entity.

World Trade Organization (WTO) An international organization dealing with rules of trade between nations.

Yield to maturity The rate that discounts all future periodic coupons and principal at maturity to the current asked price.

Yuan Reminbi, the Chinese currency.

Bibliography

CHAPTER 1: AN OVERVIEW OF CHINA'S POWERFUL AND GROWING ECONOMY

Abrami, R. "China and the WTO: Doing the Right Thing." Harvard Business School Case 9–704-041, 2005.

China Business Review. Various issues.

Clark, D. C. "China's Legal System and the WTO: Prospects for Compliance." *Washington University Global Studies Law Review.* Vol. 2 (2003), pp. 97–118.

Dayal-Gulati, A., and A. Y. Lee. *Kellogg on China: Strategies for Success* (Evanston, IL: Northwestern University Press, 2004).

Denend, L. "The Competitive Advantage of China." Stanford Graduate School of Business Case IB-57, 2004.

Harvard China Review. Various issues.

McKenney, K. I. "An Assessment of China's Special Economic Zones." Executive Research Report S94, Industrial College of the Armed Forces, National Defense University, Washington, DC, 1993.

Morrison, W. M. "China Economic Conditions." CRS Issue Brief for Congress, Foreign Affairs, Defense, and Trade Division, 2005.

Prasad, E. ed. *China's Growth and Integration into the World Economy: Prospects and Challenges.* Washington, DC: International Monetary Fund, 2004.

Republican Policy Committee. "China and the WTO: Chinese Legal Commitments and Their Effects on the U.S.-China Economic Relationship." Washington, DC, December 2005. http://rpc.senate.gov/_files/Dec1405ChinaWtoJT.pdf.

Tseng, W., and M. Rodlauer. *China: Competing in the Global Economy.* Washington, DC: International Monetary Fund, 2003.

Yusuf, S., K. Nabeshima, and D. H. Perkins. *Under New Ownership: Privatizing China's State-Owned Enterprises.* Washington, DC: The World Bank, 2006.

Wu, J. *Understanding and Interpreting China Economic Reform* (Mason, OH: Thomson, 2005).

CHAPTER 2: OPENING FINANCIAL MARKETS THROUGH WORLD TRADE ORGANIZATION MEMBERSHIP

China Securities Regulatory Commission. *China's Securities and Futures Markets* (Beijing, China: 2006).

Euromoney. *China Capital Markets Handbook* (London, 2005).

KPMG. "Foreign Insurers in China: Opportunity and Risk." 2005; http://www.kpmg.com.cn/en/virtual_library/Financial_services/Foreign_insurers_in_China0507.pdf.

Moreno, R. "Reforming China's Banking System." *FRBSF Economic Letter* (May 31, 2002); http://www.frbsf.org/publications/economics/letter/2002/el2002–17.pdf.

Prasad, E. ed. *China's Growth and Integration into the World Economy: Prospects and Challenges* (Washington, DC: International Monetary Fund, 2004).

PricewaterhouseCoopers. "Asia Financial Buyer: A Bulletin for Financial Investors in Asia Pacific." January, 2006; http://www.pwchk.com/webmedia/doc/1137382517118_asiafinancialbuyer_jan2006.pdf.

PricewaterhouseCoopers. "Foreign Banks in China." September, 2005.

PricewaterhouseCoopers. "NPL Asia." No. 6, November, 2005.

Walter, C. E., and F. J. T. Howie. P*rivatizing China: The Stock Markets and Their Role in Corporate Governance* (Hoboken, NJ: John Wiley & Sons, 2003).

World Trade Organization. "Report of the Working Party on the Accession of China." 2001.

CHAPTER 3: HUGE OPPORTUNITIES AND UNIQUE CHALLENGES OF INVESTING IN CHINA

Abrami, R. "China and the WTO: Doing the Right Thing?" Harvard Business Case 9–704-041, 2005.

Bhattsali, D., S. Li, and W. Martin. *China and the WTO: Accession, Policy Reform, and Poverty Reduction Strategies* (Washington, DC: The World Bank, 2004).

China Netcom. *Annual Report.* 2005.

China Telecom. *Annual Report.* 2005.

Denend, L. "The Competitive Advantage of China." Stanford Graduate School of Business Case IB-57, 2004.

Fung, K. C., L. J. Lau, and J. S. Lee. *U.S. Direct Investment in China* (Washington, DC: American Enterprise Institute, 2004).

Huang, Y., and W. Kirby. Ed. *Selling China: Foreign Direct Investment during the Reform Era* (Cambridge, UK: Cambridge University Press, 2005).

KPMG. "Coming of Age: Multinational Companies in China." 2005.

KPMG. "Investment in the People's Republic of China." 2005.

Lo, V. I. *Law and Investment in China: The Legal and Business Environment after China's WTO Accession* (Oxon, UK: RoutledgeCurzon, 2005).

U.S. General Accounting Office. *World Trade Organization: U.S. Companies' Views on China's Implementation of Its Commitments* (Washington, DC: U.S. General Accounting Office, 2004).

Zinzius, B. *Doing Business in the New China* (Westport, CT: Praeger, 2004).

CHAPTER 4: NAVIGATING CHINA'S BUSINESS CULTURE, POLITICAL RISKS, AND CORRUPTION

Begovic, B. "Corruption: Concepts, Types, Causes, and Consequences." Economic Reform, Washington, DC: Center for International Private Enterprise, March 2005.

Fan, C. S., and H. I. Grossman. "Entrepreneurial Graft in China." *The Providence Journal* (May 3, 2001), p. B5.

He, Q. "The Evolution of Corruption in China." August 13, 2004. http://www
.theepochtimes.com/news/4–8-13/22861.htm.

Kennedy, S. *The Business of Lobbying in China* (Cambridge, MA: Harvard University Press, 2005).

Lautt, K. "Corruption and Market Reform in China." University of California, UCLA International Institute, Los Angeles, 2000.

Leung, T. K. P., Y. H. Wong, and C. T. W. Tam. "Guanxi and Favor in the People's Republic of China." Working paper, Hong Kong Polytechnic University, Department of Business Studies, 2003.

Orts, E. W. "The Rule of Law in China." http://law.vanderbilt.edu/journal/34–01/orts.html.

Stuttard, J. B. *The New Silk Road* (New York: John Wiley & Sons, 2000).

Sun, Y. *Corruption on Market in Contemporary China* (New York: Cornell University Press, 2004).

Thun, E. *Changing Lanes in China* (Cambridge: Cambridge University Press, 2006).

Tjoa, L., O. Jianyu, and L. Pykstra. "Complying with PRC Antibribery Laws." *China Business Review* (March–April 2005). http://www.chinabusinessreview.com/public/0503/wong.html.

CHAPTER 5: CHINESE BUSINESS AND FINANCIAL LAW

Ministry of Commerce of the People's Republic of China. "Detailed Rules for the Implementation of the Law on Wholly Foreign Owned Enterprises." http://english.mofcom.gov.cn/aarticle/topic/lawsdata/chineselaw/200301/20030100062868.html.

CHAPTER 6: GREASING THE WHEELS AND ENTERING THE CHINESE MARKETS

China-Britain Business Council. *Market Intelligence-Establishing a Presence* (London: Publisher, 2006).

Dong, J. *China Business Laws and Regulations* (Saratoga, CA: Javvn Publishing, 2005).

Gamble, W. B. *Investing in China: Legal, Financial and Regulatory Risk* (Westport, CT: Quorum Books, 2002).

Kluwer Law International. *China Business Law Guide* (New York: Aspen Publishers, 2005).

KPMG. Investment in the People's Republic of China. 2005.

Ministry of Commerce of the People's Republic of China. "Detailed Rules for the Implementation of the Law on Wholly Foreign Owned Enterprises." 2006.

Ministry of Commerce of the People's Republic of China. "Law on Wholly Foreign Owned Enterprises." 2006.

O'Melveny & Myers LLP. *Reorganizing Foreign Invested Enterprises in China: The New Merger and Division Regulations* (Shanghai, China: O'Melveny & Myers LLP, 2000).

Plante & Moran. *Strategies for Entering the Chinese Market* (Shanghai, China: Plante & Moran, 2003).

Trade and Industry Department of the Government of Hong Kong Special Administrative Region. "Mainland and Hong Kong Closer Economic Partnership Agreement (CEPA)." 2006.

CHAPTER 7: OPPORTUNITIES AND CHALLENGES FOR FOREIGN FIRMS IN CHINA'S FINANCIAL SYSTEM

Allen, F., J. Qian, and M. Qian. "China's Financial System: Past, Present, and Future." Working paper, University of Pennsylvania, Wharton School, Philadelphia, 2006.

Bank of China IPO Prospectus.

Dipchand, C. R., Y. Zhang, and M. Ma. *The Chinese Financial System* (Westport, CT: Greenwood Press, 1994).

Langlois, J. D. Jr. "The WTO and China's Financial System" (*The China Quarterly*, 2001), pp. 610–629.

Ma, W. *Investing in China: New Opportunities in a Transforming Stock Market* (London: Incisive Media Plc., 2006).

McGeehan, K. *China's Banking System and How Citibank Can Capitalize on Its Liberalization.* Master Thesis, Tufts University, The Fletcher School, Medford, MA, 2005.

Prasad, E. "China's Financial Sector Challenge" (Washington, DC: International Monetary Fund, May 10, 2005).

Tam, O. K. *Financial Reform in China* (London: Routledge, 1995).

Tsai, K. S. *Back-Alley Banking: Private Entrepreneurs in China* (Ithica, New York: Cornell University Press, 2004).

Watanabe, M. (ed). *Recovering Financial Systems: China and Asian Transition Economies* (New York: Palgrave Macmillan, 2006).

CHAPTER 8: PRIVATE EQUITY FUND MANAGEMENT AND INVESTING

Amihud, Y. *Leveraged Management Buyouts: Causes and Consequences* (Frederick, MD: Beard Books, 2002).

Asia Private Equity Review. Various issues.

Asia Venture Capital Journal. Various issues.

Baker, C. P., and G. D. Smith. *The New Financial Capitalists: Kohlberg Kravis Roberts and the Creation of Corporate Value* (Cambridge, MA: Cambridge University Press, 1998).

Batjargal, B., and M. M. Liu. "Entrepreneurs' access to private equity in China: the role of social capital." Working paper, Stanford University, Stanford, CA, 2002.

Camp, J. J. *Venture Capital Due Diligence: A Guide to Making Smart Investment Choices and Increasing Your Portfolio Returns* (Hoboken, NJ: John Wiley & Sons, 2002).

China Venture Capital Research Institute *China Venture Capital Yearbook 2006* (Hong Kong: China Venture Capital Research Institute, 2006).

Fernadez, J. A., and L. Underwood. *China CEO: Voices of Experience from 20 International Business Leaders* (Hoboken, NJ: John Wiley & Sons, 2006).

Journal of Private Equity. Various issues.

Lerner, J. *Venture Capital and Private Equity: A Casebook* (New York: John Wiley & Sons, 2000).

Neftci, S. N., and M. Y. Menager-Xu. Eds. *China's Financial Markets: An Insider's Guide to How the Markets Work* (Oxford, UK: Academic Press, 2006).

Sullivan, M. K. "Segmenting the Informal Venture Capital Market: Economic, Hedonistic, and Altruistic Investors." *Journal of Business Research.* Vol. 36 (May 1996), pp. 25–35.

Venture Capital Journal. Various issues.

CHAPTER 9: THE GROWING MARKET FOR MERGERS AND ACQUISITIONS

Baker and McKenzie. *Guide to Mergers & Acquisitions 2005/2006* (Hong Kong: Baker and McKenzie, 2005).

Baldwin, C. Y, C. E. Bagley, and J. Quinn. "M&A Legal Context: Standards Related to the Sale or Purchase of a Company." Harvard Business School Case 9–904-004, 2003.

Burrough, B., and J. Helgar. *Barbarians at the Gates* (New York: Harper Perennial, 1990).

Cullinan, G., J. M. Le Roux, and R. M. Weddigen. "When to Walk Away from a Deal." *Harvard Business Review* (April 2004), pp. 1–9.

Lee, C. F and K. T. Liaw. "Mergers Can Reduce Systematic Risk." *Advances in Financial Planning and Forecasting.* Vol. 6 (November 1994), pp. 347–353.

Lipin, S. "Takeover Premiums Lose Some Luster." *Wall Street Journal* (December 31, 1996), pp. 13–14.

Lipin, S. "Closing Loophole Puts a Chill in Tax-Free Deals." *Wall Street Journal* (April 21, 1997), pp. A3, A13.

Mergers and Acquisitions Journal. Various issues.

Piskorski, M. J. "Note on Corporate Strategy." Harvard Business School Case 9–705-449, 2005.

Securities Regulation Institute. "The Evolving M&A Market." Northwestern University Law School, Evanston, IL, January 2005.

CHAPTER 10: UNDERWRITING STOCKS

Bethel, J. E. and L. Krigman. "Unallocated Shelf Registration: Why Doesn't Everybody Use It? Equity Issuance, Managerial Choice, and Market Reaction." Mimeo. Babson College, Babson Park, MA, 2004.

China Securities Regulatory Commission. *China's Securities and Futures Markets* (Beijing, China: China Securities Regulatory Commission, 2006).

Chi, Jing and Padgett, Carol, "The Performance and Long-Run Characteristics of the Chinese IPO Market" (April 23, 2002). U of Reading, ISMA Centre Discussion Paper No. 2002–09. Available at SSRN: http://ssrn.com/abstract=309931 or DOI: 10.2139 /ssrn.309931.

Deloitte. *Going Public (China).* 2006.

Kanatas, G., and J. Qi. "Underwriting by Commercial Banks: Incentive Conflicts, Scope Economies, and Project Quality." *Journal of Money, Credit and Banking.* Vol. 30 (February 1998), pp. 119–133.

Krigman, L., W. H. Shaw, and K. L. Womack. "The Persistence of IPO Mispricing and the Predictive Power of Flipping" *Journal of Finance* Vol. 54 (June 1999), pp. 1015–1044.

Liaw, K.T. *The Business of Investment Banking: A Comprehensive Overview* (Hoboken, NJ: John Wiley & Sons, 2006).

Linebaugh, K. "Goldman to Reap Handsome Profit on Chinese IPO." Post-gazette.com. http://www.post-gazette.com/pg/06271/725840–28.stm, September 28, 2006.

Kursman, S. C. "Recent developments regarding regulation of initial public offerings." *Securities Industry Association Reports.* Vol. 5 (April 2004).

PricewaterhouseCoopers. "Greater China IPO Watch." 2006.

CHAPTER 11: UNDERWRITING FIXED-INCOME SECURITIES

China Securities Regulatory Commission. *China's Securities and Futures Markets* (Beijing, China: China Securities Regulatory Commission, 2006).

Fleming, M. J. and K. D. Garbade. "Repurchase Agreements with Negative Interest Rates." *Current Issues in Economics and Finance.* Vol. 10 (April 2004), pp. 1–7.

Gu, G.Z., and A. G. Frank. *China's Global Reach: Markets, Multinationals, and Globalization* (Palo Alto, CA: Fultus Corporation, 2006).

Kluwer Law International. *Foreign Exchange Control in China* (London: Kluwer Law International, 2005).

Liaw, K. T. *The Business of Investment Banking: A Comprehensive Overview* (Hoboken, NJ: John Wiley & Sons, 2006).

Ma, W. *Investing in China: New Opportunities in a Transforming Stock Market* (London: Risk Books, 2006).

McDonald, R. L. *Derivatives Markets* (Boston, MA: Addison-Wesley, 2002).

Neal, R. S. "Credit Derivatives: New Financial Instruments for Controlling Credit Risk." *Economic Review,* Federal Reserve Bank of Kansas City (Second Quarter, 1996): pp. 15–27

Neftci, S. N., and M. Y. Menager-Xu. Eds. *China's Financial Markets: An Insider's Guide to How the Markets Work* (Oxford: Academic Press, 2006).

Phillips, A. L. "1995 Derivatives Practices and Instruments Survey." *Financial Management.* Vol. 24 (Summer 1995), pp. 115–125.

Soeder, G. A. "High Yield Bonds and Movement in Interest Rates." *Market Week in Review.* (February 6, 2004), pp. 1–5.

Stigum, Marcia. *The Repo and Reverse Markets* (Burr Ridge, IL: Irwin, 1989).

CHAPTER 12: DERIVATIVES MARKETS AND RISK MANAGEMENT

Chacko, G., A. Sjöman, H. Motohashi, and V. Dessain. *Credit Derivatives: A Primer on Credit Risk, Modeling, and Instruments* (Philadelphia: Wharton School Publishing, 2006).

Davison, A., L. L. Wolff, and A. Sanders. *Securitization: Structuring and Investment Analysis* (Hoboken, NJ: John Wiley & Sons, 2003).

Fleming, M. J., K. D. Garbade. "Repurchase Agreements with Negative Interest Rates." *Current Issues in Economics and Finance.* Vol. 5 (April 2004), pp. 1–7.

Graveline, J. J., and M. R. McBrady. "Who Makes On-the-Run Treasuries Special?" Working paper, Stanford University, Stanford, CA, 2005.

Jordan, B. D., and S. D. Jordan. "Special Repo Rates: An Empirical Analysis." *Journal of Finance.* Vol. 52 (December 1997), pp. 2051–72.

Liaw, K. T. *The Business of Investment Banking: A Comprehensive Overview* (Hoboken, NJ: John Wiley & Sons, 2006).

McDonald, R. L. *Derivatives Markets* (Boston, MA: Addison-Wesley, 2002).

Neftci, S. N. *Principles of Financial Engineering* (Oxford: Academic Press, 2004).

Shearman and Sterling. *Securitization and Derivatives.* 2005.

Stone, C. A., and A. Zissu. *The Securitization Markets Handbook* (New York: Bloomberg Press, 2005).

Walmsley, J. *The Foreign Exchange and Money Market Guide* (New York: John Wiley & Sons, 2000).

CHAPTER 13: ASSET MANAGEMENT BUSINESS

Bogle, J. C. and P. L. Bernstein. *Common Sense on Mutual Funds* (New York: John Wiley & Sons, 2000).

Chandler, B. *Investing with the Hedge Fund Giants.* 2nd ed. (Upper Saddle River, NJ: Prentice Hall, 2002).

Darst, D.M. *The Art of Asset Allocation.* (New York: McGraw-Hill Companies, 2003).

Investment Company Institute. *2006 Investment Company Fact Book* (Washington, DC: Investment Company Institute, 2006).

Liaw, K. T. *The Business of Investment Banking: A Comprehensive Overview* (Hoboken, NJ: John Wiley & Sons, 2006).

Mazzli, P., D. Kittsley, and D. Maister. *Exchange-Traded Funds* (New York: Morgan Stanley, 2005).

McCrary, S. A. *How to Create and Manage a Hedge Fund: A Professional's Guide* (Hoboken, NJ: John Wiley & Sons, 2002).

Xu, X.E. "Performance of Securities Investment Funds in China." Working paper, Seton Hall University, South Orange, NJ, 2004.

CHAPTER 14: PROFIT FROM INVESTMENT OPPORTUNITIES IN CHINA

Bodie, Z., A. Kane, and A. J. Marcus. *Investments* (New York: McGraw-Hill, 2004).

Howie, F. J. T., and C. E. Walter. *Privatizing China: Inside China's Stock Markets* (New York: John Wiley & Sons, 2006).

Knee, J. A. *The Accidental Investment Banker: Inside the Decade the Transformed Wall Street* (London: Oxford University Press, 2006).

Link, M. *High Probability Trading* (New York: McGraw-Hill, 2003).

Ma, S. *The Efficiency of China's Stock Market* (London: Ashgate Publishing, 2004).

Ma, W. *Investing in China: New Opportunities in a Transforming Stock Market* (London: Risk Books, 2006).

Pring, M. J. *The Investor's Guide to Active Asset Allocation* (New York: McGraw-Hill, 2006).

Stigum, M. *After the Trade* (Burr Ridge, IL: Irwin Professional Publishing, 1988).

Tinic, S. M., and R. R. West. "The security industry under negotiated brokerage commissions: Changes in the structure and performance of New York Stock Exchange member firms." *Bell Journal of Economics* (Spring 1980), pp. 29–41.

CHAPTER 15: INVESTING IN GROWTH SECTORS

Dubil, R. *An Arbitrage Guide to Financial Markets* (Hoboken, NJ: John Wiley & Sons, 2004).

Eng, W. F. *The Day Trader's Manual: Theory, Art, and Science of Profitable Short-Term Trading* (New York: John Wiley & Sons, 1993).

Equity Analytics. *Technical Analysis* (New York: Equity Analytics, 1997).

Fernald, J., and J. H. Rogers. "Puzzles in the Chinese stock market." *Review of Economics and Statistics.* Vol. 84, No. 3 (August 2002), pp. 416–432.

Green, S. *China's Stock Market.* (London: University of Cambridge, 2003).

Kirkpatrick, C. D., and J. R. Dahlquist. *Technical Analysis: The Complete Resource for Financial Market Technicians* (Essex, United Kingdom: FT Prentice Hall, 2006).

Kleinman, G. *Trading Commodities and Financial Futures: A Step by Step Guide to Mastering the Markets.* 3rd ed. (Upper Saddle River, NJ: Financial Times Prentice Hall, 2004).

Liaw, K. T. "Book review: The Day Trader's Manual: Theory, Art, and Science of Profitable Short-Term Trading." *Journal of Finance.* Vol. 50 (June 1995), pp. 758–761.

Ma G., and B. Fung. "China's Asset Management Corporations." BIS Working Papers No. 115: Bank for International Settlements, 2002.

Shanghai Stock Exchange. *Fact Book 2005* (Shanghai, China: Shanghai Stock Exchange, 2006).

Tengler, N. *New Era Value Investing: A Disciplined Approach to Buying Value and Growth Stocks* (Hoboken, NJ: John Wiley & Sons, 2003).

World Bank. *China: The Emerging Capital Market* (Washington, DC: World Bank, 1995).

CHAPTER 16: INVESTING IN VALUE SECTORS

Damodaran, A. *Investment Valuation: Tools and Techniques for Determining the Value of Any Assets* (Hoboken, NJ: John Wiley & Sons, 2002).

English, J. *Applied Equity Analysis: Stock Valuation Techniques for Wall Street Professionals* (New York: McGraw-Hill, 2001).

Fabozzi, F. J., S. M. Focardi, and P. N. Kolm. *Financial Modeling of the Equity Market: From CAPM to Cointegration* (Hoboken, NJ: John Wiley & Sons, 2006).

Gray, G., P. Cusatis, and J.R. Woolridge. *Streetsmart Guide to Valuing a Stock.* 2nd ed. (New York: McGraw-Hill, 2003).

Hoover, S. *Stock Valuation* (Hoboken, NJ: John Wiley & Sons, 2005).

Paulos, J.A. *A Mathematician Plays the Stock Market* (New York: Basic books, 2004).

Penman, S. *Financial Statement Analysis and Security Valuation* (New York: McGraw-Hill, 2003).

Porter, M. *Competitive Advantage: Creating and Sustaining Superior Performance* (New York: Free Press, 1998).

CHAPTER 17: INVESTING IN CHINESE COMPANIES LISTED ON U.S. EXCHANGES

Aggarwal, R., S. Dahiya, and L. Klapper. "American Depositary Receipts (ADR) Holdings of U.S. Based Emerging Market Funds." World Bank Policy Research Working Paper 3538, 2005.

Bank of New York. *The Depositary Receipt 2006* (New York: Bank of New York, 2007).

Bank of New York. *The Global Equity Investment Guide: The Case for Investing in Depositary Receipts* (New York: Bank of New York, 2004).

Bank of New York. *Worldly Choices: Overseas Investment Opportunities Grow* (New York: Bank of New York, 2004).

Desai, M. "Cross-Border Listings and Depositary Receipts." Harvard Business School Case, 9–204-022, January 2004.

Lang, M. H., K. V. Lins, and D. Miller. "ADRs, Analysts, and Accuracy: Does Cross Listing in the U.S. Improve a Firm's Information Environment and Increase Market Value?" Research Paper (New York: New York Stock Exchange, 2002).

Liaw, K.T. *The Business of Investment Banking: A Comprehensive Overview* (Hoboken, NJ: John Wiley & Sons, 2006).

Muscarella, C. J. "Stock Split: Signaling or liquidity? The case of ADR Solo-Splits." *Journal of Financial Economics.* Vol. 42 (September 1996), pp. 3–26.

Pagno, M., A. Roell, and J. Zechner. "The Geography of Equity Listing: Why Do Companies List Abroad?" *Journal of Finance.* Vol. 57 (2002), pp. 2651–2694.

CHAPTER 18: INVESTING IN CHINESE MUTUAL FUNDS

Benz, C., P. D. Teresa, R. Kinnel, and D. Phillips. *The Morningstar Guides to Mutual Funds: 5-Star Strategies for Success* (Hoboken, NJ: John Wiley & Sons, 2004).

Bogle, J. C. and P. L. Bernstein. *Common Sense on Mutual Funds* (New York: John Wiley & Sons, 2000).

Gremillion, L. *Mutual Fund Industry Handbook: A Comprehensive Guide for Investment Professionals* (Hoboken, NJ: John Wiley & Sons, 2005).

Investment Company Institute. "2006 Investment Company Fact Book."

Liaw, K.T. *The Business of Investment Banking: A Comprehensive Overview* (Hoboken, NJ: John Wiley & Sons, 2006).

McCrary, S. A. *How to Create and Manage a Hedge Fund: A Professional's Guide* (Hoboken, NJ: John Wiley & Sons, 2002).

Nicholas, J. G. *Market Neutral Investing: Long/Short Hedge Fund Strategies* (New York: Bloomberg, 2000).

Pozen, R. C. *The Mutual Fund Business.* 2nd ed. (Cambridge, MA: MIT Press, 2002).

CHAPTER 19: INVESTING IN CHINESE EXCHANGED-TRADED FUNDS LISTED ON U.S. EXCHANGES

Downes, J., and J. E. Goodman. *Finance and Investment Handbook* (New York: Dow Jones & Company, 2003).

Gastineau, G. L. *The Exchange-Traded Fund Manual* (Hoboken, NJ: John Wiley & Sons, 2002).

Meziani, A. S. *Exchange Traded Funds as an Investment Option* (Hampshire, United Kingdom: Palgrave Macmillan, 2005).

Morgan Stanley. *Prospectus of Morgan Stanley Capital Protected Notes Based on Value of AMEX China Index* (New York: Morgan Stanley, 2005).

Morgan Stanley. *Prospectus of Morgan Stanley China A Share Fund, Inc.* (New York: Morgan Stanley, 2006).

Morgan Stanley. "Exchange-Traded Funds." 2006.

Morningstar. *Morningstar ETFs 100: 2006* (Hoboken, NJ: John Wiley & Sons, 2006).

Morris, V., and K. Morris. *Standard and Poor's Guide to Money and Investing* (New York: McGraw Hill, 2005).

Murren, C. *Comparing the aspects of ETFs vs. Mutual Funds for the Personal Investor.* Masters thesis, St. John's University, Queens, NY, 2005.

Vomund, D. *ETF Trading Strategies Revealed* (Columbia, MD: Marketplace Books, 2006).

Index

About the Author

K. Thomas Liaw is a professor of Finance and chair of the Economics and Finance Department at St. John's University, New York. He speaks on investment banking and capital markets at executive programs, APEC and World Bank symposium, and Harvard China Review and Harvard Asia Business conferences. He travels to China, Hong Kong, and Taipei regularly on various assignments. He recently authored *The Business of Investment Banking: A Comprehensive Overview* (John Wiley & Sons, 2006). His principal areas of teaching and research include capital markets, risk management, and investment banking. Professor Liaw served as president of the Chinese American Academic and Professional Society for 2005. He is a director of the State Bancorp, Inc. and State Bank of Long Island. He also is a member of the board of trustees at Taylor Business Institute. He is an associate editor for *Review of Pacific Basin Financial Markets and Policies*. He serves as an adviser to several companies. Professor Liaw holds his doctorate from Northwestern University.